Planning in the UK

Planning in the UK

An Introduction

Clara Greed

with David Johnson

palgrave
macmillan

First published 2014 by
PALGRAVE MACMILLAN

Palgrave Macmillan in the UK is an imprint of Macmillan Publishers Limited,
registered in England, company number 785998, of Houndmills, Basingstoke,
Hampshire RG21 6XS.

Palgrave Macmillan in the US is a division of St Martin's Press LLC,
175 Fifth Avenue, New York, NY 10010.

Palgrave Macmillan is the global academic imprint of the above companies
and has companies and representatives throughout the world.

Palgrave® and Macmillan® are registered trademarks in the United States,
the United Kingdom, Europe and other countries.

ISBN 978-0-230-30332-4 hardback
ISBN 978-0-230-30333-1 paperback

This book is printed on paper suitable for recycling and made from fully
managed and sustained forest sources. Logging, pulping and manufacturing
processes are expected to conform to the environmental regulations of the
country of origin.

A catalogue record for this book is available from the British Library.

A catalog record for this book is available from the Library of Congress.

Typeset by Cambrian Typesetters, Camberley, Surrey, England, UK

Printed and bound in China

Short Contents

Long Contents

PART I PLANNING AND THE PLANNING SYSTEM

List of Illustrations

Please note that there are many additional photos and illustrations to be found on the book's companion website: www.palgrave.com/companion/greed.

Textboxes

Photographs

Figures

Tables

Preface

This book builds on previous introductory texts by the author dating back to the late 1990s and early 2000s. However, given the amount of time that has passed, the changes to the planning system in the intervening period, and the opportunity to work with a new publisher, this book has been substantially re-envisioned and revised to provide a new and up-to-date introduction to planning in Britain. The book provides a comprehensive approach to most of the topics that students are likely to study at an introductory level, in an accessible style for the busy reader. The book is chiefly aimed at planning students along with those from other built environment courses, including architecture, surveying, urban geography and urban design. The book will also be of interest to planning practitioners, academics and community groups, especially in these days of community-led planning in the production of neighbourhood plans.

The book is divided into four parts. Part I describes the planning system, including the importance of planning policy-making and different types of development plans produced within local authorities and their role in controlling development in bringing these plans to fruition. There have been some major changes in the planning system over the last decade: first the restructuring of development planning under New Labour, followed by the Coalition government's greater emphasis upon the new localism and grass-roots community decision-making, arguably shifting the balance away from traditional top-down strategic spatial planning. The book outlines these changes and brings the topic thoroughly up to date.

In Part II the story of planning is told through the history chapters. There is also a planning theory chapter at the end of Part II which will help the reader to look 'behind' the development of planning, to understand the concepts, ideas and beliefs that have shaped planning policy past and present.

Part III is devoted to current planning policy topics, including rural planning, sustainability, regeneration, transport planning, housing and urban design, all of which students are likely to find comprise modules on modern planning courses. As will be seen there is no one 'planning' but several types of planning with different specialisms often taking different approaches to urban problems, especially in respect of planning for (or against) the motorcar.

Part IV focuses on the social aspects of planning. The relationship between urban sociology and planning will first be discussed, followed by a chapter which provides an alternative 'minority' perspective on planning policy. Nowadays there are many more ingredients, beyond gender, that make up the equality and diversity agenda, such as age, sex, religion, ethnicity and age, but gender is still used as a well-worn example (and as yet unresolved issue) to illustrate the eternal urban question of 'who gets what, where, why and how'.

In terms of specifics, the UK remains the main focus and examples will be highlighted of current interesting developments, types of plans and ongoing planning debates. However, an international approach has been included for comparative purposes, because many planning issues are global in extent, for example the environment, poverty and population.

Whilst the book is up to date at the time of going to press, inevitably changes are still taking place. Therefore readers are advised to consult the internet for a range of excellent central and local government planning websites, such as the government's

Planning Portal. But a special feature of the book is that it is accompanied by its own web page, where the reader will find a series of e-supplements, providing more detailed and updated coverage of key topics, along with additional resources and reference material.

The book seeks to point the reader in the right direction towards useful examples and helpful material on the web and through further reading, rather than to include detailed case studies or specific details on planning rules and policies. The book seeks to make readers aware of what is important, and to discuss, reflect upon and explain key issues. It seeks to provide a pathway and direction in amongst the overload of material that is now available through the internet.

A set of three types of tasks is provided at the end of each chapter to further the reader's understanding. These comprise, firstly, information-gathering tasks which can be undertaken on the internet or by site visits and local investigation; secondly conceptual tasks asking the reader to explore and discuss different aspects of planning theory and policy (including some essay exam-type questions); and thirdly reflective tasks requiring the reader to give their views and opinions on particular planning topics, as informed by their studies and their own life experience as a citizen living within the built and natural environment.

Illustrations have been included, for planning is a visual subject as well as a statutory process. The emphasis is upon choosing photos that highlight significant points, rather than seeking to provide a tourist guide to spectacular buildings, or a developer's guide to significant new projects. Be very wary of convincing websites and for that matter television documentaries on planning, which, in reality, are strongly biased and only tell part of the story. So always check your sources carefully and compare at least three different sources when researching planning topics.

Overall the purpose of the book is to widen the readers' perceptions of what constitutes planning, and to introduce you to key debates on planning policy and priorities, rather than to provide a recipe book on 'how to plan'. Students often ask, 'but what is the right answer?' to a particular planning issue or design qustion. It all depends upon what is accepted government policy at the time of asking, and also, in terms of political power, what people need, and how they want to live. It is hoped that by reading this book students will become more aware of the intellectual challenges facing planners, but also the value of our planning system and the positive benefits that planning policy has brought to the economy, society and the built environment.

Bristol CLARA GREED

Acknowledgments and Dedication

We would like to thank colleagues from the planning school at the University of the West of England, for help and feedback on the book. In particular we would like to thank Adam Sheppard for feedback on the development management chapter and the details of planning, Andrew Tallon for inspiration on urban renewal issues, and Steve Melia for advice on shared space and traffic calming issues. We would also like to acknowledge the positive influence of other colleagues, past and present, who have all contributed to the development of planning education and scholarship in Bristol over the years, without which this book could not exist. These include, Sandra and John Manley, Nigel Taylor, Stuart Farthing, Ann de Graft Johnson, Geoff Walker, Janet Askew, Hugh Barton, Angela Hull, John Winter, Tony Paxton, Jim Claydon, Hugh Barton, Madge Dresser, Martin Boddy and a host of others.

Further afield, we would like to thank Marion Roberts at the University of Westminster for her continuing support and advice on urban design topics, and Dory Reeves at Auckland University for giving further inspiration on gender mainstreaming and equality methodologies. Thanks go to Michelle Barkley and John Griggs for their help on Building Regulation and British Standards and Jo-Anne Bichard and Barbara Penner for their encouragement on sanitation, accessibility and equality issues.

In particular, David thanks Tessa Coombes for her support, and Clara is eternally grateful to John Greed her late husband, who initially encouraged her, by his example, to write.

CLARA GREED
DAVID JOHNSON

List of Abbreviations and Acronyms

AONB	Area of Outstanding Natural Beauty
BCSC	British Council of Shopping Centres
BIDs	Business Improvement Districts
BME	Black and Minority Ethnic
BREEAM	Building Research Establishment Environmental Assessment Methods
BSA	British Sociological Association
BSI	British Standards Institute
CABE	Commission for Architecture and the Built Environment
CAD	Computer Aided Design
CAE	Centre for Accessible Environments
CAFOD	Catholic Agency For Overseas Development
CAG	Cooperative Advisory Group
CAP	Common Agricultural Policy
CAPG	Conservation Area Partnership Grant
CBA	Cost–Benefit Analysis
CBD	Central Business District
CBR	Cost Benefit and Risk
CCT	Compulsory Competitive Tendering
CCTV	Closed Circuit Television
CDA	Comprehensive Development Area
CDP	Community Development Programme
CEC	Commission of the European Communities
CFCs	Chloro-Fluoro-Carbon gases
CIB	Construction Industry Board
CIBSE	Chartered Institute of Building Services Engineers
CIC	Construction Industry Council
CIH	Chartered Institute of Housing
CIL	Community Infrastructure Levy
CIOB	Chartered Institute of Building
CLA	Country Landowners Association
CLG	Communities and Local Government (or DCLG)
CPRE	Campaign to Protect Rural England
CPRE	Council for the Protection of Rural England
CRE	Commission for Racial Equality
DAS	Design and Access Statement
DBIS	Department of Business, Innovation and Science ('Biz')
DCLG	Department for Communities and Local Government ('Communities' or CLG)
DCMS	Department for Culture, Media and Sport
DDA	Disability Discrimination Act
DECC	Department of Energy and Climate Change
DEFRA	Department for Environment, Food and Rural Affairs
DETR	Department of the Environment, Transport and the Regions
DfT	Department for Transport
DG	Directorate General (in European Commission)
DLR	Docklands Light Railway
DMPO	Development Management Procedure Order
DoE	Department of the Environment
DoT	Department of Transport
DPDs	Development Plan Documents
DTI	Department of Trade and Industry

DTLR	Department for Transport, Local Government and the Regions	LA21	Local Agenda 21
EC	European Commission	LCC	London County Council
EEC	European Economic Community (Common Market)	LDDC	London Docklands Development Corporation
EH	English Heritage	LDF	Local Development Framework
EHRC	Equality and Human Rights Commission	LDA	London Development Authority
		LDO	Local Development Order
EIA	Environmental Impact Assessment	LEPs	Local Enterprise Partnerships
EOS	Equal Opportunities Commission	LGMB	Local Government Management Board
EPA	Educational Priority Area	LLDC	London Legacy Development Corporation
ES	Environmental Statement		
ESDP	European Spatial Development Perspective	LMS	London Midland and Scottish
		LNER	London and North Eastern Railway
ESRC	Economic and Social Research Council	LOCOG	London Organising Committee of the Olympic Games
EU	European Union		
EZ	Enterprise Zone	LTGDC	London Thames Gateway Development Corporation
FSA	Food Standards Agency		
GIA	General Improvement Area	MAFF	Ministry of Agriculture, Fisheries and Food
GIS	Geographical Information System		
		MCC	Metropolitan County Council
GLA	Greater London Authority	MCZ	Marine Conservation Zone
GLC	Greater London Council	MDGs	Millennium Development Goals
GM	Genetically Modified	MoD	Ministry of Defence
GMCA	Greater Manchester Combined Authority	MPs	Members of Parliament
		MPG	Minerals Planning Guidance note
GPDO	General Permitted Development Order		
		NAEA	National Association of Estate Agents
GWR	Great Western Railways		
HAA	Housing Action Area	NDO	Neighbourhood Development Order
HMI	Houses in Multiple Occupation		
ICE	Institute of Civil Engineers	NEA	National Environment Agency
ICO	International Committee for the Olympics	NEET	Not in Employment Education or Training
IDC	Industrial Development Certificate	NFU	National Farmers Union
		NGO	Non-Governmental Organisation
IDS	Inclusive Design Standards	NHS	National Health Service
INTERREG	European Community Initiative for Trans-National Policy	NIA	Noise Impact Assessment
		NID	National Infrastructure Directorate
IPC	Infrastructure Planning Commission		
		NIMBY	Not In My Back Yard
IRRV	Institute of Revenues, Ratings and Valuation	NPF	National Planning Framework (Scotland)
ISVA	Incorporated Society of Valuers and Auctioneers	NPPF	National Planning Policy Framework
KICC	Kingsway International Christian Centre	NPS	National Policy Statement
		NRA	National Rivers Authority

ODA	Olympic Delivery Authority
ODC	Olympic Delivery Committee
ODP	Office Development Permit
ODPM	Office of the Deputy Prime Minister
ONS	Office of National Statistics
PAN	Practice Advice Note
PCP	Planning and Compulsory Purchase
PD	Permitted Development
PFI	Private Finance Initiative
PINS	Planning Inspectorate
PPG	Planning Policy Guidance note
PPS	Planning Policy Statement
PROW	Public Right Of Way
PSED	Public Sector Equality Duty
PTE	Passenger Transport Executive
QUANGO	Quasi-Autonomous Non-Governmental Organisation
RDA	Regional Development Agency
RGS	Royal Geographical Society
RIBA	Royal Institution of British Architects
RICS	Royal Institution of Chartered Surveyors
RNIB	Royal National Institute for the Blind
RPG	Regional Planning Guidance
RRAs	Race Relations Acts
RSPCA	Royal Society for the Prevention of Cruelty to Animals
RSS	Regional Spatial Strategy
RTPI	Royal Town Planning Institute
RTS	Regional Transport Strategy
SA	Sustainability Appraisal
SDGs	Sustainable Development Goals
SDO	Special Development Order
SEA	Strategic Environmental Assessment

SEEDA	South East England Development Agency
SEV	Sex Entertainment Venue
SIA	Social Impact Assessment
SMEs	Small and Medium Enterprises
SOBA	Society of Black Architects
SPZ	Simplified Planning Zone
SR	Southern Region
SRB	Single Regeneration Budget
SSSIs	Sites of Special Scientific Interest
STEM	Science, Technology, Engineering, Medicine and Mathematics
TCPA	Town and Country Planning Association
TfL	Transport for London
TPO	Tree Preservation Order
TVGs	Town and Village Greens
UCO	Use Classes Order
UDC	Urban Development Corporation
UDP	Unitary Development Plan
UKRC	UK Resource Centre
UN	United Nations
UNCED	United Nations Conference on Environment and Development
UNEP	United Nations Environment Programme
UNESCO	United Nations Educational, Scientific and Cultural Organization
UN-HABITAT	United Nations Human Settlements Programme
VAT	Value Added Tax
WDS	Women's Design Service
WE	Women and Environments
WGSG	Women and Geography Study Group
WHO	World Health Organization
WHS	World Heritage Site

PART I
Planning and the Planning System

Introduction: Why Planning Matters

The scope and nature of planning

The purpose of this book is to provide a comprehensive introduction to the subject of town and country planning. It covers the historical background, the development and structure of the modern-day planning system, key policy and legislative areas, along with planning theory, some urban sociology, and more reflective elements. The book seeks to tell the story of planning in an accessible manner and thus to explain how planning works so that readers new to the subject can get an idea of the scope and nature of planning, whilst giving more advanced readers an up-to-date account of planning and providing material for reflection and discussion.

Throughout the text, some key references and important websites are provided. A fuller list of references per chapter entitled Further Reading is provided on the companion website linked to this book (at www.palgrave.com/companion/greed). This provides guidance on source material and identifies key main texts plus ancillary reading. You will also find on this website a set of Tasks to undertake per chapter, including information gathering activities, essays and projects. The book is illustrated with a selection of photographs, diagrams, tables and textboxes. You will find additional illustrative material on the book's website too. You will also find a series of E-Supplements on the web which contain reference material. For example, E-Supplement 1 provides a comprehensive list of legislation, government planning policy guidance, and other official sources which is relevant to most of the chapters.

Whilst providing an accessible and descriptive overview, the book will also incorporate a discursive and conceptual perspective, so that readers are aware of the current debates, conflicts and discussions within this field. Students often ask *'what is the right answer?'* to a particular planning issue, but the nature of the right answer always depends upon what current theories, standards and ideas are shaping planning practice, and what was right in the past may not be right now. For example in the past, planners used to plan strongly for the needs of the car and this shaped the standards on road widths, housing densities and layout. At present, there is far more emphasis on the needs of the cyclist, pedestrian and public transport user, and this has reshaped our approach to road design and layout principles.

Planning by its very nature is frequently subject to philosophical trends, changes in planning theory, revisions to policy approaches, and changing political priorities. Therefore it is important not only to cover contemporary planning issues and policies, but also to give readers background, perspective and understanding of the foundations and sources of the current planning agenda. Although there have been many changes in policy approaches, the 'same' problems and issues that planners need to tackle remain, particularly those concerned with transport, land use and the environment.

In spite of all the changes in policies and approaches over the years, this book is based on the premise that planning is important and worthwhile. In the United Kingdom land-use planning is essential to help fit everything and everyone into limited space on our small set of islands, whilst retaining a balance between town and countryside. Nearly 80 per cent of the population of Britain lives in urban areas, and while there are still substantial areas of open countryside between the towns and cities, it is misleading to believe that there is room for much more house-building: the areas where there is most pressure for development are generally those areas where the availability of land is most limited. For example, South East England is much more built up than Northern Scotland and different planning policies and priorities apply.

According to 2011 UK Census results, the United Kingdom has a population of 63.2 million. Eighty per cent of the total 24,410,000 hectares of land is agricultural, although there is actually very little untouched land that is completely undeveloped (Office of National Statistics, 2012). It is not just a matter of numbers in terms of how many houses and people there should be in a particular location, there are also major planning policy issues to be taken into account. For example, policies on the environment, the countryside, transport, the inner city, development and land use, and the social aspects of planning are all within the remit of planning. For example, every time a new housing estate is built on the edge of a city for commuters working in central area offices, the cars generated by the new development will add to the rush-hour congestion in the centre. The next little site development may be the straw that breaks the camel's back. It is hoped that in reading this book you will gain a wider view of the nature of planning, and develop an informed perspective on the different policy approaches, conflicts and options that confront planners.

Rather than seeing planning as a mindless bureaucratic activity, it is hoped that readers will see the benefit and value of planning, as a constructive, beneficial influence in society, which has the potential to make people's lives better. It is envisaged that readers will get a deeper insight into key policy issues, such as environmental issues, transport planning and property development, as well as the wider social and economic aspects of planning. As a result readers will see the issues more clearly and broaden their intellectual horizons in the process, while coming to understand why planning is important and worthwhile.

What is town planning?

Common misconceptions

This section seeks to address some of the commonly held misconceptions about the nature of planning, often gained from the media, and to outline the true

---

> ### Textbox 1.1 Town Planning According to Keeble
>
> Town planning is the art and science of ordering the land-uses and siting the buildings and communications routes so as to secure the maximum level of economy, convenience and beauty (Keeble, 1969).

scope and nature of planning. People often get the impression that town planning is chiefly concerned with regulation and control. It may also be imagined that planning is chiefly concerned with building new developments, when in fact it is also strongly concerned with the conservation, improvement and management of existing areas. Planning may also be seen as being primarily concerned with built-up urban areas when in fact it is concerned with both town and country.

One type of planning or many?

The modern planning system was established under the Town and Country Planning Act 1947 as part of the wider Post-War Reconstruction programme at the end of the Second World War. At the time the primary emphasis was upon controlling land uses and development and producing actual physical plans, which showed where new building and reconstruction was to take place. This approach is reflected in the definition shown in Textbox 1.1 which was made by a prominent post-war town planner who was famous for his publications on how to build complete new towns from scratch.

So, post-war reconstruction planning was based upon a simplistic physical master plan, blueprint approach, best suited to planning new towns on green-field sites (undeveloped land). Although planning has shifted from its physical map-making origins, it is important not to forget the spatial aspects of planning. Development plans still shape the built environment. Patterns of employment, investment and social well-being continue to show distinct spatial variation between regions, and so *space matters*, that is the geographical context is still important (Massey 1984). The location of land uses and the placing of settlements have often been established for historical or geographical reasons (such as coal mining) long before modern planning came along. Planning policy, especially in respect of location policy for new housing developments, is influenced by natural factors, such as the extent of flooding, and by the increased likelihood of flooding occurring on low-lying land. But it is the role of the planner to take all these factors into account and manage wisely where and how development takes place.

In reality, planning is about more than just physical land-use control, it incorporates economic, social, environmental and political dimensions, at local, regional and national levels. The visual, architectural and urban design aspects of planning are also very important. Planning also overlaps with the discipline of geography to some degree, both in terms of physical environmental concerns, and the social geography of a highly urbanised society (Dorling 2012). For example, current planning policy is concerned with climate change, transport systems, sustainability, urban regeneration, urban design and social inclusion (Rydin 2011). So there are many different types of planners and many different specialisms within the profession.

Policies or regulations?

Planning law and regulations are important parts of planning, but this is only half the story: planners are also policy-makers. To the outsider town planning may appear to be chiefly concerned with standards and rules about the size of plots, road widths and the layout of new developments. Many people's first contact with the planners is in relation to seeking planning permission, perhaps for an ill-fated house extension proposal. So planning is often viewed in a negative light, as something that has to be overcome in order to carry out development. Many people see the planner as '*a man waiting for something to turn down*', unlike Dickens's Micawber who was always waiting for something to turn up. This is an image fuelled by media representations of the planner, who is generally seen as a white male bureaucrat, who wants to restrict the operation of the private property sector. This book argues that town planners can perform a constructive role in enabling, rather than hindering, development and urban renewal; thus

making urban problems better rather than worse (Bayer *et al.* 2010). There is room for improvement, and ways to enhance both the image and effect of planning will be discussed, but, in fairness, planners are dealing with complex issues to which there is often not one simple solution which will please everyone.

The 2004 Planning and Compulsory Purchase Act introduced by New Labour has been, until relatively recently, the main piece of legislation underpinning the planning system. This was superseded by the 2011 Localism Act as will be explained in detail in Chapters 2 and 3 (Ricketts and Field 2012). These major planning acts determine the scope and nature of the operation of the planning system, and specific types of development plans and forward planning policy documents to be prepared by local planning authorities. In addition there is a wide range of other planning legislation, case law and regulation that is concerned with controlling development. One of the main aspects of the town planner's work is the production of development plans which determine which sites can be built upon in the first place. This is likely to constitute a spatial strategy plan which is composed of both maps and a substantial policy document, and although the exact form that development plans take alters under each successive government the basic principles remain.

Development control, also known as development management, or sometimes the development consent process, is a major function of the planning system. As explained in Chapter 3, this process determines whether or not planning permission is given for development which not only includes new-build, but also substantial change to the structure or use of existing buildings (Cullingworth and Nadin 2006). In making the decision as to whether to permit development or not, planners have to retain both a city-wide perspective and a local neighbourhood awareness as to the likely effects of a particular scheme, and maintain a more critical viewpoint towards new development than the private-sector developer whose horizons may be limited to the boundaries of the site owned and the cost factor. Planning decision-making has to take into account international considerations too. Because of concerns about global warming, climate change and the environment, most major planning proposals, plans and policies are subject to environmental assessment. This reflects global concerns with reducing the carbon footprint of development, and creating sustainable human settlements.

Old or new development?

Town planning is often associated with building new towns, garden cities, and with new developments on green-field sites. In spite of their apparent importance in planning mythology, much less than 5 per cent of the population of Britain has ever lived in New Towns. No new ones have been started by the government since the 1970s, and most of the existing ones have now been de-designated. There is much interest in creating eco-towns and model communities, but little has actually been constructed as yet. Much of the modern planner's work consists of dealing with already developed older sites in which a major objective may be to incorporate existing buildings into a proposed new scheme. On such sites it may be impossible to apply exact standards or apply precise blueprints. The planner's job is to seek to be flexible in respect of planning standards when negotiating with the developer in order to get the best solution possible within what is often a difficult situation. Emphasis is likely to be put upon retaining significant existing buildings and features where possible, rather than demolition and total clearance, because of the national importance of our historical heritage.

Governments have set targets for increasing the amount of new residential development to meet the needs of a growing and changing population (Allmendinger *et al.* 2000). For example, New Labour wanted to see 4 million new houses built by 2016 (Hall and Tewdwr-Jones 2010). But much of this development was to take place within existing urban areas on brown-field sites (that is previously used, and mainly derelict, industrial sites). The Coalition government has cut back on these targets, but still wants to see a growth in house-building, both to rent and to buy, not least to facilitate the free movement of labour especially in areas where would-be home-owners are priced out of the local residential property market.

Overall, planners are much more concerned with planning for existing towns and cities, with regener-

ation, refurbishment, conservation, sustainability and urban management, and with building upon derelict and infill sites, that is upon 'brown land'. New construction represents less than 3 per cent net of the total building stock each year and indeed even less in times of recession. However, much higher rates were recorded in some regions than others, for example, in the South East of England. Urban conservation and the preservation of historic buildings and areas has become a major preoccupation of town planning. Maintenance and refurbishment of existing stock is a major aspect of the construction industry. In the public sector there has been a dramatic decline in the building of council housing, most of the new-build social housing development being undertaken by housing associations.

Rural or urban?

A major factor in keeping development at bay is the modern town and country planning system which has sought to control development and was established under the 1947 Town and Country Planning Act. The emphasis in this book will be primarily urban, that is upon *town* planning, but rural issues will be explored too, along with environmental planning and sustainability. But, the full title of the subject remains as 'Town and Country Planning' as enshrined in the many Acts of Parliament of that name. The division between urban and rural may be seen to be rather old-fashioned as modern planning policy is concerned with creating sustainable environments which are affected by overarching global factors. Indeed nowadays there is a strong emphasis upon global issues, upon sustainability, global warming, climate change and other factors that overarch UK planning, but which have to be integrated into national policy-making and legislation.

Urban or regional or local?

A key issue over the years has been the level at which planning is undertaken. Whilst town and country planning has primarily been concerned with urban areas, it was soon realised that planners needed to take into account the wider context of the geographical and economic region in which the urban area in question was located. For example, planners have attempted to balance out development within the different regions of the UK and have been particularly concerned with overpopulation and congestion in the South, and economic decline and social deprivation in industrial areas in the North. Under the Labour government (1997–2010) importance was given to regional planning. Regional Spatial Strategies (RSS) were seen as the main policy level of plan-making (Amin and Thrift 1995) although community planning was also important. Subsequently under the Coalition government (Conservative–Liberal Democratic alliance) which came into power in May 2010, a greater emphasis was put upon a new localism, community issues and neighbourhood planning, with the Local Plan becoming the main level of planning under the 2011 Localism Act.

Present or future?

Planning by its very nature is concerned with policy-making and that involves attempting to predict what future need might be, and producing plans that may cover periods five or ten years ahead. In contrast, sometimes it seems politicians, and for that matter local residents, want instant change, and there have been many attempts over the years to speed up the planning system as if complex policy issues can be solved overnight. In reality, whatever the level of planning adopted, good planning takes time to come to fruition. The results of policies may take many years to manifest their true effect. One cannot realistically plan a local area, or make snap decisions, in isolation from the city as a whole as every area is but one piece in a larger jigsaw. Each local area is linked up to other areas by transport systems, and a range of overarching policy issues in respect of the environment, the economy, and social and cultural issues and considerations.

Admittedly there might be pressing local issues that need to be dealt with as soon as possible in respect of local sites and circumstances, such as decisions as to whether to build more housing in a specific location, and pressure from private developers to get on with a particular scheme, as delay costs money. But such decisions need to take into account higher-level city-wide considerations and longer-term planning objectives such as, for example, urban

containment and green-belt protection, or getting the right balance between jobs and houses across the region as a whole.

There is also considerable difference of opinion as to what should be done. Not all local residents have equal power to shape decisions as articulate middle-class groups who know how the system runs are likely to sway the planning process more adeptly than those from poorer districts. Furthermore, too much emphasis on the new localism, on local planning, community issues, and local residents' requirements, mocked in the press as 'duck-pond planning', may lead to a situation in which there are conflicting demands between different local areas and a lack of joined-up thinking.

Policies or processes?

Town planning is not primarily concerned with imposing an instant Master Plan on our cities; rather it is concerned with gradually reshaping and controlling development. Planning has become much more of a process, or a methodology, that is a tool of urban governance (Hill 2005; Haughton et al. 2009). Senior town planners, particularly in local government, are strategic managers whose skills are valued because their professional perspective enables them to take the broader view, to see the connections between a diverse range of issues and topics in order to initiate urban renewal and economic regeneration. Modern planners are more likely to work in multidisciplinary teams, liaising with other policy-makers from the fields of housing, economic development, cultural and social policy to fulfil higher-level governmental targets. For example, planners may work alongside other professionals on policy initiatives as diverse as urban regeneration, crime and design, employment, education, tourism, ecology, power station provision and transportation networks. As a result of these changes, planning can no longer be seen as a discrete, purely spatial activity (Low 1991; Dorey 2005).

People or property?

We must not forget that planning is for people (Broady 1968) (Photo 1.1) and that social considerations are as important as environmental factors. The

Photo 1.1   Planning is for all sorts of people

Part of the queue at the London Eye. Planning policy needs to take into account the needs of all sectors of the population, old and young, male and female, abled and disabled, car driver and pedestrian.

needs, wants and activities of the population are what generate the demand for development in the first place. Thus planning has a social component too, and planners need to be aware of the requirements of 'users of land' (that is the people) rather than simply focusing on the 'land uses' in isolation. In order to develop planning policy, it is important to be able to understand what people want and also to predict changing social and economic trends. As will be explained further in Chapter 8 on planning theory, planners need to be aware of the aspatial (non-physical) factors and processes (Foley 1964: 37) such as the economic, social and political forces that determine the spatial (physical) end product of the built environment. However, modern geographers might argue that all these forces and processes are inherently spatial too, and such debates continue.

It is important, as a general principle, to plan equally fairly for everyone. To return to the above definition of town planning (Keeble 1969) one must ask for whom is it important '*to secure the maximum*

level of economy, convenience and beauty'? Different members of the urban population do not have the same needs or requirements, and planners can only hope '*to please some of the people some of the time, rather than all of the people all of the time*'. Planning for the average man may lead to planning successfully for no one at all! It is important to take into account the needs of everyone in society, including women, ethnic minorities, all social classes, all age groups, and the disabled. But this is often not the case as clearly different groups have different agendas, and, for example, developers may be more concerned with getting the best return from a site, than worrying about such social considerations.

A blessing or a curse?

In spite of its achievements, many people are of the opinion that town planning policy has been ineffective and misdirected, and that more could have been achieved with better policy in town and countryside

(Gallent *et al.* 2008). Some take the view that town planning imposes unnecessary restrictions on the property market and on individual citizens' freedom, with little of benefit to show in return. Others consider the British planning system to be the best in the world and argue that without it Britain would long ago have been covered coast to coast in housing development to accommodate a disproportionately large population relative to land surface. This book will show that planning has had its successes, but will admit that there have also been some terrible disasters and mistakes made. But it is easy to be wise after the event.

But overall, governments have continued to retain the planning system, although Conservative governments tend to have a more negative view of planning than Labour ones, which are more enthusiastic about state control and thus planning. For example, the Conservative government (1979–97) attempted to speed up the planning system, but did not abolish it. The subsequent Labour government (1997–2010) sought to modify the objectives of planning towards their own agenda, but were also quite tolerant towards reducing state control on private enterprise and development. So political attitudes towards planning are quite complex and nuanced. Many private developers also support the need for town planning because it is seen as providing a framework, a level playing field, within which the private property market can operate. But they may question the objectives upon which planning is based, and the way it is administered. The Coalition (Conservative–Liberal Democrat) government (which came to power in 2010), in spite of its emphasis upon achieving change through a greater role for the private developer, has in many respects retained much of the previous government's commitment to sustainable development.

Natural or political?

The modern nature of towns and cities is not God-given, inevitable or natural, with just one obvious right answer. The fact we have running water in every house, sewerage, drainage, passable roads, parks, libraries, sports facilities, are all the result of political reform and state intervention, often achieved after years of campaigning. They are the result of centuries of decision-making by individual owners, developers, and government bodies. Although topography and geography do play a part, they do not absolutely determine development. The nature of towns and cities, to a considerable extent, is dependent on who has the greatest influence over policy, and thus who has the strongest voice. Let us explore further the important role of politics in shaping planning.

Planning is inevitably a highly political activity. Firstly, this is because it is concerned with land and property. Planning is concerned with the allocation of scarce resources (Allmendinger *et al.* 2000). It is inextricably linked to the prevailing economic system. Planning policy change is inevitably reflective of the booms and slumps which are an enduring characteristic of the property market and capitalism itself. Planners are not free agents: they are not operating in a vacuum but within a complex political situation at central and local government levels which reflect these societal forces (Simmie 1974). But, as Rydin has commented, town planning alone cannot externally control the market, as the forces involved are immense (Rydin 1998: 6; Rydin 2011). There is much talk of partnerships between the public and private sector. Indeed, whether planners are working for the public or the private sector of development, there are certain common requirements which have to be adhered to in order to make a scheme work, such as infrastructure and transport provision.

Secondly, planning is political as it has become a component of the agenda of national party politics and political ideology. Planning is a political process, informed by a range of ideologies (Young and Stevenson (eds) 2013). It has been scrutinised by those concerned with understanding capitalism, and class and power structures within society. Urban social theory, which influences social planning, is seldom neutral. It will be seen that Labour and Conservative interpretations of the role of planning have differed considerably. Social town planning has, in particular, been associated with the Left, for example in respect of the policies of the Greater London Council (GLC) which was at its height in the 1980s (GLC 1984) or as part of full blown East European state socialism. The Greater London Authority (GLA) replaced the GLC in 2000, but put more emphasis upon economic development and the needs of the private sector, relatively speaking. However, the GLA has continued to be concerned with social issues, but this has been manifest in more planning for equalities and minority groups, rather than traditional socialist concerns with social class issues (Reeves 2005; GLA 2010), although the situation is still evolving under the Conservative Boris Johnson as Mayor of London.

Thirdly, the planning process is political at the local urban area planning level, where community politics and grass roots activity thrives, and where individual personalities, especially councillors, exert influence over planning decisions. Planning attracts interest from people across the political spectrum, and some of the most radical challenges to planning have come from environmentalists who do not fit into the conventional right/left political divisions. Planners cannot develop policies as if politics does not exist, nor can they operate as if the private sector and property ownership rights do not exist. The powers of planning and the planners are always limited and constrained by the government's approach to planning at the national level, and also at the local level by the political activities and preferences of local councillors.

Why study planning?

Tackling a challenging but interesting subject

As can be seen from introductory observations, planning is a complex subject area, but one with many different specialisms within it, and one that can provide an interesting and useful career. In discussing the topic of why it is important to study planning, at the start it has to be said that there are broadly two types of students who study planning: those who want to, and those who do not. In the first category are those who have chosen to study the subject perhaps on a planning degree, or as a module within perhaps a geography degree. On the other hand there are those who have to study to planning as part of a property development, surveying, architecture or construction degree, who may see it as irrelevant to their career, or view the subject negatively as a block on property development and their future activities. Of course there are also those who

are quite undecided, or may never have come across the subject before and are willing to keep an open mind. Indeed such students may have an open mind about the topic of planning. Let us now discuss the reasons for studying planning (and thus hopefully reading this book) from the view point of first planning students and secondly non-planning students. This section may involve the reader in some healthy self-reflection on what they are trying to get out of their course and how they see planning.

Planning students

Some students are attracted to town planning because they have a vocation to leave the world a better place than they found it. Town planning, although categorised as one of the land-use professions, has much in common with the other welfare professions and may therefore attract a more socially motivated type of student. Planning is a discipline which has links across, particularly within local and central government agencies, to the realms of social policy, urban governance, economics and political science. Others, particularly mature students, might have experienced the problems of inner-city living and have specific changes in mind which they would like to bring about by becoming town planners. Others may have studied Geography at A level and they then look around for an alternative to a geography degree and settle on town planning. In contrast, some students have a very clear idea of what they want to do, and are interested in specific aspects of planning and development, such as sport, conservation, transport, housing. It is always worth checking the RTPI website for information on careers for students, and being a student member gives access to more useful information.

Once students begin to understand the subject, they may be eager to put forward their own solutions, saying enthusiastically in tutorial discussions, '*the government ought to do something*', as if it were just a matter of realising what was needed, without appreciating the problems and tortuous paths involved in getting policy accepted and implemented on the ground. Well-intentioned policies, motivated by the best of intentions, can lead to monumental disasters unless they are accompanied by a well-informed understanding of the nature and complexity of the problems and issues at which they are directed. Therefore in parallel with looking at the planning system, the changing characteristics of the built environment, cities and urban society will also be explored. This is because you cannot plan something if you do not understand what you are planning.

Non-planning students

Many students on construction, property, and built environment courses are required to study planning but they are unlikely to become planners themselves. Increasingly all sorts of property, construction and other built environment students will be undertaking shared modules alongside planning students and will need to have a familiarity with planning issues. Some of those who want careers associated with private-sector property development may arrive on the course with fixed, and rather negative, views of planning. It is hoped that this book will broaden their horizons and demonstrate the positive value of the subject. Even if readers do not necessarily agree with the objectives of planning policy, it is important to understand the planning system because nearly all types of property development require planning permission, so you cannot escape it!

Alternatively non-planning students want a quicker, more straightforward approach to planning teaching, which just emphasises the procedural aspects of getting planning permission. Some may become bored with lectures on planning theory, urban sociology and environmentalism. Those wishing to enter the private property sector may believe that their future property development decisions will be, relatively speaking, more straightforward than those of the planners, as they will not have to worry about all the social and environmental factors which make a planner's job difficult (Ratcliffe *et al.* 2009).

The opposite is often the case. It is easy to ride on the crest of a wave and make a good investment decision which reflects current trends. But bottoms can fall out of established markets, as occurred in the recession of the early 1990s and the banking crisis which was directly related to faults in the operation of the property market and especially the subprime market in the USA. Wiser people in the private sector look into the future to try to see what is going

to be the next property development opportunity coming on the horizon, such as the growing demand for retirement housing because of the growing numbers of elderly people. To do this effectively they need to draw on the same research sources, and employ the same fields of expertise and levels of understanding towards the urban situation as the planners. Many of the large firms of chartered surveyors have their own in-house teams of planning and market researchers, and there is a thriving Society of Property Researchers which draws much of its membership from the private sector.

Property markets tend to go in cycles with booms and slumps. Foolish is the society or government which bases its land-use strategy on this lottery. Also the fact that something is financially viable or profitable does not mean in itself that it is worthwhile or good for society. Social and economic needs are often at odds with each other. There is much talk of partnerships between the public and private sector. Indeed, whether planners are working for the public or the private sector of development, there are certain common requirements which have to be adhered to, to make a scheme work. Planners are often seen as umpires, referees, that balance the contesting demands of the public and private sectors in the process of development, and far from blocking development are seen by many developers as essential to the whole process (Klosterman 2003).

Both groups of professionals, public-sector planners and private-sector developers, are making development decisions in response to the same needs of human beings, although one group may have more of an eye to the financial viability of a scheme than the other. The private sector must not neglect social factors, for if people do not like a development they will vote with their feet and not buy it. But, equally, if the public sector does not take into account the economic feasibility of a scheme or policy the venture in question may fail. Whether planning is initiated in the public or the private sector (and it is increasingly the latter) the decision-makers still need to be aware of these wider social constraints. There is, therefore, a need for students, whether destined for the public or the private sector, to study the full range of social and economic factors that affect land use and development and the operation of the planning system.

As with students, so in the 'real world' different construction and built environment professionals tend to have different perceptions of the value of planning. There is a tendency, in the more commercially-orientated land-use professions such as surveying, for practitioners to have little patience with what they may see as the 'airy fairy' policy level of town planning which they may regard as time-consuming and over-ambitious, as they want to press ahead with the 'nitty gritty' of site development and layouts. When deciding on the merits of a particular scheme, town planners look at the wider context and consider the social, economic, environmental and political aspects, because their client is society, whilst surveyors tend to look at a particular site in relative isolation and consider how they can get the best financial return from it for their client. Many other professional groups are shaping the built environment too, from different perspectives. Housing managers may be primarily interested in the social and sociological aspects, or even socialist aspects, of urban development, seeing the social needs of the people rather than the built environment as the focus of their attention. But the surveyor and the housing manager are both likely to be more concerned with the details of site layout than with the city-wide, macro-level implications of their proposals. Architects and urban designers are also concerned with 'what is built' but are likely to have a more aesthetic, visual design perspective upon the nature of the buildings and the overall layout. Civil engineers, especially highways engineers, may be obsessed with technical responses to current problems, without addressing the wider implications of their policies. In contrast, urban designers and place-makers are more concerned with the needs of local residents, pedestrian safety and the visual quality of an area than with traffic engineering solutions. Likewise environmentalists, concerned with limiting the carbon footprint of car users, may insist on strict controls with little regard to the social effects of their policies where there is no alternative viable public transport system available. Cities are shaped by all these professional perspectives in a process of negotiation and consultation. Therefore when seeking to find out about town planning, particularly in the course of undertaking project work, it is always important to check the professional or academic allegiance of the person being quizzed, or of the author of the book being read, as views vary widely.

Contents

The book is divided into four parts. Part I seeks to introduce the scope and nature of planning and explain why it is important; Part II outlines the planning system; Part III investigates specific policy areas; and Part IV deals with the more social dimensions of planning.

Chapter 2 describes the organisation and operation of the planning system. It outlines the different levels of planning, including European Union, central government, regional and local government levels. Until recently the Regional Spatial Strategies and Local Development Frameworks constituted the main operational levels of plan-making, and are still germane to policy in many local authorities. But subsequent changes brought in by the Coalition government have led to greater emphasis being put upon localism and community planning, with the introduction of the new format of Local and Neighbourhood plans under the 2011 Localism Act. The organisation and content of the planning system at all levels is strongly affected by EU level directives and requirements (EC 2010), and in some cases global commitments, for example from the UN and UNESCO, entered into by the UK, such as on climate change and World Heritage Sites.

Chapter 3 deals with the main aspects of the development control system (that is development management) which is the process of granting or refusing planning permission. This is a complex and detailed area of planning, so the chapter seeks to give the reader the main principles without getting too bogged down. E-Supplement 4 gives an account of the process of property development and the role of the planners therein, which will also be of interest to non-planning students who intend to work in the other property and construction professions and need to understand how planning fits in with their world. It is recommended that Chapters 2 and 3 are read in sequence as a pair, which deals with the two main aspects of planning practice, that is planning policy and development management, respectively.

Figure 1.1   The realms of town and country planning

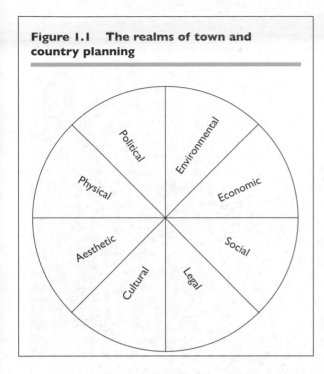

Part II recounts the Story of Planning from earliest times to the dawn of modern town planning in the twentieth century. We need to understand and appreciate the architectural heritage of the past in order to know how to plan for cities today. Chapter 4 covers the Ancient, Classical, Medieval, Renaissance, Georgian and Victorian periods. Chapter 5 describes the emergence of modern town planning, as a result of industrialisation, urbanisation and population growth, from the nineteenth century up until the first half of the twentieth century. It introduces the ideas and Founding Fathers of modern planning. These include Ebenezer Howard, the creator of the Garden City movement, and also Le Corbusier, the key proponent of the high-rise functionalist approach, and one of the main figures in the Continental and Internationalist approaches to architecture and planning. A key theme in these chapters is the evolution of city form and structure, and the implications for transport systems and housing provision. Each of the historical chapters contains a section on the parallel development of transport.

Chapter 6 charts the development of town planning in the second half of the twentieth century. It will put emphasis upon the post-war reconstruction period (1945–1960) because this was when the foundations of the modern statutory planning system and its principles were established. The chapter then outlines the subsequent development of planning under consecutive Conservative and Labour governments. For example, great emphasis was put upon planning under the Labour government of the 1960s, as a means of bringing about modernisation and promoting what Prime Minister Harold Wilson is said to have called '*the white heat of technology*'. But by the 1980s a more market-led approach to planning predominated within the thinking of the New Right, under the Thatcher and Major Conservative governments (Thornley 1991), which, arguably, has continuities with today's approach.

Chapter 7 takes the story of planning into the twenty-first century. There is a need to outline the state of play inherited, from the twentieth century, from the end of the Conservative administration under Thatcher and Major, to the policies of the New Labour government whose administration straddles the end of the last century and the advent of the Coalition government in the New Millennium. Subsequently, New Labour, which came into power in 1997, gradually developed its own approach to reshaping the planning system. Key New Labour policy areas are explained, and then current changes to the planning system introduced by the subsequent Coalition government (from 2010 onwards) are summarised which, arguably, draw from both previous Labour and Conservative governments' approaches to planning.

It is important to step back, and to look at the '*workings on the other side of the tapestry*' in order to understand the theories, beliefs, trends and ideas that have shaped and informed planners' decision-making, and their assumptions as to what is 'right' and 'wrong'. Therefore, Chapter 8 will provide an account of the main theories that have shaped modern planning from the post-war era to the present day. Planning has been influenced by a range of theoretical perspectives, originating in Britain, the USA and Continental Europe, and has undergone some quite startling paradigm shifts and pendulum swings. The extent to which planning theories have shaped planning policy and practice, and their strengths and, in retrospect, their weaknesses and blind spots will be discussed. Many find planning theory difficult, and

Photo 1.2   The modern city: Chicago

Many global cities include far more high-rise development that British ones, and also have a glamour and excitement which has not generally been a component of traditional English town planning. This is Cloud Gate by Anish Kapoor in the Millennium Park, Chicago who also designed the Orbit Tower in the London Olympic Park.

believe it to be too abstract, academic and non-practice related. But it is still a popular component of planning examinations! Beyond this it is vital to gain an appreciation of planning theory to be a credible and socially aware urban planner.

Part III, entitled The Scope of Modern Planning, takes the key policy areas identified in the story of planning as recounted in Part II, and expands them into chapters in their own right, with particular reference to present-day examples. So far much of the content has been urban-related, but the planning system is officially concerned with Town and Country Planning. Therefore, Chapter 9 will cover planning for rural areas and will first provide a brief historical account of the development of countryside planning and rural conservation, including the designation of large tracts of countryside as National Parks and Areas of Outstanding Natural Beauty (Gilg 1999). This chapter will thus lay the ground-

work for the sustainability themes developed in Chapter 10, and the changing policy agendas in respect of planning for the countryside.

Chapter 10 is concerned with the role of planning in promoting sustainable development and preventing climate change. The environmental agenda is a key driver at all levels of planning policy (UN 2009). One of the major concepts of twenty-first-century planning is sustainability, which in the UK has been interpreted to mean environmental protection in particular, even though the original Rio definition comprised environmental sustainability, social equality and economic development (that is Planet, People and Prosperity) (Brundtland 1987). At European Union (EU) level there have also been many new directives and requirements on the UK governments to introduce environmental measures such as EIA (Environmental Impact Assessment). At the global level, the UK is a signatory to a range of

Photo 1.3   People still waiting at the bus stop

Still the problems of urban transport have not been solved, especially for those without cars, who are dependent on public transport and for whom travel can be very challenging.

United Nations (UN) environmental treaties and initiatives such as the Millennium Development Goals (Leckie 2009). Global urbanisation is a relentless process, with over half the world's population now living in towns and cities. But the majority of urban dwellers are not living in the affluent areas of cities, or in fashionable districts surrounded by attractive architecture and public art (Photo 1.2) but rather in shanty towns and slums. The healthy cities movement is also an associated component of sustainability, promoted by the World Health Organization (WHO) (Barton and Tsourou 2006), and has also affected UK planning policy not least in relation to transport policy (thus also linking to Chapter 12). The impact on the UK planning systems of such UN level agreements, in relation to climate change, sustainability and equality, will be discussed (UN 1992).

Chapter 11 returns to urban issues, and is concerned with urban renewal and regeneration, and therefore with the revival of the social and economic fortunes of our towns and cities (Tallon 2013). One of the most significant changes to urban form in the last 20 years has been the regeneration of run-down inner-city areas, disused docklands and redundant industrial locations. The planning system has been central to many of these changes, both in terms of stimulating regeneration and in responding to market interest in such sites. This chapter describes these changes with reference to policy and delivery mechanisms, many of which flowed from the urban renaissance agenda championed by Lord Rogers' Urban Task Force in the late 1990s (Rogers 1999). It discusses the scale and nature of change that has occurred mainly in our towns and cities over the past ten years, through the economic boom and up to today's more difficult economic climate for development. The chapter concludes with a case study around the major development taking place on the east side of London, in respect of Thames Gateway, Cross Rail and the Olympic Park.

Chapter 12 on transport discusses the problems planners face in dealing with the continuing challenge of the inexorable growth in car ownership. The issues raised also have relevance to the sustainability agenda and to creating healthy cities, and thus to cutting carbon emissions and climate change. In the UK, for many years, planning policy sought to accommodate, even encourage, growth in car ownership and use and this approach was pursued by governments of all political persuasions. The chapter charts the growth of the pro-car transport system and considers the public transport alternatives available to the travelling public (Photo 1.3). As sustainable development has become of greater concern for government policy-makers, from the 1990s there has been a move away from the predict and provide roadbased policies of earlier years, which favoured ample parking space and motorway expansion, towards more sophisticated forms of traffic management, demand management and the promotion of alternatives to the private car. These aspects of transport policy and practice will be examined, particularly attempts to restrain car use, and the alternatives (public transport – rail, light rail and buses; walking, cycling, and so forth) will be explained. Additional details on the more technical aspects of transport planning and road design are to be found in E-Supplement 7.

Chapter 13 on urban design is concerned with a range of issues that contribute to the quality, functionality and appearance of the built environment. Cities are composed of buildings of all sorts of ages and types, both old and new, alongside each other. Therefore planners' concern with quality of place and the concept of 'making places' involves both conserving historic buildings and controlling new development whilst applying overarching urban design principles to both. This chapter will seek to provide a balance between planning for the old and the new. Increasingly two main factors are reshaping urban design and thus residential layout principles, moving away from the functionalist traffic engineering and uninspired housing layout principles of the past. Firstly there is a concern for creating sustainable settlements (Barton *et al.* 2010) and secondly a desire to create accessible inclusive design for all and (Burton and Mitchell 2006). Car-free solutions, and controversial 'shared streets' policies (in which cars and pedestrians mix), will also be discussed (Melia *et al.* 2010). Technical details on design layout may be found in E-Supplement 8.

Chapters 12 and 13 should be read as a pair, because they illustrate one of the main conflicts within planning as to how our cities should be designed. Transport planners, it appears, are still concerned with creating engineered solutions, which still take transport as their starting point (whether they are pro- or anti-car), and are concerned with enforcing national standards on road design and traffic management. In contrast urban designers, urban conservationists and many community-orientated social town planning groups are more concerned with place-making, with architectural design, housing layout, with the needs of human beings and with the visual and environmental quality of areas ... and so the battle continues.

Having presented the story of planning and identified and discussed the main aspects of modern policy and legislation, Part IV on Planning and People provides a deeper critique of the planning agenda, which is still, relatively speaking, predominantly concerned with physical land-use planning matters. Therefore, Part IV takes an alternative viewpoint and investigates the social effects of planning, drawing on urban sociology, community and user needs research, and the current diversity and equality agenda which has so challenged the status quo within local government planning departments. It also provides an opportunity to look 'under the bonnet' at the nature and influence of planning theory from a deeper academic perspective.

Chapter 14 provides an essential introductory, background chapter on what may broadly be termed the social aspects of planning, drawing on both urban sociology and social geography, and incorporating an overview of the key social theories, ideas and initiatives that have influenced planners. A summary will be given of the main components, particularly those that feature on planning courses, and which some readers may already be familiar with from A level Geography at school (albeit often in an over-simplified format), such as social ecology and the concentric zone theory. Topics covered will include the concept of community and the new towns, environmental determinism and crime, social ecology and urban structure. Many would argue that it is essential to incorporate the social perspective in order to achieve successful urban regeneration (Atkinson and Helms (eds) 2007; Panelli 2004). The Coalition government has put a great deal of emphasis upon neighbourhood planning and community involvement. But, as urban sociological studies have shown, neither of these concepts is straightforward, although they have been often used by planners in the past, with varying levels of sensitivity and success.

Chapter 15 investigates the importance of equality and diversity issues in planning. Whilst there is a considerable range of minority issues that affect planning (Reeves 2005, 2012), the theme of 'women and planning' will be used to illustrate the situation. This is because gender is one of the major overarching equality issues affecting the whole population, and also it is a field in which both planning policy and methodology is highly developed. Thus gender serves as an exemplar for mainstreaming other minority issues into planning policy and practice. Local planning authorities, along with all public and governmental bodies, now have a legal duty to assess the impact of their policies and procedures on the community and different minority groups. The various Equality Acts (now consolidated in the 2010 Equality Act) specify at least six minority characteristics, adding age, religion, disability, sexuality, but, curiously, not socio-economic group (class and social deprivation), which need to be taken into account in determining government policy, provision of public services and personnel matters.

The final chapter, Chapter 16, focuses the current and future nature of the planning profession itself, within the context of a discussion of the prospects of the wider built environment professions, whose decisions determine what is built and how towns and cities are planned. With the built environment professions, increased membership of women, ethnic minorities and people with disabilities (CIC 2009, 2010) will no doubt lead to alternative approaches to how cities are planned, and to new answers to the fundamental question of '*how do we want to live?*'. This chapter will also outline current Equality legislation that is impacting on professional practice, employment and membership issues. In the concluding section of the chapter, a plenary discussion will be given on the future of planning, and which aspects of the subject are likely to endure and predominate in the future, what issues remain unresolved and what new factors and theories are waiting to come onto the planning agenda.

For the tasks, further reading, additional photos and other resources comprising e-supplements for this chapter, please visit www.palgrave.com/companion/greed. For example, E-Supplement 1 gives details of government publications and legislation related to planning.

2 The Organisation of Planning

A game of two halves

Chapters 2 and 3 give an account of the two aspects of the planning system and should be read together. This chapter explains the development plan system and the different levels of planning policy-making (also known as forward planning). The next chapter explains the development control system (also known as development management and development consent), through which plans are implemented. Chapter 3 will also outline the process of property development which will help put planning in the wider context of the roles of the other built environment professions working in property development and construction.

The levels and scope of plan-making

In this chapter, the different levels of planning will be discussed (as shown in Figure 2.1). First we will look at international and European Union planning protocols which affect the UK. Then we will look at the UK situation in respect of the central government, national, regional, sub-regional and local levels of planning. Up until around 20 years ago one planning system covered the whole of the UK. Constitutional changes within the United Kingdom have created separate planning systems and different powers for Scotland, Wales and Northern Ireland. London may also be treated separately in many respects, the Greater London Authority (GLA) having a significantly different planning system from the rest of the UK. We will make observations and comparisons between the English system and what is happening in the other UK countries as appropriate.

In seeking to explain the planning system, we need to describe several consecutive development plan systems, including Structure Plans; Regional Spatial Strategies and Local Development Frameworks; as well as the current Local Plans and Neighbourhood Plans system. This is because there are still some local planning authorities using each of these, and approved policies from these earlier plans are accepted as legally binding, in the absence of a more up-to-date plan. Therefore information covering these previous forms of Development Plan is to be found in E-Supplement 3 on the book's website, so that this chapter can concentrate on the development plan system introduced by the 2011 Localism Act which will eventually be adopted by all local authority planning departments.

Planning has undergone some major changes in the last ten years. In 2011 the planning system was significantly revised by the Coalition government, under the Localism Act. We are still living in the overlap and many local planning authorities are in transition and still operating under the LDF (Local Development Framework) development plan format introduced by New Labour under the 2004 Planning and Compulsory Purchase Act whilst they reconfigure their Development Plan Documents (DPDs) to the new requirements.

The reader is reminded to refer to the List of Acronyms as there are very many of them in this chapter. The planning systems in Scotland, Wales and Northern Ireland are outlined in E-Supplement 2.

International levels of planning

Planning at the global level

There is no one overarching planning body nor is there a single planning document at the global scale; however there are numerous treaties and agreements

Figure 2.1   The levels of planning

INTERNATIONAL LEVEL
United Nations, UNESCO, OECD

EUROPEAN COMMISSION
Directorates-General

CENTRAL GOVERNMENT
DCLG 'Communities', Department of Communities and Local Government
Also Department for Transport, DCMS, DEFRA, DECC, DCMS, BIS

Secretary of State (a politician, MP)
Advised by planning professionals (civil servants)
Gives overall policy guidance
Overview of and Delegation to PINS

Planning Inspectorate (PINS)
Deals with appeals and Planning Inquiries
National Infrastructure Directorate
Approval of Development Plans

REGIONAL LEVEL
English Regional Planning Abolished
But Local Enterprise Panels (LEPs) introduced by Coalition
Scottish Parliament, National Assembly of Wales, Greater London Authority, Northern Ireland Assembly

LOCAL GOVERNMENT
Decisions are made by the politicians (elected councillors on council's planning committee) as advised by the professionals (planners who are employed as local government officers). Two types of development plan system are in existence, LDF (Local Development Framework, and Coalition's new Local Plan system; plus remaining Unitary Plans and some residual Structure Plan authorities and around 100 with no approved plan.

Local Development Framework	**New Local Plans**
Undertaken by Unitary Authority	District level plan
Core Strategy plus	Incorporates most of LDF
Folder of other plans	Neighbourhood Plans
Area Action Plans	Optional Parish Plans
(Previously had Regional Level RSSes)	No regional level

No county planning level unless county is now a unitary authority
Metropolitan districts abolished but GLA still produces its London Plan

RANGE OF AD HOC BODIES WITH PLANNING POWERS
Including: Urban Development Corporations, National Park Boards, Natural England, English Partnerships,
English Heritage, Social Exclusion Unit, National Infrastructure Directorate

---

at this level which have an impact on planning in the UK. The UK has signed up to many of these treaties, as a committed member of the United Nations (UN). Originally set up in 1945, the UN exists to promote peace and cooperation between all nations and to promote social progress and better living standards around the world, and particularly in developing countries. Since the year 2000 the UN has been working towards implementing eight Millennium Development Goals (MDGs) by 2015, and is extending the programme through the establishment of UN Sustainable Development Goals (SDGs). As well as being concerned with health, education, poverty and gender equality, the goals have implications for planning in respect of environmental sustainability and healthy cities. The UK is also a signatory of various international agreements on sustainability, such the Rio Declaration on the Environment (UN 1992a) and the Kyoto Treaty on Climate Change (1997) which ran until 2012. These were both foundational documents which are still being implemented across the world, and have had a considerable impact on UK planning policy and practice (see Chapter 10 on sustainability for further details). Post-Kyoto a series of international negotiations on limiting greenhouse gas emissions have been under way, for example Rio + 20 which has confirmed future commitment to sustainability in formulating the SDGs. However, global urbanisation continues apace, particularly in the Far East and many issues such as pollution, increased car ownership and control on development need to be addressed in this period of dynamic growth (Photo 2.1). By comparison many Western countries have long included within their planning system a

commitment to the provision and protection of open space within cities (Photo 2.2).

In 2012 there were 193 member states of the United Nations, including the UK. The governing body of the UN is the General Assembly; there is also a Security Council and the Secretary-General is a key figure in world affairs. Much of the work of the UN is carried out through a number of agencies, funds and programmes. Of particular relevance to planning are the United Nations Environment Programme (UNEP) and the United Nations Human Settlements Programme (UN-HABITAT). As well as developing policy and carrying out valuable work around the world, these agencies undertake research on a range of topics and produce useful reports of interest to anyone with a concern for sustainability or the management of environmental and urban problems in the developing world.

Photo 2.1   Shanghai city master plan model

All over the world with increased urbanisation, development plans are being produced, especially in China, for example in Shanghai, where there is a permanent planning exhibition for the public with models of the future city.

Photo 2.2   Urban open space gain, New York

The City Planning Commission requires that this open space area be provided for the benefit of the public.

Many local planning authorities allocate land for public open space, urban parks and leisure even within busy cities, often in agreement with developers as part of the development process.

UNESCO (United Nations Educational, Scientific and Cultural Organization) is one agency of the UN that is worth examining in a bit more detail to demonstrate how policy-making at this level can have a real impact on planning at the very local level. In 1972 UNESCO agreed the World Heritage Convention, which the UK became a party to in 1984. All states that sign up to the Convention agree to identify and nominate sites to be considered for inclusion on the World Heritage List (this process is known as inscription). Once they have obtained this status they are known as World Heritage Sites (WHS) and the member state has to

demonstrate how these sites will be protected and managed, and to regularly report on their condition. In 2009 there were 890 sites in 148 countries on the list, 28 of which were in the UK (UNESCO 2009).

World Heritage Sites can be either cultural (including built heritage) or natural sites, or a combination of the two. Cultural sites in the UK include world famous places such as Stonehenge and Hadrian's Wall, and natural sites include the Jurassic Coast of parts of Devon and Dorset and the Giant's Causeway in Northern Ireland. Planning policy at the national and local level will give the highest priority to protecting and preserving such sites, but where it becomes a little more blurred and even contentious is where the World Heritage Site status applies to part of a city, such as the historic centre and docks of Liverpool or the Old and New Towns of Edinburgh, or to a whole city as is the case with Bath. Here proposals for new urban development often come into conflict with the World Heritage Site designation and a careful balance often has to be struck to enable change to take place in a way that does not compromise the integrity of the WHS.

There are numerous other examples of policies and treaties that filter down through the many layers of governance from the UN to the local planning authority and which have to be taken into account when drawing up Local Plans and policies and in making development decisions (Amin and Thrift (eds) 1995). There is also a range of other international bodies which are concerned with planning such as the OECD based in Paris. Sometimes these place requirements on the local level that seem onerous or even unnecessary. What has to be remembered is that the government has signed the country up to these agreements and the greater good should not be lost sight of, as often happens, particularly with issues relating to the European Union, which we shall examine next.

Planning at the European level

As part of the European Union (EU), the UK planning systems are all subject to various policy directions emanating from Brussels (Devereaux 1992; Morphet 2013). EU policy directives have an important role in shaping and determining UK planning policy and legislation especially in respect of environmental controls, equality and community policy, sustainability and regional policy, as will be explained further in the various topic chapters.

The European Union has its origins in the European Coal and Steel Community which was established in 1951 as a means of encouraging economic cooperation and preventing any more wars between European countries. In 1957 the Treaty of Rome was signed by six countries (Belgium, France, Germany, Italy, Luxembourg and the Netherlands) and this established the EEC (European Economic Community), often referred to as the Common Market. The UK joined in 1973

along with Denmark and the Republic of Ireland. Since then many more countries have joined what is now the European Union (EU) and in 2012 there were 27 member states, including the UK, with more on the way.

The organisation of the EU is complex. Further information on planning, and every other subject imaginable, can be found on the EU's official website http://europa.eu/index_en.htm. The main points to note are as follows. The governance of the EU is split between the European Parliament (which is directly elected every five years), the European Council (which is made up of the Heads of State, such as the UK's Prime Minister), the Council of the EU (which is made up of Ministers from each member state with particular responsibilities, such as environment or transport), and the European Commission (made up of Commissioners, one being appointed by each member state to serve a five-year term of office). All these institutions work together in various ways to pass European laws and directives, to allocate the EU's substantial budget and to represent the interests of the EU as a whole and of all its 495 million citizens.

Each Commissioner heads up a Directorate General (or DG) and these are the equivalent to UK ministries, each with its own civil service staff responsible for advising on the development and implementation of policy. There are a number of DGs but the main ones with an impact on planning matters include the ones on Environment, Climate Action, Agriculture and Rural Development, Energy, Mobility and Transport, Equalities, and Regional Policy. DG Environment exists to protect, preserve and improve Europe's natural environment and to ensure that member states are properly applying EU environmental laws. In terms of trying to preserve nature and biodiversity there is a network of protected areas, known as Natura 2000. This network includes areas protected under the 1979 Wild Birds Directive and the 1992 Habitats Directive. Such designations have to be reflected in Local Plans and policies and development is strictly controlled in such areas.

EU regional policy also has a significant impact on certain parts of the UK. The broad intention of the policy is to reduce disparities in economic performance across the EU. This is known as cohesion and the EU directs significant levels of funding into regions and countries that are performing less well than the EU average. There are a number of funds that areas within the UK have had access to over the years, and the main beneficiaries in the 2007–12 funding period were North and West Wales and the Welsh Valleys, Cornwall, and, to a lesser extent, the Highlands and Islands of Scotland. These funds have been used to improve infrastructure such as roads and railways, to help diversify local economies and support growing sectors such as tourism, and to help invest in innovation. Some urban areas are eligible for funds to help support training programmes, particularly for groups that often find it difficult to find employment, such as the long-term unemployed, certain ethnic minorities and women. Funding is also provided to improve cooperation between parts of the EU with common interests and frontiers, known as INTERREG (which stands for the European Community Initiative for Trans-National Policy and is a translation not an acronym). As such, EU funds, which have to be matched locally, provide an important means of implementing Local Plans and policies in those areas eligible. EU Structural Funding has been distributed through INTERREG in three phases so far. For example, economically and socially deprived parts of the UK, such as South Wales and the North East, have received funding under Objective One and Objective Two funding, and currently a third Objective phase is being rolled out.

Various EU directives have an impact on the local authority planning system, for example as a result of Directives 85/337 and 97/11 all local planning authorities have to carry out Environmental Impact Assessments (EIAs) of their plans and policy decisions, and also on major development proposals and those that might affect a designated site (such as a Natura 2000 wildlife site) before they are approved. EIAs were first integrated into UK planning law under the 1990 Environmental Protection Act, and are explained in *The Good Practice Guide on Environmental Assessment of Development Plans* (DoE 1993a). The EIA was updated under the 2011 Town and Country Planning (Environmental Impact Assessment) Regulations (as explained further in Chapter 3, and Chapter 9 on planning for sustainability). This ties in with changes to the planning

system under the 2011 Localism Act, as both Neighbourhood Plans and major planning applications require SA (Sustainability Appraisal) and also SEA (Strategic Environmental Assessment).

Therefore the EU influences UK planning in a number of ways, but it is important to note that the various EU treaties and laws do not give actual spatial planning powers and competencies to the EU. These are seen as being more appropriate to the member states and local government, putting into practice the principle of subsidiarity. There is therefore no European-wide spatial plan, but there is something less directive which is known as the ESDP (European Spatial Development Perspective) (Gripaios 2005). Agreed in 1999, the ESPD sets out a number of common objectives for the balanced and sustainable future development of the territory of EU (CEC 1999).

The ESPD has promoted the concept of polycentric development; that is of towns and cities building on their specialisms in certain economic sectors and cooperating with each other in a way that would strengthen the economy of the wider region. ESPD objectives include promoting economic and social cohesion and equality, and ensuring spatial development occurs in a balanced and sustainable manner. The ESPD has identified four key policy areas, namely, urban development, rural areas, transport, and natural and cultural heritage. EU funding is distributed in the light of policy initiatives, and for example the INTERREG funding programme has tried to support the application of the ESDP and it is sometimes referred to in the policy context section of a number of UK plans (Nadin *et al.* 2010).

Regions, as defined for EU purposes, may span several countries, and can be defined on a range of overlapping criteria. For example the EU identified Eight Super-Regions including the Alpine Regions, the Central Mediterranean and the Atlantic Arc which includes part of the South West of England, Brittany in France, and part of the Republic of Ireland. One country can belong to more than one region, for example parts of France belong to five such regions, including Brittany in the Atlantic Arc, Paris in the Central Capitals region and other parts falling into both Alpine and Mediterranean regions. This is all incredibly complicated but blocking countries into these categories on the basis of shared geographical and developmental characteristics has been the basis of spatial planning at EU level. The situation is still evolving, and categories and boundaries are being rethought, as a result of the expansion of the EU to cover East European countries.

The national level of planning

The parliamentary context

The population of the UK in 2011 was around 63.2 million and growing. The country is governed by Parliament, which is made up of the elected House of Commons and the appointed House of Lords. In 2012 there were 650 elected Members of Parliament (MPs). The largest party or parties in the House of Commons form the government, who chose the Prime Minster, who in turn chooses the Cabinet. Each cabinet minister usually has responsibility for a government department and its functions and policy. The Secretary of State who heads the DCLG (Department for Communities and Local Government), and is thus the main 'minister' for the environment, has overall responsibility for shaping and guiding national planning policy, and has the final say on individual controversial planning decisions. The Secretary is advised by civil servants along with professionally qualified staff including town planners, surveyors, architects, environmental specialists and housing strategists. The Secretary of State does not have to accept their advice if it is not politically acceptable to the government. Professional town planners working in the public sector, in local planning authorities, are not the final decision-makers either. They are employees of the government, their statutory role being that of advisers to their political masters. This division of roles and powers between civil servants and politicians is central to the UK governmental system, with the former holding the expert knowledge and the latter having decision-making powers. Policy development and legislative change is further supported by a range of research undertaken both within the DCLG itself, and increasingly contracted out to academics, specialists, and planning consultancies with appropriate expertise.

Central government

The organisation of the planning system is complex. The main central government department has undergone many name changes but its functions have remained, relatively speaking, fairly continuous. Since 2006 the main department responsible for planning has been known as the Department for Communities and Local Government (DCLG), sometimes abbreviated to CLG or simply 'Communities'. Transportation planning is currently administered separately by the Department for Transport (DfT).

Under New Labour (1997–2010) a series of new departments was created which held within their remit functions relevant to planning. These included ones concerned with the natural environment including DEFRA (Department for Environment, Food and Rural Affairs) (2001 to present) and subsequently DECC (Department for Energy and Climate Change) (from 2008). DEFRA, the Department for Environment, Food and Rural Affairs, was a newer version of the old Ministry of Agriculture, Fisheries and Food (MAFF), incorporating the Food Standards Agency (FSA) concerned with food safety from 'farm to fork'. DEFRA has a major influence on the nature of the countryside, and its role needs to be linked to the planners' parallel role in seeking to conserve the landscape and achieve environmental sustainability, and the needs of the general public as consumers. (But we are all meant to be united by emphasis upon sustainability, environmental policy and conservation of the countryside and wildlife.) Concern was also raised about the coast, and indeed our offshore marine heritage. For example the 2009 Marine and Coastal Access Act raised the importance of marine conservation planning, and now Marine Conservation Zones (MCZ) are being designated; this was echoed in Scotland under the Scottish (Marine) Act 2010.

Whilst this sums up the present system, it is important to know a little about what went before (see E-Supplement 3). Prior to 1997 the Department of the Environment (DoE) was responsible for planning. When New Labour first came to power (1997) the Department of the Environment, Transport and the Regions (DETR), was created as the main central government department responsible for town planning, combining the old Department of the Environment (DoE) and the Department of Transport (DoT). This arrangement sought to relate more closely national policy-making on land use with transport. In 2001–2, the DETR was renamed the Department for Transport, Local Government and the Regions (DTLR).

Subsequently, up until 2006, the DTLR became the Office of the Deputy Prime Minister (ODPM), a title which gave little indication of its functions. John Prescott, as Deputy Prime Minister, under Tony Blair, took on a more direct ministerial responsibility for environmental policy, including planning, housing and transport. He sought to promote a more sustainable and joined-up approach to dealing with the natural and built environment (DTLR 2001a; Prescott 2009). This was replaced by the Department for Communities and Local Government (DCLG) from 2006 to the present day. Meanwhile, transport was uncoupled and is administered by a new Department for Transport (DfT). Subsequently under New Labour a series of other new departments were created which included in their remit functions relevant to planning. The Coalition has not substantially altered these departments or their names as yet.

The Ministry of Defence (MoD), although not a civilian planning authority, also has a major effect on the nature of settlement patterns. It has rights over vast areas of land used for training. It is not subject to the normal planning control for its own activities, and may, for example, build service housing estates in the countryside without going through normal planning procedures. Whilst in the past MoD sites were unlikely to be shown on development plans for security reasons (as in Wiltshire, where they comprise 10 per cent of the land surface), with the development of Google Earth, GIS and extensive satellite mapping of the UK, it is possible to 'see everything everywhere'. Likewise, because of such transparency and open government initiatives, planning departments and other land-use related government organisations are under even more scrutiny and pressure from community groups and environmentalists.

The DCMS (Department for Culture, Media and Sport) has a wide ambit including urban conservation, and incorporating within its structure English Heritage (EH) responsible for the listing of buildings, and the Historic Buildings and Monuments Commission for England. The Department is responsible for policy on tourism, urban cultural issues and sport, liaising for example with the ODC (Olympic Delivery Committee), LOCOG (London Organising Committee for the Olympic Games) and subsequent Olympic Legacy programme bodies. The Department is therefore concerned with urban design issues both in relation to historic and new developments, and, for example, public art and prestige schemes, perhaps imitating the French enthusiasm for 'grands projets' (Greed and Roberts (eds) 1998).

The DCLG's role in shaping built environment policy also had to be reconciled with the increasing role of the Treasury in influencing economic planning policy. There is also the Department of Business, Innovation and Science (DBIS) (often referred to as the Biz). The DBIS is the successor to the Department of Trade and Industry (DTI) and is responsible for commercial and business-related policies. The New Labour government under Blair (1997–2010) was characterised by the creation of a plethora of new initiatives, taskforces, and policy focus groups (Tallon 2013) targeting policy on urban regeneration, social exclusion, employment, environment and the inner city, which arguably weakened the central steer of the responsible government departments.

Functions of the DCLG

The Department of Communities and Local Government (DCLG), which is also often referred to simply as 'Communities' on government websites, is an overarching department within which many other aspects of policy-making for the built environment are carried out – beyond 'just' planning – such as matters related to housing, transportation, building and construction, inner cities, environmental health, conservation and historic buildings, urban regeneration, energy, environmental issues and many other policy areas. The situation is confusing as some of the topics and policies are also administered in part by other government departments and ministries, such as aspects of nature conservancy, road traffic, urban conservation and scientific matters related to the environment.

The DCLG is not responsible for producing development plans: there is no National Plan for the United Kingdom, nor is there one for England. But both Wales and Scotland have produced such national-level plans. Incidentally, Scotland is interesting in that it is an example of National Planning, but it also retains an emphasis upon regional planning, not least because of the considerable differences between the central urban corridor, which contains Glasgow and Edinburgh, and the underpopulated, primarily agricultural region of the Highlands and Islands. Under the Coalition this regional is administered by Highlands and Islands Enterprise. Whilst Wales does not have a secondary regional level of government it is strong on city region planning, for example in respect of the Cardiff region (Sheppard and Smith 2013).

Why have governments of all political persuasions failed to develop such a national planning strategy for England, as most other European countries have done? From a planning point of view, it could be argued that plan-making should ideally take place at every appropriate level: i.e. the international, the national, the regional, the sub-regional/city-region, the city, the town, the district and the neighbourhood or village, and even the street. Ideally, plan-making at each level would take into account the needs, problems and responses identified at all of the other levels: this is known as the vertical integration of policy. In reality, the extent to which planning can do this is determined by the way in which the structure of government is organised, and this differs from country to country. Some countries have many tiers of elected government with planning and other powers spread between the different levels. In the UK, until recently, government was heavily centralised and policy-making was very much top-down in nature. In other countries, such as Switzerland and the Netherlands, much more power resides at a local township level and is more bottom-up in nature. Many countries take an approach that seeks to make decisions at the most appropriate level of government, but guided by the principle that wherever possible this should be as near to the local level as possible: this is known as the principle of subsidiarity. Other European countries such as Germany have developed extensive protocols to ensure that

when plans are made they are negotiated and agreed with the levels above and below, creating a more cohesive system (Nadin *et al.* 2010).

In England, as against Wales and Scotland, or for that matter the Netherlands, there seems to be a fear of having a National Plan. Perhaps English politicians have been worried about the reaction that such a plan might generate; it is much easier in political terms to let the local planning authorities take the blame for what are often viewed as unpopular decisions in terms of identifying areas for growth and new development. To draw attention to this policy void, the Royal Town Planning Institute (RTPI) has launched a new initiative entitled www.mapforengland.co.uk. This is not a statutory government map, but it is produced by the professional body of the RTPI, to which most practising planners belong. The map is like a big jigsaw of the development plans and key policy designations of all the different planning authorities, comprising key planning documents and policy statements from each local planning authority as well as actual plans. It is hoped that it will contribute to achieving the requirement for greater cooperation between neighbouring local planning authorities introduced by the Coalition government in 2011. It will enable chief planning officers in adjacent administrative areas to work together better in developing shared policies and in avoiding cross-boundary policy conflicts.

Although central government does not produce an actual National Plan, it has an important role in overseeing policy and plans produced by local government planning authorities, and giving policy guidance and leadership on spatial and environmental matters of national concern. The Secretary of State produces policy guidelines at national level to advise local authority plan-making. The Secretary of State carries out consultations with the local authority planners, and with relevant professional and voluntary bodies in order to set policy guidelines. The rules governing planning decisions cannot be reduced to questions of road widths or precise land-use zonings, but are embodied in a range of strategic policy documents which are subject to interpretation. Central government has a major role in setting policy guidelines and approving plans, but it is the local authority level of counties and districts which constitutes the main plan-making level. Different governments choose to exercise a greater or lesser degree of control over the local planning authorities.

The Secretary of State is no longer directly responsible for approving Local Plans, as previously was the case. Instead the Planning Inspectorate (PINS) now has the responsibility for checking all local planning authority development plans before approval to ensure a degree of consistency and conformity with national policies and guidelines. PINS does not make policy (in theory at least!) but employs a cadre of planning inspectors to preside over the examination in public of the plan. This is an important stage in the process of approving new development plans which allows objectors and other interested parties to give their views before the plan is approved. You can access the Planning Inspectorate Guidance documents at www.planning-inspectorate.gov.uk and also you can get there through the Planning Portal. PINS will be discussed further in the next chapter in relation to planning applications.

In order to produce planning guidance the Secretary of State draws upon the advice of the DCLG's professional staff as to the objectives, priorities and required approaches to current land-use planning issues. These policies are embodied in government White Papers, circulars, consultation papers, guidance notes and directives. Planning Policy Guidance Notes (PPGs) and subsequently Planning Policy Statements (PPSs) have been produced since the late 1980s, gradually taking over from circulars and White Papers as the main basis of planning policy direction. For many years, they covered issues of national interest and taken collectively they provided an important expression of government policy that needed to be reflected in local level plans and planning decisions, and were often quoted in planning appeals.

Current national planning guidance

A major change took place to national planning guidance in 2011 (DCLG 2011a). The incoming Coalition government decided that planning had become too slow, centralised and complicated and undertook radical restructuring (Cabinet Office 2010). Nearly all the previous PPGs and PPSs were abolished, and the 5000 pages of guidance they had

constituted together was replaced by just one 59-page document entitled the National Planning Policy Framework (NPPF). In 2011 a draft version had been produced which was amended in the light of a very high level of criticism of its contents. Many saw the document as being too heavily influenced by private-sector, property development interests, providing a licence to develop basically anywhere in the countryside and on the green belts. A huge campaign was launched by the CPRE (Campaign to Protect Rural England), by the Town and Country Planning Association and many local environmental groups, with the RTPI questioning the government on the proposed changes. The final NPPF of March 2012 was a considerable improvement on previous drafts and it has sought to clarify many of the ambiguous statements that were already being pounced on by barristers specialising in planning law, and by would-be developers who imagined that local authorities' development control powers would now be weakened.

In comparison, in Scotland, as at 2013, a new version of their National Planning Framework (NPF3) (Scottish Government 2013) was produced, which draws in part on the English NPPF model, but it should be remembered that they already have a strong national level of planning to build upon.

As a result of these changes, most of the PPSs have been cancelled. Just a few remain, mainly on environmental matters such as waste, water and some mining policy issues (for example PPS10 on waste management is still in force). Planning lawyers have argued that some of the cancelled PPSs may still be admissible in courts of law as material considerations (legally valid factors), and that they should constitute an appendix to the main NPPF.

New planning guidance

A series of technical explanatory guidance notes has begun to be produced to clarify what the NPPF really means (e.g. the ones on Flooding and Minerals, March 2012) and no doubt this trend will grow given the ambiguity of some of the statements in the NPPF. Subsequently, the Coalition has been attempting to cut by half the number of other planning documents, which comprise around 7000 pages of material dating back to the 1960s (Taylor 2012).

After cancelling so much planning guidance and replacing it all with one single document, by 2013 the Coalition had backtracked somewhat in setting up a framework of National Planning Practice Guidance, which is meant to aid planners in applying National Planning Policy Guidance. This practice guidance is being delivered mainly through the web, in a revised section of the planning portal website at http://planningguidance.planningportal. gov.uk/. The topics so far bear a close resemblance to the substance of the old PPGs and PPSs. Topics covered are generally framed as policy aspirations, and cover the economy, town centres, rural areas, green belt protection, sustainable transport, housing quality, urban design, urban conservation, minerals, flooding, climate change, but also policy-making and decision-making methods in planning.

Planning for projects of national significance

There are some development projects that the government considers too important and urgent to be held up by having to go through the normal local planning application procedures. The 2008 Planning [Reform] Act established the Infrastructure Planning Commission (IPC) to try to speed up the planning process and granting of planning consent on infrastructural projects of national significance. Such projects previously had to go through lengthy public inquiries, such as the very protracted timescale taken to get the Terminal 5 development approved at Heathrow airport, and often encountered strong local opposition for instance to proposals for the construction of a new nuclear power station (BERR 2008; DTI 2007). The Commission's role was taken over by the Major Infrastructure Policy Unit within the Planning Inspectorate in May 2012 and this unit has now been renamed the National Infrastructure Directorate. It deals with applications for all major national infrastructure projects such as large wind farms, power stations, power transmission lines, new rail routes (for example the High Speed Two (HS2), the proposed new rail track from Birmingham to London (HS1 is the Eurostar) along with ports, airports and major roads in England and Wales.

In determining applications for such projects regard must be taken of the relevant National Policy Statement (NPS). Each NPS has to be consulted on and is ultimately approved by the relevant Secretary of State. The government's guidance takes the form of 12 National Policy Statements, covering issues such as energy policy; renewable energy; fossil fuels; oil and gas supply and storage; electricity networks; nuclear power; ports; infrastructure and transport networks (including rail and roads); aviation; water supply; hazardous waste and waste water treatment.

The role of special government bodies

As well as, and sometimes quite separate from, the main central and local government structure of town planning, there are many other governmental bodies that administer various other aspects of town and country planning. There has been a tradition in this country of setting up special government bodies to deal with a particular problem or policy as and when it is needed, often to be disbanded at a later date – namely the *ad hoc* body. (*Ad hoc* means literally 'to this', i.e. 'for this purpose' as a one off.) Many aspects of British town planning are administered through such bodies. For example, the New Towns were collectively administered by the New Towns Commission, and individually planned by a Development Corporation for each town. These development corporations were intended to be completely separate from the local authority administration of the area in which they were located, in order to concentrate resources and speed up development, without the problem of being slowed down by existing local government bureaucracy. Each Development Corporation was intended to have a life of 30 years, by which time it was assumed that the New Town would be thoroughly established and could then be 'handed back' to the local authority, and the Development Corporation would be disbanded, as has happened in many instances. A similar model was followed in the case of Urban Development Corporations established to plan and administer the development of special urban regeneration areas within the inner city, for example in the London Docklands, first introduced under the Conservatives in the 1980s (see Chapter 11 on regeneration). The Coalition government has created a second wave of Enterprise Zones and UDCs so it's back to the past again.

Governments often require such *ad hoc* bodies to bring about change, and many of these can be described as QUANGOs, although Labour governments tend to favour them more than the Conservatives. A QUANGO is a quasi-autonomous non-governmental organisation, that is the term used to describe any of the numerous government sponsored agencies or authorities with independent powers. For example, New Labour created, amongst other things, English Partnerships, the Social Exclusion Unit, the Urban Taskforce (Rogers 1999) and CABE (Commission for Architecture and the Built Environment). The Coalition government carried out an extensive review of such bodies shortly after being elected and many were scrapped or merged with other bodies or government departments. For example CABE became a department within the Design Council.

It is important to note that as well as local authorities the National Parks are also designated as local planning authorities in England, Scotland and Wales. Each National Park Authority has plan-making and development control powers, with each Authority having a board made up of elected councillors drawn from the National Park area and other representatives nominated by key organisations, such as the National Trust or local landowners. Each National Park Authority has a small staff who are responsible for overseeing the management of the park, and also a small planning team who are responsible for producing plans for the park and providing the system of development control/management. Under the Coalition, greater emphasis has been put upon National Parks cooperating on policy-making with the local planning authorities in whose area they are located (see Chapter 10 on rural planning).

There is also a range of non-governmental organisations (NGOs), which may appear to be 'official', but are separate from government. For example, the Town and Country Planning Association (TCPA) is a voluntary body, whilst the Royal Town Planning Institute (RTPI) is the main professional planning body. The National Trust, which has vast land holdings, and innumerable conservation, community and environmental groups are keen to influence planning but are not government bodies. Rural bodies concerned with planning policy (both pro and anti) include the National Farmers Union (NFU), Friends of the Earth, the Country Landowners Association (CLA), the Countryside Alliance, and the CPRE, the latter having a major role in campaigning to modify the NPPF. However, it is generally considered that consumer and community groups are underrepresented in the planning decision-making process and that there is an underrepresentation of women and minorities too (cf. Part IV on social aspects of planning).

The regional planning level

As will be explained in Part II (on the history of planning), varying amounts of emphasis have been put upon the regional level of planning over the years, as an intermediary tier between central government and the local government level which has traditionally been the main level of development-plan creation and development-control operation. Regional planning has mainly been favoured by Labour governments, especially in the post-war reconstruction period, possibly because of its tradition of support from the Northern industrial working class areas and their Trade Unions. For example, as will be explained in Chapter 6, under Harold Wilson in the 1960s, regional economic policy was particularly important, shaping physical land-use planning in depressed areas, with its emphasis on new housing, new towns and industrial development. But little importance was given to regional planning under the Conservative governments of Thatcher and Major, who put more emphasis upon the needs of inner-city areas and urban regeneration, particularly within the South and Midlands (Dungey and Newman 1999)

After coming to power (1997), New Labour soon set about putting its policy proposals into action (Labour Party 1996), rebuilding regional planning, with Regional Development Agencies for England being created under the Regional Development Agencies Act 1998 (Swain *et al.* 2012). Their role is seen to complement the established Regional Planning Guidance (RPG) produced by the government, in the drive for economic change, regeneration and regional competitiveness. Subsequently the revision of PPG11 *Regional Planning* issued in 1999 set out the principles for the resurrection of the regional level. The topics listed in this document as worthy of consideration at regional level are as follows: economic development, housing, transport, retail, hospitals, leisure and sports uses, rural development, biodiversity and nature conservation, the coast, minerals and waste.

Under New Labour, the 2004 Planning and Compulsory Purchase Act increased the importance of plan-making at the regional level by introducing a new type of plan known as the Regional Spatial Strategy (RSS). As outlined in the section on local authority development planning and explained in more detail in E-Supplement 3 on the companion website, the RSS comprised the high-level policy component of local authority development plans under New Labour, forming a bridge between the strategic regional level and the more detailed local area planning level more commonly found at local authority level.

Regional planning already existed to some degree through the Government Offices in each region and in the form of the Regional Development Agencies (RDAs). These were made up of elected councillors appointed by the local authorities in each region along with representatives of business and other sectors. They were responsible for drawing up the old regional planning guidance under the 1998 Regional Development Agencies Act, but under the 2004 Act they were tasked with producing the Regional Spatial Strategy for their region. The RSS was seen as providing the spatial development plan for the region, produced in association with the intended Regional Planning Boards, which would sit alongside the Regional Economic Strategy produced by the RDA (Regional Development Agencies established in 1998). The regional planning bodies, which were more like standing conferences, were reconstituted in 2004 and renamed Regional Assemblies, whose members were, again, nominated not elected. It was the duty of the regional assembly to produce the RSS, setting out the economic and spatial strategies for each region. Each Regional Assembly was supported by a small dedicated team of planners and other regional policy specialists who were responsible for drafting and consulting on the RSS prior to its approval by the Regional Assembly. The RSSs, along with the LDF (Local Development Framework, that is the main Local Plan) produced at the local authority level, comprised the new suite of development plan documents, as will be explained further in the section on local planning.

According to the Barker Review of Housing Need (Barker 2004), commissioned by New Labour under the direction of John Prescott, 4 million houses were needed by 2016. A subsequent Barker report (Barker 2006) concluded that it was the role of the local planning departments to facilitate this process, over and above local concerns. The RSSs provided the vehicle to allocate new housing development within each region. Many local authorities did not like being dictated to as to what should be built in their own area. The new arrangements were much criticised in terms of the increasing centralisation of policy with little allowance for local geographical and social differences. PPS3 on Housing (as produced in 2003) was instrumental in conveying New Labour's housing policy to the local planning authorities, and their role was now to implement, rather than create, policy. PPS3, and the overall New Labour stance on housing policy, seemed to be based on assumptions that all local authorities were dealing with highly urbanised situations in which the emphasis was upon infill and use of 'brown land' (derelict land sites previously used for industry), sometimes referred to as 'previously developed land'.

There were many other criticisms of New Labour's regional level, particularly that it was seen as being too distant from the local planning authority level and that the regional authorities were not democratically elected but comprised nominated members of the great and the good. There was a widespread perception that they were unaccountable and driven more and more by national policies and targets rather than by the views of local people. A stronger sub-regional planning level was needed to link local and regional together. The process of drawing up and approving each RSS was slow one and took a number of years to complete, but it was stopped in its tracks when there was a change of government in 2010. The newly elected Coalition government abolished the RSSs and initially devolved decision-making over housing numbers and targets to the local planning authority level. It also returned to local authorities the powers to set their own residential density standards and car parking requirements.

On the positive side, the RSSs did try to draw up meaningful and relevant plans for their regions. They sought to identify land for new development in the most sustainable locations, usually looking to expand existing large towns and cities and seeking to protect important areas of landscape or nature conservation interest. They looked to coordinate development with plans for new road, rail and other infrastructure, and to integrate the planning of the region with the economic strategies of the Regional Development Agencies. They also set out plans at the sub-regional level, providing broader planning guidance for natural city regions and enabling the growth of towns and cities to be tackled and planned on a more rational and coherent basis. The plans they came up with though were not always popular, particularly in the south of England, where there was much opposition to the scale of new development proposed, and as we have seen they were scrapped before they were finalised.

Planning at the sub-regional level

It is always difficult to decide at what level to plan within local authority structures at the local planning authority level. Local authorities have traditionally been divided between counties and their districts, providing a workable two-tier system under which to operate the planning system, with the former being the strategic development plan and main policy level and the latter being the Local Plan and implementation level. Admittedly there have been attempts at combined 'unitary plans', but these too have been structured internally around a distinction between strategic and localised policies. In the following section on local authority planning, we will highlight the role of the different levels, and consider how successive changes in the planning system have sought to make this distinction.

A key question has always been whether a county, although a large unit, is big enough to be used as a basis for high-level policy direction, whereas in comparison the regional level may appear just too large and remote. Plan-making at the sub-regional, intermediate level (between region and county level) is a vitally important element of an effective plan-making system, particularly in relation to the planning of a city-region or a town and its immediate hinterland. Such areas are often defined by travel-to-work catchment areas: these identify patterns of economic activity and travel quite well, and enable the plan-makers to direct growth in ways that can best be supported by existing or new transport provision, such as roads or, more sustainably, by new or improved public transport links. This level of plan-making is often referred to as strategic planning, and it is concerned with broader issues such as population changes, housing provision, economic development, transport and environmental protection.

Much depends on the actual size and delineation of the regions, counties and districts themselves, and, as will be explained, there have been attempts to redraw historical boundaries to reflect modern travel and activity patterns. There have also be attempts to augment the two-tier system by the introduction of a range of extra categories of local area for plan-making purposes within the main divisions, such as Action Areas, District Plan and thematic subject-based plans (such as on regeneration), as will be illustrated in the following account. The periods when the sub-regional and strategic component was stronger will be highlighted, such as under the Structure Plan system. The question of how to divide up the planning system, both horizontally and vertically, continues today with the 2011 Localism Act opting to go back to a more localised solution with relatively little regard for regional planning considerations. But before discussing the present situation we need to fill in some detail on the nature of development plans in recent past.

Planning at the local level: development plans

Endless changes

The development plan system has also undergone several major changes in form and content over the last 40 years. Here is a brief summary.

The modern planning system was established in the post-war reconstruction period, under the 1947 Town and Country Planning Act. Local authorities were required to produce zoning maps that were seen as fairly inflexible and overly land-use based with little allowance for the consideration of chang-

Photo 2.3   City Hall, London Assembly

This is the headquarters of the London Assembly of the Greater London Authority which has extensive plan-making powers rather like a small country in its own right.

ing social and economic forces. Subsequently a new type of development plan system was established under the 1971 Town and Country Planning Act, comprising a high-level strategic Structure Plan with secondary level detailed Local Plans.

A recognition of the increasing complexity of urban planning resulted in the introduction of Unitary Development Plans (UDPs) under the 1986 Housing and Planning Act. The new UDPs sought to combine the best of the structure and Local Plan approach from the old system. Part I of the UDPs was devoted to strategic policy statements, like the old Structure Plan, and Part II dealt with detailed land-use issues and planning in specific areas like the old Local Plans.

Whilst such plans were geared to the traditional county/district division found across England in the provinces, particular problems arose in trying to deal with the intensity of concentrated development

within London and other large cities. London may almost be seen as a country in its own right and has been used to having its own metropolitan powers, previously under the Greater London Council (GLC) and now under the Greater London Authority (GLA) which produces the London Plan, which is effectively a Development Plan (or RSS) for the whole conurbation, and has considerable spatial power in its own right (Photo 2.3).

The third main change to the development plan system came under New Labour under the Planning and Compulsory Purchase Act of 2004. A new Regional level of planning was introduced, with Regional Spatial Strategies (RSSs) providing the main strategic 'development plan' level (as explained in the previous section). These were accompanied by Local Development Frameworks (LDFs) that provided policy at the urban and district levels. Instead of consisting of one plan (that could take a long time to amend) the LDF constitutes what is termed a Folder of documents. The key policy document within this was the Core Strategy: this set out the broad framework and strategy for the future development of the local planning authority's area over a 20-year period, as well as Area Action Plans (not Action Area plans note) for particular localities.

The new planning system

Having described the sequence of recent development plan systems, some of which are still in operation in different localities, we will now explain the current system. The proviso is that the situation is still evolving so the emphasis in this section is upon trying to set out the main principles and issues.

2011 Localism Act: Back to the Future – the return of the Local Plan

No sooner had local authorities got their teeth into working on the new LDF system, than they were challenged with a whole new ball game. The Coalition government (combining Conservatives and Liberal Democrats) came to power in 2010. Initially they appeared to be quite antagonistic towards planning because of its slowness and what was seen as its negative approach to new development. The perceived problems were summed up in the Green Paper, *A Broken System* (2010). Therefore it was decided to undertake a major overhaul and simplification of the planning system.

Whilst an earlier section explained the Coalition's changes to National Planning Guidance, this section is specifically concerned with the implications for local plan-making. The Coalition cancelled nearly all previous Planning Policy guidance documents and instead introduced the NPPF (National Planning Policy Framework). Also they removed the national and regional housing targets and housing stock policy was devolved to local authorities. Early drafts of the NPPF caused alarm bells to ring. At first it seemed the NPPF gave carte blanche to developers, allowing them to build anything anywhere. A massive counter-attack was organised by the radicalised CPRE (Campaign to Protect Rural England, previously the more sedate Council

for the Protection of Rural England), marshalling many other pressure groups to lobby the government against the changes. Gradually retrenchment set in and the NPPF was rewritten to espouse a more moderate and better informed approach. A 'presumption in favour of sustainable development' has become the keystone of the revised NPPF and 'sustainability' was defined therein to include social, economic and environmental factors (for more on sustainability see Chapter 10).

In terms of plan-making the LDF was replaced (in name at least) by the Local Plan (which in spite of its confusing name is actually the new form of Development Plan) (Ricketts and Field 2012). But, the Local Plan retained much of the content of the LDF, but with a more readily understood name, it has to be said. Government guidance encouraged the integration of existing planning policy documents, as widespread abandonment of the LDF system was not seen as practical. Within the Local Plan the Core Strategy retained its key importance in terms of the overall vision and direction of the area into the future. For most local planning authorities this meant a quick change of name while work continued on plan preparation and the production of more detailed development management policies.

With the abolition of the regional tier of planning policy (under S.109 of the Localism Act) in England the Local Plan alone became the statutory development plan, except in London, where the London Plan also has to be taken into account. This meant that outside London there was no larger strategic plan-making level, which is, arguably, so essential in developing county, sub-regional, urban hinterland and metropolitan planning policies. For example, many policy issues cannot be resolved purely at the local planning authority level, such as transportation and highways policy that may stretch across several adjacent council areas. Likewise there are many land-use location and zoning issues that have to be dealt with at a wider urban level, such as decentralisation and relocation policies on housing, employment and retail development. Whilst there was no longer any requirement to implement nationally-set house-building policies, each local planning authority needed to sort out where new development could be built, based on an identification of need within the area.

Thus arose the vexed issue of likely conflict between importing and exporting authorities. Typically a heavily populated inner-city district with little brown-field land available for further housing development might request an adjacent suburban or indeed rural district to be allowed to accommodate some of the demand for new housing, which in turn would ensure the wider economy of the area was supplied with the necessary workforce. But such outer authorities might be in a strong position to object because of a valid desire to preserve the green belt, or because of local political pressures to keep the developers out of their area and preserve house prices and perceived amenity. In the absence of either a regional plan or a traditional county structure plan it is easy to see how an impasse could arise.

Therefore the government introduced, under Section 110 of the 2011 Localism Act, a 'duty to cooperate' between adjacent local authorities, and evidence of this is required within the Core Strategy policy statements, and in order for the plan to be accepted. When testing the plan, the Planning Inspector will apply a test of soundness (Section 112 of the Act) which should include evidence that cooperation has been undertaken. (Previously under the LDF the soundness test investigated whether the plan was justified, effective and consistent with national policy.) The emphasis on cooperation has created all sorts of uncertainties and legal scenarios as to what might happen if a particular local authority refused to cooperate, or to what extent one might judge that the best intentions of the duty have been followed. For example, there is the issue of local authorities that have already completed their Core Strategy and have not yet submitted it, as to whether they will be given a period of grace or will be required to go back to square one and seek cooperation with their neighbours.

The lack of a regional level has been acknowledged as a problem by the Coalition government itself because of its importance to business and enterprise. But this weakness has been compensated for by two strategies. Firstly Local Enterprise Partnerships (LEPs), have taken on, to some degree, the role of the Regional Planning Bodies in giving regional guidance, although the LEPs are not charged with producing actual plans but rather overseeing the regional situation. Secondly, the Localism Act has reintroduced the sub-regional element in stipulating the duty to cooperate with each other by local planning authorities. Many central area districts in large cities are quite small in area and may need to export business parks, housing, out of town centres, airports, to surrounding suburban and rural local authorities, but they may be rebuffed by these potential importing authorities who, no doubt, will seek to protect the quality of their local area. Thus the importing/exporting (of development) is a crucial issue in this new cooperation scenario, and, for example, Manchester has a multi-authority arrangement in place to deal with such issues.

Neighbourhood plans: community planning?

The Coalition government has sought to augment the Local Plan (which is the equivalent of the main Development Plan) with a new type of plan: the Neighbourhood Plan. This arises from the government's commitment to putting localism into place by giving Parish Councils and, in cities and urban areas, recognised neighbourhood forums, the power to draw up these new neighbourhood-level plans. An important decision was made by the government when they stated that such plans had to be in general conformity with the Local Plan, though where it was agreed locally higher numbers of new housing units could be included. This at least introduced a level of coherence into what otherwise could have been a free for all at the local level. A number of pilot projects were identified as official front-runners in 2012 to test the development of these new Neighbourhood Plans and a few frontrunners were completed (Backwell 2012). The ultimate intention is that Neighbourhood Plans are developed across the country, but the process is onerous. When the Neighbourhood Plan has been completed there must be an Independent Examination (and a public hearing at the discretion of the examiner) and a final Referendum in which 50 per cent of the relevant population must be in favour of the plan. It remains to be seen if local communities have the skills, time and energy to fully engage with the process. It is likely that the process will place further demands on already stretched local planning authorities, but it does offer local people a new and perhaps more inviting opportunity to become involved in local planning matters. But they are unlikely to have the resources or resilience of major developers wanting to build in their area, and for that matter the local community may be weakened by internal divisions on proposed planning policies.

This new localism, with its emphasis on the parish and community level and enabling local people to have more say in planning matters, embodied the Coalition's idea of communities having the power to shape development in their area (often dismissed as mere 'duck pond planning') (Farnsworth 2013a, 2013b). Suggestions are that the Neighbourhood Plan will with time increase in importance whilst Core Strategies will diminish in role.

Clearly the emphasis has shifted from the regional level, and indeed from the high-level urban policy level, to the non-strategic community level (BDOR 2011). Neighbourhood Plans are now a statutory component of the Local Plan, but with an emphasis on more flexibility with the local community having a more proactive and creative role rather than just having formal public participation. The main community body preparing the plan will be a neighbourhood forum group which should be composed of 21 members, and in the case of parished areas (such as rural areas) the local parish council. In the case of non-parished areas such as much of the London boroughs, where there is high density population, wards may be used instead, and as the basis for the creation of neighbourhood forums produce the plans (Morphet 2010).

After all this talk about parishes and local empowerment, it was subsequently decided that Parish plans, whilst they can still be prepared, do not form a statutory component of the new planning system (as originally implied). However, they can be one of the building blocks of the Neighbourhood Plan. In spite of this rather surprising emphasis on community empowerment and local democracy from the Coalition government, including its old-time Tory members, all is not quite as it seems. Producing Neighbourhood Plans is not an option, entirely up to enthusiastic community groups. In fact it is a statutory duty for Neighbourhood Plans to be produced and for the local planning authority to assist the community in this process. Therefore there is a fair amount of 'steer' from the planners to

make sure they are produced and in a manner that is acceptable to the planners. It is not a free for all, as Neighbourhood Plans must conform to EU law, national UK planning law, NPPF guidance and the Local Plan, so they do not 'trump' other levels of planning. Neighbourhood Plans must be supportive of sustainable development just like Local Plans which in turn should contain a 'model statement' on sustainability to pass the test of soundness. But they should be 'positively prepared' with an emphasis upon responding to local needs and economic demands too. Whereas the Local Plan Core Strategy will still set the numbers of houses to be provided in an area, the Neighbourhood Plan can give guidance on where they are to be located and how they are to be planned. All this is not optional or voluntary; there is a duty to agree on the part of community groups, and a duty to support on the part of the local planning authority (Urban Vision 2012; Ricketts and Field 2012). Whilst *horizontally* across boundaries local planning authorities must show a duty to cooperate, *vertically*, community groups 'have a duty to agree' with Local Plans and national planning guidance. There are other strange anomalies at the local level. The 2011 Localism Act has given local level councils, such as town councils, 'General Powers of Competency' to 'do anything', whereas previously their ambit was restricted. But there is no extra money for them, say, to build schools or provide recreation facilities, and this power, no doubt, has to be reconciled with the requirements of the Neighbourhood Plan. At the same time the Coalition is still talking about freeing up the planning system to encourage developers to build more houses in order to get the economy going, which does not tally well with promises of greater community autonomy and power.

But it still seems a lot of work to be expected of community groups. The emphasis is upon local plans produced by local people, and not just on passive public participation. This seems to be a further development of New Labour's front-loading of an emphasis upon community involvement consensus in plan-making, which was much criticised at the time for the ambiguity of the term 'community' and the unpaid work and time expected of local residents. There has been much criticism of the whole idea, as clearly some neighbourhoods and communities are in a better position to be involved in the production of such plans than others because of differences in people's socio-economic resources, free time, education and general know-how. Local businesses may be involved too, in support of community interests, but again this assumes the area in question contains such economic resources. Likewise many other ideas of Cameron's Big Society have been criticised for ignoring the huge differences in power and influence held by different groups in society. For example, with the cutbacks in local services and facilities, middle-class communities are in a much better position to take over the running of libraries and other public facilities than people on deprived housing estates who are more concerned about personal survival in adverse times (Morphet 2010).

However, Planning Aid for England and other voluntary planning groups are supporting communities producing Neighbourhood Plans (for example see *Town and Country Planning Association Journal*, July/August 2012 on neighbourhood planning; and 'A Quick Guide to Neighbourhood Planning' (Urban Vision 2012). The plans can be quite flexible, varying in area size and number of policies, and can cover both urban and rural, affluent and deprived areas. Local neighbourhood groups may have considerable powers, not only can they produce plans but they can also produce NDOs (Neighbourhood Development Orders) which can increase or reduce the level of accepted planning control in the area. The NDO also usually enables the granting of planning permission for development identified within the Neighbourhood Plan. But again there is some contradiction as it is unclear how many of these promises can be fulfilled when the local authority still has overall control as to development policy within the Neighbourhood Plan. As has been commented, the planners specify how many houses will be built in the Neighbourhood Plan area, but the community can have some say as to where exactly they will go.

Updates on the operation of the neighbourhood planning system

The situation is still evolving and at the time of completing this chapter, further clarification of the question of '*How* to do a Neighbourhood Plan' has been emerging, as local authorities, parish and community groups, and developers try to make sense of it all. It has become clearer that Neighbourhood Plans should not been seen in isolation or as the only way of achieving local level policy objectives. Rather they should be seen as part of the wider concept of 'neighbourhood planning' as a manifestation of the new localism and greater community involvement. Neighbourhood Plans should not be seen as a creating a clean break with previous local authority planning department work at the local level. Rather previously approved Local Plans, initiatives and community policies are now to be seen as potential building blocks in creating sound Neighbourhood Plans. Many local authorities already had a great deal going on at the local policy level as encouraged by New Labour. For example, existing Action Area Plans (from the LDF system), Parish Plans, Village Design Statements, Town Plans, Master Plans, Traffic Plans, Site Briefs and Local Facilities Audits (and so forth) might all contribute to the development of the new Neighbourhood Plans.

The other key question is '*who* is meant to produce the Neighbourhood Plan?' There has been a great deal of talk of handing powers back to the local community. But as already discussed in this chapter it is the local planning authority that has ultimate power, as Neighbourhood Plans must conform to the policies and requirements set out in the new Local Plans. They cannot contradict existing policy or regulations (for example on sustainability) from EU, UK and local authority levels. Parish councils and the newly emerging neighbourhood forums (in non-parished areas) initially were likely to see themselves as actual policy-makers with considerable power. However, it now emerges that their role is to lead and manage the planning process at the local level, by harnessing and co-ordinating the community, but they only have limited decision-making powers. For example, as stated earlier, they cannot decide the amount of housing to be built in their area, but they can have some say in its overall design, location and other site details. So many local residents have become rather disappointed that Neighbourhood Plans are not all they seemed to be initially. Local communities also lack the financial

Photo 2.4   Revamped St Pancras Station, London

Whatever the planning system adopted it is vital to fund, maintain and improve the transport infrastructure, especially the railway system, which was originally developed in Victorian times and is now being upgraded in many parts of the country. But local road and bus service improvements are as important at the neighbourhood level too.

power, influence and know-how of would-be developers from property development companies.

The scope and extent of Neighbourhood Plan designation is also now beginning to become clearer. We are not talking about a universal two-tier system of Local and Neighbourhood Plans being rolled out across the country. Rather we can see a scatter-gun approach developing, in which only a relatively small number of local areas are opting to produce them – a couple of hundred so far – from the pool of around 17,000 potential areas (including parishes and other neighbourhood-able areas). Generally it has been the rural parish areas that have made the most

progress, but even then, so far, examples are few and far between. For example, Backwell, Much Wenlock and Upper Eden, are all local communities that have already produced Neighbourhood Plans. If you access such plans from the internet you will see how very varied they are, generally quite short and very specific in their policy statements. The Coalition always said that they could be very flexible, and there was no one approved format, or required number of policy topics to be covered. This is quite a difference from the 'one size fits all' approach found in previous local planning systems over the years (for example the local plan level of the Structure Plan, UDPs and LDF systems as already outlined in this chapter). Size-wise a Neighbourhood Plan can relate to just one parish, or as is already emerging such a plan can be produced by a small consortium of parishes or local wards that share the same planning problems.

Within cities the situation is more complex, not least because many urban areas are non-parished. For example, London and Bristol are not parished, but curiously Milton Keynes is heavily parished! Milton Keynes is using the Neighbourhood Plan to push through policies on the modernisation of its city centre. In contrast, the City of Bristol has decided to encourage the production of Neighbourhood Plans in some of the more deprived areas of the city, drawing heavily on its pre-existing neighbourhood planning initiatives and networks. Bristol's planning authority is not encouraging the production of such plans in the more affluent areas. It believes the NPPF wants Neighbourhood Plans to be used to bring forth 'growth and development' and there is very little space for any new development in already built-up middle-class areas, such as its urban conservation areas. However, nationally it is noticeable that the more affluent, articulate, middle-class areas, rural or urban, are certainly more equipped to produce such plans. Deprived areas lack the resources, know-how and time to be involved, unless their local authority actively supports them.

This brings us to another very fraught issue – the relative lack of financial and administrative support to enable local communities to produce neighbourhood plans. Central government is providing really quite small sums of money (of a few thousand pounds at most) to support local community groups for publicity, administration and consultation. But it can be an expensive business; for example running a Referendum is not cheap, and is likely to cost around £15,000 per area (as at 2013), as it is necessary to set up a proper polling station and the full rigmarole of organising and counting votes. However, as explained further in the next chapter those areas that do have a Neighbourhood Plan will be entitled to a greater level of central government funding, in particular from the Community Infrastructure Levy (CIL) (as explained further in Chapter 3). This will pay towards infrastructural improvements and community amenities (Photo 2.4). Furthermore it is the duty of the local planning authority to support local communities in the production and implementation of Neighbourhood Plans, but, of course, in these days of government cutbacks many are very stretched in having the staff resources to do so. So, what started as a relatively simple idea of giving power to the people is turning into a much more complex and costly exercise than the Coalition ever imagined. The first Referendum on the adoption of a completed Neighbourhood Plan took place in Upper Eden, at Penrith in the Lake District in February 2013 and revisions were subsequently made in April 2013 in the light of the referendum and consultation process.

For the tasks, further reading, additional photos and other resources for this chapter, please visit www.palgrave. com/companion/greed. E-Supplement 3 provides information on recent UK planning systems, and is particularly useful in relation to this chapter. Also E-Supplement 1 lists government publications, legislation and policy guidance. E-Supplement 2 describes the planning system in other UK countries, including Scotland, Wales and Northern Ireland.

3 Control of Development and the Development Process

Introduction

The purpose of this chapter is to introduce development control, which is also called development management. Development management is one of the main means whereby development plans and related planning policies (as outlined in the last chapter) are implemented both at city-wide level and in relation to 'place-making' and urban design at the local level, through the control of the development of individual sites and schemes.

First the legal definition of development is given. Then the relationship between national planning law and local-authority level planning control is explained. Whilst the rules may appear inflexible, say to the householder applying for an extension, in fact there is a considerable degree of negotiation and preliminary discussion between the developers and the planners when dealing with major development projects. Then the two key sets of criteria which set out when planning permission is required are described, namely the Use Classes Order (UCO) and the DMPO (Development Management Procedure Order). The complexity of what constitutes permitted development is investigated. Following this additional levels of control are explained with reference to urban conservation areas and listed buildings. E-Supplement 4, on the process of development, describes the wider context of the property development process within which planning control takes place, and introduces the reader to the other actors involved in the development process. Later in this chapter Figures 3.1 and 3.2 (pp. 55–6) summarise the development control process and the wider property development process.

This chapter seeks to give you the reader an idea of how the system works, and what to look out for; to provide a potted outline of what is a very complex field. There are exceptions to almost every rule, as decisions are frequently challenged by planning appeals and the legislation and case law is constantly changing. There is also a range of other controls on development, parallel to, but not strictly part of, the statutory planning system that may delimit the nature of development. These are in relation, *inter alia*, to public health, building control, highways, water supply, toxic waste, noise, disability, nature conservation, licensing laws, military defence and environmental requirements.

Development control

Overall considerations

As explained in Chapter 2, the planning system may be divided into two aspects, development plans and development control, also known as development management. The current development plan documents and accompanying maps provide policy direction, for example in relation to how many houses are permitted overall in a particular locality. Development control management provides the means to control development to fulfil the requirements of the development plan, to conform to national planning law requirements, and to deal with the details at individual plot level, in terms of the use, design and location of the building in question. Overall development management should not be seen as a negative activity but as a means of implementing and achieving such goals as creating and managing liveable cities, supporting sustainable development initiatives and contributing to the attainment of transport policy objectives. The planning system seeks to maintain a balance between

Photo 3.1   Demolition of property: Bexhill on Sea

When at the end of their usefulness many buildings need to be demolished, or perhaps refurbished for new uses. But most demolition now counts as a form of 'development' and requires planning permission.

reasonable legal control over development and providing the means for appeal and consultation, thus endorsing democratic principles. Likewise in operating the development management system planners are not just unthinking bureaucrats following rules, because even dealing with the simplest application may require a high level of understanding and the exercise of discretion to achieve the best outcome.

Definitions of development

Development is defined in planning law under Section 55 of the Town and Country Planning Act 1990, as '*the carrying out of building, engineering, mining, or other operations in, on, over or under land, or the making of any material change in the use of any buildings or other land*'. Therefore development means two main activities: firstly, physical change

such as the development of new buildings and other works; and secondly the material (significant and legally enforceable) change of use from one use to another, for example an existing building changing from residential to commercial use. Demolition may also require planning permission especially in urban conservation areas (Photo 3.1).

For the purposes of the planning system, not all development requires planning permission if it is Permitted Development (PD), such as, for example, minor alterations to property or temporary uses. But development is taking place all the time, and the ground rules of planning law are frequently changing. Therefore, it may be that an applicant does not require planning permission. An applicant can apply for a certificate of lawfulness, or may be able to regularise the situation by gaining retrospective permission. These are of two types: The Certificate of

Photo 3.2   House extension on older property

Dealing with domestic house extensions forms a major aspect of development control, and for ordinary people this is what planning is seen to be.

Lawful Use or Development for existing development, and The Certificate of Lawfulness for proposed use or development for proposed development, which establish the legality of the use or development in question.

If permission is refused dissatisfied applicants may appeal their planning decision. Procedural routeways are available to unsuccessful applicants through the DCLG, with some cases ending up being determined in the law courts. But many appeals are dealt with through what are known as 'written representations', without anyone actually meeting face to face. (See the Department of Communities and Local Government (DCLG) and the Planning Inspectorate websites for statistics on these matters.) Here we get into complex legal distinctions, as one can appeal against a decision to

the Secretary of State at the DCLG, through PINS (the Planning Inspectorate), if it is considered that the decision was determined (decided) wrongly on planning grounds. Cases can go all the way to the High Court or even to the Law Lords (renamed the Supreme Court) if the decision can be challenged on a complex legal point or procedural technicality.

Planning applications

Planning applications are generally submitted electronically, through the Planning Portal at http://www.planningportal.gov.uk. The fees for a planning application are frequently revised upwards and readers should check current costs on the Portal. These can be around £150 (at time of writing) for small domestic householder applications and into thousands for large-scale development. There are two types of planning permission, outline and full (detailed). Outline permission establishes the broader principles that development of a certain type is allowed on a particular site, whereas the full application deals with all the specifics. Normally small householder-type applications, e.g. residential extensions, go straight to the full stage. Most fairly straightforward planning permissions, including householder applications, are known as 'express planning permissions'. As will be explained later in the chapter, many minor changes or actions are permitted development and come under 'deemed consent' as not requiring planning permission.

To submit a householder application, or a full planning application for other uses, the applicant has previously been required to complete four copies of the forms supplied by the local planning office, and supply four copies of the plans. Applications for house extensions are one of the most common forms of domestic property application (Photo 3.2). In the recent past planning applications were submitted on paper forms by post. Nearly all planning authorities now do all their development management activities online. The plans that must be submitted consist of a site plan, normally to the scale 1:1250, showing the existing buildings in and around the site where the development is proposed to take place, with a red line around the whole plot. Detailed plans should be to 1:50 or 1:100 using the metric system of measurement. An Ordnance Survey grid reference may be required which is shown as follows. First (with the north at the top) the 'easting' is given which is the number (found on the top or bottom margin) of the vertical line to the left of the site, followed by the 'northing' which is the number of the nearest horizontal line below the site (shown on the sides of the map). In other words the figures along the bottom of the map should be read first followed by those up the side of the map. Building plans should also be provided, showing the floor plans and elevation of the building, plus a section through the building showing annotated details of the construction and materials to the scale of 1:50 or 1:100. The North point, the scale, and a key should be included on every plan or map.

The planning authority is required to keep a register of planning applications which is open to the public and which they may consult without charge, and which is likely to be published online. This is a separate register from the Local Land Charges Register which gives information on other matters relevant to the area, such as road widening and planning matters, which would affect a piece of land or the sale of a house. This is separate from the Land Registry which records the ownership of all registered land and property, covering the majority of the country. The local authority is likely to store the details of the application on computer using GIS software (Geographical Information Systems) that can display both map details and information about the application. Advanced 3D imaging, CAD (Computer Aided Design) software and indeed Google street-view all enable individual buildings to be shown in greater detail. Local planning authorities have access to all sorts of data related to the area in question in a GIS format, including land-use, population, car ownership, employment, environment, crime, housing demand and so forth. The whole system has moved over to what is called e-planning as part of e-government as the web and e-communication has vastly expanded. What was seen only ten years ago as ground-breaking stuff on e-planning (Allinson 1998) is now seen as commonplace as if it had always existed (DCLG 2005).

When submitting a planning application, one of four certificates must be completed by the applicant, which records the ownership of the property. Complete Certificate A if one is the sole owner. Complete Certificate B if the ownership is shared with others, and then send in Notice 1, which is given out as part of the application form, to each owner. Certificate C is used where the applicant is unable to discover all the names of the owners, and Certificate D where the applicant is unable to discover any of the names of the owners. Publicity of the application will be required in cases C and D. This procedure is under review. In general, at present most planning applications are advertised by the local authority in a local newspaper, and by site notices, and 21 days is given for people to inspect the plans at the local planning office if they so wish, and to submit objections if they are unhappy with the proposal. But there has been a move to abandon newspaper advertisements and provide online announcements instead which has caused great concern as many people still do not have access to the web or cannot use computers, especially the elderly, the poor and those in the countryside who do not have the benefit of broadband access. However, 'immediate neighbour notification' is also carried out by most local authorities for next door neighbours. The 2011 Localism Act made compulsory pre-application community consultation on major local schemes, as part of its commitment to local empowerment and neighbourhood-level planning.

When submitting a planning application, applicants are also usually required to fill in an online Equality Monitoring Form. This is because of perceptions of a greater refusal rate being applied to applications from ethnic minority householders and businesses. In the case of larger developments careful consideration will be given to whether the proposed development might adversely affect certain minority groups, under the operation of the PSED (Public Sector Equality Duty) of the 2010 Equality Act. Equality has become an important issue in local authorities and most will have produced a Single Equality Scheme governing their approach to personnel matters, working practices and policy matters (including planning). Accessibility for people with disabilities is particularly important and covered by disability legislation requirements both in relation to the internal design of buildings and increasingly the external environment, so a Design and Access Statement (DAS) will be prepared as part of the development management (such as CABE 2006a).

Once submitted electronically the application may be passed to other relevant departments such as conservation and highways. For example, in the case of an application for a housing development, it is likely the application may be referred to the highways department, and to other departments responsible for providing services and infrastructure in the district, such as education and social services. The local planning authority is not necessarily a free agent to determine all aspects of the application. Highways are still a function of the county council, although the situation is complex according to whether the development abuts a trunk road, or certain categories of classified road. There is normally a system in place for parallel consents in relation to highways matters. But as discussed further in the transport and urban design chapters

(Chapters 12 and 13) the planners and highways engineers do not always see eye to eye, because of different priorities in terms of the needs of the motorcar and the need to create sustainable urban environments.

The highways authority will be concerned with traffic generation, parking, access and road safety, and with the question of whether new road development is needed. Developers have entered into an agreement under Section 38 of the Highways Act 1980 (still current) which allows the developer to undertake the construction of the roads in return for the local authority adopting them and maintaining them in the future, or alternatively advance payments are made by the developer to the local authority under Sections 219 and 228 of the Highways Act before the site is 'released' for development, with Sections 38 and 278 also allowing for an element of 'highways gain' over and above the minimum to facilitate site development. The New Roads and Street Works Act 1991 modified the legal mechanics of these methods to a degree (Section 22) but the principle remains the same. Under Section 104 of the 1991 Water Industry Act a sewage undertaker can agree with a developer to adopt the new development's sewers. Other significant water acts include the 1991 Water Industry Act and the Flood and Water Management Act 2010. With changing weather patterns and global warming, flooding has become a major consideration in siting new development. Under the 2010 Act a sequential test is now required as to the areas least likely to flood. Of course insurance companies and local businesses are also very concerned about the cost implications of flooding events. As an elderly planner once advised me when I was starting out on my planning career, 'it all comes down to sewers in the final analysis'.

Any development, however small, which requires access onto a trunk road, or classified road, requires permission from the county highways authority. However, if permission is given for car access the local authority may be happy to permit access by dropped kerb on the site. But the highways authority must be notified before work commences, and the householder would be expected to pay for the works involved. Classified roads are A and B roads, but also C roads which are not shown as 'special' on ordnance survey maps, but are coloured in yellow along with ordinary small non-classified roads. Most bus route roads are classified roads. Trunk roads are roads of major national importance and include most A roads and also motorways, and are managed by the highways authority which may also be involved in major development proposals affecting its road. However, as will be explained in Chapter 12 on transport, there has been a major move away from automatically providing for the motorcar (predict and provide) on new developments to a more restrictive approach for environmental sustainability reasons. Thus much of the old guidance on housing densities, levels of car parking and width of roads has gone by the wayside.

Building Regulations consent may also be required if the planning proposal involves new build or physical alterations to an existing property. Forms for building consent are also to be found on the Planning Portal. British Standards (produced by the BSI) may also be cited in terms of official guidance on accessibility, safety and design. Sometimes strange anomalies occur in that a building may meet the requirements of planning law but fall foul of Building Regulation control, for example in relation to fire exits and safety. Properties that are Houses in Multiple Occupation (HMO) are particularly complex in this respect and a HMO licence is required. Sustainability initiatives may also conflict with planning, for example, in 2012 the government introduced the Green Deal whereby money was made available for external insulation (that is on outside walls) that could be held up by requiring planning permission (as reported in *Construction Manager*, September 2012, p. 6). Whilst in some local authorities there are still strong links between planning and building departments, in others Building Control functions may have been privatised and are undertaken by external accredited agents. Building Control is quite separate from the planning decision process, although there is often need for liaison between planning and building officers on the details of a scheme.

The relationship between national planning law and local planning policy

After all this is done, the local planning committee (the councillors) decide whether or not to approve the scheme in question, taking into account the professional advice of their planning officers, written representations, and feedback from the community. Neighbour notification is required with 21 days for responses, and this is very important when dealing with householder applications on what are often quite high-density housing layouts, where immediate neighbours are worried about being overlooked or blocked by neighbouring development. The council is bound by national legal and policy requirements in making their final decision. However, on certain minor planning applications that are not seen to be of strategic policy significance or of major public interest, planning officers themselves can determine (decide) some applications under what are known as delegated powers, to save bringing every single application to the planning committee. However, if there are a significant number of objections (ranging from 3, 6 or more depending on the local requirements) from the public the case may go to the councillors in the planning committee to decide.

Thus the planning authority makes its decisions on the basis of national planning law, that is the Planning Acts, and rules of the Orders, such as the Use Classes Order (UCO) and Development Management Procedure Order 2010 (DMPO) and upon various other directives, policy guidance statements and White Papers (command papers). As explained in the last chapter, until recently Planning Policy Statements (PPSs) provided a key source of national planning guidance, but most were replaced in 2012 by the new National Planning Policy Framework (NPPF). This guidance is now being delivered mainly through the web, in a revised section of the planning portal website at http://planningguidance.planningportal.gov.uk/

Central government planning policy documents are the embodiment of the Secretary of State's approach. Therefore should a particular planning decision go to appeal the decision may be determined in accordance with specific aspects of their contents. In addition to these ministerial documents, existing case law and appeal decisions are major indicators of current policy as to what is permissible: perhaps more so than all the other factors mentioned. It should be stressed that case law is a very major consideration in determining planning decisions on appeal. As explained in the last chapter, the Planning Inspectorate deals with all planning enquiries and appeals, including those who consider their applications were unfairly refused from a planning perspective. It is a complex system, with many decisions being given in writing without an actual 'hearing'.

As well as the complying with the details of national planning law, an application must also be in accord with local planning authority policies. Whilst national planning law and policy requirements relatively speaking trump local considerations, nevertheless Section 38(6) of the Planning and Compulsory Purchase Act 2004 requires planning decisions to be made in accordance with the development plan unless material (significant) considerations indicate otherwise. City-wide level policy statements found in the Development Plan Documents, be they Structure Plan, UDP, Core Strategy within the LDF Folder, or the new Local Plans (that is whichever is the current approved plan in the local authority in question) are of major importance. They should be taken into account when deciding if a development should occur at all in a particular location, and in the case of the larger planning applications, as proposals must tie in with agreed development allocations for the area.

Many planning authorities produce design guides, which set out the accepted standards of design, car parking, density and estate layout guidance and so forth for different types of land-use such as residential business parks, retail development and conservation areas. These, too, are taken as accepted policy documents, that is as being of material consideration (as having legal authority as approved policy) in the development management 'determination' (decision-making) process. The application of planning standards and design principles in respect of a particular site should not be seen as absolutely fixed, but as subject to a certain amount of negotiation to get the best solution for that site, all things being considered. There may also be practical barriers arising from the nature of the site in question. For example, on some small inner-city sites the planners and developers may find their decisions are constrained by the presence of underground sewers, unstable land, soil contamination, restrictive covenants, the height and effects of neighbouring

development, and the existence of archaeological remains (see Chapter 12 of the NPPF document). The Coalition government has been very keen to speed up development and reduce red tape. For example, in the case of retail and town centre development 'sequential tests' were required under the previous Labour government, by which the developer, wanting to develop out of town, had to prove that no other suitable sites were available closer in. The Coalition government abolished retail sequential testing as bad for business, whilst still endorsing the importance of town centre development to revitalise rundown areas and encouraging less harsh central area parking restrictions (Portas 2012).

Negotiations and planning gain

In the case of larger developments, even before an outline planning permission is submitted, the developers may enter preliminary negotiations and discussions with the planners to sound them out, and either side may produce a planning brief, a document for discussion setting out how the area is envisaged as developing. For the planners the location of large housing estates might have strategic implications for the future structure of the whole urban area, future infrastructure, bus routes, schools, and generation of increased traffic volumes. Developers stand to make or lose millions of pounds depending on the planners' decision. Thus, developers will try to speed up the planning process, for example by discussing Heads of Terms (agreed principles as to what is being offered) in advance of entering into a Section 106 Agreement and sorting out planning gain. For larger, more complex and controversial schemes, such as the building of a housing estate, or a new out-of-town shopping centre, it is normal to agree the principles at the outline stage.

The planners and developers will meet for pre-application discussions long before the actual planning application form is filled out. It is likely that what are known as 'reserved matters' will be held over for consideration at the detailed stage. These usually are shown under five headings on the planning application forms: appearance, access (including car parking), landscaping, layout, and scale of development. These criteria will embody both national planning guidance and local planning standards. For example, until recently car parking provision on residential developments was limited by central government guidance, but the Coalition has now delegated the power to decide parking standards back to local authorities

The issue of planning gain is likely to be an integral part of pre-application discussions with the planners. It is an integral part of the planning application process, because development of land and property is a major financial activity, and thus commercial considerations are always on the agenda. The local authority is also keen to maximise the benefits for the community arising from new development. Therefore developers may be willing to enter into a planning gain agreement to get planning permission. The phrase 'planning gain' is a non-statutory term which covers additional 'concessions' which the local authority derives from the developer in entering into an agreement to provide certain amenities in return for a more favourable planning permission. Planning obligations (yielding planning gain) are entered into under Section 106 of the Town and Country Planning Act 1991. Circular 16/91 (which updated 22/83) set out the parameters of what the Department of the Environment considers to be 'reasonable' factors germane to a planning gain agreement. Planning gain is not a bribe as it is done for the benefit of the community, and has to be directly related to the development in question. *Planning Obligations: Delivering Fundamental Change* (DTLR 2001a) further clarified the situation. Circular 05/2005 was the last circular on Planning Obligations which was cancelled in 2010 with the introduction of the NPPF.

Typical examples of planning gain might be the provision of public conveniences, a crèche in a shopping centre, affordable housing, landscaping, seating and street improvements. The stakes get much higher with some London boroughs who might seek to get contributions out of the developer for community centres, local schools and sports facilities. This has antecedents under the (still in force) Open Spaces Act 1906, whereby a developer can (still) agree to lay out, plant and maintain an area of public open space before handing it over to the local authority for adoption. But few new housing schemes contain even a small park or open

space. But they may contain 'leftover' bits of green space which the local authority may not want.

In theory planning gain had to relate to the site being developed but in reality it often provided a source of income for infrastructural services and road development too, and even funded new schools, roads and amenity schemes far from the site. But the overall requirement was to demonstrate that the planning gain proposed had a link to the site, albeit often tenuous. In fairness this is one of the few means left to local authorities to make the social aspects of planning a reality in view of the cutbacks in local government finance. A planning gain component is often to be found on new housing developments, or even individual new houses. Increasingly 'planning gain' is being augmented by more formal arrangements.

Under the Coalition, the Community Infrastructure Levy (CIL) has been introduced as a new form of planning gain but based on a more formalised, regulated and less discretionary system. CIL was first introduced in 2010 and now features in the NPPF and the 2011 Localism Act. CIL has a chequered history, dating back to earlier attempts to introduce a roof tax on new housing developments under previous governments. (The roof tax system is still in force in Milton Keynes under its new town development corporation powers.) CIL calculations are now a major part of the planning permission process. The CIL regulations require developers to make a statutory contribution towards off-site provision of roads, sewerage, water and other infrastructural provision that will serve their new development and join it up to the main services and road system. CIL is based on a percentage payment per square metre (or per unit of development) and must be in accord with an approved charging structure. It is a highly complex and evolving topic. Any new building development over as little as 100 square metres, even residential building, is now likely to be subject to the CIL Community Infrastructure Levy. S106 agreements can continue for on-site additional facilities and, for example, affordable housing, as before.

Planning decisions

Local authorities are required to make a decision within eight weeks of the application being received, but on average decisions are given within 15 weeks. There have been many attempts to speed up the system, by means of setting targets, undertaking audits and creating more efficient office systems. For example, under New Labour there was a flurry of monitoring initiatives (Audit Commission 1999) with an emphasis on customer rights, speed, efficiency and Best Value, but most of this is now abolished. If an applicant is unhappy about the decision they have, in some cases, six months to appeal to the Secretary of State. Applicants also have the right to put in an appeal upon the expiry of 12 weeks if they have not got a planning decision by then. The major developers have used all sorts of ways of putting pressure on the small local authority, such as twin tracking whereby developers put in multiple applications for the same site to push the planners to make a decision. Likewise the local authority can create delay by means of bureaucratic procedures, or they may simply want to sit on a major application whilst they await imminent changes in central government policy. This is all in a quite different league from ordinary householder applications. Planning consultants and planning lawyers working for the private sector know how to play the game and get the best return for their clients.

Any objections to a planning application can be submitted during the determination process. But they have to be material planning considerations, significant changes, which relate to highway safety, parking, road layout and highway access, traffic growth, noise, design and layout, density, disabled access, layout, and effect on historical buildings and conservation areas, that is mainly physical issues. The planners are not allowed to take into account moral issues, property values, competition with existing businesses, and private real property law matters. But under the 2009 Policing and Crime Act, Sex Entertainment Venue Policy (SEVs), moral and public order issues may be taken into account, for example in the case of the siting of lap dancing clubs. Noise can be dealt with under the 1996 Noise Act which includes provision for NIA (Noise Impact Assessment). For commercial premises the Licensing Act 2003 also comes into play in controlling noise from clubs, pubs and other entertainment facilities.

Planning applications will receive one of four answers: yes, no, wait, and yes but with conditions. Planners are entitled to impose '*such conditions as they think fit*' (Section 70 of the 1990 Act). Circular 11/95 (previously Circular 1/85) set out the six tests as to the validity of conditions of permission and this was subsequently incorporated in planning guidance (for example PPG1) but the NPPF has not been particularly supportive on this matter. The basic principle is that the conditions must have been imposed for a planning reason related to the site, and not for some broader environmental or social policy reason. The local authority may accept the development in principle but require modifications, or they may choose to limit the permission to a period of years. This is a growing trend in the case of a change of use to allow the local planning authority an opportunity for future review of the situation in the light of changing circumstances. In the case of new building development, matters such as landscaping, car parking and access may have to be altered, for example tree screening might be required. Overall it is very important to stress that in spite of all the recent changes, the NPPF 2011 endorses and continues the principle of a plan-led system. The most important principle in determining applications is 'a presumption in favour of sustainable development' which is strongly promoted with the NPPF.

Planning applications from central and local government departments, and those concerned with land owned by the state, may be seen as falling into a different category from regular private-sector applications. Some buildings have 'Crown Immunity' and therefore the planning acts do not necessarily 'bind' the Crown (Part 7 of the 2004 PCP (Planning and Compulsory Purchase) Act). However, Permitted Development (PD) rights for these bodies are increasingly limited. Similar exemptions may apply to land and properties under the control of Ministry of Defence, the Police, and a range of statutory undertakers, or their privatised successors, related to gas, electricity, water, as well as the NHS (with its vast estates) and education departments too. However, there is provision that on the disposal of land from these bodies, planning permission can be given before the sale which enhances its value in the market, for example, in the case of property in the green belt. Special arrangements were also made in the disposal of forces housing (and army camps), much of which is in located in attractive countryside areas. Local authority departments themselves are technically required to apply for planning permission like anyone else when dealing with their own land and property.

The government has been particularly concerned about how long it can take to get approval for major, infrastructural projects of national significance. The topic of transportation infrastructure policy is discussed further in the transport chapter (Chapter 12). The Infrastructure Planning Commission was set up at the end of the Labour administration under the 2008 Planning [Reform] Act, to try and speed up the planning process for projects of national significance which were likely to create a high level of opposition. This was a reaction to the very protracted timescale taken to get the Terminal Five development approved at Heathrow airport and ongoing local opposition to proposals for the construction of a new generation of nuclear power stations. The Commission's role was taken over by the Major Infrastructure Policy Unit within the Planning Inspectorate, and this unit is now renamed the National Infrastructure Directorate. There are major democratic considerations to be taken into account, as the UK system currently allows for a high level of participation, consultation and the making of representations against a proposal. Good planning is not necessarily quick planning, indeed it may be slow planning after all the relevant bodies have been consulted and all the key policy issues and impacts have been addressed.

Planning policy and development management decisions ultimately have to be backed up by 'enforcement' measures against those who do not comply with planning decisions regarding their property. Sometimes development goes ahead in spite of the refusal of planning permission, or the scheme built differs from what was agreed, in which case a stop notice may be issued to prevent further works being undertaken on the building in question. Whilst in some cases negotiation and discussion may result in a way ahead, in others stronger measures are needed including fines, the demolition of the offending property, and even criminal prose-cution. This is a specialist area of planning, with its own enforcement officers and planning lawyers. The situation is highly complex. For example, in some cases, if development has not come to the local authority's notice, unauthorised development may be immune from enforcement after four to ten years, depending on the nature of the breach. However lack of compliance and regularisation through gaining retrospective planning permission, or leaving unauthorised development unchanged, may affect the subsequent saleability of the property.

On the other hand, development may not take place after planning permission has been obtained for a variety of reasons including financial circumstances. A completion notice may be issued by the planning authority. Indeed a local authority itself may fail to implement a particular scheme, on its own account or in partnership with a developer. But they may have already used their considerable compulsory purchase powers to assemble the site ready for development. According to what are known as the Crichel Down Rules (after the site in question), since 2004 land and private property previously compulsorily acquired which is found to be surplus to requirements can be offered back to its former owners rather than going onto the open market.

The criteria for change of use

Planners base their decisions as to whether development, including change of use, has taken place with reference to the different categories of land use known as the Use Classes Order. Not all changes require permission, for as stated some count as PD (Permitted Development), the general principle being that if the change is from something 'good' to something 'worse' then it will require planning permission, such as going from a shop to a house. (But beware local policy may seek to protect shopping provision so this is not always so). If a building changes from being a house to an office that counts as development even though no actual new building has taken place. The original UCO Order of 1987 has been tweaked and amended many times over the years. The UCO as amended in 2010 is as follows:

> ### Table 3.1   The Use Classes Order
>
> - A1: shops
> - A2: financial and professional services
> - A3: restaurants and cafés
> - A4: drinking establishments
> - A5: hot food takeaways
> - B1: businesses (offices, light industry)
> - B2: general industrial
> - B8: storage and distribution
> - C1: hotels
> - C2: residential institutions
> - C2A: secure residential such as prisons
> - C3: Dwelling houses
> - C4: Shared multiple occupation
> - D1: non-residential institutions (schools, libraries, surgeries)
> - D2: assembly and leisure (cinemas, swimming baths, gymnasiums, including churches and other religious buildings)

UCO amendments May 2013

The Coalition government revised the UCO again in 2013 for the purposes of freeing up the planning system and encouraging business ventures, both in respect of urban regeneration and re-use of redundant agricultural buildings. Please note some of these changes are time-limited.

Premises in B1a (office use) can change to C3 (residential use) without requiring planning permission.

Premises B1, C1, C2A and D1 can change use permanently to be a state-funded school.

Buildings with A1, A2, A3, A4, A5, B1, D1 and D2 uses will be permitted to change use for a period of two years to A1, A2 and B1 uses to help new and start-up business enterprises.

Agricultural buildings under 500 square metres can change to a number of commercial uses A1, A2, A3, B1, B8, C1 and D2 (note not C3 residential).

In addition four new class categories were introduced, J, K, L and M, which have caused considerable controversy.

The new classes added in May 2013
- Class J allows the change of use of any building from its previous use to change to a residential use. In particular this allows for a change from offices to dwellings to count as permitted development.
- Class K allows for a wide range of types of buildings to be converted into schools.
- Class L automatically permits a building to revert to its previously approved use.
- Class M makes it more flexible for agricultural buildings to be converted to a range of business uses, including shops and cafés (but not dwellings).

These changes were introduced under the *Town and Country Planning (General Permitted Development) (Amendment) (England) Order* of May 2013.

Sui generis

Many uses do not fall into any class and are therefore in a class of their own (*sui generis* means of its own kind). Theatres, car hire, petrol stations, car showrooms, and lap dancing establishments and various innovative uses have been seen to be *sui generis*. This leaves the planning office discretion to decide on the basis of planning policy whether the change is acceptable and how it should be managed. They must also take into account the policy use allocations (zonings) shown on the approved plans for that area. Also the extent and intensity of the change has to be taken into account to determine if it is a material change of use or just a temporary or ancillary (secondary) use, whether it generates more traffic or causes a disturbance and so forth. If all changes of use were set out in the UCO then planning would become mechanical and there would be no professional judgement involved. As time goes on new 'uses' and categories develop which require amendments to planning law. For example, there are proposed changes to split the A category again to include various leisure and entertainment uses that are seen to affect the character of the surrounding area, such as lap dancing and also 'vertical drinking' establishments. Likewise there are proposals to take religious buildings such as churches and mosques out of D4 because of the problems, and high levels of refusal, encountered by ethnic minority, faith groups, applying for permission to house their expanding congregations (as discussed further in Chapter 16 as a social aspects issue) (CAG 2008). It would seem that planning law can deal with straightforward land uses but always has difficulties dealing with social changes, especially those involving entertainment, morals, religion and large crowds of people! Technological changes also create development management pressures, such as the expansion of the mobile phone network and the need to build antennae (Askew 2009).

Advertisement control

The display of advertisements is another category of control, and requires a special planning application under the Town and Country Planning (Control of Advertisements) (England) Regulations 2007 (previously the 1984 Town and Country Planning (Control of Advertisements) Regulations). There are currently 16 categories of types of advertisement, most of which are covered by deemed consent. Local authorities also have the right to designate areas of Special Advertisement Control in areas where greater levels of control are needed, for example to protect the amenity of an area. Unfortunately previous guidance on Advertisements such as PPG 19 and Circular 3/7 were cancelled by the Coalition government, when all previous guidance was replaced by NPPF, which contains very limited reference to advertisement control in Section 7. Subsequently in 2011 a guidance document to local planning authorities in the series, *Letters to Chief Planning Officers*, at https://www.gov.uk/planning-guidance-letters-to-chief-planning-officers, entitled *Advertising Control – Provision of DCLG Guidance*, sought to clarify the government's policy on this topic.

The Development Management Procedure Order

The Development Management Procedure Order (DMPO) sets out what counts as 'Permitted Development'. In 2010 the DMPO replaced the General Permitted Development Order (GPDO) (Ricketts and Field 2012, 137–8). The GDPO was introduced in 1995 (Grant 1998, 2014) (previously known as the General Development Order) and is often still cited. The GDPO is a lengthy document, but, for example, Part I of the DMPO deals with various small-scale aspects of householder development which do not require express planning permission (which is known as Permitted Development). For example, one can build a porch provided it does not cover a ground area of more than three square metres.

Until relatively recently, house extensions could be up to 15 per cent of the original current cubic volume on a semi-detached or detached property or 70 cubic metres, or 10 per cent on a terrace or 50 cubic metres, whichever is larger, both up to an overall maximum of 115 cubic metres. No extension could butt out in front of the front wall of the house except where the house is set further than 20 metres from the boundary. Neither should it go above the ridge of the roof. No part of the extension should be higher than four metres and it must lie within two metres of any boundary. Along with outbuildings the extended house could not occupy more than 50 per cent of the area of the garden. Subsequently the regulations were altered to be more dimensions-based. However the old rules still give a good rule of thumb. As a general principle the regulations seek to minimise the impact of extensions whilst adopting a proportionate approach to control. Note that in respect of getting permission for extensions all measurements relate to the house as originally built, or as it stood at 1 July 1948, and are related to the external cubic volume. Even if Permitted Development, all such improvements are still likely to require Building Regulation consent in relation to construction, materials, electricity supply, water supply, insulation and so forth. Remember that even if the house improvements are within the GDPO it may fall in an area of additional special control as explained above.

Until May 2013 the main rules were as follows:

An extension is counted as Permitted Development if:

1. It covers no more than half the area of land around the original house
2. No part must be higher than the original height of the house
3. A single storey extension must not extend beyond three metres of the rear wall of the original house or four metres if it is a detached house
4. Extension of more than one storey must not extend beyond three metres of the house
5. Two storey extensions must not be within 7 metres of the rear boundary.

There are several additional rules about height of eaves, side extensions, use of windows and so forth, so it is quite complicated and you may have already noticed that if you do not have a long back garden you are unlikely to take advantage of the above rules. There are separate rules for flats, apartments and maisonettes. There are all sorts of other considerations, for example you cannot necessarily demolish a property, or part thereof, and assume it does not require planning permission.

Changes to the GPDO

On 30 May 2013 the Coalition government made some major, but temporary, changes to these regulations as follows:

- Rear extensions can now extend beyond the rear wall of the original dwelling house by up to eight metres (26 feet) in the case of a detached house, and up to six metres for any other dwelling house subject to the following conditions:
- The extension must be single storey and not exceed four metres in height.
- The house must not be in a Conservation area or other protected category land.
- The local planning authority must be notified before work commences, who then have 21 days to consult neighbours.
- It should be stressed this is not a planning application as such but the local authority does have the power to refuse prior approval (but no fees are charged).
- The works must be completed before 30 May 2016.

In other words the owner of a detached house may be able to extend the property an incredible 26 feet (eight metres) out into the back garden, but is only required to give the neighbours 21 days' notice for consultation.

Many planning authorities have expressed concern about this new arrangement because of the time and money involved in dealing with the notifications, and the fact that during three years very major permanent changes could take place in residential areas with people building over their back gardens. The system is also likely to lead to neighbour disputes and arguments over 'rights to light'. But the Coalition sees these measures as a means of stimulating the economy through the increased activity of the construction industry. However, any extension built under these temporary provisions will still themselves be permanent and irreversible.

Ancillary development

Students always ask about that hypothetical carport without walls in the front garden. If it is joined to the house and permanent it is development in any case. But the question is whether it is Permitted Development, and the local planning authority may treat it as an extension. If it is in front of the front wall of the house, and/or over the building line, the local authority are likely to act on it (if they notice it). Some local authorities have additional controls about parking cars and caravans in front gardens, and any caravan which is permanently occupied within the curtilage (surrounding plot) of a dwelling is bound to attract of the attention of the local authority. Working or running a business from home may be construed as a 'change of use', unless the use is 'ancillary' to the main residential use. 'Ancillary' means some use or activity that is incidental to the enjoyment of the house as a dwelling. There is the principle that the 'intensity' and 'predominance' of the use should be taken into account, and a use which is ancillary or secondary to the main use is not necessarily a change of use. Planners are more concerned about external effects such as generation of car parking, noise and disturbance, than about the turnover of a business or how much disruption it causes within the household.

Certain minor house improvements and changes, such as painting the outside of a house, count as 'Permitted Development' and normally do not need planning permission, but there are numerous 'exceptions' and 'buts' on other little changes. For example, satellite dishes, decking, solar panels and carports do not necessarily count as not requiring permission. Many urban authorities expressed concern at the loss of front gardens which are paved over for car parking, thus affecting the water run-off situation, visual appearance and traffic management of the area and so introduced special controls. Subsequently amendments to the GDPO in 2008 removed Permitted Development rights for hardstandings in front gardens.

Photo 3.3   Front garden parking issues

For many householders the front garden is an essential parking space, particularly when surrounded by double yellow lines. Many local authorities have sought to control the concreting over of gardens.

The DMPO does not apply everywhere. Under an Article 4 direction the Secretary of State and the local planning authority can withdraw some or all Permitted Development (PD) rights, for example to retain the quality of a residential area or to add controls over an urban conservation area. Local Authorities also have powers to suspend rights in cases where the development proposed would be detrimental to the proper planning of the area, or a threat to the amenities of the area, but this direction can only remain in force for six months, unless approved by the Secretary of State. In recent years new types of development orders have been added, including Special Development Orders (SDOs), introduced in 1990, applicable by local authorities in special circumstances. The Local Development Order (LDO) introduced under the 2004 Planning and Compulsory Purchase Act improved on the SDO. The LDO gave the local planning authority itself powers, as the name suggests, to exert greater control over a particular local area (for example in the case of urban renewal areas). The 2011 Localism Act introduced Neighbourhood Development Orders (NDOs) which, along with the introduction of Neighbourhood Plans, enable local communities to exert greater control over the planning of their local area. Compensation is payable in some cases for loss of Permitted Development rights under the DMPO.

Gardens and vegetation

Subject to any special provisions such as Article 4 Directions, one can plant anything in the garden, provided it is 'incidental to the enjoyment of the dwelling', but even these factors may be covered by special controls. Householders must take responsibility for unauthorised flora such as Japanese knotweed which is a 'notifiable' illegal plant, known for spreading rapidly and destroying the foundations of buildings.

Another tricky issue is that of incidental buildings such as greenhouses, outbuildings, garages, sheds, tree houses, lean-to's and conservatories within the curtilage of a dwelling (the plot on which the house stands, usually the garden). Garden sheds should not normally be more than two metres high, but may be counted in the volume of the house as a whole when dealing with future permissions. The matter of greenhouses in residential areas should not be confused with that of glasshouses, which are horticultural greenhouses and permitted in agricultural areas and green belts. But greenhouses are accepted as part of the enjoyment of the curtilage of the dwelling and may be permitted under the GDPO subject to the allowances for outbuildings. Conservatories are often advertised by double-glazing firms as exempt from planning control if they do not have solid brick walls and are seen as temporary structures. However, they are actually development, but usually Permitted Development. It is important to check with the relevant local planning authority. Garages are also exempt unless they give access to a classified road or are more than five metres from the house. Dormer windows and roofs in general can be tricky too. In the case of listed buildings additional restrictions exist. Parallel listed building approval will be required for any change to a listed building that is not like-for-like change. Unauthorised change to a listed building is a criminal offence, unlike unauthorised development which only becomes a criminal matter if enforcement action is not complied with adequately (Sheppard and Britnell 2013).

Hedges have not traditionally been subject to control. Around 20 per cent of the population, at any one time, are having neighbour disputes over rights to light, to retaining a view, overhanging trees, tree roots, high hedges, noise and anti-social behaviour. There are some legal remedies such as tort of nuisance, trespass of roots and overhanging branches, and infringement of restrictive covenants,

which may be invoked in a limited range of cases (under private Real Property law as against state Planning law). The problem of controlling neighbours' leylandii (fir trees) has been the subject of a national campaign and a consultation briefing note by the government (DETR 1999c). Measures have now been introduced to require householders to cut down high hedges, especially of leylandii trees, which block out the light and cause nuisance. Significantly this was introduced under the 2003 Anti-Social Behaviour Act, Part 8 (of ASBO fame), not through a planning act!

Hedge and plant height is not otherwise controlled by planning law, but they may be the subject of other local authority controls if plants affect people's use of the adjacent pavement. Because of unsuitability, height, loss of view and light, and neighbour nuisance, some countries have banned the use of certain non-indigenous species. For example, eucalyptus and leylandii are banned in some Canadian states, and there is much stronger 'tree control' in relation to private gardens, boundaries and hedges than found in Britain. Likewise Australia, home of the eucalyptus, exercises a range of flora (plant) planning controls over foreign species, because of the fragility of the local ecology.

In contrast, individual and groups of native trees may be protected under Tree Preservation Orders (TPOs) under the 1999 Town and Country (Trees) Regulations (Tree Preservation Orders). Planning permission is required to lop such a tree, and if felled, it must be replaced with a tree of similar species, and heavy fines are available for non-compliance. Article 4 directions may be used to impose controls on planting in open-plan estates, and in conservation areas trees and hedges are subject to special controls. In contrast, man-made fences and walls are normally permitted development up to a height of two metres, or one metre if adjacent to a classified road (except in conservation areas and other areas of special protection where controls are greater). Confusion as to what is or is not allowed under planning law arises because some local planning authorities enforce the rules more rigidly than others. Indeed if they are short-staffed and no one 'notices' unauthorised development, it may appear that it is permitted. But it should be pointed out that planning authorities do have powers to require the demolition of unauthorised developments, and it is a criminal offence not to comply with an enforcement notice. This includes controlling unauthorised use of existing buildings. For example, there has been a spate of people in London renting out their garden sheds as basic housing, especially to new immigrants; therefore the Coalition government set up a taskforce in 2012 on the 'beds in sheds' problem.

The Planning and Compensation Act 1991 increased the penalties and related enforcement powers, and they have subsequently been updated in line with inflation. However, if, for example, the alterations to a house would have been permitted in any case had the owners applied for planning permission, then there are means of granting retrospective permission. This may be necessary if these irregularities show up at the time when a house is being sold; in this age of do-it-yourself conveyancing it may go unnoticed, with dire consequences for the next owner down the line when a new keen planning officer does track it down. Under the 1991 Act, the four-year rule giving immunity to development without permission (which has not been challenged in that period) is now accompanied by a ten-year rule which gives immunity for uses carried out without planning permission.

Caravans and campsites

There is a range of controls over caravans and campsites. There are over half a million caravans in Britain, a third of a million mobile homes, and 150,000 motor homes. Indeed the difference between and mobile home and a caravan is a moot point. Many caravan sites are temporary and permission is often granted on a seasonal basis. But the gradual build-up of the use of seasonal holiday facilities as year-round housing is problematic. Mobile homes are a particular problem. Temporary uses such as fairs, circuses, sport-related marquees and markets may be exempt from planning permission but are sure to involve other local authority departments such as health and highways. Powers are administered in conjunction with the magistrates and public health officials. Legitimate traveller groups and Travellers and traditional gypsies have some rights as to where they camp and perhaps settle, but allocating an area as a permanent gypsy site is always controversial with local residents. These matters are complex and controversial as they impinge upon legislation related to housing, vagrancy, gypsy sites and anti-racism policy, going beyond the scope of town and country planning alone. The legislative situation is in transition, and readers should check the professional press for future developments. From time to time the news features major confrontations between the planners and the gypsies but it is important to look carefully into the full picture on these occasions as to whether planning permission to settle exists or whether trespass is being committed.

Environmental assessment

EU directives require Environmental Impact Assessments (EIA) to be undertaken to ensure new developments are environmentally sustainable, and thus to measure the 'carbon footprint' before giving planning permission (see Chapter 10 on sustainability). These first came into force in 1985 under EEC Directive 85/337, and directions were given to local planning authorities to undertake this process, as part of planning, in the Town and Country Planning (Assessment of Environmental Effects) Regulations, No.1199, 1988, updated with assessment categories extended in EEC Directive 97/1. The Planning and Compensation Act 1991 further integrated the process into the statutory planning system. Environmental Impact Assessment is required under the 2011 Town and Country Planning (Environmental Impact Assessment) Regulations, and also the 2011 Infrastructural Planning (EIA) (Amendment) Regulations. Normally an Environmental Statement (ES) (showing the results of the EIA) would be required if the development was considered to fall into a qualifying Schedule. In the case of large developments it is likely that the developer will submit an environmental assessment as part of the initial stages of the proposal. However, it must be stated that some developers, and, significantly, some local planning authorities, have been slow to take on board the need for environmental assessment and this has led to legal challenges in some cases. Sustainability Appraisals (SA) may also be required in some instances under the Local Planning Regulations introduced in 2012.

Figure 3.1   The development control process

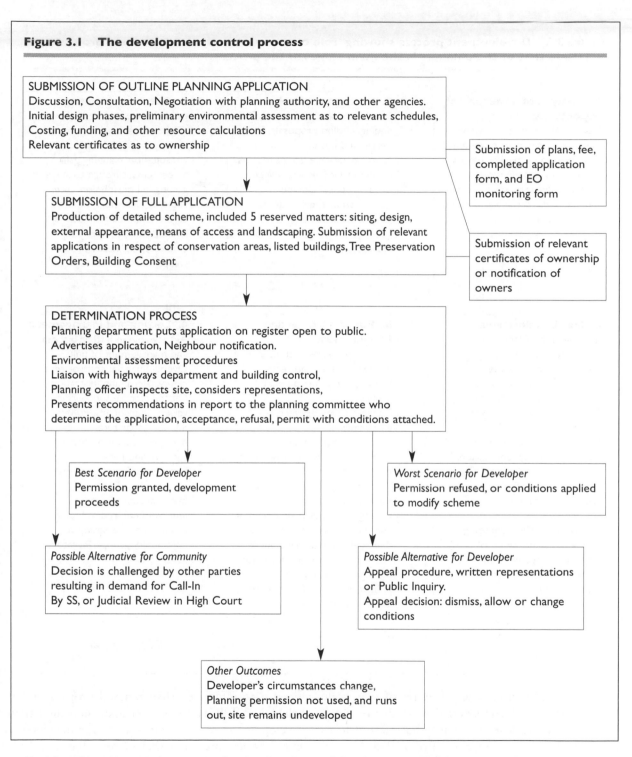

Local authorities are also required to undertake an environmental assessment of their development plans (originally introduced in the UK under PPG12 on Development Plans, now cancelled). Schedule 1 of the above Local Planning Regulations lists all the types of development for which assessment is compulsory, as part of the development control process, and Schedule 2 lists those which may have

Figure 3.2   Development process showing role of the construction and property professionals alongside that of the planners in the main stages of the process

1. Analysis of development opportunity
Review of property portfolio
Existing portfolio management
Examination of market trends
Accountants, economists, financiers, bankers, stock market specialists, the developer as client, commercial and residential chartered surveyors, valuers

2. Decision to develop
Feasibility, location analysis, Site finding, outline proposals, Draft design and layout
Town planning specialist surveyors, private sector planners, valuers,
Initial costings, Outline construction specifications, project management
quantity surveyors, construction managers

3. Obtaining planning permission
Client represented in *private sector planning* in negotiations, consultation, planning gain agreements, through to stage of gaining full permission. *Local authority planners, highways engineers, building controllers involved along with lawyers, engineers, architects, community groups,*

4. Site Development
Investigation of land rights, covenants, easements, constraints on scheme
Legal factors and contract issues, Capital investment,
Lawyers, chartered surveyors, valuers, accountants
Site analysis and setting out
Landscape design and liaison,
land surveyors, landscape architects, planners
Detailed costing design and specification
Bills of quantities, tendering agreements setting up of project management and site teams, *quantity surveyors, construction professionals*

5. Building Design and Development
Liaison on design with user groups, business interests, highways and environmental groups
Planners, urban designers, environmentalists
Costing, procurements, tendering, project management, contracting
Construction professionals, quantity surveyors, architects, accountants
A range of generic management and business roles and tasks, overseeing the project, public relations, arbitration, negotiation
Managers, construction professionals, workforce providers, local labour initiatives

6. Letting and Management
Agency role in letting, disposal and management of units.
Overall financial control, rent reviews, legal administration.
General practice surveyors, valuers, accountants, lawyers
Services, structural management, maintenance, security and repair
Facilities managers, property agents
Eventual refurbishment, improvement, redevelopment
Planners, conservationists, community groups, investors, surveyors

Back to Stage 1

environmental consequences because of size, scale location and other characteristics. A scheme which does not require assessment may be referred to as having 'Schedule 2 exemption' (Rydin 1998, 238 and Rydin 2003; McGillivray 2006). The uses requiring environmental assessment range from rural uses that would not normally require planning permission under the British system, such as salmon fishing and

forestry, to intensive urban renewal projects under Schedule 2. Likewise even non-toxic, non-industrial developments, new housing estates, even new forests and fisheries, may nonetheless be subject to EIA because of possible emissions and overall impact on the environment.

As will be explained in Chapter 9 (on rural planning), planning control was not extended to farming in the post-war era because it was considered that farmers needed the freedom to produce food at that time, and because it was considered that there was little need to control the countryside (which was seen as 'good') as against the need to control the evils of urban development. Therefore, under UK town planning legislation, Agriculture (Class VI) has been subject to fewer planning controls than urban development. Farm buildings come under control if they are near an airport (if they are more than three metres high within three kilometres of an airport or 12 metres elsewhere), but the trend is towards growing control in view of pressure from environmentalists and the green movement in general. But please note the recent changes to the UCO described above which now allow some redundant farm buildings to be used for a range of commercial purposes. Areas of Outstanding Natural Beauty (AONBs) and National Parks are subject to somewhat different GPDO rules, and the controls on village buildings can be as strong as those found in an urban conservation area. The current emphasis upon sustainability and environmental issues applies equally in town and country. Environmental assessment regulations do not, significantly, make the same sharp division between urban and rural development, or between industrial and agricultural uses, rather the emphasis is upon scale, size and likely impact of the development (as explained further).

Listed buildings and conservation areas

Listed buildings are subject to a higher level of planning control. A full application must be submitted in the case of listed buildings (not outline) because the planners will want to know what the scheme will look like, in terms of façade, townscape, and also matters of car parking, access, etc. Listed building consent will also be required in cases of alterations to the building which are not like-for-like changes. Conservation area consent is required for demolition of an unlisted building in a conservation area above a certain size. In sensitive cases, the developers will need to produce a small report, in addition to the application, and include annotated diagrams and plans, photographs and further explanation of exactly what is intended, for example, whether a significant wall is going to be demolished, and how

landscaping will be dealt with. The planners and developers are likely to have a meeting about building materials at the detailed stage, and samples of different materials will be discussed. Conservation areas provide a means of additional development control beyond normal planning powers. For example, the whole ring around Bristol city centre is now covered by over 22 conservation areas. Conservation areas continue to proliferate; indeed local planning authorities can now 'self-designate' without being statutorily required to consult the Secretary of State to do so under 2004 Planning and Compulsory Purchase Act.

The DCLG, and to some extent the Department of Culture, Media and Sport (DCMS), provides guidance to local authorities on the listing of buildings and on control to prevent demolition or alteration without notice, to prevent neglect by owners and to benefit the general public. English Heritage (EH) advises the DCLG on listing, finance, conservation areas and town schemes. See the EH website on listed buildings at http://www.english-heritage.org.uk.

The DCLG coordinates conservation with policy related to inner-city initiatives, city grants and housing improvement funds, all of which also deal with 'old' buildings. Private development companies themselves often have a conservation section and seek to liaise with the DCLG, English Heritage and the relevant local authorities on larger schemes, to keep a 'good image' with the planners and the grant-givers.

The Historic Buildings and Monuments Commission for England established in its present form under the Ancient Monuments and Archaeological Areas Act 1979 is responsible for a wider range of historical buildings including castles, cathedrals, churches, and many of the main national treasures and tourist attractions. Those associated with Royalty (having Crown immunity) and the Church (the Anglican, Roman Catholic and Methodist buildings are specified as protected) are not subject to normal conservation policy and with which agreements are made to conform to accepted planning and conservation policy. The National Heritage List, drawn up by English Heritage, comprises 410 sites and buildings of high national importance, such as Stonehenge.

Buildings are listed if they are seen to be of outstanding historic or architectural interest. All buildings built before 1700, most 1700 to 1840, some 1840 to 1914, a few 1914 to 1939 and even a few after that are listed. Buildings from the 1960s and later into the second half of the twentieth century are increasingly listed, because of their significance to modern architecture. For example, Sheffield Park Hill, a 1960s 'streets in the sky' council flats development, has been listed and is now being completely refurbished and turned into private apartments by the regeneration company Urban Splash. In some countries, such as Japan, buildings are given the equivalent of a listing 'at birth', if they are considered to be of exceptional architectural merit, although these are likely to be the least endangered. Being listed may increase the value of the property but may restrict the owner's freedom of use, and cost of building repairs. In England and Wales, there are three main categories of listing. Grade I should not be removed in any circumstances as they are are of national, even international, importance. They must also not be altered, or their original character changed. Grade II comes in two sub-categories. Grade II* (starred) which means they have an asterisk * beside them on the list. Such buildings cannot be removed without a compelling reason, and are usually of significant regional, if not national, importance and include set-piece Georgian houses in some of the main terraces and squares in cities such as Bath.

Grade II non-starred are more ordinary buildings such as typical Georgian or Victorian town houses of more local importance. There is also a non-statutory category, Grade III, which is not actually on the central government list, but on a list composed by the local planning authority. This list is advisory, but there are powers to upgrade such buildings to Grade II if they are threatened. Conservation control is particularly concerned with the external appearance of buildings but in the case of Grade I and Grade II* there are additional controls on internal features.

According to English Heritage, in 2012 listed buildings comprise 3,750,000 properties (including 15,000 church buildings). 2.5 per cent are Grade 1, 5.5 per cent are Grade II starred and the rest are ordinary Grade II. There are 9080 urban conservation areas, 17 World Heritage Sites and 19,717 ancient monuments. As stated, National Parks also constitute a form of conservation with buildings within their boundaries being protected (but often also listed too). New forms of control continue to emerge. For example, the 2006 Commons Act has enabled the registration of Town and Village Greens (TVGs), in order to protect the local character, but has been used to block new development as in the case of a village green being designated on the site of the proposed new Bristol City football stadium at Ashton Vale in Bristol. Subsequently under the Growth and Infrastructure Act 2013, such use of village green rights was blocked on sites already under determination for development, along with other vexatious methods by local residents to block major development (Herrington and Parker 2012).

Preservation conjures up images of buildings turned into museums and put in mothballs. Conservation contains the idea that the buildings in question remain as part of the living fabric of the city in daily use, for example, as houses and offices (Photo 3.4). Conservation should not be seen, either, as just being applicable to stately homes, palaces, tourist destinations or simply to the 'Country Life' type upmarket private houses. There are many working-class areas and terraces which are conserved because they too are part of our heritage, and in such areas conservation policy can often be linked to urban regeneration programmes, and more collaborative approaches to undertaking urban renewal (Punter 1990, 2009). For example, back-to-back housing Birmingham is listed (for example at Hurst Street crossing with Inge Street) and is now a tourist feature run by the National Trust. In the countryside the Campaign to Protect Rural England (CPRE) is concerned with both natural and built environment issues and has campaigned to retain planning controls over green-field sites and village development.

A listed building cannot be demolished or altered without listed building consent, but in the past some people just left their buildings to fall down 'naturally', particularly if they were right in the way of a new development scheme. To prevent this a Repairs Notice may be issued if a building is not properly maintained, and two months after its receipt the owner may serve a compulsory purchase notice on the local authority. On the other hand the owner can issue the local authority with a listed building

Photo 3.4   Urban conservation control

Even though housing provision demand is high, urban conservation policy still seeks to control the design of residential conversions, infill and improvements within sensitive village locations.

purchase notice to buy the property if the upkeep is too much. Although there are considerable negative powers associated with conservation, there are limited positive financial incentives to encourage conservation. There is also the questionable assumption that listing will increase the value of the property, which does not necessarily follow in all parts of the country. Nevertheless the local authority may impose additional burdens by stipulating in renovation work the use of genuine slate tiles on the roof, or traditional hard wood sash window frames, rather than condoning the use of aluminium frames or plastic double glazing.

As more and more Victorian and Edwardian areas come under conservation policy control, some people on low incomes may find they are faced with impossible choices and may simply move out of the area to avoid the costs of upkeep. But unaffordable housing is a national issue affecting all sorts of homes too, as average house prices are now more than ten times average salaries. So those who can buy prestigious homes that are listed are likely to be more affluent and already well ahead on the housing ladder. In London they are increasingly likely to be foreign investors and businesspeople. Further, some of the design controls on listed buildings actually contradict the rules under public health and building regulation controls, e.g. on the heights of ceilings and the design of windows in relation to conversion and modernisation work. Basically there is more flexibility if it can be shown that the developer is seeking to return the building to, what is agreed as, its original design. A building can be listed without the owner's consent and there is no appeal procedure against this. Most buildings have been listed by government experts who literally have been going around the country listing properties from the 1970s onwards when listing first came in. A building may also end up listed because it is recommended by the local authority, or perhaps the local residents group, conservation society and sometimes the owner. Whilst conservation is a worthy objective in protecting the visual quality of the townscape, many would argue that it involves greater infringements on personal freedom and rights over one's own property than ordinary planning law.

There has been limited financial aid available under the Historic Building and Ancient Monuments Act 1953, still in force as the Ancient Monuments and Archaeological Areas Act 1979, which empowers the Minister to make grants for maintenance and guardianship of properties which are of national touristic importance. Under this Act the Minister can also designate 'Town Schemes' which are usually small areas such as a town square, a high street or village green, for which the following grants are available: 25 per cent from central government and 25 per cent of the cost from local government, the rest being supplied by the owner. Conditions regarding town schemes, and the limited availability of grants and loans related to conservation, are set out in Sections 77–80 of the consolidating act on conservation, namely the Planning (Listed Buildings and Conservation Areas) 1990. City grants have been available in some cases under Part III of the Housing and Planning Act 1986 and that were part of the Action for Cities programme and such measures turned the tide of previous demolition. Under the Local Authorities (Historic Buildings) Act 1962, local authorities were first able to make grants and loans towards conservation, but in view of the present nature of local government finance and cutbacks, this is rare. However, many listed buildings are also used as houses and therefore people have been able to claim Housing Improvement Grants under the Housing Acts (1969 onwards). As will be explained in later chapters, over the years a plethora of grants, loans and initiatives were introduced to conserve, improve and protect older property under urban conservation, renewal and regeneration programmes.

In the 1970s this was easier and more money was available for a range of improvements and alterations. Indeed this provision contributed towards the process of gentrification, although the original intention was to help poor working-class areas. The term gentrification describes the process in which middle-class people move back into the inner city and renovate property, thus causing a rise in the property values in the area. In some cases areas worthy of conservation were also designated as General Improvement Areas or Housing Action areas. There are so many listed buildings that buildings are no longer considered so special and worthy of financial support just because they are listed. But housing grants are only available for a more limited range of improvements. Another bone of contention has been the question of Valued Added Tax (VAT) on listed building repair and/or renovation. This is a detailed taxation and legal question. Readers should check the professional press for the current state of play at the time of reading this book. As at 2011, the Coalition government proposed making VAT chargeable on church and cathedral renovation, a measure that was subsequently dropped owing to public outcry.

In the 1990s a range of new possibilities for funding listed buildings opened up under the Listed Buildings and Conservation Area Act 1990, which are still in force. Conservation Area Partnership Grants (CAPGs) are also available for selected properties as a result of Lottery funding, and especially Heritage Lottery Funding. Additional assistance may be available at local authority level, for example in Bristol, from the City's Wanted Homes Team which seeks to bring empty property badly in need of repair back into the housing stock. Also liaison with housing associations, educational establishments, letting agencies and charitable bodies all provide means of funding such property, particularly in conservation areas. English Heritage (EH) is now the government body responsible for listed buildings and some grants are available through EH for buildings of historical significance. Listed buildings do not only comprise housing, but offices, shops and all sorts of other uses, being part of the living fabric of the city. For example, there have been several programmes to revitalise shopping streets, for example by means of the Town Centre Shop Front Improvement Scheme in London run by the GLA. Following the major inner urban riots of 2011 there was a campaign to get planning law changed to allow for shopkeepers to install security shutters over their windows (to prevent looting) without the need to get planning permission. But in the end this did not go ahead, partly because of concerns about the visual impact, and the defensive, alienating evening environment this might create. But many Chambers of Commerce representing small businesses, concerned about their members' livelihoods, are not happy about this.

Increasingly planning policy and development control are concerned with managing entire conservation areas, giving attention to the surrounding townscape, trees, street appearance and incidental non-listed buildings which together formed the backcloth against which the listed building stood. The Civic Amenities Act 1967 established the category of 'Conservation Area'. These are designated and controlled through the local planning authority. The aim is to maintain the overall visual quality and character of the area. New buildings can be constructed in a conservation area but they must fit in with the historical style of the area. Thus there has been a proliferation of neo-Georgian office buildings with modern 'historic style' sash windows and mansard roofs. But 'conserve and enhance' is the key objective, and there are many good modern, contemporary infill schemes in sensitive historical locations.

The Town and Country Amenities Act 1974 gave increased powers of control in conservation areas, preventing demolition of all buildings and also giving further protection to plants, trees and other townscape and street features within conservation areas. As indicated above, all the conservation legislation is now consolidated in the Planning (Listed Building and Conservation Areas) Act 1990, which is still in force at the time of writing. This did not, of itself, introduce any significant new measures but tidied up existing legislation. Many planning authorities found that the designation of conservation areas (often on the rather questionable pretence of protecting marginally important buildings) was a means of increasing development control and reducing rights under the (then) General Development Order (GPDO), for example, in respect of demolition which heretofore has not counted as 'development'. But, under Section 13 of the Planning and Compensation Act 1990, the demolition of a building may count as 'development' in certain complex circumstances. In fact control within conservation legislation is not as strong as it might be, and many local planning authorities add an Article 4 direction to increase their powers within conservation areas.

When designating a conservation area, the local authority needs to be concerned about traffic movement, parking, and pedestrian circulation within the area. In some cases streets are blocked off, or one way systems introduced to control traffic movement. The environmental effects of modern traffic have to be taken into account both in terms of the effects of attrition on the building fabric, and also the overall visual impact. Most conservation areas are localities where people live and work, and so a compromise must be reached between the need to protect the area and the need to enable people to carry out their businesses and lives in the area. In some cases urban conservation areas have also been designated as Local Plan areas in the overall Development Plan, as well as aligning the area in question to any housing improvement area designations that might result in an increased chance of housing grant money. This enabled the comprehensive planning of the area on the statutory basis of the approved policies enshrined in the plan's written statement and land-use plans. There has been much controversy about car parking restrictions and through traffic controls in conservation areas. Whilst these no doubt improve the quality of the conservation area, some community groups living in nearby working-class inner areas are of the opinion that such policies can be class biased, pushing the commuter traffic and on street parking into poorer areas where residents are less articulate. Furthermore, from the viewpoint of the suburban commuter faced with reduced car parking space in central areas, residents of conservation areas are often seen as projecting a fortress mentality in protecting their areas from urban transportation pressures generated by adjacent central business district expansion. Yet again planning for the needs of one group may disadvantage another (Photo 3.5).

In addition to the governmental bodies concerned with urban conservation, such as DCMS, DCLG and English Heritage, there are several non-governmental bodies which have acted as powerful

Photo 3.5   House building pressures

One of the greatest challenges for the future is the demand for more house building. In order for new housing to be developed, planning permission must be given, and this needs to ensure that the location, type and density of housing conforms to development plan policy requirements, as well as parking, infrastructure and design criteria.

pressure groups in bringing about the current emphasis on conservation, and which exert a continuing powerful role. These voluntary bodies include the National Trust which is, among other matters, concerned with the fate of stately homes, large country houses and large rural estates, and its urban relative the Civic Trust founded in 1957 but sadly disbanded in 2009 owing to financial problems. Both of these bodies are entirely independent from the government. As indicated above, there is a series of voluntary bodies representing the needs of buildings from different historical periods, such as (in chronological order), the Georgian Society, Regency Society and Victorian Society, and increasingly societies concerned with each decade of the twentieth century, for example defending buildings from the 1920s and 1930s and now the 1960s onwards. There are other government bodies such as the Royal Fine Arts Commission and various other design bodies, including the Design Centre, which may be consulted on visual townscape issues. CABE (Commission for Architecture and the Built Environment) was set up under New Labour in the 1990s as an important player in everything to do with townscape, urban design and urban conservation. Under the Coalition government it was merged with the Design Centre and is now known (somewhat unimaginatively) as 'Design Council: CABE' and its role and staffing levels are likely to be reduced further. When dealing with aesthetic issues, national expert advice and local opinion both play a part, over and above the strict interpretation of planning law. Overall, the objective of preserving the 'amenity' of the area is central in many a planning controversy. 'Amenity' is an extremely elastic and much used word in the world of planning. It does not have a strict legal definition, but nevertheless carries considerable power as a material consideration in determining a planning decision.

For the tasks, further reading, additional photos and other resources for this chapter, please visit www. palgrave.com/companion/greed. E-Supplements 1, 2 and 4 provide information on legislation and government plan- *ning guidance, planning systems for Scotland, Wales, Northern Ireland and London, as well as information on the process of property development, respectively, and will be particularly useful in relation to this chapter.*

PART II

The Story of Planning

4 The Historical Roots of Planning

The influence of the past

The purpose of this chapter is to give the reader a summary of the main historical phases of the development of urban planning. The main emphasis in this chapter is chiefly upon the development of European architecture and planning, although reference will be made to international influences. In the first half of the chapter, the Ancient (Egyptian), Classical (Greek and Roman), Medieval and Renaissance stages will be summarised. In the second half, emphasis will be given to the development of more modern planning in Britain with reference to the Georgian and Victorian periods.

Emphasis is given to the visual and physical aspects of planning, such as urban design and architectural style, because these have been so important in shaping the nature and appearance of the built environment. Many buildings still survive from the past and great emphasis is put upon urban conservation and the listing of buildings of architectural and historical importance, and therefore it is important to be familiar with the different styles of architecture found in each historical period. The social, economic, political and cultural factors will also be highlighted in explaining why planning developed in the way it did to meet the needs of different societies. For example, changes in class structure, as a result of the Industrial Revolution, had a major effect on urban form and housing. The final section is devoted to the development of the parallel transport revolution which was to have widespread social, economic and land-use implications. The social aspects of planning are discussed in more detail in Chapters 14 and 15.

The ancient world

Architectural features and town planning principles from ancient times have been a continual source of inspiration to designers. For example, neo-Egyptian influences can be seen in 1930s architecture, and today in post-modern architecture. In the ancient world of Egypt town planning and architecture had the role of reinforcing the power of the ruling elite. Public buildings often had a mystical rather than practical purpose by modern standards. For example, the pyramids were built for the dead, not the living, and for the upper class at that (Photo 4.1). Planning can be use for a wide range of political, religious and ideological purposes. In comparison it is interesting to observe that both Hitler and Mussolini favoured heavy classical architectural styles for public buildings. Totalitarian regimes, whether they are political or otherwise, seem to favour megalithic architecture on a gigantic scale. Large cities, such as Thebes in Ancient Egypt, with great processional routes and geometrically laid out streets were designed chiefly to meet the religious and governmental role of the state. Harappa and Mohenjo-Daro in the Indian Sub-Continent were designed as religious cities, but also manifested a high level of functionality in their design. Likewise in the Far East, Angkor Watt in Cambodia comprises an extensive ancient city laid out on religious principles. Planning does not have to have a social welfare function, nor be associated with the modern concepts of equality and democracy, but may serve the requirements of the ruling elite or religious requirements.

Many of the early settlements were located where there was a plentiful water supply, good transport routes, and fertile ground to support the population (Mumford 1965). A river valley was an ideal location,

Photo 4.1   Pyramids mobbed by tourists

Contrary to the image given in many a television documentary, the Pyramids do not stand in splendid isolation surrounded by desert but are increasingly near to the outskirts of the city and the ring road, and under threat from increased tourist overload.

with the town sitting at the narrowest bridging-point of a river. In the modern world towns and cities can be located virtually anywhere provided there is adequate technology to overcome natural disadvantages and enough money to pay for it. In Britain, the development of the national electricity, gas and water grids and road systems reduces the geographical restrictions on location.

Most of the ancient civilisations built their main public buildings in stone or other local materials. Until the Industrial Revolution every region in every country had its own local architecture distinguished by its local building materials and its own style which developed in response to the needs of the village culture and the constraints of the local climate. This raises the classic geographical determinism debate: Is it the geography of the areas which makes the people the way they are, or the people who shape the built environment? With the coming of mass-produced materials and the spread of the International style of architecture, building materials have become much more similar in different countries in the twentieth century, and may be supplied by the same multinational suppliers.

It is often quite difficult to get hold of the original materials for restoration work. Maintenance has always been a major problem in respect of ancient historical buildings the world over. The present-day emphasis on conservation has broadened the emphasis to not just preserving buildings as historical monuments but also restoring the surrounding context of the buildings which form the backcloth and setting to the main attractions. In the case of more recent (rather than ancient) historical buildings the aim is to ensure that they are conserved as part of the living fabric of the city, and are used rather than being just preserved as antiquities.

Classical Greece

The Greek civilisation is the source of many of the ideas and philosophies of Western Civilisation. The classical style of architecture with its use of columns, topped by capitals in the three main Greek orders, Doric, Ionic and Corinthian, are still seen by many as the only real architecture'. The Doric has what looks like a spare tyre on the top of the column; the Ionic has 'two eyes on it': a stylised depiction of curled rams horns; and the Corinthian has decorative acanthus leaves above the column. The Greeks developed theories on Town Planning, many of which they put into practice in the building of their city states and colonial towns.

Most Greek settlements were based on a grid layout (streets at right angles to each other) but they combined this with a flexibility of design which took into account site characteristics. Greek settlements centred on the Agora (market place) which was surrounded by the main public buildings such as the Stoa (town hall). Not only did the Greeks build magnificent streets and buildings but they took into account the needs for sanitation, drainage and water supply. Lewis Mumford (1965) stated that the quality of a civilisation should be judged by the way in which it disposes of its waste material. The architecture of Athens has acted as a model for generations of architects. The Parthenon (a temple) on the top of the Acropolis (a large natural hill in the centre of the city) has inspired many travellers and is considered to embody perfect harmony of proportion. It became fashionable in the eighteenth and nineteenth centuries to make the Grand Tour of Europe, and many of the features of Greek architecture were copied back in Britain, adding a touch of class to the new industrial cities, e.g. Birmingham Town Hall (Briggs 1968), for example in the use of classical features such as Doric, Ionic and Corinthian capitals. Some of the buildings on and around the Parthenon are being restored, and this is the subject of much controversy. People are often startled by the fact that many of the Greek temples would have originally had red Roman tile roofs and that the walls and sculptures were decorated in bright colours.

Roman planning

Rome completes the classical period with the emphasis shifting to a relatively more decorative and ostentatious style, Greek architecture being purer and more simple. Throughout history it is noticeable how architectural styles go in cycles from pure classical simple buildings into more and more ornate styles → ostentatious styles → mixtures and novelties → over-decorative → reaction → return to classical simplicity. Some would say the Modern Movement of plain abstract architecture was a reaction against the over-decorative styles of Victorian times. The present emphasis on Conservation and Neo-Vernacular and generally more historical styles may be leading to another Decorative phase of architecture. Rome was a vast empire which extended across Europe even as far as that backward third world country of Ancient Britain – which soon became a profitable agricultural colony. The Roman Empire was a city-building enterprise and '*Every Roman soldier had a town plan in his knapsack*', the Army did most of the construction and many of the town planners, civil engineers and architects were military men. Roman towns were more standardised than Greek ones, and were based on a simple grid layout with a square in the centre, called the Forum, and several other standard public amenities were provided around the town such as baths, latrines, an arena, etc.

There was an element of land-use zoning in both Greek and Roman cities, which was based on different criteria from today. Zoning was a mechanism to create order, often undertaken to enforce the separation of the sacred and profane; and thus clean and dirty categories for religious and cultural reasons (Douglas 1966). For example, areas were designated where women, slaves and foreigners were not admitted, such as certain public squares and temple precincts. In ancient societies only a small percentage would belong to the ruling and priestly castes and the majority of citizens were likely to be slaves and workers (Boulding 1992). Likewise when the Greeks talked about the ideal city consisting of 5000 people they included only the people that mattered, discounting slaves, women and trades people. Distinct residential zones and districts were created for people of different social rank and occupation. This resulted in an early form of land-use zoning, in that there were distinct areas for merchants (and thus retail development) and artisans (and thus industrial development), in a society where people tended to live in the same buildings as they worked. This historical legacy was undoubtedly to influence the founding fathers of modern town planning many centuries later such as Geddes, Howard and Abercrombie (Geddes 1915).

The greatest engineering achievements of the Romans were the perfection of the Arch and the Dome. The Coliseum in Rome is of Arch construction, as are the many aqueducts and viaducts dotted throughout the Empire. Fresh water, good sewerage, drainage and good roads were all features of Roman development, and in many respects they were never surpassed for many centuries until the time of the Industrial Revolution. The Roman town was an important colonising tool in the Empire, acting as a garrison and an administrative centre in order to subdue the local population. Defensive walls were an essential feature of many Roman settlements. Town Planning was part of a military exercise to ensure effective defensive measures. The Roman towns and interconnecting roads established the national land-use and settlement pattern for Britain's subsequent development. Today many main roads, such as the A1, follow Roman routes. Many of the main towns and cities (especially those ending in 'chester', or 'cester') are of Roman origin. Some believe the Romans were following earlier roads related to ley lines (prehistoric lines of alleged terrestrial power) and that many of their settlements were based on ancient religious or tribal centres in what was a sophisticated, but predominantly rural, society that predated urban civilisation.

Medieval development

In the centuries after the Romans left, there was a series of invasions, for example, of Angles, Saxons, Jutes and Danes, but none of these were great city-building civilisations. Britain reverted to a rural society in which towns were market centres and local administrative nodes. The Norman Empire, which was extended to Britain by William the Conqueror in 1066, had a major effect on the land-use patterns of Britain. It influenced the class structure and feudal foundations of society. The Church was the main administrative arm of the state. The establishment of Abbeys and the endowment of cathedrals led to a new spate of construction, and the development of new market places and squares and related buildings administered by the ecclesiastical powers (as illustrated by Photo 4.2). There were some New Towns built by Edward I, and castles built mainly for defence, but in general towns grew and expanded naturally in an unplanned organic manner (Bell and Bell 1972).

In medieval times the main architectural styles were of two types. First there was the official architecture of the Church. The Norman style (with a rounded arch) predates the Gothic style (pointed arch) which went through various phases from a

Photo 4.2   Chartres Cathedral, Rose Window from outside

The main investment in urban form in the Middle Ages was in cathedral and church architecture. Such buildings were often hidden away within the tangled street pattern as they were designed for the glory of God rather than the human eye.

Photo 4.3   Organic street pattern, northern Italy

Whilst planned cities were generally based upon a grid layout, naturally evolving settlements tended to be more random, organic and human-scale in their development patterns.

simple basic style to a very decorative exaggerated style. The Gothic style was much copied in later centuries, especially by the Victorians. Local vernacular styles developed in different parts of the country, dependent on availability of materials and local weather conditions. Thatch and half timbering were not universal; indeed slate and stone was probably more common in some areas, and cob in others. Neo-vernacular is still a popular style. Mock Tudor, also known as Pseudo-Tudor, is a variation of Neo-Veo (neo-vernacular) which has always been scorned by architects and loved by the people.

Travel in the middle ages was undertaken on land by foot or by horse, mostly for religious purposes, such as pilgrimages, or for trade. Apart from the occasional stone bridge, the routes used by the trav-

ellers of the time were poorly constructed and maintained; so much so that in 1555 a Highways Act made every parish in the land responsible for the maintenance of the roads that passed through it, and required the annual election of a Surveyor of Highways to oversee the work (Bodey 1971).

A small settlement would develop beside a river and gradually tracks would develop into roads that meandered down the valley side to a bridge. Houses would be built alongside the roads where and when the residents felt the need. Bit by bit other facilities, artisan quarters, houses, paddocks and market places would develop, often centring around a well or a crossroads. Roads would follow footpaths, creating the typically irregular street pattern characteristic of medieval towns. This contrasts with the predesigned, premeditated plan characteristic of Roman towns, and other periods of history when the design has been imposed from above by a powerful Empire, military force or ruler upon the subject population.

Left to themselves towns and cities tended to evolve naturally, that is organically, if somewhat chaotically, and not necessarily in the ideal interests of all the residents. In recent years, almost in reaction against over-planning, there has been a return to enthusiasm for organic natural town forms (Photo 4.3), as against more formal grid layouts, and road layouts designed to serve the motorcar (refer to Chapter 13 on urban design). Paradoxically, to achieve this effect today, for example on a new housing layout, requires a fair amount of forethought and planning to create a genuine quaint townscape! Another effect of current planning emphasis on the virtues of the past and on conservation in particular, has been to stop the natural change that would normally occur. Any ordinary street scene is usually made of buildings from different historical periods cheek by jowl; some clashing and some complementary. An emphasis on design policy controls may lead to an artificial sterilisation of a quality townscape.

Vernacular building

Before the mass production of bricks, and their nationwide distribution by rail in the nineteenth century, each region of Britain had its own distinctive style, reflecting the availability of local materials and climatic factors, e.g. houses in areas of heavy rainfall such as West Wales had a steeply pitched roof, and the roof would be built of local slate rather than thatch. One of the most common styles in the south east and midlands was half timbering. This was originally introduced by the Anglo-Saxons, who originated in areas where there was ample supply of wood in Central Europe. The areas between the wood were filled in with wattle and daub and with other materials which were locally available, e.g. flints. In areas where stone was available this became the main material; different qualities were given to the buildings by different building materials, e.g. hard stone and granites in the Pennines (which weathered to black) as against soft golden stone in parts of the South West. The colour and texture of the materials used were important factors in creating the townscape and atmosphere. Cob, a mixture of clay, sand and mud, was a material used in areas such as Devon where neither stone nor wood were plentiful local materials. Walls were built up about two feet thick to create a flexible load bearing material which stood by its own weight, as is found in Dorset. Gable ends of the cob and half timbering were sometimes decorated by pargetting, with folk art patterns and mouldings raised in stucco.

Clunch consists of blocks of chalk which are used like stones. Chalk is porous, so a damp course of hard stone or brick was often inserted first, whilst tar was used in some seaside areas from the boat building industry along the south coast of England. Weatherboarding is an attractive form of exterior cladding often found in seaside areas, and apparently copied from the design of ships. It consists, in England, normally of horizontal slats of wood used to clad wattle walls. But in North America wood boarding and wooden shingles are frequently used on their own as the main structural material, particularly in New England. In Britain, tile hanging on walls was often used as another form of weather protection on the windward end of the building, often in conjunction with weatherboarding. Bricks were not a native material, but were imported from Holland, although there are earlier examples left by the Romans. They were used for expensive public and royal buildings, Hampton Court in Kingston upon Thames in London being a classic example from Tudor times. During the Industrial Revolution there was a boom in factory made bricks which replaced most of the traditional building materials, and bricks became commonplace. Likewise mass produced roof tiles replaced traditional materials such as thatch and slate roofing (Prizeman 1975; Munro 1979; Oliver 1997).

The Renaissance

Towards the end of the Middle Ages in Europe the sway of the Church began to become less dominant in the prosperous city states which were developing particularly in Italy, where self-made business men and merchants, rather than traditional feudal powers, took control. There was a rebirth (re-naissance) of interest in the ideas and culture of the Classical civil-isations of the Greeks and Romans, which were considered more appropriate to then modern values than the mystical emphasis of the Middle Ages. There was enthusiasm for the use of classical features in new public buildings and palaces to express the wealth of the merchant princes, e.g. the Medicis in Florence. Splendid new town planning features were introduced to Italian cities, which were in effect where major central area redevelopment occurred. Emphasis was put on the creation of a formal central square (along the lines of the forum, or agora), namely the piazza. Most Mediterranean settlements have squares which often act as outdoor living rooms where people meet and eat in the pavement cafés, and walk around in the cool of the evening. Many Italian cities of the late Middle Ages had been built at fairly high density owing to the need for defensive city walls. It was dangerous and expensive to extend them even if population growth occurred. The layout was shaped by the need for defence. Many examples can be seen in Italy, and in the planning books of geometrically laid out military settlements with octagonal, star shaped and circular forms. The outdoor squares acted as important safety valves in providing communal open space, and areas for military parades and carnivals. Later Renaissance piazzas often incorporated a colonnaded walkway in the classical style along one side, and fountains and statues in the centre.

The use of perspective techniques to create space and depth in paintings was carried over into town planning. Long narrow squares with a statue or townscape feature placed strategically at the vanishing point drew the eye into a greater perception of three-dimensional space. Making the windows on a building progressively, but imperceptibly, smaller as the upper floors were reached gave an illusion of height. Town planning and architecture had more in common with theatrical stage set design and art, than with modern-day practical, functional land-use planning.

Venice is a renaissance city of particular interest to modern planners. It had all the features of piazza planning but also serves as an ideal example of complete pedestrian–vehicular segregation as there no roads in Venice, only canals. Originally Venice consisted of a series of swamps and small islands that were reclaimed by the construction of drainage canals. Each small artificially-constructed island was centred on a well in a piazza, in which fresh water rose up naturally from the artesian basin under the sea bed. A natural 'neighbourhood unit' developed around each well. Another interesting feature of Venice is the unique architectural style – a combination of Classical, Gothic and Eastern Mediterranean Moslem influences. This style was much copied, particularly by the Victorians.

The Renaissance style developed on a more magnificent scale known as the High Renaissance style, quickly followed by the Baroque and the Rococo styles. Various Popes in conjunction with leading artists and architects of the time, such as Michelangelo and Bernini, progressively redeveloped the centre of Rome, creating magnificent squares and processional avenues. St Peter's Basilica was rebuilt in a style that resembled a pagan Roman temple, replacing the Gothic structure which was destroyed in a fire. The Baroque style of planning and architecture made much of the space around and between buildings. An obelisk (pointed stone column monument) was often used in the centre of a square to act as a central pivot to the geometrical layout of avenues and buildings radiating from it. No expense was spared, but the aim of this type of town planning was not to rehouse the poor, or to zone industry or to solve the traffic problems; indeed these matters were of little interest. The Grand Manner of Renaissance Planning gradually spread throughout Europe. It was the ideal style to express the power and magnificence of the ruler and the state. Many European cities were replanned (some several times over) with boulevards, squares, fountains, statues and triumphal arches. Town Planning was essentially a form of art and aimed at meeting the aspirations of the rising merchant classes and affluent bourgeoisie.

Georgian planning

The development of Georgian planning and architecture resulted from the influence of the Renaissance on Britain. The style and scale are significantly different from the Grand Manner in Europe (Summerson 1986; Kostoff 2009). The

Georgian style is so named as it developed at the time when a series of King Georges were on the throne between 1714 and 1830 (George I–IV). It is a mixture of classical Italian renaissance features and other influences from Northern Europe. In particular the Dutch had developed (with their usual enthusiasm for frugality, cleanliness and Puritanism), a distinctive domestic (housing) architectural style as expressed in the neat but restrained symmetrically-proportioned brick town houses in Amsterdam with sash windows and gabled façades. Brick was a relatively expensive building material in Britain and was usually only used in great houses, being imported from the Low Countries (Holland and Belgium), although it was also made in small quantities in London, Luton and Bridgwater too. Following the Great Fire of London in 1666 there was an opportunity to rebuild the capital with a Grand Manner Comprehensive Master Plan approach to planning. But there was much opposition from individual landowners. The Monarchy did not have the power of some of its European counterparts to impose a Plan from above. Individual real property rights and increased parliamentary democracy meant that redevelopment was inevitably going to be piecemeal.

A series of individual speculative developments emerged, many of which took the form of town squares with Georgian town houses facing onto grass and trees in the middle of the square. The houses themselves, aimed at the new affluent middle classes, were a mixture of Dutch features and classical elements with an emphasis on symmetry, sash windows and Greek pediments, and columns, rather than traditional gables. The squares were no doubt inspired by the Italian piazza but had a soft grass centre rather than a hard paved surface, thus prefiguring the garden city movement's love of grass and trees. Individual front gardens were not favoured, being considered rather rural and peasant-like, but there were often long walled back gardens, and separate mews at the back for the servants and the horses. Names such as Bedford Square, Grosvenor Square and Sloane Square bear witness to the property development abilities of the ducal landowners who possessed estates in what are now the West End, Kensington and Chelsea. The main city churches and St Paul's Cathedral were rebuilt by Sir Christopher Wren, following the Great Fire of London in 1666. St Paul's is in the style of St Peter's in Rome, whereas many of the other Wren churches are more English yet still classical in design.

In Georgian and Regency times a large number of provincial towns and resorts were developed to meet the needs of the new affluent leisured classes. The early resorts were mainly inland and centred on spas where people could 'take the waters', e.g. in Bath, Cheltenham, Harrogate, Epsom complete with racecourse, Hotwells in Bristol, and Brixton in South London. Later sea bathing became the fashion, and a second series of resorts was developed, including Brighton with its Regency Pavilion, Skegness, and later Weston-super-Mare. It was not until the development of the railways that these became more working-class resorts. Bath is one of the most famous spa towns. Its importance was established when Queen Anne took the water there for her rheumatism in the 1720s. But Beau Nash really popularised and publicised the city when he was made the Post Master for Bath. He has been compared with Billy Butlin in creating the holiday industry, in this case encouraging wealthy people to come for the season. Bath is composed of a series of terraces, squares and crescents, all designed in the Georgian style. Even the smaller houses, back streets and mews buildings are designed in a similar style, creating a totally coordinated designer environment. Houses in those days were built to different maximum sizes which were taxed at different levels of 'rates' and this was a considerable constraint on the design and density of the housing planned. In Bath there were six main rating levels in operation. Thus the phrase, 'it's only second rate', originally meant it was not quite the best type of housing. Nash worked in conjunction with the two architects named John Wood the Elder and John Wood the Younger (father and son), who created an atmosphere of refinement and classical culture in designing a city of Georgian town houses. But Bath does not only consist of the grand squares and crescents, it is held together by all the small backstreets, small terraced houses and incidental features in the same style. This account has centred upon English towns, but it should be noted that both Dublin and Edinburgh in the 'New Town' also provide magnificent examples of classical development.

Prior to the Fire, Inigo Jones, the King's Surveyor, had built the Covent Garden scheme, just

Photo 4.4   Regency housing, London

In between and overlapping with the Georgian and Victorian periods, the Regency style of Architecture brought a greater level of ornamentation and additional 'Quality Street' urban design elements to major cities, especially London around Regent's Park.

outside the City of London. This was designed along the lines of an Italian piazza with a colonnaded walkway and town houses facing the square. An opera house and theatre was provided for the leisure and pleasure of the residents. A small market was held on the square from time to time. Over the centuries the market became the main fruit and vegetable market for London and the area went down socially. In the early 1960s the market was relocated at Nine Elms, Vauxhall, and the area seemed threatened with demolition. The area eventually became a conservation area and an upmarket tourist attraction. Many of the original working-class residents despaired that they no longer fitted in the area and could not afford to live there any more. London continued to grow throughout Georgian times, to develop as a prosperous capital and eventually in the nineteenth century as a world capital of

the Empire. This role was reflected in the architecture of individual buildings in Georgian and Victorian times. Yet, there was no comprehensive replanning of the whole London in the Grand Manner. But in the early nineteenth century in Regency times (named after the Prince Regent) part of the Crown Estates just to the north of the centre of London, namely Regent's Park, was developed as a series of upmarket town houses by John Nash (Photo 4.4). Further developments occurred down Regent Street to Clarence House, a north/south axis on the boundary between Soho and Mayfair. Trafalgar Square, the Mall, Piccadilly Circus, Oxford Circus and Buckingham Palace were all part of this grand design. In fact the scheme developed over many years, the Victorians altering and enlarging various elements of the original Regency scheme.

Industrial Revolution

New concepts of town planning

At the beginning of the nineteenth century Britain was undergoing major economic and social change. The demand for town planning was called forth by a combination of the effects of three main factors, namely, industrialisation, urbanisation and population growth, and the related problems of overcrowding and disease (Ashworth 1968; Briggs 1968). As outlined in the first part of this chapter, town planning, prior to the Industrial Revolution, was based on quite narrow objectives, such as the desire to create beautiful architectural set pieces, and providing housing for the more affluent classes. Nineteenth-century town planning was more down to earth in its concern with public health, social reform, sanitation and with meeting the functional requirements of industry and transportation.

Industrialisation

The Industrial Revolution, as its name suggests, transformed Britain from a predominantly rural agricultural society to a modern industrial urban society (Ryder and Silver 1990). There had been changes in agricultural methods in the eighteenth century which led to greater yields with fewer agricultural labourers. In some areas this created a surplus of workers, leading to migration to the towns, thus providing the necessary workforce for the Industrial Revolution.

The development of new forms of technology, and in particular the creation of machinery which could produce manufactured goods more quickly than the human hand, led to major changes in the nature of work, and the duties of the workforce. Originally, for example, textiles had been produced by hand, by individuals sitting at their looms and spinning wheels in their separate cottages. The introduction of mechanical forms of power which drove several machines at once required the assembly of many workers (called 'factors') and machines, all together in the same building which became known as the 'factory'. At first industrial development occurred on a fairly small scale, fitting in with the surroundings with little disturbance because the early woollen mills and factories were powered by water power. The early industrial settlements were relatively rural, being placed alongside fast-flowing streams in hilly countryside.

Later coal was used to fuel steam engines which could power many more machines at once, by means of connecting drive belts running throughout the factory. New industrial settlements grew up located alongside the coal mines particularly in the North, Midlands, and South Wales. The emphasis shifted from the production of textiles in rural areas, to iron and steel, and then manufactured goods in highly urbanised areas, as a result of technological developments. These were aimed at the home market, and at the expanding overseas markets which resulted from the growth of the British Empire in the nineteenth century. People flocked to the newly industrialising areas resulting in rural depopulation and a complete regional redistribution of the population broadly from the South towards the North and across from the West Country to South Wales.

In the later stages of industrialisation other forms of power were developed which could be transmitted anywhere nationally, such as gas and electricity. In theory anything could be developed anywhere, provided there was the financial backing to do so. This led to the phenomenon of footloose industry which went wherever it was the most economic to locate. Nevertheless, development was inevitably attracted to locate in areas which had already established themselves as industrial centres, because they offered concentrations of skilled workers, the necessary infrastructure, and the commercial expertise to help run the businesses and market needed to sell the products. Nowadays access to transport routes for distribution purposes, especially the need to be near motorway junctions, or within prestigious motorway corridors such as the M4, is likely to be more important than being near sources of local power because of the ubiquity of the national grid.

Changes in city form and housing development

Not only did cities expand, but new concentrated forms of urban land use developed, as distinct factory areas and working-class housing areas grew up side by side. Not only were there changes in the quantity of people in towns and cities, but inevitably there was a decline in the quality of their lives owing

Table 4.1   UK population growth 1801–2012

Date	Total Population
1801	8.9 million
1851	17.9 million
1901	32.5 million
2010	60.0 million
2012	62.0 million
2014	63.2 million

(See Ashworth 1968, 7 for fuller details for 1801–1901; ONS website for later years)

Table 4.2   England: urban growth 1801–1901

Date	Birmingham	Manchester	Leeds
1801	71,000	75,000	53,000
1851	265,000	336,000	172,000
1901	765,000	645,000	429,000

(See Ashworth, 1968 for fuller details of many towns)

to disease and overcrowding (Cherry 1981; Ravetz 1986). These problems could not be solved by personal individual efforts but required civic initiatives and national solutions, as explained in the second part of this chapter.

Whilst there was an overall growth, and natural increase, there were also large movements of population from one part of the country to another, both on a regional basis, and a migration to the towns from the countryside. This may be summed up in the following statement:

1801 – 80 per cent of the population was rural.
1991 – 80 per cent of the population was urban.

Housing problems occurred in the nineteenth century chiefly in areas where there was a concentration of large numbers of working-class people in poorly built housing around the new factories and mills. They located there because at the beginning of the Industrial Revolution, there was very little money or time for commuting and the transport systems had not yet developed, so people were huddled together in proximity to their workplace. At first it was a matter of converting existing housing. For example,

larger inner-city town houses were subdivided into separate dwellings; in some cases whole families were living in one room or in cellars (Ashworth 1968). Some of the factory owners provided cheap housing for the workers, although they might deduct the cost from their wages: the philanthropic factory owners were the exception to the rule.

Many local builders cashed in, building substandard tenements and terraces, which were known as 'jerry built' (apparently a phrase deriving from the reputation of the work of a particularly bad builder of that name). Houses were often '*half a brick thick*' (i.e. thin, substandard walls) and 'back to back'. This means that what appeared to be a terrace of ordinary houses in fact contained twice the number of dwellings, because the houses were divided at the ridge of the roof, backing onto each other: creating two rows of houses, one facing on to the street and the other facing onto the back alley way. However the housing situation was soon to change as a result of further improvements in transport, private enterprise and social reform.

The effects of the Industrial Revolution were not limited to the North of England. In Southern cities, especially within London, large amounts of manufacturing industry developed within inner-city areas, often as back-street business in erstwhile residential areas. Many houses on main roads were converted into shops or businesses. One can quite clearly see that the shop fronts were added, looking down on the buildings from the top of a double-decker bus. Urban development spread out, in all directions with hardly a break, over many miles in the London region. Some of the most industrialised, urbanised, as well as commercialised, areas of Britain were in the South, for example, in the inner London boroughs with large working-class populations to match. In the south the office and commercial revolution followed hard on the heels of Industrial Revolution, creating a new employment sector made up of clerks, typists, service industry workers, and service workers.

Wonderful architecture or terrible slums?

How bad was it really in the Industrial Revolution? It gives a false impression to suggest that the entire population at the time of the Industrial Revolution worked in factories, lived in the North, and lived in poor housing. In fact conditions varied considerably according to people's social class and the region in which they lived. Not all residential development consisted of substandard working-class housing and slum properties, but of town houses and villas. The nineteenth century was a period of the most prolific amount of house-building, and this included the construction of middle-class villas, town houses and substantial terraces which still occupy large tracts of our cities, and comprise the Victorian and Edwardian inner rings of the suburban development. Suburban growth continued into the twentieth century as people sought to live further away from their work, as was possible with the expansion of tram, rail and subsequently bus services. There were also large areas of better quality, skilled artisan and respectable working-class housing consisting of miles of little terraced houses built on a grid layout. Many Victorian residential areas have been recolonised (gentrified) by the middle classes. Erstwhile 'slum' houses within the inner city such as Islington, London are now areas of some of the highest property values in Britain.

Although much is made of the poverty, overcrowding and bad housing that resulted, paradoxically this was the most prosperous era in history with increased wealth (for some) which led to a building boom and the construction of many magnificent buildings, both public and private. Relatively speaking, there was an increase in overall national prosperity, which itself funded the highly-decorative Victorian style of architecture. There was a tremendous amount of building of commercial premises, town halls, libraries, law courts and the beginnings of modern High Street development with large rows of individual shops, early department stores, purpose-built offices, banks and other business premises: all these buildings together creating the foundations of the modern Central Business District (CBD). There was also emphasis on the building of town parks and playing fields, which are often seen as a luxury by both developers and local authorities. Many such open spaces are today in danger of development, as they are often located in what are today central area sites with high land values.

Victorian architecture was decorative and 'heavy' in style. It was eclectic, that is it incorporated features from a range of historical styles, in particular the Gothic and the Classical. But also with the expansion of the British Empire, a range of features from all over the world were incorporated too, including Indian, Egyptian and Chinese features. This type of architecture fell out of favour whilst the Modern Movement held sway, in which the emphasis was on clear-cut lines and 'honesty' in building style. Victorian architecture and townscape has made a valuable contribution to the urban fabric, as reflected in the listing of many buildings from this period.

The Victorians liked to build solid, enduring public buildings using stone and often a range of marble, e.g. Portland stone brought in from Dorset on the railways for use in London. Civic pride and public building works went hand in hand with reform which often took the form of what was called gas and water socialism, that is investment in public works to build up the necessary infrastructure (Dixon and Muthesius 1978). A vast amount of investment was put into 'under the city streets' in the form of sewers and drains (Bell and Bell 1972). The new wealth derived from the Industrial Revolution was used by the City Fathers and urban benefactors to add prestige and respectability to the new industrial cities such as Manchester, Leeds and Liverpool to build magnificent town halls, museums, libraries and art galleries.

Many industrial buildings, particularly warehouses, were given the full architectural treatment and there were many examples of magnificent buildings in commonplace industrial settings, amongst declining docklands and industrial zones, although many of these have since been renovated and incorporated in the new gentrified schemes. Railway stations and other public buildings, work houses, police stations, asylums and public conveniences were all however more humble in design, but still given some architectural embellishment. In the case of workhouses and prisons the style of architecture was intended to give the inmates a sense of the overpowering fortress-like strength of the buildings and the harshness of their circumstances. Also because people were unsure about travelling on the new railways it was thought that if they were made to look like great cathedrals people would be less afraid because they thought they were going to church.

Towards the end of the century a reaction was setting in to the excesses of Victorian architecture. Magnificent new structures in the form of factories, bridges, warehouses and engine sheds (built by people such as Isambard Kingdom Brunel) were still seen as engineering although they proved to be the true ancestors of modern architecture.

Social change

Employment structures

Not only were the settlement pattern and the nature of cities changed as a result of the Industrial Revolution, there were also major changes taking place within the nature of urban society itself and the patterns of daily life. The changes which occurred in the nature of social class divisions, the family and community, and the relationship between home and work, male and female, and in people's daily lives, will now be discussed. All of these were manifested in the nature of the layout and zoning of towns and cities.

As a result of the Industrial Revolution, the structure of society changed. New types of class divisions and occupations emerged as a result of new technological inventions, and wider changes in the economy itself. In the traditional rural society of the past, a relatively feudal static social system existed, the inhabitants of a typical village consisting of the landowners and the agricultural labourers, with a vicar and a few skilled trades people in the middle, but without an intermediate middle class or large numbers of working-class people, who worked in factories rather than on the land. People did not have a social class as such, but rather were endowed with a certain status, which they were born with, and all human relationships were governed by this. The static and deferential nature of pre-industrial social attitudes is summed up in the following ditty:

> God bless the squire and his relations,
> And keep us in our proper stations.
> (Anon.)

With the coming of the Industrial Revolution social structure was transformed, as large numbers of people moved from the villages and set up home in the new industrial cities, swelling the ranks of the new working classes. It now became accepted to classify people in relation to what their work was, rather than what they were born as. Most noticeable was the development of a new industrial working class, or rather working classes as they were many and varied. However, in spite of all these changes, a small minority of landowners continued to own the majority of the wealth and land (Norton-Taylor 1982).

Relationship between work and home

As a result of the Industrial Revolution, changes occurred not only in the range of occupations, and related class structure, but in the nature of work itself with more people working outside the home. Home-based craft industries were abandoned as workers flocked to the new factories. Workers' lives were increasingly controlled as they were required to attend for a long and fixed period of hours every day. In contrast the traditional agricultural worker's life was governed by the seasons, and by the amount of daylight. For women, in particular, 'work' had not been rigidly divided between work in the home and going out to work elsewhere; many tasks which were eventually industrialised, such as weaving, were originally carried out within the home (either working in their own home, or as a servant in someone else's home) along with everything else, such as cooking and childcare.

The factories were all dependent on the same sources of power to drive the machines, and so were often clustered together creating distinct factory zones, with the housing huddled around the factories. With time the early planners sought to segregate out the land uses, creating separate industrial and residential areas, which, as has been explained, were increasingly located further and further away from the workplace. As increasing numbers of women worked in factories and went out to work like the men, they too were affected by these land-use trends. All this tended to segregate women's lives, for the zoning whilst hygienic and efficient, made it very difficult for women to combine work and home, and it was none too convenient for men either, as well as creating the 'journey to work' and subsequently all the commuter traffic problems of today. These social issues are discussed further in Chapters 14 and 15, whilst Chapter 12 focuses on transport planning. But in this introductory chapter the important point to grasp is that the way society is organised shapes urban form and land-use patterns.

Family structures

The traditional rural family in pre-industrial society was fairly large by modern standards. Most families are what are called 'nuclear families', which means they consist of the nucleus of the mother and the father and the immediate offspring, classically of 2.4 children on average, and is nothing to do with nuclear war, or explosive family relationships! This image may be based more on myth (as represented in the 'Cornflakes Family' seen on television commercials) than on statistical reality, as the situation has gradually changed in the second part of the twentieth century (Hamnett *et al.* 1989). In pre-industrial societies, and indeed in third world agricultural societies today, families were more likely to be 'extended families' which meant that they consisted of the nucleus of the parents and children, but vertically might also consist of grandparents and grandchildren, and horizontally might extend out to include uncles and aunts, nephews and cousins. Indeed the borderline between the extended family and the concept of the tribe, and the village in which everyone is related to everyone else, is a matter of degree.

During the Industrial Revolution it was generally the younger people who moved to the new industrial towns and cities, leaving the older people behind, although sometimes sending money back to support them. Birth rates were high in the new industrial towns with many families having six or more children. This was in spite of the small size of the housing which consisted of two up and two down terraced houses, and high infant mortality levels (Whitelegg *et al.* 1982; Lewis 1984). As time went on families became smaller, and paradoxically housing for the working classes became somewhat larger.

Transport revolution

Let us now return to the transport aspect of the Industrial Revolution, as transport was to become such a major issue for modern planners dealing with towns and cities shaped by previous land-use transportation systems (as discussed further in Chapter 12). In the nineteenth century Britain was a major maritime power and trading nation and this affected the settlement pattern and nature of urbanisation at home. The goods produced had to be transported to their markets both within Britain and to the expanding markets at home and overseas. In order to export goods, the building of new docks became a very important form of development throughout this period as can be seen in the extensive areas today such as in London, Liverpool and Bristol. By the eighteenth century the need for investment in the country's roads was widely recognised, and the Turnpike Trusts were set up to levy a toll on the users of a stretch of road, the funds raised being used by the Trust for its repair and maintenance, and in many cases to make a profit. The growth of towns and the improved condition of the roads led to more comfortable forms of travel, such as the coach or the carriage, and this in turn promoted travel for leisure pursuits as well as for mail, trade and business. The quality of the roads improved as surveyors such as Telford and Macadam became more skilled in engineering (Bodey 1971) and new processes and materials became available as the Industrial Revolution gathered pace. The need to move much greater quantities of material to feed the ever growing demands of industry initially led to the development of canals in Britain in the latter half of the eighteenth century.

The turnpike road system served the early years of the Industrial Revolution, but this proved to be an expensive and bumpy way of transporting manufactured goods. It was soon overtaken by the development of the canal system, which was especially backed by the Staffordshire pottery manufacturers to ensure fewer breakages en route. At its height this provided an extensive system connecting the main industrial centres, markets and ports throughout Britain, but it was soon upstaged by the development of the railway system. Canal building in Britain really took off with the construction of the Bridgewater canal by James Brindley in 1760. While many rivers had previously been made more navigable, the coming of the canals changed the nature of transport in Britain and left a lasting mark on its

Photo 4.5   Industrial settlement with steam train

Both urban and national structure was transformed by the development of mills and then the new railway system that served to distribute their goods, and of course the people. The industrial and transport revolution are inseparable.

landscape. The canals had to be kept as level as possible and along with the construction of their towpaths came much greater feats of engineering such as locks, tunnels, basins and aqueducts, such as the magnificent Pontcysyllte aqueduct, constructed by Telford and completed in 1805. At 37 metres above the river Dee, which it crosses, it has been described as 'perhaps the greatest monument in stone of English canal engineering' (Hoskins 1985, 251) and was designated as a World Heritage Site in 2009. By 1840 there were an estimated 4500 miles of canals in Britain, which made it possible to transport bulky and heavy materials great distances at a much reduced cost.

Yet the age of the canal was short-lived and eclipsed by the development of the railways. The canal system provides a valuable leisure and environmental asset which is painstakingly being restored in many parts of the country, mainly through voluntary initiatives which have only latterly attracted government support, as in the case of the Kennett and Avon Canal which links London to Bristol. Thus our historical transport systems, as well as the buildings and land uses from the past, have become part of our historical, national heritage and are the subject of conservation and leisure policies, as discussed in later chapters in Part III.

The first main passenger railway was the Stockton to Darlington Railway, opened in 1825. The opening of the Liverpool and Manchester Railway in 1830 heralded a fundamental change in the way in which people and goods were transported and had a marked effect on the growth and spread of urban areas in Britain. Railway locomotion was based upon harnessing the power of steam. Whilst

Watt's steam engine was stationary and revolutionised factory production, driving the machinery, George Stephenson's steam engines were developed to pull along trains along metal rails (Photo 4.5). Horse-drawn rail transport had previously only been used to a very limited extent in coal mining areas. With the growth of the railways entire industrial settlements grew up around the stations serving the factories and mills.

Between 1830 and 1840 nearly 2400 miles of railway track were built, connecting London with the great new industrial cities such as Birmingham, Liverpool and Manchester. A second boom came in the 1840s and by 1848 there was around 5000 miles of track connecting most of Britain's towns and cities to London and to each other. As well as the huge economic changes which the spread of the railways brought about, they symbolised the conquest of space and of parochialism (Thompson 1955) and facilitated a number of significant social and political changes. The engineers behind the construction of the railways, such as Stephenson and ultimately Brunel, were to become world famous and the scale of change brought about by their works to the fabric of Britain's towns and country was enormous (Hoskins 1985). New lines required parliamentary approval, and a total of 93 Railway Acts were passed by parliament between 1825 and 1837 alone (Thompson 1955). A number of railway companies grew up to finance, construct and run the railways; they were built by thousands of labourers, many Irish, who were known as 'navvies' (from their earlier role constructing the *navi*gation canals). By the 1860s a national network of routes had been established in Britain, run by about 15 railway companies (Bradley 2007) which, perhaps for the first time, helped to create a fully integrated national economy (Matthew 1993). Growth continued, and by the 1870s there were nearly 16,000 miles of railway. In comparison there were 30,000 miles of track in the whole of Great Britain in 1960. There are only 10,000 miles today, as a result of the cutbacks ordered by the Beeching Report (Beeching 1963) and subsequent rationalisations and cutbacks, but England, in particular, still has one of the highest levels of track provision in the world. But times were to change, with the invention of the internal combustion engine and the growth of mechanised individualised road transport in the twentieth century. But our rail system still has a huge effect on the shape, extent and layout of our urban areas and national settlement pattern.

For the tasks, further reading, additional photos and other resources for this chapter, please visit www.palgrave. com/companion/greed. In particular you will find many more photos of historical buildings and diagrams of different types of city form and structure and a table charting the historical development of architectural styles.

5 Industrialisation: Reaction and Reform

Rising to the challenge

Modern town planning arose in the nineteenth century in response to the problems and conditions outlined in the latter part of the last chapter. Early reforms simply sought to deal with the worst effects of disease, overcrowding and slum development. Later the emphasis moved towards seeking to create, more positively, whole new ways of living, through the founding of model communities and development of new concepts and theories on how to plan cities.

This chapter takes us from the great reform movement of the nineteenth century up to the middle of the twentieth century before the Second World War. It discusses both legislative reform and new approaches to urban planning, the two chief influences being the Garden City Movement and the Modern Movement in architecture with its emphasis upon high-rise city development.

Legislative reforms

Local government reforms

To implement reform there was a need for an effective, administrative structure, and a series of acts of parliament were passed. The Municipal Corporations Act 1835 laid the foundations for this, making possible the creation of locally elected urban councils, i.e. local authorities, which had the powers to levy rates from householders and businesses, and to use the money to employ professional and administrative staff, in order to carry out these improvements and building programmes (Ashworth 1968). Initially town planning housing and public health reform went hand in hand but they became separated out into distinct departments within the new local government system.

State intervention gradually built up pace through the nineteenth century as each subsequent act increased state control over the built environment. In 1840 a Select Committee, headed by Edwin Chadwick, on the *Conditions in Towns* had been established, leading to the *Report on the Sanitary Conditions of the Labouring Population, and on the Means of its Improvement* in 1842. In 1843 this was followed by the establishment of a Royal Commission on the Health of Towns, and in parallel the Health of Towns Association was founded. The Sanitary Act 1847 required sewers and drains to be provided in all new residential areas. The spread of cholera and other waterborne diseases made intervention necessary. There were major outbreaks in 1832 and 1849. It might originate in working-class districts, but could spread anywhere, and to anyone, along the insanitary water systems of the city. In 1854, a Dr Snow showed the relationship between a major cholera outbreak and a single polluted pump in the Soho district of London (Hall 1992: 18; Hall and Tewdwr-Jones 2010) (Photo 5.1).

The realisation that disease was waterborne rather than existing in the miasma (poisonous smell) of the atmosphere was a great leap forward for sanitary engineering (Greed 2003a). Increased state intervention to provide sewerage and drainage systems was needed, along with both domestic and public toilet provision (Briggs 1968; Cherry 1988).

The Public Health Act 1848 went further, being one of the first Acts intervening in *how* houses were constructed, and therefore potentially added to the cost for the developers. This Act required that all ceilings must be at least eight feet high. Low ceilings had health implications as they reduced the

Photo 5.1   John Snow's water pump, Soho, London

This pump was identified by John Snow as the source of a cholera epidemic. This pump still stands, but no longer works, and is now in a busy part of central London, surrounded by offices and not far from Oxford Street. It is just across from a pub called the John Snow.

likelihood of light penetrating the building, and reduced the circulation of air, leading, it was thought, to the lurking of germs and diseases in the dark corners of badly ventilated rooms. Many of the newcomers to the industrial towns would live in lodging houses and other forms of temporary accommodation, until they had established themselves and were able to rent a terraced house. The Common Lodging Houses Act and the Labouring Classes Lodging Houses Acts of 1868 were passed, introduced under the sponsorship of Lord Shaftesbury, which enabled the inspection and better provision of lodging houses.

Gradually controls moved from dealing with individual properties to planning whole areas. The Artisans and Labourers Dwellings Improvements Act also of 1868 (the Torrens Act) increased powers in dealing with insanitary buildings and the area surrounding them (Ashworth 1968). The Artisans and Labourers Dwellings Improvement Act of 1875 increased local authority powers to deal with whole areas, as against individual buildings, giving them compulsory purchase powers, and the powers to build schemes which provided accommodation for the working classes. This was a major step towards the modern-day powers of local authorities to carry out compulsory purchase and to take control of the planning of an area themselves. The Public Health Act 1875 set minimum standards on the design of houses and also on the layout of streets, so it is in a sense one of the first true town planning acts. The implementation of these standards was achieved by giving local authorities the power to introduce by-laws to control the layout of new streets and housing schemes in their districts. These standards required that every house should have a rear access, which was meant to solve the problem of back-to-back houses, which shared a common party wall. To summarise, in these acts the three functions of local authorities were to clear existing substandard housing, to carry out building works themselves, and to control the nature of construction built by private builders and developers (Photo 5.2).

Normally, under the by-law regulations, the width of the street had to be at least the same dimension as the height of the building's front wall up to the eaves. This created a rather enclosed, reassuringly human scale to such areas. This sense of

Photo 5.2   Small terraced housing, Easton, Bristol

Many such 'by-law' houses were built in towns and cities all over the country, to the minimum standards set by the reforming housing acts. They are still solid valuable homes today.

human scale in residential areas was lost with the introduction of much wider streets to make way for the motor car, and more generous front gardens in housing estates in the early twentieth century. In 1890 the Housing of the Working Classes Act increased local authorities' power to build new houses themselves, thus creating an early form of council housing. By this time developers were losing interest in building cheap housing for the working classes to rent, and were turning their attention to the more affluent emerging owner-occupied middle-class suburban housing developments. Council housing was to go on to become a major feature of our towns and cities in the twentieth century. It is only since the 1980s that this sector has been in decline, being overtaken by owner-occupation.

Social constraints on reform

All this legislation was chiefly aimed at the working classes (M. Smith 1989). It was considered politically unacceptable to control the design of middle-class housing – indeed it was not needed, with high ceilings and large rooms – although the sanitation often left much to be desired (Rubenstein 1974). Indeed *'an Englishman's home is his castle'* and the government had no right to intervene, as yet. Nevertheless these early acts paved the way for later, wider controls over all classes of housing and types of land uses by means of town planning. There were already some limited controls on middle-class housing and commercial buildings in London that had existed ever since the Great Fire of London in 1666. By the end of the century many of the larger Northern cities such as Manchester, Liverpool and Newcastle had also increased their controls on urban development by means of private acts of parliament, before the main national town planning acts of the early twentieth century came into being. The importance of well laid out cities and town planning was widely accepted as a boost to commerce, and a benefit to the citizens.

Government initiatives were augmented by a range of private reforming endeavours. There were a number of housing societies concerned with improving the conditions of the working classes, such as the Peabody Trust. This was set up in 1862 by George Peabody, an American philanthropist. Many of his Peabody Buildings can still be seen today in areas of London such as Islington, Whitechapel, Vauxhall and Bethnall Green, and most of them are in the style of walk-up tenements. There were many other schemes, many of which were based on sound commercial principles, in that subscribers to the scheme received what was then a reasonable rate of interest on their investment: that is '5 per cent Philanthropy'. Many of these schemes look fairly grim, judged by today's standards, but they were better than existing alternatives.

The attitude towards the nature of housing provision for the working classes had come a long way from the poor law philosophy of the first half of the century which actively discouraged people from seeking help. Official attitudes were strongly influenced by the theories of Malthus (1798), who took the unenlightened view that overpopulation was caused by the poor themselves. He suggested that nothing should be done to ease the conditions of the poor, as this would only cause them to 'breed' more and thus make the problem worse. But, poverty was more often caused by low wages or unemployment. Rich men had many children in Victorian times and did not become poor as a result.

Ever since the Law of Settlement and Removal Act 1662, the homeless and 'sturdy beggars' had been seen as a burden on the parish. The belief in a division between the deserving poor and those who could work if they so chose, was fundamental to much reform thinking and indeed is to be found today in modern condemnations of those who are perceived as work shy, as *'chavs'*, and living off benefits (O. Jones 2010). The problem became greater with the movement of people generated by the Industrial Revolution, and by more people being pushed off the land as a result of modern farming methods, this being reinforced by the various enclosure acts such as that of 1801. In 1832 the Royal Commission on the Poor Law investigated the whole situation, resulting in the 1834 Poor Law Amendment Act, which actually reduced the level of help in spite of growing demand. In order to reduce numbers looking to the parish for relief (help), the view was taken that conditions should be so harsh in the workhouses that people would only seek admission as a last resort. This attitude still pervades aspects of the housing benefits system even today by making it really difficult for people to claim.

Model communities

Private initiatives

Whilst much of the new legislation was concerned with controlling development in cities, modern town planning owes much to the visionary forces of those who wanted to create completely new settlements (Bell and Bell 1972). Various factory owners, often of Quaker, non-conformist, or socialist persuasion, sought to change society, at their own expense. Whilst some critics would accuse them of being paternalistic in their approach, others would argue that there was no compulsion on them to improve workers' conditions. There was a surplus of workers and high unemployment during much of the nineteenth century, so, presumably, they were operating out of the best of intentions and a sense of public duty. Some, however, may have been motivated by more businesslike, utilitarian, principles, which may be summed up in the principle that happy workers are good workers and loyal to the firm.

New Lanark

Robert Owen (1771–1858) was one of the earliest town planners and an early socialist, who had many new ideas, and tried them out, in respect of just about every aspect of human society, including education, housing, health, trade unionism and even birth control. Like many of the reformers, Owen came from humble origins. From working in a draper's shop, Owen rose to be manager of a Lancashire cotton mill, and then married the daughter of David Dale, the owner of the New Lanark Mills in Scotland. New Lanark was already a self-contained and planned industrial village when Owen arrived, the first buildings having been completed in 1786, and by 1790 the population had reached 2000. In 1800 the mills were taken over by Robert Owen from David Dale, who had set up the original scheme.

During the next 25 years Owen developed his schemes on community living and education. The Institution for the Formation of Character was established, which included nursery schooling and adult education, as well as school provision for children. The town included Britain's first co-operative store. However, the housing provision constituted tenements with minimal plumbing with shared kitchens and communal WCs. It was all rather grim by today's standards, and somewhat regimented with regular inspections of the dwellings being undertaken by Owen himself, to look for bedbugs. New Lanark was set in a narrow valley along a fast-flowing stream which provided water power to run the machinery. New Lanark is not really very industrial to look at. Owen wanted to spread his ideas by setting up 'villages of co-operation'. Several Owenite communities were set up by his followers,

both in Britain and in North America, such as New Harmony in the USA. Also he wrote *New View of Society* in 1813 and *Report to the County of Lanark* in 1821, and his ideas spread widely. New Lanark is a heritage village attraction open to tourists.

It should be noted that New Lanark was not just a one-off exception in Scotland, but was but one manifestation of a long-running and extensive industrialisation period, which saw the growth and urbanisation of existing cities, especially Glasgow. An expansion of dock construction, shipbuilding and mercantile trade was generated by the need to export manufactured goods across the world. Likewise in Northern Ireland, rapid expansion and industrialisation of Belfast, manifested in the large areas of terraced housing for the workers, the expansion of the docks (best known for the construction of the Titanic at the Harland and Wolff shipyard in Belfast) and the investment in high-quality public buildings (Purdue 2013). Meanwhile Wales, especially South East Wales and the Welsh Valleys, was hugely impacted by the Industrial Revolution and areas that previously comprised small rural villages became major centers of coal mining and manufacture. Architecturally the industrial heritage is still to be seen in Cardiff in the large districts of terraced housing built for the workers (but occupied by students today) and in the magnificent City Hall, Civic Centre and other public buildings.

Bradford-Halifax school

The next phases of model community building occurred in West Yorkshire, where rapid industrialisation was taking place. Colonel Akroyd, a rich mill owner, built two model communities, the first at Copley in 1849 in the Calder Valley near Halifax, and then Akroydon in 1859. George Gilbert Scott, the great Victorian architect, was employed to design Akroydon, which consisted of fairly modest terraced and town houses for the workers, with the main family Hall of the Akroyds' set on the hillside above, so that he could look down and see his experiment at work (a common Victorian preference). This model community is now surrounded by subsequent suburban development, and does not look particularly innovative, but at the time the layout and design were seen as quite innovative. Akroyd pioneered the concept of home-ownership for his workers, by means of establishing the Halifax Building Society in 1845.

Another key figure in the Halifax school of model industrial town planning is Titus Salt (1803–76), who founded the village of Saltaire in 1851, on the River Aire. His business was based on producing cloth from the wool of Alpaca goats, which was imported from overseas. Saltaire is protected by conservation area policy. Salt is famous in the history of industrial relations for being the first factory owner to introduce an official tea break for his workers. Salt was generally seen as a benevolent employer but he organised the housing allocation strictly according to the seniority of the workers' jobs, with overseers receiving substantial double-fronted houses, and factory hands only getting small terraces. However no expense was spared in terms of architectural detail, a classical Italianate style, known as Tuscan, being used for all the buildings, including the factory, all built in a soft golden stone, similar to Bath stone.

Salt did not entirely understand the difficulty people had in carrying out their essential domestic tasks. He banned housewives from hanging out their washing across the backs, and apparently would gallop down the back lanes on his horse, sword drawn to cut the washing lines if they did so. However, he did provide communal wash houses, and social amenities such as libraries, canteens, allotments, schools and almshouses. Saltaire was a relatively small scheme with only 800 houses, but many public buildings and amenities. It had a strong influence, disproportionate to its size, on many subsequent model towns in North America and Europe, especially on the Krupps model town at Essen in Germany, and on the Pullman railway towns in the United States.

The Garden City movement

The ideas

There is a marked change of style from the relatively high-density utilitarian developments of the early nineteenth century to the lower-density, more luxuriant Garden City schemes of the latter part of the century in which the housing consists of traditional cottages with gable ends and front gardens, rather than tenements or plain terraces (Cherry 1981; Hall 1992). Designing ideal housing for the working classes became a very popular branch of architecture, although some of the schemes were so expensive that they contributed more to the development of fashionable middle-class domestic architecture, than providing a model for cheap mass-produced housing, for example Bedford Park, London (Bolsterli 1977). There had always been a tradition in the large country estates of designing quaint little cottages for the agricultural workers, often in the picturesque style, which in themselves would provide an interesting feature in the landscape when viewed from the windows of the stately home (Dresser 1978; Darley 1978).

Famous architects such as Unwin, Parker, and Lutyens were employed in the design of Garden Cities and garden suburbs, developed towards the end of the century (Service 1977; Dixon and Muthesius 1978). Raymond Unwin, in particular, was in favour of low-density housing with gardens and coined the phrase 'nothing gained by overcrowding' (Unwin 1906). He sought to demonstrate in his plans that high-density grid layout of terraces was not necessarily the best way to save space, recommending 12 houses to the acre (30 per hectare) was the best solution (Hall 1992). Notable literary figures and members of the upper classes were involved in campaigning for better conditions, such as Beatrice Webb, Ruskin, William Morris, Charles Dickens, William Booth, Cardinal Manning, Charles Kingsley and Henry George, all of whom were connected to the Garden City movement, and the early town planning cause. Many women were active in the early housing movement, the most well known being Octavia Hill, who in 1875 wrote the book, *Homes of the London Poor*, and who went on to set up many housing initiatives and arguably influenced the nature of the whole modern housing management profession (M. Smith 1989; Macey and Baker 1983).

Ebenezer Howard wrote the book *Tomorrow: A Peaceful Path to Reform* in 1898, which was renamed *Garden Cities of Tomorrow* in 1902, in which he put forward his main town planning ideas for the creation of an ideal community (Howard 1974, originally 1898). Howard believed that although the

Industrial Revolution had been accompanied by great problems of overcrowding, bad housing and environmental problems, it had also brought many benefits. Therefore he sought to combine the best of the modern town and the new industrial society with the best of the countryside and the traditional way of rural village life in the town-country or garden-city, as he called his ideal community.

Howard was part of a wider group of men and women concerned with urban conditions in the wake of the Industrial Revolution. He had visited the USA where he had seen Owenite communities, and a range of religious communities such as the Mormon settlement of Salt Lake City, and various Mennonite communities founded in the land of freedom, which sought to create heaven on earth (Hayden 1976; Kanter 1972). Howard envisaged the creation of Garden Cities of a population of approximately 30,000 each, divided into smaller neighbourhoods of 5000, acting as counter-magnets to existing conurbations, and together forming larger 'social cities' linked in a complex regional network across the country. He envisaged this network as being joined together by the most modern public transport railway systems (he was truly living in the age of the train in Victorian England), with new settlements being formed as and when the population expanded.

This would result in planning on a national scale with a complete network of interconnecting cities covering the whole country, whilst existing cities would return to a more manageable size and pleasant environment. Howard is often misrepresented as favouring an escapist folksy way of life based on green principles. In fact he was advocating a very realistic way of restructuring the economy and community of Britain, by means of creating a complete network of Garden Cities which would act as counter-magnets to the existing conurbations, and which would re-establish the urban–rural balance which had been shaken by the Industrial Revolution.

Howard, therefore, was not only planning cities at the macro level but had a complete regional and national land-use strategy, and also had thought through how the cities would be subdivided at the micro neighbourhood level. The idea of dividing the cities into neighborhoods of 5000 people was realised in the neighbourhood units which formed the basic structural component of the post-war British new towns developed from 1946 onwards. The magic figure of 5000 was seen as an ideal size for a group of citizens to possess a sense of community, a questionable concept, going back to the times of the Greek city state of antiquity (see Chapter 4).

Transport played a major part in structuring the garden city, which would be connected to the outside world and to other settlements by a railway system. Internally tramways would provide transport along the main boulevards that delineated and connected the main sectors of the city. But, the newly invented bicycle would be the main form of transport over short distances around the neighbourhoods, between home and work, and for leisure journeys to recreational areas and the surrounding agricultural green belt. Howard put forward many innovative ideas on zoning the different land uses and activities within the Garden City. He also put all the industry on the outside ring, on the periphery of the city, this being another feature which was followed in much post-war town planning. He proposed relatively low densities within the residential areas, with plenty of trees, open spaces and public parks, as well as generous private gardens around each house, all essential features of creating the Garden City layout. But he was not just playing at creating beautiful stage sets, as some of his critics imagined, as everything had a scientific purpose to reduce disease, encourage people to grow vegetables in the gardens, and create a sense of well-being, harmony and community spirit.

He proposed that there should be a green belt around the city, to be used for agriculture: it was not a mere buffer zone between town and country in the modern usage of the phrase. He sought to reunite the relationship between town and country in the economy of the Garden City and in the division of labour and nature of the work options which people had. Indeed he wanted to create a complete lifestyle package. In order to unite town and country in everyday life, as well as on the plan, he saw the town's citizens working in and controlling the agricultural land around the city as well as running modern industrial activities (Howard 1974, originally 1898).

Clearly, Howard was not just concerned with the physical town planning of his developments, but had ideas for every aspect of the social and economic characteristics of the community at every level, from city-wide down through the local neighbourhoods to the family level, relating to how people lived, and how land and property were owned. He did not see himself as a socialist but came from a more liberal tradition which advocated communitarianism rather than communism *per se*. He envisaged much of the land being owned cooperatively where that might be the best solution, but also allowed for private ownership of shops and businesses, very much what today would be called a mixed economy approach. In his book on *Garden Cities* (Howard 1898) he included three chapters on the financial arrangements for the development, explaining that agricultural revenues and urban rents from the housing schemes would be used to fund the infrastructure, including the transport network, and community amenities such as schools, parks, hospitals and so forth (Hardy 1991). So all revenue was to be ploughed back into the community and was not to be seen as speculative profit as was the case in later private suburban developments.

Likewise the idea of dividing the city into distinct neighbourhood communities was not only a practical solution to the phasing and development of the town, and the provision of essential amenities and facilities in a logical manner. He wanted to engender a sense of community amongst the residents, and believed that by dividing his Garden City into identifiable neighbourhood sectors, each with its own school and shops, this aim would be best achieved. This theme was to re-emerge in post-war British new towns. His interest in 'community' also reflected the influence of the sociologists of the day who were concerned with the 'problem' of the decline of traditional communities and the potential breakdown of society in the large impersonal cities, as will be discussed in the social aspects chapter, Chapter 14, in relation to the concept of the neighbourhood unit in modern New Towns.

Unlike many modern town planners, Howard's vision was not limited to the 'big issues' of the public realm of life, for he did not despise the domestic and private realms of the family as trivial; arguably the whole concept of the Garden City was a celebration of domestic petit bourgeois virtues. He was aware of the problems of the burden of domestic work and

family care, which had been publicised by the feminists of the time. Therefore he sought to incorporate attempts at cooperative housekeeping into the layout and running of Garden City (Pearson 1988). At that time many men and women were looking at ways of rationalising domestic work in the same way that production outside the home had been industrialised, and apparently rationalised. The issue had become pressing in many households as women sought greater emancipation.

The 'servant problem' was a middle-class one, but cooperative housekeeping would also alleviate the toil of working-class women, both in their own households and as servants in those of others. All sorts of other ideas were put forward to reduce the problems of housework, especially in North America. For example, it was suggested that there could be a conveyor belt running round the town, from which individual households would collect their meals, replacing their washing up to be done in the communal kitchen in the centre of the town (Hayden 1981).

The garden city concept was intended to provide an alternative form of settlement for the working classes who formed the bulk of the overcrowded population of existing cities, although paradoxically it reflected many middle-class attitudes on how to solve the servant problem. As will be seen, Garden Cities were later regarded as being mainly for middle-class people, with disparaging images of Fabian intellectuals, and liberated women on bicycles being seen in the popular press as the main inhabitants of these rarified communities.

Howard was not only a theorist but a man of action. In those days there was no adequate state system of town planning, and so whatever was to be done had to be achieved through private investment and development. He set up the first Garden City Company Limited before the First World War and started developments in Letchworth in 1903, and later in Welwyn Garden City in 1920, both on the edges of London at the time, and now well and truly within the commuter belt. (Interestingly in 2013 Welwyn was identified as a site suitable for fracking activity, resulting in considerable concern amongst local residents and Garden City enthusiasts.) Both Welwyn and Letchworth, with its own Garden City Museum, remain substantial and important examples of garden city town planning and architecture. The other sites Howard had recommended for the rest of his proposed ring of Garden Cities were not taken further because of business difficulties, but were later adopted by the planners under the New Towns Act 1946 as the location of the first phase of British New Towns.

Howard's influence was greater in what he wrote than in what he built. Aspects of Howard's work continued to be very influential in the development of modern town planning, including the subdivision of settlements into neighbourhoods, the creation of local and centralised hierarchies of amenities and facilities, green belts, land-use zoning, approaches to public transport, and an enthusiasm for bicycles which were (at that time) a recent innovation; hence the provision of cycle paths in many post-war new towns. Possibly most influential of all the aspects of the garden city movement was the emphasis on traditional small cottage-style housing with gardens at medium-to-low density as the main form of residential development in the Garden City. This contrasts with the emphasis on model tenements for the labouring classes, as found in much early charitable development and some model communities within inner-city Britain and within Continental Europe, such as, for example, the Peabody Buildings tenements in South London.

Many other aspects of Howard's ideas have been lost with time. For example cooperative housekeeping was soon abandoned by later planners. The variety of ideas about creating a new economic order based on cooperation and reconciling the town and the country were reflected, but weakly in the state planning system with its emphasis on control and sterile land-use zoning. The desire of the Garden City architects, and subsequently the speculative builders, to recreate the English village led to the revival of many of the traditional styles of domestic architecture (Munro 1979; Prizeman 1975). His ideas were copied in the building of many garden suburbs, most of which favoured the Mock Tudor (half-timbered with gabled ends) Garden City architectural style. This style of housing became even more popular in the 1930s and came to represent the epitome of home-ownership for the new middle classes, being popularised by speculative house-builders and estate agents' advertisements of the

time (Betjeman 1974). In the 1990s there was a considerable revival of this pseudo-Tudor style. Many architects look upon this style as artificial and generally as bad taste, but the majority of the population now live in suburban development. It has endured the test of time better than the so-called modern movement of impersonal functional glass and concrete, which has never been popular with the people, who are the ones who live in the houses.

Garden City communities

Howard drew encouragement from a range of like-minded people, and also influenced the work of many of the later model community builders, who built in the Garden City style. For example, George Cadbury (1839–1922) moved his chocolate factory out of Birmingham to Bourneville in 1879, and built the main settlement around it from 1895, at the same time as Howard was writing his book. W. Alexander Harvey, who was employed as the architect, designed the layout in sympathy with the topography, believing it was better to use the contour of the land, taking a gentle sweep in preference to a straight line (Gardiner 1923). This contrasted with the grid-iron type layouts of many of the earlier settlements, and is a precursor of the trademark of much, especially English, town planning of meandering and curving roads, and a generally natural appearance. The houses were built at a very low density of seven or eight houses to the acre (less than 18 houses per hectare), with large private gardens for horticulture, lots of trees and open space, and wide roads, plus adequate provision of schools and shops. Some of the houses were for sale to the general public from the beginning, but the whole settlement was strongly linked to providing for the workforce of the factory. The style was in the Mock Tudor, medieval cottage style so favoured by the reformers. George Cadbury was a supporter of Ebenezer Howard's ideas and was on the first board of directors for the first Garden City built by Howard in Letchworth, which is between Luton and Cambridge (Gardiner 1923).

Port Sunlight was built by Lever the soap manufacturer, across the Mersey from Liverpool. Lever (1851–1925) (and brothers) started in business as a grocer, making soap and candle-making in the back

Photo 5.3   Mock Tudor housing

Both Port Sunlight and Bourneville, built at the turn of the century, used the Mock-Tudor style, which was subsequently to become a major influence in the creation of pseudo-Tudor private suburban housing developments.

room of his shop. Lever bought 52 acres of land on Merseyside and started building his factory there in 1888, and then started his model village in 1889, which was not completed until 1934. Again the scheme is low density with five to eight houses per acre. The houses were mainly grouped in blocks around allotment gardens without any private back gardens, much to the annoyance of many generations of residents. He employed a range of architects, but was himself the main influence on both the architecture and the town planning, and also endowed the first Chair of Town Planning at Liverpool University (Cherry 1981; Ashworth 1968).

Joseph Rowntree (1836–1925) built a model community at New Earswick near York. He employed Unwin and Parker as architects, developing Garden City type houses grouped around culs-de-sac. The style and space standards of the houses were to act as models for the council houses introduced under the Housing and Town Planning Acts 1909 and 1919, and in particular the Tudor Walters standards (1918) for council housing design (later to be superseded by the Parker Morris standards in 1961). The architectural style at New Earswick was to be influential in the developments of Hampstead Garden Suburb, Wythenshawe in Manchester, and the first garden city at Letchworth, albeit in a slightly more attractive upmarket way. There were smaller garden suburb type schemes throughout the country, but by the early twentieth century these had often become nothing more than an architectural shell used by developers to sell houses to the new middle classes, and many of the original communitarian ideals had long since been forgotten.

Model communities do not have to be built for philanthropic or utopian reasons. There were several purely commercial Garden City type experiments in North America, and in the 1980s in Britain, there were proposals for a ring of entirely private upmarket new towns, within the London green belt put forward by Consortium, the development group, which is strongly influenced by the heritage of the Garden City concept. But the proposals met with considerable opposition from both the central and local government, and such pressure groups as the Council for the Protection of Rural England (CPRE), so that the idea was abandoned.

The influence of the garden city movement reverberates right through the twentieth century, influencing the style and layout of interwar 'semi-detached suburbia', albeit in a debased form (Photo 5.3). It also fed into the post-war New Towns programme. Garden City ideas spread worldwide, and schemes can be found in Japan, Australia, North America and Germany and many other countries. Indeed it may be argued that a parallel movement in Germany pre-dated the English Garden City movement.

Some have considered the Garden City principle over-simplistic, with an emphasis upon architectural and physical planning solutions to complex social and economic problems. But it is argued that Howard, as against his imitators, sought to provide a holistic approach to planning, which incorporates both spatial and aspatial issues. His designs are arguably environmentally sustainable, although developed at a time when industrialisation and exploitation of natural resources were the rule.

The modern movement

New horizontal theories of city form

A major constraint on the development and nature of cities is the level of construction and transportation technology available. Cities can grow upwards and/or outwards, or they can be very close-knit and compactly built, with everything based on walking distances. The Garden City approach had used traditional forms of low-rise construction in the form of Mock-Tudor cottage style houses, but it, nevertheless, adopted some of the latest developments in transportation to enable the city to spread outwards, horizontally, utilising trams, trains and bicycles. Inspired by the transport revolution, by the dawn of the twentieth century, urban thinkers were coming up with all sorts of other ways to design cities in relation to how they are laid out horizontally alongside linear transport routes. Changes in transport technology had changed the form, extent and structure of cities.

To recap, for centuries, cities had been relatively close-knit because the extent of cities, and the distances between different land uses and amenities, was governed by the distances which people could comfortably walk or go by horse. With the introduction of mechanical means of transport, people could travel further and more quickly than they could walk, and cities began to spread out horizontally. With the development of the railway system, those who were more affluent moved further out and commuted into the town centre, starting the trend of suburbanisation and decentralisation which has been such a major feature of urban development in Britain over the last 150 years. Many small towns owed their very existence and prosperity to the development of the railways, being blessed with a station which brought with it potential customers for local goods and services. Other towns were more directly involved as major interchange points on the railway system, e.g. Crewe, or major producers of rolling stock, such as Swindon. As motor cars grew in number, public transport declined. People without cars in some areas are worse off in terms of transport than their ancestors were in the nineteenth century. The motorcar soon became popular in the USA even amongst relatively low-income people, thanks to the cheap mass-production methods of Henry Ford. One of the main concerns for planners in the twentieth century has been the problem of planning for the motorcar.

Tramway systems contributed to decentralisation, and were popular for many years. In Britain they were removed by the middle of the twentieth century, but many European cities have kept their trams. The first line of the London Underground was opened in 1863, namely four miles of the

Metropolitan line from Paddington to Farringdon Street. With the invention of the internal combustion engine, public transport was augmented, particularly after 1918, by omnibuses, which were not limited to a fixed linear track and could go anywhere. The buses, and of course the subsequent development of the private motorcar, led to a veritable explosion of suburbanisation, for, provided there were passable roads, people could for the first time in history travel anywhere they wanted at considerable speed. The bicycle became popular in the late nineteenth century and is having a comeback today. These changes in transport technology further encouraged cities to grow and to segment into distinct land-use zonings, and in particular for the industrial and residential (the work and the home) areas to separate out (Greed 1994a).

The logical conclusion of all these changes, in order to create maximum efficiency, for cities based on public transport, was to abandon the traditional radial, circular form of cities and build linear developments along the main routes, with concentrations of housing ideally located at relatively high-density clustering around each railway station or tramway stop. It was important to have enough people living close to each stop, within walking distance, in order to make the developments viable in enabling passengers to reach them without them having to use a secondary form of transport each time. For example, in Spain, Arturo Soria y Mata suggested the concept of the linear city 1882. He visualised it stretching right across Europe from Cadiz in the South of Spain across to Leningrad (now St Petersburg) in the North West of Russia (Hall 1992)! The linear form could be joined up to form a circular 'ring' city, or turned in on itself as a figure of eight such as in Runcorn New Town Plan, near Liverpool, in the 1960s. Soria y Mata only succeeded in building a few kilometres outside Madrid (Hall 1992, 1996). This is not to be confused with ribbon development.

Frank Lloyd Wright (1869–1959), an American architect, developed the idea of a city planned entirely for the growing popularity of the motorcar, 'Autopia', as proposed for Broadacre City in the 1930s. This was to be based on a very low-density grid with every house being like a homestead with a one-acre plot in which they would grow their own food. The settlement would not have a centre in the traditional sense but the districts would be focused around the gas station (petrol station). This vision is what some American cities actually became like, such as Los Angeles where everybody drives rather than walks. Those who do not have cars, including the poor, or who are unable to drive such as the young and old, are at a severe disadvantage, and have to depend on limited public transport or the goodwill of others. Such ideas were to influence the development of British town planning, although totally inappropriate for a small, and relatively poor, set of islands! The impact of the motorcar on our approach to urban planning is discussed further in Chapter 8 on planning theory, and in Chapters 12 and 13 on transport planning and urban design.

New vertical theories of city form

The garden city movement may be seen as a reaction to the Industrial Revolution, as going back to the past to reclaim traditional values, and re-establish harmony with nature and the countryside. This is not to discount the importance of the garden city movement as it is still strongly reflected in what Hall has typified as the Anglo-American approach to planning, which is characterised by an emphasis mainly low-rise, low-density, individual family housing development, and the acceptance of suburbanisation, zoning and motorcar use (Hall 1996). However, the concept of the garden city was also highly influential in Germany, popularised by the architect Camillo Sitte. Garden cities, or rather *les cités-jardin*, were also an idea taken up by the French to a small degree, limited to a few experimental communities in the Ile de France near Paris. Garden city ideas were spread by the International Federation for Planning and Housing which celebrated its centenary in 2013 (see special issue of the journal, *Town and Country Planning*, May, 82(5), 2013).

However, what Hall (1996) calls the European town planning movement was more influential on the Continent, with its emphasis on functionalism, modernity, futurism and high-rise development. Why was the vertical extension of cities as expressed in the high-rise movement essentially a European rather than English trend? In many European countries there has been a need, right up until the last

Photo 5.4   Moscow housing factory

It was found to be more efficient to mass-produce pre-fabricated housing components in factories and then assemble them on site. This form of housing was also to prove popular in the UK with local authority housing departments (but not with residents) in the 1960s when skilled labour was in short supply and there were pressures to built fast and high.

century, to provide defensive measures, particularly city walls around individual city states, because the political situation was far less unified than in Britain. It was not until the beginnings of aerial warfare that walls became redundant. The Garden City movement reflected a trend throughout English history to have undefended open cities which were fringed by low-density urban sprawl and suburban villages around the main urban centres. In Europe the need for defence had led to a greater acceptance of living at higher densities, with buildings packed closer together, often consisting of apartment blocks of several storeys (Sutcliffe 1974). It was generally accepted that the natural limit to upward or vertical growth was about six storeys, as this was the maximum practical height the average person was willing to climb in what were effectively walk-up tenements.

To call the high-rise approach to town planning purely 'European' may be a misnomer, as in fact it was part of a wider international architectural movement which particularly flourished in North America, the home of the skyscraper. Indeed Le Corbusier, the famous Swiss-French architect who popularised the modern movement, had himself been inspired by the skyscrapers and technological progress found in North America, especially in New York and Chicago. With the development of new forms of power, namely gas and electricity, and new technological inventions and machinery, it was possible by the late nineteenth century to build much higher. Steel-framed structures enabled high-rise buildings to be built. Previously most building had been held up by load-bearing walls which stood by their own weight. In a steel-framed structure the wall and windows effectively are curtains hung from the steel skeleton. The invention of the mechanical lift, particularly the electric elevator in North America, meant that people could live higher without walking

Photo 5.5   Moscow apartment blocks

Impersonal high-rise blocks are a feature of many previously Communist East European countries, but the high-rise movement was also popular amongst Western architects and planners, as a means of housing the working classes in a modern, functional manner. The only trouble was nobody asked the would-be residents whether they wanted to live this way.

up all the stairs; in fact the sky was the limit. The social results of this when applied to cheap state council housing, where the lifts do not work and people have to walk up all the stairs, is a different matter altogether from the situation in a cared-for expensive block of private flats. High-rise was also popular in the Soviet Union, albeit for a different set of reasons, with its emphasis upon industrial development, mass forms of housing provision and lack of private-sector development (Photos 5.4, 5.5).

It is significant that the European high-rise movement went hand in hand with the functionalist style of architecture. New movements, such as functionalism and futurism, arose to meet the needs and mood of the new (twentieth) century (Pevsner 1970). The concept of functionalism was based on the design concept that 'Form follows function'. 'Beauty is function' and 'Function is beauty' became the battle cries of a new generation of architects, who tried to create a new non-decorative, honest, 'style-less style' known as functionalism, promulgated by Walter Gropius in Germany. He was an internationally famous architect and principal of the Bauhaus, a highly influential experimental school of architecture, art and design which was active in the interwar period. An emphasis on clean-cut, uncluttered designs and the use of pristine white concrete, glass and steel, represented a reaction against what was seen as the chaos of traditional cities, and against the sentimentality of Mock-Tudor and other traditional styles (Pevsner, 1970). The influences of the functionalist style and the Bauhaus on interior design are still to be found in a faint echo in Heals, Habitat and Ikea furniture today.

The concept of Futurism went beyond a specific architectural style. It was seen as a way of changing society. Disciples wanted to create a space-age society, using the new technology and materials to the full. For example, the Italian architect, Sant 'Elia, proposed a multilevel city of 1914 that looked like something out of science fiction or a Star Wars film, consisting of huge apartment blocks more suitable for androids than humans. Such an approach was not particularly popular in England. But after the Second World War, some of the European functionalist architects came to Britain and worked in the London County Council (LCC), contributing their designs to the post-war reconstruction planning and housing programme. And some were responsible for the building of some of the first high-rise council blocks of flats, such as at Roehampton in West London. These blocks were of a higher standard than what was to follow as other councils sought to solve their housing crises by building substandard high-rise blocks. Much of this architecture subsequently proved not to function well, and was in need of maintenance within a short period of being built: it was certainly unlikely to last into the future. The concrete discoloured, reinforcements deteriorated, window frames rusted, lifts broke down and flat roofs leaked. Traditional vernacular styles of building proved in the long run to be more functional, but had been dismissed as sentimental, old fashioned and bourgeois by the *avant garde*. Building styles that utilised local materials such as stone and slates took account of the local weather conditions by evolving different pitches of the roof etc., which had often been developed by trial and error over the centuries by local builders and carpenters. Details like ensuring the window sills are set out from the wall, thus preventing any water dripping off them running straight down the wall and causing discolouration, were observed by traditional master builders, but were ignored in the streamlined buildings of the modern movement.

So the twentieth-century architects of the 'Modern Movement' wanted to create a new way of designing buildings and indeed cities, and generally reacted against the excesses of decoration, eclecticism (Victorian copying of historic styles such as Neo-Gothic and Mock-Tudor), and urban chaos of the nineteenth century and sought to create a 'style-less' modern movement, which was entirely based on function and the application of science and technology in the form of new building materials and methods. Mind you, not everyone wanted functionalism and simplicity and there was always a battle of the styles going on. In the first part of the twentieth century, there were a variety of other contending architectural styles, such as 'Art Nouveau' and Art Deco, which drew much from trends in art and painting, and from the broader 'Arts and Crafts' movement. This was characterised by an emphasis on using traditional materials in an original manner, especially ornate ironwork. Other architects sought to return to a restrained, classical style, after the fussiness of Victorian architecture. For example, Lutyens favoured a modest neo-Georgian style using traditional brick in the building of many town halls and public buildings. His architecture also shows evidence of Indian influences, which he became interested in while he was designing the new state capital of India, New Delhi. Paradoxically the early American sky scrapers so admired by Le Corbusier, were, in many cases, quite decorative, both inside and out, with neo-Egyptian, neo-Gothic and Art-Deco features to be found in both New York and Chicago sky scrapers.

Le Corbusier

The high-rise functionalist approach is epitomised by the ideas of Le Corbusier, who saw the ideas of the past as outdated and sought to create a new age of progress, based on the conquest of nature by means of science and technology. Le Corbusier (1887–1965) (Pardo 1965), a Swiss architect working mainly in France, popularised the ideas of the international style. He was influenced by his visits to New York where he first saw the massive scale of modern high-rise buildings. He was also influenced by ancient mystical ideas in architecture, such as the Golden Rule, which relates to correct proportions in buildings (Birkstead 2009). Le Corbusier did not invent a new building style; rather he made the North American style acceptable in Europe as the way ahead, as the new 'international style', which encompassed the ideas of functionalism, futurism and an enthusiasm for high-rise development, along with new technologies and materials. On his visits to the USA, Le Corbusier had been impressed by Henry Ford's approach to the mass-production of motor cars, and believed dwellings could also be mass-produced on an assembly line and then the components slotted together on-site. Le Corbusier sought to use modern building technology to enable his cities to spread upwards vertically, even suggesting the idea of mile-high skyscrapers. There was little attention given to the needs of ordinary people, and their existing way of life. Le Corbusier showed little understanding of the daily lives of men and women, or the daily round of family life (Greed 1994a: 121–2). Rather than being seen as possessing worthwhile homely values and a well-ordered sense of domesticity, the urban masses were seen as ignorant, backward, and therefore uneconomic. The working classes were seen as in need of re-education and reorganisation to best serve the needs of the new industrial society, with its harsher, no-frills, streamlined view of life. And this could be achieved by redesigning their built environment.

Living in France, Le Corbusier's concept of housing tended to centre on the apartment or flat. He envisaged multi-storey living, high-rise blocks of flats in which each individual dwelling unit was to be based on scientifically worked out dimension – a modular unit to meet the needs of the average man. He said, 'a house is a machine for living in' (*une machine à habiter*) (Ravetz 1980). This is a limited view of a house and presumes that the architect can produce a standardised unit for the needs of the standardised human being. Clearly a house was not a home!

He had grandiose ideas for replanning European cities. His solution to the congestion and problems of modern industrialised urbanisation was to knock it all down and start over again. He wanted to demolish and rebuild Paris, but the city authorities fortunately did not go along with his ideas. Housing, and other land uses too, were to be piled one on top of the other to create the vertical city in high-rise blocks with vertical neighbourhoods in each. These blocks were to stand on pillars, thus freeing the space at ground level for expanses of landscaped public areas of grass and trees. He even suggested that 90 per cent of the ground could be left free, by piling the people up in these blocks (Le Corbusier, 1971, was 1929). There are curious similarities with

the Garden City approach in the emphasis on open space, but it was to be provided communally and not in the form of individual personal gardens. Le Corbusier did allow for some low-rise housing in some of his schemes, but not for all. Le Corbusier is often accused of being totalitarian in his views. He said, 'we must create the mass production spirit' by creating a mass-produced housing environment. This is a far cry from participatory planning; rather the architect was part of the priestly caste of experts who believed, because of their superior intellect, that they knew what was best for the people.

Modern architecture in general is often accused of creating impressive massive buildings from a visual and townscape aspect, but lacking sensitivity and awareness as to how individuals and families actually live in the buildings, leading to the classic problem of where to hang the washing, where to let the children play, where to spread out the bits whilst repairing the motorbike without them being stolen, to name but three normal functions of modern family life. But his followers would say that the high-rise buildings of today bear no relation to Le Corbusier's original ideas and noble plans. For example, in Britain at the height of the 'high-rise movement' in the 1960s, the average tower block would reach around 12 storeys at the most, their design and quality being limited by financial constraints, and by the fact that such blocks were mainly built to house council tenants, as speedily and cheaply as possible. In other parts of the world, especially North America, and increasingly in South East Asia, buildings are on a much bigger scale. High-rise development can be either a luxury form of housing or a cheap means of housing the poor, depending on the locality and political context. High-rise is the dominant form of new urban development in the Far East. Entire mega-cities are being built in China on the high-rise principle, but they owe little to the ideas of Le Corbusier and more to the demands for growth and urbanisation created by its centrally-planned economy.

Le Corbusier also had a flourishing architectural practice and is well known internationally for a range of individual building commissions. In fact he was one of the first internationally-famous 'starchitects' (star architects) and his influence is still immense today. The high-rise element was only one aspect of a whole range of other town planning ideas put forward by Le Corbusier. Like Ebenezer Howard, he believed in the importance of land-use zoning (vertical as well as horizontal in his case), and the centrality of transportation, even suggesting an early form of urban motorway to weave between his blocks to allow for the new invention, the motorcar. Most of his plans remained as ideas in books rather than actual schemes, but nevertheless he greatly influenced succeeding generations. He never had the opportunity to build one of his cities in Europe. Nevertheless, somewhat inappropriately, he was responsible for designing the new state capital of the Punjab in India at Chandigargh: a fairly conventional medium-rise scheme. Western architecture, with the emphasis on scientific land-use zoning, and the ample provision of wide roads for the motorcar, may have been ideal solutions to the problems which existed in Europe, but the city seems out of context and out of place in India, with limited motorised traffic and a more rural way of life.

Le Corbusier is probably better remembered for a much smaller scheme in the South of France: the *Unité d'Habitation* apartment block development, built in 1947, near Marseilles, which consists of a medium-rise apartment development with the main building combining social and commercial uses, including a nursery, shops, common rooms and a rooftop sports area, alongside the dwelling units. Inspired by such concepts, the idea of a high-rise block being like a vertical city, containing the full range of land uses, became more popular internationally in the 1970s, by which time the technology was available to build much higher. For example, the John Hancock Building in Chicago was built in 1970 as a mixed-used vertical city of 1500 feet on 100 floors with 40 floors of offices below, a middle section of retail and leisure facilities and the rest of the building above comprising condominium apartments. Apparently this building was the inspiration for the classic disaster movie, *Towering Inferno* (essential viewing for all planning students). Likewise the new Shard building in London comprises mixed uses. The destruction of the World Trade Centre (9/11) (that is on 11 September 2001) in New York does not seem to have diminished people's enthusiasm for tall buildings.

Meanwhile in British domestic housing architec-ture, pride of place was given to the Garden City Mock-Tudor style in the interwar period. There were attempts by more daring local builders to apply the ideas of the modern functionalist movement to domestic housing in Britain, creating 'sugar lump houses', white concrete houses with flat roofs, and functional metal window frames in the modern style. Examples of these can be found in many British cities, but they never became as popular as more vernacular styles of suburban housing, such as Mock-Tudor.

The creation of modern bureaucratic planning

A new century

Away from all the high-jinks and ego trips of the 'starchitects' of the international movement, town planning was becoming a recognised municipal func-tion within British local authorities, closely identified with the practical work of surveyors and public health professionals. By the start of the twentieth century town planning was being recognised as a higher profession in its own right, separate from surveying and engineering. The Royal Town Planning Institute was established in 1914 (Ashworth 1968, 193). The Town and Country Planning Association had been founded as a major pressure group which grew out of the Garden Cities movement. Planning was becom-ing increasingly professionalised. The Sex Disqualification Removal Act of 1919 enabled women to enter the professions for the first time, because of manpower shortages after the high death rates of the First World War (Lewis 1984; check the Centre for Accessible Environments website and their magazine *Access by Design* (for example, Special Issue, 130, 2012, p. 2) which discusses the implica-tions of the Localism Act).

In fact there were no 'town planners' as such; most of the new practitioners were architects, surveyors and engineers. Professional staff were needed to 'man' and operate the new planning system. Women who had previously been involved in voluntary and charitable work dealing with hous-ing, public health reform, and town planning were not given paid employment. Because of the marriage ban in local and central government preventing women working upon marriage (which was not completely removed until the early 1960s) few women achieved senior planning positions.

Several progressive local authorities had already produced their own plans, and had built social housing schemes (Cherry 1981; Ashworth 1968). Plans had already been produced in some urban areas in relation to the extensions of sewerage, drainage and road systems which would serve new privately-developed housing areas and urban improvement schemes. Early town plans were also undertaken in order to show the location of new social housing estates which were introduced in some cities before the subsequent national acts of the early twentieth century. For example, the Boundary Estate in Shoreditch, in inner London, is generally considered to be the first 'council housing estate' built in 1893 and comprising 23 tenement blocks arranged around a small park with a central bandstand (Collins 2011). In 1909 the first Housing and Town Planning Act was passed. This was to set the agenda for the future path of the scope and nature of town planning in Britain. The act, introduced under a reforming Liberal government, made possible the creation of a much extended mass council housing system, which coincided with the decline of the private rented housing sector. Under this Act local authorities were expected to produce 'schemes', as town plans were called in those days, showing the location and layout of these new developments. In the process of planning these individual schemes, they were inevitably moving towards considering questions as to the layout and design of whole towns and their likely future growth. They often put the housing estates out on the edges of cities where the land was the cheapest and in areas where they were less likely to cause conflict or reduce the property values of middle-class suburban areas, storing up transport problems for the future.

After the First World War (1914–18) the Housing and Town Planning Act 1919 introduced a massive council house building programme specifically aimed at providing 'Homes for Heroes', that is for the soldiers who returned from the Great War. Under the 1919 Act, 213,000 houses were built, then the first Labour government introduced the Wheatley Act, that is Housing Act 1919, which gave greater emphasis to the state provision of housing

(Macey and Baker 1983; and M. Smith 1989). One of the largest council housing estates of the time was the Becontree Estate in Essex, built between 1921 and 1932. Design standards were based on the Tudor Walters report in 1918, and influenced by Garden City ideas and the work of the architect-planner Raymond Unwin. The occupiers of the early council houses were chiefly respectable skilled working men and their families who had to undergo various tests to judge their suitability, so the aim was not primarily to provide for the poor, homeless, elderly or otherwise disadvantaged.

The 1919 Act required local authorities to produce schemes that are town plans, for settlements of over 20,000 people, showing the overall land-use zonings and the locations of the new housing estates in particular. This part of the Act, like most of the planning acts right up until after the Second World War (1939-45), was weak and difficult to administer and enforce, because of lack of resources and skilled personnel. The town plan was only advisory, or illustrative, in that it was often no more than a land-use map showing what had been already developed rather than what was proposed for the future, but it was a beginning. Nevertheless the foundations of the modern scientific approach to planning were laid through this early legislation. In particular Patrick Geddes, one of the founding fathers of the modern planning movement, promoted a scientific approach to planning, based on the mantra of Survey, Analysis, Plan, along with the collection of detailed statistics. He also promoted the separation and zoning of different land uses in the name of functionality. Geddes' ideal rational city was divided into three types of zones, based on 'home, work, and play' (Geddes 1915). This zoning triad was to be much criticised in later years, not least because it excluded several other land-use activities, and because it contributed towards the increasing separation of residential and employment areas, and therefore the creation of the 'journey to work' and therefore all the problems of modern-day commuting, congestion and the unsustainability of increased car use.

The inter-war period and housing growth

The Industrial Revolution had changed the face of Britain; by the Victorian times the economy and the population was largely urban-based and great new towns and cities had grown up in the industrial areas of Britain. The railways had a huge impact on these urban areas and the people who lived in them. The trains brought noise and dirt into the city and considerable amounts of land were needed by the railway lines themselves and their associated embankments, bridges, marshalling yards and stations. The rapid growth of the city was dependent on the parallel development of new railway lines as the principal means of commuting (Mumford 1965). Poor living conditions and industrial pollution led to the middle classes moving to the suburbs, using the very railways that had created such change (Mumford 1965) and the Underground in London.

The first underground railway in the world opened in London in 1863. By 1882 an inner circle line had been constructed and by the start of the new century underground lines were already beginning to snake into the countryside around London. In some cases they served the newly established suburbs, in other cases the extension of the lines was a deliberate strategy by the underground company to facilitate the growth of new suburban development and generate additional custom (Bayman 2008). For example the extension of the Metropolitan Tube Line through the north-western suburbs of London in the early part of the twentieth century gave rise to the term Metroland (Jackson 1992; Betjeman 1974). This combination of new suburban housing and easily accessible underground stations fuelled the further growth of the city, in some cases the developer being the underground company itself! This is a good, if rare, example of private-sector housing development and public transport being planned and provided at the same time. Of course, the underground company had its own profit-making motives, and the housing was relatively low density, which subsequently encouraged car use rather than public transport, but this level of *integration* of development and public transport has been sadly lacking in British planning.

The 1920s and 1930s were also times of extensive private house building across the more prosperous areas of the South and Midlands. Vast areas of private speculative housing estates were built around towns and cities and people escaped out of the urban congestion into the fresh air and sunshine of the Home Counties. As more people had the where-withal to make their own choice as to what they wanted, many opted for owning (or renting) an individual house rather than living in a crowded flat or terraced house. With increased affluence amongst large groups of the population the planners became concerned with protecting the countryside from the suburban sprawl of the expanding towns.

It was speeded up by another transport revolution, namely the invention of the internal combustion engine. The motorised bus (omnibus) with its new bus routes into the suburbs gave far greater mobility. But private car ownership never topped 2 million before the war and then actually went down again after the war until economic recovery occurred in the late 1950s.

Another economic revolution was taking place, as far-reaching in its effects on society and urban development as the Industrial Revolution, namely the development of commerce and office employment. This has continued to the present day. It created a new middle class of office workers, administrators and managers in the 1920s and 1930s. These were the new commuters living in the new sprawling suburbs. In 1910, 90 per cent of all housing was rented, owner occupation being limited to the more affluent classes (Swenarton 1981). Even in the interwar period the vast majority of people rented their housing either from the council or from private landlords, with owner-occupation accounting for one-quarter to one-third of the housing tenure depending on the locality, whereas today it is approaching 70 per cent. The building society movement was growing amongst the new middle classes, the mortgagariat who were able to buy their house with a building society mortgage (Merrett 1979).

Between 1930 and 1940 alone, 2,700,000 houses were built, and much of this development was occurring as urban sprawl. The Town and Country Planning Act 1932, in an attempt to control this expansion, required local authorities to produce zoning maps designating restricted areas for housing development, and requiring developers to get a rudimentary form of planning permission. But planners' powers were very weak. Many developers ignored the legislation as the penalties were minimal and difficult to enforce. The local authorities were also required to pay compensation if permission was refused which naturally discouraged them from making refusals. If there was no plan available when developers wanted to build they were granted what was known as 'Interim Development Control' permission. In practical terms all this meant was that the planners often drew the land-use zoning plan after the developers had built – hardly positive town planning!

Developers often built houses along existing roads to save money, creating long ribbons of development cutting into the countryside on the outskirts of towns. Agricultural land was cheap as a result of overseas food imports and so farmers were keen to sell their land to developers. Visually this housing blocked the view of the landscape although there might be fields behind the houses. Long spread-out rows of houses made the provision of schools, shops and social amenities difficult. From the traffic aspect, as car ownership grew, a whole series of garages and driveways going straight onto the main road caused major traffic problems. The Restriction of Ribbon Development Act 1935 attempted to control this unnecessary linear development, and required developers to build in more compact units with integral estate roads off the main road. This Act covered many other aspects of land use and development and was in a sense another early town and country planning act in all but name.

Amenity and rural preservation groups were springing up who feared the spread of suburbia and the loss of valuable agricultural land. The building of electricity pylons across the fields and extensive road-building also meant that there were fewer and fewer unspoilt beauty spots. But with the coming of the Second World War, all private building ceased. In those times of shortages and national crisis, utility and functionalism came firmly into fashion; the Anderson air raid shelter was probably the most representative architecture of the time. No homes were built during the war.

Thus, to conclude, we can see different strands and types of town planning emerging. The main types were:

1. The Anglo-American, Garden City approach whose principles predominantly shaped the early town planning acts and policies in the first half of the twentieth century.
2. The European high-rise movement, whose principles had little effect on England until the 1960s but which were to prove very influential internationally.
3. The international 'Starchitect' (star architect) type of planning (usually part of type 2). Urban planning and design were an extension of architecture and were associated with big names and large prestige schemes. Big-name architects are still prominent in planning such as Richard Rogers and Norman Foster.
4. A wider strategic policy-related form of planning, manifest in early stirrings of the regional planning movement and in a national land-use perspective that took into account both urban and rural planning issues.
5. An institutionalised, bureaucratic municipal and local authority form of planning which in reality was the main manifestation of the subject in Britain, whose role was to deal with everyday issues, planning for real cities, old and new, with all their problems and far less glamour.
6. Planning theorists and thinkers who were not practical planners but who reflected on the problems of cities and urban society, and who were to find a place in the new planning schools and universities of the post-war period.

For the tasks, further reading, additional photos, diagrams of Howard's Garden City concept and other resources for this chapter, please visit www.palgrave. com/companion/greed.

6 From Industrialisation to Globalisation

Planning in the second half of the twentieth century

This chapter gives a potted history of the development of planning in the second half of the twentieth century. The chapter will illustrate the different approaches to planning that have been adopted, and will identify the changing levels (national, regional, local) at which planning was undertaken, and the changing focus of planning, in terms of physical, economic and social policies, and the types of plans that were produced. The changing nature of the policy agenda can be observed with some issues that were initially seen as of little relevance, such as the environment and transport, increasing in importance, whilst others fall by the wayside.

This chapter illustrates the political nature of planning, for example how policies can shift from one extreme to the other depending on the nature of the government in power. Labour governments generally favour greater levels of state intervention and a stronger role for local authorities, and Conservative governments usually emphasise the importance of stimulating the private sector through tax breaks and incentives to carry out development. However, paradoxically the actual planning policies, relatively speaking, have not been that different, as both Labour and Conservative governments have aimed at increased house-building, greater protection for the country-side, economic growth and urban renewal. In particular one can see history repeating itself if one compares the Conservative policies of the 1980s under Mrs Thatcher and the present-day Coalition government's policies, especially in relation to freeing the market from the fetters of planning.

Knowing the historical background is important for as the saying goes, '*we should learn from the lessons of history or we will be condemned to repeat our mistakes again*'.

Post-war reconstruction

The Second World War

The Second World War (1939–45) was a watershed in the development of British town planning. A range of social, economic and land-use issues that might benefit from state planning were already in evidence in the interwar period, such as poor housing and unemployment in the North, and suburbanisation and sprawl in the South of the country. As was seen in the last chapter, an elementary form of regional economic planning already existed, and some restrictions on house-building in relation to ribbon development had already emerged. The war effort had required a greater level of state intervention and planning than was previously acceptable in controlling industrial and agricultural production, and in setting up regional and national government agencies to coordinate the effort. Following the war there was a general acceptance that in order to re-establish the economy and reconstruct society, there was a need for as much overall government control and planning as there had been during the war effort. The widespread bombing of large areas of housing and industry, and the flattening of many historical town centres and inner housing areas, made comprehensive redevelopment and planning a necessity. Therefore a powerful range of new planning legislation was introduced between 1945 and 1952 (Hall and Tewdwr-Jones 2010).

Reconstruction planning 1945–52

As with the First World War, there was considerable unrest, and demands were strong for a better society to compensate the workers for their contribution to the war effort. The Labour Party was elected to government after the war (taking power between 1945 and 1951). They were in a strong enough position to carry out extensive reform, to implement a nationalisation programme of basic industries, and to build the Welfare State. Overall, there was also a general consensus amongst all political parties that there was a need for modernisation and planning was welcomed as the logical way to rebuild Britain.

The wartime Coalition government had set up various committees to consider the future planning of Britain. The Scott Committee reported in 1942 on Land Utilisation in Rural Areas and linked to this the Dower Report on National Parks was produced in 1945, followed by the Hobhouse Committee on national park administration in 1947. The Uthwatt Committee produced a report on the vexed question of compensation and betterment in 1942. The Reith Report on New Towns was produced in 1946, being preceded by the Dudley Report in 1944 on the Design of Dwellings which had a particular bearing on the New Towns (Cullingworth and Nadin 2006). The 1944 White Paper, *The Control of Land Use*, set out the agenda for future planning control. Also during the war in 1943 the Ministry of Town and Country Planning was set up, to be replaced in 1951 by the Ministry of Housing and Local Government.

Town planning was one component of a much broader social and economic programme of post-war reconstruction aimed at creating a better, more rationally organised Welfare State, which covered health, welfare and education. Though there was a strong emphasis on greater equality the aim was not to create a socialist state, but rather the goals reflected the typically British compromise of creating a mixed economy (combining the best of the public and private sector), and reform rather than revolution, in which both private enterprise and state intervention could play a part. Overall there was an emphasis on trying to create greater efficiency, order and progress by providing modern facilities, planning having an important role in coordinating all this. Indeed planning became the philosophy of the post-war period, the spirit of the age. The aim was literally to '*Build a Better Britain*'.

New beginnings: the 1947 Town and Country Planning Act

The foundation of the modern planning system was the Town and Country Planning Act 1947 under which all development had to receive planning permission (Cullingworth and Nadin 2006). This is such an important act as it is the very foundation of the modern planning system. Local authorities had to prepare Development Plans showing the main land uses by means of coloured zonings. The system was based on a physical 'master plan', or blueprint approach. The plans were to be prepared on the basis of the survey, analysis and plan approach originally promoted by Geddes (Geddes 1915). Emphasis was put upon zoning land uses, clearing mixed-use areas, moving industry to new estates, and creating separate residential areas. The main types and levels of plans to be prepared under this Act were to be county maps which were produced to an Ordnance Survey base to one inch to the mile; county borough maps which covered the main urban areas at six inches to the mile; and supplementary town maps showing details of smaller towns and specific urban areas. Therefore planning was essentially spatial with a strong emphasis upon urban areas. Comprehensive Development Area (CDA) plans were produced which dealt with town centre redevelopment in detail. The plans were meant to have a five-yearly review, but the amendments system proved lengthy to implement, and the plans were seen as slow and inflexible in responding to change (refer to Chapter 2 on the development plan system).

To make the new planning system work there had to be strong powers of control. The private property market had been suspended during the state of emergency created by the war and right into the early 1950s rationing and state control continued, not only over food and clothing, but also in relation to construction materials and the right to develop. Planners were given extensive powers of compulsory purchase, land assembly and decision-making: often against the wishes of the remaining residents. Many of the areas that the planners would have never been able to get demolished had been removed for them by the bombing and the opportunity had at last arisen to put planning theory into practice.

Total land nationalisation was certainly contemplated but instead it was decided to impose a betterment levy (a development tax) on developers who benefited from an increase in land value because of a planning decision or land-use zoning. For example, if agricultural land were zoned as residential land this would vastly increase its value. Originally the betterment levy was at 100 per cent, but this was later reduced and then abolished under the Conservative government of the 1950s. The 1975 Community Land Act was one of the last attempts by a subsequent Labour government to tax development profits as part of the planning system, as subsequently any profits were taxed through the mainstream capital gains tax regime. As for compensation, in certain circumstances, in locations where there was likely to be no financial gain in small-scale development, a compensation payment was given if a planning refusal deprived a developer of his natural right to develop. People who did not make any profit from their land but whose property was adversely affected by planning decisions were also eligible for compensation. From these beginnings, over the intervening years compensation and betterment has become a controversial, specialist area of planning law which is still with us today, for example when a person's land is taken for new highways or airport runway development. This is a very fraught subject, which you should be aware of, entailing issues such as what is the true market value of a property, especially when the area has suffered from 'planning blight' (that the value has been lowered by the uncertainty of demolition or delayed planning proposals hanging over the area).

Much of post-war planning was concerned with towns and cities. There was little interest in controlling the countryside, at a time of national food shortages, when it was believed 'the farmer knows best'. In fact the countryside was heavily protected, and many development planning policies were concerned with keeping urban sprawl out of the countryside, through the enforcement of strict zoning and green belt designation. The National Parks and Access to the Countryside Act 1949 established a range of protected rural areas, within the context of a national land-use strategy for Britain (Hall 1992). However, as will be discussed in Chapter 10 (on rural planning), there were as many unrecognised problems and planning issues in the countryside as in the town, that were yet to be addressed under modern environmental and sustainability policies.

Housing provision: the new towns programme

After the war, there was a need for 'Homes for Heroes' for returning servicemen and their families, and to provide for civilians made homeless by the bombing. Town planning and housing policy and legislation worked in tandem. London already had a more advanced planning system than other provincial cities and the London County Council (LCC) (1889–1965) had considerable independent planning powers at the sub-regional, pan-urban level. London's problems were so much greater, with its population of around 8 million, having experienced major bomb damage in the Blitz with over 600 acres of the city destroyed, thousands of houses bombed, and over one and a half million people homeless. The 1944 Greater London Development Plan was produced by the prominent planner Patrick Abercrombie, and this formed the basis of much post-war town planning in London (Abercrombie 1944). Prior to the war, London had already designated its own green belt under the Green Belt (London and Home Counties) Act 1938. Abercrombie's plan also made proposals for a series of inner and outer ring roads around London to cope with imagined future levels of traffic, which, in retrospect, were totally underestimated. It was envisaged that new expansion would occur in a series of satellite new towns outside of the green belt, in locations comparable to Howard's original ideas and as part of the overall strategy for the London conurbation and the South East. Frederick Osborn, a disciple of Howard's ideas, had a key planning role in adapting garden city ideas for the more pragmatic requirements of the government new towns programme (Osborn and Whittick 1967; Armytage 1961, 2007).

Following the war there were continuing shortages and rationing of building supplies, resulting in a functional, modernist style being adopted, based on faster construction, system building and pre-fabrication. The 1944 Housing (Temporary Accommodation) Act gave local authorities the powers to build pre-fabs (pre-fabricated housing units) which were only intended to be temporary structures, and 156,632 were built. They were greatly admired for their mod-cons and modern style, and many remain today and some are even listed buildings. The 1946 Housing Act increased house-building subsidies to local authorities for council estate building. The 1949 Housing Act gave local authorities greater powers to build council houses for the population as a whole. Unlike the situation under earlier housing acts (of which there are many), recipients of state housing were no longer required to be in work, that is members of the 'working classes', a term which had been legally specified under previous key housing acts of 1909, 1919, 1924 and 1930. In fact by 1970s over a third of the population still lived in council housing.

Whilst new council housing estates were more numerous, the building of prestige new towns attracted more attention and was a key plank of post-war reconstruction planning and housing provision. The New Towns Act 1946 in many respects fulfilled the original dreams of the late Ebenezer Howard. The new towns were managed by the New Towns Commission (Alexander 2009). Individual towns were run by Development Corporations which existed quite separately from the local authority in whose area they were located. The new towns were developed in three main phases; the first – Mark I – were built immediately after the war. This was followed by a much reduced second phase of Mark II new towns under the Conservatives in the 1950s, comprising only one new town, Cumbernauld in Scotland; and then a third extensive Mark III phase built under the Labour government in the 1960s (Aldridge 1979).

The majority of Mark I new towns consisted of satellite settlements around London on sites which were very similar to Howard's original ones. They were aimed at skilled workers, and, for example in the case of Stevenage New Town, were also in already-prosperous parts of the country, with great demand for the industrial estates being built in parallel with the housing. But, a few were built in the depressed regions, such as Cwmbran in South Wales

Photo 6.1   A typical neighbourhood shopping precinct

The post-war new towns were designed in a community-focused manner, on the assumption that few residents would have a car and most people would shop locally within walking distance of their home.

and the North East. Cwmbran's function was to act as a growth point for revitalisation of that side of the Welsh valleys. It may be argued that concentrating investment in one new town at the expense of existing settlement is not the best way to regenerate a region, and may in fact lead to the further decline of some of the poorer settlements. New towns were seen by politicians as a tangible mark of progress, that they could point to, and say that they have achieved something. Piecemeal small-scale development in and around existing urban areas was far less politically attractive although arguably socially more worthwhile. Many would argue that the new towns programme actually starved existing inner-city housing areas of funding and thus sowed the seeds of the social problems that were to emerge by the 1970s (Ravetz 1980), as discussed in Part IV on planning and people (see Part IV on the social aspects of planning). But its ideas and vision were very influential, albeit often flawed (Photo 6.1).

Regional planning

The post-war planning system also sought to address the regional inequalities that had already become marked in the 1930s. Whilst the South of England had prospered, and experienced much suburban housing building, the interwar period had been characterised by periods of depression and high unemployment in the older industrial areas of the country, especially in the North and Scotland in areas of declining heavy industry. There was a need for planning to take a wider remit and deal with national regional inequalities, and to create a more balanced distribution of jobs and people, and thus to help break down the 'two nations' division between North and South which became more noticeable as the Depression of the 1930s deepened. The government had made their first attempt at regional planning with the Special Areas Act 1934. This set the principle of designating specific areas of unemployment and economic decline for special treatment, namely the North East, South Wales, Cumberland, Glasgow and deprived Scottish districts, all of these being areas which had experienced decline in heavy industry. It should be noted that in those days regional planning was still driven by the assumption that London and England were central to policy and that Wales, Scotland and Northern Ireland were peripheral regions, not countries in their own right with their own economies and national policy objectives.

Following the 1934 Act, in 1937 the government set up the Barlow Commission, namely The Royal Commission on the Distribution of the Industrial Population (Ravetz 1986). Therefore planning had become increasingly concerned with national and regional level economic issues, as well as with producing physical land-use plans within each local authority area. But, unemployment and many other social and economic problems were temporarily disappeared overnight with the coming of the Second World War in 1939, which required the call-up of the majority of the male workforce, leaving the women to man the factories and armaments work.

The Distribution of Industry Act 1945 gave grants and incentives which encouraged firms to move to depressed areas, indeed, new trading estates were often based on munitions factory sites, empty after the war. Housing policy was not only concerned with rehousing people after the war, mainly in new housing estates, it was strongly linked to regional employment strategies, to facilitate mobility of both labour and capital. The overall policy was to attempt to take 'work to the workers' rather than the opposite of taking 'workers to the work' (the 'on your bike' philosophy). The latter was discouraged because of the massive level of population migration to the South which was putting great pressure on the housing, services and infrastructure (as it still does today). It was considered bad economics as some areas in the North were taking on the form of ghost towns as everyone moved out, leaving empty houses, disused factories and neglected roads and public facilities, i.e. wasting existing facilities. However, this approach penalised businesses that wanted to develop and expand in existing areas and reduced local employment opportunities. For example, in inner London, there were distinct areas of unemployment and poverty which needed investment and could not compete with the more favoured areas (Balchin and Bull 1987). The regional policy was mainly manifested physically in new purpose-built industrial estates in the depressed regions. However, such was the lack of resources that several previous wartime munitions factories were converted into new industrial use (which had, conveniently, been located in the regions to avoid being bombed), such as in Treforest in South Wales. Subsequently many manufacturing firms settled in South Wales which remained a popular location, although the Banking Crisis from 2008 resulted in many closures in recent years.

The return of the private property market

Planning under the Conservatives 1951–64

A series of shortages, cold winters and political reaction against continued rationing meant that the Labour government which had been elected after the war and established the planning system, only lasted a short time. But, the Conservative government which came back into power in 1951 only repealed the more extreme aspects of the Labour government's planning legislation and continued with the town planning and state housing policies of the day, and, for example, more houses were built per year under Harold Macmillan's government than has ever been achieved subsequently. However, the Conservatives lifted many of the restrictions on private businesses and property development. Only one new town was commissioned, Cumbernauld in Scotland. Instead the Conservatives favoured a policy of developing 'expanded towns', based on existing provincial towns such as Swindon and Andover to take 'overspill' from the large conurbations under the Town Development Act 1952.

The Conservatives retained regional planning policies, albeit more targeted to specific areas, with more emphasis upon tax incentives to business than direct grants to local authorities. The 1958 Distribution of Industry Act extended regional aid to areas where unemployment was high. Subsequently the 1960 Local Employment Act replaced the existing extensive Labour system of regional aid, with development districts which covered less than 10 per cent of the country but targeted aid more directly in giving 20 per cent grants on plant and machinery in these areas. The Local Employment Act 1963 gave building grants of 25 per cent on new industrial development in development districts, and also tax allowances and 10 per cent grants for plant and machinery. Also a range of grants were introduced for the improvement of derelict land of up to 85 per cent of the cost, plus special grants for provision of infrastructure and the attraction of key workers to development areas.

Property boom

Overall, planners had not predicted, and were unprepared for, the rapid changes which occurred in the post-war period, in particular the growth of the use of the private motorcar, the increase in private house-building and owner-occupation in the 1950s when the building licence controls and rationing were removed under the Conservatives. The pent-up demand of the private sector was given free play and vast numbers of new houses were constructed, testing the new restrictive planning system to the full. But the most significant change was in the growth of the commercial property market, and the development of office blocks and retail development.

Local authorities were overwhelmed with the task of reconstruction and entered into partnership schemes with developers to rebuild bombed town centres, for example in Plymouth, Birmingham and many other urban centres. However, design standards were poor. Shoppers complained about the unfriendliness of the design of many of these new centres, because of excessive numbers of steps, escalators which seldom worked, lack of public conveniences, and a lack of sitting areas and meeting places. The needs of the main shoppers, namely women (that is housewives often with pushchairs and small children, but certainly not cars) were not taken into account. Initially there was little understanding of the effect of motorcar use. For example, when the bombed centre of Coventry was redeveloped, it was assumed that just a few car parking spaces would be needed and they could park on the reinforced roof of the new shopping centre (Tetlow and Goss 1968).

In the late 1950s and early 1960s the private property sector came into prominence again, after the building controls of the 1950s, resulting in town centre redevelopments, new office blocks and high-rise housing schemes. There was a growing demand for office space, and high-rise office blocks were seen as assets valuable to pension funds and insurance companies, often being worth more empty for investment purposes than occupied in those days when rates were not payable on empty buildings (Marriott 1989). High-rise office blocks dwarfed historical town centres and church spires as in Manchester and in Birmingham where the city centre was circled by a ring road and pedestrians were pushed underground. The property boom benefited the land-use professions, creating a demand for a greater range of property-professional specialisms and levels of expertise (Marriot 1989). As time went on, retail developments also became more sophisticated. In the 1950s and 1960s the shopping precinct was in vogue, basically a pedestrianised shopping street which was open to the elements. By the 1970s enclosed shopping centres were being built by companies such as Arndale. These were an improvement on the windswept facilities of the 1950s. From the outside these often looked like medium-rise office blocks. Inside they consisted of multilevel shopping malls, such as the Whitgift Centre in Croydon. In recent years such schemes have been subject to remodelling and expansion, as they look very old-fashioned compared with modern developments such as the two Westfield Shopping developments in London, one alongside the Olympic Park and one in Shepherds Bush.

Labour and the white heat of technology

Planning under the Labour government 1964–70

The Labour government under Harold Wilson sought to modernise the country and put much emphasis upon rational state planning and upon harnessing the 'white heat of technology'. In parallel there was an enthusiasm amongst architects, local authorities and building contractors for building high-rise development as this was seen as a way of solving the housing crisis, rapidly and highly visibly. Other key features of planning at the time were new town building, regional planning, planning for the motorcar, and overall a more scientific approach to urban policy-making, based on the systems view of planning (McLoughlin 1969), as will be explained in Chapter 8 on planning theory. For a government that was meant to be concerned with the working classes, there was a surprising lack of understanding of the needs, and housing requirements, of ordinary people, with limited public participation.

High-rise development

Town planning took on a new impetus in the 1960s with an emphasis on high-rise developments (Sutcliffe 1974). However, many would argue that it was not actually the planners who were at fault as many of them, along with local authority housing managers, had advised against such development. But many local councillors welcomed such a quick, visually impressive and prestigious solution to the housing problem (Coleman 1985). Also, high-rise approaches to planning were seen as the way ahead by many architects and some planners. The influence of Le Corbusier and the modern movement was strong, particularly in the London County Council (LCC) architects department. The development of a large complex of council housing at Roehampton, near Richmond Park, in London, was very influential, consisting of pristine white blocks of flats on a green landscaped slope with the buildings raised up on pillars. The high-rise movement went on to be promoted throughout the country, but the standard of the blocks varied. They attracted publicity levels disproportionate to their numbers as less than 5 per cent of the population live in blocks of flats of six storeys or more (Photo 6.2).

It was imagined that by building high it was possible to get the same number of people back on the site housed in the modern blocks as had existed in the small cramped terraced housing of the inner-city areas before the site was cleared. However this was not feasible because sunlight and daylight regulations were applied which required the buildings to be spaced out to ensure that they received adequate light and did not overshadow other buildings (DoE 1970). By the time provision (even inadequate provision) had been made for play space, landscaping, and increasingly the demand for car parking around the base of the blocks, the density was not that much greater than that attained by building high-density low-rise development.

It was often argued that it was cheaper to build high rise, but this depends on what is included in the cost. All the services, pipes and cables had to be carried up into the building vertically to provide water, gas, electricity and waste disposal for the flats, which increased the cost. Studies showed it was marginally cheaper to build up to a certain point but beyond this the cost increased, usually floor six, and definitely floor ten was when the 'threshold' was reached and costs climbed rapidly (DoE 1993b). The Labour government of the day encouraged high rise as the solution to the nation's housing problems by giving subsidies to local authorities to build blocks of flats, thus distorting the argument as to whether it was cheaper than conventional housing. Harold Wilson, the Prime Minister, was a great believer in the '*white heat of technology*' and favoured the fast pre-fabricated techniques of systems building. The schemes were never popular with the residents and the collapse of Ronan Point, an inner London residential tower block, in the late 1960s confirmed their fears. A lady on one of the top floors got up in the morning and switched her gas oven on, there was an enormous explosion, and the whole of the side of the building collapsed like a pack of cards. The public outcry which followed helped swing the pendulum back towards traditional construction (Ravetz 1986).

There were the practical problems of young families with children living in small flats, without the overflow space of a back garden, for play, storage, and somewhere to put the washing. There were structural

Photo 6.2   Roehampton flats development

The Roehampton development is to the West of London near Richmond Park, and comprises a range of high-rise blocks of flats, inspired by Le Corbusier's ideas, and built by the council to provide social housing from the late 1950s onwards.

problems of faulty construction, condensation, noise between flats with thin party walls, smelly, inefficient waste disposal chutes, and expensive communal heating systems. There were psychological problems of the effects of height. Socially, people felt isolated because there was no longer any street life to walk out into, people were filed away in their little boxes along each corridor. People felt unsafe, and unable to achieve adequate 'surveillance' of the area around their dwelling. They could not see who was going along the corridor from inside their flats, and many of the lifts, communal areas and entrances were heavily vandalised, with strangers wandering in and out (Coleman 1985).

Most of the high-rise flats in the UK were built by local authorities, that is they were council housing and built 'on the cheap' at that. But high rise can work well in some situations. For example, there are high-rise blocks in the upmarket area of Mayfair in central London; and along the south coast, in which the retired elderly predominate. Apartment living is also commonplace in many European cities for all social classes. In contrast, most of UK housing is low-rise and increasingly suburban.

Much depended upon the quality of construction, level of back-up services, and lifestyle and income of the residents. Many council blocks of flats, built to provide an alternative to nineteenth-century slums, have themselves become slums. Some local authorities have adopted drastic measures, 'beheading' them, turning them back into lower-rise housing or maisonettes, at considerable expense. Some have simply been blown up, having become uninhabitable, whilst others have been entirely refurbished and sold to the private sector. Some would argue that it is not just the form of construction but also

Photo 6.3   Dwarfed by the buildings in Chicago

Whilst in the UK high-rise building has always been the exception rather than the rule, and seemingly out of place, in many North European cities, high-rise development was seen as a sign of progress and the cutting edge of technology early on in the twentieth century.

the poor quality of housing management and estate supervision which are at fault on rented social housing, high-rise estates where nobody has a sense of ownership or belonging, and which are still used to provide accommodation for the poorest and most deprived groups (Cockburn 1977; Roberts 1991). In contrast a new generation of luxury apartment development has sprouted up in many cities, such as in the London Docklands, aimed particularly at single, childless people working in the city centre in business and management occupations, which saves them the need to commute. Indeed under New Labour high rise has even been promoted by government policy (PPS3) as a form of sustainable development, mainly built on brown-field sites. However, as shown in other chapters, such accommodation may

be ideal for this new type of resident but offers little provision for those with families, the poor or the traditional working-class populations that used to live in such areas (Ravetz 1980; Greed 2011a).

As time went on, the quick and cheap building approach to much council house high-rise construction began to show its weaknesses, with maintenance problems, condensation and structural factors soon merging. The type and range of tenants also became more diverse. Initially would-be tenants were carefully chosen, had to be in full-time employment and were subject to suitability tests, and were grateful to be living in flats with inside toilets and bathrooms. But following a major change in Labour housing policy with the 1977 Housing (Homeless Persons) Act, council housing lists were opened up to more needy groups,

Photo 6.4   Petronas Towers, Kuala Lumpur, Malaysia

The Petronas Twin Towers in Kuala Lumpur are amongst the tallest in the world, funded by one of the major petro-chemical companies in Malaysia. One needs to get up close to appreciate the scale of the development, whilst inside there is a huge shopping mall, then a succession of apartments and offices further up, and, of course, a mosque.

including the homeless, single-parent families, the unemployed and others suffering social deprivation. High-rise buildings were increasingly associated with drug-dealing, vandalism, graffiti and violence. There were also accusations of racism and social stereotyping in that many so-called sink estates were used to house predominantly ethnic minority tenants, whilst many of the original white tenants had long since moved out. Although high-rise development never really caught on in the UK at the time, internationally it has been a key characteristic for both residential and commercial development in many emerging economies and megacities internationally. There is a race on to build the world's tallest building.

Global high-rise comparisons

Whilst in Britain high-rise housing never really caught on, during the second half of the twentieth century the high-rise city had already emerged in North America, particularly in New York and Chicago. However, in the UK high rise has mainly been a feature of commercial, and mainly office, development, because it enables a large amount of usable space to be built on a small building footprint in city centre areas where land values were very high. Subsequently entire megacities in the Far East have chosen the high-rise option. So let us look at some examples of what is happening internationally, where high-rise development is in a different league in terms of height, imagination and level of investment (Photos 6.3 and 6.4). More photos may be found on the website of what is happening elsewhere in the world chiefly because of population growth, migration from countryside to town and also the modernisation and replacement of existing housing stock.

1960s Labour new towns

In the 1960s there was a return to greater emphasis being put upon another new towns programme. The Mark III new towns, built by Labour, consisted both of regional growth centres in depressed areas which were meant to act as growth poles for the surrounding area, and also a further phase of overspill new towns in prosperous areas in the Midlands where they were intended to take the pressure off existing cities and provide new opportunities for investment and growth. In Mark III new towns neighbourhood design and overall planning structure had become more sophisticated. For example, one finds arrangements based on new towns being divided into intermediate districts of say 15,000 people, these being subdivided into smaller neighbourhoods and local areas, each with their own centre (Photo 6.1). The assumption that people would walk to the local shops and mainly use public transport was a thing of the past. Some would subdivide the Mark III new towns further, and designate Milton Keynes: Mark IV. This is virtually a city rather than a town, and had a target population of a quarter of a million. The design of Milton Keynes was conceptualised primarily as a transportation grid. It had some similarity with Broad Acre City, Frank Lloyd Wrights 'autopian' dream. There was a high level of good quality, dual-carriageway standard roads provided, but pedestrians took second place. This was a reflection of the central fixation of 1960s planning with the motorcar.

There have been no new towns designated since the beginning of the 1970s. When recession set in, in these artificially-created settlements, economic and social problems were amplified, particularly in the more vulnerable new towns located in the North and Midlands. Many of their industries were multinational and had no local ties, and so they simply moved out to catch the next government grant elsewhere. Whilst some of the new towns, especially in the South, including Milton Keynes, have gone from strength to strength, others are the worse for wear. Most of the housing in the Mark I new towns was rented, but by the time Milton Keynes was built, over 70 per cent of the housing was owner-occupied. Although the official government new towns policy has been wound up, there has been interest in recent years in the development of private new towns, especially eco-towns.

Regional planning under Labour

Economic and physical planning took on a central importance under the Labour government of the 1960s. In 1965, Regional Economic Planning Boards, and related advisory Councils, were established. These formed the institutional framework for the intended development of a much more carefully organised regional strategy, although their executive powers were fairly limited. As under New Labour, these regional bodies were to provide a strategic policy level above local planning authority level on housing and employment-related development. Attempts were also made at a National Plan (an economic one, and short-lived) and a whole series of national economic planning bodies was created to oversee economic development in the different industrial sectors. A particular problem as perceived by the Labour government was the concentration of office development in London. The Control of Offices and Industrial Development Act 1965 introduced Office Development Permits (ODPs) for all new office development in the South East and Midlands over 3000 square feet, and the Industrial Development Certificate (IDC) system was also made stricter for these areas. The Industrial Development Act 1966 tidied up what had by now become an unwieldy system, creating five large development areas which covered 40 per cent of Britain, introducing a range of grants and incentives. The Special Development Areas Act 1967 introduced further refinements to the delineation of areas worthy of funding. Wherever the boundaries are drawn, and whether the areas are large or small, there will always be some resentment that some are in and others are out. Following the Hunt Report in 1969, the Local Employment Act 1970 was introduced which designated a further series of intermediate areas with their own grade of grants and incentives.

However, a gradual shift was in evidence away from this obsession with defining depressed industrial areas as the main, and only, recipients of government funding. There was a gradual realisation that inner-city areas, even within otherwise prosperous cities, were also suffering from high levels of social deprivation, unemployment and deterioration of the building stock. As indicated above, the emphasis on new development, new towns and new housing estates during the immediate post-war reconstruction period had diverted resources away from helping existing areas. Householders had found their properties were condemned without prior consultation as 'unfit for human habitation' under the still extant 1957 Slum Clearance Act. More properties were destroyed under this act than by aerial bombing in the war. One and a half million homes were demolished under slum clearance between the end of the war and the start of the 1970s. As a result 3.7 million people were made homeless and relocated (Ravetz 1980). People wanted housing improvement and modernisation rather than clearance. The Denington Report (1966) reflected public concern, and proposed a change of direction away from clearance towards comprehensive improvement of both older housing and the surrounding environment. Therefore the Housing Act 1969 established a programme of General Improvement Areas (GIAs), giving grants to renovate existing properties rather than demolishing them.

Whilst this opened up a new lease of life for many of the older housing areas, it had not necessarily solved the related social problems. Indeed existing residents were often being pushed out of their home areas as a result of these policies, for as an area went up in the world, rents increased for private tenants, and pressures to sell were strong amongst previously impoverished owner-occupiers. In 1968 the Home Office had initiated the 'Urban Programme' with 34 pilot local authorities to investigate the emerging problems of the inner city. This project was as much concerned with rising crime as it was with wider social issues. In 1969 the Community Development Programme (CDP) was set up. CDPs ran in 12 areas to begin with, with social workers rather than town planners taking the leading role. It was fashionable at the time to see the problems 'spatially' (in terms of the built environment) as a set of factors that were found in, and could be dealt with in, the framework a specific geographical area: without necessarily considering the social forces that brought people 'down' into these areas in the first place. In the 1970s

Educational Priority Areas (EPAs) had been established in areas where positive discrimination was needed, interestingly towards the white working class, rather than ethnic groups at this stage, as in the case of a scheme which was established in Everton in Liverpool.

There was considerable opposition to all these changes in the built environment and to the planning system itself, especially from those concerned with the protection of historic buildings, especially local housing areas, from yet more demolition. Urban conservation groups became increasingly concerned at the visual effects of high-rise 'modern' architecture (until then the highest buildings had been the church towers) and at the wanton demolition which was occurring (Esher 1983). Many Victorian town halls narrowly missed destruction, and many a Georgian terrace was sacrificed. The government had introduced subsidies for some categories of high-rise buildings in the late 1960s, leading to a spate of high-rise development of hotels, council blocks of flats and offices. Towns throughout the country were becoming similar to each other with the 'same' shopping centre, high-rise blocks and traffic problems. People felt the new planning system had destroyed much that was valuable from the past. Looking back it is astounding how much power planners and local authorities had to demolish, condemn and redevelop cities, all without much consultation, participation or involvement in democratic processes. It is even more astonishing when one realises many of these decisions were made by planning officers whose background education was limited to technical subjects, such as building and surveying, who could condemn a property as a slum 'just like that' with little awareness of the social, cultural and economic implications of their actions.

A desire to return to more traditional values, and disillusionment with the Brave New World of the planners and the property developers, led to a great emphasis on improvement and conservation policies. The beginnings of the reaction were manifest in the Civic Amenities Act 1967 that gave powers for the creation of Urban Conservation Areas, and the listing of buildings of historical and architectural importance became a major issue. Developers adapted to these changes. One development company set a trend, namely Haslemere Estates, specialising in the refurbishment of historical town squares and prestige buildings for offices. This form of accommodation soon became more upmarket and fashionable than an office suite in an impersonal concrete block. Likewise in the 1960s we see the first stirrings of the environmental movement that was concerned with conservation, sustainability and green issues, the Friends of the Earth being established in the late 1960s. In 1970 the first European Conservation Year was declared, and the Environment Action programme began in the following year, but the UK was barely catching up with these changing priorities. The topic of urban conservation is discussed further in Chapter 13.

Transportation planning

In all this flurry of development plan-making and reconstruction planning, little thought was given to the transport implications, for example of how zoning, and separation of residential and employment areas, would extend the journey to work, and encourage the development of a new generation of car-borne commuters. As explained in Chapter 12 on transport, there were less than 2 million cars on the road after the Second World War and most people travelled on two wheels or by public transport. Increased prosperity in the 1950s meant that car ownership gradually began to rise and by 1958 this figure had risen to 4.6 million and by 1968 to 10.8 million, with a further 3.5 million lorries, vans, motorcycles and buses giving a total of 14.4 million vehicles licensed for use on the roads in 1968 (Bodey 1971). Car ownership was beginning to put huge pressures on existing urban areas, contributing to ribbon development, increased suburbanisation, and dispersal and decentralisation of uses (Headicar 2009; Banister 2005).

The government and the planners welcomed the growth of motorcar ownership in the 1960s and a nationwide system of motorways was begun, along with all the paraphernalia of service stations, slip roads, underpasses and flyovers. New motorway interchanges were built such as Spaghetti Junction in Birmingham and a new form of concrete traffic architecture was hailed as a sign of modernity. Travel between towns and cities by motor vehicle undoubtedly improved as a result of the new motorways and

improvements to other main (trunk) roads. However, this was at the expense of the railway network, and following the publication of the infamous 'Beeching Report' in 1963 the government, which had taken over the railways in 1947, decided to close what were seen as under-used (mostly cross-country and rural) routes and around 5000 miles of track (just under a third of the network) and over 2000 stations were axed (Beeching 1963; Jones 2011). The glories of the Victorian age of the railway system as described in Bradshaw's Railway Guides, which had enabled people to travel far and wide, had been lost for ever (Bradshaw 2012, originally 1863). Many would say the car manufacturing lobby was influential in these decisions, at the expense of the train-using population. It was naturally assumed that the car was obviously good and that everyone would soon have one. In fact less than 40 per cent of households had even one car at that time. But there were less out of town shopping developments, or decentralised schools, hospitals and business parks in those days, and one could still go about one's daily life without the use of a car, using the bus or simply cycling or walking. However, there had always been a problem of the lack of adequate transport for people stuck out on housing estates be, they private or council.

The 1950s were very much the age of the bicycle as well as the train, bus, motorcycle, moped and scooter. Initially very few people had cars, but by the 1930s there were around 2 million cars in Britain. In 1951, 86 per cent of households had no car (Mawhinney 1995), as against virtually the reverse today. Increased prosperity in the 1950s meant that car ownership gradually began to rise and by 1958 this figure had risen to 4.6 million and by 1968 to 10.8 million, with a further 3.5 million lorries, vans, motorcycles and buses giving a total of 14.4 million vehicles licensed for use on the roads in 1968 (Bodey, 1971). Car ownership was beginning to put huge pressures on existing urban areas, contributing to ribbon development, increased suburbanisation, and dispersal and decentralisation of uses. Meanwhile the railways were gradually losing their importance. The railways were grouped into four large companies in 1923, Great Western Railway (GWR), London Midland and Scottish (LMS), London and North Eastern Railway (LNER) and

Southern Region (SR). They were not nationalised and unified until after the Second World War under the Labour Government which came to power in 1945. The problem of how to plan for the motorcar continues into the next chapter and is a major consideration in Chapter 12 on transport planning.

However, the massive growth in vehicle numbers taking place at this time resulted in many problems within Britain's towns and cities. Entire parts of cities were demolished to make way for new urban motorways that would (in theory) reduce congestion and enable the commuter to get to the city centre more quickly. But the more roads that were built the more cars came along to fill them up (Parkinson's law), and congestion became a serious problem in most urban areas, especially during the rush hour. Traffic speeds in some cities were reduced to that of medieval times. As time went on increased levels of traffic management, traffic signals, signage and road markings were introduced to better manage these increasing numbers of vehicles. Stationary cars were to become as much a problem as moving cars, indeed cars spend most of their day dormant in car parks and garages. Car parking became an increasing problem in London where parking meters were first introduced in the late 1950s. As city-centre parking pressures grew cars were directed into multi-storey car parks, usually made of concrete; badly lit and poorly designed, they hardly provided a welcoming place for the car drivers once they left their vehicles. Pedestrians were to be kept separate from the busy roads; railings herded them into unpleasant underpasses or along tortuous footpaths and bridges in an attempt to reduce accidents.

The root causes of many of these problems, the ever increasing numbers and use of cars, were rarely confronted and a 'predict and provide' approach was adopted at national and local level (rather than the more restrictive 'let the polluter pay' approach in later years). In the 1960s planners were strongly influenced by transportation planning theories and policies from North America where mathematical models were extensively used to calculate the scale and location of new highways and interchanges to allow the traffic to flow freely (see Chapter 8 on planning theory). Much emphasis was put upon calculating the needs of facilitating 'the journey to work' (by car), using the newly invented computer,

to show trip generation, origin and destination, and trip allocation (Roberts 1974). There has been much subsequent criticism of such models especially from non-car users and those that questioned the long-term effects of such an emphasis on the motorcar and the related decline in public transport. While this approach may have been appropriate in the USA, where scarcity of land is not really a problem and petrol was cheap, its application in the UK led to many of the problems mentioned above.

But the financial climate was changing and petrol costs rose steeply in the 1970s as a result of an economic downturn and unrest in the Middle East affecting oil imports. Reaction to the massive housing clearance programmes that had been undertaken to build new urban motorways was also growing among grass-roots residents groups and urban conservation societies, and newly-formed environmental groups (such as Friends of the Earth, founded in the late 1960s) resisted the plans for more and bigger road systems (such as the Hammersmith Flyover). Significantly many of the views expressed by environmentalists were echoed by those concerned with the social aspects of town planning, especially those representing minority groups and those with limited access to the use of a motorcar, such as women with small children. Health concerns were also expressed regarding pollution, and the use of leaded petrol which was increasingly linked to cancer.

After many years of transport policy being unquestionably concerned with catering to the needs of the motorcar, gradually in the 1960s we begin to get a separate strand of a more sophisticated approach to transport planning emerging. A major landmark was Colin Buchanan's report for the Ministry of Transport entitled Traffic in Towns, often referred to as the Buchanan Report. Published in 1963, the report aimed to balance the need for efficient traffic management with the need to provide a satisfactory standard of environment in our towns and cities (Buchanan 1963). It proposed that to do this a hierarchy of distributor roads should be created, with primary distributors carrying the bulk of through traffic and smaller, local distributors serving what were described as 'environmental areas' – these were the areas where, as Buchanan put it, 'daily life is carried on' (Buchanan 1963, 44) and while they would not be traffic-free in these areas, traffic considerations would be secondary to environmental concerns. Buchanan was a Scottish civil engineer and a town planner and the report generated much interest; it was even published in reduced form in 1964 as a paperback book which became a surprising best seller. The report and the book are well worth reading, both for a historical perspective on transport planning and because many of the issues and options are just as relevant to planning in our towns and cities today. Under the Localism Act 2011 Neighbourhood Plans are being produced based on identifiable local areas, and in some cases, such as in Bristol, previously used 'environmental area' designations are proving a useful starting point.

Many of Buchanan's ideas were not new: the notion of creating environmental areas free from through traffic had also been tried out in the post-war new towns. These were generally designed on the neighbourhood unit principle with a cul-de-sac system providing limited access for traffic off the bigger distributor roads. This approach was in turn inspired by an idea from the USA and used in a new development in the late 1920s at Radburn, New Jersey, which employed a hierarchical arrangement of roads that separated traffic from open space, which was used for pedestrian and cycle routes, all in a very natural setting (Hall 1980) (see Chapter 13 on urban design for further details). A further idea in the Buchanan Report took this concept even further by suggesting a multilevel split between vehicles and pedestrians in the most built-up urban areas. Roads, car parking, bus stops and servicing would take place at ground level and pedestrian decks would be built above for the pedestrians. A number of UK towns and cities took up this idea but extensive schemes were rarely carried out in full: Cumbernauld New Town in Scotland is one example, and the main campus at Bath University demonstrates the principle well. The Bath campus was designed in the late 1960s and Colin Buchanan was the traffic consultant. The buildings are arranged around a raised central pedestrian spine with the service road below it at ground level (Forsyth 2003). Buchanan also wanted to drive a tunnel right under the historic centre of Bath and create a peripheral road system, involving demolition of secondary historical areas, but this was opposed and never happened. These

were interesting ideas, but for many planners and highway engineers the report was interpreted as a green light for ever more complex and intrusive road layouts, and many towns and cities were subjected to such schemes throughout the 1970s and 1980s. It appeared that Buchanan's emphasis on the environment, what we would refer to today as sense of place, and the need for traffic restraint in such areas, was lost in a rush to build more and more roads.

As the years progressed, traffic problems increased along with car ownership and higher petrol prices, and gradually there was a move from an unquestioning approach to planning for the motorcar towards a greater emphasis upon its control, and upon finding new ways of enabling people to move around urban areas by other means, such as by public transport, walking or cycling. Much of this change was inspired by the rise of the green movement and wider concerns over the negative impacts of car use, whether these be noise, safety, pollution, the depletion of fossil fuels, the effect of CO_2 on the environment and the very future of the planet. Many of these issues are discussed in Chapter 10 on the environment and sustainability.

As sustainable development became more of a concern for government policy-makers, and as protests against new road proposals mounted in the 1990s, there was a move away from the 'predict and provide' road-based policies of earlier years towards more sophisticated forms of traffic management, demand management and the promotion of alternatives to the private car. We have not reached full road capacity or saturation point yet in terms of the number of vehicles on the road but many areas are already subject to heavy congestion and delays, so alternatives must be found to mass car usage. Yet the use of the car is still very popular. In 2012 there were 28.6 million cars and a further 5.7 million other vehicles licensed for use on the roads in Great Britain (Department for Transport 2012a). This is within the context of a UK population of 26.3 million households, and over 61 million people, with some households having more than one car, but still a significant minority of up to 30 per cent of households in some areas having no access to a car (check for updates when you read this on the ONS and DfT websites).

More change in the 1970s

Conservative government 1970–74

A Conservative government, under Ted Heath, was returned for a brief period, and interestingly many of the Labour government's policies on regional policy, urban regeneration and renewal were maintained and expanded. In 1971, Comprehensive Community Programmes were introduced in a range of areas, with a broad brief to include education, health, social services and housing policy. In 1972 the emphasis shifted more towards special policies within the realms of town planning itself, and the Department of the Environment established its Six Towns Study, focusing on areas such as Lambeth in southern inner London, and at last publicly recognising that there was poverty near at hand. The Housing Act 1974 established another category of special housing areas, that is Housing Action Areas (HAAs). These were smaller than GIAs but in which the emphasis was upon more concentrated immediate attention. However, regional policy was also still ticking over, and the Industry Act 1972 further developed a complex hierarchy of aid and control based on several categories of area, consisting of development areas, special areas, intermediate areas and derelict land, but the emphasis was again more on helping local businesses and offering tax concessions, rather than giving direct grants (Hall 1992; Heap 1996). This was a time of trade union unrest, three-day weeks and all sorts of other problems so there seemed to be little time to give much attention to the planning system.

New development plan system

The traditional approach to plan-making, based principally on simplistic land-use zoning, was inadequate to deal with rapid change. The planners wished to incorporate advances in planning theory, and more public participation into the plan-making process. Therefore, a new development plan, the Structure Plan, had been introduced in the late 1960s, under Labour and then consolidated into the Town and Country Planning Act 1971, interestingly under the Tories. Paradoxically the diagrammatic nature of the new plans, and the jargon they were written in, were even more confusing for the general public than the 1947 version.

In summary, the 'plan' now consisted of both a written policy statement and diagrammatic plans of the policy directives as described in Chapter 2. The system was meant to be based on planners continuously monitoring change in the urban system (using their new computers) to see how, for example, economic changes would affect the demand for new industrial sites, or how changes in family structure were to affect housing demand. The planners sought to identify goals and objectives which they wanted to achieve as the basis of the plan, rather than drawing out a rigid, once-and-for-all master plan. These goals, relating, for example, to the expansion of a particular area, or the provision of a certain level of facilities, could be reached in a variety of ways. Structure Plans were meant to be able to accommodate rather than restrict change provided it tied in with the urban goals that were set. They allowed for a more flexible approach based on negotiation and agreement, rather than preconceived land-use plans. So a more 'incremental', that is a step-by-step, approach was adopted in order to achieve the long-term objectives. Ironically the new system proved even more long-winded and inflexible than the previous system, with local planning authorities taking many years to produce the initial Structure Plan. Many local authorities had great difficulty producing the new local and Structure Plans, let alone carrying out continuous monitoring. In these cases planning continued, regardless, on the basis of existing plans, with non-statutory plan updates taking effect as approved 'adopted plans' of the planning committee and therefore, in the interim, having the force of law.

Labour government 1974–79: disillusionment with planning

The Labour government returned under Harold Wilson in 1974, who was subsequently replaced by Jim Callaghan, but by then there was a growing disillusionment within society with both planning and modernisation. A period of public reaction to the Modern Movement in architecture grew apace not least because of the unpopularity of the high-rise movement. Traditional values, architectural conservation and appreciation of classical and historical vernacular styles were all coming back into favour. In parallel there was an increased interest in the social aspects of planning and demands for the problems of the inner city to be addressed (see Chapter 14 on social aspects).

In 1975 the Urban Aid programme enabled money to be allocated to other inner-city schemes including community centres, and later Law centres. In 1977 the Manpower Services Commission was set up with particular concern for enabling employment in inner areas. This was followed by the Inner Urban Areas Act 1978, which established special inner urban area policy programmes, this time under the control, chiefly, of the town planners. Thus the tide had turned from a regionalist approach to one which put greater emphasis upon targeting specific urban areas and this policy was to be continued and amplified throughout the Thatcher administration of the 1980s. In addition in 1975 the Labour government introduced the Community Land Act, which was yet another attempt to cream off the profits from property development for the benefit of the community, by means of an updated version of the betterment levy, but full-blown nationalisation never happened.

However, the Labour government continued to update regional planning policy, but it appeared to be increasingly detached from the changing needs of society, because of increasing affluence, social mobility, car ownership, owner-occupation and educational aspiration, especially in the South. But, at the same time, there were greater levels of deprivation, racial conflict, unemployment and decline within inner-city areas. These were, arguably, equally as dire as the problems encountered in the economically depressed areas of the North. Traditional Labour-voting areas were experiencing decline in the heavily unionised sectors of mining, shipbuilding and heavy industry, and the classical Labour emphasis upon the needs of the historical working class and traditional industry-based economic policies seemed strangely out of date. Indeed old-time socialism had an image problem, being seen as too elitist and out of touch with the needs of the workers who simply wanted to have a decent job, house and car. Neo-Marxist theory and discussions of capitalism and state control, which were a popular inclusion in many an academic planning course, arguably did not resonate with the needs or aspirations of ordinary working people (cf Chapter 8 on planning theory).

The Conservative years 1979–97

Laissez-faire or state intervention?

The new Conservative government under Mrs Thatcher, which came to power in 1979, sought to encourage private business investment rather than direct state intervention, as a means of building up the country and ensuring new development. They were in favour of a *laissez-faire* approach, which literally means 'free for all' ('allow [them] to do'), and thus promoted an unfettered property market (Lavender 1990; Myers 2008). The Conservatives saw this as the way of creating jobs and eradicating poverty and deprivation through private enterprise, rather than through the state welfare programmes previously favoured by Labour (Thornley 1991). But both administrations were concerned with economic planning, albeit informed by totally different images of the economy and society (Atkinson and Moon 1993).

However, there was really a considerable degree of state planning, in all but name, as growth was not left purely to a free for all. Rather government policy supported growth in specific sectors and regional localities. The emphasis shifted towards supporting the needs of the tertiary and quaternary sectors of employment (office, service and knowledge-based sectors) and away from seeing the old primary and secondary industries of the past such as heavy industry, engineering and manufacturing. The workers were now more likely to be perceived as those employed in offices, retail and service sectors, as industry-based, working-class jobs declined. Traditional regional policy was seen as supporting 'lame ducks' in the North, thus penalising growth in other areas. Instead there was an emphasis on urban regeneration, and the redevelopment and renewal of towns and cities, particularly in the southern part of the country, and especially London. Attention was given to the growing financial, business and service sectors of the economy (Oatley 1998). Likewise there was considerable emphasis and increased support given to urban conservation policies, which supported the gentrification of inner-city areas within the context of urban regeneration (cf Chapter 11).

Factors including the globalisation of economies, international market trends, immigration of new reserve labour forces, more women working, indus-trial decentralisation, unemployment and a growing proportion of elderly population (9.3 million) have all redefined the nature of the available workforce and of the economy itself (McDowell 2013). During the 1980s, in the Thatcher era, town planning took on the values of the Enterprise culture, inspired by monetarism and the work of the American econo-mist Milton Friedman (1975, 1991). Friedman remarked, '*there's no such thing as a free lunch*', imply-ing that everything had to be paid for somewhere along the line by someone, even in a Welfare State. Prior to the Thatcher government, it was generally accepted by all governments that there was a need for some measure of state intervention in the econ-omy and in the built environment. Government policy was still based on a 'mixed economy', that is of a combination of a state control and free enter-prise. So there was a measure of planning but there was also private ownership of property and an active property market running in parallel.

In Britain it has traditionally been considered vital for government to take over the provision of non-profit making – but nonetheless essential – urban amenities and infrastructure, and to provide for those sectors of the population who cannot afford to meet their needs through the market place. In recent years there has been a breakdown in this consensus, and a more market-orientated, profit-making emphasis has been applied to public services. However affluent people are at an individual level they still need certain social goods and services such as roads, sewers, fire services and local facilities. These commodities are aptly described as 'social capital' (Saunders 1979). Otherwise one ends up with a situation, as in some of parts of North America, where people have enormous houses but no mains drainage and every house has its private septic tank. It may be more economical and in soci-ety's and industry's interest to provide these utility services on a non-profit-making basis to reap the returns in the long run. But the Conservative government began to change this consensus.

Acts of Parliament were seldom used (except for Consolidation Acts) to bring in changes in the plan-ning system, as the Conservative government gener-ally introduced change through amendments, statutory instruments and orders, and circulars, making subtle alterations in past legislation, rather than introducing clear-cut new Acts of Parliament. In other words a 'non-plan' approach to planning was practised (Greed 1999a, 1999c). This tied in with the Conservatives' distaste for state intervention and bureaucracy and their preference for a *laissez-faire* approach (Brindley *et al.* 1996). Both the Community Land Act 1975 and Office Development Permits (ODPs) were abolished by the Control of Office Development (Cessation) Order in 1979. In 1981 IDCs were completely suspended. In 1979, 47 per cent of the population had been covered by some form of regional aid. By 1982 the extent of coverage was reduced to 27 per cent of the working population. A three-tier system was estab-lished of special development areas, development areas and intermediate areas, in which grants were available for plant and machinery at the rates of 22 per cent, 15 per cent and on a discretionary basis respectively. But in 1984, aid was further dramati-cally reduced, which led to a situation of *'less jam spread more thinly'* as the late John Smith, then Shadow Labour Trade Secretary, described it. Further changes in 1984 introduced a two-tier system with development areas which qualified for 15 per cent grants towards new plant and machinery and intermediate areas which were eligible on a discretionary basis, with the areas themselves being greatly reduced. The emphasis had moved away from regional planning to inner-city regeneration. In parallel, ideologically the population was no longer seen as comprising capitalists and oppressed workers, but as individuals who all, in theory, had the same chances in life, provided they 'got on their bike' to find work.

At the same time that new categories of area were being created, existing planning departments, and the local authorities to which they belonged, were being reorganised. Some would say that the aboli-tion of the Greater London Council (GLC) (which was established in 1965 and ran until 1986), along with the large first-tier strategic Metropolitan County Councils (MCCs) in 1986, and the subse-quent creation of second-tier district and borough authorities was done intentionally because these big authorities were predominantly Labour-held, with the GLC carrying out what were seen as left-wing policies right on the doorstep of Parliament.

Subsequently the GLA (Greater London Authority) was established in 2000 under the 1999 Greater London Authority Act. Far from reducing government controls, a great deal of state intervention and centralisation of policy-making was needed to sustain the free market and related enterprise culture. As the years went by the government was faced with a range of urban problems and policy issues that required intervention and control, such as, for example, increased traffic congestion, an overheated property market and increased demand for green-field site development. The latter incensed traditional Tories in the shire counties, who did not want the urban masses impinging on their territory. Indeed members of the new Conservative government were referred to as '*just a bunch of estate agents*' by some hereditary peers who had a more paternalistic, less commercial view of government's duty to its people.

Other forces of change and new trends were coming to bear upon planning. These factors included the environmental movement (see Chapter 9 on sustainability) and the requirements of the European Union (as described in Chapter 2). New alliances were developing between radical environmentalists and shire-county conservatives, for example, on the preservation of green-belt land and the restriction of urban growth (Shoard 1999). But demands for environmental sustainability sat uneasily with the enterprise culture of the 1980s. The demand for sustainability was influencing the design of the built environment as well as the countryside. There was a reaction against much of so-called Modern Architecture, which was seen in retrospect as being ugly, energy-inefficient and socially problematic. By the 1980s contemporary architecture took two main forms. First, there was a growth in traditional, and some would say reactionary, neo-Georgian styles, which were much used in office and residential buildings in areas where urban conservation policy was in force. Secondly, a range of new High-Tech styles were developed, as used, for example, by Richard Rogers in the Pompidou centre in Paris, Lloyds of London and subsequently the Millennium Dome under New Labour (renamed the O2 Centre). Whilst conservation policy controlled the march of high-tech buildings in many provincial city centres, the development of science and business parks on the

city's edges, beside the motorways, allowed free rein for the new 'shed' architecture which has developed in the name of progress and technology. But it was also easier and cheaper to develop on edge-city and green-field sites, and to build minimum quality industrial units to use as retail premises.

Enterprise planning

A range of initiatives was created to bring back business to the inner city, and to facilitate urban renewal. The Local Government Planning and Land Act 1980 consolidated previous legislation and provided the enabling powers for a range of other programmes and measures. For example, Enterprise Zones (EZs) were intended to attract investment to run-down areas by means of reducing planning controls and suspending ordinary planning law within their boundaries. Urban Development Corporations (UDCs) were established in inner areas (Cullingworth and Nadin 1997 edition, 238–9). Various other grants, loans, rates holidays and incentives were introduced, including the City Grant for the redevelopment of areas and repair of buildings which were too deteriorated to be of interest to the developer.

EZs are relatively small areas, the size of a small industrial estate, and are administered via the existing local authority, whereas UDCs are much larger areas, for example the Bristol Development Corporation area and the London Docklands Development Corporation area (LDDC). The London body was established separately from the existing local authorities in their area (much to their chagrin) and employed its own army of planners, surveyors, architects, etc. Its main aim, however, was not so much to build new development itself, but to make land readily available, to provide the infrastructure, especially roads, and the famous Docklands Light Railway, and to encourage private developers to come in and build and invest in the redundant docklands to the East of London. This is a different approach from the New Town Corporations which always took a much more active role themselves in building both housing stock and industrial units for rent.

Both the EZs and the UDCs had a limited life expectancy, of around ten years, when they would be de-designated. The aim was simply to give critical areas special status whilst they are finding their feet and getting established. Considerable investment has been put into infrastructure, as in the case of the Docklands Light Railway (DLR) in East London. Although many firms took up the offer, as with old-fashioned regional planning it is debatable as to whether new jobs and new prosperity were really created, or whether firms simply moved across the boundary in order to catch the grant, and thus deprived other areas of existing employment. Enterprise zones have come back into favour under the present Coalition, and Heseltine has had a new innings advising the government on rolling out another phase of EZs.

There were also some spectacular, but short-lived, cultural projects embarked upon under Michael Heseltine, the Secretary of State responsible for planning at the time, such as the International Garden Festival programme. For example, in 1984 the first festival took place on a newly reclaimed dockside piece of derelict brownfield land in Liverpool. Subsequent festivals took place in other depressed areas such as South Wales. Millions were spent on land reclamation, planting and landscaping, in order to help revitalise the area. But it had little impact on local long-term employment prospects, and there was not the money to support the scheme. For many years it remained derelict and at present is to be redeveloped for housing.

Under UDC policy, vast areas were reclaimed for upmarket residential and business use within the old London Docklands, in close proximity to the City of London, attracting a new social class to the old 'East End', and gentrifying the area. But this process created considerable resentment amongst some of the original working-class residents. Although the inner-city legislation was originally, purportedly, meant to be on their behalf, it has benefited the middle-class groups more. People remember how difficult it was in the past even to get the council to put on an extra bus service to get them to work, whereas now expense is no object. Meanwhile, because of high house prices and lack of council or cheap rented accommodation, many working-class people who also have jobs in central London (on the Tube, in the hospitals, cleaning in the offices, in the shops) find they have to commute further and further out, whilst many managers wonder why there is no longer a ready supply of working-class labour to do all the essential, yet low status, jobs upon which the running of the capital depends.

In 1985 the government introduced the White Paper, *Lifting the Burden*, which emphasised minimising perceived restrictions on economic growth created by planning controls. Heseltine is rumoured to have castigated the planning system because of the delays it caused, resulting in '*jobs locked up in filing cabinets*'. Subsequently the Housing and Planning Act 1986 introduced Simplified Planning Zones (SPZs) which supplement the EZs and UDPs, but are smaller and the criteria for their location are more flexible. Rydin notes that these were part of a move towards a blanket zoning approach to planning in which permission for development was inherent in the area designation of SPZs (Rydin 1998, 212; 2003). Around 13 SPZs, as against 35 EZs, were designated. The need for their designation was subsequently superseded by the introduction of a range of other measures which sought to 'lift the burden' from developers. The UCO and GDO categories were revised and liberalised somewhat to enable greater flexibility between uses (especially among 'B' uses) to encourage new business development.

The principle of such initiatives was to attempt to simplify and speed up the planning system, and to create an organisational framework tailor-made for the special circumstances of a particular situation without disrupting the existing planning system. Meanwhile, in non-special category areas planning law became more complex, and the Conservatives introduced planning charges for applications in the late 1970s. The proliferation of ad hoc bodies only served to weaken the existing planning system, and increased the powers of central government. In spite of other regeneration schemes such as 'Garden Festivals', and various other inner-city initiatives, unemployment continued to rise, inner-city problems continue and regional disparities became even greater. Many argued that it was time to bring back regional planning (Hamnett *et al.* 1989). But it needed to be based upon more sensitive criteria than last time; for example, it should take into account women's employment as well as men's, and demonstrate awareness of the great social disparities which can exist within a region such as the South East between run-down inner-city areas and the more prosperous suburbs and market towns.

The Major government: a softening of attitudes?

As the years progressed a gradual warming towards the traditional objectives of town and country planning was observed within the Conservative government, under the leadership of John Major (1990–97), although there also remained a commitment towards the needs of the developer at the local level. Gradually there was a move back towards a 'plan-led' as against developer-led approach to planning. In particular, successive Secretaries of State for the Environment put their mark upon the Department of the Environment. Development plan policy was reaffirmed as a 'material consideration' in determining planning applications, reinforcing the principles of Section 54 of the Town and Country Planning Act 1990. Different Secretaries of State took varied approaches to planning. For example, Michael Heseltine was keen to promote a range of initiatives which incorporated a greater sensitivity to the environment, whereas, subsequently, Nicholas Ridley was much criticised for favouring several controversial developments on green-field sites. John Gummer was generally seen as the most sensitive towards town planning issues, and became such a convert to the cause of town planning that he continued to write a weekly column for the RTPI in *Planning* many years after leaving office.

Members of the Conservative government did not comprise a unitary group with identical values, and under John Major's administration there was a gradual softening of the hard-line values adopted during the Thatcher years. Reasons for this softening included Major's new style of government motivated by his stated desire to create 'a nation at ease with itself'. The libertarian strand of Conservatism overcame the more authoritarian strand represented by Thatcher herself and hard-liners such as Norman Tebbitt. The need to capture the 'green vote' was also crucial as the green movement and concerns with environmental sustainability grew stronger amongst the electorate. Around 15 per cent of voters were voting green and this was seen as a serious

threat to retaining a Conservative majority. Pressure from traditional shire county conservatives to protect the countryside, along with new green interests, plus pressure from Europe together led to a measure of 'greening' of Tory policy under Major. The interests of conservative NIMBY voters were in an uneasy coalition with 'eco-warriors', for example in the battle over the building of the Newbury bypass in Berkshire. At an international level the government had made commitments to a range of treaties and agreements concerned with the reduction of pollution and the conservation of the natural environment, such as the Rio Treaty on Sustainability (UN 1992). This all made for a more environmentally-friendly, and less developer-led, form of town and country planning more acceptable (Barton 1996). Even property developers had begun to realise they really needed their old enemies the planners. Town planning was re-embraced for the traditional reasons that it actually helped the market, in creating a level playing field, and as a means of regulation and control that could be used to serve the requirements of established property interests.

Inner-city problems continued, and the housing market went through a series of booms and recessions in the 1990s. Homelessness was a continuing problem, with large numbers of people sleeping on the streets. Housing issues were frequently featured in cutting-edge documentaries on the television. The housing situation has become increasingly topical in the light of the swing of government policy away from state provision of council housing in the 1980s. There was a greater concern with social issues in the dying years of the Conservative government, which contrasted with the harder line adopted by Mrs Thatcher, who famously had declared that there was '*no such thing as society*', thus rendering valueless the work of generations of sociologists and social policy-makers.

The planning system was becoming more developer-friendly too. Emphasis was put upon more positive, proactive initiatives as well as amending restrictive controls on property development. For example, The Leasehold Reform, Housing and Urban Development Act 1993, Part III facilitated the creation of the Urban Regeneration Agency, and a more entrepreneurial approach to local government policy. In addition to the UDCs, there was a range of other programmes and initiatives in which private developers directly dealt with central government to obtain funding as under the City Grant provisions introduced in the late 1980s. Because of the increasing diversity and complexity of government schemes, attempts were made to coordinate the various policies, firstly under headings, such as Action for Cities, the Urban Programme, and City Challenge. All these programmes were subsequently combined and reorganised under the Single Regeneration Budget (SRB) in April 1994. The SRB, initially, combined over 20 existing programmes, such as Estate Action, City Challenge, Urban Programme, Safer Cities, TEC Challenge, *inter alia*. The SRB seeks to coordinate the input of different government departments, such as the DETR, Home Office, Employment Department, local authorities, and other bodies concerned with the social, economic and physical regeneration of inner-city areas, through a system of integrated regional offices. The SRB programme is continuing at the time of writing, but will soon be likely to be wound up.

The role of the state was receding, with greater emphasis on privatisation of erstwhile public functions and bodies. As stated earlier, under the Housing Act 1980, Thatcher had given tenants 'the right to buy' their council houses. A series of subsequent Housing Acts, such as the Housing Act 1985, further marginalised the role of public sector housing management, reducing the amount of stock available for people on the housing lists. Very little new council housing has been built since. There had been, however, a revival of interest in the voluntary housing sector and the government favoured contributing financially towards the building and management programmes of housing associations (M. Smith 1989). This has all reduced the local authority housing department's role in the provision of social housing. Rather than providing blanket housing provision for around a third of the population as in the peak of Labour times in the 1960s, a more selective approach developed. Generally the government has prioritised a more targeted approach to the provision of special housing and

planning schemes within the inner-city and problem estates, in terms of finance and support, arguably thus reducing local government's say in the management of their locality. The Local Government and Housing Act 1989 introduced the concept of 'Renewal Areas' which are like the old GIAs and HAAs (which they replaced), but the emphasis was on partnership with the private sector in renewal, and grants to individual householders were means tested.

As for the development plan system itself, there was a series of consolidatory Town Planning Acts in the 1990s, mainly dealing with the format of the development system and the enforcement of planning control (refer to Chapter 2). There does not appear to have been, at first sight, any strong policy statement on national town planning policy as one would have expected from governments in the past. It seemed as if the government was marking time, unsure what to do with the planning system next. The Town and Country Planning Act 1990 and the Planning and Compensation Act 1991 tidied up the system but did not introduce any new radical change to the development plan system.

In conclusion, although the Thatcher and Major Conservative governments were committed to reducing state intervention and regional and urban planning, by the mid-1990s the government had created a large collection of new initiatives and programmes which together de facto comprised a significant new block of planning policy in all but name. Looking back with the benefit of hindsight one can see that signs of a new agenda were emerging based on a more selective, rather than comprehensive, approach to planning, and an emphasis on local-level issues. These new directions in planning were to develop further, first under New Labour and subsequently by the Coalition (as discussed in the next chapter).

For the tasks, further reading, additional photos and other resources for this chapter, please visit www.palgrave. com/companion/greed-planning-in-the-UK. See, especially, E-Supplements 1 and 3, a table of the tallest buildings in the world, and a map of UK new towns.

7 Planning into the New Millennium

Bringing planning up to date

All change

This chapter charts the development of planning in the UK under New Labour, and then up to the present day under the Coalition government. Following the period of Conservative government first under Thatcher and then Major, the period to be discussed commenced with the election of the New Labour government under Tony Blair in 1997, continued through the premiership of Gordon Brown (2007–10) to the early years of the Coalition government formed by the Conservative and Liberal Democrat parties following the general election of 2010. The chapter embraces the onset of the new millennium, and although a largely symbolic moment in time, there were some very significant changes that took place in the ten years before and after 1 January 2000. This 20-year period saw the fall of communism in Russia and Eastern Europe which may be seen as discrediting the idea of state planning. Market forces and consumerism soon took over (Photo 7.1). International changes such as the growth of the European Union, the rise of globalism, and the emergence of developing countries such as China, India and Brazil as major economic powers in their own right have all impacted on Britain (Boym 1994). The huge growth of information and communications technology across the world with the expansion of the internet has led to a completely new world, not least in enabling you the reader to find information on all sorts of planning topics from your laptop without having to struggle to find a relevant book in the library. The global economic crash of 2008 and its aftermath has also had a major impact on the economy and society, not least resulting in major government cutbacks in the employment of planners and in reducing the amount of new development. All these events of the recent past have helped to shape the policies and practices of planning in the UK which are now examined in more detail in this chapter.

The majority of the chapter explores Labour's three terms of office. The first term of the New Labour government (1997–2001) was characterised by an increased emphasis on regional planning in England and the far-reaching devolution of powers to Scotland, Wales and Northern Ireland. The government's attempts to combine land use and transport planning and to tackle emerging global environmental issues such as climate change are also examined. The second term of New Labour's office was characterised by fundamental reform of the planning system. The third term under Tony Blair and then Gordon Brown as Prime Minister resulted in further reforms to the planning system, but also major economic challenges to the whole 'New Labour' philosophy.

The final part of the chapter moves on to the election of the Coalition government in June 2010 and its rejection of what was seen as an overly top-down style of planning under New Labour and the introduction of a new approach known as localism. Despite this break with the past, the Coalition government continued to see the planning system as a barrier to growth, a view which characterised the latter part of New Labour's period in office. How the planning system will respond to these changes in national government policy remains to be seen, so the chapter concludes with some informed speculation on the ever-changing and more immediate future of planning in Britain.

Photo 7.1   Post-Communist consumerism in Moscow

Modern Russia is very different from Soviet times; with the abandonment of state planning, global consumerism has taken over, with a new oligarchy emerging, along with new extremes in wealth and poverty.

Thus this chapter may be seen as a bridge that continues the sweep of the story of planning up to the present day. Thus this chapter touches up, and contextualises, a range of current planning issues and policies, which will be covered in more detail in the various topic chapters in Part III, for example on the development plan system, transport planning, urban regeneration, sustainability, and to the social aspects of planning in Part IV. Whilst giving an account of the changes, the chapter also seeks to show the workings behind the changes in the planning system, with particular reference to political and economic factors. It emphasises the evolution of the policy areas of regional planning, infrastructural provision, housing and sustainability under the Coalition, which were fundamental considerations under New Labour.

Labour's first term

A new start?

The election in May 1997 brought a change in administration following 18 years of Conservative government and potentially to market-led approaches to planning (Thornley 1991). The landslide electoral victory for Tony Blair and 'New' Labour signified a real desire for change in the country. New Labour reflected this mood for change. Its leaders were predominantly young and fresh to government, 'modernisation' of the country and its institutions was their driving principle, 'New Labour, New Britain' was their banner. The industrial sector was declining, and this particularly reduced employment for manual workers in traditional, male, unionised occupations. Yet despite this apparent seismic shift in government, there was a considerable degree of continuity in terms of policy from the previous Conservative administrations (Allmendinger 2001). This can partly be explained by the particular nature of the New Labour project and by the prevailing economic conditions of the time. In the early years of John Major's government, the country experienced a period of serious recession, followed by a gradual recovery that was still under way when New Labour was elected in 1997. The favourable economic climate meant that unemployment was relatively low, new sectors of the economy were growing and greater public investment in the nation's infrastructure was possible. Gordon Brown, Labour's new Chancellor of the Exchequer, promised responsible and prudent management of the economy, and later went on to famously predict an end to the cycle of 'boom and bust' that had so damaged the British economy in the past.

While New Labour also embraced the free market it was committed to giving everyone in society a better chance in life through the creation of a modern Welfare State (Labour Party 1996) underpinned by the notion of rights and responsibilities for all. This combination of free-market economics with a belief in social justice was described by Blair as 'the Third Way' (Rawnsley 2001). Blair's pursuit of this Third Way – a balance between the roles of the state and civic society, and between state intervention and the operation of a competitive market economy (Giddens 1998) – manifested itself particularly in an attempt to apply the practices of the free market to a reformed public sector. Although there was a lack of willingness by many in government to adopt the term Third Way, the approach could be seen in many of the actions of the New Labour government for the next 12 years (Morphet 2010).

Despite a growing awareness of environmental issues amongst the electorate in the 1990s, there was very little attention given to planning matters by the new government. Tony Blair himself as leader of the party 'seemed ambivalent to environmental concerns' (Tewdwr-Jones 2002: 61). There was no new significant planning legislation as the government's priorities for reform lay elsewhere. The creation of the new Department of Environment, Transport and the Regions (DETR) could be seen as one of the few significant acts of Labour's first term in office to address environmental and broader plan-

ning issues. The formation of the DETR combined two existing government departments: The Department of the Environment (DoE) and the Department of Transport (DoT), and added a new function to oversee the delivery of Labour's plans for a new regional framework of governance. The combination of two such well-established departments was welcomed by some as a means of better integrating transport and land-use planning. However, it was inevitably fraught with many political and administrative difficulties. With a commitment to strengthening regional governance (against a wider policy and legislative background to modernise government itself, including a significant devolution of power to Wales, Scotland and Northern Ireland) the challenges that faced the new department were considerable. The new department's Secretary of State, John Prescott, MP for Hull, had a long-standing interest in transport and local government. One of Prescott's first tasks was to take part in the negotiations which culminated in the Kyoto Conference on climate change, held in Japan in December 1997. The conference agreed binding targets for a number of industrialised countries, including Britain, to reduce their emissions of greenhouse gases (UN 2009; Wilson and Piper 2010). The importance and implications of the Kyoto agreement are explored more fully in Chapter 9.

The first two years of the new government concentrated on social policy and constitutional change and there seemed to be no real agenda for planning at this time (Hall and Tewdwr-Jones 2010). But, there was a reversal of the previous Thatcherite emphasis upon solving society's problems through a belief in the economic benefits of supporting big business 'trickling down' to the rest of society. Local authorities' role and powers were being reinstated, and greater state support and intervention at the local level began to be established again. There was an increasing interest in the regeneration of Britain's cities and urban areas. As traditional centres of Labour support this was hardy surprising, and along with the generally favourable economic climate of the time and investment in cultural facilities through the National Lottery, city living once again became fashionable. The government, in 2000, through a revised Planning Policy Guidance (PPG) note, PPG3: *Housing*, made a commitment that the majority of new development in urban areas should take place on previously developed 'brown-field' land (Cullingworth and Nadin 2006: 209–13; Ratcliffe *et al.* 2009). This approach took forward the recommendations of the Urban Task Force's report *Towards an Urban Renaissance* (Rogers 1999). This focus on regenerating cities culminated in the publication of the Urban White Paper in 2000, which set out the government's urban regeneration policy of the time. The millennium saw a number of regeneration projects come to fruition, including the controversial Millennium Dome at Greenwich (now called O2), which represented signs of growing confidence and investment in Britain's towns and cities (see Chapter 10 on the renewal of Britain's cities for a wider discussion of regeneration).

A new regionalism

A significant development at this time was the government's commitment to devolution in Wales, Scotland and Northern Ireland and to regionalism in England. The devolution of planning functions is described in Chapter 2. While the Labour Party has had a traditional commitment to regional planning it has not been shared by Conservative governments, who in the past had tended to favour regional guidance and the production of various advisory reports and policies such as Regional Planning Guidance documents (RPGs). A renewed commitment to regionalism in England emerged in 1997 under New Labour. A new Planning Policy Guidance note was issued, PPG 11 *Regional Guidance*, in 2000, and along with the consultation paper which preceded it entitled *The Future of Regional Planning Guidance* (DETR 1998a) set out the agenda for the future within the context of modernising planning (DETR 1998b). Greater responsibility was to be placed upon regional planning bodies, working with regional Government Offices, and key regional stakeholders. These included public and private bodies which played a role at the regional level in terms of policy or investment in infrastructure, for example. PPG11 outlined the need to put greater regional focus on strategic issues, the adoption of a spatial strategy which extended beyond land-use issues, and the creation of an integrated transport policy at the regional level (Haughton *et al.* 2009).

As part of this revised system of regional planning the government, under the Regional Development Agencies Act 1998, established Regional Development Agencies (RDAs) in each region of England. An emphasis within this new regional planning approach was put on working in partnership with the private sector, and upon developing links with business. The RDAs represented an ambition by Labour to create dynamic new bodies capable of driving forward economic change and progress in each of the English regions. Though there was considerable opposition within government to more far-reaching regional devolution (Dungey and Newman 1999), the establishment of the RDAs satisfied both a desire for greater government intervention in the management of the economy at a regional level and to provide a means of engaging the private sector in modernising the country's economic infrastructure. The RDAs were therefore set up with a private-sector ethos, each one being headed by a Board, appointed by government, consisting largely of leading industrialists and business people from the region, along with a minority of representatives from local government and interest groups.

Reform of public services

New Labour's search for the 'Third Way' could also be seen in the government's approach to the delivery of public services over its first term in office. The previous Conservative governments of Thatcher and Major had introduced compulsory competitive tendering into the provision of many local government and other public services. This approach was criticised for concentrating purely on cost, and for ignoring issues of quality. New Labour's answer was termed Best Value, a regime set up by the 1999 Local Government Act that combined cost with other considerations in the provision of public services, such as value for money, efficiency and effectiveness. This was to be achieved through a series of targets, monitoring and annual reporting, overseen by the Audit Commission, and which was also applied to a number of areas of planning and transport, such as recycling rates of household waste, satisfaction with public transport services, the percentage of development on brown-field land and the introduction and monitoring of timescales for determining planning applications (ODPM 2001). This desire to monitor the performance of local planning authorities in terms of implementing national policy was reflective of a wider concern in some government circles that viewed planning as a constraint on growth. This was to become a continuing theme throughout the next Labour government's term of office.

Labour's second term

Building up momentum

The general election held on 7 June 2001 saw the re-election of the Labour government, with a clear, though slightly reduced majority (down from 179 seats in 1997 to 167 in 2001). The election had taken place against the backdrop of a major outbreak of foot and mouth disease which severely affected the country's more rural areas and the rural economy in general. The subsequent election of New Labour for a second term with a clear majority was a historic event, something that had not happened before in British political history, yet the mood of Tony Blair and the new government was much less euphoric than four years previously. The re-elected government took an approach that sought to build on the foundations of their first term and to concentrate more on delivery rather than chasing headlines in the press (Rawnsley 2001), a conspicuous criticism of New Labour's first term in office.

In terms of town planning, this was manifested in a departmental reorganisation which saw the break-up of the Department of the Environment, Transport and the Regions (DETR), and a focus on the role of planning in delivering nationally-led targets for increased housing numbers and economic growth. This led to a major shake-up of the planning system in 2004 which replaced the long-established system of Structure Plans and Local Plans with new Regional Spatial Strategies and Local Development Frameworks to guide planning and development at the local level (Rozee 2008). The changes to the development plan system are set out in Chapter 2.

Environmental concerns, particularly the growing awareness of climate change and the need to respond to it, represented a continuing theme in planning policy over New Labour's second term in office, as did the need to tackle the growing rural 'crisis' (see Chapters 9 and 10).

A departmental reshuffle immediately following the election saw the creation of two new departments: the Department for Transport, Local Government and the Regions (DTLR) preserved much of the former DETR. Environment was combined with agriculture to form a new department, called the Department for Environment, Food and Rural Affairs (DEFRA) which was designed to show that the government was giving greater priority to rural affairs and to tackle the inherent problems facing Britain's farming sector (Rydin 2003). In 2002 a further reorganisation took place, this time the DTLR was split into two, with a new stand-alone Department for Transport being created. This left John Prescott in charge of housing, planning, regeneration, local government and the regions in a new department called the Office of the Deputy Prime Minister (ODPM). The break-up of the DTLR represented a setback to those who favoured the closer integration of land-use and transportation policies. The decision was made by Tony Blair without any consultation with Prescott and appeared to have been the result of a Cabinet reshuffle, though there were those in the government who had been seeking its break-up (Prescott 2009).

It could be argued that this was a turning point in terms of the New Labour government's view of the planning system, which was starting to be seen by some in government as more of a problem than as a solution to a number of the problems facing the country. This can be seen in one of the newly re-elected government's first actions, which was to initiate a review of the planning system at the regional, county and local level in England. This resulted in the publication in December 2001 of a Green Paper entitled *Planning: Delivering a Fundamental Change* (DTLR 2001b). The Green Paper set out a number of familiar criticisms of the planning system, stating that it was too complicated, inflexible, legalistic and bureaucratic, and had led to a system that was too slow and unpredictable and blocked rather than encouraged development. This proposed a number of significant changes to 'modernise' the operation of the planning system, a number of which took many years to eventually be implemented. These included the abolition of Structure Plans, Local Plans and Unitary Development Plans and their replacement in England with a new system whereby Regional Spatial Strategies and Local Development Frameworks made up the statutory local plan. The Green Paper envisaged that development control would become more responsive and customer focused, with tighter targets being imposed to attempt to speed up the determination of planning applications. The system of Planning Policy Guidance (PPG) notes would be updated and a new set of shorter, simplified Planning Policy Statements (PPS) introduced giving greater emphasis to policy, as opposed to guidance and advice. Further reforms were suggested to speed up the process of dealing with major infrastructure projects. Taken as a whole, the sentiments of the Green Paper represented a move to 'change the very culture of planning' (Cullingworth and Nadin 2006: 118; Healey 2006, 2007).

Creating sustainable communities?

At the same time the government continued to address the urban renaissance as advocated in the report of the Urban Task Force (Rogers 1999). A major Urban Summit took place in Birmingham in November 2002, at which the then Chancellor, Gordon Brown, made a commitment to introduce a new programme of enterprise areas, interestingly an approach previously used by the Conservative government of Mrs Thatcher. Other government ministers made commitments to increase housing supply, and particularly the provision of affordable housing, and to a continued emphasis on the development of brown-field land, with higher densities of new development and the proposed designation of a number of new 'growth areas'. Ministers used the summit to announce their commitment to a long-term plan for sustainable communities (ODPM 2003a).

This document emerged in February 2003 under the title *Sustainable Communities: Building for the Future* (ODPM 2003b). The status of this publication was a little ambiguous; it was described as a 'programme of action' (ODPM 2003a, 5) and it spelt out a number of policies and financial commitments that had already been made public, such as the target for 60 per cent of new housing development to be on brown-field land and for larger housing sites to achieve a minimum density of 30 dwellings per hectare. Yet the document can be seen to represent perhaps the first real attempt to set out a spatial strategy for the country as a whole (it should be noted that the document applied only to England). Despite a failure to describe itself explicitly as a spatial strategy, the document became known as 'the sustainable communities plan'. Though it lacked any binding policy status it did provide an overview of the government's housing, planning and regeneration agendas, along with an indication of priorities for action, the resources needed to deliver these, and the identification of the key partners needed for the effective delivery of sustainable communities over the following 15–20 years (ODPM 2003b).

A broad spatial concern identified by the document was what is often described as the 'North–South' divide. Though this is a crude description, in general terms it sums up the economic situation that has faced the country for a number of years, within the 'North' (Photo 7.2). This could also be seen to include the industrial and rural areas of Scotland, Wales and Northern Ireland, suffering economic decline and the collapse of traditional manufacturing industries, while the 'South' (essentially London and the South East of England) experienced substantial economic growth and employment creation in the high-tech and services sectors. This divide was characterised by areas of industrial dereliction, high unemployment, low housing demand and vacant homes in many of the Northern towns and cities; while in the South the demand for new housing far outstripped supply, thus pushing up house prices, increasing densities and pressure on open spaces and the green belt. Both of these situations were seen as unsustainable. Instead, the notion of sustainable communities was articulated in the plan through a number of key criteria, such as the need for a flourishing economy, good public transport provision, and a mix of decent homes of different tenures that combined would create places where people would want to live (ODPM 2003b).

Photo 7.2   Housing disparity in the North

Whilst there has been great prosperity and astronomical house-price rises in London and the South East, there remain longstanding areas of deprivation, poverty, unemployment and even empty housing, in erstwhile industrial areas in the North. Truly 'two nations'.

The Sustainable Communities Plan attempted to address the under-supply of housing in London and the South East through a 'step-change' in housing provision, focusing new development on four major growth areas. These were identified (along with projected potential new housing numbers) as:

- Thames Gateway (120,000 new homes to be built between 2001 and 2016)
- Ashford in Kent (potential for 31,000 new homes by 2031)
- The London–Stanstead–Cambridge corridor (potential for 500,000 new homes by 2031)
- Milton Keynes/South Midlands/ Northamptonshire (potential for 370,000 new homes by 2031).

The identification of the Thames Gateway (including the subsequent development of the Olympic site at Stratford) as a major growth area resulted in it becoming one of the largest regeneration initiatives in Europe. Thames Gateway will be discussed further in the case study in Chapter 11. As shown above, the growth areas represented a commitment to provide substantial numbers of new housing in the South East which were much higher than were set out in the existing Regional Planning Guidance for the areas concerned. The plan was to result in the setting up of a number of new delivery mechanisms to see through the implementation of the key proposals. These took the form of non-statutory partnerships in some areas, such as in Ashford in Kent, through new Urban Regeneration Companies in places such as Southend-on-Sea and Peterborough, and through the return of the Urban Development Corporations in areas where increased planning, and particularly compulsory purchase powers, were seen as essential for regeneration, such as parts of the Thames Gateway and West Northamptonshire.

The plan also set out how the areas of low demand and vacant homes in the North of England would be tackled. This was to be done by directing increased investment into areas of poor housing and greatest need through the establishment of nine new Housing Market Renewal Pathfinders (ODPM 2003a). New partnership organisations were set up in each of these nine locations with the responsibility to develop strategic plans for housing in their areas, which would include new building, refurbishment and, in some cases, demolition. New resources were promised to help implement these plans.

A further key action identified in the Sustainable Communities Plan was the need for reform of the planning system to facilitate this level of growth. A new system, called the 'plan, monitor and manage' approach, would replace the previous approach to planning for housing growth, known as 'predict and provide' as embodied in the revised PPS1 entitled *Delivering Sustainable Development*, on the general principles of planning (ODPM 2005). This called for a much more flexible system, with local planning authorities taking a more facilitative approach to proposed new development where that was in line with government policy and with a revised system of regional and local plans. This would require the integration of plans for new development with the provision of new transport and other community infrastructure and the identification of the necessary resources to ensure smooth delivery on the ground. This represented a move to a system of spatial planning rather than the more traditional focus on purely land-use matters.

The Planning Green Paper of 2001, on Delivering Fundamental Change, had paved the way for the introduction of a new planning Bill which subsequently became the Planning and Compulsory Purchase Act, 2004, which brought about a fundamental reform of the planning system in England, as covered in Chapter 2. In summary, under this new system, Regional Spatial Strategies would set out the housing requirement for a period of approximately 20 years for the region concerned, and these would be translated into local targets to be met through policies and proposals in Local Development Frameworks. Some of the reasons for its introduction have been discussed earlier, and with the benefit of hindsight, the question can be asked whether such fundamental change was actually needed to achieve the government's objectives. It was clear at the time that the government felt it necessary to have a new system of spatial planning with an emphasis at the regional level on responding to the demand for new housing growth, as identified by the government in its Sustainable Communities Plan.

The issue of housing provision, and particularly the mismatch of supply and demand, assumed a considerable degree of political prominence around this time. In April 2003 the Treasury commissioned an economist, Kate Barker, to undertake a review of the housing situation, resulting in The Barker Review of Housing Supply (Barker 2004). It is interesting to note that this review was initiated by the Treasury, demonstrating the key role it and the Chancellor Gordon Brown played in much of the government's domestic policy at the time. Barker identified a major gap between housing need and supply. This was largely due to the changing demographics of the UK, particularly the large increase in the number of single households. To address the need for new housing, Barker estimated that on top of the 125,000 private-sector completions achieved in 2002–03, a further 120,000 new completions per annum would be needed to limit the growth in future house prices to a rate of 1.8 per cent per year. The report also identified the need for 26,000 social homes to be built each year. The report did acknowledge the limited and finite nature of Britain's land supply and recognised that there would be public concern at the loss of open space if these rates of new house-building were to be achieved. The review concluded that sufficient land could be identified, avoiding the most environmentally sensitive areas, through the use of brown-field sites.

Barker also stated that the operation of the planning system needed to be speeded up, that infrastructure provision needed to be properly addressed and phased, and that additional resources should be found from capturing the increase in land values that planning permission for housing, particularly on green-field sites, brings with it, through the introduction of some form of development gain levy. The government's response to Barker accepted the case for a step change and showed support for most of the key findings of the Barker Report, including increasing its housing targets from 150,000 new homes per year to 200,000 per year by 2016; establishing a number of new growth points; and pursuing further reforms to the planning (HM Treasury and ODPM 2005). These would be issues that would prove controversial in Labour's third term of office.

Despite facing much criticism for its commitment to substantial housing growth and new development, government policy did set out to ensure that such growth would be more sustainable than that achieved in the past. In early 2005 the Office of the Deputy Prime Minister published a new Planning Policy Statement 1 (PPS1) *Delivering Sustainable Development* (ODPM 2005) which set out the government's overarching principles for the planning system. At its heart was a continued emphasis on sustainable development; it even went so far as to state that sustainable development was 'the core principle underpinning planning' (ODPM 2005, 2). Drawing on the four key aims of the government's 1999 sustainable development strategy, *A Better Quality of Life*, PPS1 related each of these to the remit of town planning, as follows:

- The promotion of social cohesion and inclusion, through a better mix of housing types and tenures, for instance.
- The protection and enhancement of the environment, and particularly important natural and historic environments.
- The prudent use of natural resources, by achieving higher densities in new housing developments, by using brown-field land for most new development, and through the promotion of renewable energy measures.
- The achievement of sustainable economic development, recognising the importance of economic growth, the provision of sufficient new housing and reducing the need to travel.

The PPS went on to state the importance of taking a spatial planning approach when drawing up regional and local plans and policies. This would mean plan-makers having to take greater account of other issues and services, such as health and education, which have an impact on land use and the provision of infrastructure, such as roads and public transport. The PPS stressed the need to consider sustainable development in an integrated manner, taking into account social, environmental and economic matters. It also highlighted the need for good quality design and the active involvement of the community in the development of plans and in the planning process in general (ODPM 2005).

The growth of regionalism halted

New Labour's first term of office saw the devolution of considerable powers to new governmental arrangements in Wales, Scotland, Northern Ireland and London. This, however, left an anomalous situation in England. While Scotland, Wales, Northern Ireland and London had their own directly elected bodies (the Scottish Parliament, the Welsh Assembly, the Northern Ireland Assembly and the Greater London Assembly and Mayor) the regions of England had no such arrangements. Regional Planning Conferences, made up predominantly of elected councillors representing their councils within each region, had been set up previously to draw up the Regional Planning Guidance for each region. However, these were not directly elected bodies, nor did the English regions have any powers or tax-raising ability, as was common in most other European countries. The exception was London, which had its own directly elected Mayor and Assembly (set up in 2000) and which had responsibility for strategic planning, environment, transport and housing matters for the capital.

The drive for stronger regional government for England had been promoted within government particularly by John Prescott during New Labour's first term, and this resulted in the establishment of the Regional Development Agencies in 1998. There was also considerable interest from the regions themselves, particularly in the North of England, which needed regional structures to better access and oversee European Union regeneration funds, and who felt that their needs and concerns had been largely overlooked, particularly by the previous

Conservative government (Fenwick *et al.* 2009). Labour's aim following the general election of 2001 was therefore to seek to establish a directly elected regional tier of government for England during this, their second term of office. This was to be done following the approach that set up the devolved governments in Wales, Scotland and London, that is the people of each region in England would be asked, through a referendum, whether they supported such a proposal. The public enthusiasm may have been strong for Scottish, and, to a lesser extent, Welsh devolution, but the likely support for devolution to the English regions was felt at the time to be much less assured. As such, the government decided to hold its first referendum on this matter in the North East. This was seen to be a region with a strong identity, far removed from London and predominantly Labour in its politics. Following a lively campaign, the referendum was held on the 4 November 2004. Just under a half of the electorate took part and decisively rejected the proposal to establish a directly elected regional assembly for the North East. 77.9 per cent of people voted against the plans, while 22.1 per cent voted in favour (Electoral Commission 2005). If the result had gone the other way, the government would have held further referendums in Yorkshire and the North West. As it was, the decisive result in the North East caused the government to abandon plans for any further referenda, and effectively the result put a stop to the development of greater regional empowerment in England (Fenwick *et al.* 2009). This lack of a directly elected and accountable mechanism at the regional level was to prove a major issue in Labour's third term of office in respect of the role of regional planning, which has continued to be a highly contested area of public policy for over a century (Glasson and Marshall 2007). Likewise there was considerable concern at the local level about the effects of New Labour Policy in spite of new programmes on urban design and urban regeneration. In spite of New Labour politicians including the words 'community' and 'social inclusion' at every opportunity, they seemed increasingly unaware of growing dissatisfaction and potential unrest in inner-city and deprived residential areas (as discussed further in the regeneration chapter, Chapter 11, and social chapters, Chapters 14 and 15).

The close of New Labour's second term

Planning issues became a much more important aspect of government thinking and action during New Labour's second term of office. Primarily this was driven by economic imperatives, often initiated by the Treasury in seeking to respond to messages from the markets, developers and the volume house-builders. Government politicians accepted the need for much higher rates of house-building, as advocated by the Barker Review, and, as mentioned above, introduced the new system of Regional Spatial Strategies and Local Development Frameworks as a means of translating this demand into delivery on the ground through the designation of more land for housing in local-level plans. The Sustainable Communities Plan (ODPM 2003b) had established the notion of major growth areas in the South East of England, and planning for huge developments such as the Thames Gateway were well under way by the end of New Labour's second term. The commitment to much higher levels of new development was matched by a desire to see this take place in a more sustainable way than previous growth through developing predominantly on brown-field land and by increasing housing densities, as set out in PPS1 (ODPM 2005).

The general economic boom of the period was represented in ever-increasing house prices and higher returns for housing developers. This in turn created an acceptance amongst the house-builders of government policy for higher levels of affordable homes as a proportion of all new large housing developments and for the need for developers to contribute more to the provision of essential new infrastructure, such as community facilities and public transport. With much development also taking place in city centres, and a greater emphasis being given to higher environmental and design standards in new building, it seemed that government planning policy was finally delivering the urban renaissance articulated so convincingly by Lord Rogers five years earlier (Rogers 1999). There were some concerns raised by environmental organisations at the scale of development proposed, but these were generally overwhelmed by a wave of mass consumerism and overconfidence generated by the continuing economic boom. However, this situation was to not last, as the next section of this chapter, on New Labour's third term, explains.

New Labour's third term

Regional planning in England

The 2005 general election was a curious one, in that the sitting Prime Minister, Tony Blair, led the Labour Party into the election with a promise that it would be the last election that he would fight as party leader and Prime Minister of the country (Labour Party 2005). The election itself took place on 5 May 2005 and New Labour was returned for a historic third term, this time with a much reduced majority of 66 seats. Blair remained as Prime Minister for two years, being replaced by Gordon Brown in June 2007. Brown as Chancellor and as Prime Minister took a much greater interest than Blair in issues such as housing growth, regional planning and the broader role of the planning system in delivering higher economic growth.

New Labour's third term saw efforts to properly implement the new system of planning brought in by the 2004 Planning and Compulsory Purchase Act. As stated, the main aim of the Act was to introduce a new system of spatial planning based on Regional Spatial Strategies and Local Development Frameworks (LDFs). Yet many local planning authorities struggled to come to terms with the requirements of the new system. By 2010 there were only around 50 approved LDF Core Strategies, a disappointingly low number given five years had passed since the Act came into force (PINS 2010). Indeed at present over 100 local planning authorities have failed to produce up-to-date development plans.

However, it was the emerging regional spatial strategies that became the focus of much public and political attention between 2005 and 2010. The introduction of a more robust planning framework at the regional level was welcomed by many in the planning profession, but the lack of a directly accountable regional level of governance was to prove a major weakness. The levels of housing growth set out in the emerging Regional Spatial Strategies caused a considerable adverse reaction from many local people and organisations opposed to further urban encroachment into the countryside and the loss of green belt. This polarised political opinion at the national level, with the government continuing to push for higher housing numbers through the emerging Regional Spatial Strategies while the Conservative and Liberal Democrat parties adopted policies to abolish the whole tier of regional planning in England. By 2010 a number of Regional Spatial Strategies were held up awaiting the resolution of legal challenges while others had been temporarily sidelined until after the general election which only served to add further uncertainty into the role and operation of the planning system in England.

The economic downturn

By 2008 such arguments about housing numbers became largely irrelevant because of the financial crisis which brought about economic catastrophe across the world. Much of the boom had been built on debt, and it subsequently transpired that a large number of banks and financial traders had been making excessively high-risk loans to people and organisations whose creditworthiness was not particularly secure. This was particularly true of the property sector, where land and housing prices has risen to unsustainable levels, not just in the UK, but in the USA and particularly the Republic of Ireland, where economic dependency on the property and construction sectors had reached dangerous proportions (O'Toole 2009). The subsequent financial crash exposed these dangerous levels of often hidden borrowing and debt that had spiralled out of control in many countries during the mid-2000s. The global interconnectedness of the financial system was cruelly exposed as banks and financial institutions around the world collapsed. Governments had to step in to prop up the financial systems of their own countries, and the subsequent lack of available capital fuelled an economic downturn, major job losses and recession.

In the UK one of the first casualties was the property market. Mortgage funding dried up, housebuilding suddenly came to an abrupt halt, and many of the larger house-builders laid off large numbers of employees or even went bankrupt as the value of their land and their sales income plummeted.

Funding for commercial development became equally hard to obtain as the banks tried to rebuild their assets by cutting down drastically on loans, despite government urging them to keep the funding to business flowing. From 2008 to 2011 new development in and around Britain's towns and cities showed very limited signs of recovery. While some major building projects did manage to continue, particularly in parts of London, it is unlikely that the record levels of investment in new shopping centres and housing developments seen in the first decade of the new millennium will be reached again in the foreseeable future.

Further changes to the planning system

In the years immediately prior to the economic crash of 2008 the planning system across the whole of the UK was trying to come to terms with the booming economy, the demands for more housing and commercial development and the need for more sustainable forms of development. As can be seen in Chapter 11, the planning system played a largely positive role in helping to facilitate such development. Yet New Labour's third term in office saw further reforms of the planning system to tackle what the government saw as a continuing barrier to the delivery of economic growth, as investigated by Barker's report of 2004. In 2005 Brown again invited Kate Barker to lead a review, this time into the operation of the planning system itself. This resulted in a 226-page report entitled *Review of Land Use Planning: Final Report* (Barker 2006). The terms of reference for the report were to examine how planning policy and procedures could better deliver economic growth alongside wider sustainability goals. While recognising the valuable and necessary role of planning, the review once again raised a concern over the responsiveness of the planning system and questioned its transparency and efficiency. The review concluded that a more positive attitude to development was needed and that a wide-ranging package of reforms was necessary, especially to deal with the provision of major infrastructure projects. The report's recommendations responded to a number of these issues. It suggested that the delivery of development planning documents (in Local Development Frameworks) should be speeded

up; that the national policy for economic development should be updated to reflect the importance of this aspect of planning; that the boundaries of green belts and the quality of green-belt land should be reviewed; that a new system should be introduced to deal with major infrastructure projects; and that sufficient resources should be provided to support the planning system and to improve the skills of planning officers and councillors. Most of these recommendations were acted upon by the government over the two years following the publication of the report and are referred to again in the appropriate policy chapters in Part III.

The most significant of Barker's recommendations related to the way in which the planning system, along with other consent regimes, dealt with proposals for major infrastructure projects. While recognising that proposals for such projects were inevitably complex, and that it was hardly surprising that their consideration through the planning system (and often other consent regimes, dealing with transport or pollution matters, for example) would be time consuming, the review questioned whether the length of time involved was excessive. The report highlights a number of examples such as Heathrow Terminal Five, which took just over seven years to finally reach a decision, including a four-year Inquiry; and the proposal to expand Southampton Docks into Dibden Bay, which took nearly four years for a decision to be made, including a 13-month-long Inquiry. The report concluded that there needed to be a more effective way of making such decisions. It therefore recommended that there should be clearer national policy, a more joined-up national framework for infrastructure provision and a new 'independent Planning Commission' (Barker 2006: 78) to consider and determine applications for new major infrastructure projects. The government were quick to support the report's recommendations. They appeared to agree with Barker that the planning system was acting as a constraint to delivery of infrastructural projects considered to be of national importance. As a result the Planning Reform Act 2008 introduced major changes to the planning system in respect of procedures for approval of major new infrastructure projects.

The Infrastructure Planning Commission (IPC) was established in October 2009 to deal with planning applications for major new infrastructure projects, such as new nuclear power stations, ports and airports. The Act set out a number of thresholds, above which a particular proposed project would fall within the definition of a nationally significant infrastructure project and be dealt with by the IPC. Such projects, which include the expansion of ports and airports, new nuclear and other types of power station, on-shore and off-shore wind turbines and wind farms, major road and rail schemes, and water treatment facilities and reservoirs, would require approval from a new body, the Infrastructure Planning Commission (IPC). The IPC's powers to determine applications came into force on 1 March 2010, initially only for the energy and transport sectors. The operation of the IPC only applied to England and Wales. The 2008 Planning Act also allowed the government to publish a series of new policy statements to provide a policy framework within which the IPC could base its decisions on individual applications, along with other more local factors which would have to be considered. The legislation required the National Policy Statements to be drawn up following public consultation, a sustainability appraisal and parliamentary scrutiny. Following the general election of 2010 the IPC was merged with the Planning Inspectorate, as described in further detail later in this chapter. Once again, Brown had seen reform of the planning system as necessary for the increased growth of the economy. By 2013 the IPC had been renamed the National Infrastructure Directorate (NID).

Ministerial changes

The third term of the New Labour government saw a number of changes to the organisation of planning functions at central government level. At the same time as Blair resigned as Prime Minister in June 2007, John Prescott also stood down as Deputy Prime Minister. Prescott had lost most of his departmental functions a year earlier in 2006 in a previous government reshuffle which had led to the creation of the Department for Communities and Local Government (DCLG), or Communities and Local Government (CLG) as it preferred to be known. Prescott continued for a year as the Deputy Prime Minister, but without a departmental portfolio. Most of the functions of the former Office of the Deputy Prime Minister (ODPM), including housing and planning, were transferred to the new department. These changes of responsibility between departments are a continual feature of government.

Apart from a short spell in the 1940s, town planning has always been combined with other functions, such as housing and local government, in terms of its departmental home. As previously discussed, during New Labour's first term of office, planning sat alongside transport in a government department that sought to better integrate these two inextricably linked activities. However, political considerations led to the break-up of the department, and by the end of New Labour's third term in office, planning was subsumed into a department that had communities and local government at its core. Following the general election of 2010 the new Coalition government kept the departmental structures unchanged.

Retrospect: planning and New Labour

From a planning perspective, it is possible to discern two broad phases of New Labour's period in office between 1997 and 2010. The first phase could be seen to cover the years from New Labour's first electoral victory to the publication of the Sustainable Communities Plan in 2003. This period saw a number of fundamental changes to the way Britain was governed, with the establishment of the Scottish Parliament, the Welsh Assembly and the Mayor and Assembly in London (Hambleton and Sweeting 1999, 2004). This will perhaps be seen as New Labour's most lasting legacy, and has created the opportunity for Scotland, Wales and London to develop their own spatial plans and planning policies. The setting up of the Regional Development Agencies in England had started a similar process of devolution to the English regions.

The publication of the Rogers' report (*Towards an Urban Renaissance*) in 1999 had produced a framework that was to help shape and direct much of the private-sector-led growth that took place in the boom years of the mid-2000s and led to the substantial regeneration of many of our towns and cities during this time. This was perhaps the high point of John Prescott's influence over the planning and urban regeneration agendas. During this period new policies were developed on increasing residential densities and building on brown-field land and other practical changes in planning policy (which are discussed further in Part III). His Department of the Environment, Transport and the Regions (DETR) had tried to integrate land-use and transportation planning within a revitalised regional context. Sustainable growth, as represented by sustainable communities, was seen as the goal to be achieved and this was widely embraced by the planning profession at the time. During these first six years of New Labour's period of office it could be argued that planning was regarded by government as being part of the solution to a number of the problems facing Britain.

A second phase of the New Labour government could be characterised by their view that planning had become 'part of the problem', particularly in terms of blocking the delivery of new housing that was seen by some in government as the embodiment of Britain's growth and prosperity. This phase was signalled by the breaking up of the DETR and the rejection (initially by the voters of the North East) of elected regional government in England. As the economy continued into a period of boom, the planning system was identified, particularly by the Treasury, as a barrier to its continued growth. Gordon Brown had made a commitment that 3 million new homes were needed by 2020, and to help achieve this economist Kate Barker's reviews into the supply of housing and the operation of the planning system were to lead to significant changes to the operation of the planning system.

However, the degree of change to the planning system at the local level required a culture change in local authority planning departments that was more difficult to achieve than the government anticipated, despite the imposition of numerous targets, penalties and incentives to 'encourage' them to produce the new types of plans required. Simpler reforms to speed up what was a somewhat inflexible system of local plans could have achieved the government's aims a lot more effectively, but major reform was seen as necessary. This overly 'top-down' approach could be seen as a factor in the limited success of the government's reforms. Likewise, as discussed further

in Chapter 11 (regeneration), in spite of a plethora of local-level initiatives concerning social inclusion, urban deprivation, equalities monitoring, and community initiatives, many urban problems persisted (as will be discussed further in Part IV on the social aspects of planning. Indeed local authority planners appeared overwhelmed by the mass of new initiatives, plans and programmes they were expected to implement. The subsequent setting up of the Infrastructure Planning Commission in 2008 to deal with major projects of national significance, while welcomed by many in the planning profession, nevertheless had given rise to a perception that too much power was being centralised and that a greater degree of local control was needed. These would be issues that were subsequently resolved by the 2010 general election.

A new localism

The 2010 general election

The general election of 6 May 2010 resulted in the first 'hung' parliament for over 30 years. The Conservative Party emerged with the largest share of the popular vote and the largest number of MPs, at 306 just short of the 326 needed to command an absolute majority of the 650 MPs that make up the House of Commons. The Labour Party lost nearly 100 seats and was reduced to 258 MPs. Despite losing a handful of seats, the Liberal Democrats, with 57 MPs, found themselves holding the balance of power. For a few days following the election the outgoing Prime Minister, Gordon Brown, sought to enlist the support of all the non-Conservative parties to form a grand coalition but the electoral arithmetic was clear: Labour had lost the election and the Conservatives under David Cameron had won, albeit without a clear majority. The Liberal Democrats, despite being seen by many as a 'left of centre' party, quickly realised that the creation of a stable government through a formal coalition with the Conservatives was their best option and preferred choice. A few days later Britain's first Coalition government for generations took office under David Cameron as Prime Minister and the Liberal Democrat's leader Nick Clegg as Deputy Prime Minister.

A new ideology

Both parties (Lib-Dems and Conservatives) seemed to find some common ground in terms of their attitude to the role of the state and its impact on the individual. Conservatives have generally been opposed to greater state intervention, or 'big government' as it is referred to in the USA. Cameron tried to articulate an alternative approach known as 'the big society'. This strategy sought to achieve a shift in power and responsibilities away from government at all levels and instead to empower ordinary citizens, community and voluntary groups to build a stronger society and help modernise, even run, public services (Cameron 2011). This approach, which advocates the importance of society, family and community, appears to have rejected the traditional market versus state choice that characterised more traditional Conservative politics. This may be seen as a further development of Giddens' idea of the 'Middle Way' and arguably a return to the principles of a mixed economy, with a lighter touch towards planning control. Thus the government adopted a neo-liberal approach to government and thus to freeing up the planning system (Morphet 2010; Rydin 2011).

The necessity of being in coalition with the Liberal Democrats also meant that some of the more traditionally right-wing policies of previous Conservative governments had to be softened, and common ground was established particularly around the Liberal Democrats' long-standing commitment to individual rights and the importance of the environment. These values were reflected in a joint policy statement issued by the new government shortly after its formation. Formally entitled *The Coalition: Our Programme for Government* (HM Government 2010), this statement set out a number of commitments that both parties would work towards over the five-year term of the parliament. These included a number of planning and related issues which are explored in further detail below.

More changes to the planning system

In terms of town planning the election of the new Coalition government resulted in some significant shifts of policy and direction. In the run-up to the election both the Conservatives and Liberal Democrats had supported campaigns to oppose the Labour government's house-building plans. They saw these as top-down targets, imposed by unelected regional bodies that did not have the support of local people. The Conservatives in particular advocated major reform of the planning system. They wanted to see a planning system that would engage local people much more in the planning process. This would be achieved by taking a more bottom-up approach, known as localism, and by opening the system up to all. Their proposals were set out in a document called *Open Source Planning* and many of the ideas in this paper informed their early actions in government.

One of the first acts of the new Secretary of State for Communities and Local Government, Eric Pickles MP, was to announce the abolition of the Regional Spatial Strategies which were either in place or being progressed for each of England's regions. Instead, the government stated its intention to give local planning authorities a much greater say in determining new levels of housing growth. Though this was challenged in the courts by a housing developer on the basis that it needed new legislation, the writing was on the wall for the future of Regional Spatial Strategies. The government made clear its intention to introduce such legislation in the form of a new Localism Bill which subsequently became law in 2011. Following Pickles' announcement to scrap the Regional Spatial Strategies, a number of local planning authorities immediately revised the housing numbers in their emerging Local Development Framework core strategies downwards, resulting in a considerable loss in provision from that set out in their original plans.

Research carried out in September 2010 estimated a reduction of around 160,000 proposed new homes in emerging Local Development Framework Core Strategies, eventually rising to around 300,000 by the end of the following year (Tetlow King 2011). It could be argued that this was a purely political exercise given the collapse in new house-building as a result of the economic crisis, but it did highlight a criticism of the new localism approach. It was argued that the more strategic response to housing need (as had been set out in the Regional Spatial Strategies) was being replaced by the power of the NIMBY

Photo 7.3   London housing pressures

Every square inch of London that can be used for residential, commercial or other uses is in demand, and many people live in small, high-density expensive private flats (apartments) as near as possible to their work to avoid the horrors of commuting. The same type of property in London as in the North East can cost many times more.

lobby to restrict levels of new housing on the ground. This loss of a more strategic perspective was much criticised at the time (RTPI 2010). Indeed the decline in the housing market was not equally experienced throughout the country, as in London there was still a great deal of demand for places to live (Photo 7.3).

The Localism Act introduced some significant changes to the planning system (see Chapter 2). It abolished the Regional Spatial Strategies and has given more say over housing numbers to local planning authorities, removing national targets and restricting the powers of the Planning Inspectorate to impose changes to local planning documents. This approach sought to tackle the criticism that strategic planning would be lost by imposing a 'duty to cooperate' on neighbouring local planning authorities. Somewhat surprisingly, the Act maintained the previous government's commitment to

introduce a local charge on new development to help fund infrastructure, known as the Community Infrastructure Levy.

The move to greater localism in the planning system has been demonstrated in the new emphasis on neighbourhood planning, with parish councils and neighbourhood forums being encouraged to draw up their own plans. A critical concern is the relationship between the proposed neighbourhood plan and the planning policies of the local planning authority as set out in its Local Development Framework and Core Strategy. If the neighbourhood plan could contain its own housing and employment numbers for its own local area it was argued that this would make the Local Development Framework practically worthless. This was subsequently clarified by the government in the National Planning Policy Framework (DCLG 2011a) which states that neighbourhood plans must be in general

Photo 7.4   Sheffield Park Hill

Rising above the railway station, these are the infamous Park Hill Flats, once famed for providing 'streets in the air' that were meant to generate a sense of 'community'. Long since vandalised and neglected, they are now undergoing major refurbishment and renewal – mainly for sale and private renting – through a mixture of government grants and private investment and are likely to prove popular with young professionals.

conformity with the strategic policies of the Local Development Framework. In spite of the Coalition's commitment to speeding up planning it has set a rather onerous process for the adoption of these neighbourhood plans, including an independent inspection and a local referendum on the plan. This might put off all but the most determined of local community organisations from undertaking this exercise. As a result of lobbying from the business community, the government also decided to widen the scope of its neighbourhood planning proposals to allow business representatives to take part, and even for businesses to draw up their own plans for business districts such as industrial estates or retail centres. A number of locations were identified in 2010 to pilot these proposals and at the time of writing right across the country neighbourhood plans are under production.

The Act also gave local communities powers to determine (decide) the nature and amount of development schemes in their area through new Neighbourhood Development Orders and Community Right to Build Orders. Taken as a whole these proposals represent a potentially serious loss of power for the local planning authority. They also seek to bypass the planning profession itself and instead give more of a say on planning matters directly to members of the community. While most planners recognise the importance of community engagement in the planning process, there is a danger that objectivity and balance may be lost if particular groups or interests have an undue influence over these new methods of local planning. Some observers even believe that the many practical problems these new processes will throw up will actually lead to a reduction in the level of community-led planning (BDOR 2011). Only time will tell whether there is such a desire for this level of public engagement with the local planning process. However, it is already emerging that there is a greater level of control on what local communities can really do, as their decisions must not trump either national policy direction or Local authority planning policy. This has not been the case in some recent regeneration programmes, such as in Sheffield (Photo 7.4), where many local people felt somewhat marginalised by the new pressure for modernisation of their areas.

National planning policy and other changes

The new government made a number of decisions that had a significant impact on the operation of the planning system, particularly as it operates within England. As a result of the poor state of the country's finances, major reductions were made to the budgets of many public sector organisations, including local authorities (and their planning departments) and other planning-related bodies such as English Heritage, the Environment Agency and Natural England. These budget reductions led to the loss of many experienced staff and along with a general cull of many semi-government bodies (known as QUANGOs) that had grown up under previous governments, such as CABE (the Commission for Architecture and the Built Environment), represented a serious loss of capacity across the planning and environmental sectors.

The government also announced that it would reintroduce Enterprise Zones (EZs) across the country, as discussed further in Chapter 11. These are site-specific and seek to encourage new development through a mixture of simplified planning regulations, new broadband access and some limited financial support. Alongside this initiative the government set up a number of new Local Enterprise Partnerships (LEPs) to take forward economic development in their areas, constituting a

weak substitute for Regional Spatial Strategies. Normally covering the area of a county or a group of local authorities, these LEPs are supposed to be business-led, and are intended to replace the Regional Development Agencies set up by the last government. The remit of the LEPs could easily lead to them play a role in more strategic planning, transport and infrastructure matters in their local areas over time. Along with EZs and LEPs, the Coalition government has also introduced ancillary funding under Regional Growth Funds (Tallon 2013) and City Deals targeted at major regional cities (see Chapter 11). (See Photo 7.5.)

In terms of Nationally Significant Infrastructure Projects, the government decided to essentially retain the system set up by the previous government through the Planning Act 2008. This, as previously stated, set up the Infrastructure Planning Commission (IPC) to determine applications for the development of proposed major projects, such as power stations and airports, for example. The government did make a number of significant changes to the way the system would operate. It abolished the IPC and transferred its functions to the Planning Inspectorate (PINS), giving the Secretary of State for Communities and Local Government the power to ultimately decide all applications in accordance with any relevant national policy statements, which are gradually being introduced. For example, the government approved six such National Policy Statements in July 2011 on energy matters. Increasingly PINS seems to be picking up the slack and taking over planning roles previously carried out by the Secretary of State and the DCLG.

At the same time as pursuing changes to the planning system, the new government also set out to streamline planning policy at the national level. National planning policy (in England) had previously been set out in a number of Planning Policy Guidance (PPG) notes, which were gradually being updated and replaced by Planning Policy Statements (PPS). In 2011 there were a total of 25 PPGs and PPSs covering a wide range of planning issues, including sustainability (PPS1), housing (PPS3), transport (PPG13), renewable energy (PPS22) and flood risk (PPS25), along with a number of supplements addressing more pressing policy concerns such as climate change, eco-towns and coastal change. Many of these policy documents were also supplemented by guidance and advice notes, leading to a situation where planning policy was spread over 40 documents and 1000 pages. The government felt that these policy documents should be consolidated into one much simpler document – and published the National Planning Policy Framework for England (DCLG 2011a).

The National Planning Policy Framework (NPPF) sets out the government's principles which would underpin the operation of the planning system, along with more detailed policies covering many of the key issues previously addressed by the PPSs and PPGs. It managed to do this over 51 pages (instead of the previous 1000 pages of guidance) with sections on housing and transport, for example, covering no more than three pages each. The rationale of the document was that it was a framework, leaving considerable flexibility for its interpretation and application to the local level. The overarching theme of the document was a commitment to delivering sustainable development. It reiterated previous planning policy (PPS1) by stating that sustainable development is the core principle underpinning planning (DCLG 2011a, 3). The document then set out a range of policies under the three broad components of sustainable development: economy, society and environment. The provision of transport infrastructure is an increasingly important component of both regeneration and sustainability policy in which public- and private-sector interests need to work together, as in Sheffield.

The Localism Act has come in for criticism, particularly in that it would make it easier (and more likely) for local people to block proposed new development 'in their back yards'. The publication of the National Planning Policy Framework therefore took many by surprise with its forthright commitment to growth. The document made it very clear that the planning system should be about supporting sustainable economic growth and that there should be a *'presumption in favour of sustainable development'* in local plans and in the consideration of planning applications (DCLG 2011a, 3). New development should be allowed unless there would be significant adverse impacts which clearly outweighed the potential benefits. Some observers maintained that

this was not that much different from the existing system, but the apparent emphasis on sustainable economic growth worried many conservation bodies. For instance, the National Trust roundly criticised the document, claiming that the default answer to all development proposals would in future be 'yes' and immediately organised a mass petition against it (National Trust 2011).

The government has sent out mixed messages through the National Planning Policy Framework and the Localism Act. For example, while the former stressed that local plans should meet the 'objectively assessed need' for new housing in their areas (DCLG 2011a, 31), the latter appeared to be giving much more say over such matters to local communities. At first it seemed that local planning authorities could take the opportunity genuinely and responsibly to plan for the needs of their area, free from interference from Whitehall. This would have heralded a resurgence of interest in planning at the local level as local communities, business groups and elected politicians grappled with the challenges facing their areas and sought to take responsibility for finding genuinely sustainable solutions. In fact many in the planning profession, developers and the public saw the new system as only bringing yet more unnecessary change and complexity in a time of stretched public resources and limited new development. Furthermore, it would seem that there is still a considerable amount of central government control and 'steer' on local communities and councils. As the saying goes, *'You can do anything you want as long as you do what we want you to do'*. Some major contradictions have developed in terms of different pronouncements by the government on planning policy. On the one hand the government say they want to speed up the system, but on the other hand they are making the planning system more complicated with a time-consuming new neighbourhood planning level. At the same time, they are promoting the 'presumption towards development' which has given some developers the idea that they can develop anything anywhere. But, in reality, they are introducing considerable constraint on this process and in the NPPF, stressing the cardinal rule that to gain permission, development must be sustainable (an ill-defined term indeed). Again they say they are giving the local community greater control over local facil-

Photo 7.5 Birmingham Bull Ring undergoing change

In the early twenty-first century planners were still grappling with the planning mistakes of the past as illustrated. In Birmingham the centre has now been redesigned in favour of pedestrians (see Chapter 11, Photo 11.4).

ities, but are reducing local services and facilities and still carrying out further cutbacks.

The apparent conflict in Coalition policy between speeding up development to release jobs, houses and infrastructure, and its support of the new localism, giving local communities and cities more power through the new local planning system, became more stark in 2012. The 2013 Growth and Infrastructure Act, arguably, gave central government powers to override local concerns, property rights and householder objections to major new development and infrastructural development. But it became apparent that the new local powers given to local communities under the Localism Act, through Neighbourhood Plans and parish powers, were in fact fairly limited and subject to the control of the Local (development) Plan. The changes to the planning system seemed to be driven by the Treasury, not by the DCLG, with little understanding of the true nature of the development process and the role of planners and developers in bringing forth large-scale development (Herrington and Parker 2012; Taylor Review 2013). But then the government's main reason for the changes to the planning system has been to foster growth and development, especially of new housing. Likewise, there has been a gradual volte-face (policy turnaround) regarding housing numbers.

Although Regional Spatial Strategies were abolished by the Coalition and therefore top-down new house-building targets were no longer to exist, the Coalition still maintained requirements for a five-year housing land supply, and an overarching ten-year plan too (Lock 2012). Much of this has been driven by the Treasury, not the DCLG, and seems to demonstrate little spatial awareness of the geographical, physical land-use planning of such policies. Proposals to resurrect the New Towns programme and build a new set of garden cities around London, as announced by the Coalition in December 2012, may have excited some planners but the proposals lacked any consideration of the realities of where to put them in our modern, intensely developed land.

Nevertheless, regional planning seemed to be creeping back into the Coalition's agenda, in spite of their apparent aversion to state intervention. This was because of the huge economic disparities between North and South, and the differences between London and provincial cities. But a concentration on urban renewal was also under way, with 20 City Zones covering provincial cities established in early 2013 which involve devolving some powers to local municipalities, along with the creation of City Mayors, who are effectively City Managers, in some cities. Major cities, such as Birmingham (Photo 7.5) and Manchester, which previously suffered 'modernisation' and demolition under 1960s planning (see last chapter), were now being 'made over' and regenerated in a manner which put greater emphasis upon the needs of pedestrians, and less upon the motorcar, and also sought to create a sense of urban design and distinctiveness. So there is hope for the future.

For the tasks, further reading, additional photos and other resources for this chapter, please visit www.palgrave. com/companion/greed.

8 The History of the Theories behind Planning

Planning theory matters

The importance of planning theory

The purpose of this chapter is to identify the theoretical perspectives behind the development of planning and to enable the reader to identify the way it has influenced planning policy and practice. The first part of this chapter explains the different aspects of planning theory and introduces research activity upon which it is based. The second part of the chapter identifies the changing theoretical perspectives that informed planning in each main epoch.

Planning may appear to be an uncompromising, definitive activity, as its policies are backed by legislation and its operation is based on enforcement of laws, standards and regulations. Yet, planning policy and theory are not fixed and have manifested some quite extreme paradigm shifts as to what is right or wrong according to the fashions, conditions and politics of the time (Young 2008a). A paradigm may be defined as the prevailing, dominant set of theories and ideas that inform a subject area, and the term was originally derived from science (Kuhn 1962): that is a totally different way of seeing things.

Planning theory is an elastic term which may be used to describe a variety of intellectual activities. The word theory comes from the Greek *thereo* which means 'I see', so planning theory may be defined as the way in which planning is seen, and understood. Many dictionaries make the distinction between conceptual theory being based upon abstract conceptualisation and conjecture which is aligned to philosophy, as against empirical theory which is based upon gathering data through research, experimentation, observation and applying scientific methods and which may be used to directly underpin policy-making (Taylor 1998; Allmendinger

2002). For example, much governmental planning research involves the preparation of surveys and forecasts. It is statistical, that is quantitative, and is concerned with investigating how many, what and where. In contrast, qualitative research is concerned not only with what but why and who in particular (Silverman 1985). It is concerned with understanding (*verstehen*, Weber 1964) and making sense of the city, rather than with trying to prove a scientific hypothesis. For example, there is a great deal of modern urban geography research concerned with understanding, and developing theories of, the city (Pacione 2009; Hall 2006; Panelli 2004). As will be seen in Chapter 14 on people and planning, many of these concepts and approaches are integral to urban sociology too. There is a need to take into account both quantitative and qualitative factors when developing planning theory and policy.

Students often say, '*why do we have to study planning theory?*' It has to be conceded that some local authority planners seem to be completely oblivious to all this intellectual activity and just want to get on with their job. They carry on planning and operating the development control system as they think best, unaware of the fact that their actions and decisions might be seen by some academic researchers as manifestations of a particular theoretical approach to planning. Nevertheless, all those who wish to become planners must study at least some planning theory to complete the course. It is hoped that a more reflective and reflexive practitioner is emerging who is more aware and conscious of the implications of professional policies upon society (Schon 1995; Hillier 1999). In order to develop high-level planning policy and to occupy senior posts in planning it is vital to have a grasp of the planning theories that inform policy.

Definitions of planning theory

There are two types of planning theory: theories about the nature of planning and theories on how to plan better (Taylor 1998). Firstly, planning theory may be seen to refer to those theories, political ideologies and philosophies which have sought to define the function, role and nature of planning and planners within society and the economy. These may be categorised as theories *of* planning, which have been developed mainly by non-planners, especially by urban geographers and sociologists, many of whom have been highly critical of both planners and planning policy (Faludi 1973; Campbell and Fainstein 2003).

Secondly, planning theory may more broadly be construed to include all the theories which have shaped planning policy and practice (Fainstein and Campbell (eds) 2011; Taylor 1998). These may be termed theories *for* planning, which have been developed by planners in order to facilitate better planning policy and processes, such as how to produce new types of development plans (Allmendinger *et al.* 2000; Feinstein and Campbell 2011).

Further divisions must be made between substantive, procedural, normative, explanatory and causal planning theories (Taylor 1998). To explain, substantive theory is concerned with the substance and content of planning, that is with the scope and nature of planning policy issues. Procedural theories are concerned with the process of planning, that is how it is carried out, the organisational structures which are used to deliver planning, and the skills, methodologies and techniques required to operate the planning system, and draw on wider management and organisational theory (Thornley 1991; Brindley *et al.* 1996). Normative theory is concerned with norms, that is with how planning ought to be, in terms of standards and objectives, and embraces the issue of how to plan 'better' and is often linked to more prescriptive recommendations for legislative reform. In contrast, definitional theory is concerned with explaining what planning is, whilst explanatory theory seeks to explain why it is so. Causal theory seeks to unravel the causes of the problems encountered. These aspects of planning theory are often linked to a more critical,

---

Textbox 8.1   Key dualisms in planning theory

Empirical/conceptual
Empirical/normative
Causal/normative
Substantive/procedural
Definitional/critical
Quantitative/qualitative
Spatial/aspatial
Planning/geography
Theories in (for) planning/ theories of planning

---

analytical and often sociological and political perspective on what is wrong with planning, and about planning's failings in addressing, or indeed creating, the problems of the modern city. Planning theory of all types does not exist in isolation from the rest of the academic world. The planning discourse may be seen as a hall of mirrors reflecting back a range of theories coming from outside the subculture (cf. Greed 1994a, ch. 1), including geography, economics, sociology, philosophy, management studies and science. In the next section we will look at some of the questions with which planning theory is concerned, drawing on the various branches of planning theory outlined above. Some of the key dualisms (contradictory dimensions of planning theory) are listed in apposition in Textbox 8.1.

Key theoretical questions

What is planning?

This question is both definitional and substantive. Most of the categories of types of planning identified by commentators fall either into the spatial or aspatial category (Foley 1964), as explained in Chapter 1. Spatial matters are those concerned with physical land use and development. Aspatial matters are those social, economic, cultural, managerial and political forces and decisions which generate the need for development in the first place and which shape what is built. Much of post-war planning has been dealing with the spatial end product, that is with the built environment, rather than with more radical policy concerned with shaping the forces that determine the nature of the built environment in the first place (Massey 1984).

British town planning has generally prioritised spatial physical land-use planning. However, planning can also be aspatial in that it deals with economic, social and cultural factors too. For example, Healey, a modern urban theorist, stresses the importance of economic planning (Healey 1997; Rydin 2011). Inevitably aspatial planning has spatial outcomes in terms of meeting demands for employment premises, providing housing for the workers, and dealing with the needs of depressed regions by means of regional planning and addressing inner-city decline through urban regeneration. Economic planning has generally been concerned with state intervention within a mixed economy situation, and has been primarily favoured by Labour governments. Healey argues that planning has been construed as a management tool, as a form of urban governance and as a process (Healey 2007). In this procedural perspective on planning, the substantive, policy content is secondary. Planning has become a management tool aimed at increasing efficiency, equally applicable to large private-sector organisations and to government agencies and public administration departments. Conservative governments have been particularly keen to speed up planning, often seeing it as an outdated bureaucratic activity that holds back market forces. The current Coalition government also appears to be concerned with procedural issues such as simplifying the planning system and reducing planning controls, but, paradoxically, also has a strong green agenda, which, to achieve, will inevitably require increased planning controls.

What is the relationship between planning and politics?

A distinction must be made between what a planner actually 'is' and what planners can really 'do' within the British system. One should not assume that just because some idealistic academic planner has written about planning as if it is all powerful, and can do anything, that it actually is in the real world, as there is a strong element of wishful thinking and bravado

at work within academic circles. Whilst the political system gives the planners a measure of power to put planning theory into practice through policy-making, the ultimate power resides with the politicians, for planning is a political process, and also exists in an uneasy relationship with market forces within the property sector too (Ratcliffe *et al.* 2009). To recap planning is political for three main reasons. In summary, first planning is political because it is concerned with controlling property and land, and therefore with money and power. So, it is inevitably a highly controversial activity, inextricably linked with the prevailing economic system, and with the allocation of scarce resources (Simmie 1974, 1981). Planners operate the statutory framework as an arm of the bureaucracy of government and therefore it is inevitably political. Secondly, it is political because it is a component of national politics and political ideology (Montgomery and Thornley 1990; Tewdwr-Jones 1996). Thirdly, the planning process is extremely political at the local area plan level, where community politics and grass-roots activity thrives, and where individual personalities, especially councillors, exert influence over planning decisions.

In comparison, Rydin gives a different set of three reasons for viewing planning as political (Rydin 1998: 6; Rydin 2003). First, it is concerned with the allocation of scarce resources, especially land and the right to develop, and thus it can alter land values and the cost of development. Secondly, she argues that it is political because it involves struggle and negotiation between conflicting interest groups, such as developers, environmentalists and local communities. Thirdly, she argues that planning is political because it is shaped by ideology. The operation of the planning system is influenced by the perspectives of the government in power, and by power politics at the local government level. Planning is a public sector activity seeking to regulate and control the activities of businesses, households and citizens. Thus planning theory has always had to incorporate and evaluate the role of political considerations in the planning process, which may not necessarily support the planners' aspirations regarding creating, say, sustainable cities (Rydin 2011) or for that matter socially equitable society.

Paradigms and paradigm shifts

In each generation, theory and philosophy undergo a paradigm shift (as defined by Kuhn 1962), that is a major shift in theoretical perspectives. A paradigm shift describes the situation when existing paradigms are replaced by a completely new way of seeing things, that is when a sea change occurs (Taylor 1998: ch. 9; Guba and Lincoln 1992). In the field of town planning, there have been a series of paradigm shifts (Innes 1995). Taylor highlights two shifts in particular, namely, from planning being a design discipline to becoming a science in the 1960s, and from the planner being a technical expert and scientist to becoming a communicator and negotiator in the 1980s (Taylor 1998). The red/green shift that is from socialism to environmentalism, manifest in planning priorities in the latter half of the twentieth century, has been quite drastic too. But then planning can be anything you want it to be (Greed 1994a), as manifested in the chameleon-like changeability of the modern planning profession, and the policies and standards it has recommended, over the last 100 years. However, the term paradigm shift should be used sparingly, as planning is a very broad church, and there are all sorts of planners and *plannings* as manifest, for example, in the different planning specialisms found within local authority departments. But a new specialism in planning does not constitute a paradigm shift. On the other hand, some major movements within society itself such as the rise of feminism, and arguably the wider equality and diversity agenda, and the rise of religion in the twenty-first century (Baker and Beaumont 2011; Sandercock 1997), whilst affecting the overall culture, have not had a particularly great effect on the planning profession to shift it to a new paradigm. New paradigms such as the concept of the Healthy City (Barton and Tsourou 2006) and the Culturally Diverse City (Sandercock 1997; Young 2008b) inevitably reshape the role of planning in response to these changes.

The story of planning revisited

The story of planning will now be revisited in order to highlight theoretical underpinnings and the main

---

Textbox 8.2   In summary planning theory is concerned with:

Scope and nature of planning
Types of planners
Nature of the planning process
Political, economic, social and cultural context
 Planners' views of reality and priorities

Textbox 8.3   Key questions in studying planning theory

What form did planning take in each stage of development?
Who were the planners and what skills did they require? Architects, economists, scientists?
What theories informed planning? Marxism, market economics, sustainability?
What was the planners' view of reality, and what there their priorities?
What function did planning perform? Regulation, regeneration, enablement?
How was planning done? And in what organisational and procedural structures?
What were the implications for the real world and our cities?
Who were the stakeholders the receivers, that is the planned?

---

paradigm shifts which have taken place over the years. This section also provides a summary overview of the whole story of planning for revision purposes. In seeking to develop an understanding of theories **in** planning and theories **of** planning readers are advised to bear in mind the following Textbox (8.2) and questions (Textbox 8.3), which are broadly covered in the text.

The nineteenth and early twentieth century

The Industrial Revolution, and the accompanying urbanisation and population growth, in the nineteenth century precipitated the development of modern town planning and related state intervention and organisational structures (see Chapter 4).

Embryonic town planning was closely linked to the public health and housing reform movements. Ideologically and politically the early town planning initiators were motivated by a range of reformist principles. The Liberal reforming governments headed by Gladstone in the second half of the century introduced a foundational range of housing, planning and public health acts. The local government reform movement was strongly linked to concepts of citizenship and civic pride, epitomised, for example, in Manchester and other major civic centres, in gas and water socialism.

The late nineteenth century and early twentieth century may be characterised as an era when spatial planning predominated, and planning was conceptualised as urban design, or simply as Big Architecture (Greed and Roberts 1998). Emergent planning theory, such as it was, may be characterised as being positivist and scientific in character, often engineer-led and concerned with the basics of sewerage, drainage, public health and housing issues. Planning itself appeared relatively crude and simplistic in its lack of understanding of complex urban forces. Theoretically, the early planning movement can be seen as being focused around the powers of environmental determinism, that is salvation by bricks, hence the belief in building model towns and promoting housing reform (as illustrated in Chapter 5).

Architects, engineers and surveyors staffed the new local authority planning departments. Planning was seen as both a design discipline and as a component of the public health movement, which itself had a positivist scientific approach to problem-solving. There was limited space for a consideration of social planning factors within the new local government-based regulatory system, which was obsessed with producing planning schemes based on physical land-use zoning. In the aligned area of housing policy there remained a greater social awareness, albeit often tinged with paternalism towards the working classes, and also this was one of the few professional areas where there were a significant number of women involved (Greed 1999a). But many of the utopian planning projects, academic treatises and ideals of the time were more holistic and aspatial (social) in approach, dealing with social, economic and environmental issues too. Non-governmental and more radical strains of planning developed,

expressing their aspirations in imagineering ideal urban communities. For example, Howard sought to create sustainable settlements in which social, economic, environmental and aesthetic factors were integrated. Subsequent development of speculative garden suburbs and state new towns were travesties of Howard's original concepts, by putting an overemphasis upon physical layout and architectural considerations.

At the dawn of the twentieth century a more sophisticated theoretical perspective, albeit still positivist, was being developed by geographers, sociologists and earth scientists who were taking an interest in the urban situation. Early contributors to the theory of how to plan included Patrick Geddes, who was one of the founding fathers of the modern town planning movement. Geddes promoted a scientific approach to the planning process, based on the principles, survey, analysis plan. Also a range of theorists, writers and researchers developed theories of urban geography (Von Thunen 2009; Christaller 1966 (was 1933)); history (Mumford 1965); zoning (Geddes 1915) and sociology (Rowntree 1901). As explained in Part II, zoning was a particularly strong theory in the development of the modern planning movement under the influence of Patrick Geddes (Geddes 1915). Other early planning theories related to ideal forms of residential layout and recommended densities and also linked across to architecture and house design. Overall, planning was suffused with ideas of order, modernity, functionalism and a scientific spirit.

Although emphasis was put upon use of scientific and unbiased methods, it is of note that many such theories were heavily laden with racial, sexist and classist ideology (Rydin 1998: 17; Matless 1992; Greed 1994a). In contrast, ideal community design based upon utopian socialist principles often manifested links with first-wave feminism. As detailed elsewhere, much of this foundational work was conveniently lost and forgotten as the century progressed (Hayden 1976). After the First World War a separate town planning profession gradually developed. With the establishment of the RTPI in 1914 it was possible to be a town planner without also being an architect or a surveyor. The Housing and Town Planning Acts of 1909 and 1919, introduced again by Liberal governments, established a rudimentary development plan system. The first Labour government came into power in 1924 but did not major upon town planning issues. Subsequent acts in the 1930s increased the sway of the planners. But it was not until the 1947 Town and Country Planning Act that physical land-use planning enabled national blanket coverage of development plans and development control. In the interwar years physical town planners were mainly concerned with designing new council housing estates or were working for the private sector building suburbia, with nearly 3 million houses being built between the wars. But planning controls were limited and ineffective, and concerns were expressed about the loss of the countryside to urban sprawl.

Whilst physical land-use planning remained in the doldrums, in contrast, economic planning gained momentum. Emphasis was being put upon regional planning as a means of ameliorating high levels of unemployment in depressed areas. Labour governments took charge between 1929 and 1935, and introduced rudimentary regional planning legislation. Culturally employment problems were primarily perceived as consisting of unemployment among male workers in primary and secondary industries, where the main trades union support for the Labour Party was to be found. Whilst at the time the Labour Party might have seemed new and radical, in fact by today's standards the agenda was essentially Old Labour, non-sustainable and low on gender awareness, and primarily concerned with production, industry, and male employment.

Post-war reconstruction planning

The 1947 Act established the modern development plan and control system which was focused upon the objective of controlling land uses, by means of zoning and other physical planning measures (see Chapter 6). Planning, like rationing, was seen as a logical process, simply concerned with the allocation of resources, in this case land uses, in a no-nonsense military manner. There was little space for doubt, for citizens' viewpoints, or for the fact that there might be a plurality of conflicting needs within society. Planners were both state bureaucrats and urban managers, albeit with a strongly spatial (physical), rather than aspatial (socio-economic), brief. 'The

new Britain must be planned' was the slogan of the day as declared by the *Picture Post* Editorial (Lake 1941) and planning was the *zeitgeist* (spirit) of the age.

In retrospect, the planning system that was established in the post-war reconstruction period (1945–65) appears a disjointed mixture of components, fired by conflicting ideologies, within a tangle of diverse theoretical perspectives and paradigms. Nationalisation of development rights, through a complex system of betterment levies, and an enthusiasm for economic planning measures reflect an apparent longing for a form of state socialism, as was current in Soviet Bloc countries at that time. State planning, and in particular the creation of Five-Year Plans, were the main means of the Soviet Union achieving its goals for creating a socialist state, and spatial planning was an important means of modernising its housing stock, albeit with little concern for the social aspects of planning (Attwood 2011). In contrast, the UK development plan system, with its emphasis upon control, required a private sector to control, and its establishment was reflective of a typically British compromise, the maintenance of a mixed economy, shored up by welfare economics and a Welfare State. As Rydin (2003, 2011) notes it was assumed that the economy could be directed externally, and that a range of regional economic planning policies could redirect investment without any more structural measures being required. But, planners underestimated the economic forces involved and held an oversimplified view of the relationship between aspatial (economic, political, social) forces and the spatial (physical) land uses and developments they generated. Likewise the 1949 National Parks and Access to the Countryside Act evidenced the combination of a patrician (upperclass) concern for preserving the countryside, and an unquestioning support for farming interests, with a leveller's (ordinary people's) concern for rights to roam, and an embryonic concern with environmental conservation. Many strands and potentially conflicting elements comprised the span of post-war planning legislation.

As outlined in Chapter 6, a very extensive programme of demolition, decentralisation, new town building and new housing development took place in the post-war period. Planners were increasingly, by default, taking on the role of social engineer (Carey and Mapes 1972) but both planning and the government of the time were fairly theory-free and did not appear to be particularly conscious or reflective of the effects of their drastic spatial policies. In retrospect it is astounding how much power local planning and housing departments had in the post-war years, to demolish entire tracts of historic cities and to place thousands of people in distant housing estates, and in the 1960s into tower blocks. But, there was growing criticism of the activities of the planners, both from the community and from academics. Traces of critical theory perspectives *of* planning may be seen in planning literature of the later 1950s and 1960s as a new breed of urban sociologists investigated the experiences of new town and inner-city populations and the overconfidence of the planners (Broady 1968) (see Chapter 14).

The role of the town planner was seen as being similar to that of the referee, or umpire, who sets out the pitch, resolved conflict between opposing teams, and enforced the basic ground rules and framework for fair play, within which the game of property development was carried out. With the wisdom of hindsight, this appears a strangely apolitical and sanitised view of the planner's role. The planner's brief was to ensure that towns and cities developed logically and conveniently, with an emphasis being put upon zoning. This provided a framework for the design of the road network and the provision of other infrastructural services, and gave the market confidence in the future security of the area.

Whilst the emphasis was upon the planner as controller, such power could be positive in its effects in ensuring that space was available for the non-profit-making and more social uses which were essential to the urban population but which were not attractive investments for the private sector itself. These included recreational space and facilities, schools, health and community buildings, and sewers and drains, all of which were provided by other local government departments and statutory undertakers. In those days there was more money available from the state for the provision of infrastructural services, and many of the public utilities had been nationalised in the immediate post-war period. Looking back across the wake of privatisation and widespread cutbacks in the 1980s and 1990s, it is astonishing how many such social goods were provided free in the 1960s without the need for planners to enter into protracted planning gain negotiation and to adopt a more entrepreneurial role as is the case today. It is also astonishing how much power was wielded by the planners, especially their powers to demolish large tracts of our cities and to replan Britain, most of their decisions being based on common sense rather than upon planning theory.

The planner was seen as a generic decision-maker, exercising procedural control over a whole range of human activities through the insensitive instruments of land-use zoning, demolition and redevelopment policy. The planner was a generalist, who apparently could plan anything, and was to be credited with great knowledge about a great range of human activities. Planning was seen as a relatively straightforward procedure (Rydin 1998: 37; Rydin 2011). The presumed objectives of planning were so obvious that they did not merit special attention or justification in the new development plans and instead emphasis was put upon implementational policies. The emphasis was upon producing the Master Plan, a highly prescriptive and absolute document covering planning for the area in question for the next five years or more. The master-plan approach to planning contrasts with the more incremental approach which was to become popular in later years (Taylor 1998). An incremental approach to planning is based upon a more gradual evaluation of all parameters and an acceptance of continuous change within what is being planned, so that policy adapts to change. Broad goals and objectives are set, but a variety of ways of achieving them is accepted as the only realistic way to achieve policy implementation.

The post-war planner was likely to be equipped to do all this with only a diploma in surveying or a highways engineering qualification, and probably no urban sociology or planning theory background whatsoever. (It was a different age; less than 1 per cent of the population had degrees in the 1940s (Millerson 1964).) But the power and role of the planner was increasingly being questioned (Simmie 1974; Goldsmith 1980; Montgomery and Thornley 1990). Planning was based upon a top-down rather than bottom-up approach to planning with very little involvement of, and hardly a word of protest from, the people, who were meant to be the beneficiaries of the planning system.

Systems or society?

From 1964 to 1970 a Labour government took charge under Harold Wilson, who believed in planning as a key tool of government, and guidance of the economy, and who put much emphasis upon progress being fired by the white heat of technology. In parallel, an expansion of higher education in the 1960s resulted in the creation of more full-time planning degrees, and thus planning took on a more academic persona than previously (Schuster 1950; Greed 1990). Planners needed to find a theory that would enhance and legitimate their role as technical experts and academic thinkers, in the wake of continuing criticism of their role as urban designers. Systems theory met this requirement. A major paradigm shift occurred within planning, as planners moved from being urban designers and master planners obsessed with physical land-use planning, to becoming scientists, technical experts, and managers of both spatial and aspatial urban systems. A range of new ostensibly scientific theories of the city as a system, mainly from North America, began to shape planning theory in Britain (McLoughlin 1969). The city was seen as a gigantic system, made up of human activities and economic forces, which generated the need for different types of physical land uses and buildings. Whatever your view of planning theory at the time, or of Wilson's policies, it is astonishing in retrospect that planners had so much of a higher status and power, compared with today.

The purpose of planning was to solve the problems of the city by bringing back harmony and balance to the urban system, which had been disrupted by rapid change. It was believed that it was possible to measure and track the economic and activity changes that created demand for new developments and especially for highway networks with the growth of motorcar travel, so that the planner could control the future state of the city (Eversley 1973; Faludi (ed.) 1973). Therefore planning was seen as constituting the application of scientific method to decision-making, rather than primarily being concerned with designing towns and cities (Davidoff and Reiner 1962; Faludi (ed.) 1973; Hall and Gieben 1992). Systems planning was more concerned with large-scale quantitative data and seeing the large-scale picture rather than with the

details of everyday life at street level (Greed 2013). Also it was not much concerned with substantive policy issues, or with qualitative matters such as whether a policy was right or wrong or unjust, in the eyes of the people being planned, as planning was essentially positivist and objective in approach (Amin 2006).

The planner was seen as the helmsman guiding the city into the future, and he needed all this information to steer a straight course (McLoughlin 1969). As outlined in Chapter 2 (and Textbox 8.1), the scope and format of the new type of development plan, called the Structure Plan, introduced under the 1971 Town and Country Planning Act, was strongly influenced by systems planning. For planning to be effective there was a need to understand the activities and changes which create a demand for the land uses in the first place, in order to make a pre-emptive strike through anticipating what was about to happen next. Thus the plans were underpinned by extensive research and forecasting, and alternative strategies were subject to much evaluation prior to their approval. As a result there was less emphasis on traditional physical land-use plans and more on policy statements to guide the ever-changing city system.

Much of the rightness of planning was taken for granted as unquestionable, and the planners manifested high levels of self-confidence as the scientific experts of the time. Planning theory at this time was, therefore, concerned with procedure, and number crunching using the new age of computers, rather than with substantive or social policy issues. There was a danger in treating society as a gigantic scientific tidy system, which apparently operated according to neutral scientific laws, rather than seeing it as a disorganised, somewhat chaotic result of competing interest groups and political factions trying to get their way, as critics were already warning at the time (Foley 1964; Alexander 1965). Looking back, the amount of power and authority held by the planners at that time is astounding.

A scientific planning process?

In the 1960s, computers were introduced to the planning process for the first time in Britain; enormous   machines   that   filled   entire   rooms!

Consequently, much use was made of mathematical models and scientific prediction methods for developing and justifying policy, especially transportation planning which lent itself well to computerisation with all those quantifiable trips, and cars! Inspiration and technology transfer from the space race was to influence approaches to urban planning characteristics. Retail gravity models were very popular: and still live on in parts of the private property sector. These are used to predict the likely demand for new floor space in shopping centres in relation to the size of the population in the surrounding catchment area and the distance they have to travel to reach the centre, relative to the attraction that other existing centres offer. Such approaches have been much criticised, not least by women who constitute the bulk of shoppers. Not all retail space is of the same quality, or of the same use value to a particular individual. Secondly, the calculations were usually based on assumptions of people travelling chiefly by car, when many women did not have access to a car during the daytime. The frequency of public transport, the availability of facilities such as crèches and public conveniences are far more likely to act as inducements to use the centre. But, planning was now seen as a rational scientific process, with an emphasis upon objective and quantitative considerations, which contained little space for such qualitative or minority considerations. But so many of these factors could not be readily quantified. Indeed, as I was told by my supervisor when I entered planning, '*If you can't count it, it doesn't count*'. Therefore it is important to be aware of what is left in or out of the survey in question. Planning for a scientifically constructed average resulted in planning successfully for no one, and excluding the needs of many from the decision-making agenda. In spite of this weakness, there was also a proliferation of mathematical models and methodologies for predicting urban change, and as aids to decision-making, e.g. cost–benefit analysis (CBA), threshold analysis, network analysis, etc. (Mishan 1973; Lichfield 1975; Roberts 1974). By the way, CBA should not be confused with the Coalition's emphasis on evaluating CBR, that is Cost Benefit and Risk, as a factor in determining the soundness of Neighbourhood Plans.

All this did not go unchallenged, and a range of urban sociologists were highly critical of UK planning policy and the planners, thus developing their own theories *of* planning (Simmie 1974; and see also E-Supplement 3). Planners were seen as powerful urban gatekeepers ensuring unequal distribution of urban resources, and increasingly a conflict-laden interpretation of the situation was adopted. Scientific objectivity was not seen to be practised by planning authorities, and by their planning committees, in areas where the property boom of the 1960s was in full swing, where the financial stakes were high, and where in some instances subsequently bribery and corruption came to light. Increasingly grass-roots community groups mobilised in relation to the effects of planning on their area. With the rise of the second wave of feminism in the 1960s, the civil rights movement, and the drive for equal opportunities, specific critiques of the planning system were emanating from the different minority groups. As discussed in Part IV, a new wave of urban sociological literature, urban feminist literature, and ethnic minority studies was bubbling forth, some of which was co-opted by planning academics as a component in courses at planning schools. Thus a range of critical theory perspectives on planning were emerging.

Marxists or managers?

By the 1970s some planners within academia, seeking a more critical intellectual basis to their study of urban issues, had become enamoured by Marxist theory, and were known as neo-Marxists (Harvey 1975; Taylor 1998). Marxism was more than an academic theory; it has also been seen as a programme of political action and revolution to intervene in history and bring about the ideal new society of the future (McLellan 1973). Marxists argue that many of the problems and inequalities of society derive from the nature of the economic system underpinning society, in particular the development of modern industrial capitalism as had emerged in the nineteenth century. Basically Marx saw only two classes, the capitalists (bourgeoisie), i.e. the owners of production and the factories, and the workers (proletariat), the producers, whom he saw as having a fundamental conflict of interest (Gabler 2010). Until this was resolved by the future revolution, there would always be problems in society and undertaking reform, for example through town planning, would be as useless as *rearranging the deckchairs on the Titanic*. Marx described the economic base of society as the substructure of society, and above this is the superstructure which consists of the social and cultural institutions, the built environment and everything else which makes up our civilisation. Marxist theory is strongly determinist in that it says that the superstructure takes the form it does in order to facilitate the continuance and maintenance of the social relations and means of production which enables the capitalist class to get the most work out of their workers at the lowest wages possible. Therefore, simply seeking to change the nature of the built environment was seen as pointless and superficial. Thus the planners were seen by his followers as the lackeys of the bourgeoisie, tinkering with the superstructure. Therefore, for example, it was argued there was little point in carrying out improvements to the built environment if people could not afford to benefit from them. If their wages were too low (because of the structure of society) they would simply move elsewhere, rather than pay higher rents for the improved property. As Engels, Marx's colleague, said, '*You don't solve the housing problem, you only move it*', alluding to fact that there would always be slums until people had the means to afford better housing. All this is very different from the current Coalition government's perspective, and indeed that of most previous governments, in which it is believed that the way to create equality and reduce poverty is to let the market improve everyone's lot.

Rejecting the importance of spatial issues, and over-stressing the aspatial factors, especially material economic prime causes, led planners into an impasse, which undermined their authority to exert control over the built environment (Taylor 1999). Indeed Marxism, which condemned private property (that is most of the built environment!) was difficult to translate into spatial planning policy. Many of the problems which are related to physical land use, design practicalities, infrastructure, sewers, roads, drains and the provision of basic facilities always exist in society and have to be dealt with, whether that society is capitalist or socialist. Women in particular were critical of the abstract nature of neo-Marxist planning, and its disregard for the daily problems and realities of urban life, such as housing problems, childcare, personal safety and accessibility. But such matters were likely to be seen as domestic, selfish, bourgeois and capitalistic (Attwood 2011) and would have to wait their turn. But some neo-Marxist planning theorists, taking what is known as a materialist stance, argued that space matters and that the study of the city was important because it provided the basics of life including shelter, and the localities where economic activity, that is work, took place (Taylor 1998; Harvey 1975; Castells 1977; Massey 1984).

Neo-Marxists believed it was essential to deal with cause rather than effect, namely to change society, rather than changing the built environment. Marx believed that society could only be transformed by adopting a socialist mode of production in which the private ownership of capital and indeed all private property was abolished. If the people themselves were running and owning the system (on the basis of the principle, from each according to his ability and to each according to his need) then no one would be poor again: indeed there would ultimately be no need for money or profit in a truly socialist state. But, as has been seen in respect of Eastern Europe, it is easier said than done, because of human nature, corruption and power politics. Followers of Marx believed that the revolution was too important to leave to the workers. There needed to be an elite cadre, the Party leaders who would take the lead in creating the new society (parallels with some British town planners?). Like any elite group, with time they lost touch with the people and pursued their own interests at the expense of the masses, without even being answerable to the requirement of accountability which democracy gives. Alonso (1965: 170) noted that the urban planning profession, like most adolescents, likes to revolt, to strike a pose, and to rapidly adopt and discard heroes (Greed 1994a: 30). But each generation of planners tends to produce its own brand of angry young men who challenge the authority of the elders of the planning tribe, gain power, but in the process mellow and become like their forebears. Again in retrospect, it is astonishing that local government town planners believed they were one of the elite groups that had so much power. Was this justified at the time or just bravado?

Another problem with neo-Marxism was the assumption that the proletariat whom the revolution was for consisted mainly of male workers occupied in heavy industry and mining, which seemed rather old fashioned, given the decline of traditional industries and the growth of service industries and office-based employment as the largest sectors of the economy (Davis 2009). Many groups felt disenfranchised by Hard Left politics that seemed to exclude women, ethnic minority groups, and anyone who was not in employment, who were likely to be seen as part of the *lumpen proletariat* (an ancestor of the chav of today). A softer New Left was developing concerned more with community issues, women's rights, the inner city, equal opportunities, and ethnic minority issues. Rather than class and work (and the working class at that) being seen as the sole determinant of oppression, a plurality of factors could now be taken into account, including gender, ethnicity, sexuality, age, disability, religion and cultural difference. Much of the pioneer work to bring these perspectives into the world of town planning was carried out by enlightened minority planners, supported by more progressive metropolitan authorities, in particular by the example of the GLC in London. Thus progressive planners became concerned with community participation, acting as enablers and advocates (Rydin 2011). The socially-concerned planner might act as advocate as in the case of Planning Aid for London or as champion of equal rights as included in the publications of the radical GLC planning department (GLC 1984). The danger of a participatory approach to planning is that it can appear enlightened and inclusionary and yet prove merely to be a mechanism to control rather than empower minorities, as set out by Arnstein (1969) in her ladder of participation diagram. All this will be explained further in Part IV.

Although Marxism was undoubtedly a strong influence in shaping planning theory in the past, there have always been those who question its assumptions and today a more balanced approach is prevalent. Marx saw unresolved conflict as essential to class struggle in generating revolution and thus change in society. In contrast, others who subscribe to the concept of Agonism question this. Agonists argue that conflict is not an end in itself but a natural, productive component of decision-making within a pluralistic, democratic society. In the case of planning proposals, different groups within society and the community need to argue it all out and come to a consensus, in order to move forward to deciding what should be done, as explained by Allmendinger and Tewdwr-Jones (2002).

Entrepreneurial planning

The planning pendulum was swinging in another direction again by the late 1970s, by which time neo-Marxism had run its course. A more subdued, middle-of-the-road version of planning developed, under the Callaghan Labour government. Local government reorganisation in 1974 provided the opportunity for planners to take a new role within the corporate affairs of the local authority, but this role was not sustained in all cases as a result of subsequent political, financial and organisational changes in local government. Planning gain and bargaining became the main way to tax the developers, as the vestiges of development land tax had been repealed by the 1974 White Paper. Land was issued as a last forlorn attempt at tackling the land value issue and the question of development gains tax. Planners were increasingly seen as managers within the local government system, not revolutionaries, or even reformers. Relatively speaking, greater emphasis was being put upon short-term problem-solving through incrementalism as against long-term planning, and a greater emphasis was put upon planning at the local level, after the impersonal scale of systems planning. Overall the emphasis was more upon speeding up the planning process than with the policy aspects of planning. Within the less pro-planning political climate of the 1970s, planners recreated themselves as negotiators, networkers and coordinators, rather than as controllers and gods.

Gradually past incarnations of planning began to spring back into life. For example, urban design had never gone away, and was still a component of local authority planning, although not a hot topic in academia at the time. The production of the influential Essex Design Guide in 1974 brought this aspect of planning back into the fore (see Chapter 13 on design). Likewise the urban conservation movement continued apace. These more aesthetic dimensions of planning may be seen as relatively apolitical and espousing traditional conservative values of a bygone England, receiving royal support (Prince of Wales 1989) and embodied a renewed concern for our

Photo 8.1 The importance of urban human interaction

Cities are not just inanimate objects; they are major meeting points, melting pots, and places where ideas, entrepreneurial activities and community identity are generated, as here in Chicago.

historical heritage, which in subsequent years was to grow apace, as planning became more concerned with preserving the familiar past, than creating a revolutionary new future. Planners recreated themselves as protectors of our historical heritage, as urban renewal experts.

The Conservative government gained power under Mrs Thatcher in 1979, and it would have seemed that large-scale state planning was doomed, as described in Chapter 6. The New Right government arguably lacked the paternalistic custodial attitude towards the people and the land that had been found to a degree in previous more gentlemanly Old

Right Conservative governments. The New Right appeared much brasher, more business-like and commercial in demeanour, and was inspired by New Right American economic theory (Friedman 1991). Social awareness was not a feature of this group, and Mrs Thatcher herself is rumoured to have declared, *'there's no such thing as society'*. Instead emphasis was put upon the individual, who apparently could shape his or her own destiny by hard work, enterprise and initiative (Photo 8.1). Those planners who had pioneered a greater emphasis upon the social aspects of planning, and who had brought equal opportunities issues into the foreground, were to find that equality was now redefined as '*anyone can succeed in business*'. But not everyone started from the same advantageous position in the first place. In fact lack of economic well-being and unemployment were seen as the planners' fault. Michael Heseltine, Thatcher's Secretary of State for the Environment, spoke of jobs being locked up in filing cabinets, presumably in dusty planning departments. But, as explained in Chapter 6, by the time of the Major government, attitudes had mellowed with time, and the traditional role of the planner as arbitrator and umpire came to be recognised as of value to the private sector, if only to help oil the wheels of capitalism.

Environmental planning

The planning kaleidoscope was being shaken again; new forces were at work, at an international level, that were to reshape and dominate planning for many years to come. As we move into the 1980s, we see a paradigm shift from red (economic) to green (environmental) planning issues. Great concern was expressed about the future of the planet, global warming and the possible destruction of Planet Earth by its own people. The Rio Declaration (UN 1992a) of the United Nations required all signatory member-states to integrate environmental controls and policies within their own respective planning systems. Great emphasis was placed upon the concept of sustainability of leaving the planet in good shape, with adequate natural resources, for future generations. But planning policy actually obstructed the chances of producing a next generation, because of its disregard of family needs, women's issues and childcare needs. Sustainability originally had three dimensions to it: environmental sustainability, economic viability and social equality, that is Planet, Prosperity and People, as promoted by the female chair of the influential Brundtland Report (Brundtland 1987). When these principles filtered down into the UK planning system, given the cultural values of the planning tribe (for more on professional subcultures see Chapter 16), greatest emphasis was given to the physical environmental aspects, and little emphasis was given to either the economic or social equity dimension, let alone the relationship between gender and sustainability. But

in other European countries, especially in Scandinavia, sustainability policy integrated equality issues to a far greater extent (Skjerve (ed.) 1993).

However, significantly the environment, indeed the whole planet, was also seen as a system which was out of balance because of mankind's actions, and had to be rebalanced through ecologically-informed policy. So to some extent the concept of environmental sustainability took on some of the idea of harmony and balance (Gore 1992, 2006) also found in earlier systems planning theory (and for that matter in Buddhism, management theory, and early computer theory (Rand 1943), as discussed in depth in Greed 2013). Environmentalism became the new gospel of redemption and *raison d'être* for planners; this built up into another major paradigm shift. Green politics, and the related environmental movement, challenged both capitalist and socialist politics. The greening of planning was seen by some as its depoliticisation because there appeared to be little emphasis on traditional economic concerns. But, the principle of let the polluter pay repoliticised the agenda (Rydin 2011; Barton *et al.* 1998). Once big business realised that the new movement had legislative and fiscal power, much of which emanated from the European Union, corporate interests sought to absorb rather than ignore the green movement.

Planners have often been criticised for suffering from 'cultural lag', that is not keeping up with the times (Ogburn 1922) and not spotting significant changes in society and theory. Because of the over-emphasis upon market considerations it took a while for environmental issues to be taken on board by either the UK government or the planners. When Major replaced Thatcher as Conservative Prime Minister some softening towards the planning system and warming towards environmental issues was to be found. Changes had to be made in the scope and nature of planning legislation as a result of UN agreements and EU directives, as Britain, and its planning system, became increasingly subject to the effects of globalisation. The new environmental agenda had some quite drastic effects on planning policy. For example, it provided the impetus for a shift in attitudes away from planning for the motor-car, to restrictions on car use.

As for the process of planning, environmental planning has been better at dealing with quantifiable data, using EIA (Environmental Impact Assessment) methods to test the likely sustainability of new development proposals. But little has been done about SIA (Social Impact Assessment) – in the UK at least – in spite of a range of qualitative methodologies being in existence (RTPI 2003; Greed 2005b). Arguably, much of environmental planning seemed to be more concerned with the planet and as people-less in their perspective as previous generations of planners. Many environmental planners seem to be totally unaware of the difficulties and rigours of everyday life for ordinary people. Prioritising environmental concerns about individual carbon footprints, without linking this to the social, economic and spatial realities encountered by ordinary people, leads to further oppression in the name of the environment (Uteng and Cresswell (eds) 2008). Likewise scant attention is given to women's different travel needs and thus to the challenges the sustainable city presents to women, such as the very tight time-budgets, and complex trip-chaining patterns, that women have in order to carry out all their home and work tasks (as pursued further in the equalities chapter, Chapter 15).

Collaborative community-based planning

Many imagined that New Labour, which came to power in 1997, would re-establish the power of town planning and adopt a more socially and environmentally aware programme of urban policy than its Conservative predecessors. At first little happened except for some restructuring of government departments responsible for planning, and the publication of a series of consultative documents on the importance of urban renewal, socially inclusive policies, joined-up thinking and community development; and a great deal of spin. It was time for planners to recreate themselves again and no longer be seen as the enemy of the people. A new power base and agenda were needed. So, planners began to take on the role of champions and advocates of the community, minorities and inner-city residents, that is the very groups which had been so critical of planning policy in the past. Many minority and community groups had been empowered by their experiences, and have been setting the agenda for change within society and for the built environment professions

from the bottom up. The planners' image was now cast as enablers and regenerators rather than as bureaucrats.

A whole new set of planning theories, methodologies, organisational structures and ways of doing planning have been developing in the 1990s to justify this shift towards a collaborative, communicative approach to planning (Healey 1997). As mentioned, a key theoretical strand in this direction has been an agonistic perspective in which consensus rather than conflict is seen as the more dominant force (Allmendinger and Tewdwr-Jones 2002). This reorientation reflects a wider paradigmatic shift within academia towards the importance of the micro level of society and cultural issues (Williams 1981). There was a greater emphasis upon the qualitative side of sociological research and upon the individual, the local community and social interaction; and away from the heavy, positivist, macro-level structural theories of society and the economy of the past (Guba and Lincoln 1992). It was now acknowledged that there was a range of groups within society, and that one right answer for the average man in the street was not adequate to meet people's needs. This stance reflects wider changes in sociological theory, towards post-structuralism, post-scientific, post-modernist, post-materialist, post-Fordist and post-positivist perspectives which acknowledge the importance of diversity, for example in relation to ethnicity, gender, locality and culture. Rigid structuralist theories of the past which were based on crude class divisions were no longer appropriate as a basis for policy-making. It was acknowledged that there is a diversity of interest groups each with their own viewpoint on the city and their own experiences of life, so there is unlikely to be one scientifically proven right answer to specific planning policies. This diversity has been manifest and recognised in the new rights and equalities agenda as discussed in Part IV. This new diversity led to the acknowledgement that there was a range of right answers but such relativism was difficult for some planners to cope with, who previously believed there was only one right answer to many urban issues. This diversity could also lead to conflict rather than consensus as it should not be assumed that all minority groups agree with each other.

Nevertheless, planners need to muddle through and do their best in increasingly difficult circumstances. As a result an institutionalist approach to planning has been seen as one way forward. An institutionalist approach is one in which greater attention is given to working with and through social and community networks, agencies and other social *institutions* to facilitate policy change (Healey 1997, 5). It thus provides a depoliticised Third Way between the rocks of the Left and the Right. Giddens gave academic support to Blair's Third Way approach to government, which envisaged a more interactive model of society and social empowerment. (Giddens is also known for his work on the structure and agency debate, as to what caused what, top-down or bottom-up influences (Giddens 1989).) Habermas has also had a major input on these new theoretical perspectives (Habermas 1979, 1987) through his work on how participatory democracy might be extended as a means of enabling citizens to engage in debate and to open up the public arena of decision-making in a more inclusionary manner. The Third Way was meant to facilitate a communicative approach to the design of governance systems and practices, focusing on ways of developing collaborative and consensus-building practices. The institutionalist approach also allowed for diversity and the participation of a range of stakeholders in the planning process. The emphasis was upon participatory democracy within a pluralistic society. Thus collaborative planning was to be based upon negotiation, networking, and liaison with community groups, rather than upon autocratic direction and coercion. Both institutionalist and collaborative planning theory may be seen as procedural planning theories.

But there are considerable problems with the collaborative planning approach. Minority groups have expressed reservations about the process, because the stakeholders are not necessarily represented in such a way that would allow space for the consideration of the differing needs within the community on the basis of class, race, gender, age and so forth. Concern was expressed that many planners are ill-equipped to operate a more communicative egalitarian planning system, when they have clearly not all taken on board the basic principles of equal opportunities and lack social awareness or understanding of the needs of the planned, and still lived in a world of no-nonsense physical land-use planning. There is also the major problem of differential levels of power between planners and planned. Although the theories are widespread within academic planning circles at local government level there is little training or preparation for planners to take on this new softer role. Indeed in many a local planning authority planning practice has changed little, although now a new socially-inclusive script can be recited to legitimate planning decisions which are not necessarily in the interests of the planned.

Real collaborative planning requires accountability because the planned are now to be seen as citizens, customers, clients and stakeholders, rather than as the masses who have to be planned 'for' rather than 'with' (Reeves 2005). Statutory planning is now seen as a service, and one that must be shown to be efficient, economical and rapid. Therefore in this vein a series of initiatives have been introduced to speed up and improve the planning service, such as Audits and Best Value initiatives. Policy statements such as the Citizen's Charter have sought to provide guidance on this more accountable form of government service. But theory and practice are not necessarily in harmony, according to feedback from minority groups. Overall, more inclusionary and sensitive mechanisms of governance have been promoted. Emphasis is put upon developing webs of communication (Healey 1997, 58–9). But such are the barriers between planners and planned that, as Hillier states, the two groups tend to '*talk past each other*' even when they wish to communicate (Hillier 1999). Yet planners are now portrayed as communicators, networkers and facilitators. So the necessary skills to be a planner are those of communication and negotiation. But they are also, and conflictingly, required to be assessors, auditors and financial managers, in an audit culture in which everyone is now checking on everyone else. Needless to say, many minority-group individuals would argue that traditional planners are in no position to take on this more interactive, communicative role, having previously proved themselves incapable of communicating with ordinary people and having a very limited sociological background.

Coming up to the present day, one can see in the collaborative and institutionalist approaches to planning, a prefiguring of the neo-liberal ideas subsequently taken up by the Coalition government in terms of the Big Society, the New Localism and the active citizen. All of these concepts have the same problems associated with them, namely the differential levels of power possessed by different groups in society and the lack of time, resources and expertise found in many areas which are so necessary to enable the community to participate meaningfully in decision-making processes (Morphet 2010). Under the 2011 Localism Act, the concept of cooperation and collaboration has been taken even further, with adjacent local planning authorities being expected to cooperate with each other horizontally, as well as their being expected to collaborate and work with local communities vertically to produce the new Local Plans at neighbourhood and parish level (see Chapter 2).

Cultural geography meets planning theory

Planning theory is still undergoing change, and has been strongly influenced by the surrounding intellectual climate, as mediated through the work of urban geographers and cultural philosophers who are looking at the city with fresh eyes (Panelli 2004; Pacione 2009; Fainstein and Campbell 2011). In the Noughties (2000s) there has been a return to the importance of space, that is the physical built environment. But this time around it is conceptualised as a product or manifestation not just of social and economic factors, but cultural values too. You may remember that earlier on in the chapter, I referred to the work of Massey, Castells and Harvey on the concept of the reproduction over space of social relations, that is the ways in which social factors imprint themselves on the built environment, the city being seen as the end product of such aspatial forces (Massey 1984). One could be cynical and say that planning theory, like fashion, goes in cycles, and if you wait long enough a particular theory will come back into vogue, albeit in a somewhat different format. There seems to be no corporate memory or institutional knowledge within the profession, planners know little of their past, and so rehashes of old theories are often met as new revelations, when in fact someone has probably already written all about the new idea in question back in the 1930s or even 1850s!

Culture became a consideration in creating urban regeneration, with support for the arts and creative industries, and every provincial city undergoing renewal had to have its own iconic landmark building (Photo 8.2). But culture is now a key word in planning theory and theorists seem to be more influenced by the humanities than by science. Raymond Williams defines culture as a phenomenon (force) appertaining to a whole way of life, including material, intellectual and spiritual (Williams 1981). Culture may be defined as what is seen as normal and obvious in society, everywhere and nowhere like the sky (Barthes 1973). Having tired of scientific approaches to planning theory and North American theorists, there is now considerable interest in Continental European theory and philosophy. Planning theories have taken inspiration from the writings of the French philosophers Cixous, Foucault, Irigaray, Lacan, Bourdieu, Sartre and Lefebvre (Gunder 2009; Merrifield 2006). Please note, there is some unavoidable overlap here with the end of Chapter 14 on urban sociology, especially for Bourdieu (1970). Since the translation into English of the work of Henri Lefebvre, in particular *The Production of Space* (*La Production de l'espace*) and *The Right to the City* (*Le Droit à la Ville*) (Lefebvre 1991; Mitchell 2013), a whole new generation of urban theorists has taken an interest in his work. At a very practical level, following Lefebvre's concept of the right to the city being applied to the equality agenda by the Socialist government in 2013, one interesting example has been the decision to make all public toilets in the city free to both tourists and residents.

Lefebvre's work is quite complex (Lefebvre 1968, 1974). Lefebvre was originally a neo-Marxist, but he evolved into a situationist, that is a materialist realist (basically he was dealing with the real issues that confronted him rather than just theory). He is most well-known for his writings on the city, and especially for developing a Triad (Three Key Issues) relating to conceptualising space. Lefebvre distinguishes between social and physical space, as have many urban social geographers over the years (Panelli 2004). He is also concerned with the processes that create space, perceptions of space, representations of space, and the space people actually live in and how they imagine it to be (Qvistrom 2010).

Photo 8.2   Salford Quays Cultural Centre

Culture and other touchy-feely aspects of urban society were often neglected by planners in the past. In contrast, today arts and culture are seen as major ingredients in urban regeneration as here in Salford, near Manchester, where the Lowry Museum is housed.

The three factors in the Triad essential to understanding space are:

Spatial practice (perceived space), that is *l'espace perçu* = production and reproduction of space, that is process, empirical measurements of space

Representations of space (conceived space), that is *l'espace conçu* = conceptualisation, theory, abstract, but also plans, official documents, planning

Representational spaces (lived space), that is l'*espace vécu* = lived in spaces, actual spaces, social space, emotional space, everyday life, creative space, artistic space

Perhaps the third category, lived-in space, is the most interesting in that it relates to how people actually live in different spaces, how they create, adapt and relate to those spaces. Other theorists have been investigating the process of planning, and how control, regulation, zoning and conformity have been the main characteristics of planning, and have created formalised space, whereas others want to foster freedom, creativity, flexibility, positivity, ownership, *inter alia*, but also maybe some variety, chaos and difference within lived space (Qvistrom 2010; Hughes and Sadler 1999).

If this last section does not mean much to you, do not worry, but just be aware that such theories exist. One of the key attributes of planning theory is that it should be difficult and esoteric, that is understood by only a few, but that because it is elite knowledge it lends its weight to the status of the profession. In any case much of this will not be of much relevance to work in a local planning department, although you may need some of it to pass your planning theory exams. But the true value of theory is to get planners thinking about cities and urban space, in particular to help them appreciate how diverse

Photo 8.3   Which way the Frisbee?

Beware the Frisbee of life! What is the next new great idea, paradigm shift or theory that will catch us all unawares and influence future planning policy?

perceptions of space exist for different sorts of people. Planning policy and development plans cannot hope to approximate or encompass all this variety and complexity. But at least there is some hope, through public participation, consultation and a more collaborative approach to planning of developing an appreciation of different people's spatial needs and the cultural, emotional and social characteristics they associate with different types of spaces.

Indeed, the ideas of Lefebvre and other cultural geographers and urban philosophers chime well with the current emphasis upon seeing cities as places of culture (rather than just work), where the arts thrive and dynamic communities and distinct cultural quarters are encouraged, themes that are discussed further in Chapter 11 on urban regeneration and Chapter 13 on urban design, place-making and culture.

However, looking to the future, many feel that there is a danger that planning both as a government function and as a concept is under threat and this fear has generated a new spate of theories concerned with resistance, resilience, uncertainty, and a questioning of the given priorities and assumptions within existing planning theory. A much more subtle, less linear, more complex field of theory is now emerging. Much of the new theory is quite difficult to understand and readers who are interested should consult the May 2013 edition of the journal *Planning Theory and Practice* for a range of papers on the topic of resilience (for example, Davoudi 2012). But trends in planning theory can be fickle so who knows what will come next? (Photo 8.3.)

For the tasks, further reading, additional photos and other resources – including explanatory diagrams charting the development of planning theory particularly useful for this chapter – please visit www.palgrave.com/companion/greed.

PART III

The Scope of Modern Planning

9 Planning for the Countryside and other Green Areas

The rural realms of planning

This chapter provides, first, a background description of the historical development of the countryside, landscape and garden development, followed by an account of rural conservation policy, including the designation of large tracts of countryside as national parks or areas of outstanding natural beauty. The countryside may appear natural, unchanging and placid, but in fact it is subject to many forces, pressures and policy demands over the years. The chapter will look at large-scale landscape within rural areas and also at changes in domestic and urban garden design: both of which are manifestations of human intervention in, and 'planning' of, the natural environment (that is broadly non-built upon 'green areas'). En route, issues concerning farming, minerals, leisure, tourism, recreation, gardening and the coast (the seaside) will be touched upon (Photo 9.1).

In the course of this chapter we will inevitably not only look at policy issues but at the different sorts of people affected by planning policy. These include residents, farmers, business people and tourists, in terms of their livelihoods, housing, transport and environmental impact. Voluntary bodies and user groups campaigning for changes in policy will also be highlighted. So, as can be seen, rural planning is concerned with many of the issues with which urban planning is concerned, echoing parallel social, economic, physical, political, environmental and cultural dimensions. The urban and rural aspects of planning are always linked, and impact upon each other. The full titles of many planning acts include the words 'town and country planning' as one of the concerns of the planning system, established in 1947, has always been to control urban development in order to protect the countryside.

Country Life magazine, and television programmes such as *Escape to the Country*, may give the impression that everyone is rich in the countryside and lives in large houses. In reality many people living in villages and declining market towns suffer from rural deprivation, manifest in lack of local bus services, closure of shops and minimal medical, educational and social services provision as identified in the Taylor Review, entitled *Living Working Countryside: The Taylor Review of Rural Economy and Affordable Housing* (Taylor 2008) (Photo 9.1). The rural population contains a higher proportion of elderly people than the national average because of the popularity of countryside and coastal areas, such as in the South West, for retirement. But young families and local workers seeking housing in the countryside may find they are unable to afford a home there because of spiralling house prices fuelled by second-home ownership and people moving from London and other urban more expensive urban areas.

There are links between this chapter and several others. The countryside needs to be seen within the context of the environmental sustainability agenda discussed in Chapter 10, and to wider town and country planning policy considerations of land use, development, housing, green belt and urban containment. As explained in Chapter 1, the UK comprises a small set of islands in which land is very precious, and so protection of the countryside and of agriculture has always been important. Every square inch has been surveyed, scrutinised and carefully planned over the years. For example, in the 1960s the geographer Dudley Stamp undertook a national land-use survey of the countryside (Stamp and Coleman 1960; Stamp 1962).

Photo 9.1   The importance of agriculture

Post-war planning protected the countryside and assumed the farmer knew best. But even today, with so much food being imported, agriculture is still a major component of the economy, with much of the countryside being used for livestock grazing.

Historical development of the landscape

Much of what appears today to be natural in the countryside is in fact the result of human intervention. As the demand for greater planning control in the countryside, and especially conservation of what are imagined to be traditional natural features, increases, it becomes vitally important to understand the historical nature of the factors which have shaped the present-day countryside. There is hardly any part of Britain's landscape which has not been touched in some way by human activity, often more so than in the urban areas. Many complain about the removal of traditional field patterns and hedgerows, but in fact those hedgerows were not always there, and much of the land has been brought into cultivation either from forest or from heathland. Likewise there is much concern about wildlife habitats being destroyed as a result of the draining of the wetlands in Somerset and also of the fenlands in East Anglia, but again these only exist in their current form because of drainage schemes being built in the past, to which wild animals have adapted.

Before the Romans arrived, there was fairly limited cultivation in Britain, settlements tended to be on the higher land and lowlands were left undeveloped. One can still find many examples of hill forts, standing stones, ancient trackways (often aligned along ley lines), and earthworks from earlier times, some of which are protected as ancient monuments. The Romans had a tremendous impact on land use, urbanisation, road construction, land drainage, and cultivation patterns. The decline of the Roman Empire was followed by a series of invasions by European tribes, each contributing in their own way to farming and to place names and local cultures.

The Normans arrived in 1066, and established a programme of colonisation and plantation development. The land and society itself was divided up and organised on the basis of the feudal system. In the Middle Ages the population was over 80 per cent rural, mainly located in small villages with agricultural activity based on what was known as the three-field system of crop rotation, typically of wheat, barley and fallow, on a three-year cycle. Each peasant farmer had his own strips of land in each field within this framework. Increasingly the more remote areas were brought into cultivation by the monasteries who introduced sheep to the Pennines. Other improvements were made by the monks, for example the Abbots of Glastonbury in Somerset had Sedgemoor in Somerset drained. In those days, Britain was relatively peaceful, allowing expansion of agriculture into the more remote areas, whilst many other European countries were not as unified, with walled cities providing shelter from which the inhabitants would cautiously venture forth to tend the adjacent farmland.

By the Renaissance, greater emphasis was put upon horticulture, and gardens were increasingly designed for leisure purposes. The wealthier classes were able to turn their attention away from pure survival towards embellishing their houses and cultivating their estates. The rich city states in Italy contained formal gardens of huge dimensions, which were laid out according to classical architectural principles, purely for the pleasure of their owners, and as a sign of conspicuous consumption (wealth). Flowers and vegetables had little place in these gardens, and were relegated to the servants' area. These ideas spread to Britain, but had to compete with an already established traditional form of garden which was on a more intimate and functional scale, as typified by the Shakespearean knot gardens consisting of box hedges containing beds of herbs, flowers and vegetables.

There was a gradual move towards a more Grand Manner approach to gardening which in Britain took the form of the Landscape movement with its emphasis on earth modelling on a huge scale, creating lakes and vistas, accompanied by extensive tree planting. This was linked to the growth of the English country house set in its own grounds, without fortifications, and without the estate farm, kitchen gardens, or tenants in sight. There had always been a great interest in arboriculture (tree cultivation), as evidenced by the cultivation of the Royal forests of oak for ships and also as hunting parks. In 1664 John Evelyn wrote *Sylva* on tree cultivation which was highly influential (Evelyn 2013). Art and literature influenced people's ideas about the landscape too. Milton's poem, *Paradise Lost*, describes a beautiful natural wilderness. French artists, such as Claude, Poussin and Lorrain, painted 'naturalistic' landscapes, presenting an idyllic image of pastoral life. This romantic view of the countryside was chiefly for the upper class and bore little relationship to the harsh realities of farming for the ordinary people. In 1720 Bridgman designed a country estate at Stowe in Buckinghamshire in which he created '*a little gentle disorder*' as he put it, thus rejecting classical principles and purposely designing a more natural-looking layout.

One could look out of the windows of the Big House and see the pastoral landscape stretching into the distance with cows grazing and 'figures in the landscape', that is picturesque peasants going about their work. But they were prevented from straying up to the house by Bridgman's invention of a hidden ditch, which was called a 'ha-ha'. Other landscape architects of this time include William Kent who was, it is said, 'the first to leap over the fence and to show the whole of nature', and Lancelot Capability Brown, the most famous of the landscape gardeners responsible for schemes such as Blenheim Palace, and Longleat in Wiltshire. Humphrey Repton created a more contoured approach and incorporated artificial grottos and 'follies' (pretend ruins). In all these estates emphasis was put upon grass and trees and features in the landscape rather than on details of flowers and colours. But outside these developments, the countryside remained a patchwork of villages with their cottage gardens, and large communal fields, and open woodland beyond, prior to Enclosure taking place.

The Agricultural Revolution preceded the Industrial Revolution and was based on many innovations in agriculture by people such as Jethro Tull (1674–1741), Turnip Townsend who perfected crop rotation, and George III who was known as Farmer George. These changes increased yield whilst reducing labour. The need for larger units for efficient rotation, and the extension of sheep farming, led to the General Enclosure Acts of the early nineteenth century, further reducing grazing and common land rights for the rural population who increasingly migrated to the towns. The Industrial Revolution itself, and the urbanisation, canal and railway building, mining and factory development which accompanied it, had a major impact on land-use patterns, and created large amounts of derelict land, spoil tips and pollution.

The Victorians were keen gardeners. The science of horticulture and cross-breeding developed, accompanied by the introduction of exotic species from all corners of the Empire. Botanical gardens and greenhouses, such as Kew Gardens, became popular. Formal Victorian parks were developed in the new industrial towns for the people. These were characterised by formal beds containing flowers in primary colours, floral clocks as in Edinburgh, and also adjacent playing fields for recreation. Domestic gardening by individual households also became popular now that most people no longer worked on the land. The urban garden was a little bit of the countryside that people could enjoy within the new towns and cities. The development of the garden city movement enabled the provision of large individual flower gardens for each house for the masses. Those who lived in high density houses and flats might have no gardens but would usually be able to rent an allotment locally. Private gardens, playing fields, parks and other green space within towns and cities still constitute a considerable amount of 'urban countryside', providing refuge for birds and other wildlife, as well as providing a much needed relief from the pressures of urban life for humans. Together back gardens constitute an area the size of an average county, such as Dorset, and are also a source of wildlife, urban foxes, birds, newts, frogs, and all sorts that have escaped from the pesticide in the towns. Low-density suburban gardens can provide a more welcoming environment for wildlife than modern agricultural land with its lack of hedges and high use of chemicals.

Carefully designed cottage gardens for the more discriminating affluent members of society became fashionable, as popularised by the work of Gertrude Jekyll (1834–1932) (Massingham 1984) who in conjunction with Lutyens, the famous architect, developed several gardens around large country houses at the turn of the last century. Jekyll's hallmark was the use of subtle blue, silver and white flowers and foliage, as at Sissinghurst, and at Hestercombe in Somerset. In contrast, in the early twentieth century there were still landscape architects, such as Jellicoe, designing in the Grand Manner. Jellicoe even admitted he knew nothing at all about flowers but he was a founder of the Landscape Institute.

As the twentieth century developed, the emphasis upon the cultivation of individual domestic gardens, particularly in the suburbs, continued. The development of large new public parks was less common, although there were many sports facilities, and public recreational areas developed. In the post-war period, landscaping was required for municipal and public sector schemes, rather than for private estates. For example, landscaping for the new universities in the 1960s, the New Towns, and modern-day motorways, rather than for large individual houses, became the main career opportunities in the post-war period.

In more recent years a concern with the environment and nature, rural estate management, afforestation, and planning for recreation and leisure in the countryside are all leaving their mark on the nature of the countryside. Most large developments are 'landscaped' but if it is done well people will not even notice. There was also a tremendous growth of interest in gardening for the masses, as evidenced by the proliferation of television programmes, books and gardening centres. However, as a result of the environmental movement, and greater awareness of green issues, there has also been greater criticism of rural policy, and of the use of pesticides, and of so-called scientific 'modern' horticultural practices. In conclusion, it can be seen from this chapter, that neither urban nor rural areas are entirely natural; they are all the result of centuries of human activity and intervention.

State intervention in the countryside

Designated areas

This section outlines the main types of area control over the countryside with reference to the system created as part of post-war reconstruction, which still today structures the countryside, in terms of protection and rural conservation. All the areas described below have special controls over them in terms of getting planning permission, with strict controls on new housing development, so, in many ways, the situation is similar to that found in urban conservation areas (see Chapter 3).

Development control (planning law) is surprisingly limited in terms of control of development in the countryside itself. Many people believe that there should be controls on the use and development of farm buildings, field patterns, ponds and farm-related businesses, particularly in respect of industrial-type agricultural buildings such as silos and battery hen units. But many of these matters were deemed to be outside the scope of planning law when it was first developed, because of a belief in the post-war reconstruction era that food production was paramount and that 'the farmer knows best', which still broadly applies. Again it is a complex situation with a mixture of restrictions and freedoms. Rather than including details that might soon go out of date, it is recommended that readers check the current situation on the web on matters such as the construction of solar panels, wind farms, vast plastic cloches, and other man-made manifestations that farmers are increasingly keen to cover their fields with, as a more profitable crop than food or animals. You may also find it useful to check the National Farmers Union (NFU) website and the views of other agricultural groups on these matters. In contrast, there are very strict controls on house-building in the countryside, and on non-agricultural building in the countryside.

National Parks

Post-war reconstruction planning was more concerned with keeping the town out of the countryside, and protecting remote and scenic areas from development, than with worrying about extending development control to cover the activities of farmers. The provisions of the Agricultural Act 1947 were based on the assumption that the farmer knows best and should not be hindered in increasing agricultural production by any means. There were demands from the urban population, and from pressure groups such as the Ramblers Association, to open up the countryside more for recreational purposes.

The National Parks and Access to the Countryside Act 1947, as its name suggests, set up a series of National Parks and also opened up a series of footpath networks throughout the countryside. At present there are over 118,000 miles of footpaths and bridleways to which the general public have access, with footpaths comprising the majority with a total length of 91,000 miles (146,000 km). In particular coastal footpaths already exist over around a third of England's coastline, with much work previously being undertaken by the National Trust, through the Enterprise Neptune programme from the 1960s, to open up coastal areas.

The National Parks were administered by ad hoc bodies, by means of joint boards and committees, and overseen by the National Parks Commission. In 1968 this became the Countryside Commission with a broader role, including within its ambit concern for agriculture, leisure, recreation and landscape, as well as the National Parks (Countryside Commission 1990). In the post-war period car ownership was low and some areas were still fairly inaccessible by road, and so the Bank Holiday traffic jams found on Dartmoor or the Lake District were not dreamt of in those far-off days. The aim of the National Parks was to preserve the natural beauty of the countryside and provide access for the general public, along the lines of the recommendations of the Scott, Dower, and Hobhouse Reports, and so were part of the overall national land-use planning strategy of the post-war period described in Chapter 6. The initial designation in the 1940s concentrated mainly on mountainous and moorland areas. Subsequently, less remote areas such as the Norfolk Broads (1989), New Forest (2005) and South Downs (2010) were added. For a complete list, look at the National Parks website.

As noted in Chapter 2, the National Parks now have independent plan-making powers and are comparable to local authorities in terms of being required to produce development plans and currently Local Plans, and in operating a full development management system. However under the 2011 Localism Act, National Park Authorities are now required to have a higher level of cooperation and liaison with the counties and districts which they overlay in developing Core Strategies. One should be aware that the situation is complex and not necessarily the same for each National Park, with some having additional delegated planning powers, and controls over minerals extraction and infrastructural developments. Each National Park has its own website but make sure you put the word 'planning' into your search to avoid landing on local tourist websites.

AONBs

The 1949 Act also established Areas of Outstanding Natural Beauty (AONBs), which are smaller, more accessible areas than the National Parks, e.g. the Quantock Hills in Somerset. Seventy-five per cent grants were made available to the local authorities whose job it was to administer them for maintenance and improvement of amenities, and they still benefit from a range of grants and subsidies. Both in National Parks and AONBs there are strict planning controls on new and existing development. This is comparable to the situation in urban conservation areas. (For legal details see Cullingworth and Nadin 2006.) The overall principle is to be aware that the government over the years has introduced an increasingly complex range of 'special areas' in the countryside and a complex range of planning controls.

Country Parks

Continuing pressure for rural recreation, combined with growth in car ownership, led eventually to another category of special area being introduced in 1968 under the Countryside Act. This followed the recommendations of the White Paper, *Leisure in the Countryside* (1967), which marked a change of attitude in putting more emphasis on non-agricultural uses and ecology in the countryside. Country Parks are meant to enable people to enjoy the countryside

without having to travel too far, to ease pressure on remote and solitary places and reduce risk of damage to the countryside. This was achieved by creating small, managed park areas near to urban concentrations with ample provision of car parks, toilets and amenities such as picnic sites and transit sites for campers and caravans. Local authorities received 75 per cent grants from central government to create Country Parks, which were seen as 'honey pots' drawing people away from a more dispersed use of the countryside. The building of car parks and public toilets in the Country Parks was seen as a means of attracting people out motoring. (Incidentally, the Countryside Act is the only piece of planning legislation requiring public toilet provision, a point which will be of significance when we discuss the social aspects of planning in Part IV.)

SSSIs

Greater emphasis was increasingly put upon the need for protection of smaller 'special' areas within the countryside, for example where a rare wild flower, or species of butterfly, was found. Under the 1949 Act provision had been made for the identification of Sites of Special Scientific Interest (SSSI). But it was not until the 1980s that greater awareness of SSSIs developed among both the public and affected landowners, as a result of the environmental movement, and they came under the control of the Nature Conservancy Council. Many of these sites were right in the middle of farmland and it was difficult to enforce these controls, indeed a site could be ploughed up before anyone even realised. Farmers were however given compensation for the loss of their right to farm parts of their land where SSSIs were located. Such sites could also be endangered by careless tourists, and according to the Department of the Environment (in 1991) by the increasing popularity of war games! Greater controls were introduced both for SSSIs themselves and also Nature Reserves, and a range of other ecological issues under the 1981 Wildlife and Countryside Act and the 1990 Environmental Protection Act. In fact, as time has gone on, there have been so many environmental and sustainability-related measures covering the 'ecosphere' as a whole, that the idea of separating off special little areas for extra protection

Photo 9.2   Nibbling away at the green belt

There may appear to be lots of land, according to the Coalition, that can be built upon, but in reality many of the previously protected areas around cities are very vulnerable to new housing development, and along with this comes more infrastructural work, roads, sewers, and all the other trappings of civilisation that further eat up our surroundings.

may be seen as somewhat dated, albeit still necessary. There are a vast number of EU directives and regulations on water, wildlife, flora, fauna, and so forth, which would fill a book in themselves, so check updates on the internet (and see Chapter 9 on sustainability).

Green belts

Around the edges of urban areas there are additional controls within the ambit of the green-belt legislation. Green belts were given a new impetus in the 1960s by Duncan Sandys, the Conservative minister then responsible for town planning under Section 4 of the Town and Country Planning Act 1962, and

have gone from strength to strength ever since. Green belts are not designated for their landscape value, but to prevent urban sprawl in areas of development pressure, but, more broadly, they have also been seen as the 'green lungs of the city', and as having recreational and agricultural value.

The idea of the green belt was popularised by Ebenezer Howard (see Chapter 5), although earlier historical versions existed for military, religious and agricultural purposes (Elson 1986). Howard had a more social and functional approach to the green belt. He located agricultural smallholdings, 'asylums' (hospitals) and recreational uses in his green belt circling the Garden City, but in general he envisaged the green belt to be much more agricultural than the present-day version. In the present day, substantial parts of approved green belts are not really very green, more 'brown' with a whole diversity of gravel workings, glass houses, and infill sites. Green belts, of which there are 15 in all in England, contain 20 per cent of all agricultural land and constitute 13 per cent of the land area of England. Certain uses are seen as being suitable for green-belt location, such as golf courses along with hotels and leisure facilities. Golf courses are one of the largest sports land uses in the country (area-wise), covering both outer urban locations and 'links' coastal locations; but they are only used by a relatively small proportion of the population. Although green belts are intended to be permanent, occasionally bits are chipped away on their inner circumference, and extensions to the green belt are not infrequently made on the outer edge (Elson 1986; Herrington 1984). In fact in recent years there have been tremendous battles to develop in the green belt and to protect the green belt (Photo 9.2) and other 'extra-urban' and 'edge city' locations (Garreau 1991), where town meets country.

White land

White land is an old-fashioned term with no legal significance. It just means land that was not designated a particular land use under the old style of development plan. White land is also referred to as undesignated land. It is often on the inside edge of the green belt. Developers saw these areas as ideal for housing, and in some cases the government appeared to go along with this presumption in the past. Most white land areas have subsequently been covered by development plan policies. In addition there are often wedges of white land marooned on the urban–rural interface which would cut into the countryside if developed. For example, awkward little bits are often left between the edge of an urban area and a passing motorway: a prime site for development if there is also a motorway intersection nearby. Motorways cut right through established green belts often attract a corridor of planning applications alongside their path. Some would argue that green belts do not prevent development in any case. All that happens is that development 'leapfrogs over the green belt', leading to a second ring of housing,

and greater commuting distances for its inhabitants further out into the countryside (Pahl 1965; Newby 1982). Arguably, with some relaxation of planning controls under the Coalition government, any left-over bits of land that have not been designated are up for grabs by developers looking for land to build housing, out-of-town retail, and business parks, in spite of New Labour putting great emphasis on using up brown land first within urban areas (see Chapter 7). Even village greens are under threat, but, until recently, it was possible to register existing ones and to create new ones as protected space. But this right can be used, some would say inappropriately, to block unwanted development. For example, a village green was created and registered, giving protected status, right in the middle of the proposed location of the new Bristol City football ground in Long Ashton on the edge of Bristol. Subsequently under the Growth and Infrastructure Act 2013 the Coalition reversed this right, because of its determination to push through new development and related infrastructural schemes. Some would say this top-down approach does not sit well with the Coalition's previous support for local-level planning and community empowerment.

Conflicts in the countryside

Different ministries

There has always been controversy about the role of public bodies and private owners within the countryside (Norton-Taylor 1982). The situation has not been helped by the way in which different rural planning functions have been divided up between different ministries. The Department of Communities and Local Government has overall national planning control, but other government departments also have a major role to play. For example, previously the Ministry of Agriculture, Fisheries and Food (MAFF), which was replaced in 2001 by the Department for Environment, Food and Rural Affairs (DEFRA), has in its various incarnations had a major role to play in shaping agriculture and rural land use. Arguably, there is currently greater concern for the needs of the general public as consumers of farm produce, as visitors to the countryside, and as citizens concerned with the environment and ecology, than with farmers and agriculture.

The MAFF, for example, gave grants for ploughing up the moorlands, and for the grubbing out of hedgerows, as was common, for example, in the 1970s, contrary to the policies of other government departments (Shoard 1981). (MAFF was subsequently amalgamated into DEFRA along with the Food Standards Agency (FSA) within the division concerned with agriculture and food production.) Recent governments have attempted to take into account more the links between agricultural production, food quality and environmental concerns and to address policy mistakes of the past. In the past subsidies to promote industrialised farming methods led to the creation of prairie-like, flat scape created in some lowland areas, and the subsequent demise of various species of wildlife. All this was done in theory to increase food production, but until relatively recently there were much criticised food mountains, and wine lakes, in warehouses within the European Union as politicians sought artificially to keep the price of produce high (Shoard 1987). Indeed debates about CAP (Common Agricultural Policy) and of subsidies and artificial controls on food production within the EU continue although much-promised reforms are being introduced from 2013. But, regardless of EU problems, UK food production now needs to be put within the context of international trade, as much of our food is freighted in by air, being grown in developing countries where labour and production costs are low. So one can eat anything at any time of the year, regardless of seasonal availability, and this has decimated many of the traditional fruit and vegetable growers and often undercut UK producers economically.

Rural social change

Once upon a time farming was very important and many people worked in agriculture, and this was how the plan-makers saw the world during the post-war reconstruction period, during which the foundations of the modern planning system were laid down. With increased agricultural mechanisation, Massey Ferguson tractors etc., people abandoned rural villages to move to towns for work and decline set in. In the 1960s, because of the decline in rural population, some county planning authorities, such as Durham, had designated villages to 'die' as Category D villages, the view being that it was better to concentrate resources in the more populated Category A villages, and not invest further in Category D villages. The process of rural decline had been precipitated by the Beeching cuts to the national railway system in the 1960s when many branch railway lines and stations in rural areas had been closed (Beeching Report 1963). Houses in similar villages nowadays are expensive, very sought after for retirement and second-home purchase.

But by the 1970s population growth and change was occurring in the countryside. Mainly middle-class urbanites were attracted to country living and the availability of cheap cottages that they could do up and still be able to commute by car to work in the city. In 1981 the Census showed for the first time that rural villages were actually gaining population rather than suffering from migration. When the availability of rural dwellings began to dry up they moved on to farm buildings and a spate of barn conversions began. This created problems for the planners as technically any new or converted residential building in the countryside had to be occupied by proper agricultural workers. People have spent years trying to find ways around the controls on residential development in the countryside, there being several examples of spurious agricultural workers, and people building rather large 'stables' complete with horse which can easily be converted into a house, thus getting around restrictions on house-building on farmland. But less than 1.5 per cent of the population work in the countryside and seasonal crop-picking requirements are augmented by the labours of temporary and migrant workers.

Many people have since moved into the countryside, either to retire, or because with the development of the motorway system they are happy to commute longer distances to work. It is the fashionable thing to do and television programmes like *A House in the Countryside* promote the rural idyll. Ironically, although the properties may be wonderful, many of the local facilities and shops in villages are in decline, or have closed completely. Whilst many villages have subsequently experienced 'rural gentrification' as new affluent householders move in, those without cars in the countryside are suffering from 'rural deprivation' because of lack of public transport, local shops, closure of post offices, pubs, churches and community facilities which can be as devastating as the deprivation experienced by their urban cousins. Many low-income people in rural areas felt compelled to move out, particularly young couples who could not possibly compete with the newcomers in the housing market. Also the retirement of many elderly people to the countryside and the seaside puts considerable burdens on local health and care services. Even affluent people have suffered telecommunications deprivation in the countryside, as some remote rural areas still lack decent broadband speeds or indeed any internet access at all. Mobile phone signals are available across most of the country but still there are areas of bad reception in the countryside in spite of carefully disguised radio masts in the countryside (on church steeples and masquerading as tall trees) (Stewart Report 2000; Askew 2009). The Sustainable Communities Act introduced by New Labour in 2007 has sought to strengthen and support local communities, including rural ones, and is, in a sense, a precursor to aspects of the 2011 Localism Act. The Coalition government has introduced rural social enterprise grants to help local businesses, which in a sense are the rural counterpart of business enterprise initiatives (and zones) in the cities.

In parallel many traditional seaside areas are not only attracting the elderly but they themselves are in decline, and many of the country's piers have fallen into disrepair. On the other hand there is growing demand for more recreational access to the coastline, through footpaths skirting the entire coast, and for unspoiled natural areas to be preserved. Under the 2009 Marine and Coastal Access Act, the previous government was committed to improving access to the coastline. In 2010 the Coalition government introduced the Coastal Access Scheme with the objective of creating a continuous footpath around our coasts to be administered by Natural England. Implementation is already underway 'filling in the gaps' in Somerset, Kent, Norfolk, East Riding and Cumbria.

Housing in the countryside

In the past most village housing was occupied by locals, especially those in agriculture. Availability of housing was reduced by the planners' policies of restricting growth in rural settlements to limited infill. Subsequently under the Conservatives in the 1970s and 1980s greater freedom was given for a 'presumption in favour of development' within the planning system, and Circulars 14/84 on Green Belts, 15/84 on Land for Housing, and 22/84 on Structure Plans and Local Plans set policy directives which leaned towards allowing development in the urban–rural fringe. But there were still many restrictions and much opposition at local plan level to more housing in the countryside. Indeed it was often the local Conservative councillors and affluent residents on the local planning committees that opposed development in their villages as they feared that their areas would be swamped by townies. What was needed was not just more housing, but affordable housing for those who had been priced out of the local housing market.

Planning law sought to ensure that any new housing built on farmland had to be occupied by agricultural workers. But with the surge of gentrification many local people were priced out of the market by incomers, many of whom are second-home owners. There is no provision in planning law for specifying the tenure or category of occupants of housing developments. But attempts have been made at tenure control on Exmoor, Somerset, restricting second homes as a form of development (which has proved a controversial planning law issue). However, Circular 7/91 *Planning and Affordable Housing* stated the provision of low-cost rural housing for *local* needs should be taken as a material consideration in development control. Even if people can get low-cost housing in the countryside they still need shops, schools and jobs. Employment, for some, might consist of working the night-shift in the local chicken processing plant – which hardly ties in with the romantic ideal of agricultural life. Subsequent PPG3s (and subsequently PPS3) on Housing further elaborated this aspect of tenure control, and the issue remains controversial. Likewise the Environment Agency includes sustainability within its policy agenda (Chapter 10).

Under New Labour from the 1990s, the need to build more houses became a major priority, with the Barker Commission stating that 4 million new dwellings were needed nationally over the next 20 years. Much of this development was to take place on brown-field and infill sites and at relatively high densities. As explained in Chapters 2 and 7, this policy was to be implemented via a new regional level of planning, which would allocate specific numbers of housing to be built in each region. As a result many market towns, small country towns and large villages found that they were expected to build more houses, and generally to locate them as 'infill' at higher densities than the surrounding properties (as specified in PPS3, which stressed the use of high-density brown-land infill). This might have been appropriate in London or Birmingham but proved controversial in many rural settlements, being a challenge to historic village layout patterns, established densities and vernacular design principles. PPS3 (now cancelled) applied to all areas, both urban and rural, resulting in accusations of town cramming, such as in Dorset where there is no need for more housing and probably no jobs either. Likewise in Wiltshire a high percentage of the population are already retired, and so both employment and housing strategies were quite inappropriate. In contrast the development of purpose-built, accessibly-designed rural retirement villages may be more appropriate in meeting such housing needs.

Subsequently, the Coalition government abolished the regional level of planning and handed backed the decision as to how many houses should be built and where, to the local planning authorities themselves. In fact the Coalition appeared to be in favour of reviving the new town idea, albeit in a privatised form, concentrating new development in purpose-built small towns with modern services and facilities rather than dotting housing about in existing settlements. There has been talk of building such developments on the green belt and reducing and reconfiguring the green belt in areas of population pressure around the main conurbations, and even to use up another 3 per cent of rural land for housing.

The Localism Act 2011 put considerable emphasis upon the role of parish councils in producing neighbourhood plans, and it is in rural areas where local government is most likely to be 'parished', with administrative areas often corresponding to village boundaries. However, rural areas are also some of the most contentious when it comes to battles over house-building and so Neighbourhood Plan proposals are more likely to be concerned with controlling, or limiting, rather than welcoming new development. Indeed there are many pre-existing approved plans and policies regarding rural development, such as Village Design Statements, village fence policies, and previous Action Area, Conservation, and Traffic Plans. All of these may be seen as the building blocks to be utilised in the new Neighbourhood Plans. Parish Plans, themselves, can also feed into Neighbourhood Plans, but are, as originally proposed, statutory plans in their own right. Ironically the new localism legislation has increased parish-level 'general powers' (see Chapter 2). But at the same time many parishes simply have no money to implement policies, or to provide local amenities and facilities, although, in theory at least, CIL (Community Infrastructure Levy) should benefit them (DCLG 2011b). But, it is significant that many of the front-runners in the production of Neighbourhood Plans are rural authorities, such as Backwell, a village in Somerset (see www.backwell-pc.gov.uk/backwell-draft-neighbourhood-plan), Upper Eden in Cumbria, and Much Wenlock in Shropshire. Policy issues in such locations are generally concerned with making more housing available to locals, with provision of local shops, schools and other amenities, and also with ensuring that broadband facilities are available to villagers, as the digital divide has badly disadvantaged many rural areas.

Environmental movements

One of the reasons building more housing in the countryside became more acceptable from the 1970s onwards was because many believed farmland was no longer needed and the countryside was becoming redundant. Less land was considered to be needed for agricultural production, because of the enormous surpluses of farmland which had built up in the EU as a whole. By the 1990s in the United Kingdom 2.5 million acres, that is an area the size of Devon and Cornwall, were seen as no longer needed for agriculture (Gilg 1999). This was a very different situation from the post-war period when the government put great emphasis upon the UK being self-sufficient in food because of the experience of the Germans blockading ships bringing food imports in from the Commonwealth.

From the early 1970s, a growing environmental movement challenged this assumption of overproduction and less need for farmland. This was also the time when Friends of the Earth was establishing itself as a pressure group. Environmental issues were first coming to the fore in the media, and journals such as *The Ecologist* were established. In 1972 *Blue Print for Survival*, a foundational environmental document, was published (Goldsmith 1972) which argued for better use of the Earth's resources, and a removal of artificial market controls on food production and distribution. Please refer to Chapter 10 for the continuing story of the growth of environmentalism and the demand for sustainability and the influence on planning policy.

The emphasis gradually shifted from seeking to protect the countryside for the sake of agricultural productivity to protecting it for its own sake as an environmental resource, and as landscape and habitat. Farmers felt they were being expected to take on the role of park keepers rather than food producers (Haskin 2003). Farmers increasingly entered into land management agreements in relation to the preservation of certain sites for which they are compensated. Related to this, 'set aside' policy, derived from controversial EU policy, enables farmers to take land 'out' of agricultural use – and be paid to do so – with the proviso that interim uses should not in the long term negate the return of land to full agricultural use. UK and EU taxation and agricultural subsidies policies affect what the farmers grow, or whether they grow anything at all. The 'green and pleasant land' of the countryside may appear far from green, as farmers grow whatever crops catch the subsidies, such as what look like inland seas of blue linseed in early summer, preceded by yellow deserts of rape seed in late spring, plus miles of plastic sheeting.

Of course environmentally sustainable uses of the countryside are not necessarily attractive in the traditional sense, as many farmers are very keen to use their fields for wind farm development, with huge wind vanes, and an equally impactful change in terms of roads, construction sites and cabling at ground level. As indicated above, some farmers make more money covering their fields in acres of solar panels rather than actually growing any crops. Those who do grow crops may not be doing so for

human consumption but to provide the raw plant material for bio-energy generation that may one day provide an alternative to petrol. Even pleasant fields of apparently traditional crops may not be as they appear, but rather they may comprise GM (genetically modified) produce. Currently the establishment of test sites has caused great opposition, not least because of fears of the impact on surrounding organic farmers' land and the declining bee, butterfly and insect population (as predicted by Rachel Carson in *Silent Spring* (Carson 1962). Whilst one still sees the traditional scene of cows and sheep grazing in fields, in fact there has been a massive movement of animals indoors, not just chickens and pigs, but currently there are applications for 'super-farms' on a North American scale where the animals are intensively farmed and stay indoors all year. On the more positive side there has been a growth in organic farming and animal husbandry and increased animal welfare controls on factory farming methods. This is to be welcomed in recreating natural habitats and woodlands lost in during past phases of farm modernisation.

Some farmers have given up growing crops or keeping livestock altogether. In the 1980s further relaxation of controls was proposed to enable farmers to carry out countryside-related businesses to enable them to stay on their farms. Circular 16/87 *Development Involving Agricultural Land* and PPG7 *Rural Enterprise and Development* reflect this new philosophy, and farmers were encouraged to diversify within the rural economy. Business activities were still meant to be related to agriculture. There is a fine dividing line between selling home-produced jams in a farm shop, and setting up an industrial plant on the farm: although some saw the latter as a logical progression, and argued that such industrial activities would also ease rural unemployment. Increasingly, farmers have diversified into all sorts of different business activities, and have latched on to the tourist market in providing farmyard attractions and children's play facilities, and agricultural museums and all sorts. All this provides a good day out for the highly mobile modern car-borne family. The leisure industry has grown in parallel with increased car ownership, affluence and mobility within society. But rather than this leading to greater levels of recreational activity in the countryside itself, people are more likely to head for heritage-based locations, leisure parks with children's facilities, and special interest activities. Indeed many prefer to use their leisure going shopping in out-of-town retail developments, such as Clark's Village near Glastonbury in Somerset.

Countryside bodies

The Countryside Commission

There are many other governmental and voluntary government bodies which have a continuing impact on the nature of the countryside, but are 'above' or separate from the main planning system, but which still have an input to the process of property development and upon economic and employment policy in the countryside. In recent years these rural bodies have increasingly emphasised the importance of both the environmental and the social aspects of the countryside, as against simply supporting the farmers. As will be seen, some of the bodies named in this section were superseded by more modern versions, but their foundational work is still so influential that they are worthy of discussion.

For example, the Countryside Commission (1999–2006) operated under the auspices of the DoE, and produced two significant documents reflecting a new more entrepreneurial strategy towards development in the countryside, namely *Shaping a New Countryside* in 1987, and *Planning for a Greener Countryside* in 1989. The Commission believed that the old reason for adopting a negative restrictive approach to development in the countryside, namely shortage of agricultural land, no longer held good in the light of changing economic circumstances. There was a need for acceptance of the principle of some development in the countryside provided it was done in a constructive and controlled manner. This approach raises the question of whether development in the countryside can actually enhance the rural scene with suitable landscaping. The Countryside Commission proposed that green belts should be seen as having a wider purpose and be viewed more positively in their own right. The government produced a consultation paper early in 1991 which proposed that fewer limitations should be put on the re-use of redundant buildings such as

mental homes and hospitals in the green belt. For example, business uses would be acceptable provided the development fitted in to the 'footprint' of the existing building stock and site layout.

The Countryside Commission also recommended that the idea of new settlements in the countryside should be viewed more positively and has been, to a degree, in favour of accepting more 'urban' development in the countryside, provided adequate design and landscaping measures are guaranteed. But it has also emphasised the importance 'greening of the city' in the sense of bringing the countryside into the town, thus breaking down the urban/rural dualism further. The creation of new 'countryside' on derelict land is suggested and also the development of new urban forests on the edge of cities. Special areas for horses might also be considered, indeed there is already a thriving unofficial 'horsiculture' sector on the edges of many cities, providing grazing and shelter for ponies and horses. Many of these proposals and issues remained on hold under the New Labour government. Increased pressure from environmental groups and demands for the creation of sustainable agriculture and rural communities have all further politicised the situation. By the late 1990s rural communities, farmers' organisations and pro-hunt groups were mobilising to protect what they saw as the 'traditional rural way of life'. However, this lifestyle was hit by several events in the new millennium: the foot and mouth outbreak in 2002, which prevented the movement of livestock and severely affected many farms, and the abolition of fox hunting with hounds in 2005.

English Heritage is the government's statutory adviser on the historic environment. Officially known as the Historic Buildings and Monuments Commission for England, they are an executive Non-Departmental Public Body sponsored by the Department for Culture, Media and Sport. Their principal powers and responsibilities are set out in the 1983 National Heritage Act. English Heritage, although mainly responsible for conservation and listed buildings, was also producing key countryside policy documents, such as *Countryside Quality Counts* in 2004, and *Heritage Counts* in 2005. It was also a longstanding supporter of sustainability (English Heritage 1994). New voluntary groups were also being established such as the Countryside Alliance.

This brought together a range of country interest groups to combat the perceived anti-rural bias of New Labour. In part this was because DEFRA (compared with the old MAFF) was seen as putting more emphasis upon the consumerist viewpoint on food production 'from farm to fork' rather than promoting the traditional agricultural farmers' interests. New Labour also sought to promote the rights of poorer residents in the countryside (as against just farmers) and promoted 'Social Justice for All' in combating rural deprivation. Even within apparently wealthy groups such as landowners and farmers there may be considerable variation in incomes (asset rich, income poor) according to market situations. Also variations may occur on the basis of gender, age and family structure. For example, not all farmers are male (Little 1999). Events far away can affect farming incomes, for example it is only recently that those Welsh hill farmers have had restrictions on their land lifted, arising from the nuclear explosion in Chernobyl in Russia over 20 years ago. In contrast, most hill farmers do receive EU subsidies, so it is swings and roundabouts. Therefore one must be very careful when discussing farmers, farming policy and planning controls on the countryside not to succumb to generalised media images of who farmers are and what they do, as there is considerable local, regional and demographic variation amongst their numbers.

From Countryside Agency to Natural England

The Countryside Commission was merged with the Rural Development Commission in 1999, creating a new statutory body called the Countryside Agency, tasked with conserving and enhancing the countryside, but also spreading social and economic opportunity to the people who live within it. Under New Labour, the Haskin Report (2003), entitled *Review of Rural Delivery Arrangements*, looked at the various bodies responsible for countryside policy and management and led to the creation of Natural England. This was formed in 2006 under the Natural Environment and Rural Communities Act 2006 by bringing together English Nature, and the landscape, access and recreation aspects of the Countryside Agency, and the environmental land management functions of the Rural development Agency.

Natural England's aims are to work for people, places and nature, and to enhance biodiversity, landscapes and wildlife in rural, urban, coastal and marine areas, to promote access, recreation and public well-being, and to contribute to the sustainable management of natural resources so they can be enjoyed by future generations. In all these worthy policy objectives, access to the countryside (and to urban parks) for people with disabilities needs to be taken into account too. Many of these objectives were initially reinforced in PPSs produced under New Labour, such as PPS7 Sustainable Development in Rural Areas (2004), and PPS9 Biological Diversity and Geological Conservation (2005) and previously Coastal Planning (PPG20 in 1992). These documents were cancelled in 2011, as were all PPGs and PPSs, and replaced with the National Planning Policy Framework (NPPF) which still stresses sustainability but gives far less attention to the countryside.

New Labour also created the Commission for Rural Communities in 2005 which was formed as part of the Countryside Agency with a focus on disadvantaged rural settlements, acting as an advocate for rural people, businesses and communities, giving expert advice, and acting as an independent watchdog. Under the Coalition these policies have continued, and it is significant that the NPPF has very little to say about rural issues specifically, as the emphasis within that document is generally upon urban issues. However, there has been a move towards a relaxation of planning controls on the use of agricultural buildings. From 30 May 2013, agricultural buildings up to 500 square metres are covered by Permitted Development rights, allowing them to be converted to a variety of alternative commercial uses, such as shops (A1), restaurants and cafes (A3), hotels (C1), light industrial (B1), offices (B1) or storage (B8), without the need to apply for planning consent for the change of use.

Forestry Commission

The Forestry Commission, which owns 2 million acres of land, has had a powerful role in protecting the countryside, but is currently subject to being broken up for privatisation. However, the Forestry

Commission's preference for coniferous, rather than native broadleaf, trees has been the cause of much criticism from environmentalists in the past, especially since native species provide habitat for indigenous wildlife. On private land likewise tax incentives encouraged landowners to plant coniferous rather than deciduous trees. Much re-afforestation consists of miles and miles of unnatural standardised plantation only relieved by linear fire breaks. On the positive side, there have been attempts to support the restoration of ancient and historical woodlands and the related habitats for local fauna, such as brown squirrels, as people appreciate the value of such areas. There has also been a series of urban forests developed, and a strong emphasis on new tree planting as part of sustainability policy. For example, the Olympic Park was carefully landscaped using native species.

Statutory Bodies

Various statutory undertakers, including electricity and water authorities in the past, have had the right to develop in protected rural areas. Water authorities have been infamous for 'screening' their reservoirs with trees, and painting everything 'green' which draws even more attention to the developments. The situation has not improved markedly with the privatisation of utilities, and, for example, there has been a decline in the attention to the clearing out of all the little water courses on the Pennines in the North; and to 'keetching the rhynes' on Sedgemoor, in the lowlands of Somerset. Arguably, lack of such maintenance contributes both to falling water levels in reservoirs and unseasonal flooding.

Under Thatcher a major programme of privatisation of state providers began and has continued, so most of the utility undertakers are now run by private businesses. Nevertheless they are still subject to planning controls, and also frequently the subject of environmental group protests. Because of concerns about the visual impact on the countryside, electricity companies are now routing many cables underground, particularly in environmentally sensitive areas. But in the days of nationalisation the Electricity Board was notorious for building pylons right across the landscape. Advances in technology and the development of the internet have resulted in

a whole new range of planning issues and conflicts regarding mobile masts and broadband connections. In fact around 20 per cent of the population, mainly in rural areas, lack any, let alone fast, broadband connections. Leaving the task of creating a national broadband grid to the private sector is not wise. It is likely to result in a concentration of services in more populated, and thus profitable, areas, and very low speeds in rural areas. Arguably, an emphasis upon profit, efficiency and cost-cutting usually results in hard-to-reach rural areas receiving a lower level of service and utility coverage.

Other bodies that affect the countryside include the MoD. As stated in Part I, the Ministry of Defence (MoD) owns over 90,000 acres of forestry and also they own vast amounts of land, for example over 10 per cent of Wiltshire is MoD property.

Voluntary bodies and user groups

In this section some of the main pressure groups and rural interest bodies are briefly covered because of their importance in shaping the countryside, both through direct landownership and through campaigning.

Landowners and farmers

The Country Landowners Association, which was founded in 1926, is a powerful pressure group supporting the needs of its members which no doubt influences legislation through its historic links with the House of Lords, and with the National Farmers Union (NFU). In 1986 it produced 'Land: New Ways to Profit: a handbook of alternative enterprises' which echoed many of the government's own proposals. The emphasis in this document is more on clay pigeon shooting and golf courses than on small farm shops or crafts.

National Trust

The National Trust, founded in 1895 (Gaze 1988), is completely independent of the government but has a powerful role in countryside matters, and in the protection of both individual houses and areas of landscape. The National Trust, and other such groups, have become much more politicised, for example over the question of the abolition of fox hunting. In 1999 a huge demonstration march took

Photo 9.3   Tourist pressures: volcano

With increased affluence and leisure time, everyone is travelling everywhere, and historical sites are constantly under threat of numbers. Note the warning sign from this site in New Zealand threatens Divine Retribution for misbehaviour!

place in London, composed of members of a wide range of countryside pressure groups, including farmers and landowners, to protest against what they saw as increasing pressures on their livelihoods and the rural community.

Enterprise Neptune is a branch of the National Trust which offers protection to over a third of the coastline. The Council for the Protection of Rural England (CPRE) was founded in 1926 and seeks to campaign for the preservation of rural amenities and scenery. There are many other local voluntary bodies which all play their part in influencing policy at both the central and local government level. In recent years, urban bodies concerned with food production and prices from the shoppers' viewpoint have also had an increasing influence on rural matters, and in particular the National Consumers Association (which produces *Which Magazine*).

Access groups

Ramblers groups are constantly vigilant concerning the maintenance and extension of access to the countryside through a national footpath system. The Open Spaces and Footpaths Preservation Society, founded in 1865, the Youth Hostels Association, and the Ramblers Association continue to press for better access. Farmers, on the other hand, express concern about the damage that dogs can do to flocks and seek to control the general public walking over standing crops. The effects of human attrition can be even greater on internationally important sites, be they mountains, lakes or volcanos (Photo 9.3).

Environmental groups

Many environmental groups such as Friends of the Earth, and the Soil Association, are concerned about the use of chemical fertilisers and pesticides on crops. Animal welfare groups, including the long-respected Royal Society for Prevention of Cruelty to Animals (RSPCA), are concerned about factory-farming methods, and the quality of life of farm animals in general, especially battery hens. Also, in respect of pet animals, welfare groups are concerned about the increasing trend to ban dogs from public parks and beaches. This policy contributes to the likelihood of dogs being locked in hot cars on family outings, a potential cause of death. Whilst this is understandable because of perceived health hazards to young children, it reduces domestic animals' access to the countryside. (Farmers have already put increasing numbers of farm animals inside.) If there is meant to be a surplus of agricultural land it would seem logical to solve the growing problem for dog owners of where to exercise their pets by introducing 'dog only' exercise fields and areas of public open space, as are found in other countries. Planning must take into account the needs of all users, human and otherwise, and introduce policies which provide for greater differentiation between types of open space areas, for specialist use by potentially incompatible groups, rather than having a blanket 'open space' or 'countryside' policy. Arguably, all these matters are planning matters, because they affect the way people use and enjoy land, and are all part of the often neglected 'social aspects of planning'.

Animal charities

It is estimated conservatively that there are 8.3 million cats and 6.5 million dogs in Britain. Yet there are over 5 million dog-owning households, and nearly 6 million-cat owning households in the United Kingdom. In some North American and also Australian states, including Victoria, because of fears about conservation of local wildlife, domestic cats are subject to a night-time curfew. In some areas under zoning planning regulations cats are only permitted if kept inside the house, and can legally be shot if found out on the street. Heated debate has ensued. A similar, but less emotive, situation has arisen in Britain in respect of grey squirrels. These were originally introduced from North America and are defined as pests and competitors to the indigenous brown squirrel. However, they are much loved by many, and are a major tourist attraction in the London parks. Likewise mink and other non-indigenous small mammals which have

escaped from fur farms may be seen as causing a threat to native fauna, or as exercising their hard-won freedom. Another so-called pest, the pigeon, is a major concern to those concerned with the conservation of historic buildings. But pigeons are what many tourists go to Trafalgar Square to see and feed them. These are the nitty-gritty issues that local authorities have to face, hardly the glamorous side of town planning, or indeed of environmentalism. But a holistic view of sustainability includes concerns for animals as well as humans, indeed for all flora and fauna.

Rural change

Not the countryside: land in transition

In this final section, some of the wider land-use issues and trends which affect both town and country are discussed. There are vast areas of spoilt and under-used land, both in urban and rural areas, which is increasingly the subject of a range of planning initiatives. The government, and indeed the EU, appears to favour the use of existing wasteland within cities for new development, rather than spreading out new green-field sites, as set out in the European Commission Green Paper on the Urban Environment. There is a range of policies, incentives and grants to encourage the re-use of derelict land. The use of brown land rather than green-field sites for new development has been for many years a major governmental objective. However, Coalition policy gradually weakened control over green-field site development in favour of housing development and the CPRE has led a major campaign to protect the countryside. Arguments range from stating there is 'too much countryside' and taking some more for house-building will do very little harm, to counter-arguments that in reality all land is very precious in such a crowded land as England and we cannot let our countryside be concreted over.

There are many different versions of 'how much land is available to build on'. The DoE established a register of publicly-owned under-used or under-utilised land under the 1980 Local Government, Planning and Land Act, and currently the Homes and Communities Agency seeks to identify and bring forth development on under-utilised public land.

Photo 9.4   Wind farm footprint

Wind turbines create a good deal more change to the surrounding area, because there is a need to provide construction support sites to build them and roads to access them, as shown here in the case of Central Wales.

This particular register is not to be confused with other registers, such as the register of planning applications, or the Land Registry which records the ownership and transfer (e.g. house conveyance) of land. On average per year there are 100,000 acres, on around 8000 individual sites, of under-used and vacant land identified on this register, and this level has been maintained (source: DEFRA Web Page www.defra.gov.uk).

Around 25 per cent of this land has been vacant for over 20 years. Interestingly, much of this land is owned by statutory undertakers, local authorities. Nationalised industries and their privatised succes-

sors have a particularly bad record, especially in respect of railway land.

Under Section 215 of the Town and Country Planning Act 1990, local authorities have had powers to require the proper maintenance of land by private owners, and there are additional powers under the Public Health Acts. But, if the owner considers his land has been blighted by adverse planning decisions, he has the right to serve a Blight Notice for the local authority to purchase the land under Section 150 of the Town and Country Planning Act 1990. Some areas can become neglected and fall into a state of dereliction because of lack of management, without any actual mining or industrial activity taking place.

Under the Derelict Land Act 1982, money was made available to improve such areas, this money being augmented by urban development grants, and urban regeneration grants under the Inner Urban Areas Act 1979 and Local Government, Planning and Land Act 1980. In 1988 these grants were replaced by one category of City Grants. Money is also available within the ambit of the enterprise zone, urban development corporation legislation, Single Regeneration Budget programme, urban conservation, and EU programmes, as discussed in earlier chapters. As a result many erstwhile docklands, derelict harbours and old industrial land has become valuable residential, employment and recreational land (Photo 9.4).

Mining controls

The National Land Utilisation Survey, originally undertaken by the geographer Sir Dudley Stamp and continued by Professor Alice Coleman, has shown, in spite of the introduction of town planning over the last 40 years, that the rate of loss of agricultural land to development has not been reduced, indeed it has continued to grow (Stamp and Coleman 1960). In order to prevent at least some types of dereliction increasing in the future, the government has sought to increase controls over mining activities, especially opencast mining which causes some of the most visible problems. Mining counts as a form of development, and is therefore subject to control under the planning acts. County councils are required to include policies on mineral extraction, a county function, in the Structure Plan. The planners are concerned about how extraction will limit other future uses, for example opencast mining can 'sterilise' wide areas for future development, whilst underground mining may burrow under surrounding sites which will subsequently be unsuitable for development because of the threat of future subsidence. Both types of mining will also create major environmental problems, as does quarrying. Heavy lorries create wear and tear on local roads and communities.

Planners are concerned with ensuring long-term supervision of mining activities. A site will need to be reinstated after mining has ceased, perhaps in 30 years' time, and planning conditions may be made to this effect with varying success. In the past some successful agreements were entered into with the National Coal Board, which were subsequently honoured, ensuring a measure of landscaping and environmental control. The Town and Country Planning Act 1947 first introduced controls over mining. Guidance on the control of minerals was found in what were known as 'The Green Books' produced by the (old) Ministry of Housing and Local Government in the 1950s and 1960s, whose influence is still to be felt. From the 1970s minerals control became the responsibility of counties and other first-tier authorities. The Town and Country Planning (Minerals) Act 1981 increased planning authorities' powers of enforcement. An important feature is the need for 'aftercare' of the site.

Where local government reorganisation has taken place, for example in Wales in 1995, the new unitary authorities became responsible for minerals. In Wales this was by virtue of the Local Government (Wales) Act 1994, but further changes evolved as a result of the creation of a separate Welsh Assembly and related governmental restructuring. All minerals authorities are required to prepare Mineral Subject Plans alongside their other statutory development plans. Under the Town and Country Planning (Minerals) Act 1981 powers were increased, especially in respect of restoration and aftercare of sites, and limitations on the duration of planning permission. Typically mining permissions will contain far more 'conditions of permission' than other planning permissions, and generally take longer to go through the system. In 1988 Minerals Planning Guidance Notes (MPGs) were introduced and controls were increased because of European Directive 85/337 requiring environmental assessment of all minerals applications.

Although there has been an improvement in modern controls, there still exist many pre-1947 permissions, with estimates of over a thousand nationwide. Such permissions were meant to be registered formally with the local planning department by March 1992, for consideration of imposition of modern conditions on the permissions, or they would cease to exist. In fact, in spite of considerable pressure from environmental groups, the process has not been straightforward as there are legal complexities involved in determining whether permission is still extant or can be extinguished, and in some cases reliable records no longer exist. Such sites find themselves alongside gentrified rural settlements or in what are seen as environmentally sensitive areas. Such environmental considerations must be weighed against the importance of ensuring adequate provision of raw materials for industrial and construction purposes.

Minerals are a very specialist aspect of development management, previously covered by MPGs (Mineral Planning Guidance) from the government (the Planning Portal includes detailed information on minerals planning matters). Complex legal matters include the revocation, modification, discontinuance, suspension, intensification, reclamation and conditionality of planning permissions (Senior 1996). Most mining is likely to be based on surface extraction than on 'mining' as existed from the Industrial Revolution. But at an introductory level you only need to know it exists. Recently concerns about new forms of 'mining' have arisen in respect of 'fracking', that is removing gas from shales with concerns about polluting water courses and even causing mini earthquakes. As at the time of writing, the government has given the go-ahead for fracking in England, in spite of considerable opposition. But in retrospect it is probably industrial activities that have caused more environmental problems in the countryside because of the polluting and carcinogenic effects of manufacturing practices (Carson 1962; Griffin 1978; Parkin 1994).

The future countryside agenda

As can be seen from this chapter (and the next too) there are many different, and often conflicting, interest groups concerned with rural planning, including residents, landowners, farmers, developers, environmentalists, promoters of tourism and the leisure industry, and those concerned with energy generation, be it from traditional mining, wind turbines or solar panels. The Coalition government may have altered the power balance to some extent, in promoting local, and especially parish-level, planning. But at the same time the government's main intention is to speed up planning and to free up more land, even green-field land, for development. So it will be interesting to see how the situation develops into the future.

For the tasks, further reading, additional photos and other resources for this chapter, including a map of rural control areas, please visit www.palgrave.com/companion/greed.

10 Sustainable Development

Planning for sustainability

This chapter provides both a historical background and a current overview of the subject. It traces the sustainability agenda which has so reshaped the scope and nature of British town planning over the last 20 years (Blowers (ed.) 1993; Blowers and Evans 1997). First, definitions of sustainability will be given, along with meanings of climate change and global warming. We will discuss how sustainability links to, and is part of, other global policy priorities, as set out in the landmark UN Millennium Development Goals, illustrated with reference to the problems of rapid urbanisation, and secondly global water crises. We will then outline the growing influence of the sustainability agenda on UK planning legislation. We will chart the build-up of UN, EU and UK treaties, directives and regulations (respectively) that have sought to mainstream sustainability considerations into environmental policy and thus eventually into UK planning law and plan-making.

The way in which these changes have been integrated into UK statutory planning at the local plan level is then discussed, with particular reference to the Local Agenda 21 programme and to Environmental Impact Assessment (EIA) requirements (McGillivray 2006, 646–82). By way of illustration we will discuss how energy policy, infrastructural development and waste disposal initiatives have all been shaped by UK sustainability policy. There is a great deal more to environmentalism than recycling cans (important though this is, Photo 10.1). At the end of the chapter, to balance the overall emphasis on environmental issues, we will then return to the social aspects of sustainability, again at a global level, with reference to the MDG goals and the question of population growth. In conclusion we will pose the question: is the sustainability agenda sustainable for the future?

All these are highly emotive topics, resulting in a range of definitions, reasons for their cause, political attitudes towards the issues, and varied policy solutions being put forward. Therefore this chapter approaches the topic from a discursive perspective, including both opinions and observations to encourage readers to delve deeper in order to be able to justify where they stand on these matters, rather than just accepting what is given out by the media. The importance of sustainability and the environmental agenda as key drivers at all levels of contemporary planning policy not only underpins the chapter, but also relates to other chapters such as transport (Chapter 12).

Definitions

Definitions of sustainability

Much of the environmental policy agenda is driven by the need to achieve sustainability. But what is it? At the broadest level, sustainability may be defined as the process of reaching a state where global ecosystems are capable of absorbing human impact without deterioration (Barton *et al.* 1998; Barton 2014; Layard *et al.* 2001). There are two main perspectives on the significance of sustainability. One perspective is human-centred: we must be kind to the Earth so that the Earth is kind to us. The other is nature-centred: we must respect the Earth because the Earth and its creatures have as much right to exist as we do. The health of the biosphere, and the health of humanity, are indivisible, that is one is nature-orientated and the other is concerned with the social aspects of planning.

187

Photo 10.1   Can recycling cans make a difference?

Whilst recycling is now popular with many shoppers, more fundamental structural environmental issues such as decentralised retail location, non-recyclable and excessive packaging and non-returnable bottles remain unsolved.

The original definition of sustainability was promoted at the Rio UN Conference on Sustainability (UNCED 1992; Keating 1993) as previously defined in the Brundtland Report (Brundtland 1987; UN 1992). According to Brundtland (1987) sustainability comprises three components, namely social equality, economic self-sufficiency, and environmental balance (that is People, Place and Planet). Brundtland defines sustainable development as that which meets the needs of the present generation without compromising the ability of future generations to meet their own needs. In comparison, sustainability, according to Blowers (1993), is generally accepted as having four recognised elements: conserving the stock of natural assets; avoiding damage to the regenerative capacities of ecosystems; achieving greater social equality; and avoiding the imposition of risks and costs upon future generations.

Definitions of climate change and global warming

The terms climate change and global warming are frequently used, often almost interchangeably. Climate change relates to long-term changes in the global climate system, rather than short-term changes in the local weather. (In summary 'climate' may be defined as a long-term phenomenon and 'weather' as a short-term factor.) Such changes are observed statistically and manifest in lasting shifts in long-term weather patterns, including increasing extremes in climatic conditions, which are seen as taking place slowly over centuries, even millennia. Climate change can be attributed to a range of natural factors such as solar radiation, plate tectonics and ecological changes. But it is often used in a disapproving way, as a pejorative term, implying that the cause of the speeding up of change is due to human activity. Global warming relates to the rise in the

Figure 10.1   Circles of sustainability

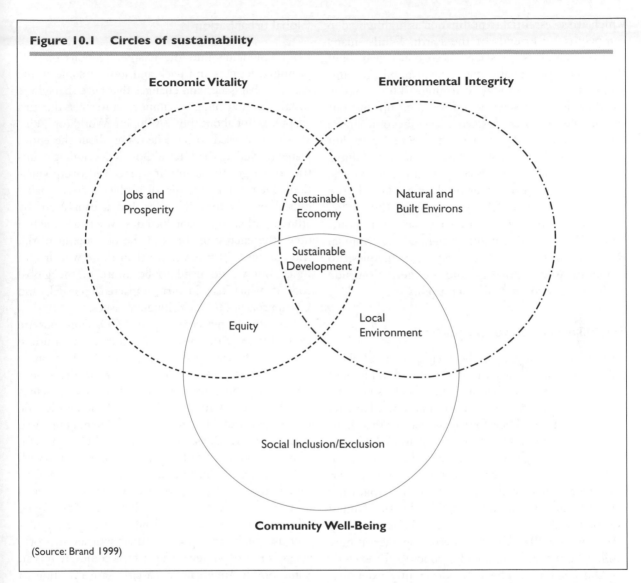

Economic Vitality

Environmental Integrity

Jobs and
Prosperity

Sustainable
Economy

Natural and
Built Environs

Sustainable
Development

Equity

Local
Environment

Social Inclusion/Exclusion

Community Well-Being

(Source: Brand 1999)

average temperature of the Earth's atmosphere, surface and oceans. Global warming is seen by some as a component of climate change, although the climate can be observed to both heat up and cool down over the centuries. This is evidenced by receding glaciers, melting of the polar ice caps and major weather events. Human contributory causes are seen to include (variously) industrial pollution, car ownership, domestic heating, rampant consumerism, the burning of fossil fuels which releases carbon dioxide (CO_2), the release of CFCs (Chloro-Fluoro-Carbon gases) that attack the ozone layer, and, in fact, modern living in general! All these human-generated causes are also seen as contribu-

tory factors in the depletion of the ozone layer, along with natural forces. But, it should be stressed that the links between climate change, global warming and holes in the ozone layer are complex and not necessarily causative. The hole in the ozone layer does not directly affect air temperatures or trigger global warming, but it is one contributory factor, and the release of excess CO_2 and CFC gases are seen as the main human culprits in exacerbating the situation. Whatever the arguments, increased pollution makes life on Earth more problematic in any case, affecting human health. Pollution and climate change also affect flora and fauna. For example, there has been a major decline in the bee population, which are so essential to pollination as highlighted in campaigns by Friends of the Earth. Whilst many environmentalists and scientists are concerned about these changes, arguably the general public remains sceptical about global warming. The English weather does not seem to be warming up, but our seasonable weather patterns have become more unpredictable, and we have had some very hot summers and very cold winters. But as outlined above this is not necessarily significant, as the processes take place over millennia. The Kyoto Treaty on Climate Change established in 1997, which ran until 2012, was also a major milestone. The 2012 Rio+20 Summit reiterated the original Rio commitment, and the Kyoto principles, to reducing world poverty and hunger, alongside achieving environmental sustainability.

The Millennium Development Goals

Sustainability should not be seen as a stand-alone policy but rather as part of a wider development agenda concerned with global issues such as poverty, population, health, water and sanitation, education and urbanisation. Therefore at the start of this chapter the Millennium Development Goals (MDGs) are listed below, and two aspects, namely urbanisation and the global water crisis, will be discussed next. They were introduced by the UN in 2000, following the Millennium Summit organised by the United Nations in New York. They are to be achieved by 2015, but by 2013 this was becoming increasingly unlikely and there are already proposals for extending the deadlines. The UN is currently extending the MDG programme through the establishment of Sustainable Development Goals (SDGs) which were drawn up at Rio+20.

The MDGs are eight in number:

- Eradicate extreme poverty and hunger
- Achieve universal primary education
- Promote gender equality and empower women
- Reduce child mortality
- Improve maternal health
- Combat HIV/AIDS, malaria and other diseases
- Ensure environmental sustainability (links to Rio)
- Develop global partnerships for development.

Global urbanisation

Before plunging into the chapter sections on UK planning, let us stand back and look at some of the major global issues and changes that have shaped the sustainability agenda. It is important to stress that this chapter is not about the Developing World (or Third World, as it used to be called) but about the entire planet (including the UK), although developing countries often get the blame for perceived overpopulation. But many of the global problems are arguably caused by Western lifestyles and urbanisation, by affluent rather than poor societies. Americans use five times the energy of those in the developing world, and consume 20 times more than those who live in India. But we do need to be aware of the global context, which has, in turn, impacted upon EU and UK approaches to environmental issues.

Seventy-five per cent of global CO_2 emissions are from cities, not the rural areas, so cities are a prime factor in achieving sustainability, not the Amazon or the ecosphere. Over 80 per cent of the South American population is urbanised, with mega-cities such as Mexico City, and also San Paolo and Rio de Janeiro in Brazil. However, Africa is catching up, with Lagos and Kinshasa experiencing huge growth. Urbanisation is a fact of life, but it is how we deal with it that matters. Whilst China has moved from a bicycle-based society to one of massive cities gridlocked by a vast increase in car ownership, Japan has taken a different route. In Tokyo 78 per cent of the population use public transport for their journey to work, whereas in Los Angeles 80 per cent commute by car. Some South American mega-cities are investing in public transport such as Bogota, whereas in contrast San Paolo is becoming gridlocked with motorcars used by the affluent sectors of the population whilst the 60 per cent who live in the surrounding slum areas lack access to public transport. So town planning has a major role in trying to sort all this out.

As explained above, the 'sustainability' agenda contains a major social policy component along with environmental dimensions. Many modern-day social problems of poverty, famine and lack of sanitation are found amongst the growing urban populations in developing countries, although they are more commonly associated with rural poor (as portrayed in the often misleading photographs used by some

Relief Charities). Burdett and Sudjic (2011, 2012) observe that 53 per cent of the world's population is urban and will be 75 per cent by 2050, but 33 per cent of urban dwellers are living in slums. There have been huge movements of impoverished populations from the countryside into cities, creating major pressures in terms of housing, water supply, sewerage and drainage.

One of the largest cities is Mumbai (Bombay) which is 19 million now and will be 35 million by 2050 (see E-Supplement 1: Table of the World's Largest Cities), with 60 per cent living in slums, often in close proximity to new middle-class apartment complexes. The image of the glamorous, trendy, cool, rich modern city is widespread, often used in global advertising for luxury goods. But wealthy urbanites comprise just a very small part of the world's global population. Although there is a new mega-rich class of billionaires in many developing and erstwhile Communist countries, there are also vast numbers of people living in very poor housing, shanty towns and informal settlements. In fact there are 1 billion urban squatters worldwide (out of a world population of approaching 7 billion). For example, Durban in South Africa is a city of 4 million people but 1 million comprise the inhabitants of the surrounding, and ever-growing, shanty towns. The rich/poor divide, in such cities, still corresponds broadly to the white/black division of the apartheid era, and crime and personal safety is a very major issue, with many houses in affluent areas being surrounded by razor wire, armed response guards and high walls. Whilst in some Western cities there are some 'no go' areas where it is wise not to walk around at night, in some developing-country cities it is not advisable to walk around any part of the city in a carefree manner, not even in broad daylight.

Given that there are famine and food shortages in many parts of the world, it is of great concern that so many people are migrating to the towns, leaving farmland untilled and unproductive. Control of food production, distribution and marketing by multinational companies is of growing concern. It is estimated that 10 per cent of the Earth's surface is actually used for agriculture, and that much of this is used for grazing. New intensive forms of agriculture may help to feed the world's population but often at the cost of loss of local landownership and the rural way of life. There are also debates about the growth of GM (genetically modified) crops and the role of multinationals in 'copyrighting' seeds, so that the local farmer loses control over crop production. At the other end of the process, in terms of consumption, the global spread of fast-food outlets is also replacing local culinary traditions and methods. All these issues need to be taken into account when discussing whether the world is overpopulated and what the ideal population size might be. In many countries it is not lack of food that is the problem but rather lack of money to buy it because of extremes of wealth and poverty among the local population. Also it is often more profitable to export food products to Western countries than use the produce for the needs of the local population.

Closely aligned to ideas of the sustainable city is the concept of the Healthy City as promoted by the WHO (World Health Organization) (Barton and Tsourou 2006; Falk 2012; WHO 2011 and www.who.int). There is a policy emphasis upon encouraging people to walk and cycle, with reduction in pollution, and in developing countries with the provision of water supplies and sanitation services. In fact lack of water resources is a major issue internationally which will also feature frequently in this chapter. There are 2 billion people without toilets and also without reliable access to water and electricity. Two-thirds of the world's population lack access to the internet, but many commercial companies and governments are keen on solving this problem. But in comparison toilet provision is not very glamorous. More people on Earth own mobile phones than have private toilets. But if we look back to Chapter 4 you will recall that baths, toilets and aqueducts providing water supply were key features of many ancient and classical Greek and Roman cities. The stark contrast in sanitation, water supply and building standards is shown in the many photographs in Burdett and Sudjic's books (2011, 2012). But, flies are no respecter of class or wealth, and if you have open defecation and no sanitation system working in poor areas, then airborne and waterborne disease will soon spread to rich areas, as, for example, flies that have been feeding on open pits of human waste drop in on the kitchens and food of the rich.

A digression into water

We have included a separate section on water, because providing adequate and reliable water supply, and also sewerage and waste disposal, are at the very heart of dealing with the problems of urbanisation and disease. But the availability of water is also linked to the wider environmental agenda of global sustainability. There is said to be a global water shortage and a major crisis looming, especially in sub-Saharan Africa, although over two-thirds of the planet is ocean (albeit saline) and many inhabited parts of the world are blessed with heavy levels of rainfall. According to traditional water cycle theory, it rains, the water is soaked up by the ground, goes into the rivers, down into underground aquifers and is drawn upon as domestic, industrial and commercial water supply, and for agriculture, and eventually goes back into the ocean and then through evaporation goes back into the clouds to rain again. So where does the water go?

It is debatable as to whether water is being lost for ever as some television documentaries suggest, categorising it as a non-renewable resource like coal or oil, but it can't fall off the planet. However, what is happening is that in some areas the underground aquifers and artesian basins are not being replenished because of major weather changes and increased water usage because of industrialisation, urbanisation and modern intensive agricultural practices. Water is also running off paved, man-made surfaces, with increased urbanisation, and not soaking back into the ground because of increased urbanisation and the destruction of natural water tables, basins and feeder-stream systems. Also some argue that global warming is speeding up the water cycle and preventing adequate cloud formation and so more water is being deposited back into the sea rather than returning as fresh water over the land.

Deforestation has also contributed, leaving many areas without any ground cover, so previously wooded, wet and fertile areas are becoming deserts. Deforestation may be on a large scale as in the case of logging companies in the Amazon rainforest, or on a small scale through the daily actions of needy villagers collecting wood for domestic fuel in developing countries (Photo 10.2).

The human element is at work here too, as issues of water ownership, distribution and infrastructural provision also determine who has the right and opportunity to access a reliable and cheap water supply. For all these global issues, it is strongly recommended that you look at articles from the *New Internationalist*, international development magazine, at www.newint.org. Many countries, such in South America, have no national grid or services infrastructure and increasingly private water companies control the supply in the cities. Water companies may not consider it is financially worthwhile to extend their services to poor and deprived neighbourhoods. Buying bottled water is seen as an unsustainable lifestyle choice in those countries where the public water supply is quite safe to drink (potable). But in many developing countries safe drinking water is not available on tap, and has to be bought, with supplies being delivered (like milk) door to door from a water tender, or for the more affluent in bottled form.

In spite of increased urbanisation, still over 80 per cent of water goes into agriculture in the Global South (Developing World). But even in agricultural areas the demands of modern irrigation methods may mean that water is not readily available to farm workers in needy villages. Likewise building major dams may help provide water to new large cities but may also deprive local farmers around the dams of water for their crops. The old ways of building earth terraces and small retaining pools saves water for local farmers' use. Thus the natural water cycle is being disrupted in so many ways. Therefore one must always remember the human factor when discussing sustainability and environmental issues. The true situation in a particular locality is often far more complicated than simply blaming global warming. Local politics, human greed, power and financial considerations (such as paying the shareholders of privatised water companies) have a major role to play in who benefits and who loses out.

Sustainability does not exist in a vacuum, whether in the Amazon or in the Thames Basin. Thus, in the UK, climate change, especially the lack of, or overabundance of, water, has had major implications for land-use planning and the location of new residential development because of rising water levels, increased flooding and sea defence issues. Both

Photo 10.2   Wood storage on a South East Asian street

Many of the poor are very careful in their use of natural resources, such as wood, and therefore their lifestyle is, of necessity, more environmentally aware than in rich countries, where coal is still the dominant form of fuel.

households and businesses are criticised for using too much water in spite of Britain's wet climate. Local authorities have been criticised for selling off disused waterworks and reservoirs, especially around London, which with population growth are now needed again to build up water reserves in the Thames Basin. Domestic water metering and rationing have been proposed for the UK.

Over 80 per cent of UK water is used by industry and commerce, and many water authorities since privatisation have appalling levels of maintenance, for example, approaching 50 per cent of water is lost by Thames Water serving London through its anti-quated leaking pipe system, and emergency storage reservoirs have been sold off. Water conservation is becoming a more important issue and the amended Part G of the Building Regulations (2011 Water Efficiency Requirements) has included water saving measures in the overall design of plumbing and water supply systems in domestic housing. There is also much enthusiasm for using grey water, that is previously used water from baths, washing machines and such like, for flushing toilets. Toilet cisterns now use lower volumes of water for flushing and many have dual flush arrangements. Wasteful water-based sewerage works are also subject to modification and reed-bed filtration systems are more widespread. However, we still discharge sewage out into the sea in some areas and we still depend upon a Victorian system of sewers and pipes, many of which need renewing. But we have not moved, yet, to a greater emphasis upon recycling human waste, to be used as fertiliser as found in some developing countries. Indeed some developed countries, such as Australia, which is a relatively waterless continent, are very keen to use solar power to decompose human waste, whilst entire sewage works in Japan utilise sustainable methods to break down, separate and recycle human waste using high-tech computer-controlled methods. In the UK the Machynlleth Centre for Alternative Technology in Wales is a major centre of green technology and innovation. So as illustrated with reference to 'water', global sustainability issues impact upon urban planning, and indeed the nature of daily life, at both international and UK levels.

UK environmental sustainability policy

Reinventing the wheel?

The scale of modern environmental planning is so much wider than that of traditional British town planning, because it is concerned with global issues that require international solutions. The green movement has drawn attention to the fact we all live on a fragile planet and from this wider perspective, town/country divisions become meaningless, because environmental issues overarch national boundaries and statutory land-use planning divisions. The globalisation of economies, coupled with an increasing awareness that we are all thrown together in the same 'Spaceship Earth', has led some to argue that the nation-state (such as the UK) is no longer the key level at which to plan. Many of our economic, environmental and social problems require international cooperation and global solutions. For example, concerns about global warming and the discovery of holes in the ozone layer have united the world's population across national boundaries, for example to limit CFC gas emissions which are believed to be a causal factor. Whilst these insights have led to a more holistic view of planning for the environment, they have also led to criticisms of what may be seen as the narrower and less enlightened agenda of British town planning.

Many planning historians would argue that a concern among planners with the environment is not new. Precedents for modern environmental policies can be found in an early commitment to reducing urban sprawl and to protecting the countryside through the development of town and country planning in the last century. For example, Ebenezer Howard's concept of the garden city was, in its original form, a sustainable community (Chapter 5). All that has happened is that the wheel has been reinvented by a new generation, and a new eco-language is being used to describe the age-old and well-acknowledged problems, which inspired the founding fathers of the modern town planning movement. Whilst the global perspective is vital, it is argued that many town planning issues are best still dealt with in a detailed way through local planning for specific sites and geographical localities, and other issues need to be tackled from a wider regional, national or European Union policy level.

More fundamentally the environmental *green* movement has challenged the basic assumptions which have informed much socialist *red* movement thinking previously associated with planning, in respect of the emphasis upon production and thus upon the centrality of economic growth and employment policy in planning policy. But sustainability policies have wide political and economic implications, beyond purely environmental objectives. Taking a sustainable perspective reveals the hidden costs of 'production' and 'consumption' and the costs and benefits of 'decomposition'. Decomposition is the next essential stage towards restoring environmental assets and balance through recycling, that is decomposition and recomposition of natural materials. The importance of dealing with the entire ecosystem and thus with all these three components in the cycle has been stressed particularly by those working in the fields of ecology, rural planning and landscape design (Turner 1996: 30).

Influence of UN and EU policies

UK environmental policy has been strongly influenced and determined by international trends. Concern with sustainability had become a higher governmental priority by the 1980s as a result of international influences such as the Brundtland Report, *Our Common Future* (Brundtland 1987). Friends of the Earth and other pressure groups had drawn attention to deficiencies in policy and legislation in Britain, and internationally groups such as Greenpeace alerted people to the global implications of the greenhouse effect, the depletion of the ozone layer, increased pollution, and diminishing natural resources. International-level policies have been introduced in many countries to limit CFC gas emissions which are believed to be a contributory factor. The Montreal Protocol of 1989 established the requirement, internationally, that there should be a phasing out the manufacture of materials that contribute towards the depletion of the ozone layer. The Environmental Protection Act 1990 consolidated and expanded pollution controls introduced under earlier public health and clean air acts, but now with greater emphasis upon chemical pollution. The (original) Clean Air Act 1956 was repealed under this Act. By this time coal fire derived pollution, and many of the traditional heavy industries which contributed to London smog, had long since declined.

Many would argue that pollution is just one small part of the total environmental cost paid by the planet. Over the last 20 years there have been moves to make the developer contribute more towards the true cost of development. For example, the Water Act 1989 enables water companies to levy an infrastructural charge on developers of new housing estates. Such measures may be compared to earlier attempts to tax the developer, for example by the betterment levy in the post-war years (Chapter 6) or under planning gain (Chapter 3). Such regulation was influenced by the German-derived concept of the 'precautionary principle'. This sought to prevent pollution at source, whatever the cost to the producer, to avoid society and the environment paying greater costs later. The precautionary principle may be equated to the sentiments embodied in the saying 'a stitch in time saves nine'.

The agenda of the new 'green' environmental movement gradually began to impact on the scope and nature of mainstream town planning, rather than just pollution (Blowers 1993). In the early 1990s, under the Conservative government headed by John Major, the UK's environmental policy agenda was set out in the White Paper *This Common Inheritance: Britain's Environmental Strategy*, Cmd. 1200 (DoE 1990a). Early signs of policy change included the content of the revision in the 1992 PPG9 on Nature Conservation which went beyond a limited concern with local, 'special site'-related issues to consider wider ecological issues, but both

were subsequently cancelled by the Coalition in 2010.

In 1992 the Earth Summit on 'The Environment and Development' took place in Rio de Janeiro which introduced defined sustainability as a high-level international objective (as described at the beginning of the chapter). Following this the policy document *Sustainable Development: The UK Strategy* (DoE 1994a, 1994b) was produced by the government, which covered a range of topical issues such as global climate and air quality, and discussed policy in relation to non-renewable resources such as water, earth (soil) and minerals. Setting a future agenda for government, business, non-governmental organisations (NGOs), and individual men and women, it stresses partnership approaches (DoE 1994a). This strategy is paralleled by equivalent documents in other EU states, which have all been produced within the framework of the EU's Fourth and Fifth Action Programmes on the Environment (CEC 1990, 1992).

All the international resolutions and goals on sustainability soon filtered down to the European Union level. Much was being learned from what had been achieved in other European countries, and from already established EU environmental policy programmes. Partnership opportunities developed within European Union initiatives on the environment (CEC 1990; and Williams 1999). A main goal of the Fifth Environmental Action Plan produced by the EU (CEC 1992) was to raise awareness of environmentally friendly behaviour amongst three identified groups of actors – government, consumers and the public. A major objective of the European Union is to achieve 'sustained and non-inflationary growth respecting the environment'. Initiatives such as the European Spatial Development Perspective (ESDP) (as discussed in Chapter 2) seek to develop policy perspectives that relate the needs of specific cities and regions in the EU to wider environmental policies from the global and panEuropean level arena.

Integration of sustainability into UK planning

The foundations of planning for sustainability were established by the end of the 1990s. But there were marked inconsistencies in policy as not all approved plans and planning permissions embodied pro-environment objectives. Sustainable policies were recommended in revised PPGs such as PPG12: Development Plans and Regional Planning Guidance, produced in 1992, which highlighted the importance of taking into account the relationship between climatic change and land use and transport policy. In general the emphasis in planning had shifted from the old adage of 'project and provide' (or predict and provide) in respect of meeting demands for more roads, houses and commercial developments, towards a more cautious approach to permitting new development, where other more sustainable solutions might be implemented. Likewise there has been a move away from the old 'announce and defend' approach to policy-making towards a more collaborative, consultative approach, particularly in environmentally sensitive situations where there is likely to be considerable opposition.

Advisory bodies, such as the UK Round Table on Sustainable Development (UK Round Table 1996) and the House of Lords Select Committee on Sustainable Development (House of Lords 1995), were also established in the mid-1990s. A number of existing QUANGOs were given enhanced statutory duties in respect of environmental responsibilities. The Environment Act 1995 tightened and extended environmental controls (Ball and Bell 1999; Lane and Peto 1996; Grant 1998). It increased local authority powers to control pollution, strengthened recycling measures and increased grants for conservation (Brand 1996, 1999). The 1995 Environment Act introduced measures relating to abandoned mines and contaminated land, and a new regime for reviewing and updating longstanding mineral permissions. The act introduced changes in the responsibilities of National Park authorities, strengthened control over water resource management, flooding and pollution, and established a National Environment Agency (NEA) for England and Wales in 1995, the Scottish Environment Protection Agency, and separately the Alkali and Radioactive Inspectorate in Northern Ireland. It should be noted that the Environment Agency incorporates the National Rivers Authority (NRA). The Environment Agency (previously called the NEA) is responsible for dealing with flood risk, climate change and coastal erosion amongst other topics.

Tighter controls and penalties under this Act raised the political profile of environmental issues among developers and within industry (Rydin 1998, ch. 11). This was because of the application of the principle 'let the polluter pay', a concept which rested uneasily in the entrepreneurial climate of Thatcher's Britain. Subsequently in 1996, environmental taxes on landfill were introduced, and now it is considered quite normal to recycle, both at household level, and in terms of disposing of demolition and building waste within the construction industry. Nuclear waste was also subject to additional controls under Her Majesty's Inspectorate of Pollution. But there was not, as yet, an integrated approach to environmental issues, because, historically, different issues were dealt with by separate and diverse departments.

The Amsterdam Treaty of 1997 further strengthened the importance of environmental considerations in EU planning policy. Under New Labour (1997–2009) there was a flurry of papers and legislation regarding sustainability. Greater emphasis was put upon applying sustainability principles to urban form and new development, for example, the 2003 ODPM document, *Sustainable Communities: Building for the Future*, recommended 60 per cent of all new development was to be on brown-field infill sites. PPG1 (of 1997) on general planning principles included reference to the Rio definition of sustainability. PPS3 on housing likewise put a considerable emphasis upon urban containment, the compact city and building at higher densities of 30 dwellings per hectare, and the utilisation of infill and brown-field sties. In 1999 the EU Directive on Integrated Pollution and Prevention Control Directive Number 96/61 came into effect, extending the precautionary principle. In the process the traditional role of British town planners was being extended, along European lines, towards that of 'environmental police'. The principle of the polluter paying was further promoted in PPS23 Planning and Pollution Control, 2004.

Planners were required to integrate Environmental Impact Assessment (EIA) into the development control process as required under European Directives that were being embedded into UK and other member states' legislative systems. Many local planning authorities introduced EIA systems into their development management procedures and inserted policy statements and specific sections on sustainability into their Unitary Development Plan documents and local plans. With the coming of the Coalition government in 2010 most of the PPSs were cancelled. The new National Planning Policy Framework reaffirmed sustainable development as a key component, with stronger legal backing as its materiality in determining planning decisions. The 2011 Localism Act requires environmental assessment when testing the soundness of plans, as explained in Chapters 2 and 3 on the current planning system. As introduced in the development management chapter (Chapter 3) there is a range of procedures required, under the SA (Sustainability Appraisal), SEA (Strategic Environmental Assessment) and EIA (Environmental Impact Assessment), now consolidated under the Local Planning Regulations 2012. Meanwhile sustainability had spread through the construction industry and built environment professions and the revised Building Regulations, Part L on sustainable construction was reinforced by using improved BREEAM methods on evaluating whether sustainable materials from sustainable and renewable resources were being used, for example endangered hardwoods were now no longer acceptable. (Building Research Establishment Environmental Assessment Methods = BREEAM). Eco-building, creating green construction and sustainable buildings, has become a major preoccupation of the construction industry and an integral component of good architectural practice and modern design. Reducing dependence on carbon fuels also continues to be a policy priority. Thus, central government has increasingly supported sustainability policies. For example, in 2012 the government produced the UK National Renewable Energy Plan to conform to the requirements of the EU European Renewable Energy Plan, which requires 15 per cent of our energy consumption to be from renewable resources by 2020 (DECC 2012). There are a growing number of policy initiatives arising from the sustainability agenda affecting the everyday work of the ordinary local authority urban planner.

However, arguably, in Britain sustainability, environmentalism, and especially green issues, are often more likely to be associated with countryside issues and nature, than to be applied to addressing the problems of urban areas. This attitude can depoliticise the agenda and leads to a predominantly physical, land-use based approach to environmental issues, which conveniently fits in with the traditional spatial emphasis within UK town planning (Brand 1996, 1999). Indeed planning for the environment has often conveniently slotted into the pre-existing 'country green dimension' of town and country planning. This gives it 'space' on the existing UK planning agenda, but creates limitations. However, the original Rio definition of sustainability comprised environmental balance, social equality and economic development (that is Planet, People and Prosperity). However, it is true that many of the sustainability issues in Britain are played out within the countryside or at least in less-urbanised areas, especially in the media, for example in respect of battles over the location of wind turbines. Rural planning has been strongly affected by many aspects of the sustainability agenda, including the need to grow more food locally to cut down on food miles, the need to protect agricultural land from housing and the need to conserve the natural environment and conserve biodiversity (see Chapter 9). In parallel in the UK debates about the pros and cons of genetically modified (GM) food production, organic farming, or industrialised forms of food production all impact on planning for the countryside. Whilst all these rural issues are of great concern, it is within the towns and cities, at the local community level, that progress in the implementation of sustainability policy has been the more marked.

Local level application of sustainability principles

The Rio Declaration on sustainability arising from the 1992 United Nations Conference provided the basis for the establishment of the Agenda 21 programme as a key means of policy implementation. This required all signatory states to draw up national plans for sustainability. Agenda 21 is a lengthy document, with 40 chapters split into four sections, which has been extensively analysed and critiqued (Blowers 1993; LGMB 1995). In summary, from the 1990s emphasis has been placed on the social and economic dimensions of sustainability, including the need to combat poverty, strengthening the role of major groups (including women, local authorities and NGOs) in the process of implementation (Brand 1996: 60).

Thus, the community is seen as having a key role in achieving sustainable development. Chapter 28 of the Agenda agreement required local authorities in each state to produce 'Local Agenda 21' initiatives for their areas. Local Agenda 21 provides the basis for a comprehensive programme and framework for action into the twenty-first century for governments and development agencies (UNCED 1992; Keating 1993). Chapter 28 calls upon each local authority to undertake a consultative process with its citizens. It is as much concerned with the process of 'planning' as it is with policy. It puts the onus upon local authorities, with their communities, to design and deliver (DOE 1994a, 1994b, 1994c). Throughout Agenda 21 there are calls for new approaches to decision-making, emphasising intersectoral cooperation, local consultation and greater democracy within the community. This may be described as a collaborative approach to planning (Healey 2007).

Subsequently, a UK Local Agenda 21 Steering Group was established and the Local Government Management Board took on the role of disseminating guidance throughout the UK (LGMB 1993). Within the context of their national strategies for sustainable development, central governments may help the local process. Given the complexity of Agenda 21 and the need for the commitment and cooperation of UK local governments for its fulfilment within the Local Agenda 21 process, various national bodies have responded by offering guidance to the more local level. So the environmental movement is having a growing effect upon the operation of the day-to-day statutory planning system in the UK, through development control. Likewise development plans must also be environmentally appraised, as must any major planning policy document, such as the Structure Plan or Unitary Development Plan. In other words, environmentalism has become embedded and mainstreamed within the national planning system.

As a result most development plan policy statements have large sections on environmental policy within them, and many cross-references to wider sustainability goals and policies. Development control (management) also has a duty to undertake

EIA on a wide range of schemes, not necessarily just the real big urban developments, but anything that is likely to have a major impact on the environment, even forestry and industrial farming applications. Progressive local authorities have produced Agenda 21 policies and cross-referenced them to their forward planning policy documents. For example, the London Borough of Wandsworth's adopted UDP plan of 2003 stated, 'the council will promote sustainable development in the borough to protect and enhance quality of life, to improve economic and social opportunities, and to contribute to the council's Local Agenda 21 programme'. Such statements have become increasingly common in subsequent development plan and local plan statements and you will be able to find many yourself by checking the websites of local planning authorities.

Local Agenda 21 assumes it is not only desirable but possible to achieve a high degree of collaborative action in a community by voluntary agreement. There is a strong emphasis upon the process of involvement (collaborative planning) rather than upon rules. It is a matter of building up cultures and changing attitudes. LA21 committees involving the public, private and voluntary sectors would enable a discussion of sustainability issues to take place, to produce together an integrated plan. The UK government required every local area to produce such a plan by the end of 1996. But the process and requirements presented a challenge to those involved, and the process is by no means complete at the time of writing. The holistic approach of Local Agenda 21 offered a cultural and organisational challenge to authorities, which are traditionally organised on sectoral lines. Several authorities have developed cross-cutting departmental arrangements. All have appointed a Local Agenda 21 coordinator. They are located in various departments, with the Chief Executive Office, Environmental Health, and Planning Departments being the most common locations. All this emphasis on community involvement ties in well with the Coalition's emphasis on localism and community involvement in the planning process, and to New Labour's 2007 Sustainable Communities Act. But in reality planning is political and quite complex at the local parish council and community group level, so we have yet to see how all this works out. After all, sustainability is in fact quite a complex technical issue which requires a considerable amount of technical knowledge rather than simply enthusiasm about saving the planet.

The hope is that by involving different interests – e.g. the local Chamber of Commerce, utilities, environmental pressure groups and the local authority – insights will be shared and a coordinated strategy will emerge. This is an idealistic adventure, and has given a culture shock to many of those involved, as international level 'top-down' influences impinge upon the various British town planning systems.

By the new millennium there was an even greater emphasis upon localism and the role of the community being involved; indeed the 2007 Sustainable Communities Act enshrined the importance of local participation and involvement in creating environmentally sustainable communities. By the time of the Coalition in 2010, under the Localism Act 2011, there is now a duty for local planning authorities to involve parish councils, neighbourhoods and local community groups in the planning process, and to produce Neighbourhood Plans which will have a strong environmental component in them.

It is noteworthy that the 2011 Localism Act has taken a more enlightened view of what constitutes sustainability, beyond the usual environmentally-loaded agenda. The Act requires economic and social, as well as environmental, issues to be taken into account in the test of soundness of the plans produced at both local and neighbourhood level, embodying the principles of the Circles of Sustainability diagram (Figure 10.1). However one must be cautious as 'economic' could mean 'pro' potentially polluting industry, or urban sprawl. It does not necessarily mean 'economic well-being' but nevertheless potential for a more inclusive approach to sustainability is to be welcomed.

So to conclude this section, sustainability and especially environmental considerations have been mainstreamed into both development plan policy-making and into development control through EIA but also moved 'down' more to a grass-roots community level too. Both the global and local commitment was reiterated in the 2012 UN Conference Rio+20 which seeks to move the old sustainability debate forward into the new century. One manifestation of this great community emphasis is the importance given to neighbourhood forums and town and parish councils under the 2011 Localism Act.

A digression into energy and local planning

Energy is worth exploring further as a key planning policy area that has particularly affected local-level planning and which often leads to conflicts between local communities and the planners. Historically the Industrial Revolution and most industrial development into the twentieth century was fuelled by coal, and the composition of our towns and cities was shaped by industrial land uses surrounded by working-class housing areas, with little consideration of the pollution aspects.

Concern with reducing the carbon footprint has shaped recent transport policy, by restricting car use, improving public transport and reducing the need to travel in the first place through changes in land-use zoning and location policy. Climate change, and measures to combat it, also has major implications for land-use planning and the location of new residential development because of rising water levels, increased flooding and sea defence issues. For example, an international system of carbon credits and carbon sinks has been introduced whereby carbon is meant to be paid back into the environment by the planting of new trees and forests, albeit this approach is questioned by many critics for not really solving the problem. Likewise policies concerning renewable energy, nuclear power and wind turbines all have major infrastructural and spatial planning implications in terms of policy and development control. Overall power is derived from the following sources in these percentages:

71 per cent fossil fuel
16 per cent nuclear
1.3 per cent hydroelectric
0.2 per cent wind
0.029 per cent solar

(*Source*: the CIA World Fact Book at https://www.cia.gov/library/publications/the-world-fact-book/.)

Not everyone is so keen on community sustainability policy when environmental planning decisions affect them personally at the local level, as sustainability policy can sometimes conflict with other traditional town and country planning objectives. Whilst people happily subscribe to the abstract ideas of community, sustainable development and reducing the carbon footprint, it is another matter if they fear that wind turbines will be located near their village, for example, and then a NIMBY (Not In My Back Yard) attitude is likely to take over. Alternative sources of energy, such as vast areas of solar panels, are seen by some conservationists as a blot on the landscape, whilst many locals are worried about the noise, hum from turbines and disruption caused by green energy schemes. The government has encouraged, and subsidised, private investment in building off-shore wind turbines along the coast of Britain, and in windy areas inland which are mainly on agricultural land. Such schemes are wildly expensive but ensure fuel security in the light of increased international tension affecting fuel imports. But aesthetically such structures have caused much opposition and people living nearby are distracted by the hum of the turbines and the effect on migratory birds. Likewise policies concerning renewable energy, nuclear power and wind turbines all have major infrastructural and spatial planning implications in terms of policy and development control. The 2008 Climate Change Act established a commitment to reduce CO_2 emissions by 34 per cent and wind turbines were seen as a way of achieving this. But they are heavily subsidised with 120 billion pounds committed to their continuing construction, ten times what it would cost to build modern gas-fuelled power stations to achieve the same energy output. Individual wind turbines can cost between 50 and 150,000 pounds to construct depending on their location, and may only work at 15 per cent of their capacity over the year as a whole to raise around 100,000 pounds worth of energy per year. Are such expensive devices are really sustainable in terms of their social and economic impact as well as their environmental record? Wind turbines have received a great deal of opposition at local level because of the noise and the general disruption caused by the construction of roads and site works to install them.

The Infrastructure Planning Commission (IPC) was established in 2009 to deal with controversial types of development, such as nuclear power stations, new airport development and other major schemes. In 2010 it was abolished by the Coalition government and its role was returned to a branch of the Planning Inspectorate and now it has been restructured and named the National Infrastructure Directorate. There have been some strange situations arising with adversaries both citing environmental considerations. For example, the move away from fossil fuels and coal-fired power stations has let in by the back door a return of a new enthusiasm for nuclear power stations, a strategy much favoured by the government, as the new clean source of energy that does not affect the ozone layer. Many campaigners argue that these are not environmentally sound, because there is the small matter of radioactive waste that will not degrade for many centuries. So they suggest that what is needed is more power saving measures, less wasteful heating and lighting and everyone to wear more winter clothing. In contrast some environmentalists are now in favour of nuclear power because it is seen as clean and less polluting of the environment. But of course, it takes thousands of years for nuclear waste to degrade and become safe. Can you be green and in favour of nuclear power? (A good essay question!) The energy industry is now looking at other alternatives such as fracking, which is getting methane gas out of the fissures from underground geological strata, mainly trapped within shale deposits, a highly controversial activity said to cause earth tremors and contamination of groundwater, but which causes very little visual intrusion on the landscape compared with old-time mining activities. As explained in Chapter 2, the Coalition government has been keen to invest in major infrastructural projects including building new power stations. It has also given the go-ahead for widespread fracking, although most of the project work is investigative at the moment. But, it should be noted that most power stations are still fuelled by coal in spite of all the innovations in fuel types.

There are all sorts of proposals for alternatives to petrol for cars, including processed chip fat and solar panels. The government has been supporting the development of electric cars but at present they are very expensive and have a limited mileage range. Of course they still draw on fossil fuels as electricity comes from gas and therefore require increased production from power stations, which might, actually, be a less green solution than carrying on with petrol. If we solved the petrol crisis and had cheap fuel for all everyone, all that would happen is that Britain would grind to a halt, traffic jams would be far worse than today and town planners would have to rethink transport and road-building strategies. The quest for new cheaper forms of electricity is intense. There seems to be no one simple solution. For example, using bio-fuels, that is petrol created from growing sugar beet and other crops, only contributes to the world food crisis. Lateral thinking is required. For example, a small British company has come up with idea of turning air into petrol (Google 'Air Fuel Systems'), as reported in October 2012. Closer to home, science colleagues at the University of the West of England, Bristol, in the Robotics Laboratory, are generating electricity from urine which can be scaled up for commercial use (Ieropoulos *et al.* 2012). All over the world keen environmentally-minded scientists are looking at other sources of power and electricity, often using small-scale, micro-processes integrated into everyday life objects and activities. This would also help deal with the question of what to do with human waste as sewage is a huge component of waste disposal policy.

Recycling and waste disposal

Another sensitive issue that affects people's way of life is the task of recycling. Waste control and recycling is affecting our daily lives, but which has global implications and where every little helps. For example, at a very practical day-to-day level, plastic carrier bags are not generally biodegradable, and plastic bags, bottles and bits from the Western consumer societies now end up, taken by the oceans' currents, on the distant sandy shores of the tropics and distant islands all over the world. The National Assembly of Wales, to counteract this, now requires all shops in Wales to charge 5 pence for a bag, whilst many supermarkets in the UK offer reusable fabric bags to shoppers. The environmental movement has become popular among the general public and a new 'green consumer' movement was created. It was disconcerting that environmentally aware shoppers often seemed more concerned about wanting recy-

clable carriers rather than plastic bags from their local hypermarket, than about questioning its out-of-town location and the farming methods involved in producing its goods and this was noted early on by German environmentalists (FUN 1998). In fact environmentalism can deteriorate into a lifestyle choice, and even a fashion statement, rather than being seen as a major structural, strategic factor in shaping the whole of land use and planning policy.

Waste management remains a county function under the Coalition government and waste management and recycling have been a major factor. EU regulations have sought to reduce landfill and encourage recycling, whilst local authorities are subject to fines if they do not reduce their waste totals progressively each year. Waste is still a county role of strategic importance but no longer part of the development plan. Local authorities are required to produce Waste Plans at county level. Waste plans are not separate from mainstream planning. Waste-related land use, including disposal sites, landfill locations and recycling facilities, is one of the most prominent topics causing disagreements between adjacent local planning authorities seeking to undertake their 'duty to cooperate' in the production of the new Local Plans under the 2011 Localism Act (see Chapter 2 on development plans).

The government is particularly keen to reduce landfill so that only 10 per cent of waste goes to this destination (at present it is nearer 50 per cent) and has been imposing increasingly higher recycling requirements on local authorities. These can only be achieved by more intensive recycling measures. But domestic waste only accounts for around 20 per cent of all waste, so clearly more needs to be done by industry and commerce too. Sorting and recycling household waste (into paper, plastic, metal, glass and so forth) is now a major preoccupation of the nation, with separate containers usually provided by the council. From an urban design and local residential planning perspective, wheelie bins and the whole paraphernalia of refuse collection has become a visual factor in design (see Chapter 13 on urban design). In some local authorities a very officious approach to recycling has been adopted and people are fined for minor infringements such as over-filling their bin, or leaving their bins out too early. Waste collection, which residents pay for through their rates, is no longer seen as a public right. Many commuters have to put their rubbish out early as they are going to work, and many houses and flats do not have external storage and have to save it all in the kitchen. Particular condemnations seem to be reserved for people who put out piles of disposable nappies and in general housewives are seen as wasteful, although few local authorities run nappy washing and recycling units (Oates and McDonald 2006). The recycling industry is global, with much of the UK rubbish being put on container ships to be sorted in developing countries, especially in India. Likewise clothes from charity shops are exported to Africa and have become a major component of the local economy and street markets there. Nothing is wasted in other parts of the world. Many developing countries are not only dealing with processing all the rubbish of the rest of the world that has been sent to them, but also they are trying to cope with very primitive human and community waste disposal systems in their own villages.

Socio-economic aspects of sustainability

Planning for people and the planet

The majority of this chapter has been concerned with the more environmental aspects of sustainability as this is the aspect that is prioritised in UK statutory planning. However, sustainability always had three components, environmental, economic and social. At the 2012 Rio+20 UN conference the lack of success in reducing world poverty was seen as a major barrier to progress in bringing about environmental sustainability. Saving the rainforest remains more 'sexy' than dealing with the starving millions or dealing with enduring poverty. But there are many international agencies, such as UNESCO, non-governmental organisations (NGOs) such as Oxfam, and many national bodies that are seeking to deal with the social aspects of population, human suffering, poverty, disease, famine and drought, which affect millions in developing countries (what used to be called the Third World and is now often called the Global South or the Developing World). The main topic categories set by Rio+20 were food, water, energy, jobs, disasters and oceans, but poverty

cross-cuts many of these issues. As stated in the introduction, the UN Millennium Development Goals have identified many key social issues alongside environmental sustainability objectives, as the two are strongly linked. The subsequent Sustainability Goals Programme will seek to make these links stronger.

Over 300 nations have committed their governments to contributing towards the achievement of these MDG goals and they may be seen as being as important as the Rio Declaration. Environmental sustainability is inseparable from social and economic conditions. For example, in some developing countries, well watered and fertilised crops may be grown for Western markets in heavily guarded farms, whilst local peasants do not have access to water supply and live in arid conditions. However, such matters cannot just be dealt with through changing the environment. In many cases the physical conditions people endure are the result of unstable governments, corrupt officials, wars, great extremes between wealth and poverty, the lasting effects of colonisation, and the overall dominance of Western countries in trade and investment. All these factors result in people in the Global South (including Africa and South America), especially in predominantly agricultural areas, being affected far more by climate change and natural disasters. In contrast, in developed Western democracies, building construction is generally to a higher standard, and there is a higher level of medical and emergency services. So when disasters hit, the impact is less and the governments and the populations are more able to cope and rebuild.

New forms of international urban planners have emerged to deal with these issues. Disaster planning has become a professional field in itself, concerned with both predicting disasters and dealing with them on the ground, often having additional expertise in water supply, drainage, crisis housing, sanitation and emergency health facilities. Architects, planners, civil engineers and urban designers have important roles in ensuring that buildings and cities are designed and built in a manner that is more disaster-resistant, for example by not building on land that is likely to flood and not zoning essential farmland for housing. In areas prone to earthquakes (such as Pakistan and Turkey) the government needs to

Photo 10.3   Workers' housing, Seoul, South Korea

Many countries use the high-rise solution to dealing with urban migration and population growth. Is high-rise more sustainable than low-rise housing? The social cost is lack of individuality, privacy and space. They may lack individual comforts but they benefit from a high level of infrastructural investment in South Korea. But all these apartments have access to the highest internet speed in the country and good public transport.

ensure that the building regulations, construction codes and standards are sufficient to minimise structural damage, especially in poor, unregulated settlements. The location of nuclear power stations in areas hit by these natural forces in Japan in Fukushima in 2011 made the situation even worse. Whether at home or abroad, urban planners also have a major role in helping to prevent disasters in the first place, by promoting policies concerned with reducing the carbon footprint of cities, and thus supporting sustainable development.

Population policy

Whilst it is fashionable to blame overpopulation and the Third Word for so many problems, in fact Westerners consume more, create more waste and have a larger carbon footprint than the poorer populations in the Third World. But the problem of 'too many people' being seen as 'destroying the planet' are catchphrases often spouted, particularly on tele-vision documentaries by elderly upper-class white males (who usually have produced a fair number of offspring themselves!). Planning has always been linked to demographics and population predictions, and it is no accident that birth control is called family planning, reflecting a scientific bent of mind that everything can be solved through planning based on statistical analysis. This goes back to the work of Malthus which argued that population growth would not be sustainable (Malthus 1798), disregarding the fact that more people did not just mean more mouths to feed but more hands to work. Toffler (1970), in his hugely influential book *Future Shock*, argued that the world was heading for over-population and advocated family planning and increased controls, particularly in the Third World. But overpopulation is a relative term as population densities are much lower in Africa than in Western Europe. It has been shown that there is enough food to go around in the world (Bandarage 1997). It is argued that shortages, famines and high prices are caused more by government policy and social inequality than by people having large families. This is particularly so in developing countries where infant mortality is high and life expectancy is very low, so net population gain is low. Such issues are frequently discussed in campaigns and publications by Oxfam, CAFOD and the *New Internationalist* monthly magazine. Whilst strict family planning policies were advocated in the past to reduce population growth, it has been found that when people, especially women, have better education, employment prospects and an improved standard of health then family sizes tend to reduce accordingly. The introduction of GM (genetically modified) crops as the great technological solution to famine has also been questioned. Multinational companies have introduced patents on seeds in many areas and distributed non-fertile varieties of some food crops. This goes against the sustainability principle of biodiversity and if all the crops are standardised they are more vulnerable to disease. But, many see the main population problem as not one of numbers but rather one of the changing composition. In many developed countries the population is ageing, with few children being born (the opposite of the situation in the developing world). Centrally planned economies such as China which has operated a one-child policy for 30 years now finds it has a huge population imbalance without enough young people to support a growing elderly population. Population issues will be discussed more fully in Chapter 14. China needs to house vast numbers of people coming into the cities as do many other developing countries. For example, in South Korea high rise seems to be the most efficient solution and perhaps in the circumstances it is the most sustainable too as it concentrates infrastructural provision and new development within high-density areas, rather than spreading outwards from the cities (Photo 10.3).

Conclusion: is sustainability sustainable?

We need to ask what the overall impact of sustainability has been on town planning and on the UK. As with most urban policies, change has been gradual and long term, as it is no simple task to change urban structure, provide people with a viable alternative to motorcars, and deal with all the related social and economic effects of environmental change. Nevertheless, British town planning's encounter with the international sustainability movement has led to culture change, if not shock. In particular, it has opened up the door for more collaborative approaches to the planning process, contributed to a greater emphasis upon community involvement and a local planning approach, and it has challenged the narrow physical land-use basis of British planning. Also it has created new synergies and connections in respect of defining the ambit and boundaries of what might validly count as part of 'town and country planning'.

One spin-off from a more sustainable perspective on urban planning has been the growth of the healthy cities movement. Awareness of the interrelationship between the urban environment and health issues has been marked, both within the sustainability movement and increasingly within central government policy statements from New Labour (cf. Fudge 1999). For example, *Our Healthier Nation* (Department of Health 1998) recognises the relationship between health and the quality of the environment and the social and environmental causes of ill-health. It offers a commitment to targeting inequalities in health, proposes a UK strategy to tackle poverty and social exclusion and has clear implications for urban policy and local transport policy. Overall sustainability policy has become increasingly linked to creating healthy cities, and to the social equality agenda too.

Local Agenda 21 programmes have contributed towards achieving these objectives in developing countries. The original Agenda 21 document acknowledged the importance of poverty and health issues, and states, 'good health depends on social, economic and spiritual development and a healthy environment, including safe food and water' (Keating 1993, 11). Previously, the World Health Organization (WHO) had established the Healthy Cities Project internationally (WHO 2011; Barton and Tsourou 2006). This was designed to promote good health and prevent disease, and was seen as a means of legitimising, nurturing and supporting the process of community empowerment (Brand 1999). It is significant that Mrs Gro Harlem Brundtland,

Photo 10.4   Questioning suburbia

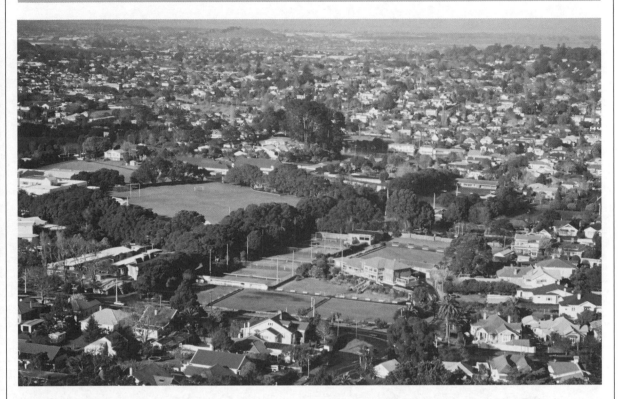

What is the future of traditional suburbia, parks and green spaces? Retrofitting, increased densities? Auckland, New Zealand.

the author of the 1987 Report, became the chair of the WHO (1999–2003). The WHO covers 51 nations and 870 million people. It is significant that health, along with social equity, were key themes in the United Nations Conference, Habitat II, held in Istanbul in 1996 and subsequently in Nanjing China. The human element, and thus the 'social aspects of planning', is being given greater attention in the international sustainability debate, as well as the natural environment component, which has, arguably, dominated British town planning. If 'predict and provide' is no longer to be the guiding principle in town planning and car-focused transport policy, more proactive and better-funded alternatives must be found to meet people's needs to go about their daily round of work, home-making and other essential activities. Back in the UK, the 2012 Health and Social Care Act, although mainly concerned with the reorganisation of the NHS

(National Health Service) also has implications for planning policy in terms of creating a more healthy population through urban policy and less car-based transport policy.

Thus, both the sustainability and the healthy cities agendas have had an increasing influence on the design and layout of cities, and as will be discussed in Chapter 13 on urban design, new forms of residential layout, and a more flexible approach to district and local area design follow naturally from a greater emphasis upon walking and less car usage. To achieve sustainably planned settlements the planners would need increased powers to achieve the fundamental structural shifts in land-use patterns, densities, traffic management, and layout patterns (Barton 1998). These issues affect every aspect of UK planning, not just new eco-towns but our approach to urban regeneration and renewal. We need to create the compact city, maybe to increase densities and to

Photo 10.5   A traditional Indonesian village

In contrast this is a pre-industrial, traditional rural settlement in central Java, where local building materials are still used, and it is so untouched by 'progress' that it is extremely green and environmentally sustainable.

consider retrofitting the suburbs to achieve environmental targets (Tallon 2009, 163–4). But, there are still major barriers to change. Unless there is a tremendous shift in central government attitudes, funding, and regulation regarding public transport, motor car usage, pollution control enforcement, building design, energy policy and waste disposal practice, the planners, alone, have inadequate powers to achieve sustainable cities. There are many other debates around the pros and cons of environmental policy, which in some cases arguably contradicts or works against other social, design and accessibility considerations (Greed 2011a, 2012). Likewise sustainability has become so holy and above reproach that few dare question it (Madariaga

and Roberts (eds) 2013). For example, increasing densities in the suburbs and building over gardens might help the housing crisis but it would have a negative effect on the natural environment in terms of water run-off, habitats for local fauna, and major political problems in terms of our whole attitude to owner-occupation and privacy, for culturally, 'An Englishman's home is his castle'. Many of the new environmentally designed architectural eco-buildings such as the BedZED development in Beddington, Sutton, is, arguably, not that attractive visually. BedZED stands for the Beddington Zero Energy Development, London Borough of Sutton, and was built in 2000, and can be accessed from Hackbridge Station and by taking the Croydon

Tramway system. Much of such architecture is certainly a culture shock to those whose ideal house is more traditional in design (for example Photo 10.4, suburban housing in the same area), and one needs to respect the needs and wants of the population. It is important to work with people, and see their point of view, rather than judging them (Hague (ed.) 2006). In planning all one can hope is to do the lesser of a choice of different evils. But in the final analysis pre-industrial villages in the developing world (Photo 10.5) may be more sustainable than modern Western cities (Photo 10.4).

For the tasks, further reading, additional photos and other resources for this chapter, please visit www.palgrave.com/companion/greed. E-Supplement 1 provides information on legislation and government planning guidance, and will be particularly useful in relation to this chapter (there is a chronological list of sustainable development events and a table of the world's largest cities).

Regeneration, Retail and Renewal

A new urban dynamism

One of the most significant changes to urban form in the last 20 years has been the regeneration of run-down inner-city areas, disused docklands and redundant industrial locations. The planning system has been central to many of these changes, both in terms of stimulating regeneration, responding to market interest in such sites and managing change. This chapter traces this transformation with reference to the recent history of policy approaches, policy priorities and delivery mechanisms. We will examine the scale of change that has occurred in towns and cities. During the last 20 years cities have been shaped by economic boom but we have now entered a more difficult economic climate for development, following the banking crisis of 2008.

In the course of this chapter we will cover some of the main components of urban regeneration development. In particular, three key elements, namely employment, housing, and retail development, will be discussed. Each of these have already cropped up in preceding chapters in the course of the 'story of planning' but it seems appropriate to deal with them again in more detail. In the final section of the chapter case studies will be given of some of the most important examples of urban renewal which are reshaping the eastern extension of London, namely the three major, and linked, developments of the Olympic Park in Stratford; the massive Thames Gateway development, where half the new houses in London are currently being built, stretching out to the estuary of the Thames; and the Cross Rail which joins it all up with the rest of London and actually extends from near to Reading in the West right across to the new developments in the East and is expected to be completed by 2019. In the conclud-ing section of the chapter, certain key themes evident in urban regeneration policies and developments are identified, namely the importance of branding, legacy and culture.

In discussing regeneration there is a need, throughout the chapter, to ask 'of what and for whom?' Regeneration policy may be seen as proactive in terms of facilitating the renewal of our urban areas, and bringing forth retail, commercial, residential and leisure developments. But it is also reactive in seeking to respond to long-term issues such as unemployment, inadequate housing supply, and the perceived problems of the 'inner city' (Tallon 2013). Thus much of this chapter is strongly linked to policy issues and problems introduced in previous chapters (especially Chapters 6 and 7), including housing policy, regional planning and employment. Urban regeneration also links to other urban policy agendas such as urban design, place-making and culture (Chapter 13); and to transport and infrastructural development (Chapter 12). Many issues particularly link to the content of the social aspects of planning chapters, especially Chapter 14. But in the real world all these factors are combined together in the planning and design of particular schemes and project locations, as illustrated in the case studies.

Employment and economic development

It took a long time for the problems of the declining inner urban areas to be recognised and acted upon. As described in Chapters 6 and 7, there has been a tradition of regional planning in which successive Labour governments, in particular, have given financial aid to the economically depressed regions and have sought to control and move new development from the prosperous South East to the North. One of the fundamental components of post-war reconstruction planning legislation was the 1945 Distribution of Industry Act which enacted regional policies concerned with supporting declining Northern industrial areas as described in Chapter 6. There was, arguably, a somewhat anti-urban, anti-Southern bias towards regional policy, which was to continue for many years. This approach was pursued in spite of the fact that around 30 per cent of the population has always lived in the South East, including large numbers of working-class people within the inner London boroughs. But they were not socialist heroes such coal miners or steel workers, but more likely to be bus drivers, health workers, cleaners and low-paid office and shop workers. Inner-city areas were seen in a negative light as overcrowded and in need of clearance. Subsequent post-war governments sought to move people out of the inner city to new towns, new housing estates, and other regions to create a more balanced distribution of population, housing and employment. As explained in other chapters, such policies deprived inner-city areas of investment and contributed to the inner-city problems of today.

Conservative governments also supported new house-building on green-field sites in the post-war period but were less enthusiastic about regional development. Giving regional development grants to depressed areas in the North was seen by the Conservatives as supporting lame ducks and suppressing essential new financial development and job creation nationally. For example, a particular problem as perceived by the Labour government of the 1960s was the concentration of office development in London. The 1965 Control of Offices and Industrial Development Act introduced ODP (Office Development Permits) for all new office development in the South East and Midlands over 3000 square feet, and the IDC (Industrial Development Certificates) system was also made stricter for these areas.

The Labour governments of the early 1970s began to shift policy gradually towards the acknowledgement of the needs of what had by then become known as the inner city, through emphasising hous-

ing improvement rather than demolition. But it was not until the Conservative government came to power under Mrs Thatcher in the 1970s that attention was strongly diverted to inner-city areas, and old-fashioned regional policies based on dealing with heavy industry and manufacturing became increasingly irrelevant. The reality was that the whole global economy was changing and Britain was no longer the workshop of the world, with stiff competition from emerging economies in the Far East, such as China, where wages and production costs were so much lower. Major international changes were resulting in the de-industrialisation of Great Britain. Increasingly it was realised that Britain's economic future no longer lay in manufacturing but rather in service industries, in financial services, retail, expansion of the knowledge industry (including higher education), and in business investment and enterprise. All of these activities were likely to result in office jobs rather than factory jobs, and women workers were more employable and docile than men used to working in mines, mills and factories. Many of these jobs did not have high salaries, were part-time and fairly exploitative (call centres etc.), although greater social inequalities began to emerge with some, such as bankers, earning millions a year. But they were all factors in changing the face of Britain, not least regionally, as most of these jobs were not tied to a particular raw material or industrial site but could be undertaken anywhere, although preferably in cities where the financial infrastructure and a suitable workforce already existed. Gradually, it was accepted that decline in the UK had to be 'managed' by accepting it as a fact of life and that in some areas it was necessary to plan for 'degrowth', that is decline (Photo 11.1). As time went on, as described in the sociological chapters in Part IV, the old working class ceased to exist and the whole economy moved towards providing financial services, especially after the Big Bang and the deregulation of financial services. Whereas in the 1970s around 75 per cent of the population proudly self-identified as belonging to the working class, the same percentage see themselves as middle class and are nowadays likely to be employed in office and service sector jobs (see Chapter 14).

Photo 11.1   Decline never goes away

There is still a north–south divide and still pockets of housing decay in inner cities, usually made up of both old council blocks of flats condemned for redevelopment and, astonishingly in view of the national housing shortage, empty private property suffering from planning blight and compulsory purchase threats.

As described in Chapter 6, when the Conservatives came to power in 1979 a sea change took place. The Conservatives clearly saw the inner city as a greater problem than the regions, although there was clearly a north–south divide (Photo 11.1). They also had little time for the Unions whose heartlands were in the old mining and manufacturing areas. UK coal mining was in decline and, according to Mrs Thatcher at least, the Trade Unions had to be 'faced down' during the Miners' Strike as they were asking for exorbitant pay increases without increased production. The Conservatives' strategy was based (increasingly until their defeat in 1997) on the idea that there should be encouragement of the private-sector business investment and the growth of commerce and financial services, located mainly within London, the South East and major provincial cities. The Conservatives saw private enterprise, rather than state intervention and the welfare programmes favoured by Labour, as the vehicle for eradicating poverty and social deprivation: through the creation of new jobs.

Under the Thatcher Conservative government, the emphasis moved right away from regional planning to inner-city regeneration, with new legislation heralding in Enterprise Zones (EZs) and Urban Development Corporations (UDCs) (introduced in 1980) (see Chapters 6 and 7). Arguably, the primary objective of all these initiatives was not (really) to solve the social problems of inner-city residents, but rather to see the run-down and derelict urban areas as having huge potential for investment, development and renewal. The Conservative government built up an array of policy programmes aimed at the inner city, including Action for Cities (1988), City Challenge (1991), English Partnerships (1993) and the Millennium Partnership Programme. The Single Regeneration Budget (SRB) introduced in 1994 by the Tories was taken over enthusiastically by New Labour and only abolished in 2007.

Hence under Michael Heseltine, the minister responsible for planning under Thatcher, a vast array of Enterprise Zones and Urban Development Corporations and special investment areas were created in major cities. The redundant London Docklands become one of the first areas to be so designated, namely the London Docklands Development Corporation (LDDC). This was accompanied by major supporting infrastructure improvement such as the London Docklands Light Railway. All this has been a major driver to new development, such as the extension of the 'City' to a new international financial centre around Canary Wharf (previously part of the derelict London docks and wharves area alongside the Thames). There were many other EZ and UDC schemes throughout the UK and some rather innovative ideas to kick start renewal that did not always work, for example in 1984 the International Garden Festival in Liverpool was opened, masterminded by Heseltine who spent millions on reclaiming derelict land along the Mersey. After the festival closed the area became neglected and run-down owing to lack of further funding and little luck in attracting businesses to the area, and it was closed in 1997. However, it was refurbished and reopened in 2012, almost as a sign to the world that the Coalition government were following the earlier Heseltine–Thatcher approach to regeneration.

The Conservatives also freed office and retail development from Labour controls and favoured the free play of the market. The Office Development Permits system was abolished (introduced in 1965) by the Control of Office Development (Cessation) Order in 1979, along with Industrial Development Certificates in 1981. This resulted in the growth of commercial development within city centres, on a scale not experienced before. This trend has continued ever since, to meet the needs of a changing office-based workforce. There has also been a return to enthusiasm for high-rise buildings, but they are usually office blocks, or private apartment blocks, not council blocks of flats, which have never had been popular with the public, indeed ever since the collapse of Ronan Point on 16 May 1968. The Shard, the tallest building in Western Europe, was completed in mid-2012 and along with the Gherkin and Canary Wharf creates a new high-rise skyline for London. Retail development has also changed vastly over the years.

The New Labour government, which came to power in 1997 (lasting until 2010), continued commitment to further development on this new 'East-side' of London with the building of the Millennium Dome (now called the O2 Centre and proving a major entertainment venue). As Tallon explains (Tallon 2013), New Labour put so much emphasis upon business and enterprise that some have seen Blair as the true son of Thatcher. Nevertheless New Labour continued the socialist tradition of its forebears in resurrecting the regional dimension of planning under the RSS (Regional Spatial Strategies). But even when dealing with the traditional depressed regions such as the North East, the means of creating change was more likely to be by trying to attract business through the RDAs (Regional Development Agencies), rather than getting the state heavily involved in direct subsidies and grants. But Labour's commitment to mining and heavy industry was still evident, albeit on a much smaller scale. For example, the English Coalfields Regeneration Programme (Tallon 2009: 93) seemed to be a way of paying lip service to traditional Labour voter needs, but through regeneration rather than coal industry subsidies. But most new jobs were in the financial sector, computer technology, retail, the service industry and office work (Jones and Evans 2008).

Whilst the domestic UK-related regional level of planning had changed, Britain was playing a longer game on the international and European economic stage. A new transnational urban region now stood out, namely the Golden Triangle drawn between London, Paris and Brussels, further linked by the Channel Tunnel (opened in 1993). But, it is over-simplistic to say that 'everyone' was now middle class. Even in London, which is one of the wealthiest cities in the world, with one of highest levels of people with degrees employed in the business and finance sectors, at the same time there continue to be large pockets of poverty within the inner London boroughs. Significant proportions of the workforce were still employed in manufacturing industry across the Greater London region, contrary to images that 'everyone' worked in high-paying office jobs. But a substantial low-paid, and less-unionised, working class still existed within these sectors, including cleaners, care assistants, bus drivers, junior teachers, administrators and unskilled manual workers, and there was also a growing non-working class (as discussed further on the social aspects of planning in Part IV). The challenge of this class system, with its extremes of wealth and poverty, was reflected in the 1995 Tory revision of RPG3 (Regional Planning Guidance Note 3) Strategic Guidance for London Planning Authorities.

The Coalition government, elected in 2010, has since it has been in power, demolished many of the more generous state-funded aspects of New Labour regeneration policy but has kept those aspects which encourage partnership between the private and public sectors. It has resurrected the idea of the Enterprise Zone and is in the process of designating a range across the country. It has also committed to increased investment in infrastructure and transport, as a means of generating the conditions for more economic activity. It has continued to support New Labour's Cross Rail, Thames Gateway projects and continued the funding and fully supported the Olympics developments, as this was seen as a cross-party initiative above national political interests.

By the new millennium Britain had become a post-industrial society, in which the composition and culture of the workforce had changed completely. Tallon discusses the move from Fordism to post-Fordism, because it has so fundamentally affected employment, business and the approach to urban regeneration in our post-industrial society (Tallon 2009, 133). Fordism was a capitalist mode of production associated with a high level of regulation of the workforce, by the use of assembly lines, manned, I would add, by a fairly uniform workforce, comprising male skilled workers. In contrast, under post-Fordism, the workforce is more diverse, creative, consumption-related, localised, and self-employed, and both male and female. In parallel the whole class

structure changed, and the service and financial sectors employ far more people than manufacturing (ESRC 2012 which has some good diagrams of changing class composition and see the ONS national statistics website).

Housing and people issues

The housing and planning policies of the past have continued to have a major impact on the type of inner-city housing available today. Many of the inner-city areas that have been the subject of regeneration previously comprised historical terraced housing for the working classes, or, in areas where this housing had been demolished, high-rise council blocks from the 1960s. Increasingly redundant churches, educational establishments and commercial development have also been used for new housing too. Much of this refurbishment is aimed at middle-class occupants. But, until the 1970s, much housing policy and related inner-city planning work was motivated by providing 'housing for the working classes', not planning for the needs of the new urban middle class which subsequently gentrified these areas.

As described in Part I of the book, in the history chapters, the main concern amongst housing reformers was with dealing with the slums and the needs of the poor, and with the labouring classes in general. These were not only located in the depressed Northern industrial regions, in substandard terraced houses, but poor housing had been a component of London life in the metropolis, ever since Booth's street survey of London. In 2012 the historical background to erstwhile working-class streets in London that have now been heavily gentrified, with properties each fetching millions, was featured in the television documentary *The Secret History of Our Streets* (BBC 2012), which can still be obtained through the Open University publications and check on the BBC website iPlayer. Substandard housing in the metropolis consisted both of terraced housing in the East End, and also subdivided mansions and run-down town houses, in what had once been good quality middle-class housing areas further West in the city. But there was no concept of the 'inner city' as yet in British planning. In contrast to all the money and attention going to propping up industry, during the 30 years after the war, there was little financial or positive help for poor inner-city areas. Rather the policy was one of destruction rather than support.

The post-war period was a time when a great deal of house–building took place. During the war, 50,000 civilians had been killed in the bombing; 40,000, the majority, in London. One and half million people had been made homeless, and around 4 million houses were damaged (to varying degrees, with over a quarter being destroyed). In London a total of 600 acres of inner-city housing was reduced to rubble. Initially housing policy was concerned with new house-building and repair. 500,000 new houses were built in the immediate post-war period by the Labour government, half of which were council houses, plus 157,000 prefabs). This pace of development continued under the Conservatives (1951–54) who achieved 300,000 houses per year, a figure never yet exceeded. The bandwagon of housing demolition continued long after the main war damage had been dealt with. A series of Housing Acts, culminating in the 1957 Slum Clearance Act, focused on the condemnation and demolition of vast tracks of the inner city, including historically important residential buildings, as 'unfit for human habitation'. In fact more houses were demolished under this legislation than were bombed during the war (Ravetz 1980). As explained in Chapter 6, over 1.5 million houses were demolished under slum clearance programmes, which affected 3.7 million residents. They were relocated either in distant, new council housing estates on the edge of urban areas, new towns, or piled up in blocks of high-rise flats, with drastic social consequences. This freed up a large amount of land around city centres for future development.

Significantly, all the local economic activities, the shops, businesses, back-street industry and workplaces were swept away too as clutter to make way for the pristine zoned city of the planners (Young and Willmott 1957) (see Chapter 14 on the social aspects of planning). Thus the seeds of future inner decline were sown. Rather than seeing all this enterprise, local employment and community activity as the 'mulch' out of which new industry and businesses would arise, to the benefit of the economy, they were devalued. In particular, planners voiced a disdain for shopkeepers and anyone else in 'trade', including all the self-employed SMEs (Small and Medium Enterprises) that today are seen as the lifeblood of the nation (Portas 2012). Indeed planners seemed to be quite dismissive of small shopkeepers and had little idea of their role and importance in the local economy and community.

There was a gradual move towards renewal rather than demolition. Under Labour (1964–70), as described in Chapter 14, there was more awareness of the importance of the community and tenants' rights, and the destruction that slum clearance wrought. The 1969 Housing Act, which gave improvement grants to older properties, opened up a new lease of life for many of the older housing areas, and established General Improvement Areas (GIAs) for comprehensive refurbishment of areas. But this legislation did not necessarily solve the related social problems; indeed as we have seen earlier the existing residents were often being pushed out of their home areas as a result of these policies. In 1968 the Home Office had initiated an Urban Programme with 34 pilot local authorities to investigate the emerging problems of the inner city: note that this project was as much concerned with rising crime as it was with wider social issues. In 1969 the Community Development Programme (CPD) was set up, with CDPs running in 12 areas to begin with, with social workers rather than town planners taking the leading role. However, it was fashionable at the time to see the problems 'spatially' as being contained within a specific geographical area, without considering the wider social factors that brought people 'down' into such areas in the first place. For example, in 1970 Educational Priority Areas (EPAs) were established in areas where positive discrimination was needed, interestingly towards the white working class, rather than ethnic groups at this stage, as in the case of a scheme which was established in Everton in Liverpool. All this prefigures area-based approaches that were adopted by New Labour and are still popular today. By the 1970s the problem of the inner city had become firmly established in the public's conscience, and it was another area where the government could introduce yet another set of confusing categories and area classifications.

In 1971 Comprehensive Community Programmes were introduced in a range of areas, widening the concern to include education, health, social services and housing. In 1972 the emphasis shifted more towards special policies within the realms of town planning itself, and the Department of the Environment established its Six Towns Study, focusing on areas such as Lambeth in southern inner London, and at last publically recognising the poverty near at hand. The 1974 Housing Act established another category of special housing areas known as Housing Action Areas (HAAs), which were smaller than GIAs but adopted a more concentrated immediate attention. Such schemes often seemed separate or insensitive to other social problems in the areas chosen. For example, in one black inner-city area in Birmingham where unemployment was high, white workmen were brought in by the council from outside to repair black tenants' houses, causing considerable tension in community relations. In 1975 the Urban Aid programme enabled money to be allocated to other inner-city schemes including community centres, and later law centres. In 1977 the Manpower Services Commission was set up with particular concern for enabling employment in inner areas. This was followed by the 1978 Inner Urban Areas Act, which as its name suggests enabled the creation of special inner urban area policies, this time under the control, chiefly, of the town planners. The 1989 Local Government and Housing Act has introduced the concept of 'Renewal Areas' which are like the old GIAs and HAAs (which they replace) but the emphasis is on more partnership with the private sector in renewal, and grants to individual householders are means tested.

Whilst major urban regeneration had taken place, in spite of all this change, there was still social deprivation and many problems had not been conquered. Back in the 1970s inequality was visibly re-emerging in society and the economy, and also social unrest was manifest but not just in the historically poor industrial areas of the North. Poverty and new forms of urban deprivation were developing, which could not simply be explained away by unemployment, but were the result of other social problems such as racial discrimination, family break-up, disability and an ageing population. The 'inner city' became the catch phrase to describe the collection of spatially identifiable groups and problems located broadly within the poorer inner urban area neighbourhoods, corresponding to what traditional urban sociologists called the zone of transition (see Chapter 14). Riots took place in inner-city areas, in the 1960s and 1970s, such as in Handsworth in Birmingham, Everton in Liverpool, St Pauls in Bristol, Tottenham in London, and Sparkbrook in Birmingham. These early riots were generally seen to be 'race riots' mainly undertaken by young black males as protests against heavy policing, and lack of education and jobs (Scarman Report 1982). At that time there was little concept of the importance of ethnic minority communities, and the fact that they comprised all sorts of people, families and age groups, not just 'young males'. In contrast some London boroughs comprise more than 60 per cent ethnic minority populations, and have done so for over ten years, so they are hardly a minority any more (Onuoha and Greed 2003).

Under the intervening Conservative government, Mrs Thatcher famously introduced the 'right to buy' in 1979, by which council tenants could own their own home, and at a discount too. This was a hugely popular policy but it completely decimated national social housing stock. Housing Associations increasingly stepped into the breach. However, under Major there was some softening of attitudes and greater support for those seeking housing, and paradoxically a growth in range and complexity of government policies on those without housing, the unemployed and single parent families. However, this was a period of considerable private-sector house-building and the promotion of Britain as a property-owning democracy. This was also the period in which increased gentrification of inner-city properties was taking place, as historically working-class areas were colonised by young affluent office workers tired of commuting, seeking a more urban lifestyle and reacting against the silence of the suburbs. As a result it was also the start of the rise in house prices that would soon prevent working-class and low-income people living in the inner city, unless they were council or housing association tenants.

When New Labour came to power in 1997, as stated above, it wound down the Enterprise Zone programme. It created a myriad of new measures and programmes to deal with urban deprivation, poverty, social exclusion, crime and housing problems throughout out its period in office (1997–2010). To start off it published the policy document, New Deal for Communities, in 1997. Key programmes centred on neighbourhood renewal and urban regeneration using various tools, such as regeneration companies, partnerships, SRB, and special ad hoc bodies. Many of these initiatives were inspired by the 'urban renaissance' agenda championed by Lord Rogers' Urban Taskforce in the late 1990s (Rogers 1999) and politically from New Labour's 'Third Way' philosophy, which sought to use both state intervention and the market to push forward policies concerned with tackling urban deprivation and social exclusion. However, some policies solved one social problem and created another. For example, the popularity of policies aimed at boosting the evening economy, 24-hour city and 'cool' cultural areas whilst creating more vibrant cities (for some) do so at the expense of others, especially the working-class families remaining in such areas.

The New Deal for Communities, Neighbourhood Renewal, BIDs (Business Improvement Districts), Urban Regeneration Companies, Training and Enterprise councils, and the Social Exclusion Unit sought to tackle social disadvantage through encouraging new investment in run-down areas. UDCs and Enterprise Zones also quietly finished their lifespan under Blair, and were not seen to be contrary to New Labour policy. Whilst all this appeared to offer more money and attention to inner-city issues, New Labour's funding regime was increasingly based upon different local authorities and communities bidding and competing with each other to get resources, under a peculiar funding regime driven by a Lottery Fund mentality. There were so many urban initiatives under New Labour that the reader is advised to check those of interest to their area or project work on the internet. But the reality is that most are now on the way out because of the changes being brought about by the current Coalition government.

New Labour also made major changes to housing policy guidance as described in previous chapters (and in the topic chapters on transport, sustainability and urban design). PPS3, on Housing, required higher residential densities (of 30 dwellings per hectare), and that 60 per cent of new housing development should take place on brown-field land. The government set much higher building targets of 4 million houses to be built in the next 20 years (Barker 2004). Barker wanted 60 per cent of new housing to be built on brown land and delivered through the Regional Spatial Strategies. There was particular concern over lack of housing in the South East and in 2003 the Sustainable Communities Plan set aside 610 million pounds to build an extra 200,000 houses in this region, a drop in the bucket. The required rate of building to reach 4 million houses was never achieved with, for example, 175,000 new houses being built nationally in 2007. Labour governments always have had high aspirations regarding 'solving the housing crisis' through new house-building. In comparison, under the Labour government, led by Harold Wilson 1965–79, 2 million houses were constructed, half of which were council houses (Dunleavy 1980). Rather than really solving the housing crisis, this resulted in massive amounts of high-density, medium-rise, executive apartment blocks being built in the derelict land around city centres. These were convenient for single people or childless couples but not for families with children, and were occupied by 'the single socially-mobile white-collar' worker, and mainly male at that. Such apartments were expensive and were often bought as investment properties and rented out, or used by international business people, so none of this benefited local people with families. In these new residential areas, there was little provision of local infrastructure, such as schools or local community facilities, but restaurants, wine bars, gyms and Metro supermarkets proliferated. This has been a very strong trend in London but also in Manchester and Birmingham. Whilst this has worked well in areas such as Canary Wharf, the London Docklands and Thames Gateway, the effects of the financial collapse from 2008 onwards has resulted in many of these properties remaining vacant with negative equity, particularly in provincial cities.

One finds huge social contrasts within inner-city areas, sometimes in the same street, of very rich people living in gentrified properties alongside very poor people living on housing benefit, as in

Bermondsey and other erstwhile working-class East End districts. As the saying goes, *'you have to be very poor or very rich to live in London'*. This process had begun back in the 1960s with the gentrification of Georgian and Victorian properties. But London is a global city and part of an international property market which has inflated prices vastly. However, the situation is complex as whilst there are both very rich and very poor areas in inner cities, there are other new factors at work too, such as the proliferation of student housing (Tallon 2009, 213) where occupants are seen as temporary, and often resented by the existing working-class neighbourhoods they have colonised. Large-scale immigration, for example from the Indian subcontinent, Africa and Eastern Europe, has also changed the housing dynamic in many areas. Overall the American 'social ecology' theories, such as the concentric zone concept that many of you readers were taught at school, proved inadequate to explain or map what is happening in modern British cities. (Global population was discussed in the last chapter, and the UK situation is discussed further in Chapter 14.)

In spite of assertions that community and social considerations were important under New Labour's regeneration programme, many questioned whether it was really reaching those in need. The pressure for middle-class housing in inner areas, and the whole gentrification process that has totally transformed so many erstwhile working-class districts, has, in part, been driven by this massive office development growth, along with the desire to live near to one's work and not to have to commute or use the car. All this could be justified in the name of sustainability, because the residents could commute to their jobs in the city by public transport, along the Docklands Light Railway for example, but it has had disastrous social consequences for working-class people trying to buy into the inner-city housing market.

Regeneration is big business. Vast amounts of public money were put into all these projects by New Labour, even though, in theory, it was private-sector business activity that was meant to revitalise the areas. PFI (Private Finance Initiative) schemes were used to fund public works such as hospital and school building, by which the private sector actually made a profit out of funding public works, often costing more than direct public sector funding

approaches. It is rumoured that over 60 per cent of grant money was going to planning consultancies advising on urban regeneration rather than directly to the people in need. Many community groups felt there was so much emphasis on bringing new business and enterprise into run-down areas that often struggling small local shops and businesses were swept away in the process. In some inner-city housing estates, and outer council estates, food deserts now exist with few local shops, nowhere to buy fresh food and vegetables, and perhaps just fast-food takeaways (Shaw 2006).

However, in larger housing schemes there was requirement for 20 per cent social housing to be included. This was usually in the form of housing association provision, along with some dedicated accessible housing for the disabled, creating a semblance of some social diversity in the area. But overall there was little consideration of social facilities and requirements. In spite of the frequent use of the word 'community' in New Labour policy documents, in reality many local residents felt they had little say in what was happening. From an equality perspective, the overemphasis upon economic issues and especially unemployment when discussing 'social exclusion' resulted in inadequate attention being given to social issues and support services. These are the very factors that would enable people to get into work in the first place, such as better public transport, childcare provision and investment in local schools (Greed 2011a, 2011b). However, 'Sure Start' programmes did provide coordinated childcare provision in some areas. But promises of the upgrading of school buildings (including the ones that still had outside toilets and ancient boiler heating systems) are not yet fulfilled .

When the Coalition came to power in 2011 they immediately cut back many of the programmes, along with public sector spending in general, to deal with the deficits and debts arising from the Banking Crisis which had started in 2008 (which arguably was the fault of millionaire bankers not the public sector, humble local government employees or the inner-city poor). A leaner more directed approach to inner-city regeneration was heralded by the return of the Enterprise Zone and the Urban Development Corporation, but this time areas covered were to be smaller and more focused than under the

Conservative government. For example, the Royal Docks in London are now an EZ which is in an area that has already received a great deal of regeneration support and policy attention. The Coalition has reiterated a commitment to new house-building, arguably with a greater emphasis upon green-field sites than inner-city locations. Initially there was much fear that the Coalition would allow a 'developers' free for all' to be set in motion by the NPPF (Chapter 2). Further proposals to reduce planning controls (Chapter 3) to stimulate the house-building market have been much criticised, even by the property industry itself. There are already half a million agreed planning permissions for housing development in existence, but developers cannot afford to build because of the financial crisis and lack of lending by banks and financial institutions. In 2010 only 102,500 houses were built, the lowest figure since 1923. In 2011 only 110,000 new houses were built, mainly by the private sector, but 1.8 million households (5 million people) remain on housing waiting lists (Hanley 2012). Around a million houses are always empty, for a variety of reasons, such as ownership transfer, compulsory purchase, abandonment, second homes and so forth. There are around 250,000 second homes, some of which may be empty most of the year, comprising around 1.5 per cent of the housing stock, see www.savills.co.uk. For all these figures look at House Building Statistics, which are released on a quarterly basis (go to www.communities.gov.uk and look for 'housing'). As discussed in Chapters 2 and 3, there are around half a million houses ready to be built which have planning permission but whose developers cannot go ahead because of lack of finance.

In comparison, in 2007, 175,000 new houses were built each year. But the whole tenure situation has changed over the years, and many young people cannot possibly afford a mortgage and for the first time for a hundred years owner-occupation is declining slightly relative to renting. Today, around 74 per cent of households are owner-occupied, 9 per cent are council rented, 5 per cent housing association and 12 per cent (and growing) are privately rented. There have been seismic changes in housing tenure over the last century. In 1901, 90 per cent of all housing was privately rented, the complete opposite of today. In contrast, council-rented property reached a peak of over 30 per cent in the 1970s. Private renting is becoming a growing sector because young people cannot afford to take out mortgages which may be several times their income. Check the 2014 Census data, especially on housing and population which was published by the Office for National Statistics.

The social component of urban regeneration is no longer as strong under the Coalition, and indeed the government is determined to 'get people back into work' and to discourage 'social security scroungers' and a 'culture of worklessness'. But many of the poorer people living in inner cities and other deprived areas *are* in employment but cannot hope to buy property and have found the whole gentrification and regeneration scenario has made it too expensive to live in the areas where they were born. So people doing low-paid essential work serving the needs of the city centre, such as cleaners, drivers, teachers, security staff and so forth find they have to live further out and commute in. There is huge pent-up demand for more housing, and yet options are limited. The Barker Report on Housing of 2004 had identified that increased demand was down to 39 per cent population growth; 28 per cent falling mortality; 22 per cent migration and 11 per cent higher headship rates (especially more single person households). These trends have continued, with London and other large cities being particularly pressurised in terms of housing stock. But in contrast, some economically depressed regions have a surplus of housing and low house prices. Surprisingly slum clearance is still taking place. For example, under New Labour 500 million pounds was set aside to tackle the problems of housing abandonment and low demand in Liverpool and Hull. It so happened that Ringo Starr's childhood home was caught in the net of the slum clearance area in Liverpool, known as the Welsh Streets, leading to Beatles fans demanding the terraced house should be spared and become a listed building. The long-drawn-out battle continues under the Coalition.

In spite of the apparent lack of sympathy of the plight of ordinary folk, and all the cutbacks to the public sector, as it turned out the new government has promoted itself as being concerned with 'society', promoting a new localism and enthusiasm for community involvement (see Chapters 2 and 7).

Significant investment was allocated to specific projects such as New City Deals in July 2012, and six such deals were given to key cities, along with greater powers and funding to enable a freeing from Whitehall control. Cities included are Birmingham, Newcastle, Nottingham, Leeds, Liverpool, Manchester and Bristol. Bristol received approval and funding for the go-ahead of the much longed-for Bristol Metro, a rapid transit tramway system connecting up key points in the city. But overall, aside from prestige projects, there were such major cutbacks in public funding and support services that The Big Society and new localism seemed very limited in many areas. All this is very confusing, as the government is sending out mixed messages, but by the time you read this book the situation may have become clearer.

Another interesting development is the apparent lack of appreciation the Coalition government has for the planners, who are seen as slow and holding back development. As a result 'planning' may no longer be seen to be as important to the process of urban regeneration. The planners have always worked with a range of other policy-makers and urban managers in the field of health, education, social services, transport and, of course, housing, often taking the lead as facilitators and coordinators. But increasingly it seems that policy is being directed more centrally with the Treasury having a growing role, or ad hoc bodies such as Enterprise Zone bodies are being introduced that circumvent the powers of local authority planners. Indeed the very term 'town planning' has become outdated and discredited, and a 'dirty word', which has been replaced by urban regeneration as a profession and a means of urban governance. Tallon has discussed the expansion of area designations and related policy initiatives under New Labour (Tallon 2009: see his list of initiatives on page 105), entitling the section describing this progression as 'From Patchwork to Spaghetti', and an area-based approach seems to be continuing under the Coalition. In spite of New Labour's assertion that they wanted more joined-up thinking, in reality there seemed to be little coordination between policies in many areas. Tallon also discusses the importance of inter-city collaborative networks to make it all work, and this concept echoes Patsy Healey's emphasis upon collaborative planning with the community (see Chapter 8 on planning theory). This approach has resurfaced under the Coalition as 'the duty to cooperate' both horizontally across adjacent local authorities, and vertically between the local community and the local authority under the new planning system brought in under the 2011 Localism Act.

The whole neighbourhood planning agenda, and related new localism, should not necessarily be seen as a means of benefiting the community and bringing planning closer to the people. Rather we should always remember, as outlined in the NPPF and in numerous Coalition policies, that the purpose of the changes is to speed up the planning system, and to bring forth growth and development. However, in this process, both the community and the developers are apparently coming closer, ostensibly working together for the regeneration of cities, without the interference of the planners. Indeed some would argue that planners are being increasingly excluded from planning. But in all this plethora of activity, there is still a need to restore the strategic spatial dimension of planning, to avoid an uncoordinated scatter gun approach to site development. Also there is a need to remember the social purpose of regeneration too (Grindrod 2013).

Many things have not changed. Riots have continued sporadically over the years, since the days of Brixton and Toxteth, and have developed into new, more aggressive forms in the new millennium, with a whole different scale of intensity and extent. For example, the summer of 2011 was marked by rioting on a massive scale across inner London and within other large cities, but they involved a wider range of types of people in terms of age, gender and ethnicity. They were apparently sparked off by the police handling of a shooting incident but they may owe much to a general sense of despair and social exclusion. But these were not 'race riots' as they were called in the media. In fact people from different ethnic origins were both the perpetrators and the victims in many areas, with Asian businesses being targeted. Whether these recent riots were actually 'caused' by where people live, a typical spatial planning explanation, is also open to question, as with Facebook, Twitter and SMS, large numbers of people can be rapidly alerted to be mobilised from outside the area in question, with looters and organised gangs commuting into the area in question. So the debate continues as to what extent such occurrences were down locational factors, such as living in deprived areas in poor housing, in which case the planners have a major role to play in 'planning out crime', as discussed in the social aspects chapter on environmental determinism (Chapter 14). Such 'consumer riots', in which branded sports goods and designer labels were looted, need to be distinguished from the 'human rights' demonstrations for democracy that spread across the Middle East in 2011–12 as the Arab Spring, and the more intellectually motivated demonstrations such as Occupy sit-ins in London and New York which were protests against the banking system.

Retail and commercial development

Commercial developments, including office and retail development, have also been key components of urban regeneration. Shopping development has been a major force in reshaping the inner city, in terms of input to both the economy and jobs market. Eleven per cent of all enterprises and Small and Medium Enterprises (SMEs) are retail businesses: that is shops. But, as mentioned above, regeneration does not necessarily benefit traditional small shops as it can be used to clear out local traders in order to acquire land and premises and bring in national chains. Furthermore, web-based internet shopping is also a growing challenge to the whole retail sector. Let us briefly summarise the history of retail development and its effect on land use and city form.

Traditional corner shops, parades of 1930s shops and long-established High Streets, were soon competing with new shopping centre development in the 1950s. For example, Broadmead in Bristol was completely rebuilt after the bombing. Town Centre Redevelopment and Comprehensive development schemes were taking place all over the country, aided by extensive compulsory purchase powers, and slum clearance legislation which freed up land in the city centre and surrounding 'zone of transition' (Saunders 1979). As described in Chapter 12 on transport, shopping precincts, early enclosed centres such as Arndales and eventually out-of-town shopping malls developed over the years. Planners tried to reduce pedestrian–vehicular conflict and investors

sought new ways of maximising floor space and increasing the attractiveness of their scheme to consumers. The harsh, non-user-friendly, concrete architecture of such precincts was the result of the influence of the modern movement, and the ideas of planners such as Lord Holford who was responsible, for example, for redesigning the bombed area around St Paul's Cathedral and also many town centre modernisations and suburban precincts across the Commonwealth. As described in Chapter 8, by the 1970s a range of 'retail gravity models' were developed which measured the likely attractiveness and 'pull' of new retail centres in regard to the journey distances from the surrounding hinterland by car. As explained in Chapter 15, this ignored the fact that most shoppers were women, travelling by public transport, and their idea of 'attraction' was much more to do with accessibility, provision of toilets and other amenities, personal safety, and good public transport.

As the years rolled by a new wave of decentralised mega-retail developments took place, such as Bluewater south of London and Cribbs Causeway in Bristol. Many such did provide the facilities women wanted, as it was almost impossible to take a toddler and pushchair to some existing, inhospitable city centres, with poor bus services and limited parking. But out-of-town development, especially new hypermarkets, certainly undermined many local centres, but provided convenient food shopping for working women. Traditional Labour governments had been well known for their contempt for 'shopkeepers', and lack of understanding of shopping needs, because of their emphasis on production (industry) rather than consumption (retail and marketing) (McDowell 2003). However, this was to change under New Labour, and a series of retail reports were produced mid-term, including *Ghost and Clone Town* by the New Economic Foundation, 2004; *Driving Change: Retail Strategy* by the DTI in 2004; and *High Street 2015* in 2006 by the all-parliamentary small shops group of the House of Commons. Subsequent planning requirements brought in under New Labour, such as the sequential test which required developers to prove they could not find a suitable site nearer to the city centre, before making an application for an out-of-town retail scheme. This resulted in a halt on decentralisation and the development of new mega-centres within city

Photo 11.2   Cabot Circus, Bristol

Whilst Bristol has out-of-town retail development, it has also focused on reviving the city centre, where the new Cabot Circus development has been built to link to the renewed Broadmead shopping centre.

Photo 11.3   Changes on the high street

Whilst many traditional high streets are in decline, some with 30 per cent of shops being empty, others, especially historic towns, market towns, and more affluent areas, have survived. But even the remaining high streets are likely to contain an increasing number of charity shop and hot food takeaways, whereas banks and traditional shops such as butchers, ironmongers and greengrocers are in decline.

centres, such as the Westfield centres in Shepherd's Bush and Stratford in London, and Cabot Circus in Bristol (Photo11.2). Such schemes have been major components in urban regeneration programmes.

Retail remains an important sector of the economy and workforce (Gibbs 2012). Over 2 million people are employed in the retail sector, far more than are to be found in manufacturing and industry. But not all work in new shopping malls and as Napoleon once said, England is a 'nation of shopkeepers' and self-employment offers many redundant workers new opportunities. Whilst the Coalition government has supported Small and Medium Enterprises (SMEs), including shops and local businesses, and even commissioned the Portas Report (2012), at the same time the banking crisis, and the restrictions on lending to small firms, along with reduced consumer demand, has resulted in a 14 per cent vacancy rate in shop premises, and many bankruptcies. In 2013 the Distressed Town Centre Property Taskforce was established, which has argued that town centres should be designated as key national infrastructure and funded accordingly. Whilst big national retailers can survive and have strong lobbying powers, for example through the British Council of Shopping Centres (BCSC), those essential small traders in local shops cannot hope to compete. But they are necessary to the social and economic well-being of local areas, and particularly vital for food shopping, where there is low car ownership, and residents are on low incomes, elderly or unemployed. Many high streets and shopping parades now comprise charity shops, fast-food takeaways, and a few bargain Pound shops, and increasingly pawn brokers premises.

Photo 11.4   Rebirth of Birmingham Bull Ring

In recent years this centre has undergone major refurbishment with a greater emphasis upon not just fancy architecture, but also upon the prioritisation over pedestrian flows and needs over that of the motorcar.

On many a high street, banks have closed their local branches, but not everyone has access to the internet, and everyone needs a Post Office (Photo 11.3). Whilst much is made of exciting new retail experiences, 'pop-up shops' and new smart cafés, such premises are generally only catering to the more affluent, younger and fashionable shopping public. Age is an important factor in inner-city regeneration, for as was observed earlier many of the new inner-city apartments are aimed at young professionals, whilst with 'studentification' owing to the expansion of higher education, students have colonised large sectors of the inner city around their universities at the expense of indigenous working-class communities. To conclude, overall retail has been a major driver of the economy and of employment as we have become a consumer 'throwaway society' fuelled by cheap goods from China and the Far East. Re-investment in city centre shopping malls such as the Birmingham Bull Ring suggests economic growth (Photo 11.4). But small shops in local areas are often struggling, yet they are a very important part of the local community. The Portas Review commissioned by the Coalition has identified the importance of relaxing both planning and traffic parking regulations to enable small businesses to compete with larger retail complexes (Portas 2012). This in turn will reduce traffic, and make local centres more accessible and more interesting. We have yet to see how this will work out in practice.

However there was also a move towards the renewal of existing inner-city shopping centres, such as in Birmingham where the old Bull Ring centre (see Chapter 11) was completely rebuilt, this time with more consideration of pedestrian, that is shopper, needs. In London two Westfield Shopping centres emerged, one in the West near Shepherds Bush and the other alongside the Olympic Park. At

Textbox 11.1 List of major shopping centres

Note most of these are out-of-town centres, but those marked with an asterisk * are central-area located.

Bull Ring, Birmingham*
Bluewater, Dartford, East of London
Braehead, Clydeside
Brent Cross, North West London
Cabot Circus, Central Bristol*
Cribbs Causeway, South West of Bristol
Lakeside, Thurrock, North East of London
Meadowhall, Sheffield
Merry Hill, Dudley
Metro Centre, Gateshead
St Davids, Central Cardiff*
Trafford Centre, Manchester
Trinity, Leeds (2013)
Westfield, Shepherds Bush, West London*
Westfield, Stratford, East London*
Westfield, Croydon, South London (proposed redevelopment to replace the existing Whitgift Centre, Croydon)*
White Rose, Leeds

the time of writing there are proposals for the modernisation of the Whitgift Shopping Centre in Croydon, South London, also by the Westfield group. So we have ended up with a range of types of retail facilities, all contributing to urban renewal.

Case studies of urban regeneration in East London

New horizons

In this section a brief summary will be given of three major ongoing regeneration programmes, namely Thames Gateway, Cross Rail and the Olympic Park in the Lower Lee Valley. There is a great deal of information, maps and photos of all these schemes on the internet, and they have been the subject of considerable publication, television and documentary coverage. So in this section we want to draw out some of the less evident, but actually extremely important,

aspects of these schemes, namely how they are administered in terms of planning policy direction and implementation, and also to stress the importance of the 'invisible' (and often underground) infrastructural and site preparation aspects of development. As for precise details regarding these sites, concerning population estimates, amounts of housing, land coverage, and billions of pounds, all these seem to be escalating upwards, but at least some indication will be given of the vast numbers involved.

Thames Gateway

The Thames Gateway area actually includes the Olympic site and will be served by the eastern end of Cross Rail, so let us describe it first. Thames Gateway is the largest economic development area in Europe, stretching 40 miles along both sides of the Thames estuary, covering redundant docklands, brown land, existing built-up areas, and marshland and estuarine areas. The area runs from Tower Hamlets to the Isle of Sheppey. The designated area includes both parts of London boroughs, such as Greenwich and Lewisham, and well-known locations such as Stratford and the Isle of Dogs. But it also eats into Kent and Essex and includes, for example, Southend-on-Sea, the Bluewater shopping centre, and Faversham, birthplace of Dickens. The area already contains 1.6 million people, so parts of it are already heavily populated.

Half of all London's new homes are to be built in the Thames Gateway area. Total numbers of housing to be built range up to 200,000 with 120,000 by 2016. The original proposals for the Gateway derive from Regional Planning Guidance in the 1990s, SEEDA policies, New Labour policies for major regeneration, and more specifically, Terry Farrell's original scheme for the linear expansion to the East, the 2003 Sustainable Communities Plan and the 1995 Thames Gateway Planning Framework. However, if you check the Internet you will find that some suggest the proposals go right back to the post-war period and Abercrombie's ideas on the future expansion of London. After the Coalition came to power in 2010, the DCLG continued its support for what had started as a New Labour scheme, and the Thames Gateway Strategic Group was set up to oversee its ongoing development.

The Thames Gateway scheme is delivered through the London Thames Gateway Development Corporation (LTGDC) set up by New Labour, which operates separately from the local planning authorities and London Borough authorities in the area, although there is considerable liaison between different planning bodies. The LTGDC also has to work with bodies concerned with the natural environment within the Thames Gateway Eco-Region as the estuarine flats are highly sensitive areas in terms of ecology and wildlife, especially wading bird sites. As can be imagined, there has also been a high level of consultation and participation with existing local residents, but much of this has been criticised as 'show' because a development corporation has much stronger powers to push ahead with development than a local authority. A particular concern has been about the nature of the new housing, and the future class composition of the area, because many existing working-class and ethnic minority residents feel they are being pushed out in favour of more middle-class groups who work in the City. This is a re-run of the whole Canary Wharf scenario, where offices and expensive apartments have replaced working-class housing and communities. There is however a strong social housing component in many of the schemes being undertaken. If you look on the internet you will find an area-by-area listing of all the different developments being undertaken.

Cross Rail

Thames Gateway already has strong transport links with many commuter towns for London, and also has links with the HS1 (Channel Tunnel) train system with Ebbsfleet being an international railway station. It is also one of the locations being considered for another London airport, possibly at Cliffe Marshes. Cross Rail will join Thames Gateway to the rest of London and provide a new route right across London to facilitate East–West movement.

The Cross Rail route, commenced in 2009, runs for over 100 miles, running from Maidenhead near Reading to Abbey Wood in the London Docklands within a heavily developed part of the Thames Gateway area. Along the way, Cross Rail will link to 37 existing stations (both train and Tube), including Heathrow Terminal Four, Paddington, and, for example, Farringdon. The first phase is to go from Paddington station in the West to Whitechapel in the East. All the stations affected and their surroundings are undergoing major alteration. There are additional plans for further off-shoot connections to Chelsea, Hackney, Gravesend and Shenfield. The trains will consist of 10-car trains running 24 times an hour.

This is Europe's biggest construction project costing more than 20 billion and counting, and should be completed by 2019 (estimated in 2012). Originally a form of Cross Rail was proposed by Abercrombie in the 1944 London Development Plan, and then recommended again in 1974, but after several other versions being cancelled it was not actually approved until 2005 and started in 2009. This is a massive, infrastructural civil engineering project. Five sections of the route, 14 miles (21 kilometres) in total, are to be deep tunnels, 6 metres (20 feet) in diameter. Huge boring machines are achieving a rate of 100 metres per week of completed tunnel. A vast list of firms and contractors are involved, employing the full range of built environment professional expertise in the process, such as the work of civil, structural and electrical engineers, construction managers, surveyors, transportation experts, and of course town planners (see the last chapter for more on the role of the different built environment professionals). Environmental Impact Assessments of the various stages of the work are being undertaken because although all this is underground it does affect the surface. For example, millions of tons of waste excavated material have to be disposed of, and in some cases the material is being used for sea defences within the Thames Gateway region. Accessibility and equality issues also come into the mix, as many have been critical that in spite of all the refurbishment of existing stations, many still lack good access, with steps, changes of level and lack of adequate lifts, and such basic facilities as public conveniences for the travelling public. Building the Cross Rail is only half the battle, as its future efficient and safe running will depend upon Transport for London (TfL) which will operate Cross Rail, along with all its other connecting stations and lines.

Olympic Park site development

Naturally, there was a great deal of media coverage about the Olympics during 2012, and the internet is still full of information about the Games themselves. But, in this section, there is a need to go behind the scenes of what was actually built, and explain some of the less visible aspects, such as site preparation, planning control, workforce composition, and future legacy issues. In addition to the Olympic Park, the Olympics took place at 15 other venues along the Thames and within London such as at O2, Excel Exhibition Centre, Horse Guards Parade and Greenwich Park. Nearby areas such as Newham, Dagenham, Redbridge, Waltham Forest and Greenwich were also drawn into the development proposals for the provision of ancillary sports pitches and facilities. There were also 13 venues outside London, including Manchester, Birmingham, Glasgow, Newcastle, Cardiff, Weymouth and Portland. It took over seven years to prepare the Olympic Park, and the speed of development was record-breaking for such a major construction project. The project was delivered on time, as discussed in a special issue of *Construction Manager* July/August 2012.

As stated above, the Olympic Park site is part of the wider Thames Gateway area (Hopkins and Neal 2012). It is located in the old East End at Stratford in the Lower Lee Valley, and covers 750 acres (3 square kilometres). Site assembly and preparation were major issues. The site was heavily polluted and obstructed by centuries of industrial activity adjacent to the London Docklands. It comprised areas of derelict, polluted brown land, previously covered by old factories and large areas of unauthorised waste tipping. Two hundred existing, and mainly derelict, buildings had to be removed. There were many legal, property law issues to resolve and compulsory purchase powers were used to gain control over land and property on the site on adjacent areas in the Lee Valley location. There are also many social, economic and, of course, sporting issues to consider (Poynter and MacRury 2009; Gold and Gold 2012).

To make the site usable, 2 million tons of soil (*Guardian*, 28 July 2012, page 41) had to be cleaned, as was explained in detail when I attended a CIOB-hosted meeting at the London Olympics site when the initial groundwork was under way. The soil was literally taken away by the lorry load and put through a cleaning machine and returned to site (also check the CIOB website on this). Eight kilometres of polluted waterways, mainly old industrial canals, were cleaned up and restored, and 1.8 kilometres of new sewer tunnels were built to accommodate the needs of the intensive new surface development. The site was criss-crossed with all sorts of cables and services, both under- and over-ground, which all had to be re-routed and sorted out, for example 52 electricity pylons had to be removed.

To facilitate access to and movement around the site, 30 new bridges were built within the site. Major improvements were made to Stratford station to provide linkages to international railway services, through the Javelin (rapid connection) to the St Pancras Eurostar terminal, and also to improve access to the London Underground, Docklands Light Railway and mainline train services. All this transport infrastructural activity links to the ongoing Cross Rail strategy. Stratford Station links directly to the Westfield Shopping Centre, through which access to the Olympic Park could be gained. Westfield is a very major international shopping mall developer which already has an earlier 'Westfield' at Shepherd's Bush on the West side of London (and incidentally is proposing to take over the old Whitgift Shopping Centre in Croydon, in South London).

The site was designed as a self-contained Olympic village. This was partly because the ICO (International Committee for the Olympics) specified that access for athletes to the Olympic site was paramount, having experienced major problems with traffic congestion preventing athletes getting there on time in other Olympic cities. This was one of the reasons it was decided to have one self-contained Olympic Park, which included residential blocks providing athlete accommodation. But it was also decided to designate 'Games Lanes' on the main arterial roads within London, which were mainly used by Olympic officials, and caused a great deal of annoyance to ordinary Londoners and commuters, especially when London taxis were banned from using these lanes. Arguably this was all rather heavy handed, but interestingly when people found out how good the Tube and other rail systems were in London many found it easier to travel by public transport to the site.

The Olympic Delivery Authority (ODA) was responsible for the development of the site, its buildings and transport connections. The Olympics Delivery Authority Planning Committee was responsible for approving planning applications related to the Olympic development, even approving London Development Authority (LDA) schemes. The London Organising Committee of the Olympic Games (LOCOG) was responsible for delivery of the Games themselves. The London Legacy Development Corporation (LLDC) now has responsibility for the development and legacy aspects, and is again a development corporation and therefore a form of planning authority. The ODA had five objectives on sustainability: climate change, waste, biodiversity, healthy living and inclusion (ODA 2008a, 2008b). For example, water-saving technology and low-flush toilets were incorporated, as stated in the *ODA Sustainable Strategy for London* (ODA 2008b). Throughout there has been a strong emphasis on legacy, sustainability and equality issues, and this was reflected in the content of the Opening Ceremony 'Spectacular' organised by Danny Boyle. Because the Paralympics followed directly after, and used the same buildings and facilities, there was a major emphasis upon disabled access throughout.

However, there was also criticism that the strong emphasis on sponsorship, especially by fast-food companies, and multinational companies, did not send out a healthy message, and also strict rules prevented local people from advertising their businesses, including even the companies and practices that designed and built the park. There were also all sorts of problems regarding ticketing, queuing and unused seats, and complaints about the preferential treatment given to business interests and overseas dignitaries, but overall a good time was had by all.

The main contractors comprised a consortium, EDAW (not an acronym but a company name), with, for example, Buro Happold working with Arup and WS Atkins, LDA Design and Hargreaves Associates. Atkins provided engineering design services for the Games, and because the Paralympics followed, a committee was established to coordinate accessibil-

ity issues with the ODA producing its own IDS (Inclusive Design Standards) requirements. Committee members included, for example, Julie Fleck, well known for her work on planning for accessibility within the City of London, and the GLA (Fleck 2003). (Even so there were so problems; for example, at some venues wheelchair spectators complained they could not see the events because the special platforms they were on were not high enough up for them to look over other people's heads.) Thus a wide range of architectural, design and engineering practices were involved. O'Rourke were one of the main planning consultancies involved in relation to the planning, leasing, development, building and management of the park development and related transport systems.

Development on the Olympic Park included apartment-block accommodation for the athletes as well as the main Olympic Stadium and iconic buildings such as the Aquatics centre by Zaha Hadid (one of the few internationally-famous female architects). Other notable features include the Copper Box, Velodrome, and the Arcelor Mittal Orbit Observation Tower (which looks like a helter-skelter but is one of the most major expensive pieces of public art in recent times) by Anish Kapoor (who also designed the much more popular Chicago sculpture, Cloud Gate, shown in Photo 1.2). The whole area was carefully and sustainably landscaped throughout. Altogether, Europe's biggest regeneration project came in below its final £9.3 million budget, employed on average 6000 people, but this peaked to 12,000 people at certain times, including 255 women construction professionals! A further 46,000 were employed in some way or other. There was a strong emphasis on green building, and also on health and safety for the workforce, for example the athletes' village was built to Level 4 of the Code for Sustainable Homes. With so many people working on the site, there were inevitably some labour problems, mainly in relation to communication. The workforce was truly multinational with 450 different language and ethnicity groups, as all sorts of workers with specific expertise were drawn into the project, for example steel workers from Scandinavia and concrete specialists from India. Every morning site meetings would be held for the workforce at which the orders for the day were translated into the main languages represented. Although the site was surrounded by a predominantly multi-ethnic population, a low proportion was involved in the construction process. However, various training and apprenticeship schemes were established in association with the Olympic organisers and the various contractors. But many of the local population were employed in a range of other jobs such as security and services during the Games. Indeed the Games also attracted a vast number of volunteers from all over the UK, acting as 'greeters' and helpers during the Games.

Legacy

The Olympics, and subsequent Paralympics, dominated the television schedules and people's lives over the summer, and we saw sports we had never seen before. But not long after 'sport' on the television and in the newspapers reverted to the usual diet of male-dominated ball games, such as soccer, rugby and cricket, and we were seldom to see female athletes, women's hockey, disabled competitors, or for that matter show-jumping, cycling and sailing again. But this Games was dubbed the Legacy Olympics and much good did come out of it. It was also dubbed the first Sustainable Games and the first Public Transport serviced games too. It was very different from either the Austerity Games when the Olympics came to London in 1948 (Hampton 2008; Gold and Gold 2012), or the knock-out no-expense-spared spectacular of the previous Games in Beijing, China.

As stated, the London Legacy Development Corporation (LLDC) is responsible for the future of the Olympic Park and its buildings. As for the building heritage, the athletes' village has been turned into 3500 apartments to meet a combination of public and private housing need in the area. The Olympic Park comprises one of the largest city parks built in 150 years. After decommissioning from the Games, in 2013 it was reopened to the public and renamed the Queen Elizabeth Olympic Park. There have been many other spin-offs and benefits following the Olympics. The upgrading of public transport, especially the rail and Tube system, has been considerable and thus provides a valuable heritage

for the travelling public. A cable car across the Thames, from the Greenwich peninsular to the Royal Docks on the other side, built for 25 million pounds for the Games, has subsequently been running half-empty, although it was intended to contribute to the transport links within the overall regeneration programme for the East side of London. Many of the Olympic-site buildings are now occupied by media organisations, university departments and high-tech businesses, with further development envisaged as the location becomes an important regeneration hub. Gradually the remaining Olympic buildings will blend in with their surroundings.

But there is another more negative side to the legacy. Some consider the whole emphasis was too London-based and that if the objective of 'Sport for All' is to be achieved the government must allocate more money to local authorities for local swimming pools, velodromes and playing fields. For example, Bridgwater in Somerset had to close its swimming pool owing to cutbacks. In spite of promises to make good any damage done as a result of using local facilities, parks and playing fields for Olympic-related activities, many residents within the surrounding London boroughs are concerned that this has not happened yet, reducing the amount of local green space, for example the Hackney Marshes, used for generations for Sunday football. People need their green spaces, parks, commons and playing fields, at a local level, as well as the once-in-a-lifetime Olympic events. Also there is an increasing recognition of the importance of making green space and landscaping environmentally sustainable, with a growth in urban farms, and even edible landscaping, green roofs and other initiatives to green the city. All this costs money but is not particularly spectacular, but essential to creating healthy cities and healthy people.

There has also been an impact on local businesses, as industrial and commercial buildings that were previously developed as a result of earlier regeneration programmes in the East End were compulsorily purchased and demolished to make way for the Olympics. Even community buildings and some churches suffered this fate, as in the case of the famous KICC church which was promised a new site which it did not get and is still in negotiation with the council over (see Chapter 16). Strangest of all, the complete change in attitude encountered on London public transport, with guards and conductors actually being helpful and smiling, and with timetable delays being greatly reduced during the period of the Olympics, was not maintained. In particular people with disabilities soon found that the happy, helpful people who would rush up to trains with ramps and help them off, soon evaporated, making the transport system as inaccessible as ever. Clearly some aspects of the Olympics were not long term but only cosmetic and major changes in attitude to design and provision of services is needed to create a true legacy.

Concluding on culture

As can be seen from the case studies, sport has been a major factor in the regeneration of East London, because of the staging of the 2012 Olympics in the UK. But sport, recreation and leisure are also national planning policy issues, with around half a million people employed in this sector. Arts and cultural institutions and buildings can also act as catalysts for urban regeneration. Culture has become a major driver of change in the post-industrial city (Tallon 2013). In its widest sense, the word culture can be used to embrace the arts, heritage, design initiatives, museums, theatre, cinema, music, parks and open spaces, sport, recreation and a wide range of leisure activities. The benefits of cultural promotion for the generation of tourism are enormous, particularly in London. The endorsement of the 24-hour city as 'cool' has certainly benefited the evening economy although it has also brought some social problems (Roberts and Eldridge 2009). The establishment of the Department for Culture, Media and Sport (DCMS) embodies this new cultural dynamism, especially in relation to developing policy for urban locations. Indeed culture itself has become a key driver and major land use in many regeneration schemes. Nowadays both property developers and local authority planning departments are keen to make their developments attractive to tourists, residents and the wider public by branding them with distinct characteristics. For example, many cities have rebranded historic retail and residential areas as 'quarters', drawing strongly on concepts of legacy and heritage (see Chapter 13 on urban design). Likewise new housing built on reclaimed dockland sites is likely to be branded as waterfront development with allusions to the rich cultural background of the location. To conclude it would seem that culture is now seen as a major driver of development, even more important than economic considerations (Tallon 2013). Indeed it is imagined that an emphasis on arts and culture, on heritage, tourism and legacy will actually generate employment and economic recovery.

For the tasks, further reading, additional photos and other resources for this chapter, including photos of the London Olympic site, please visit www.palgrave. com/companion/greed.

12 Transportation Planning

The importance of transport

This chapter will examine the various aspects and levels of planning and transport policy and practice. Land use and transport are inextricably linked (Banister 2005; Hull 2012). Technological advances have enabled us to move around faster and travel further, resulting in changes in city form, especially the growth of suburbia (Hutton 2013). This process has had major consequences for the environment, in terms of contributing to climate change and pollution. Such changes have led to many benefits, but challenges too, for the planners and the travelling public (Shaw and Docherty 2014).

This chapter is focused upon the topic of land-use transportation planning, that is the ways in which transport systems affect urban planning policy. In the first part of this chapter, the different levels of transport policy, control and management are outlined. Inevitably the problem of how to deal with the motorcar is central to all transport planning and to this chapter. The role of planning in shaping transport policy is discussed, with particular reference to creating greener transport solutions less dependent on the motorcar. In the middle part of the chapter, alternatives to the motorcar are presented, with reference to public transport, cycling and walking. The additional problems of getting around the city experienced by those with disabilities will be raised in this chapter as an integral component of the transport agenda (I'DGO 2009). In the final part of the chapter, we return to the problem of the motorcar, suggesting ways to control it in ways that enable other transport users to move around too.

Current UK transport policy draws on international policy considerations regarding sustainability, global warming, greenhouses gases and climate change and therefore readers are advised to read Chapter 10 on sustainability for a wider perspective on this matter. The changes in the transport planning agenda are due in part to the strong influence of the sustainability agenda and to the healthy cities movement, which has demonstrated the links between increasing obesity and car usage. Far greater emphasis is now put upon the importance of walking, cycling and public transport. As sustainable development became more of a concern for government policy-makers, and as protests against new road proposals mounted in the 1990s, there has been a move away from the 'predict and provide' road-based policies of earlier years. In the past great engineering feats, including road–building, were seen as a sign of progress and a means of overcoming the challenges presented by nature (Photo 12.1). Instead more sophisticated forms of traffic management, demand management and the promotion of alternatives to the private car are being introduced (Barton and Tsourou 2006). The sustainability and environmental movements have little time for the demands of the motorcar because of its contribution to pollution, with high levels of CO_2 emissions, and may see the ideal as the car-less city (Barton *et al.* 2010; Glaister *et al.* 2006). Twenty-three per cent of the world's greenhouse gases are from transport (Burdett and Sudjic 2011, 2012). But up until relatively recently the car has been king and this inheritance is still etched into our city form and road layouts.

The chapter should also be read with reference to Chapter 13, on urban design. There is a range of professional perspectives informing approaches to dealing with traffic. In particular there is still a noticeable contrast in attitudes between urban

Photo 12.1   Mountain infrastructure

Provided the government has the money, it is possible to build anything anywhere, and many parts of Europe now have magnificent railway viaducts and motorway bridges spanning entire Alpine Valleys. Solving the transport problem is all a matter of political will and resources.

designers and highways engineers. For example, traffic engineers have traditionally designed road layouts for urban areas, which are highly formalised with investment in transportation infrastructure that has favoured the needs of cars rather than pedestrians, as in the classic guide *Roads in Urban Areas* (Department of Transport 1990). In contrast, the new urban design agenda of 'making places' and creating liveable cities generates a completely different attitude in which concepts of 'shared space' and reduction in the speed and penetration of the motorcar into residential areas prevail. Overall there is a move away from the emphasis upon car transport towards public transport, walking and cycling (DfT 2009a, 2010). The urban

design chapter, Chapter 13, will discuss the more detailed aspects of car control, including traffic calming, street layout, shared space and accessibility issues, whereas this chapter deals more with national policy issues and the transport infrastructure. Key transport concepts and theories have already been introduced, such as Buchanan's concept of 'environmental areas' (in Chapter 6) and American land-use transportation planning theories and other computer-driven approaches (in Chapter 8). This chapter is much more concerned with the actual hardware, in terms of transport infrastructure and modes of travel (trains, trams, cars, bikes and so forth) and the implications for planning policy.

What is the problem?

Why are cars a problem? In the UK, indeed in most of the West, for many years the emphasis, by governments of all political persuasions, was put upon road-building and accommodating this growth in car ownership. One of the key factors was the belief in 'progress' and that better road systems were needed to generate and support economic growth, mobility of the labour force and distribution of raw materials and manufactured goods. In spite of this mentality, increasing numbers of people still travel by rail (Table 12.1). The motorcar has given the driver flexibility to go anywhere whenever one wanted, and not to be tied to a fixed track or route as was the case with mass railway transport. Land use and transport are inextricably linked; 'planning for the motorcar' has resulted in major changes in city form and structure. These include the increased separation and zoning of land uses, with distances becoming longer between residential and employment areas, and growing decentralisation and suburbanisation, with inner-city neighbourhoods being cleared and people pushed out to suburban council housing estates (whether they wanted it or not). As a result, for many people, it is no longer possible to walk to work or to access the main functions of the city without the use of mechanised transport. The irony is that motorcar use has not necessarily increased speed or mobility. The more cars there are, the more traffic jams are created so we are not really going much faster than in the past in urban areas and the myth of the open road and individual freedom has ground to a halt as we all sit alongside each other in traffic jams.

Thus, the road infrastructure needed to be improved to meet the demand for increased personal mobility, along with a shift of freight from the use of rail to road haulage vehicles to move these goods ever-increasing distances, which has had a significant impact on Britain's towns, cities and countryside, with the development of ever-expanding suburbia. Cars were squeezed into historic streets that were never designed for such intensive use. So massive demolition and highways construction took place, with urban motorways, flyovers and car parks being built with little concern for local residents. In contrast, North American cities were built around the automobile from the outset on a much larger scale.

However, this emphasis upon structuring our cities around the motorcar has assumed that plentiful fuel, both petrol and diesel, would continue to be available and affordable. A series of wars and civil unrest in the Middle East, among oil-rich countries, has shown that our fuel supplies have become very vulnerable imports and increasingly expensive. North Sea oil will not last for ever and is not suitable for motor fuel. Therefore alternatives to the motorcar, road freight and fossil fuels are being explored and developed, with major implications for transport policy. The use of fossil fuels, especially petrol, has also resulted in increased CO_2 emissions and pollution, whilst the economic system and manufacturing base that mass produces motorcars has been questioned as non-sustainable and wasteful of non-renewable raw materials. But if a cheap alternative form of fuel was found, and if everyone in the world had a car, the situation would be unsustainable. As

Mode:	Under 1 mile %	1–2 miles %	2–5 miles %	5–25 miles %	Over 25 miles %
Walk	79	32	5	0	0
Cycle	1	3	2	0	0
Car	18	56	77	83	81
Local bus	2	6	12	7	1
Rail	0	0	1	6	12
Other	0	3	3	4	6

Table 12.1   Journeys by Mode and Distance

Source: Department for Transport (2012). The data apply to personal travel only in Great Britain during 2010.

stated in the sustainability chapter, electric cars are not really an alternative solution to the use of fossil fuels as the electricity is usually generated in coal, oil or gas powered power stations! In fact globally coal is still, by far, the most commonly used fuel to generate electricity.

The levels of transport planning and management

The relationship between spatial planning and transportation policy

It is important, from the start, to link transport policy to planning policy at national, regional and local levels. We need to identify who the main decision-makers have been in terms of transport provision, as planners do not have complete control over transport but have to work with other departments and bodies. Much of the blame for traffic jams and the woes of the motorist is laid at the planners' feet by the media. But, the powers and the culpability of the planners in dealing with urban problems should not be overestimated. Under the present statutory system, planners have considerable powers over the nature of land use and development, but they have limited powers over the transport systems which connect the land uses, and which have contributed to the outward growth of cities. There is concern nationally about the problems created by the increased use of the motorcar, and by the government's attempts to limit car use. There are demands from environmentalists for more public transport, less pollution, and generally more sustainable cities, but the responsibility for these issues often lies outside the planners' jurisdiction.

There is no doubt that planners do have a particular role in transport policy, indeed some planners specialise in 'land-use transport planning', a job description that has been around since the 1960s when 'the car' first became a major problem in cities. Planners need to take a wider, more informed view of transport problems than simply reacting to each new crisis. In trying to solve traffic problems, there is often a tendency to deal with the 'effect' rather than the 'cause' and thus to adopt negative measures that restrict and control the motorcar, parking and

goods vehicle access, particularly in city centres. But as a planner there is a need to go one step back and find out the 'cause', that is why the traffic is being generated in the first place, where it is coming from and where it is going, that is to understand the reasons for 'traffic generation'. For example, if the planners allow another residential development on the edge of the suburbs this will result in increased 'traffic volumes' and 'traffic flows' to the major centres of employment, and also will increase retail, leisure and social journeys too. The increased generation of traffic will lead to greater demands for car parking at the destination, and one of the ways to reduce car usage is to reduce car parking availability. Solutions might include improved public transport, but also more fundamental changes in city form and structure are needed that reduce the generation of commuter traffic in the first place. This might include, for example, inclusion of more workplaces within residential areas to save commuting, and a great spread of secondary centres which provide people with a viable alternative to having to go into the city centre for key services, shops and facilities. Granted the internet has reduced the need to travel to shop, work, undertake business transactions, and deal with bureaucracy (such as renewing licences and paying taxes). But still most people need to travel to work. Much focus has also been placed, therefore, on attempts to integrate transport and land-use planning over the years at a national policy level and at the more local level through local plans, strategies and numerous projects and initiatives. These will now be looked at in greater detail.

Transport and planning at national level

Transport control

What can, or should, a government do in terms of transport? Restrict it or accommodate it? The broad remit of government is to make laws, and to make policy on a whole range of issues of concern to society. In terms of transport this can become highly politicised. There has been a reluctance by politicians of all parties to do anything that might be seen as 'anti-car' and therefore potentially alienate millions of voters. In Britain over the recent past there have been a number of major, and at times very disruptive, protests, mainly against the price of petrol and the amount of tax levied on fuel. The local implementation of policies, such as car parking charges, parking enforcement, speed cameras and the introduction of bus and cycle lanes, has also proved contentious. Many government politicians have chosen to pander to the perceived car lobby rather than make the case for measures that are seeking to improve the environment or promote safety; for example, Coalition ministers announced that they were ending the 'war on the car driver' in January 2011 (DCLG 2011d) at the same time as they were developing policies to achieve a low-carbon future (DECC 2011, 2012). So, there is often a contradiction in terms of government policy when it comes to roads versus the environment; more often than not when it comes down to what governments actually do, much greater priority is given to the car, particularly in terms of spending on roads.

There is another broad remit of government, to determine how taxation is spent. This is particularly important in terms of transport as so many of the choices that people make in terms of how they travel are influenced, or even dictated, by the infrastructure available and the cost of travel. Government has a key role in determining both. Through the budget spending decisions are made on a range of options, such as new roads, rail routes and services, new or improved stations, support for public transport and a host of more local measures, such as traffic calming schemes or cycle ways, for example. Government spending on infrastructure projects such as new roads, street lighting, repairs or track and signalling for trains or trams is known as capital expenditure. The associated running costs for things such as the electricity for the street lighting or subsidies for fares on trains, trams or buses is known as revenue expenditure. This distinction is important when it comes to the allocation of funds. The government can borrow money for spending on capital items; this is a bit like taking out a mortgage to purchase a house: the total cost can be borrowed and paid back, along with the interest on the loan, over a longer period, such as 25 years. The government will have an annual cap or limit on borrowing for capital items; within this the various government departments have to battle it out for money for their pet projects – the final decision normally being made by the Cabinet and the Chancellor of the Exchequer

each year in the budget. For capital spending on projects such as new roads or rail infrastructure there is normally a three- or five-year spending plan, as these projects have a major lead-in time in terms of planning and the acquisition of the land, and the construction of the project itself can take time depending on its scale. Revenue decisions tend to be taken on an annual basis, but within a longer-term planning horizon.

Planning powers and transport

At central government level the Department for Transport (DfT) is the main UK body responsible for national transport policy; however, it has to be remembered that considerable transport powers have been devolved to the national governments in Scotland, Wales and Northern Ireland, so much of the DfT's focus is on transport in England. The department itself is responsible for policy-making and, as noted above, for allocating funds for various forms of new infrastructure. This work is underpinned by a wide range of research and the department publishes many statistics, research studies and reports that are well worth looking at. Political responsibility for the department lies with the Secretary of State for Transport and a number of deputy ministers. The Permanent Secretary is the senior civil servant in charge of the department's professional staff. Much of its work is carried out through various agencies, such as the Highways Agency, or by other arm's length bodies, such as High Speed Two Ltd (HS2) or the Civil Aviation Authority, for example. There are also numerous advisory bodies. The department also works closely with local government in England and relies on the local transport authorities to carry out numerous projects and other measures on the ground. Transport policy and its implementation is therefore very complex and there are many bodies involved. Government policy is also very compartmentalised, with policy for roads, rail, buses, ports and airports being dealt with separately, which makes integrated planning very challenging (Glasson and Marshall 2007), even more so as responsibility for land use and spatial planning lies with another department altogether (the Department for Communities and Local Government).

Whilst the DfT is responsible for everything to do with transport, the Department for Communities and Local Government (DCLG) also has a key role in shaping policy. Indeed one of the problems, at central government level, has been the separation of transport and planning into different ministries. There have been previous attempts to bring the two together, as in the creation of the Department for Transport, Local Government and the Regions (DTLR) by John Prescott in the late 1990s under New Labour. But currently 'planning' and 'transport' are in two separate departments again. However, the Department for Communities and Local Government (DCLG) also has a major impact on transport policy through national planning guidance and urban policy direction.

For many years the government used Planning Policy Guidance (PPG) notes and Planning Policy Statements (PPSs) to give guidance to local authorities on planning policy, including transport and road design issues. As a result of the combined influences of the sustainability movement, local community pressure groups, cyclist and pedestrian organisations, and the increasing level of traffic congestion, government attitudes towards 'planning for the motorcar' began to change from the 1980s. New Labour introduced revised policy guidance, strongly influenced by environmental considerations, including the desire to reduce CO_2 emissions and also to promote urban containment. This included the 1996 White Paper, Transport the Way Forward, and several new transport acts and other policy documents from 2000 (see the Government Publications E-Supplement 1).

PPG13 on Transport was published in 1994 jointly by the Department of the Environment and the Department of Transport and it represented a significant change in approach by government to transport and land-use matters (Cullingworth and Nadin 2006). The need to link planning and transport was recognised along with the need to promote more sustainable forms of transport and movement. PPG13 on 'Transport' signalled the end of high parking provision standards and also integrated environmental sustainability thinking into transport planning. PPG13 was revised in 2001 and updated in 2011.

These policy changes were to affect both residential area parking requirements and city centres and urban locations. That is both the 'origin' and the 'destination' of traffic flows. As to residential areas, for many years the planners and the house-builders were happy to agree that every house should have one if not two off-street parking spaces, and adequate garaging space. Whilst there was certainly enough space to do so, particularly in the low-density suburbs, increasingly environmentalists began to challenge the ecological and sustainability effects of this. New Labour introduced guidance on residential development, which set higher densities, requirements for choosing brown land and infill sites over green-field sites, and much lower parking standards for new residential development. These changes were contained in PPS1 General Principles and PPS3 Housing, echoed in PPS1 on the general principles of planning.

PPS3 led to the development of high-density, privately-owned, apartment blocks in regenerated areas, such as erstwhile Docklands in Manchester, London Thames Gateway, and Liverpool (as highlighted in Chapter 11 on urban regeneration) which met government targets on density and house-building, but did little for the overall housing situation. Many such dwellings were occupied by young single professionals and childless couples who wanted to live near the city, and did not necessarily need a car, because of excellent city centre transport, and in London the Tube. Whilst such measures were no doubt 'good' and needed in large conurbations, they met with considerable resistance in locations where land availability was high and traffic problems were less marked. But applying the same 'London-appropriate' carless principles to provincial areas where there was limited public transport, and people really needed a car because there was no train, underground or decent bus service, penalised residents for the mistakes and shortcomings of the local authority and public transport operators (Greed 2011a, 2011b). For many in the suburbs, where the majority of the urban population lives, cars may be the only realistic means to get to work, to reach out-of-town retail centres, and to take small children to school (ONS 2012). As a result of previous misdirected planning policy there are few retail outlets or social amenities at the local district level.

Subsequently PPG13 and PPS3 (*inter alia*) were cancelled but some of their principles were incorporated in the National Planning Policy Framework

Photo 12.2   Rail passengers at Waterloo Station

Over two million people come into London each day by public transport, and in fact, car usage is lower than in any other city. But rising rail fares, overcrowding and unreliability are making it more difficult for ordinary commuters to leave the car at home. Many commuters travel over 100 miles a day, for example from Bristol, Cardiff, Birmingham, Brighton, so going by bike is not realistic, whilst house prices are too high to move into London. Many get to the station by car as there is often no alternative in outlying areas.

(NPPF) introduced by the Coalition government in 2012. The NPPF reflected much of the thinking set out in the earlier versions of PPG13. It stated that the transport system should be balanced in favour of sustainable modes of transport and that solutions that helped to reduce greenhouse gas emissions should be encouraged. The links with land-use planning were also made: mixed-use developments should be encouraged, locational decisions for new developments should minimise the need to travel and patterns of development should facilitate more sustainable modes of transport. Previous policy guidance had set local planning standards for new development; the NPPF passed this task over to the local planning authorities. The NPPF did maintain the requirement for planning applications for new development that would generate significant amounts of movement to contain a transport statement or a transport assessment.

The Coalition government on its election made a commitment to a greener and more sustainable transport sector, including the provision of high-speed rail networks and Cross Rail (Cabinet Office 2010). But those still left standing on crowded and infrequent intercity train journeys are not convinced. However, if you look at E-Supplement 7

Table 12.2   Passenger Journeys by Rail (from Dave)

Year	Passenger Journeys Millions (Approx.)	Miles travelled Millions (Approx.)
1990	800	34,000
1995	725	29,000
2000	950	40,000
2005	1,050	45,000
2010	1,260	54,000
2012	1,480	n/a

Source: Office of Rail Regulation, June 2012 (the data have been rounded up and apply to England, Scotland and Wales only).

you will find examples of massive investment in the railway system by Network Rail and in London by Cross Rail and Transport for London (TfL). Even if people travel by train they still have to get to the station by foot, bus and car (Photo 12.2).

Sub-regional: the links between national and local transport policy

National policy works its way down to the local level through policy statements and more specifically by the allocation of funds for particular projects by the government within the local government context. This could be seen as a top-down approach, which it is, though there are good reasons for this. In the absence of any regional government in England it is only the national government that has the level of funding available to invest in large projects. However, the downside of this is that local demands often go unmet because the government and the Department for Transport in London might have very different priorities from a local council in say Newcastle or Plymouth. While local transport authorities can raise their own funds, they need to bid to government if they wish to carry out any major investments in new transport infrastructure. This process is explained below.

There is not, currently, a strong regional transport planning level. Previously, under New Labour, with its enthusiasm for regional planning, Regional Transport Strategies (RTSs) were required as introduced under the 2005 PPS11 (Regional Spatial Strategies) and subsequently strengthened under PPS13 on transport, produced in early 2011 and subsequently cancelled along with RSSs by the Coalition government. Within these plans, for example, transport planning must accommodate Environmental Impact Assessment requirements, whilst also putting greater emphasis on social considerations such as disabled access and mobility issues. In practice, urban policy-making always involves teamwork, negotiation and trade-offs between a range of professional groups and political decision-makers and those urban areas that have the best transport systems are generally those where there is a high level of cohesion and liaison between transport and planning.

But it is worth noting that in certain parts of the country there are still a number of sub-regional bodies that have been set up to coordinate transport planning. These are the Passenger Transport Executives (PTEs) and they have specific responsibility to provide, plan, procure and promote public transport in six of England's largest conurbations: Greater Manchester, Merseyside, South Yorkshire, Tyne and Wear, West Midlands and West Yorkshire (PTEG 2012). Each PTE is run by an Integrated Transport Authority, which consists of elected councillors from the local authorities within the PTE's area. The Greater Manchester PTE is part of a new statutory Combined Authority: the Greater Manchester Combined Authority (GMCA), which was established on 1 April 2011, and has additional powers to address transport and economic development issues in the area. A number of other areas, such as the West of England around Bristol, chose to work together on a sub-regional basis to address transport matters, but they do not have the powers or resources of the PTEs. They do try to plan for the city-region area, which is critical in terms of transport planning as so much travel, particularly by commuters, takes place from the suburbs and surrounding rural areas into the city where most of the jobs are. In some cases these partnerships will jointly produce the Local Transport Plan. Taking these bodies into account where they exist, it now remains for us to look at planning and transport at the local level.

Planning and transport at the local level

We have seen how important the national level is when it comes to decision-making on major transport schemes. The government sets the general policy and puts this into effect largely through the allocation of funds and through policy guidance aimed particularly at local authorities. So even at the local level the scope for action and local initiatives is somewhat circumscribed by legislation, policy and guidelines that are set down by national government. Yet within this perhaps over-centralised structure there are nevertheless many opportunities for the planner to have a greater impact on transport provision: it is at the local level that the relationship between transport and land use is perhaps most directly related, and it is at the very local level that most individual transport choices are made and are therefore subject to greater influence or even control by the land-use and transportation planners and local politicians.

It is important therefore to be clear about who exactly is responsible for making transport policy and decisions at the local level. The local transport authority (previously often referred to as the local highways authority) is a name given to those councils who have specific responsibility for transport planning and funding: in a two-tier structure, that is the county councils. Elsewhere it is the unitary authorities or, in London, the London Boroughs (although here we also have Transport for London, which is responsible for implementing the Mayor of London's transport strategy). The local transport authorities each have their own highways and transport departments which are generally separate from planning departments. However, there is a usually a strong element of liaison. It must be remembered that transport authorities are also local authorities: i.e. they are democratically elected councils, and the elected councillors are expected to set out broad transport policies and to decide on more specific proposals and schemes within their local area. This is normally done with reference to the council's wider policy framework and particularly to the planning policies as set out in the Local Plan. In theory, and mostly in practice, the transport policies and schemes should reflect the land-use and spatial strategy of the Local Plan, just as the Local Plan should take account of plans for future infrastructure and other transport initiatives. This can sometimes break down in a two-tier structure, where the local planning authority is the district council, and the transport authority is the county council. Good joint working and a commitment to shared outcomes are necessary to avoid this happening. It is common practice for a number of local authorities within a given area to work together on transport matters, and in many cases to jointly undertake transport studies and to produce joint transport plans.

At local authority level, all county and major urban local authorities have their own highways departments which are generally separate from planning departments. However, there is usually a strong element of liaison. From 1999 local authorities have had to produce Green Transport Plans showing how their policies will reduce greenhouse emissions. This has resulted in a drastic reduction in the number of workplace parking spaces specified when granting planning permission, in order to 'encourage' people to use other means of travel. This results in some workplace car parks being half empty because there is a ceiling on how many cars are allowed to park, in spite of the fact that many employees are desperate to find somewhere to park, especially those who do not have the benefit of public transport alternatives serving their area. In addition, the Transport Act 2000 required all local transport authorities in England to prepare five-yearly Local Transport Plans (Cullingworth and Nadin 2006). The Local Transport Plan is meant to consist of two parts: a strategy for transport in the area and an implementation plan showing how the strategy will be delivered (Department for Transport 2009a). The implementation plan forms the basis of any bids the local transport authority wishes to make to government for funds. The Plan is also subject to a Strategic Environmental Assessment. The first round of plans covered the period 2000–2006; the second round 2006–2011; and the third round commenced in 2012.

It must be noted that local authority powers are limited and that there are many other bodies, both public and private, involved in providing transport. But local authorities still have an important advisory role, often publicised through the planning department in association with the highways department.

Indeed the two may comprise one joint department. Even public transport, which is so essential to weaning people away from their cars, is not normally under the direct control of local transport authorities and planners have limited powers over the choice of routes provided. This has been the cause of many problems, particularly since the privatisation of train and bus operators. Most travel choices are made by the millions of people who are on the move each day, and there is only so much planners and transport professionals can do to influence these choices in a more sustainable direction, though that has been the intention of most national and local government policy for a number of years.

Within this context, local planning and transport authorities will develop their own approaches to address issues of transport, movement and development in their area. Most authorities will seek to respond to national policy guidelines, particularly in respect of reducing CO_2 emissions, and will, with varying degrees of commitment, seek to promote more sustainable forms of transportation. They usually seek to do this through a combination of policies and approaches, as summarised below:

- Reduce the need to travel through policies to influence the location of new development or to encourage home working.
- Promote alternatives to the private car: public transport (local rail, buses, trams), cycling and walking.
- Give priority to more sustainable (low-carbon) modes of travel: cycling, walking, low-emission vehicles, car-sharing and car clubs.
- Promote pedestrian-friendly areas and traffic-calm roads.
- Restrict car use through financial and other disincentives.
- Undertake education and awareness-raising to seek to change individuals' travel behaviour.
- Promote accessibility and ensure all members of society have a wide range of travel choices.

Location of new development

Local authority planners still have a key role to play in terms of thinking about how the location of new development can reduce the need to travel in the first place, or where this is not so achievable, to at least ensure that all new development promotes more sustainable forms of travel. When making plans for the future of their area, local planning authorities can promote forms of new local development that reduce the need for travel in the first place. The link between land use and transport, first highlighted by American transport planners in the 1960s (Chapter 8) should never be forgotten as, in essence, 'more houses means more cars and therefore more congestion on commuter routes'. For example, mixed-use developments can encourage people to live near the place where they work, and shop locally rather than drive to an out-of-town shopping centre. Live-work units can be planned for in new developments and encouraged through development management policies. Employers can be encouraged to support home working; working from home one day a week could make a significant difference to the number of car journeys undertaken if enough people could do this. The local planning authority can also seek to influence the location of new developments that generate large movements of people, such as hospitals, large office and retail units, etc. A more sustainable approach would be to locate such uses in town or city centres where more people can walk or cycle to them or use public transport. In terms of new housing development a key policy trend has been to promote much higher housing densities along public transport corridors; this both encourages the use of buses or trams and creates a critical mass of potential customers that can make the services more financially viable.

A way to achieve this would be to ensure that in all new developments, particularly large housing schemes, provision is made for public transport and to encourage safe walking and cycling from the very start of the planning and design process. Such provision, such as segregated bus, tram, cycle or pedestrian routes, should be in place from the early stages of building the development. In this way, as people move in to the houses the alternatives are there from the very outset. Unfortunately we are not very good at doing this in Britain; other European countries are a lot better and there are numerous examples that can be examined.

There are examples in the UK that point the way to the better integration of planning and sustainable transport in the future, for example the development of a new settlement at Northstowe, a disused airfield five miles north west of Cambridge. The County Council successfully introduced a guided bus route from the city to Huntingdon; at 25 miles in length it was the longest guided bus route in the world when it opened in 2011. The route was planned to run through the new settlement and the design of the new town is planned around it.

In the final analysis, better public transport is an absolute basic requirement needed to reduce motor-car use. But this is not always appreciated by London-based policy-makers and politicians as the capital has a very extensive public transport system, whilst the majority of provincial cities, towns and rural areas lack such provision. Local transport authorities also have limited influence over the providers of public transport in their areas. Nevertheless, promotion of public transport has been a key strand of local transport policy for many years. The powers and policies of the local transport authorities are examined in further detail below along with their scope for action in relation to the different modes of transport available, such as buses, rail, roads and so forth.

The use of different modes of transport

Heavy and light rail network provision

Let us now look at the different types of transport, or modes of transport, available: apart from the motorcar. Rail is making something of a comeback and the increased use of rail for local journeys, particularly for commuting, has been supported by many local transport authorities. Local authorities can enter into partnerships with Network Rail to invest in new or upgraded stations, which can support wider regeneration strategies or help serve areas of new housing development. Local authorities and the Passenger Transport Executives can financially support local routes which might otherwise prove unviable, and investment can also be made into new park and ride schemes and cycle and pedestrian routes to improve access to local stations. Rail therefore provides a useful alternative to the car in terms of commuting, especially in our large conur-

bations where people have to travel long distances to work in the city centre. However, rail does have its limitations as an alternative. The routes are largely fixed and the stations are not always located near enough to where people are trying to get to, such as their workplace or to the shopping centre, for example. The cost of travel is not cheap, particularly at peak times of travel (i.e. the rush hour), and trains are often overcrowded and sometimes late. Nevertheless rail needs to be an essential part of any local transport package, and the planners' role is to ensure that it is fully taken into account in plan-making and that new developments can take advantage of any local provision.

The provision and development of light rail schemes has become a key policy objective for a number of local transport authorities in Britain, especially in the larger cities. Light rail comprises modern rapid transit systems and tramways (as against 'heavy rail' which refers to old-fashioned rail systems and rolling stock). Light rail schemes are seen to appeal to the car-driving public who would never set foot on a bus to make their journey to work. They are also cheaper to build and run than 'heavy' rail and can share road space so the routes can come right into the town or city centre. Tram systems are commonplace in most cities around the world and in places such as Holland and Germany many urban areas have extensive light rail systems that are fully integrated with rail and bus routes, cycle ways and even airports. In Britain we have been slow to develop such systems. One of the first was the Docklands Light Railway in London, which opened in 1987, and which was designed to open up the docklands of east London to new development, such as that which subsequently took place at Canary Wharf in the 1990s. Since then the routes have been extended to the north and south, with a new route to Stratford International opening in 2011 to tie in with the Olympic Games. Elsewhere in London, the Croydon Tramlink opened in May 2000 serving parts of south London (Photo 12.3).

Outside the capital there are now six schemes in operation in Britain:

- Blackpool Tramway
- Manchester Metrolink
- Nottingham Express Transit

Photo 12.3   The Croydon Tramway

This is one of several new light railway solutions to modern congestion problems. Whilst it helps with city centre, and fairly localised, transport issues, unless the track system extends out into the commuter suburbs it is only likely to have a limited appeal. Indeed in Croydon commuters have found that the tram system has actually led to the diversion and reduction of existing bus routes which previously served a wider catchment area than the trams.

- Midland Metro
- Sheffield Supertram
- Tyne and Wear Metro

In 2011/12, there were 204 million passenger journeys on light rail and tram systems in England (around 2.5 per cent of all public transport journeys), as compared with just under 60 million in 1985 (Department for Transport 2012b). As can be seen, light rail has expanded considerably, though only in the large urban areas (except for Blackpool, which is a long-established tramway system – which most towns and cities had up to the 1950s). Proposals for light rail routes need parliamentary approval; the costs of construction can be quite high, as are the running costs. The complexities of developing new routes, obtaining the land and the necessary finance,

and gaining parliamentary approval have all hindered the development of trams elsewhere in the UK. There are unlikely to be any new systems developed unless there is a considerable commitment from central government to financially support such schemes. Critics argue that such schemes are excessively expensive, heavily subsidised and actually detract from providing a comprehensive bus service throughout the city. So for many towns and cities in Britain, it is buses that provide the only real alternative to the car in terms of public transport provision.

Bus services

Buses form the backbone of local public transport provision. They are the most commonly used form of local public transport. They have many advantages over other forms of transport, in that they can carry a considerable number of passengers in one vehicle, bus stops can be located within easy walking distance of large numbers of people (in urban areas) and they are relatively cheap to operate – the main capital costs are the purchase price of the vehicles themselves: the bus operators do not have to pay directly for the infrastructure that the buses run on – i.e. the roads, which are publicly funded. It can be seen from the outset that there is a split of responsibilities between the bus operators (private companies) and the local authorities. It is important to realise how these roles have changed over time, as local authorities are often 'blamed' for the poor state of public transport in their area when in fact they have important but limited powers.

Bus routes are relatively easy to establish and can be very demand-responsive, linking up the places where people live to the places where they work, shop or need to get to for recreation, leisure, education or health services. In rural areas buses are the only feasible form of public transport, and while there may only be a limited service this nevertheless provides an alternative to the car and is probably the only way that people without cars can travel around. Bus travel is often subsidised or free for groups such as the elderly or registered disabled people; these are known as concessionary fares and the bus operators are reimbursed for such passenger journeys, which made up 36 per cent of all local bus journeys in the UK, excluding Northern Ireland and London, in 2010/11 (Competition Commission 2011). In some cases concessionary fares can be extended to school students, and along with the elderly and the disabled concessionary fares provide a much needed opportunity for cheap travel. These are groups that traditionally have limited access to a private car due to limited resources or health reasons. The needs of groups such as these are sometimes met through the provision of what is known as community transport. Community transport providers are normally voluntary organisations who have to raise funds to operate their services, though in some cases the local transport authority will make some funding available to support them. They mostly run minibuses which are often adapted to carry elderly passengers in wheelchairs, for example. Such services are also provided in many rural areas where commercial provision

would be unviable. However, to put the situation in perspective, it should not be forgotten that many elderly people still do continue to drive their cars, often because of lack of any alternative, and in 2013 there were 4 million drivers over the age of 70 and this figure is growing as the population ages.

Paradoxically, in spite of rural transport needs, over half of all UK bus journeys take place within London. Pressures for bus capacity is so great in London that large, continental-style 'bendy-buses' have been tried out, though these have proved controversial. Bendy-buses have now been withdrawn from London because they proved difficult to accommodate on the city's streets, for example because of their length they blocked junctions at traffic lights, preventing traffic moving and pedestrians crossing at the lights. Some areas, such as Leeds and Cambridge (as mentioned above), have also introduced what are known as guided bus routes. These are ordinary buses that are fitted with small guide wheels at the front. These allow the bus to be driven along concrete 'tracks' at relatively high speeds and free from hold-ups as they are the only vehicles that can use the tracks. The buses can easily leave the guided routeway and operate as usual on the normal highway. This makes this option quite versatile and a lot cheaper than light rail; however it has not been widely taken up in the UK, possibly because it is seen by policy-makers and the wider travelling public as a poor substitute for a 'proper' tram system. A parallel development has been that of the driverless car, which is currently being tested on public roads both in the USA and UK, in spite of considerable reservations from the travelling public. There are all sorts of ideas about driverless pod-cars joining together on motorways and being automatically guided along, and then splitting off to their individual destinations, thus blurring the distinction between train and car, and between public and private transport.

It has to be recognised that there are a number of perceived problems with using the bus. Many car drivers in particular are put off from travelling by bus for a host of reasons, cost and convenience are obviously key, and particularly where the traveller already has a car, persuading them to use the bus instead is a very difficult task. There are many, often interrelated, factors that determine the use of buses as a method of travel. Research carried out for the Department for Transport in 2009 indicated a number of significant factors that influence bus use (Department for Transport 2009b). These were:

- The level of awareness of the services available.
- The quality of the in-vehicle experience and the information provided whilst travelling on the vehicle.
- The quality of the waiting experience (!?) and the walk to the bus stop.
- Safety and personal security issues.
- Ease of use: ticketing and seat availability.

To try to address these issues national and local government have been working together with the bus operating companies to introduce physical measures to improve reliability and journey times and to concentrate on 'softer' measures such as better information to encourage the use of buses more generally. These initiatives are explained in further detail below.

In urban areas buses provide a realistic alternative to the car for many journeys to work, particularly for getting commuters from the suburbs into city centre based jobs. To encourage this many local authorities have provided park and ride sites around the edges of their towns and cities. Drivers can leave their car at what is essentially a large out-of-town car park and use what is usually a dedicated bus service to get them to the town or city centre. Such schemes have also been pursued as part of an approach to remove cars from the centre of historic towns such as Bath and Oxford. The park and ride sites are usually linked to the town or city centre by routes which have bus priority measures such as lengths of bus-only lanes or priority at traffic lights, for example. This is all designed to give the user a faster and more reliable journey than if they had taken their car. Park and ride as a strategy has certainly proved popular for many local authorities, and the services are well used, though there are criticisms of the approach: it is still based on car use, the park and ride sites take up large areas of open space, often in the green belt, and taking cars off the busy roads only encourages other cars to use it instead. In terms of sustainability, park and ride can work if it is part of an integrated strategy. The road space 'gained' by removing cars

from the most pressurised urban roads needs to be given over to bus-only lanes or to enable environmental improvements along the route or in the town or city centre. Yet in many of our towns and cities the existing road system has little capacity for the installation of bus lanes and in such cases it is often parking spaces that have to be removed, thus making this option very unpopular with local traders and people who live along the route. A way that this has been tackled is through the provision of time-limited bus lanes, for instance the route is bus only from 7:00 to 9:00 am to give the buses priority during the morning rush hour and the rest of the day it can be used by other road users and/or for local parking.

As well as park and ride and bus-only lanes there are other initiatives that try to make travelling by bus a more attractive option than the private car. Real time information is now provided at many bus stops; this gives the passenger a degree of certainty that the bus is coming and how long they will have to wait (lack of reliability is a criticism often levelled against bus companies). Bus timetables and routes are now also available online or can be accessed through mobile phones. Many bus stops are being improved and raised kerbs make it easier for the elderly and people with prams or shopping to get on and off the bus. Bus companies are investing in new, quieter and less polluting vehicles and the idea of through ticketing is being more widely explored. Local transport authorities have entered into a range of partnerships with the bus operating companies to seek to establish higher quality standards and improved joint working. These are known as Quality Bus Partnerships.

It can be seen that bus services are an important element of local transport provision, both for those who do not have access to a private car and to help tackle congestion. Town planners therefore need to plan accordingly to meet the needs of buses and in some cases to give them priority over other road users. Park and ride sites need to be built into local plans and provision for buses can help with wider social, regeneration and sustainability strategies. Planners and transport planners have to work closely together to encourage more people to think about using the bus, but as we have seen getting car drivers to switch to this mode of transport is difficult for a variety of reasons. Local transport authorities feel they need greater powers over the bus companies, such as the ability to influence fares for instance, which was one idea looked at by the Competition Commission in their investigation into the sector (Competition Commission 2011), to enable a significant switch to what is obviously a much more sustainable mode of transport than the car. Other methods of sustainable local transport will now be examined, particularly cycling and walking.

Cycling alternatives

Before the coming of the motorcar the only 'vehicle' that provided individual freedom of route choice was the bicycle. Ebenezer Howard promoted the use of the bicycle in his Garden Cities and had little concept of the future growth of the motorcar. By the 1960s bicycles were being seen as old-fashioned and a sign of poverty and were in decline. When a family got its first car in the 1960s the adults were likely to abandon its bicycles, although lots of children still cycled to school. It was to be many years before cycling became trendy again, thanks to the efforts of campaign groups such as Sustrans (which originated in Bristol), and many other local cyclists pressure groups. These campaigned for cycle lanes and for greater space and seriousness to be given to cyclists by traffic engineers. The 1996 White Paper, Cycling in Britain, began to right the balance in official policy but there were still many conflicts and anomalies to be dealt with and subsequently local authorities were required to produce cycling and walking plans as part of their Local Transport Plans. This shift in policy represented a more inclusive approach to road space and looked to accommodate all forms of wheeled transport, not just cars.

Segregated cycle lanes provide a safer environment for cyclists and are increasingly being provided in many urban areas and built into new developments. However, in existing built-up areas of our towns and cities this is not always possible and instead provision has to be made for cyclists to share road space. This can be done through road markings and through measures that give some degree of priority to the cyclist, such as at traffic lights or pinch points that only allow cyclists and pedestrians through. Nevertheless, in 2013 in central London, the London Cycle Super Highway was created

which provides a completely segregated cycle route (for a few miles at least). But there have been several fatal accidents arising where road markings or priorities are unclear as cyclists have to merge back into car traffic at existing roundabouts and junctions.

The increasing numbers of people using bicycles has inevitably led to many clashes of opinion, with frustrated car drivers often blaming cyclists for merely being on the road. Admittedly a small number of cyclists do cycle aggressively or on the pavements, but the vast majority of cyclists are looking to get around in a sustainable manner and wish to do so safely. If cycling is to be encouraged as a matter of public policy then greater provision needs to be made in terms of infrastructure, better facilities need to be provided in the workplace (such as safe storage and showers), more training and cycle proficiency courses need to be offered, especially to schoolchildren, and attitudes towards cyclists, particularly from many car drivers, needs to change for the better.

The signs are encouraging. Sustrans, following an award of £42.5 million from the National Lottery in 1995 had by 2012 introduced over 13,000 miles of routes that together make up the National Cycle Network (SUSTRANS 2011). In London, all sorts of pro-cycling measures have been introduced, including 'Boris Bikes' which are now to be found in stands all over London, following similar schemes in Paris. Many local transport authorities around the country are introducing cycle lanes and routes that link to the national network. Measures to encourage cycling are regularly set out in travel plans for new developments and policies that promote greater cycle use are to be found in most local plans.

Walking

Many of Britain's urban areas, squares, high streets and main thoroughfares had become engulfed with traffic and parking by the 1970s. Early attempts to limit the penetration of traffic into central areas had been by means of creating new purpose-built 'shopping precincts' where cars were excluded to enable shoppers to move freely, as in the 1950s in the post-war reconstruction of many cities, such as Coventry, Bristol, Birmingham and Plymouth, although they often had to risk their lives to get across the enclosing ring road to reach the pedestrianised area. This approach of encouraging car-free shopping areas was also applied to many high streets, though an unanticipated consequence of this policy was that many people were put off walking through the pedestrianised town centre streets in the evening because they appeared dangerous, unfriendly locations after dark when all the shops closed up. In contrast, in historic tourist areas such as Exeter, Stratford-upon-Avon, Chester and many coastal villages the removal of traffic from the small-scale historical layouts made these areas much more attractive, although traffic had to be allowed back in at certain times for off-loading goods, and to give access to residents living along these streets.

Pedestrianisation of key public spaces in most of Britain's towns and cities is now commonplace and aimed at reducing pedestrian–vehicular conflict. Pedestrianisation is often part of a wider strategy concerned with place-making (see the next chapter on urban design for more on this) where well-designed and maintained buildings and spaces are carefully linked to create networks of pedestrian-friendly routes (DCLG 2009c). The public spaces are often enhanced by public art, a strategy that has been very successfully pursued over the past 20 years in the centre of Birmingham, for example, where a network of squares and public spaces has helped to transform the post-industrial past of the area and to remove many of the vast highways schemes of the 1960s and 1970s.

Many towns and cities have actively pursued strategies to promote walking, including improving signage and the information available to locals and visitors to the area to help them navigate their way around. This is often referred to as improving the *legibility* of the area, an approach that was pioneered in Bristol under the title Legible City in the 1990s where new signs and easy-to-understand maps were introduced throughout the city centre using a new lettering font and design style, such as undertaken by the Bristol Cultural Development Partnership. This approach can now be found in many towns and cities.

A key to increasing walking as a mode of transport is to ensure that the pavements and walkways are safe and properly maintained, an increasing challenge for the local authorities who are responsible for this in a climate of reduced public spending. Most public walkways will be either paved using new or historic paving stones or will be surfaced with black tarmac. Paving stones obviously look a lot nicer than the widely used tarmac, but are more expensive to replace and maintain, especially as the pavements are so often dug up by the utility companies to make repairs to underground pipes and cables, etc. Paving stones are therefore more likely to be found in conservation areas and city or town centre shopping areas and key public spaces.

In many parts of the country, especially rural areas and in the countryside, some established walking routes are designated as public footpaths. These are not usually surfaced but might need maintaining in parts, especially where they are well used and might need steps or railings to improve safety. Many of these routes will be shown on Ordnance Survey maps, and many will also be designated as what are known as Public Rights Of Way (PROW). A PROW is a path that anyone has the legal right to use on foot; the Local Transport Authority has the power to make an order creating a right of way over a piece of land where they think it would add to the convenience or enjoyment of the public (Ramblers Association 2012). There are often conflicts between landowners and the public who wish to walk over their land. The PROW legislation and designation process are meant to be the ways that such conflicts are resolved, but they can become mired in legal and procedural issues. The network of public footpaths is a great resource and many are signposted or form longer, national trails which are very popular with hikers and walkers.

For many years an approach was taken in our urban areas, on the grounds of improving safety, to keep pedestrians and traffic apart; this was normally achieved though the installation of railings along the side of the street, and especially at busy junctions and road crossings. Yet this approach came in for criticism in that most of the measures appeared to be aimed at controlling the behavior of the pedestrian, who was often made to walk longer distances or was forced to use underpasses or tortuous pedestrian bridges just to get from one side of the road to the other. Pedestrians were given very little quarter and there was little consideration of the social implications of such an approach by the highways engineers

Photo 12.4   Other wheeled vehicles

If you look at the people on the streets, you will find many people with pedestrian wheeled vehicles, such as pushchairs, prams, wheelchairs, trolleys and wheeled suitcases. But all these do not 'fit' into transport policies that are based around cars and bikes. In fact pushchairs far outnumber wheelchairs, and for that matter bicycles too in many areas. To create sustainable cities planners must make it easier for all these other wheeled groups to be able to get around, without steps, steep slopes, uneven paving …

in terms of accessibility, personal safety and inconvenience. It was therefore felt that the onus should instead be put on the car driver to either slow down or to take much greater account of the needs of the pedestrian, or to do both. The installation of traffic calming measures was seen as a way of achieving this and this will now be examined, along with a more radical development of the principle, known as shared space.

Other wheeled transport and accessibility

Many user groups find that transport schemes are not designed in a way that makes them accessible and usable for everyone, for example disabled access to many facilities and transport services is poor across the country. In fact people in wheelchairs, parents with pushchairs and for that matter people pulling along heavy wheeled suitcases find that there are so many steps, changes in level and rough surfaces that they have difficulty accessing the built environment. For example, the lack of basic ancillary facilities for those using public transport, such as public toilets at bus and train stations, makes journeys a daunting prospect for those with small children, the elderly and particularly women who historically have less toilet facilities provided than men (Greed 2003a). Many of the toilet facilities that do exist are down steps and thus inaccessible to those with heavy luggage, whilst left luggage offices, staffed stations, baby-changing and disabled facilities and even ticket offices have all been cut back across the railway network, suggesting a lack of understanding of the human aspects of transport design. For many elderly people it is only the more active and able-bodied who are likely to venture forth owing to the inaccessibility of our public transport system (Lenclos 2002). For drivers with disabilities the Blue Badge system of 'disabled parking' has proved problematic. It was first introduced in1971, and demand exceeds supply, although there is also considerable misuse and counterfeiting of these permits. The increasing pedestrianisation of city centres and limitations on parking spaces make it more difficult for disabled drivers to access the city, whereas those who still walk or travel by bus are increasingly overwhelmed by complex traffic management systems and innovations such as 'shared streets', which will be discussed in the next chapter.

What are needed are more fundamental changes in the design of our cities to make them more accessible for everyone. The various Disability Acts have put greater emphasis upon the right of people with disabilities to get out and about and there have been many modifications to the built environment and transport made accordingly (CAE 2012). These range from dropped kerbs for wheelchair and pushchair access, to the 'pimples' found the pavement at road crossings, which are meant to alert blind people to imminent danger, but which have also been much criticised for being slippery and dangerous. In fact the texturing of pavements created problems for all sorts of people, as they are very uncomfortable for occupants of pushchairs and wheelchairs (Photo 12.4). The eye-catching use of different coloured paving stones to liven up a square can be very confusing to those with visual disabilities. The presence of pavement obstructions such as traffic sign poles and bollards, and the frequent changes in levels and excessive use of steps, suggests that we have a long way to go in creating accessible environments. But it is often the highways engineers, not people with experience of urban design and social awareness, that are responsible for designing pavements. Rather than having 'special' measures for people with disabilities, the reality is that many people, who are not registered disabled, experience great difficulty getting around our cities, including the elderly, those with small children, the pregnant and those lacking stamina. Whilst providing dropped kerbs is very important, there is a need to restructure entire cities to increase accessibility and convenience for those with mobility needs. This may involve rethinking land-use patterns and reconfiguring transport routes (I'DGO 2009). Therefore, a more inclusive universal approach to transport planning is needed, which will actually make life easier for everyone (Goldsmith 2000; TCPA 2005; Greed 2011a, 2011b).

The demise of the private motorcar?

Car controls

All the above can be seen as very positive alternatives to car transport, in comparison with slavishly following North American trends and catering for the motorcar without question. Indeed a whole new attitude and approach to 'planning for the motorcar' had emerged by the new millennium. PPS3 had set a new policy regime in intensifying controls on the motorcar, especially in respect of 'destination' areas including city centres. This was a major turn-about: a volte-face. Whereas for 50 years local authorities had torn up whole tracts of cities to make way for the car, now they exercised their powers to restrict car use. Whilst many of the changes were introduced under New Labour (from 1997), the preceding Conservative government under John Major took a more understanding attitude towards environmental sustainability (see Chapter 7) and, in spite of being in favour of free enterprise, were already introducing greater traffic controls. For example, the Road Traffic Act 1991 gave London special traffic control powers such as road pricing and enforcement powers.

As car ownership grew into the new millennium a whole range of car control mechanisms are in existence, with the purpose of increasing the capacity of existing roads, making the traffic flow more efficiently, reducing accidents, but also, arguably, increasing revenues too. Historically, motoring became controlled, first with the introduction of driving tests in the 1930s, then over the second part of the twentieth century, gradually seat belt laws, reduced speed limits, MOTs, and restrictions on drinking and driving, were introduced. Vehicle engines became more efficient but also subject to a whole range of environmental controls which resulted in catalytic converters being required, lead petrol being banned and braking systems being improved and air bags being introduced.

A variety of new fiscal and physical measures were introduced to control the motorcar. Arguably people have already paid for the right to drive through their licence fee, so one can either see these measures as a means of enforcing controls, or more cynically as a means of increasing revenue in these days of government funding cutbacks. For example, fuel and vehicle duties have been increased, but the proportion of this revenue reinvested in the road system has been reduced– 82.2 per cent of the average price of petrol is taken in tax and other ancillary charges! (Check this for yourself on the internet but be careful to check 'who' is putting forward a particular point of view.) But only 20 per cent of that amount is used for road improvements, yet Middle Eastern oil exporters are conveniently blamed for the rise in fuel prices. Clearly the aim is to price people off the road, so that the ability to pay rather than the necessity, or the social usefulness, of the journey becomes the main criteria of car use. As raised in Chapter 10 on sustainability, finding alternative cheaper fuels than petrol would not necessarily solve the problem. Cheap fuel, or perhaps electric cars, would lead to far more vehicles on the road, and thus greater traffic problems. So it is in the interest of both the oil companies and the government to adopt a cautious approach to such innovations.

As the years went by the competition for on-street parking became intense and less and lessspaces and more and more controls reduced parking availability. Over the years the perceived 'war against the motorist' has increased, with parking meters first being introduced in the 1950s. But it was still relatively easy to park then in provincial towns and cities because few people had cars and there were many empty bomb sites to park in. As city-centre parking pressures grew cars were herded into multi-storey car parks. There is a vast array of parking controls, fines, and confusing regulations. If too much control is enforced then this can affect the local economic viability of shops and town centres. Whilst such an approach was helping to 'solve' the city centre traffic problem in some cases, especially in smaller towns where public transport was limited, it actually led to a decline in retail turnover, thus endangering local businesses.

Parking control

Road markings (single and double yellow lines) are frequently used to limit parking and in busy shopping areas, town and city centres there is usually a charge for on-street parking through the use of parking meters. Local transport authorities have the power to designate such charging zones and the provision of parking meters usually provokes opposition from local traders who fear it will deter trade, though the meters are really 'rationing' the use of a very limited commodity (i.e. the parking space) and ensuring that the same people, or the people who work in the local shops and offices, do not park there all day. The other option is to provide dedicated car parks; in our town and city centres these are normally multi-storey car parks and can be provided by either the public sector (i.e. the local council) or the private sector. For the majority of the day and night most commuter cars are actually static, either sleeping in their garages at home, or sitting in work-related car parks, and most are only on the road for about an hour or two a day. Some authorities are looking at introducing a charge on workplace parking as a less direct method of limiting car use (as well as limiting available spaces), but again this is not politically attractive and has practical and economic barriers that need to be overcome. But there are lots of other cars moving around and needing parking on journeys related to shopping, childcare, hospital appointments and leisure activities.

The provision of car parking and parking spaces is a key consideration when it comes to planning for our high streets, in-town shopping areas and town and city centres (Portas Report 2012). A balance has to be struck between encouraging more sustainable patters of transport while at the same time recognising that many people will want to drive by car to do their shopping. A criticism of out-of-town shopping is that it not only discourages travel by public transport (as it is not in a central location) but actively promotes car travel through the provision of huge areas of free parking. In the past, government planning policy has sought to restrict the number of parking spaces in new developments by setting maximum limits in its Planning Policy Guidance Note for transport, PPG13. These nationally set parking standards were removed by the Coalition government in 2011 and the responsibility was given to the local planning authorities instead to set their own standards on new residential and other forms of development through their local plans.

It is often the case that the motorist will choose to avoid paying for parking altogether by using a street that is not too far away from where he or she is seeking to get to. This normally means a residential area close to the town or city centre, and such locations are often full of commuter parking between the hours of 8:00am and 6:00pm on working days. This obviously upsets local residents who see the spaces in their street or outside their house as being exclusively for them, though they certainly have no legal basis for this view. Similar conflicts can occur around developments that generate large numbers of cars at certain times of the day or week, such as football grounds. Some local councils have sought to address this issue through the introduction of residents' parking schemes. Zones are established where only permit holders (local residents) can park at certain times of the day. There is normally a charge for this to help cover the cost of administration and enforcement. Again, the introduction of these measures often proves controversial; some residents see it as an additional tax on them rather than as a benefit. The creation of such zones around the town or city centre can also be used as a means of deterring commuter traffic as part of a wider strategy to reduce car use. Further developments of car control such as Home Zones, Shared Streets and carless residential areas will be explained further in the next chapter.

Road charging
The final issue to be considered here in terms of seeking to restrict car use is possibly the most controversial, that of charging the car driver either directly for using their car through some form of 'congestion charging' or less directly through taxation. The latter power is already extensively used, and while in the past the government has been keen to point out that road tax and tax on petrol are forms of general taxation and are not directly linked to the provision and upkeep of the roads, for example, higher rates of tax have been introduced on vehicles with larger engine sizes in an attempt to 'make the polluter pay' and to encourage the take-up of smaller cars. This is a good example of using fiscal policy measures to seek to influence public behaviour. There is also the whole issue of speed cameras, which are meant to increase safety, but which bring in a substantial revenue and also control, or possibly deter, motorists in their use of road space and driving behaviour.

In terms of local transport policy and practice in the UK, the scope for using financial measures to explicitly restrict car use has been limited essentially to the setting of parking charges and here the objective of deterring car use has only been an indirect one, it being a brave politician who would advocate such a thing! National government has only relatively recently given local government the power to introduce measures such as road-user charging and workplace charging through the Transport Act 2000 and it has only been in London that a form of local road-user charging was successfully introduced in 2003 in the form of the Congestion Charge. This proved very controversial at the time and needed a considerable degree of leadership by the then Mayor of London Ken Livingstone to see it through. The scheme is still in place and while there have been political differences over the extent of the charging zone it is widely seen as being a success.

Two other UK cities have tried to introduce congestion charging and have failed. In 2005 Edinburgh City Council asked its citizens to approve a package of measures designed to improve public transport in the city based on increased revenue generated by a congestion charge. The proposal was rejected by 75 per cent of those who voted and was dropped. A similar initiative in the Greater Manchester area was put to local people in another referendum in 2008. The government promised a substantial amount of funding for new public transport infrastructure but required the local authorities to also make a financial contribution, and a congestion charge was put forward as a way to doing this. Over 1 million people voted and the proposal was decisively rejected with 80 per cent of voters being against the idea. Road-user charging is therefore a difficult measure for local transport authorities to introduce as it is so politically controversial, as we have seen. For many local authorities it is a case of seeking to persuade and encourage car users to switch to more sustainable methods of transport rather than through coercion – using the 'carrot' rather than the 'stick'. This approach will be briefly considered next.

Overall there has been a considerable increase in the micro-management of road space. Traffic control measures include bus-only lanes, red routes and priority routes where absolutely no stopping is permitted, and also 2+ only lanes which generally operate during the rush hour and also 2+ parking spaces at the workplace. The Congestion Charge in inner London has been the subject of much debate, as proposals have been introduced to extend it to cover residential areas beyond the West End of London, whose residents are more articulate and powerful. This was going to be rolled out to other cities if it worked in London, but so far this has not happened. Most of these measures are policed by CCTV cameras and automatic fines. But those who 'trip chain' on their way to work may start with several passengers, such as taking children to school, or spouses to the railway station, but by the time they have reached the 2+ lane they are alone. Further, many people have quite varied hours, may travel for their work and may not have nearby co-workers who they can travel with. And the 'white van man' is not taken into account either. Even the introduction of car clubs cannot always link everybody up, because of the very varied nature of people's work and journey requirements. There are also several companies that will loan out cars for the day, or by the hour, which are more community-based than the more 'executive level' likes of Avis for business customers.

However, negative controls on the use of the motorcar are proving impractical for many people, because the government is not offering them any public transport alternatives to car travel in their particular area (Uteng and Cresswell 2008; Greed 2011a, 2011b). For many in the suburbs, where the majority of the urban population lives, cars may be the only means to get to work, to reach out-of-town retail centres, and to take small children to school (ONS 2012; check for up-to-date figures by referring to the ONS website http://www.ons.gov.uk/). If there is no public transport available in many areas, with no train stations, and bus journeys are slow, infrequent, indirect, complex and unreliable, then they do not provide a realistic alternative in terms of personal time management, accessibility and practicality, then people will resort to their cars. Policies which work in London where there is an extensive public transport system do not work in the depths of Somerset. As a result of previous misdirected planning policy there are few retail outlets or social amenities at the local district level. So there has been a continuing resentment that people are penalised for using their cars when it is not their fault the planners moved everyone out in the past. Also however much you interfere in people's lives, they cannot do anything about it, as people do not have the individual power to build new railway stations. Furthermore, lack of available, reliable and regular transport adds many hours to the working day and costs the economy millions. Meanwhile some groups actually need to use car transport such as the elderly, those who cannot walk far, the disabled and those with small children, who find it difficult to struggle through the assault course that public transport constitutes in many cities.

Conclusion: mind the gap

Many have heeded the government's call for people to leave the car at home, but they often find that the alternatives available are slower, unreliable and not designed to go where they need to get to. So there is a major credibility gap between what the government says can be done to improve the transport situation and what is actually available to the travelling public. The transport issue illustrates, par excellence, many of the controversies and dilemmas surrounding planning policy-making in general. Everything is highly political, and different groups benefit or lose out according to what policy is adopted. Planning is not a straightforward subject in which there is one right answer or a fixed set of rules; it all depends on the answer to the question *How do you want to live?* (DOE 1972b). Planning is a messy, complicated, never-ending and time-consuming process. Ad hoc solutions, glib sound bites, or false 'instant' solutions are not the answer;

rather a fully integrated, and carefully structured, land-use and transportation strategy is needed. Clearly revenue and funding are key issues in the success of bringing schemes to fruition, especially in times of recession and government cutbacks.

Other European countries seem to be doing better at dealing with their transport problems and 'planning for everyday life' in meeting the needs of ordinary people (Skjerve (ed.) 1993) in a more progressive and socially aware manner. As explained in Chapter 2, membership of the European Union (EU) has opened up alternative ways of planning for all (Cullingworth and Nadin 2006; Nadin *et al.* 2010). European women planners have described the ideal city as the city of short distances, mixed land uses and multi-centres (Eurofem 1998; Skjerve (ed.) 1993) (and see Chapter 15). This vision happens to coincide with the idea of the sustainable city, and the healthy city too. Significantly, many of the views expressed by environmentalists are echoed by those concerned with the social aspects of town planning, especially those representing minority groups and those with limited access to the use of a motorcar, such as women with small children. There is a need to change the car culture, but also to provide reasonable alternatives such as much better public transport and improved infrastructure to enable people to live, work, travel and get on with their lives.

Much has been made of the Coalition's commitment to investment in new infrastructure but whether prestige projects such as HS2 and airport termini are going to have any effect on the daily needs of commuters is open to question. New forms of funding such as CIL are much vaunted but the reality is that there have been major government cutbacks at local authority level, which have affected new local infrastructural investments, as well as the staffing of local planning authorities and other service providers. Meanwhile train fares continue to rise way above inflation, driving people back to their cars, but then petrol prices continue to rise too. So we await what will happen next.

But we are living in the overlap, between the rebuilding of public transport and the decline of the motorcar. Whilst the government goes on and on about the importance of sustainability, cycling and public transport, the reality is that in many areas public services and the public transport infrastructure is so run down, especially outside London, that they are no help. So the real issue is how to deal with the continuing use of the motorcar by the majority of the population in a way that is more civilised and controlled than in the days when the car was king. Please now go to the next chapter on urban design where the issues of traffic calming, shared streets and accessibility will be discussed.

For the tasks, further reading, additional photos and other resources for this chapter, please visit www.palgrave. com/companion/greed. E-Supplement 1 provides information on relevant legislation and government transport policy, whilst E-Supplement 7 provides a fuller coverage of the more technical aspects of transport planning and will be particularly useful in relation to this chapter.

13 Urban Design, Place-Making and Culture

Creating the places we live

Investigating urban design

The purpose of this chapter is to familiarise readers with key themes, principles and changes at the local design level of planning. Indeed, as with much of planning, there may be no one right answer, but there is likely to be a widely-used set of principles which work for most situations. Previously urban design has been tackled in two edited collections by the author and colleagues (Greed and Roberts (eds) 1998; Roberts and Greed (eds) 2000 with a Chinese language edition 2010) which you may still find useful. Emphasis is given to residential development in this chapter, which comprises over 70 per cent of all development, and has also been the focus of government commitment to increase provision. In this chapter, in the introductory section, the new urban design agenda is heralded. Alternatives to car-dominated design are then discussed, starting with the influence of Radburn layouts, and moving on to traffic calming, and shared approaches to design, in which the pedestrian and the residents of an area are likely to benefit. The social, human aspects of urban design are then discussed further in terms of user needs, mobility and disability. The chapter concludes by discussing the emergent trends towards a more cultural approach to urban design, including urban renaissance, place-making, and generally a more visual, arts-based approach towards designing cities (Carmona and Tiesdell 2006).

As will be seen, there is an increasing tension between planners and architects concerned with 'place-making' and an enlightened approach to urban design; and highways engineers and other wielders of regulatory and statutory power, who, arguably, have a more technical and less socially-based agenda. But they still have a tremendous influence on shaping what can be built through the enforcement of technical requirements and standards. One must also take into account the power of private-sector property developers, particularly those concerned with new housing estate development. Their views on questions of density, house type and road provision and design are likely to be motivated by the cost factor, the need to meet market demand and make a profit. Urban designers and planners share control over the design of the built environment with all these other actors in the development process (as indicated in Chapter 2).

A new urban design agenda

The objectives and scope of urban design have changed considerably over the last 20 years (Carmona *et al.* 2010; Punter 2009). In the past, 'housing layouts' were generally designed according to fixed rules, often by people with an engineering background who prioritised the needs of the motor-car (Roberts and Greed 2000). Great emphasis was put upon setting standards as to road widths, densities and building styles, especially in the post-war period when over 30 per cent of housing was council built. The emphasis on standards was accompanied by a practical concern for the provision of sewers, drains and other infrastructural services. Even more socially-motivated early planners favoured a pattern book approach. For example, Louis Keeble's books provided instant recipes and layout patterns on how to plan new towns, new housing estates, town centres and industrial estates (Keeble 1969, 1983).

Today, there is a greater emphasis upon 'place-making' rather than upon 'highways engineering'

Photo 13.1   Marina waterfront housing, Portishead, Bristol

Many derelict docklands have been redeveloped as marinas with new housing alongside, often in the form of high-density modern apartment blocks. But owing to its proximity to Bristol, here the Georgian townhouse style found in the Clifton conservation area has been mimicked albeit for much smaller houses.

when shaping urban areas and designing residential layouts which take into account the needs of pedestrians rather than just the motorcar (Brown *et al.* 2009). So there is a clash of cultures! Whilst urban designers discuss permeability, legibility, shared spaces and sustainability, traffic engineers still talk about visibility splays, traffic speeds, road capacities and road widths. So 'housing layout' is now a 'contested space' in itself. But, in the real world, local planning authorities still have to produce clear guidelines and requirements as to what is expected of house-building developers, and therefore many have produced their own design guides. The 'Grandfather of them all' was the 1975 Essex Design Guide that has achieved cult status (Essex 1973; updated Essex 2005). Look online at www.the-edi.co.uk/downloads/19715_essexdesignguide.pdf. As the guide evolved it took on board national shifts towards environmental policies which have sought to restrict, rather than cater for, car usage.

In contrast to post-war planning, four key factors dominate current urban design practice. These are the importance of creating sustainable settlements; designing socially-inclusive environments, especially for the disabled; the importance of urban design in 'place–making'; and the valuing and conservation of the historical built environment as a cultural artefact. For example, 'place-making' may be applied to residential development, commercial schemes and to leisure and recreation (Photo 13.1).

Overall there has been a move towards higher densities, restrictions on motorcar use and parking, more social awareness, an emphasis upon sympathetic treatment of historical areas, and a preference for brown-field infill development, rather than building upon green-field sites on the edge of town. At the same time there has been a resurgence of a more architectural and aesthetic approach to urban design. This has been linked to the enthusiasm for conservation as manifested in the creation of many urban conservation areas and the listing of buildings. It should be noted that the nitty-gritty of the legal aspects of listed buildings and conservation area controls were covered in Chapter 3 as part of the 'development management' agenda, whereas in this chapter it comes in to the discussion as one of the components in the urban design agenda, particularly in relation to the visual architectural heritage.

Urban design has its roots both in the grand historical designs of the past and in a more visual, design-orientated, cultural approach to planning (Kostoff 2009; Doxiadis 1968). But the Grand Manner tradition of European planning, manifest in the great squares, boulevards and avenues of many capital cities, was essentially an artistic rather than functional exercise, with a God's eye view looking down on the drawing board from above (Gibberd 1970) rather than looking at the situation of the pedestrian battling through the city at street level. In contrast, as will be explained in the second part of this chapter, urban design is more concerned with user and resident needs at local level (Burton and Mitchell 2006). Thus there is a new socially-focused approach to functional urban design.

Fixed standards or flexible policies?

The local design level is still the area of planning that many newcomers to the subject assume is the 'real planning'. They may imagine the planners' work to be centred upon following fixed rules as to road widths, densities, plot ratio and so forth. Students often imagine that there must be one right technical answer to the question of how to do a housing layout. But, as with much of town planning, 'the right answer' depends on what the planners wants to achieve, and where the development is located. In fact the situation is not straightforward. Whilst it is true that there are national planning standards such as on major arterial roads, in relation to traffic engineering and highways design (DfT 2011a, 2011 b), local planners and urban designers can have more discretion into how infill sites and local residential schemes are designed to meet local needs. They will also have an element of flexibility, according to local circumstances and topography, as to how they meet higher-level government policy objectives on, for example, reducing global warming,

creating inclusive healthy environments, and designing attractive settings for everyday life: through the way they design a particular layout (Barton and Tsourou 2006). Local design and layout decisions will also be shaped by the policy statements and guidance found in the development plan, and now, as the new planning system comes into effect in the Local Plan, and neighbourhood plans for the locality as a whole. Although different local authorities may adopt their own approaches, albeit informed by national policy, once their policies are adopted they do have a legal status in the area in question. Private-sector, nationwide, mass house-builders have a very major input to the nature of modern housing estates and house types. To get planning permission they need to submit planning applications that fall within current design guidelines, and/or negotiate with the local planning authority.

Alternatives to car-dominated design

Moving on from the car

For many years nearly every aspect of housing layout and city planning as a whole was motivated by the need to make room for the car. However, even in the euphoria of increased car ownership in the post-war reconstruction period there already existed more sensitive approaches to planning that recognised the needs of the pedestrian as well as the motorcar. In particular it is worth explaining the Radburn approach which was put into practice in several New Towns from the 1940s to the 1960s, because it contained within it the seeds of ideas and principles that were subsequently to manifest themselves in modern-day planners' changing attitudes towards the motorcar, the environment and human beings. For example, in the past great emphasis was put upon creating wide roads and generously designed junctions to enable cars to go faster, whereas nowadays the emphasis is upon reducing sight lines, and actually introducing restrictions into roads to reduce speeds and 'calm' the traffic.

Radburn layouts

There is a need to control – through design – the entrance and movement of cars within residential estates for reasons of safety, environment, noise and privacy. A whole range of sophisticated road layout solutions exist, many of which still include culs-de-sac (no through roads) along with separate footpath systems. These are often called 'Radburns' (a form of cul-de-sac). Radburns are discussed briefly here because they *prefigure* so many of the issues pertinent to modern urban design of roads and pedestrian areas, concerned with controlling the car's penetration of residential areas and creating a safer, more pedestrian-dominated street environment. Also the discussion will get you thinking in design terms as to all the factors that need to be juggled and organised in your mind and thus on the plan.

In the 1920s in America, the town of Radburn was designed as a series of neighbourhoods, each of which was ringed by an external peripheral road, from which a series of culs-de-sac penetrated into the neighbourhood, providing access for residents but preventing through traffic from finding a short cut through. This is similar to the idea of environmental areas, proposed by Buchanan (see Chapter 6), in the 1960s in respect of reconfiguring road systems in existing urban areas in Britain (Buchanan 1963). Within the Radburn neighbourhood the pedestrian footpath system was designed to be completely separate from the road system. People coming to the house by car would arrive at the 'back' of the house, and park in a garage or garage court and approach the house through the 'back' door. But pedestrians would walk along the landscaped footpaths which run between the houses on the 'front' of the house. Front and back are in inverted commas, because once it is realised that pavements do not need to run alongside roads, and that houses need not face on to the street, the concept of front and back becomes almost irrelevant. Indeed, these changes to the external access to the houses did mean a major rethink of how the inside of the house should be planned. Radburns are not just a historical curiosity, they are still around, and the whole concept has deeply influenced our approach to residential layout.

The Radburn principle was adopted in many of the post-war British New Towns in combination with the neighbourhood unit concept. Such schemes often proved unpopular for whilst they were meant to increase the safety from traffic by separating the paths from the roads, many residents were unhappy with the remote, cut-off nature of some of the paths, especially lone women walking home after work in the evenings. This was particularly the case in towns where footpaths were routed through dark underpasses beneath peripheral roads. Thus road safety and personal safety were at odds. It was often expected that bicycles should share the footpaths with the pedestrians, an arrangement which has continued to prove unsatisfactory for both groups. Purists would say that if the True Radburn design had been adopted rather than cheap and nasty versions, known as Pseudo Radburns, then many of these problems could have been avoided. Most local authorities accept Radburnisation in some form or other as a basis of their design principles, with particular emphasis on the use of culs-de-sac to provide car access to the houses, and also the inclusion of footpath systems. However, there are usually also pavements alongside the roads as well.

The concept of the Radburn peripheral road can still be seen in some larger-scale developments. But on smaller schemes it is common to see the reverse, a branching 'tree' layout, with a spine road giving access into the centre of the estate and then a series of smaller distributor roads branching off from this. They, in turn, subdivide into smaller roads in the form of small access roads which serve 'clumps' of houses. In the immediate post-war period, examples of the turning arrangements at the end of culs-de-sac looked like 'lollipops', that is the road went around a little circular traffic island with a touch of greenery in the middle. Culs-de-sac normally end with a hammerhead or 'T' shaped turning space which enables adequate room to reverse around. In some cases the planners have tried to 'soften' this arrangement by creating more of a courtyard effect in which the change from road to private driveway is marked by a change in the style of paving stone. However, whilst this might look impressive, and create an urban 'mews' atmosphere when used in inner urban infill sites, many pedestrians find this arrangement ambiguous and therefore potentially dangerous.

Once traditional street patterns are abandoned, a range of layouts can be developed which set the houses in different arrangements. For example, garage courts, play spaces and communal gardens

Photo 13.2   Poundbury, Dorset

This is just one example of the many architectural styles and layout configurations found in Prince Charles' model town in Dorset. The emphasis is on creating a faux historical town, which nevertheless incorporates many modern features and has traffic calming at the core of its layout.

were often incorporated into local authority schemes at the expense of traditional gardens, pavements and garages. Some architects believed that this freeing up of the estate layout created a greater sense of space, and also got away from, what they saw as, the restrictive nature of individual house plots. Such experiments were often combined with the use of open-plan formats for front gardens, and separate 'no-man's-land' landscaped areas. However, most people prefer a private exterior zone for each house. Indeed, as has been said earlier, people want a sense of what Oscar Newman calls Defensible Space (Newman 1973). It has been found that vandalism and graffiti are reduced by such measures as clearly defining front gardens, as people think twice about stepping onto the dwelling's curtilage. With greatly increased densities in infill sites, houses often have very small gardens, and instead there may be concentrated areas of landscape located for maximum visual effect within the development. Parking is also likely to be restricted and often combined in garage courts in even quite expensive private developments. Arranging houses around crescents, circuses and squares is also coming back into fashion, perhaps because of the influence of Prince Charles' model town in Dorset, Poundbury (Photo 13.2). Prince Charles (Prince of Wales 1989) has continued to draw attention to the deficiencies of modern town planning and architecture. Yet he has arguably concentrated upon the visual aspects rather than the functional or social aspects of planning, as in his model village of Poundbury in Dorset (Hutchinson 1989), which arguably is very pretty but is actually a dormitory town for commuters and also popular with people who have retired.

Gardens seem to be on the way out, and this is of particular concern for families with small children and pets, who need 'space' to breathe and perhaps a garden shed and a bit of spare space, particularly as houses seem to be getting smaller too and the UK is

Photo 13.3   Traditional traffic calming

This first example is not a spectacular example, just one little typical urban residential road where the carriageway has been narrowed and speed bumps introduced to slow traffic. From these limited beginnings some towns have now moved on to more ambitious road closures, and designation of roadway for sharing between pedestrians, cars and cycles.

below the EU average in this respect. The average UK house has reduced in size by 40 per cent over the last 80 years. In the original Essex Design Guide (Essex 1973) it was suggested that every house should have a minimum 100 square metres (about 30 square feet) of back garden with high walls around each plot. This gave the residents a sense of private external space, but proved intimidating for pedestrians, especially women. More subtle solutions were to be found in the 'new' Essex Design Guide (Essex 1997), which also included many examples of designing in such a way that public areas and shared surfaces are integrated within housing, in the form of small squares, boulevard walkways and play space. But gardens and houses continue to get smaller and roads narrower,

even on prestigious estates. But practical standards have to be integrated to ensure for example that the fire engine can reach every house, or to enable the dustcart to get through, without the dustmen having to walk more than the distance as laid down by their union, normally set at 25 metres (80 feet). With the increase in recycling receptacles and more complicated refuse collection systems, the already crowded streets become unsightly and cluttered with 'green bins' (Greed 2011a, 2012).

Traffic calming

Planners continue to wrestle with the issue of how to control the car, and establish a fairer balance between pedestrians and vehicles in residential areas. Planners have been concerned for some time about the intrusion of our city streets by increasing levels of traffic, with increased levels of vehicular–pedestrian conflict. Whereas for 50 years local authorities had torn up whole tracts of cities to make way for the car, from the 1980s onwards they exercised their powers to try to restrict the impact of the car. The policy emphasis shifted further in the 1990s towards promoting traffic calming, facilitated under the1993 Traffic Calming Act (Photo 13.3). The movement was inspired by Hass-Klau's work in Germany, who is credited with inventing the term 'traffic calming' which has focused upon making streets safer, slowing traffic and giving sovereignty back to the pedestrian (Hass-Klau 1990, 1992).

It has been assumed that local traffic would not exceed 30 mph (the normal residential speed limit). However, 20 mph or less is considered preferable, but speeds can be brought much lower by various mechanisms. Measures included narrowing carriageways, introducing speed bumps, chicanes, and in some cases reducing visibility at junctions to make drivers more cautious. However, vehicle access is still necessary for the disabled, and for a whole range of delivery, maintenance and emergency vehicles, whilst public transport provision needs to be accessible and within walking distance. By the new millennium local authority design guides recommended much more car-restrictive layouts than found in previous editions. The aim was to create safer and more liveable neighbourhoods for pedestrians and especially children. This approach reflected a major shift in thinking by national government. But, even the most negative controls on cars were still really about traffic management and reducing traffic jams rather than thinking more creatively about designing out the car. After many years of looking to prioritise the needs of the car user, this considerable shift in emphasis was reflected in a key government guidance document called *Manual for Streets* (DfT 2007). The manual recommended that streets should be places for people to live and spend time in, and are not there just for vehicles. It called for a much higher priority to be given to the needs of pedestrians, cyclists and users of public transport. As can be seen from the last chapter on transport, things have also changed because of the campaigns by cycling groups to redesign road layouts to take into account their needs (SUSTRANS 2011).

Shared space

Whilst in the UK we were tinkering with restricting car access, a whole new way of looking at our roads and residential areas was emerging in continental Europe, and especially in the Netherlands, which was based upon redesigning the whole street as a place for living in and where the car was on equal terms with, or secondary to, the needs of the pedestrian and cyclist. This concept in the Netherlands is known as the *woonerf* and the idea has strongly influenced UK concepts such as the play street and home zones which are very plentiful in many Dutch cities, where cycling, rather than car-driving, dominates. The main characteristic of a *woonerf* is that there is little or no demarcation between the pavement and the road: instead the whole area is paved, often in coloured paving stones with subtle variations to indicate parking spaces. The streets are often ornamented with planting, seating, communal recycling and refuse collection zones and play areas. In all this there is considerable attention to detail, to road safety and to the principles of modern urban design. In some schemes there is very little or even no parking space at all, or the parking is provided in discrete areas away from the housing. The Beddington Zero Energy Development (known as BedZED, see http://en.wikipedia.org/wiki/BedZED) in the London Borough of Sutton, in South London, is an early and well-used example of such an approach in the UK, as well as being an environmentally green development (well worth Googling and visiting too). However, this is a self-contained housing development which accesses on to an existing, heavily-used and unchanged trunk road, which carries the old London to Brighton Road, as well as being served by the Croydon 'light rail' tramway system.

In many such locations, cars were not actually banned outright from entering the area; rather their penetration was carefully controlled. Bicycles, pedestrians, cars and public transport vehicles were actually coexisting, with the proviso that speeds were very low, and the only cars that were let in were ones with a destination in the area in question. But the shared street space was often very carefully designed with distinct facilities for different users, and the streets are quite wide by British standards. Purpose-built cycle track, and separate pavements, run alongside the main carriageway and in the Netherlands in particular there are complex supporting traffic management systems in place to favour the bicycle. Tramways or bus routes are often allocated a prime position in a central reservation with the cars running along either side. The principle of separation, although not sharing, is also applied on main trunk roads in many North European countries, so new intercity routes are not just designed (as with UK motorways) solely to cater for the car.

The widespread application of this approach to whole new developments has been limited in the UK. On the Continent, the leading example is found in a place called Vauban, a suburb of Freiburg in South West Germany, where there has been considerable investment and re-engineering to accommodate all users' needs: a location much visited by planners from all around the world. The whole suburb of Vauban has been built along sustainable principles, with the residential streets being largely given over to pedestrians and cyclists and car parking only available, at a cost, in multi-storey car parks on the edge of the neighbourhood (Barton *et al.* 2010). As Melia explains (Melia *et al.* 2010), some European cities have turned their historic squares into shared space. If traffic speeds can be slowed down considerably and pedestrians made aware that they are in a new type of traffic management situation then it is possible for cars and pedestrians and cyclists to share the same space (Hamilton-Baillie 2008). However, caution is advised as it all depends where the scheme is, and who is involved. Whilst it might work in large cities where people are relatively young, fleet of foot and streetwise, it may not work in small towns with a high elderly population or many families with small children. Also it depends on how carefully the space is arranged.

In Britain solutions have been generally less drastic, and less satisfactory. In many cases there has been no new road construction but rather existing space is reallocated. It is impossible to widen existing roads in many urban areas because they are flanked by rows of older housing, often with only a narrow pavement. Conflicts between pedestrians and cyclists are as marked as those between cars and everyone else. For example, problems arise if sharing means drawing a white line down the pavement and expecting pedestrians and cyclists to share the same limited pavement width. Even in pedestrianised squares and open spaces such as in the centre of Bristol outside the Hippodrome it is very unclear where the cycle paths are, in spite of the proliferation of all sorts of different paving. Many pedestrians find the situation dangerous, seeing cyclists as arrogant, as they whoosh past pedestrians without even a tinkle of their bell! In fact many of the English solutions to the needs of pedestrians, cyclists and public transport users have been fairly minimal, involving minor adjustments that adequately meet the needs of no one. But the problem is that one cannot simply knock down historic buildings and alter existing street frontages and building lines to make roads and pavements wider. There is also research under way at the Building Research Establishment (BRE) on the application of 'Dutch roundabouts' to the British situation, which allocate separate priority route ways for cycles alongside, and sometimes criss-crossing, car lanes.

Many have been quite critical of UK shared streets schemes – between cars and pedestrians – such as at Elwick Square on the Ashford Ring Road, in Kent, where there is considerable ambiguity, and therefore danger, as to who has the right of way. Apparently accidents in this location have been reduced by 40 per cent, but one has to ask who has simply stayed away out of fear of being run over. Another much-vaunted shared scheme (for cars and pedestrians) is at Exhibition Road in South Kensington, which is a heavily-used tourist 'boulevard' flanking a row of museums (Moody and Melia 2011). Some researchers have criticised this as being over-designed and providing little encouragement for pedestrians to feel confident enough to using the full width of the road, rather hugging the roadway alongside the building line, even though the pavements have now been removed. Melia found that 58 per cent of men but 98 per cent of women were against shared space. From a 'women and planning' perspective the whole shared-streets argument needs analysing, for it has long been found that 'to be male is to occupy space' (Massey 1984). Women often feel threatened in public space as it is, especially in the evenings. Having to assert themselves and walk confidentially across a challenging shared space without being threatened and shouted at by some drivers is too much for many women to face (Uteng and Cresswell 2008). There has also been much criticism of the shared streets concept (sometimes also called 'naked streets') from the Royal National Institute for the Blind (RNIB), representing people with limited vision, and from other disability groups. Mothers and parents groups are concerned about the lack of clarity as to which areas are safe and which are not, and fear small children may simply run out into the road if not strictly controlled. The elderly, anyone with disabilities, and anyone with mental or sensory problems are likely to find shared spaces confusing and frightening, much preferring clear boundaries and established rules.

As explained in the previous chapter on transport, there is increased emphasis upon walking and cycling. But conflicts between pedestrians and cyclists can be as great as existing vehicular/pedestrian (cars/people) problems. Traditionally footpaths and pavements have been 6 feet in width, this being based originally on the fact that it enables two prams to pass. Two metres (6 feet 6 inches) is taken as the minimum. Three-metre width is often designated for paths that are shared by cycles and pedestrians, with a white line drawn down the middle. This arrangement has proved both dangerous for pedestrians and unpopular with cyclists, and in an ideal situation the two should always be provided with a separate 2 metre-wide path each. Meanwhile many parents use pushchairs and baby buggies rather than prams (so they can put them into the back of the car when not walking), and their dimensions have grown with increasing affluence, creating a need for wider not narrower pathways.

A range of design devices are used to increase safety and space for the pedestrian, and to separate pedestrians from vehicles. They include the use of distinctive paving setts (pavé) and tactile paving to signal pedestrian zones, restrictive bollards, ramped kerbs, inter alia. Such uneven surfaces have proved unpopular and unsafe for pedestrians as they increase the chances of tripping up and uneven surfaces rattle the occupants of pushchairs and wheelchairs. Pedestrians may have to contend with bicycles, motorised wheelchairs and skateboards in car-free areas, such as miniature town squares provided as an interesting townscape feature or maybe a shared-space experiment within some new housing estates. Likewise many residents do not like the idea of 'play streets' where there is likely to be little escape from the noise of other people's children, a major issue when increasing numbers of people are working from home. The introduction of dropped kerbs and other grading devices which reduce the number of steps and changes of level which pedestrians have to tackle, can, if thoughtlessly designed, actually encourage cars to mount the pavement when cutting corners or looking for parking spaces.

There are arguments and evidence from both sides. What is clear is that shared-space initiatives present a radically new way of looking at a real problem, and where in the past the response has been heavy handed and led by traffic engineers and their desire to physically separate people and traffic, such an approach as shared space does start by seeking to understand how people, car drivers and pedestrians – who are often one and the same – actually think and behave. This is therefore a people-centred approach, and one that increasingly fits with modern urban design principles and the wider recognition that we need to be creating opportunities for more healthy lifestyles, especially for our children.

Social aspects of layout

User needs

Whilst in the past estate layout and road planning was dominated by engineers, particularly with the growth of women and a greater diversity within the planning profession, there is now a greater concern with social issues. Long-standing urban design principles have also been challenged, such as those found in the original Essex Design Guide, because of concerns about crime and personal safety within housing layouts. Meandering paths across open ground away from buildings, high fences alongside paths, and close planting, might according to some designers create an element of 'surprise' and 'excitement', but many ordinary people are more concerned about lack of visibility and the dangers of being mugged (Greed 2011a, 2011b). A whole new design industry has developed around the topic of 'crime and design', dating back to Circular 9/94 *Designing out Crime*, with many police forces having their own Architectural Liaison officers and reports on the topic (Thames Valley Police 2010). Likewise other users, such as women, children, the disabled and other pedestrian groups, have long campaigned for more practical and accessible layouts and some of their ideas are gradually beginning to penetrate the psyche of the designers themselves (Madariaga and Roberts (eds) (2013); Roberts and Greed 2000). For crime and design (another vast topic) (Crouch *et al.* 1999). But it should not be assumed that improvements in urban design approaches are necessarily better for pedestrians, or for minority user groups, especially not the disabled. But still the social aspect dimension of user needs is not adequately addressed; as illustrated above, modern 'progressive' solutions such as 'shared streets' can be as problematic as the solutions offered when traffic engineers dictated street design. In contrast, in Japan much higher value is given to the pedestrian experience with pavements being well designed and finished, by artists rather than engineers.

Disability

The disabled and those disenabled by the design of the built environment have had a considerable influence upon restructuring urban design (CABE 2008, 2010; I'DGO 2009). Disability has become a valid issue on the town planning, and related urban design, agenda, because of conceptual changes in how society views disability. It is also a major campaign issue in respect of inaccessible transportation planning. The Centre for Accessible Environments has produced various guides on designing accessible cities and undertaking Access Audits of buildings and their surroundings (CAE 1998, 2012).

In summary, there are three main models of disability, the medical, the charitable, and the social model, and the latter demands action (Swain *et al.* 1993). The medical model views disabled people as long-term sufferers who 'should' be confined to 'special hospitals' and homes, and therefore are unlikely to venture into the built environment (as highlighted by Damien Hirst's 'Disabled' Statue; see

photos on the book's website). However, cost-cutting 'care in the community' policies have resulted in many previously institutionalised people being 'let out' to contend with the harsh realities of modern urban society. The charitable model is based upon seeing the disabled as a group to be pitied, and as likely to be unable to look after their own affairs or lives, and as unsuitable to be out 'alone'.

The third model is based on the premise that people with disabilities are equal citizens with human rights. They may be people who were previously 'abled', who as a result of accident or illness became disabled. It also allows space for a greater range of types of disabilities, for the fact that the disabled are not a unitary group. The emphasis is shifted towards seeing society's attitudes and thus the design of the built environment as disabling, and 'making' people disabled. According to this model, town planners have a major role to play. Disability groups argue that people should be able gain access to buildings, streets and spaces as workers, shoppers, theatre goers, students or in any other capacity without fuss, on their own, and with no special assistance. It is argued that the whole structure of cities, employment, education and society needs rethinking if the third model is taken to its logical conclusion. For example, de-zoning of cities, the provision of accessible public transport, greater frequency of local centres, shops and employment, and changes in the internal design of all types of buildings are advocated (Imrie 1996; Imrie and Hall 2001; I'DGO 2009).

After many years of lobbying, a series of acts has been introduced which are meant to increase access for disabled people, and thus have implications for town planning and urban design (Davies 1999). For example, the Town and Country Planning Act 1990, Section 76, first required that local authorities give attention to the question of the level of accessibility for the disabled when determining a planning application. This particularly relates to access to individual buildings, especially offices, shops and other public buildings, by virtue of the British Standard (BS 8300) on accessible building design. In 1995 the first Disability Discrimination Act was introduced which was meant to increase access to new buildings. New access requirements began to come into force in respect of shops and public buildings in late 1999 under this Act. But it is not retrospective on existing buildings, unless they are the subject of substantial alteration. And enforcement powers are limited. The 1997 revision of PPG1 on the general principles of planning, included a good section (Section 55) on the disabled which states, 'the development of land and buildings provides the opportunity to secure a more accessible environment for everyone, including wheelchair users, and other people with disabilities, elderly people and people with toddlers or infants in pushchairs'. But subsequent versions of what became PPS1 lacked this disability element and in any case the PPSs were abolished in 2010 and the National Planning Policy Framework (NPPF) has little to say on disability access. Therefore this is a consideration that local authorities must take into account in determining a planning application (Manley 1999). Subsequently, disability became perhaps 'taken for granted' as an issue and no longer got 'special treatment', thus arguably removing it from the planners' radar. There have been a series of other Disability Discrimination Acts (DDAs), but now 'disability' is incorporated in the Equality Act 2011, along with all other so-called minority issues. However, disability requirements are also strengthened by the requirements of Part M of the Building Regulations (2004) on *Access and Use of Buildings* as amended in 2013.

But socially-aware local authorities have continued to write disability requirements into their Plans and Design Guides, with controls on unnecessary uses of steps and changes of level, and provision of dropped kerbs in all layouts, to help the disabled, the elderly, and also mothers with prams and pushchairs. All these groups may find steps an insurmountable barrier to getting about, or even to getting in and out of their own front door. Gradients on ramps should not be more than 1 in 12, but ideally there should be no steep areas throughout the housing scheme. To achieve such an objective is indeed a challenge, but one which is being tackled even in historic housing areas, for example in urban conservation areas in hilly locations within London (see CAE website and magazine). Related to this, it is now considered good practice to ensure adequate lighting and visibility within public footpath systems. Many of the principles that have been established and adopted in respect of inner-city regeneration projects, in which there has been a strong emphasis upon collaborative, participatory planning with the community, are now working their way into new developments too. In particular, the concept of 'Lifetime Housing' gradually became more widespread (Rowntree 1992; Fleck 2003).

However, there are dangers in dividing the disabled off from the able-bodied and creating special facilities or design elements for them. In reality all sorts of people have difficulty coping with the design of the built environment. For example, over 25 per cent of the population are now elderly and they comprise the majority of the disabled. Only 17 per cent of the population who are currently disabled were actually born disabled, and individuals usually acquire disabilities in their lifetime through disease, illness, accident, violence and ageing. However, many younger people suffer from a range of illnesses and accidents too, that might render them 'disabled' for a short period. There are also much larger groups of people who are 'disenabled' by the nature of the built environment. Children and people of reduced stature have trouble accessing many buildings, women with pushchairs and indeed anyone with luggage or other 'wheeled accompaniments' has trouble with all the steps, stairs and changes in level found within the average British city. Pushchairs outnumber wheelchairs at least 20 to 1, and because of steps and narrow doorways many young mothers and parents have trouble accessing public toilet provision (Greed 2003b).

Selwyn Goldsmith, a disabled architect (who died 2011), was one of the first to argue for inclusive, 'universal' design, which made it better for everyone (Goldsmith 2000). Benktzon (1993) produced a famous diagram showing the range of abilities/disabilities ranging from a broad base of the pyramid of people with some minor difficulties to those at the top of the pyramid suffering multiple disabilities. Therefore it is very important to plan and design for everyone in an inclusive manner. This may involve changing the whole way we look at cities, the relationship between land uses, the design of roads and pavements, and the availability of different transport options (Mitchell *et al.* 2004; Talen 2006; I'DGO 2009).

Cultural planning

The renaissance of urban design

Increasingly cultural factors, as well as social and engineering considerations, are reshaping approaches to urban design, and thus both to city centre and residential area design. There has always been a tradition of urban design in town planning, drawing on European civic design traditions (as described in Chapter 4). The post-war period in the USA also produced a new breed of 'urban designers' concerned with the image of the city, within the context of the modern, brash American city (Lynch 1968). Many American cities lack historical buildings, are based upon a grid layout and much larger scale, with 12-foot sidewalks (pavements) being common, and a far greater level of visual intrusion in terms of telegraph wires, poles, giant advertisements and a car-based culture. This aesthetic view of the city contrasted sharply with the scientific, technocrat perspective current in much Anglo-American planning in the post-war era. Lynch produced a set of intellectual tools for visually analysing the city. For example, he stressed the importance of identifying centres, nodal points, edges, paths and image quality as key townscape components. Urban conservation has increasingly become an international trend. For example, China is undergoing massive urbanisation, and is now giving more attention to its historic buildings and its 'hutong' (traditional housing) neighbourhoods (Photo 13.4), building on the pioneering work of Liang Sicheng and Lin Huiyin who undertook an extensive survey of China's historic buildings before the cultural revolution and whose work was continued by Chen Zhanzung at Tsingua University (Logan 2009).

In Britain there has always been a more traditional architect-led approach to planning concerned with aesthetic issues, which has gradually come back into fashion. There has long been a British tradition of aesthetic urban design, as evidenced in the work of Trystan Edwards, Clough Williams-Ellis (of Port Merion Model Village of *The Prisoner* fame) and Osbert Lancaster before the Second World War (Edwards 1921; Lancaster 1956). This movement was characterised by a concern with detailed design issues, and sensitivity to the environment, rather than with the knock-out schemes found in mainland Europe. But this tradition was overshadowed for many years by the modern movement, and by architecture and planning based on science rather than art. There was a reaction against modern architecture and a desire to return to a more human scale and the use of traditional materials from the late 1960s (Prizeman 1975). This was manifested in a growing concern for urban conservation, campaigns for buildings to be listed, and the creation of conservation areas where greater controls could be enforced to retain townscape features and the overall historical quality of the area. Increasingly there was an emphasis upon the protection of whole areas, rather than just individual buildings (under the listed building system described in Chapter 3). The listing system was extended to include a wider range of types of buildings, including ordinary houses and shops that happened to be Victorian and Edwardian, rather than just castles, palaces and churches (45 per cent of all Grade 1 listed buildings are churches). However, we have now reached the situation where in some towns 25 per cent of all buildings are covered by some form of listing or conservation area protection, with many ordinary houses being included. Arguably, many local planning authorities have seen the creation of conservation areas as a way of increasing planning control. Changes in 2012 merged conservation area control with ordinary development control but also gave local authorities greater powers over the historic core of cities.

A new urban design movement emerged gradually which incorporates a concern for aesthetic issues with an awareness of social considerations and user realities, along with a greater emphasis upon the historical built environment, and a reaction against the Modernist movement in architecture and planning, as originally inspired by Le Corbusier in the early twentieth century. Rather than seeing urban conservation areas and historic buildings as separate from the mainstream of urban development, the urban design movement takes a more holistic approach, recognising that cities are comprised of buildings of all sorts of different ages and styles, often right next to each other. Therefore old and new must be dealt with together within sensitive urban design strategies for the city as a whole. Publications such as Prince Charles' *Vision of Britain*

Photo 13.4   Hutong: traditional housing, Beijing

Urban conservation is an international issue and many capital cities are protecting their historic heritage. Whilst this is true of the main landmarks in China, many of the traditional housing areas, that is the hutongs, are being pulled down as slums to make way for modern apartment blocks. Many would argue that some should be preserved for cultural reasons and because Western tourists want to see the original architectural styles of the past.

(Prince of Wales 1989) and the architect Richard Rogers' *Report of the Urban Taskforce* (Rogers 1999) set a new agenda. Prince Charles set out ten principles which needed to be taken into account in the urban design process, namely: Place, Hierarchy, Scale, Harmony, Enclosure, Materials, Decoration, Art, Signs and Lights, and Community. The Prince was somewhat silent on the question of the effects of people's activities and town planning in terms of the generation of traffic, car parking and pedestrian flows, and there appears to be little on social inclusion, inequality or the economic aspects of planning in his pronouncements. Instead, for better or worse, he has promoted a form of architecture that is concerned with reviving traditional styles of both classical and vernacular architecture within the British urban context.

Subsequently the establishment of CABE has led to a greater emphasis upon the quality of design and a return to a greater emphasis being put upon the visual aspects of the built environment (CABE 2010). Organisations such as RUDI and the Urban Design Group have further disseminated the principles of good design and moved planning away from the twentieth-century emphasis upon science and engineering, towards traditional concerns with architecture and good urban design.

As explained in the final part of Chapter 11 on urban renewal, there is an emphasis on a return to valuing the cultural aspects of cities and creating distinctive quarters (see p. 223) and districts within the city (Tallon 2013: Hall and Falk 2013). Much of this may really be down to marketing and promoting tourism, selling heritage, and positively branding areas to increase their attractiveness for business investment. But there is also a greater awareness of the visual qualities of different areas, and the need to create attractive environments for the people who live and work in them (Johnson 2009; Bell and Jayne 2004). Overall the city is no longer seen just as a functional container for work and housing but as a cultural phenomenon, and as explained in Chapter 8 such ideas owe much to the resurgence in popularity of French urban philosophers (Lefebvre 1968, 1974; Qvistrom 2010).

The new status of urban design

Urban design has now virtually achieved the status of the 'new planning', and is strongly aligned to the sustainability movement (and thus car control), social inclusion considerations and a concern with the visual appearance of cities and thus architectural design. Because of the failures of the statutory planning system, Robert Cowan describes urban design as 'everything that planning is not' and ought to be (Greed and Roberts 1998, 5). It is as concerned with existing and historic areas as it is with new developments, regeneration and renewal. The definition of urban design used by the Urban Design Unit at the University of Westminster, developed by Professor Marion Roberts, is as follows: 'Urban design is concerned with the physical form of cities, buildings and the space between them. The study of urban design deals with the relationships between the physical form of the city and the social forces which produce it. It focuses, in particular, on the physical character of the public realm but is also concerned with the interaction between public and private development and the resulting impact on urban form' (Roberts and Greed (eds) 2000). Urban design is generally accepted to be concerned with the following factors: creating places, master planning, urban culture, sustainability, pedestrianisation, car restriction and reducing carbon footprints, disability, equality, accessibility, safety, convenience, but also landscaping, architectural design, urban regeneration and cultural vitality and creating enjoyable places. It also incorporates the concepts of management and stewardship and calls for an understanding of the processes of land assembly and building procurement. Thus 'urban design' comprises

another paradigm shift in terms of our conceptualisation of what planning is about. Arguably, urban design is town planning in all but name!

The new cultural agenda

The current enthusiasm for urban design may be seen as part of a wider trend towards a greater awareness of the importance of cultural issues, and especially aesthetic factors, within town planning. It is significant that when PPG1 was revised in 1997, for the first time a section was added on urban design, and this aspect has subsequently been amplified in later policy guidance. Urban design is now a 'material consideration' that should be taken into account in deciding planning applications. However, there is much debate as to what is 'good urban design', and what rules should be applied, and the whole topic remains controversial. More broadly, an interest in urban culture and links with the arts are to be found in the world of town planning. In recent years there has been a new interest in 'public art' in particular. This trend was accelerated in the early twenty-first century with a series of national events that promoted urban spectacles, pageants, public art, festivals, and massive commemorative building projects such as the Millennium Dome in Greenwich, London (now reborn as the O2 entertainment centre). Subsequently the development of the Olympic Park and other facilities nationwide by the ODA (Olympic Development Authority) for the 2012 Games has led to a further surge of government concern with urban design and quality architecture. The Olympic Park (as discussed in Chapter 11) was designed to incorporate the principles of sustainability, diversity, social inclusion and legacy beyond the close of the Games in 2012.

Although in many towns and cities this new agenda has been strongly related to urban regeneration and renewal, and thus with increasing economic viability, it nevertheless has embodied a desire to improve the cultural quality and attractiveness of areas. Undoubtedly much of this activity is also influenced by a desire to create the 'European City' with images of lively town squares and street cafés reminiscent of the Italian piazza or the Parisian boulevard. Linked to this is the popular concept, among planners if not local residents, of creating the

24-hour city (Montgomery 1994), and the evening economy. London is now considered to be one the 'coolest' cities for tourists and residents. There is a whole youth culture, of urban fashion, clothes, food, media, nightlife and music, which goes with this image. The Department for Culture, Media and Sport (DCMS), nicknamed the 'luvvy ministry' because of its strong links with the worlds of the arts, media and show business, has sought, in conjunction with the Department for Communities and Local Government (DCLG) to capitalise upon these aspects. Arguably, its objectives are not purely cultural, but also strongly commercial, not least in its concern to promote tourism, a major source of income. However, the emphasis upon the evening economy has not created the Continental city, but rather an increase in 'vertical drinking', street urination, and a predominantly young male-dominated evening environment. Lack of commensurate provision of policing, public transport, public toilets, lighting and taxi services has actually discouraged a whole range of other people venturing forth in the evening. For example, families, tourists and anyone going through the city on their own in the dark, for example to go to work, evening classes, church meetings, or social events, has become much more wary and cautious. So at present attempts to create the vibrant 24-hour city and the evening economy are far from socially inclusive and therefore they are unlikely to maintain economic viability either.

The shift away from new development and modern styles of architecture nationally has been accompanied by a new enthusiasm for our historical building heritage. Urban conservation may be seen on the one hand as an important component of the urban design agenda, for the movement has sought to show equal concern for both old and new aspects of the built environment. Heritage and urban conservation are by now well-established trends across the Western world. Urban design has become an international issue. Each nation's historical sites are being ranked in global importance by international bodies; for example, Bath has been designated a World Heritage Site and is visited by tourists from all over the world. Retrofitting existing cities, including the suburbs, to make them accessible is a major activity (Williams 2010; Dunham-Jones and Williamson 2011). Vastly increased numbers of people are travelling, for example air traffic has increased 75 per cent in the last ten years. Clearly urban design, tourism and sustainability are all global factors which are impacting upon British approaches to doing urban planning.

But in this process urban design is becoming commercialised and is in danger of turning our cities into mere stage sets. There is a vast heritage tourist industry in Britain in which heritage, royalty and quaintness are sold to tourists. Also there has been a growth in theme parks, and other leisure activities, all with their own architectural 'stage set' styles. The ultimate manifestation of this is Disneyland, an entirely 'artificial' creation, but one in which the architecture draws on centuries-old folkoric myths, and fairy tale images of what cities, castles, gingerbread cottages, and main streets 'ought' to be like: produced by a nation which has no history of any length of its own. Disneyfication is just part of a wider Americanisation of European culture, which is everywhere (ubiquitous), manifest in films, television and fast-food outlets. It is anathema to many architects, especially when theme park architecture influences attitudes as to how genuine historic buildings 'ought' to be restored. However, anything that relieves the boredom of life is very popular among many ordinary people trying to escape the drabness of urban Britain. But in an ideal world conservation policy would be more flexible to allow space for the design of new buildings, in a sensitive manner, alongside traditional buildings. Likewise there would be less importance given to modern buildings that are designed to shock and 'make a statement' with very little reference to their surroundings.

However, planners only have limited powers to control all these changes. A distinction must also be made as to the powers of the planners as against those of architects and developers. Planners are concerned with the overall design and appearance of the townscape of our urban areas. They can only influence the design of individual buildings within the limited parameters of their development control powers and in most cases do not have control over the internal design of buildings. Architects are the first to take umbrage if the planners try to limit their 'creativity'. Developers, architects, and the clients for whom the building is designed often have a far greater role in determining the design of the

Photo 13.5   An integrated approach to place-making

When urban conservation policy is combined with accessibility and human-scale street design and traffic planning then the final result is a liveable welcoming city.

building than the planners. For the developer, the cost factor, and the aim of achieving the greatest possible amount of lettable floorspace, are far more significant factors in the real world than the outward appearance of the design of the building.

More positively, the community, that is 'the planned', are having more input into the urban design process, and the needs of people, pedestrians and residents are more likely to be integrated into urban design, but still the needs of people with disabilities are often overlooked (Photo 13.5). A collaborative, communicative, community-based approach is in evidence in the design process, in respect of inner-city urban design projects, in which the designer takes on the role of 'facilitator' rather than that of 'expert' or 'God'. Indeed there is considerable debate as to the role of the urban designer, and whether he/she is needed at all. It is generally accepted that the urban designer, particularly the architect-designer, is essential in offering to the community the benefit of seven years of specialist

study, knowledge of the statutory context, and understanding of the system. But, ordinary people and community members, as the recipients and users of urban design, must also be involved fully. Quite how this might be achieved is a complex issue. Emphasis is put upon sustained, continuing participation, rather than 'hit and run' approaches. Also cultivation of the people's own skills and provision of education about the planning system and building design are also key issues which cannot be rushed. A variety of approaches such as 'Planning for Real', 'Plan Away Days' and 'Focus Groups' have been used to elicit people's views and to develop community-sensitive policies. Clearly the way ahead is for planners and planned to work collaboratively upon creating better urban design. In theory the new localism should facilitate such activities but disability is not a prominent component of the Coalition's changes to the planning system.

The next challenge for urban design is likely to be that of the dealing with the suburbs where around 70 per cent of the population live, to make them both more sustainable in the light of climate change, and also to facilitate less dependence on the motorcar (Williams 2010). Certainly snobbery is to be found in both architectural and sociological circles towards suburban development which is typified as bland, bourgeois and boring. In reality suburban houses come in all sorts of designs, and house a wide range of social classes and types of people. They are seen as more suitable for families with children, who need space, storage and gardens, than higher-density inner-city living. So it is an over-simplification to typify all suburbia as containing the 'same' type of housing, although certainly some modern housing estates can be fairly uniform. A more serious challenge is to retrofit suburbia to become part of the sustainable city, as many such areas lack good public transport, local shops and centres, and contain poorly insulated and ageing housing stock (Dunham-Jones and Williamson 2011).

For the tasks, further reading, additional photos and other resources for this chapter, please visit www.palgrave. com/companion/greed. E-Supplement 8 provides information on technical aspects of site development and housing layout, whilst photos of examples of urban design principles including shared streets are also available, and will be particularly useful in relation to this chapter.

PART IV

Planning and People

14 The Social Aspects of Planning

The social agenda

The purpose of this chapter is to introduce the reader to some of the main sociological theories and concepts that have influenced town planners' perceptions of the city, and their approaches to problem-solving and planning policy. The order is broadly chronological, first covering the classic historical theories of urban society, as developed, for example, by Durkheim, Weber and Marx. Next, theories that have shaped the development of British town planning at the more localised level, such as concepts of neighbourhood and community, are explained. Reference is made to the ever-popular social ecology theories which you may have already studied at school, but which have faced considerable challenge in the light of the development of modern urban society. Then the subsequent development of urban theory within Britain from the 1960s to the present is discussed, with reference to urban problems, social exclusion and the inner city. In the final part of the chapter, we look at the new sociological agenda which is characterised by a move away from stressing the importance of social class as the main determinant of societal structure, towards the acknowledgment of the importance of a range of other social characteristics including ethnicity, gender, sexuality, age and disability.

There is a danger in dealing with these topics as separate, special issues. Therefore, for example, the issue of ethnicity is woven into the account where relevant, class crops up many times, and gay issues are raised when looking at the nature of modern society. In the concluding section of the chapter the issue of population composition will be revisited. Whilst in Chapter 10, on sustainability, we looked at global population factors, in this chapter we will consider the situation in Britain, with particular reference to the demographic challenge of an ageing population. Both age and disability are factors that planners need to take into account in designing cities that are accessible and convenient for those with reduced mobility (I'DGO 2009). Because we have sought to integrate such issues into the discussion of mainstream planning policy, discussion of the different models of disability has already been included (in Chapter 12), and in respect of urban design (in Chapter 13). Gender is briefly referred to in this chapter, and is used as an example in Chapter 15 of how planners might mainstream the acknowledgement of social diversity into planning policy.

Historical sociological theory and the city

Pre- and post-industrial perspectives

The Industrial Revolution was a major turning point in the development of modern society and town planning. It called forth a new academic discipline, namely sociology, which sought to explain the new society (Gabler 2010; Fulcher and Scott 2011). Comte (1798–1857), a French academic, is generally credited with inventing the word *sociologie* (Brown 1979). Many of the early sociological theories were based upon highlighting the differences between the pre-industrial city (usually seen as good) as against the industrial city (usually seen as bad). Other countries in Europe were experiencing a similar process of industrialisation, and for example Tönnies (1855–1936), a German sociologist, wrote about the differences between what he called *Gemeinschaft* and *Gesellschaft* (Tönnies 1955). He defined *Gemeinschaft* as community, based on traditional, rural village life where everyone knew everyone else, social relationships were based on kith and kin ties, and traditional values and duties. *Gesellschaft* community (the German word for business) related to public life, where everything is based on formal and impersonal relationships, bureaucracy, law and order. Nobody knows anyone else, and people deal with complete strangers in their daily life and work. For example, in a small village you can walk down the street and say 'hello' to everyone who goes past, but in a large city it is impossible to greet everyone, and most of them you will never see again.

Durkheim (1858–1917), a French sociologist, identified the new urbanised society as being characterised by a sense of 'normlessness' and 'namelessness', that is *anomie* (literally, without a name) because, in coming to the city from their local villages, many people had lost their individual identity and sense of belonging. Note that this is a societal state; people do not catch anomie, like the flu! Nevertheless it affected individuals' behaviour within society, for he observed that this state led to increased levels of suicide, and to social unrest. Fascination with the study of the contrasts between the pre-industrial and industrial ways of life continued well into the twentieth century, whereas modern sociologists are more concerned with the post-industrial, service-industry-based, society. One of the more famous, often cited, writings is Wirth's article *Urbanism as a way of Life*, published in 1938 (reprinted in Hatt and Reiss 1963). Also the work of Sjoberg on the pre-industrial city is relevant (Sjoberg 1965). Much of sociology, right into the twentieth century, was concerned with the changes in social class that came about as a result of industrialisation, and a range of theories and categorisations developed in relation to people's economic position in society, and particularly the woes of the new urbanised, industrial working classes.

As introduced in Chapter 5, as a result of the Industrial Revolution, changes occurred not only in the range of occupations, and related class structure, but in the nature of work itself, with more people working outside the home. Individuals were no longer working in their own workshop or home, as was the case in the traditional craft industries, e.g. of weavers living and working in cottages which had large windows up in the weaving lofts to let through maximum light onto the loom, as can be seen in the architecture of these dwellings. Rather workers and their machines were concentrated in one place – the factory, which people had to attend for set times each day. The ability of the steam engine to run a large number of machines was largely responsible for this. In contrast, the traditional agricultural worker's life was governed by the seasons, and by the amount of daylight. The new industrial workforce was increasingly seen and controlled as a distinct 'class', replacing feudal and traditional pre-industrial divisions.

Class is a complex word to define. A typical twentieth-century definition of a social class is 'a number of persons sharing a common social position in the economic order', particularly in respect of to the work they do (Chinoy 1967). For the purposes of this chapter, class should be taken in the common sense of meaning of people's social position in terms of their work and way of life. As a result of the Industrial Revolution, the structure of society changed. New types of class divisions and occupations emerged as a result of new technological inventions, and wider changes in the economy itself. In the traditional rural society of the past a relatively feudal static social system existed, the inhabitants of a typical village consisting of the landowners and the agricultural labourers, with a vicar and a few skilled trades-people in the middle. People did not have a social class as such, but rather were endowed with a certain status, which they were born with, and all human relationships were governed by this. The static and deferential nature of pre-industrial social attitudes is summed up in the following ditty:

God bless the squire and his relations,
And keep us in our proper stations.
(Anon.)

The new urban entrepreneurial (business) classes had replaced the old feudal landowners as lords and masters of the working people. These new leaders of society needed to grasp the reins of society and take control. Feudal landowners had developed stable relationships with their workers over many generations, and now business managers had to do so too. Both Durkheim and Weber (separately) talk about the need to legitimate, that is justify, the new power

Photo 14.1   What class? Young office workers

Workers relaxing in their lunch hour. Prescott observed 'We are all middle class now', but 'we' are no longer working in factories and mills, but in offices, call centres, and professional practices, but we are still working. So what of class?

structures which emerged, legitimation being defined as 'the process of transforming naked power into rightful authority'. Such notions should not necessarily be seen as oppressive; as it was considered that a return to a stable situation was good for society, as well as being good for those in authority. Note the word 'legitimation' is also used in relation to town planners who seek to legitimate their somewhat questionable policies on the basis that they are planning for the good of society or for the working class.

In the workforce which emerged in the modern industrial society, workers may be classified as: Primary workers – those engaged in basic industries such as agriculture, mining, heavy industry; Secondary workers – those involved in manufacturing; Tertiary workers – those involved in office work and service industry. A further category is recognised, namely Quaternary workers who are those involved in research and development, higher professional work and the creation of knowledge. There is much debate over the use of socio-economic classifications and the occupational groupings used for government census purposes have undergone several revisions (ONS 2013). Male factory employment was the largest growing sector in the nineteenth century. Professional, office, and service industry employment have been the largest growing sectors in the second part of the twentieth century; with large numbers of women entering the office sector in particular (Photo 14.1). Of the 16 million male and female inhabitants of England and Wales recorded by the 1841 census, a little under a million were in domestic service. Throughout the nineteenth century and indeed until 1914 domestic service was the largest single employment for English women, with 1.5 million employed, and the second largest for the population, but interestingly this was of little interest to Marx or other social class theorists. Within society as a whole, traditional 'master and servant' social divisions coexisted alongside the new emerging industrial class structures.

As described in Chapter 8 (on planning theory), Marx stressed the importance of the economic (material) basis of social class divisions and divided society only into two main classes, capitalists and proletariat, and argued that when the workers rose up, Revolution, and the transformation of society, would inevitably take place. In contrast, Max Weber and more liberal-minded social theorists did not see the source of power as residing in one 'capitalist' class alone or being of only one type, but identified a range of power elites in business, politics, religion and education that together controlled society. Unlike Marx, who attributed everything to economic factors, Weber argued that a range of factors shaped society and thus facilitated a particular form of economic development, and he especially stressed the importance of the Protestant work ethic in generating industrial change (Weber 1964, originally 1905). His ideas proved popular in Britain and influenced Tawney's famous book, *Religion and the Rise of Capitalism* (Tawney 1922). Rather than focusing on class (based on employment position) as a key determinant of society's structure and an individual's power within it, Weber stressed the importance of 'status', which was based on a wider range of social, cultural, religious and political factors, as a result of which economic change was one result, but not a primary cause. Like Tönnies, Weber stressed the differences between traditional communities (*Gemeinschaft*) and the emerging public realm, preferring to use the term *Wirtschaft* (which refers to the whole political economy).

Consensus or conflict?

Many of the early theorists believed that society had been badly knocked off balance by the effects of the Industrial Revolution and that the way ahead was to re-establish consensus, balance and harmony. For example, Comte was basically what is known as a functionalist. Other functionalists who, broadly speaking, favoured a consensus view of society include such famous sociologists as Spencer (1820–1903), Talcott Parsons (1902–79), Merton (1910 onwards), Durkheim (1858–1917) and also Max Weber (1864–1920) to some extent. I mention

them because reference to their works is occasionally found in town planning books. Functionalists took the view that society was like a big machine which operated mechanically, and in which different processes and groups of people had different functions, ensuring its smooth running and the maintenance of the status quo of authority and social order. This should not be confused with the style of functionalism in Modern Architecture (see Chapter 5), although that movement, too, was inspired by similar sentiments. The Industrial Revolution was seen as a major upset to the natural order of things, which had all sorts of economic and social effects, which temporarily put the system out of sync, so that society was no longer 'harmonious' (although arguably it never had been really harmonious, but social controls had been stronger). But it was believed that this could be righted. Society would put itself back into balance again, provided the various social institutions and value systems were reconstituted to re-inspire people's trust in the system, so that business confidence, stability and law and order could be maintained. Reform and new policies were needed, and town planning had an important role to play in this process. The main rival to the consensus view of society was the belief that society was in a constant state of conflict and flux, and that it held together, not because of agreement, but because of one group actively oppressing the others. The classic example of this is expressed in Marxist theory (as discussed in Chapter 8), which centres on a perceived clash between the interests of the capitalists (factory owners) and the proletariat (workers) which could only be resolved by Revolution, ideas which, as we shall see, were to influence urban sociologists and planners in the 1970s.

However, the consensus/conflict division is not so straightforward. The functionalists accepted the need for a limited amount of conflict and unrest amongst the masses, as being functionally necessary (as a safety valve) to ensure the well-being of society. What Merton was later to term 'dysfunctions' were simply seen as healthy signs that change was occurring which required adjustment and solution on the part of society, as healthy competition between a plurality (range) of power groups at different levels of society (Bottomore 1973). Parallels to this may be seen in the theories which were developing in the natural sciences in the nineteenth century, for example in Darwin's theory of evolution. In this, natural selection, as a result of continuous aggressive competition and conflict, was seen as normal and functional in the sense that it led to progress and further evolution.

As explained in Chapter 8 (on planning theory), a conflict-based view of society, as developed by Marx, has been challenged by those who take a more pragmatic view (such as Weber) and who believe that conflict can be positive and lead to discussion, resolution and progress in society. This philosophy, known as agonism, is manifested today within planning theory (Allmendinger and Tewdwr-Jones (eds) (2002) and, as will be explained later in the chapter, in ideas of collaborative community-based planning (Healey 1997).

Planning for community and harmony

Neighbourhoods and new towns

The concepts of community and neighbourhood may seem old-fashioned and quaint in today's world. But they have often been used as identifiable units of population for the purposes of local planning and this trend continues today. For example, the Coalition government's new planning system under the 2011 Localism Act requires the production of Neighbourhood Plans. The areas may be based on parishes, wards, or in non-parished areas (such as many cities) upon the identification of specific 'neighbourhood' areas. The areas which are currently producing Neighbourhood Plans are generally of around 5–6 thousand in size population-wise, have some sense of community identity, and are concerned with shared local planning issues. Therefore it is important to understand what the terms 'community' and 'neighbourhood' actually mean, as although they started out as sociological concepts, they have been heavily drawn upon by planners.

Whilst the terms are bandied about a great deal, they still exude an element of nostalgia, as if something was lost as a result of urbanisation that needs to be reclaimed. Many of these early sociological theories, whether Right or Left in political perspec-

tive, reflected the view that something socially valuable had been lost as a result of industrialisation, especially the stability and security which apparently had existed in close-knit traditional villages and within close-knit family structures. As people migrated to the towns for work, traditional extended families in which several generations might live in one house were being replaced by 'nuclear' families which consisted of the parents and their children (only), often living in cramped terraced housing. It was argued that traditional controls over deviance (crime and social unrest) were lost, such as the role of the village elders in seeing what was going on in the neighbourhood. One of the factors behind the popularity of the Garden City movement was the desire to recreate the village community of the past, in order to re-establish the social structures which were destroyed as a result of the Industrial Revolution. Many of the ideas of the early town planners reflect a somewhat negative anti-urban attitude; a yearning to go back to an (imagined) idyllic rural past, and may be seen as somewhat conservative or even reactionary politically. Town planning could be used as one of the means of seeking to re-establish a sense of order in new urban areas, through well-planned districts and zoning controls, which, it was believed, would reduce the high levels of crime, disease and overcrowding.

Influenced by the principles of Howard's Garden City, the American architect Clarence Perry (1872–1944) devised the concept of the neighbourhood unit as a way of effectively planning new towns and communities in the New York area in the 1920s and 1930s. Perry proposed that if around 5000–6000 people were located in a neighbourhood at 37.5 persons per acre, that is at approximately 12 houses per acre allowing for three people on average per house, this would result in a neighbourhood unit of 160 acres, that is an area half a mile by half a mile or a quarter of a square mile. In this way everything could be based on walking distances of between a quarter to a half of a mile, with a community centre in the middle of each neighbourhood and shops on the edges, at the four 'corners' so they could be shared by up to four different neighbourhoods (Hall 1992). A local junior school was to be located in the centre, 5000 being considered adequate population to generate the number of children to make it viable.

The neighbourhood unit concept had many practical aspects to it, but it was more questionably associated with a mystical desire to recreate a sense of community, by influencing people's behaviour, and 'making' them mix by means of the constraints put upon them by the layout, e.g. designing the footpaths so that they ran past everyone else's front door, and putting the local community centre alongside the school.

Perry's ideas were copied in England by Parker at the garden suburb of Wythenshawe in Manchester in the 1930s and were incorporated in the Dudley Report (1944). As a result many of the British new towns built in the post-war reconstruction period were divided into neighbourhoods, or 'neighbourhood units', as they were called. This enabled the development to be phased logically and facilitated the physical provision of shops and schools with ready-made catchment areas. In the post-war period many people did not have cars, so all this worked realistically. But, the neighbourhoods had a second, more important, albeit somewhat mystical, objective of trying to create community spirit and social cohesion to stem disorder and the breakdown of traditional values. As outlined in Chapter 6, the Mark I new towns were generally divided into a series of neighbourhoods of around 5000, but the later new towns were more sophisticated in layout, with a hierarchy of intermediate districts of say 15,000 people, which were in turn subdivided into smaller neighbourhoods and local areas. Various sociological studies were carried out on both sides of the Atlantic, monitoring people's behaviour in new housing estates (Carey and Mapes 1972; Bell and Newby 1978). Not surprisingly it was found that people who lived nearer the centre of a cul-de-sac, or by a lift-shaft in an apartment block, were likely to have a higher level of contact with their neighbours than those who lived at the end of the main thoroughfare.

The planners were also concerned about the imbalanced nature of the community population, who were predominantly young families with children. The lack of age balance meant pressure on facilities as the children grew up and went through the stages of school, jobs and retirement together. This was exacerbated by the pressures of the Baby Boom which occurred straight after the war. Once the wave had passed, the facilities provided for such large numbers proved uneconomic for subsequent smaller cohorts. Later British new towns attempted to encourage a wider age range and family mix amongst applicants, but many new towns now contain large numbers of pensioners, comprising the original Baby Boom generation of residents. Class-wise, the neighbourhoods were built to house the workers employed in the new town industrial estates. Socially it was seen as dangerous politically that there were so many working-class people all together, so there were attempts to attract more middle-class people, and to encourage the employers to live in the new towns, to provide more 'leaders' for the community. Within neighbourhoods there were attempts at what was called social mix, that is mixing social classes, by means of combining house types and tenures on the same estate; which did not work well. But relatively speaking the families selected to be new town residents, and for that matter early council estates, were mainly respectable, skilled manual workers, verging on the lower middle class in identity. Single parent families, the homeless and ethnic minorities (of any class or background) were noticeably absent from these early developments (Hanley 2012).

Environmental determinism

As illustrated above, it was strongly believed that social change, stability and a sense of community could be achieved through 'salvation by bricks', that is through the way in which the new towns were designed using particular layouts, densities and design principles. The planners were criticised for going much further than just seeking to provide adequate practical facilities in the neighbourhood, but indulging in social engineering, that is seeking to control people's behaviour (for their own good) through the design of the built environment. There are many other factors which are involved in community formation. It may not be the shared locality (the fact they all live in the same neighbourhood), that engenders community. Sociologists have pointed out the importance of communities of interest, i.e. non-place-related as against place-related concepts of community are also very important. For example, people may share common interests in work, hobbies, sporting interests, and the fact that

Photo 14.2   Shuttered shops in Bedminster, Bristol

This is a retail area that has suffered considerable decline but in 2012 received regeneration funding from the Portas Fund in order to revitalise the shopping street and evening economy.

of ensuring that there is a distinct demarcation between public and private space around buildings in large housing estates, so that people think twice before crossing such boundaries and indulging in graffiti or vandalism. But more direct measures such as introducing shop shutters have become routine (Photo 14.2).

Des Wilson, one of the founders of Shelter, the housing pressure group, wrote a book entitled *I Know it Was the Place's Fault* (Wilson 1970), showing the effect the poor quality environments and substandard housing conditions could have on people's lives and misfortunes. So, there is undoubtedly some truth in environmental determinism theory, but many other factors have to be taken into account. Regardless of the theories, a whole 'crime and design' industry has grown up. There is on average one security camera every ten metres in England, although most are concentrated in large cities.

they were all young families going through the same phases of child-rearing and family development. Indeed some residents found a sense of community, of solidarity in adversity, in fighting the planners to get better facilities and amenities, or in seeking to rid themselves of some of the worst aspects of the 'plan' and getting what they really wanted instead.

Maurice Broady, a sociologist disquieted by the apparently magical powers attributed to such theories, stated, *'architectural design like music to a film, is complementary to human activity, it does not shape it'* (Broady 1968). But this does not invalidate the importance of design. Often all that are needed are quite small improvements, rather than the development of high-flown theories and complicated ideas. Most would agree that practical improvements are important, such as more lighting, less planting and thus more 'visibility' around buildings, and reorientation of pedestrian routes to make them safer, and reduce potential crime. Others would go much further, such as Alice Coleman in her book *Utopia on Trial*, who makes much of the ways in which modifications in the design of the environment can alter the behaviour of the residents (Coleman 1985). Oscar Newman (in *Defensible Space*, 1973) stressed the importance of what he called 'defensible space',

Social ecology

An influential urban sociological theory, that everyone seems to know about from Geography, is the 'concentric zone theory' and the idea of social ecology. But let us see how it fits into the consensus/conflict debate. In North America, early twentieth-century development of sociology was influenced more by conservative consensus and functionalist views of society, than by socialist conflict models as was the case in Continental Europe. North American urban sociology also adopted ideas from scientific theory. The inequalities between 'man', and even the class system itself, and the competitive and aggressive nature of the American market economy (and related political system) could be justified by Darwinism and evolution. In fact, Darwinism and the theories of evolution which developed in the nineteenth century were not 'value-free' but reflected the changing political, philosophical, social and moral attitudes of the time. Social Darwinism legitimated the power of the ruling classes, justifying it as a result of the natural process of the *'survival of the fittest'*.

The Chicago School of sociology and its theories of urban social ecology were strongly influenced by social Darwinist thought, that is 'the survival of the fittest' in the development of social ecology, with little consideration of cooperation or mutual care-sharing between different groups (Bulmer 1984; Hatt and Reiss 1963; Strauss 1968). Ecology is a term more likely to be used in relation to concerns for the natural environment and sustainability. Ecology is the study of plants and animals in relation to their environmental setting, and in particular is concerned with the process of competition for living space and territory. After the initial fight a state of equilibrium is apparently reached, with each plant or animal attaining its own little patch. It then seeks to maintain its numbers from generation to generation.

Such concepts were applied sociologically to the urban human situation, as different groups of humans sought to maintain their own locality and distinct neighbourhood within the city. Social ecology has been widely adopted and modified by geographers and town planners, and much of the original background to the theories has been discarded over the years. Studies were first undertaken in Chicago in the 1920s because of public alarm at the high levels of gang warfare in the inner city (as in the movies and Al Capone). The aim of the original study was to consider the interrelationship between the crime wave and the high levels of immigrant groups (mainly white southern and central European) moving into the poorer areas looking for housing, creating intense competition for 'space'. The research team included Robert Park and Ernest Burgess, both of whom were functionalists. Deviance and crime were analysed as symptoms of the process of the city trying to regain equilibrium after the influx of large numbers of immigrant groups, not because of underlying class conflict. It was assumed that with time the groups would assimilate and move 'up and out' to the suburbs, fulfilling the great American dream of success.

The model is not static but dynamic because the concentric zones should be seen like ripples on a pond, continuously moving outwards (see Chapin 1965: 12–25, for one of the best explanations). Immigrant pressure in the centre caused the inner area to expand and thus put pressure on the next zone out and so the city spread outwards. Burgess described the outward movement of the zones of residents into the territory of another zone as 'invasion and succession' and believed this process was one of the reasons for urban unrest. Chapin describes the processes of 'sub-dominance' and 'dominance', in which the incoming colonising group gradually takes over from the previous resident group. This process may be described by the residents in phrases such as 'the area is gradually going down', or 'the area is a lot better now'. One must realise that such theories were not value-free but reflected the race, gender and class attitudes of the time.

Since so many students have done this for A level Geography, I will only summarise the theories. Although very popular, and often used as a physical representation of a city, in fact the concentric zones model is only diagrammatic. Chicago is built alongside Lake Michigan, which is enormous, as big as the Black Sea, and thus takes the form of a semi-circular city. It is not intended to be a land-use plan of how cities should be, but rather a diagram to illustrate a theory of what cities might be like if built on a flat plain. The zone of transition around the central business district is of particular interest. This is the area where the older run-down cheaper housing is found, but it is also the area where the Central Business District (CBD) is expanding, leading to rapid changes in land values and types of development. Many British cities do indeed possess a historical central area and inner ring of housing, and may fit the description of the zone of transition. The zone of transition has become virtually synonymous with the inner city and is often associated with high concentrations of ethnic minority populations. But the situation is more complex as other inner areas consist of higher-class housing and are designated as urban conservation areas, and ethnic minority areas vary a great deal in terms of house prices and social class (Lees et al. 2008; Tallon 2013). Such complexities can readily be identified by looking at house prices in the area. But many European cities are quite different from either British or North American ones, and have much higher concentrations of people of all classes living in the centre (and less suburban development), but different districts (such as the arrondisments of Paris) still have very distinct class connotations. Meanwhile in North America's large cities, particularly in New York, the ongoing conflict for living space between competing groups can still be observed. It is made more visible by the use of graffiti to mark territories between street gangs.

The other zones on the diagram are fairly self-explanatory and were initially broadly applicable to the British situation. The zone of working men's homes might consist of small terraces around older factory areas. In Britain, because of state intervention in housing and town planning, working-class council estates are also located out on the edge of the city where the land is cheaper, or where industry has been decentralised and re-zoned. The zone of better residences is where the 'normal' average family is meant to live, in a deviance-free area. In reality, the suburbs have proved to be the source of many problems, especially for people without cars, as they are separated from the rest of the city by land-use zoning, decentralisation and poor transport links. Further, the suburbs and zoning generate traffic commuting and parking problems back in the centre of the city. The next circle, the commuter zone, is meant to be the 'best' area in the model, and is entirely dependent on the motorcar (note it has no outer boundary). In Britain a planned green belt may have been around the edge of the city, and so the suburbs leapfrog the green belt and form a secondary ring. But subsequent gentrification of the inner city, urban renewal and regeneration programmes (see Chapter 11) made all these theories seem very out of date, as a perusal of the house prices will show. Also there is pressure to move back into the city because of the cost of petrol and the greatly increased problems of commuting, plus the government's commitment to filling in brown-field sites with apartment blocks as a means of increasing densities as per PPS3, so we are getting more like European cities.

The ideas of Burgess and Park, which were based on a concentric configuration, were modified by a series of subsequent models. The Sector concept developed by Homer Hoyt in the 1930s put emphasis upon the importance of transport routes, and upon parallel linear wedges of development, superimposed over the concentric structure. Sectors of better development can develop on one side of the city because of the direction of the wind, as more affluent people prefer to live in less polluted areas. The working classes are seen as being more likely to have to live downwind from the industry with all the smoke drifting over them. Many cities have a distinct East and West End, but all areas are probably equally polluted by gases and sediments in the atmosphere. Other geographical factors such as the existence of an attractive hillside ideal for development of better housing, or the presence of a river or valley, will also create natural sectors. Roads and railways can also act as barriers. In North America working-class people are often described as living on 'the wrong side of the railroad tracks'. Lastly, the multiple nuclei concept was developed by Harris and Ullman in the 1950s. This theory reflects many of the realities of contemporary metropolitan land use, allowing for decentralisation, land-use zoning and state intervention. There has been a variety of further developments of these theories over the years, by sociologists such as Mann in Britain, and the alternatives are endless (Bulmer 1984).

Urban problem areas in Britain

Empirical studies and social reform

In the first half of the twentieth century, British urban sociological studies often appear overshadowed by the wealth of American studies, both at local and city-wide level. These run across the full spectrum of urban communities, from inner-area studies, and studies of deviant groups such as the gangs described in *Street Corner Society: The Social Structure of an Italian Slum*, by Whyte (1981 originally 1943), through to studies of more middle-class, affluent, suburban areas such in Gans' study (1967) of Levittown, a speculative private housing development (a classic, and readable). Generally the problems of the inner city appeared worse and more violent in American cities, an image still projected today via television. Likewise the suburbs always seem more claustrophobic, monotonous and more distant from the rest of the city in American studies than in Britain, where the scale is less spread out.

Nevertheless there has been a strong tradition of urban social studies in Britain going back to Victorian times. Whilst in Europe there was an emphasis on 'grand theory' in the development of urban sociology, there were two other strands particularly strong in British urban sociology in the nineteenth century. First there were empirical social studies of the poor based on statistical evidence and extensive 'field work' such as that of Lady Bell, a social reformer who made a study of factory workers' lives in Middlesbrough, entitled *At the Works* (Bell 1911). Rowntree, factory owner, town planner, and builder of New Earswick, was a pioneer in social research and wrote a study entitled *Poverty: A Study of Town Life* based on York (Rowntree 1901). He was a key figure on many government committees set up to deal with the social problems of the time. Charles Booth, philanthropic businessman and early social researcher, undertook extensive studies of social conditions in inner London backed up with detailed street-by-street maps, entitled *Life and Labour of the People in London* (C. Booth 1968, originally 1906), featured in the 2013 BBC series, *Secret Streets* which investigated the extent to which social class and housing conditions had changed in some of the areas Booth had surveyed over 100 years later (check on the BBC website and iPlayer). He is not to be confused with General William Booth, founder of the Salvation Army, who also wrote widely on urban problems, for example *In Darkest England and the Way Out* (W. Booth 1890). Secondly, there was a flourishing social policy and reform movement, supported by figures such as Octavia Hill and the Webbs in respect of housing and town planning reform. Quite apart from the work of the famous social reformers there was considerable political pressure from the people themselves for social change in the forms of Chartism, early trade unionism, and in Europe actual revolutions. The working classes were not passive recipients of theory or reform, but were active in pressing for change themselves.

Community studies

In Britain, right up until the late 1950s, the emphasis continued to be on demolishing problem areas rather than studying them, with few exceptions. Post-war reconstruction planning in Britain had no real concept of the inner city as a potential major issue for the future, and the concerns of mainstream sociology itself were somewhat different. It was assumed that all the slums would eventually be cleared and the social problems would go away in the process, and this was expressed in the town planning of the time. The 1944 Greater London Development Plan already identified and named certain areas 'inner urban' (*sic*), and recommended demolition. The problems of the zone of transition were still seen as essentially American and connected with racial tension, and, as yet, this was not seen as of relevance to England. In the immediate post-war period, planners were obsessed with the idea of creating new communities in new towns, rather than seeking to preserve existing working-class communities or addressing the difficulties encountered by newly-arrived ethnic minority communities within the inner city. A series of studies was undertaken of how the people were relating to their new housing estates, linked to empirical work on the question of environmental determinism and the creation of community spirit (Carey and Mapes 1972; Bell and Newby 1978).

There were a few sociological studies of inner areas emerging in the 1950s in the UK. Under the growing influence of the American social ecology theory, with its emphasis on deviance, it became fashionable to identify 'the criminal area' as in Morris's study of that name based on a study of an inner-city area in South London (Morris 1958). Most urban social studies of the time were related to studying the effects of slum clearance and the decentralisation of population to new housing estates and the new towns. Vast amounts of demolition were undertaken in the name of slum clearance, although many saw it as a convenient way of justifying the removal of housing in the way of new road development, or the expansion of central area schemes. In the process many valuable working-class communities were destroyed (Ravetz 1980). But the problem was essentially seen as spatial (geographical), and therefore the solution was to demolish the area.

Young and Willmott (1957) highlighted these problems in their study of Bethnall Green in the East End of London. They studied the residents before and after they had been cleared when the residents were moved out to a new council estate on the edge of London. Before the clearance the sociologists observed a close-knit community based on strong networks of kith and kin, which was demolished along with the buildings. When the people were rehoused no attempt was made to keep them together, and they were mixed up amongst complete strangers from other areas. As a result greater attention was given to the nature of working-class communities. Frankenberg's book, *Communities in Britain* (1970), gives an interesting account of a range of studies from the period. This book includes urban and also rural studies as yet again people sought to analyse the ingredients of community that made village life so different from the modern urban situation (see Rees and Lambert 1985, for further accounts of community studies). Many sociologists would question the whole idea of defining problems in relation to 'areas' rather than in relation to specific groups of people (as victims or aggressors), whilst others would argue that society itself, rather than space, i.e. the built environment, should be taken as the starting point for change. Community depends much on shared values and interests and community cohesion.

Subsequent development of urban theory

Community and conflict

This section discusses the increasing levels of tension and conflict within our cities, particularly the inner city, from the 1960s onwards. Many of the problems may be accounted for by a lack of understanding on the part of the planners of the social implications of their policies, and an ignorance of the deeper economic forces shaping inequality within urban society (Bailey 1975; Simmie 1974). In the media, race, ethnicity and immigration were closely associated with urban unrest, particularly as manifested in inner-city 'race riots', and from the late 1960s onwards a series of what were referred to by the newspapers as 'race riots' occurred in several inner-city areas including Handsworth and Sparkbrook in Birmingham, Everton in Liverpool, St Paul's in Bristol, and Brixton and Tottenham in London. But, many urban sociologists identified a range of other factors, beyond race, as contributory factors and reasons for tension and unrest, such as inequality, poverty, unemployment, lack of adequate housing and competition between deprived groups for limited resources and jobs.

Social unrest in cities has had a long history, long before immigration became an issue. Community discontent had first developed in the aftermath of post-war reconstruction planning, as people saw their familiar residential areas changed, demolished and redeveloped by the planners, in the name of progress, clearing so-called 'slums' and making way for the motorcar. Urban pressure groups began to develop to oppose the activities of the planners (Aldous 1972), especially in the inner city (Donnison and Eversley 1974). Protesters included members of early housing pressure groups such as Shelter (Wilson 1970) and many separate local groups fighting against the demolition of their local area, such as at Tolmers Square in London, and for the end of high-rise development. The beginnings of other movements which were to become central 20 years later could also be seen appearing on the horizon, such as the environmental movement (Arvill 1969) and the women and planning movement (Cockburn 1977). Dissatisfaction was felt amongst a range of ethnic groups in respect of how the planners had treated them, their areas, and their planning applications. Although in an ideal world, 'planning is for people' and the planners had immense powers, they did not necessarily use them on behalf of the local community. On the contrary, the local authority often went into partnership with the developers, using its compulsory purchase powers to assemble the site, prepare the infrastructure and generally smooth the way for the property bonanza. Many saw this unholy alliance, and tangled web of relationships between planners and developers, as the opposite of what town planning was meant to be about. In retrospect it is easy to see how they got it wrong, but it should be remembered that during the post-war reconstruction period, even into the 1960s planners were dealing with the effects of massive bomb damage to property and related housing need, throughout many British towns and cities.

Traditionally-depressed regions, such as the North East, which the post-war planning system had been geared up to deal with under the various regional planning acts, were not the only areas where there was poverty and unemployment. It was noticeable that new concentrations of poverty and deprivation were not entirely explained by economic changes. Rather they were the result of social problems such as racial discrimination, family break-up, disillusioned youth and an ageing population. The 'inner city' became the catch phrase to describe the collection of spatially identifiable groups and problems located broadly within the poorer inner-urban area neighbourhoods, corresponding to what traditional urban sociologists called the zone of transition. Both black and white groups suffered high levels of unemployment and environmental deprivation, often with run-down services and public amenities. Further, they were the ones that suffered the effects of all the commuter traffic coming through their areas from the suburbs, and who were likely to find their streets filled with parked cars belonging to office workers from the central area. Inevitably conflict emerges between deprived groups, the 'poor whites' blaming the newcomers for taking 'their' houses, and the newcomer groups feeling unwanted and discriminated against by the white population. Increasingly, urban sociology became concerned with answering the question, 'who gets what where and why'; that is with the allocation of scarce resources within the urban context (Pinch 1985).

Ethnicity issues

The theme of conflict between groups for scarce resources was first incorporated in urban social analysis in Britain in the 1960s, by Rex and Moore (1967), who made a study of Sparkbrook in Birmingham, an area with a high concentration of ethnic minority groups. Rex and Moore identified a process of conflict over the allocation of the scarce resource of housing, which they saw as leading to the development of distinct housing classes, and social unrest. They drew on Weberian concepts of the role of power elites in shaping society. Weber made much in his writings of the concept of life chances, the idea that different types of people had access to different levels of resources, opportunities, and 'chances' according to the level of 'power' and 'status' they had in society, and ethnic groups came fairly low in the pecking order (Dahrendorf 1980; Weber 1964).

To provide context to the question of ethnicity a brief background on the changing ethnicity of the UK population will now be given. It should be pointed out that everyone belongs to some ethnic group or other, and ethnic should not be used only in relation to minority groups. For example, most people in England have, historically, been Anglo-

Saxon in terms of ethnicity, whereas people in Wales may have Celtic roots. Yet globally Anglo-Saxons comprise a small minority, and 'white' people comprise less than a third of the world's population. To put things in historical context, between 1871 and 1931, during which time the British Empire was a global phenomenon, outward migration from Britain was, on average, at the rate of half a million persons per year, particularly to Australia and North America, but also to Africa and India. After the First World War the levels dropped, but gradually inward migration became more pronounced. Between 1931 and 1951 there was a net gain of 60,000 new people coming in per year. Many of these were European migrants coming for a variety of economic and political reasons. Needless to say, most of these people were white Europeans, and therefore less visible, although there was still a certain amount of racial tension in some areas of London, as in the East End of London over Jewish immigration.

The question of ethnic minority issues, or race relations as they were called back in the 1960s, did not become relevant in Britain until the immigration beginning in the 1950s of people from the West Indies, and the subsequent immigration of people from the Indian subcontinent in the 1960s onwards. Between 1951 and 1961 immigration rates started to grow, with around 30,000 to 50,000 people coming in per year, but outward movement was also high with a net outflow of 5000 people. But three-fifths of incoming peoples were 'ethnic dark skinned' (as the *Daily Telegraph* tactlessly put it in the 1960s). Many migrants arrived from the West Indies because they were invited to Britain owing to labour shortages in the post-war period (Phillips and Phillips 1998). For example, London Transport ran a bus driver training programme over in Trinidad to prepare people for the move, and guaranteed them jobs for example to work on the buses and in the hospitals. However, there was often considerable opposition and, for example, in Bristol in the 1960s what were described as 'coloured' bus drivers and conductors were not allowed (Dresser and Fleming 2007). Likewise hospitals and other public institutions sought to attract skilled staff from the West Indies, and also from India and Pakistan. Later there were migrations of relatively affluent Asian business people displaced from Uganda and other parts of the old

Commonwealth (S. Smith 1989). Parts of cities in the Midlands became popular destinations for immigrants from the Indian subcontinent, offering factory employment and obtainable housing, but also opportunities for Asian businesses, and religion, to flourish, thus revitalising run-down areas in the process.

Rex and Moore (1967) saw the problems of inner-city residents in terms of competition for scarce resources between different deprived social groups, whilst acknowledging that race was a major consideration. The problem was not seen by them solely as one of race, rather a series of factors were at work, including unemployment, lack of housing, and lack of resources. As a result, competition and so conflict developed between different sectors of the population in poorer areas for the limited pool of jobs, council housing and public resources. He identified seven housing classes which may be seen as 'class positions' or indications of the levels of life chances and therefore the relative power which each group enjoyed. They concentrated on housing rather than on race itself as the subject of conflict. Different groups found their access barred to different types of housing, because, for example, building societies would not give them mortgages, or local authorities decided they did not have enough 'points' to merit a council house. Ethnic groups could be disqualified on several grounds, including low income, inadequate residency qualifications, and lack of a conventional breadwinner or respectable family structure, none of which were technically racial discrimination, of course.

All this was played out against a backdrop of inner-city decline and lack of investment in the built environment within the zone of transition (see above). Some would say that the over-concentration on the development of new towns, and on new development in general, plus decentralisation of employment to the regions through regional economic planning policy, had taken the guts out of the cities and actually created many of the inner-city problems. Others were warning, from a variety of political perspectives, of the potential problems of concentration of deprived ethnic minority groups within inner-city areas. Enoch Powell, in 1968, gave his 'Rivers of Blood' speech, painting an inflammatory view of the future. The Commission for Racial Equality (now renamed the EHRC (Equality and Human Rights Commission)) identified the problem of 'red-lining' whereby some estate agents have discouraged ('sorry it's gone') black applicants from buying houses in white areas, because they perceive this as leading to a drop in property values (CRE 1989 and check the EHRC webpage for modern aspects at www.equalityhumanrights.com).

The planners had done a great deal and had held great power to destroy entire sections of Britain's towns and cities, since the introduction of the Town and Country Planning Act 1974. But, arguably, they had solved very few problems; in fact they had created many new ones. For example, after the inner-city riots of the 1970s and the subsequent Brixton riots of the early 1980s, Lord Scarman implied in his report on the events that the planners were to be blamed (Scarman 1982). In contrast, it was common to see the ethnic minority groups themselves as 'the problem', but many of them would comment that they find it is the white majority which is the problem for them because of discrimination. As the saying goes, 'we are here because you were there', that is over the centuries Britain built up an overseas Empire, with many British people moving to the 'colonies' as settlers (that is emigrants). Many of the ethnic groups in Britain originate from former colonies (Birmingham University 1987). Today most major cities contain a very varied range of ethnic groups (Loftman and Beazley 1993), especially London where many different languages and cultures are found.

Increasingly the attention shifted in urban sociology from looking at the groups on the receiving end, to investigating the political role of the urban professionals who decided the fate of the inner-city residents. There was already a substantial body of theory in America on the role of power elites, such as the work by C. Wright Mills on shaping society (Mills 1959). In Britain, Pahl developed the idea of 'urban managerialism', by which he suggested that the urban managers such as public council housing managers and local authority planners acted as political 'gatekeepers' and influenced the distribution and allocation of scarce resources, thus affecting people's life chances (Pahl 1977; Dahrendorf 1980). Instead of seeing the planners, and other professionals, as benevolent beings working for the good of the people, they were increasingly being cast, in urban sociological research, as biased conspirators working in collaboration with other business, governmental and professional elites actively keeping the people 'down' and under 'control'. This may not have been intentional as studies have shown that some members of the land-use professions have a very limited view of social issues, and generally do not think in terms of the social implications of their actions (Joseph 1978; Howe 1980). Town planning policy was not seen as impartial or value-free but highly biased by many of the planned. Although many urban sociologists at this time broadly subscribed to a consensus based on a liberal pluralistic view of society, inevitably there was a movement towards a more conflict-orientated perspective. Already in the late 1960s students, community activists and aggrieved groups were turning to radical politics and socialist theory for explanations of what was wrong with their cities, and with town planning itself. Others, who favoured a more left-wing analysis of events, argued that many of the problems were not just matters of managerialism or faulty professional attitudes but had deeper roots in the economic system underpinning society; typically the development of modern industrial capitalism is cited as the root of all evil by those who favoured a more Marxian approach (Bailey 1975; Simmie 1974). Urban sociological theory has been through many stages and is still evolving.

Neo-Marxist urban theory

The subsequent development of urban sociology and planning theory in the 1970s and 1980s was strongly influenced by Marxist theory (as already summarised in Chapter 8 on urban theory). Marxist theory is strongly determinist in that it says that the superstructure (including the city), that is the built environment, takes the form it does in order to facilitate the continuance and maintenance of the social relations and means of production which enables the capitalist class to get the most work out of their workers at the lowest wages possible (McLellan 1973). Therefore, for example, it was argued, spatially and socially, there was little point in carrying out improvements to the built environment if people could not afford to benefit from them. If

their wages were too low (because of the structure of society) they would simply move elsewhere, rather than pay higher rents for the improved property. As Engels, Marx's colleague, is famed to have said, 'You don't solve the housing problem you only move it', alluding to fact that there would always be slums until people had the means to afford better housing.

Urban sociology went through a neo-Marxist revival in Britain, being strongly influenced by French urban sociological thought in the 1970s. There were attempts to apply neo-Marxist explanations to real urban situations, as in the work of Saunders (1979, 1985) on the London borough of Croydon, the largest London Borough, and by Bassett and Short in Bristol (1980). But many of the ideas seemed to work better in the abstract, indeed in dismissing the built environment as merely part of the superstructure of society and giving extreme importance to underlying economic forces. As Harvey pointed out, it was as if people were living in a spaceless vacuum (Harvey 1975). The urban sociologists had dug themselves into an impasse. There was much criticism of the idea that economics determined everything, for example it did not adequately explain why black people and women were more disadvantaged than white male workers if all were 'equal' units of labour, or why some areas did so much better than others within the city.

The emphasis in Marxism on industrialisation, and production, as the path to societal transformation, did not fit well with the post-industrial emphasis within society concerned with green environmental issues and sustainability, and thus with reducing production, consumption, pollution and waste. The overemphasis in Marxist theory on production, as against distribution, and consumption gave only a partial view of urban economic systems. Saunders (1985) and others subsequently adopted a more rounded sociological viewpoint in which urban issues were looked at from the perspective of the urban resident actually living in the area, who consumes goods and services such as housing, infra-structural services, schools and retail provision within the community, rather than concentrating on the world of the worker and capitalist involved in manufacturing.

Many community groups felt that Marxist and other grand theory, socialist ideas could not help them, seeing the whole movement, like traditional town planning itself, as another elitist top-down attempt to help the working classes. Many disadvantaged urban groups started thinking and working for themselves to press for the sort of cities and society they wanted, rather than accepting the views of academics and professionals as to how they should live. Indeed the importance of their activities as pressure groups within urban politics eventually registered with urban sociologists, who sought to acknowledge the importance of these groups in their academic theories. Neo-Marxism eventually went out of fashion, and the whole paradigm (way of thinking) shifted again away from grand determinist, structural theories of the past, such as Marxism. Urban sociologists were becoming more interested in post-structuralist theory, and the *zeitgeist* (spirit of the times) was entering a post-modernist phase. (The term 'post-modernism' is also used in respect of architecture, reflecting a similar return to more traditional values, whilst Modernism had become a passing fashion, popular in the early twentieth century.)

Interestingly, a whole range of alternative, less determinist theories were coming back into fashion, for example, Weber's ideas were coming back into favour, and people described themselves as neo-Weberian with its emphasis on a diversity and plurality of power groups, and, as mentioned above, a more positive, agonistic approach to social progress (Allmendinger and Tewdwr-Jones 2002). The current resurgence of interest in the study of the professions and other decision-making groups reflects a neo-Weberian interest in the nature of power in society. This also reflects a sociological tradition of studying the 'culture' of different occupational and professional groups, using more qualitative participatory methods, and concentrating on grass-roots, people issues. This has been accompanied by a retreat from the emphasis on heavy deterministic theories, and a greater acceptance of the variety and complexity of factors, over and above economics and class, which can influence people's life experiences since the late 1980s (Hall and Jacques 1989; Hamnett *et al.* 1989). Large sectors of the population had never really fitted into Marxist theory, because it prioritised the needs and life experience of a historical male, industrial working class, which allowed little recognition or sympathy for women, ethnic minorities, the disabled, the unemployed, the elderly and the self-employed, all of whom could be worse off economically than the unionised male working class (Davis 2009).

The new urban sociology agenda

Social class or human diversity?

Diversity and minority issues, such as ethnicity, gender, disability, sexuality and so forth, have become major drivers of urban sociological theory. There is less emphasis upon social class as the one and only key determinant of social structure and division. Remarkably, class, which was the great obsession of sociology, is seldom mentioned, even though 'planning for the working class' was the great excuse for the planners to hold power. Class was not even seen as one of the main equalities categories and was not included in the list of relevant diversity issues in the 2010 Equality Act. In parallel, the New Labour government (from 1997 to 2010) moved away from a heavy emphasis upon the needs of the male working class, and stressed the importance of social inclusion, diversity and (that most elastic squishy word of all) 'community'. Nowadays the majority of members of the UK population are likely to identify themselves as middle class in surveys, and the majority of the population are owner-occupiers, and more people work in the service sector than in manufacturing. So class is no longer seen as important as a personal identifier. In fact it was John Prescott (an erstwhile traditional Old Labour politician) who, when appointed a Minister in the Blair's New Labour government, commented: *'we're all middle class now'* (Photo 14.1).

Urban sociological theory itself was shifting from its Anglo-American emphasis towards a more Continental European, and culturally-inspired, perspective. As has already been mentioned at the end of Chapter 8 on planning theory, the ideas French sociologists, such as Lefebvre, provided an alternative analysis of the city which saw the city as being shaped by cultural factors rather than purely economic forces. Other French sociologists provided an alternative perspective on class, and thus on the structuring of society. In particular Bourdieu built on the ideas of Weber, but brought in a range of other perspectives too in his work in the 1960s and 1970s. Bourdieu argued that theories of economic capital and the resultant economic classes were not sufficient to explain or define the differences within society (Bourdieu 1970 [2000 edition]). Bourdieu stressed the importance of both social capital and cultural capital, which were acquired as a result of a person's education, upbringing, connections and family background. Such factors gave a person the 'know how', what he termed 'habitus', to get on in the world. Whilst social background and economic class might generally be linked, Bourdieu argued that the mechanics of class were not that simple, or deterministic. Rather, various factions and subtle divisions existed within classes, which helped shape people's life chances, occupations and lifestyle differences. Whilst such differences might in some cases lead to the 'reproduction of the status quo' (alluding to Marxian theory), they could also lead to new types of differences, variations in class structure, and greater diversity. Overall Bourdieu promoted a more nuanced, sensitive approach to sociology than in more formal, deterministic schools of thought. In his research on reflexive sociology (Bourdieu and Wacquant 1992) he stressed the importance of a more qualitative, ethnographic approach in which the sociologist was more aware of their own social perspective and background and the realities of the lives of others. An urban ethnographic approach is widespread, which is based upon adopting a detailed, qualitative approach to studying different communities and social groups, for example the residents of a particular area, or the members of a profession, or the culture and assumptions found in a policy-making organisation (Hammersley and Atkinson 2008; Greed 1994b).

Perhaps the definition of class as one's place in society which is based upon occupation is a particularly British preoccupation given our industrial heritage. This idea of class happens to chime both with those on the Right concerned with maintaining and ordering the social structure, and those on the Left, particularly neo-Marxists, who saw the world as being divided between capitalists and workers. But many sociologists, particularly those concerned with feminist issues, ethnicity differences and with power and poverty in society, have questioned this class emphasis. In the post-industrial society, there are increasing numbers of unemployed, poor, self-employed and temporary workers, who never quite fitted into male industrial concepts of 'the working class'. Also, in these days of middle-class unemployment, forced retirement and deskilling of erstwhile white-collar jobs, there are many people whose social background, education and cultural awareness do not readily equate with the 'class' of work they do, including married women with childcare responsibilities.

Thus the pendulum has swung from emphasising large-scale, and often generalised, class divisions within society, towards studying the minutiae of individual difference and variation among and between groups within society. Likewise there has been a greater acceptance of the diversity of individuals' experiences of the urban situation, and the effects of their own personal characteristics (such as race, gender, age, disability, sexuality, culture, religion and home locality) on their status and power in society. This has led to the flowering of rainbow politics and sociology where there is a plurality of interest groups and minority interests. Whilst ethnicity, disability and gender, in particular, continue to be very important considerations in an individual's unique personal characteristics, no one factor exists in isolation and therefore new theories have evolved to accommodate this variation. In particular, the concept of 'intersectionality' (Bagilhole 2009) has sought to take into account the fact that different diversity characteristics overlap and interact within an individual's being, whilst stressing that some issues, such as gender, are likely to be more overarching in their importance than others.

In response to all these changes, in the 1990s New Labour sought to promote a more collaborative, grass-roots, community-focused approach to policy-making (Healey 2006). In part this was because the old Labour power base of unionised, working-class men employed in heavy industry had long since faded away. The new urban political movements were much more concerned with equalities and human rights. Likewise the sociological study of work itself had changed from an emphasis upon studying assembly-line workers (as in making Ford cars) and other routine occupations towards an acknowledgement of the importance of creativity, self-determination, self-employment and innovation in creating new forms of employment of value to the economy. Today the majority of workers are to be found in the service sector working in offices, shops and businesses, rather than in old-fashioned industrial occupations. Many are working in creative, self-directed employment in media, high-tech industry and entrepreneurial occupations (Tallon 2013). This shift in work patterns is sometimes called the move from Fordism to post-Fordism (Gabler 20010, 222).

New political perspectives and significant population groups

The Coalition government which came to power in 2010 appeared to be less concerned with social welfare issues than New Labour and prioritised policies concerned with economic recovery, profitability and productivity. Nevertheless, as outlined in earlier chapters, there is still an emphasis upon the importance of the role of the community and the 'Big Society' and the new localism, which has even influenced the restructuring of the development plan system (see Chapter 2). Yet paradoxically there have been major cutbacks in government funding for social welfare programmes and in housing, health and local government services. Nevertheless, the Coalition may be seen as blending liberal political views with a traditional Tory emphasis on economic growth. This has been exemplified in the Coalition's approach to gay issues in their support of 'gay marriage' as enacted in the Marriage (Same Sex Couples) Act of 2013.

Some would say that sexuality has now become a key personal identifier, and the most contested social category, more important than social class (Habermas and Ratzinger 2007). Around 5 per cent of the population identify themselves as gay (Doan 2011), whilst Stonewall estimates the UK figure is around 3.7 million people (http://www.stonewall.org.uk/at_home/sexual_orientation_faqs/2694.asp). Planners need to be aware of these issues both in terms of the overall social geography of cities (Browne et al. 2009), and in the detailed planning of specific local areas, for example in Brighton (Browne and Bakshi 2013); in relation to personal safety issues (Hanhardt 2013); and design of local facilities

(Cavanagh 2010). Around 50,000 civil partnerships take place each year, and around 1 per cent of households comprise gay couples. Same-sex marriage may perhaps lead to more households being formed, and may have implications for what constitutes a 'household' for planning law purposes (Chapter 3). In addition, 1 in 30,000 men and 1 in 100,000 women are transgender, and there are 5000 people who have undergone reassignment operations in the UK.

Population pressures: it's not all black and white

In this section two major identifiers are discussed, namely ethnicity and age, because both are reshaping modern UK society. Whilst ethnicity (and by association immigration and race) have long been blamed for all the woes in society, age and in particular the hostility towards the ageing population are relatively recent and no doubt related to the current financial crisis. Both topics have implications for town planning and housing policy.

Earlier in this chapter we discussed the impact of the initial waves of immigration in the 1960s. We will now take up the story again and bring it into the present day. As the years went by immigration continued to increase. A series of Race Relations and Immigration Acts were introduced to control the situation, such as the Commonwealth Immigrants Act 1962, Race Relations Act 1965, Immigration Act 1971 and the Nationality Acts of the 1980s. Almost every year new acts came in, containing all sorts of new complexities as to who was eligible for citizenship, work permits and residency rights. Legislation had became more sophisticated to cover Commonwealth, non-Commonwealth and asylum, and EU immigration, one example being the 2009 Borders, Citizenship and Immigration Act.

Whilst much immigration from the 1960s onwards had been limited to Commonwealth citizens, the next major change was the increase in European migration as a result of the right for the free movement of labour within the European Union. For example, mainly highly-skilled people from Poland and other Eastern European, ex-Communist countries entered Britain and readily found employment. Most were white, Christian and well educated and 'did not look any different' from the majority population. But they were not necessarily welcome and often seen as rivals to the existing residents, being accused of undercutting wage rates, increasing competition for housing and impinging on the existing culture of local areas. Resentment by white working-class groups is reported in the media, because of the belief that new jobs are taken by foreigners and immigrants, thus lowering wages and employment opportunities. However, on closer inspection many of these jobs are poorly paid and constitute the sort of work that many English people do not want to do, or they are jobs that young employed English-born people cannot do because of poor qualifications, unwillingness or lack of experience. However, many such immigrants never intended to stay long and were highly mobile, living in both rural and urban areas. Under New Labour, new categories of immigrants from overseas also increased in numbers, especially from Africa and the Middle East, especially asylum-seekers which numbered 1500 per year in the 1970s, rising to 68,000 in 1998–9 with growth continuing in the 1990s. Clearly the situation had become much more complex and the immigrants themselves manifested a wide range of social class, income levels, ethnicities, educational standards and religious affiliations.

The whole situation was accelerated under New Labour's administration, during which there was a 40 per cent increase in immigration of all the above categories. In 1997 the UK had a population of 58 million and now it has a population of over 62 million. There has been an unprecedented 7 per cent increase in the UK population since the 2001 Census, of which 55 per cent are immigrants; and 250,000 people net are added every year through immigration. At present around 500,000 immigrants enter Britain each year but the net growth in population is around 250,000 because of emigration and people returning to their land of origin. According to an Andrew Marr BBC television programme, 'This is Britain', March 2011, 580,000 came to Britain in 2011, but 364,000 left in 2011. One in eight of the population was not born in the UK: that is around 12 per cent of the population, and around 5 per cent of the population of Britain is non-white. But nationally, 80 per cent of the UK population is white British-born.

But, over half of ethnic minority people were born in Britain, for example the majority of people of Afro-Caribbean origin were born in Britain, many describing themselves as 'Black-British' or simply as 'English', now that their families may have been here several generations. Overall there has been a massive 'churn' of people coming and going from Britain, as many global forces are at work in shaping population movement. Please consult the ONS (Office of National Statistics) website for the 2014 Census report for details on the UK population. Thirty-seven per cent of the population of London (in the GLA) was born abroad. Only 45 per cent of Londoners are white British-born (that is 3.7 million out of 8.2 million total London population) with a massive decrease in the traditional white working classes. Seventy per cent of ethnic minority groups are concentrated in 10 per cent of urban areas. The growth is particularly strong in the Midlands. Leicester, Oldham and Birmingham already have majority ethnic minority populations, with over 50 per cent in many localities. Several inner London boroughs have majority ethnic minority populations, of 70 per cent or more. Nationally 45 per cent of ethnic minorities live in areas where less than half the population is British white. But they are composed of all sorts of nationalities, thus creating great diversity among the population. So it is no longer realistic to talk of 'ethnic minorities' as they form a majority in many areas. By 2051 it is likely that more than 20 per cent of the population will consist of ethnic minority groups. In 2011 a quarter of all babies born in Britain were from foreign mothers. Thus the demographic characteristics of Britain are changing both in terms of numbers and diversity. There are many newspaper and internet articles on these issues all the time, but readers are advised to check carefully the 'attitudes' expressed by journalists. Population changes, especially immigration figures, can be reported from a racist viewpoint or it can be dealt with from a more practical planning policy perspective in terms of the implications for housing, education, health, employment and land-use planning policies. In spite of all these demographic changes, a strong national identity and culture prevails, with strong support from many immigrant groups.

Whilst the government has promoted an image of diversity and harmony, and argued that multi-ethnicity is good, tension, racism and uneasiness has not necessarily abated. Various inner-city riots continued to take place over the years and in 2011 major disturbances broke out right across the country, with London and several other cities being badly affected. But were they race riots? Whilst some saw these riots as being more about organised looting and criminality, other saw them as an expression of the resentment and social exclusion of a large underclass in British cities. From a race perspective, many of the rioters were young white males (and some females). Many ethnic minority shopkeepers and business premises were looted by rioters who themselves comprised multi-ethnic groupings. So class and ethnicity are cross-cutting in new and alarming ways.

Many social commentators have identified the growth of a new white underclass, sometimes pejoratively (sneeringly) called 'chavs' (Jones 2010), who comprise a new non-working class, whose young people are generally NEETs (Not in Employment Education or Training). Chavs are typified as living in problem council estates or inner-city high-rise blocks, wearing shell suits with the latest trainers, and loving designer labels, and as being associated with drug-addiction, teenage pregnancy and living on social security. Sociologically one must always be cautious about creating stereotypes and judging people by where they live or what they look like. All sorts of other issues come in here as to the 'welfare culture' and the development of an entire subculture of people who choose not to work. But there are also many hard-working and willing people who have been thrown out of work because of government cutbacks and redundancies as a result of the financial crisis of 2008, which is still having an impact. The employment situation was not improved by the Coalition government massively reducing the public sector and its services. Therefore one must be careful not to lump everyone that lives in a 'bad area' together and also there is a need to distinguish between traditional respectable working-class families and those who lack a work-based family culture.

Whilst 'chavs' have now become an easily-identifiable and apparently homogeneous group, 'immigrants' comprise a much more diverse and complex range of people. For example, it should not be assumed that all immigrants are poor, culturally different or likely to be a burden on the taxpayer, as many bring wealth, enterprise, high levels of education, and investment to the nation. London has become a global city, attracting millionaires and even billionaires from many countries. It has become increasingly popular to own property and businesses in London but not necessarily live there. The increased levels of immigration have, at a very practical level, put many pressures on housing stock, health and education services, but not always in the way imagined. For example, 60 per cent of all new housing development in London has been bought by overseas investors, which puts a different perspective on the question of the housing crisis.

In retrospect, Ed Miliband, Labour leader (on 22 June 2012, reported in most broadsheet newspapers at the time) conceded that New Labour had not anticipated the effects of their immigration policies and acknowledged that such high levels of immigration were causing major pressures for resources and problems in the employment sector. He argued that the debate has now gone beyond issues of 'racism', given that many of the new immigrants were white and European, and was now one of sheer numbers, in terms of planning and housing a much increased population. Britain is a small country, with limited space for new housing and increasing financial pressures on housing, education, the health service, particularly since the global economic banking crisis of 2008 and the subsequent series of government cutbacks in the public sector to reduce national debts. In terms of land use, housing and planning policy, in comparison when the population was half this figure, at around 30 million in the 1940s, the early town planners were arguing that 'the new Britain must be planned' and that there was already overpopulation, overcrowding and a shortage of land with too much pressure on cities. The Conservatives have been more critical of the situation in condemning the effect of immigration on housing demand. Theresa May, Home Secretary, in December 2012, said that reduced immigration would make housing 10 per cent cheaper, and reduce the demand for new housing land. Traditional Tories have cautioned against the effect of house-building on the loss of countryside and green-belt land, whilst others have suggested that 3 per cent of such land needs to be sacrificed to meet housing demand.

Clearly everything is relative, as to what is meant by overpopulation and lack of land, and much depends on whether the economy can support greater numbers, and how they live in terms of housing densities and the sustainable design of cities. There are countries with global cities with much higher population densities than the UK (where high-rise development is the norm, so it all depends again on the answer to the question 'how do you want to live?'). Population growth has caused major challenges in terms of availability of jobs, school places and social housing, quite separately from any questions of racism. Demands for more house-building have to be set against the fact that the population is growing at the equivalent rate of the population of a medium-sized town every year, putting pressures on existing development plan land-use allocations, the green belt, and local authority services as a whole. So in calculating how many houses are needed, relatively speaking, the planners have to base their calculations on an ever-upwards-moving and uncertain target population. New Labour's objective of building 4 million new houses should be set against the fact that 3 million new people entered Britain under their administration, and that housing pressures are particularly intense in urban areas. Around 1 million people are on waiting lists across the country for social housing, now mainly only available through housing associations. Many planning authorities have found they are dealing with a moving target in terms of housing demand, as population growth continues to outstrip housing supply, whilst schools, social services, health facilities, roads and infrastructure are all also under pressure. The situation has not been helped by major cutbacks in local authority services, health, education and other services. Even the EHRC has had its budget cut by 60 per cent.

Only around 125,000 new houses are being built each year and the vast majority of these are for private ownership (Hanley 2012). Coalition proposals to speed up the planning system, build on the green belt and thus increase house-building are somewhat short-sighted and also unlikely to happen during the present economic recession. Both developers and the Local Government Association (representing local planning authorities) argue that there are already around half a million planning consents for new housing that have not been taken up owing to the financial situation and market downturns.

Further, many people simply cannot afford to buy their own house any more because average house prices are several times that of the average annual salary, whereas in the past they were seldom more than two or three times more and therefore linked to ordinary people's incomes. Paradoxically there are approaching 1 million empty properties nationwide but many are in depressed areas, some are empty for legal and financial reasons, and some are uninhabitable (for updates on all these figures look up ONS data and also many banks and building societies, and the RICS produce regular bulletins on these matters). So to conclude, it is hoped that this subsection helps to explain how complicated population issues are and how they relate to planning policy.

The age wars and changing demographics

Let us return to population issues, this time looking 'vertically' at age cohorts (rather than 'horizontally' at ethnicity and cultural divisions). Age is 'the elephant in the room' (to allude to Banksy), the great unspoken factor that might yet outrank class, gender and race in importance. The issue, as yet, has not led to riots, although there is definitely evidence of ageism and this is often linked to resentment by the younger generation who blame the elderly for taking away their inheritance and their houses (Willetts 2010). As with much of the rest of Western Europe, the problem of an increasingly ageing population is being augmented through immigration policies that provide an instant, 'ready-made' new generation of young families and skilled workers. For many years demographers and other statisticians have been concerned both with the rise in population and with the changing nature of the age structure and population composition. 'Planning for the future' may suggest shiny new space-age cities, but in reality may well mean planning for an increasingly ageing population who require accessible built environments (Age UK 2009: Gilroy 1999, 2008). The writings of Malthus, the economist, especially *Principles of Population and Colonisation* (Malthus originally 1798, 1973 edition) legitimised the need for population control. It was believed that the population of Britain was growing at such a rate that there would always be poor people as the land could not support them. In the nineteenth century, this resulted in a punitive approach to poor law relief, deterrent work-house regimes (because it was thought that charity 'only encouraged them') along with migration to the colonies (even compulsory transportation); and such attitudes persisted into the twentieth century. It should be noted that the population debate has always been suffused with social Darwinism and the very questionable topic of eugenics (which is the science of selective breeding as to who is worthy to exist and who is seen as a burden and should be elim-inated, as put into practice in Nazi Germany).

Alarm was expressed at the rise in population as a result of the Baby Boom following the end of the Second World War. Post-war town planners were concerned with population data because they needed to know how many people to plan for, in terms of growth of towns, and levels of provision of housing, schools, hospitals and so forth. Equally, private-sector developers needed to know how many people might use their retail, commercial, leisure and resi-dential developments. By the 1960s there were dire warnings about overpopulation and the chances of running out of resources, and of land. Yet paradoxi-cally there was also the encouragement of immigra-tion to fill the jobs created by the expanding economy, albeit at much lower rates than today. Some town planners wanted greater state planning controls so that rather than responding to popula-tion growth they could control it. Overpopulation was increasingly condemned by those concerned with green issues, and the ability of the planet to feed itself. Thus overpopulation has always been seen as a global issue (Toffler 1970; Club of Rome 1972; Ehrlich 1971). Family planning, along with town planning and economic planning, was strongly promoted during the second half of the twentieth century. But, it was always the poor, women and ethnic minorities that were blamed the most for overpopulation for 'having too many children'. So there was little incentive to provide childcare provi-sion, better welfare programmes, larger houses, or more family-orientated facilities. But 1960s promot-ers of family planning, in their enthusiasm for limit-ing world growth, appeared not to realise that Western European countries in reducing their already-low birth rates were in fact sowing the seeds for future population imbalance. As a result there were simply not enough children being produced to

balance and support the large numbers of now ageing people born in the post-war population boom.

Of course many of the elderly would argue that they have already contributed substantially to build-ing up the economy of the country and are arguably subsidising the younger members of society, and would expect to have their needs included in plan-ning policy. Many elderly people who have lived through the rigours, shortages, poverty and rationing of post-war Britain are very offended to be accused of having it so good all their lives, especially when such condemnation is delivered by a younger generation used to the easy-going spending of the modern consumer society. Many elderly people, who are pensioners, are in fact quite poor, and do not wish to be lumped together with wealthy home-owners and bankers, and have been seriously affected by government cutbacks. Whilst many would blame our present financial woes on the 2008 financial crisis, and especially the bankers, and other power elites and business oligarchies, the govern-ment has decided to blame the public sector for overspending, and in particular to reduce public-sector pensions, along with services to the elderly and disabled. But elderly people are becoming an increasingly significant sector of the population (Photo 14.3).

So there is blame, misunderstanding and resent-ment between old and young. Solutions include rais-ing the pension age and cutting back the Welfare State. Encouraging immigration is seen as a means of righting the population balance, and has been actively encouraged. There is now a major volte-face, a reversal of government population policy in the early twenty-first century. After 50 years of the government encouraging people to have smaller families because of fears of overpopulation, it is now realised that there are not enough young people around of working age to support the increasing numbers of elderly population, so more children are needed. However, many planners would argue that the UK is a small country and there is not the space, resources, housing or jobs for many more people. Indeed in the post-war reconstruction planners used to speak of the ideal population being around 30 million, whereas the population is now double, over 60 million. Needless to say, much of the thinking is

Photo 14.3   Planning for the future?

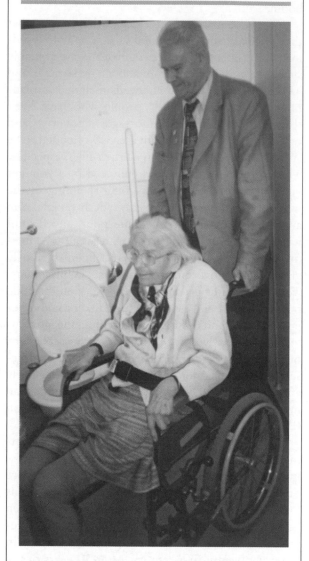

As Gilroy (2008) observes, the planner's future vision is no longer one of designing space-age cities for a young vibrant population, but rather it means dealing with the effects of an ageing population. So caring becomes an important component of planning.

numbers of people under the age of 14 has halved over the last 20 years to one in five of the population and there are actually more elderly people (over 60) than there are young people (under 18). However, the situation is not uniform across the country; in some seaside retirement areas on the South Coast and in Somerset over 30 per cent of the population are retired. But in London only one in nine of the population is retired and there is a veritable baby boom taking place.

In comparison, at a global level many countries have very large populations under the age of 30, for example around 60 per cent of the population of Middle Eastern countries, and 70 per cent of most African countries, are under the age of 30, with only around 5 per cent being over 65. Whilst Western European growth rates are declining by half in each generation (4, 2, 1), in India, for example, the population is continues to double (1, 2, 4) (as against China 4, 2, 1). In late 2013 China relaxed its one-child policy, allowing some couples to have two children, no doubt because of the demographic time bomb that previous policies had created, of a growing ageing population with not enough younger people to support and care for them. Immigration of new cohorts of younger people is often seen as a solution. But it is short term, as who is going to look

Photo 14.4   Neighbourhood play space

Whilst in the UK the population is ageing, in many countries there is a growing need to make provision for the younger generation, even in high-density areas. This is South Korea and in many Far East and also developing countries 'children' are still a very major sector of the population that planners need to take into account (Gleeson and Sipe 2006; Ward 1990, 1994).

short-sighted, as increasing the population just stores up the same problem for later generations. This is a Europe-wide problem, with most Western countries experiencing population imbalance.

According to the 2011 Census there are now 10 million people in the UK over the age of 65, whilst 16 per cent of the population is retired. But the after them when they grow old? It is important to look at population pyramids as to how changes in age cohorts will play out for the future. Worldwide major population growth is under way, and the global population has now reached 7 billion, over 50 per cent of which live in towns and cities, of which half live in poverty in shanty towns without adequate sanitation (Burdett and Sudjic 2011, 2012) and see special issue of *National Geographic*, January and July 2011 on Population. Such massive urban growth puts the town planning problems of the UK in perspective, but globally the whole situation is linked in terms of urbanisation, demographic growth, global movements of population, economic restructuring and financial crises. All this makes the 'urban sociological studies' of old a bit tame, in respect of ethnicity, class and social conflict, and we shall have to wait to see what new theories develop to interpret and understand these global societal changes. For urban planners throughout the world it brings a whole new range of issues to be tackled at a global level. So in the UK and Western Europe we need to plan for an increasingly ageing population. But in many other parts of the world planning for children and young people is important as they are the majority of the population (Photo 14.4).

To conclude, Britain has undergone some very major changes during the last 30 years and is now a multi-ethnic society, in which few people work in industry, but it is also an ageing society, one with high unemployment and a weak economy. All this is very different from the times when the first sociology theories were written, when the population was relatively young, homogenous and divided clearly into different classes. New theories and policies need to be developed to deal with the impact of the all these changes, and planners need to be at the fore-front in this process.

For the tasks, further reading, additional photos and other resources – including explanatory diagrams of the three main social ecology theories that will be particularly useful for this chapter – please visit www.palgrave. com/companion/greed.

15 Planning for Diversity and Equality: Women and Minorities

Taking an alternative perspective

In order to highlight the fact that there is no one right answer in town planning, and that it all depends on 'who you are and what you want to achieve', this chapter will first reconsider the social aspects presented in the last chapter, and secondly re-evaluate the nature of cities, from a 'women and planning' viewpoint. This perspective has arisen as a major challenge to traditional town planning as more women become town planners and as more women in the community become concerned with environmental issues. The diversity agenda has expanded to include a wider range of equality issues including gender, but also ethnicity, age, class, disability, sex, culture and religion, and has become quite complicated. This chapter will take 'women and planning' as an example, because this is a field that is well researched and also gender issues affect the whole population. One can apply the principles illustrated by gender to any of the other diversity issues too, including race and disability. However, the story of 'women and planning' is a tale that still needs to be told.

The chapter first seeks to justify the importance of gender, and thus 'women and planning'. The next section reappraises the social aspects of planning literature outlined in the last chapter, and traces the historical and contemporary evolution of the 'women and planning' movement. In the following section the land-use and planning policy implications of a gender perspective are explained, in respect of residential areas, employment policies, transport, and leisure and recreation. Then the issue of implementing gender-sensitive planning policy is discussed. It is important to explain the problems and to set out policy alternatives but the real chal-lenge is to achieve policy change. In the next chapter the theme of policy change will be discussed with reference to strategies to mainstream gender and other equality issues into planning policy and professional practice.

One could equally take the principles of this chapter on 'women and planning' and apply them, as a methodology, to other minority group needs and research the range of literature to be found. Other so-called minority topics, which actually affect millions of people, have already been discussed in other chapters, for example gay issues, ethnicity and age were looked at in the last chapter. Disability and age have also featured in the chapters on urban design, transport and the social aspects of planning. There is a considerable literature on these other minority issues, and some references have already been given in earlier chapters.

The importance of gender

Gender is taken as a key example, because it is still a primary factor within the diversity spectrum that overarches and cross-cuts with all the other diversity considerations, as will be illustrated in this chapter (Anthony 2001; Reeves 2005). As to definitions, gender relates to both men's and women's position in society. Whilst 'sex' relates to the fact that men and women are biologically different and that women are the ones who bear children, 'gender' is used to describe the package of cultural differences and distinct roles that are given to men and women in our society. 'Feminism' is the term used to describe the movement that has been concerned with promoting and achieving equality for women, albeit feminism is a very broad church containing adher-

Photo 15.1   Life's many obstructions

This shows the entrance to some very good public toilets, including accessible disabled toilets. But it is impossible for anyone disabled to get into the entrance because of obstructions on the pavement outside. This is a metaphor for many of the problems encountered in trying to access equality itself and lack of joined-up thinking between departments.

ents from right across the political and cultural spectrum. Whilst most women can give birth and men cannot, it is still women's gender role to undertake childcare, housework and caring responsibilities: as well as work outside the home (Greed 1994a).

Whilst the concept of gender, strictly speaking, relates equally to men and women, many of the problems and issues have arisen because much planning policy has been based upon the assumption, when 'planning for people', that the average citizen and worker are male. In fact there 1.1 million more women than men in the UK according to the 2011 Census, and approaching 70 per cent of mothers work. Thus women's needs and experiences of the built environment are likely to be different from men's, but those men who take on such caring roles will experience similar problems too (Jarvis *et al.* 2009; Fainstein and Servon 2005). Therefore, this

chapter presents the arguments for 'planning for women' and discusses the issues in respect of women's different needs and the obstacles encountered (Photo 15.1). In the final chapter, the implications of the equality and diversity agenda on the nature and priorities of the planning profession itself will be discussed further.

Why women?

Women comprise 52 per cent of the population (ONS 2012 and see ONS website) and since 'planning is for people', over half the attention of the planners should, reasonably, be focused on the needs of women. In comparison around 12 per cent of the population comprises ethnic minorities, 5 per cent who identify themselves as gay, 20 per cent the elderly, and, depending on definitions, at least 15 per cent suffer some form of disability (CIC 2009; Greed 2011a, 2011b). Readers are recommended to check the ONS (Office of National Statistics) website for updates and confirmation on all percentages given. In the past 'planning for people' has arguably 'meant' by default 'planning for the average man in the street', for gender considerations were not consciously taken into account in the days when the vast majority of town planners were men. But, the reader might ask, is it really necessary to plan 'specially' or 'differently' for women than for men? It is argued that women's urban needs, and the way they use the city, are different from men's. In summary, this is because they are more likely to be the ones responsible for childcare, shopping, and a range of other caring roles, all of which generate different usage of urban space. Fewer women than men have access to the use of a car, and they comprise the majority of public transport users in many areas. Women's daily activities and travel patterns are likely to be different and more complex than men's, as many will be combining work with childcare and other commitments. Therefore the classic mono-dimensional 'journey to work', upon which so much transportation planning policy has been based in the past, does not fit well with women's lives and needs (RTPI 1999; Greed 2005a, 2005b). Over two-thirds of women work in 2012, and many have great difficulty juggling their various roles and duties. Women also comprise the majority (variously) of the elderly, disabled, low paid, single parent families, carers, urban poor, and many ethnic minority populations. But women do not figure in the consciousness of the built environment and construction professions because they are a small minority (Greed 2000; CIC 2010) so their needs and different lives are unlikely to be recognised or prioritised in decision-making.

Gender cross-cuts and intersects (Bagilhole 2009; Cooper 2008) with all other aspects of diversity and needs to be taken into account in all aspects of planning policy. For example, in the past, when planning for employment and economic growth, planners tended to concentrate on the needs of the male working class, many of whom were employed in the strongly-unionised sectors of mining, heavy industry and manufacturing. Many of these employment sectors have declined, resulting in extensive unemployment, and many speak of the extinction of the male white working class (McDowell 2003, 2013). In contrast, the majority of the population work in the service sector; in offices, shops, call centres but also in high-tech industry, banking and the media. Over 40 per cent of all workers are female, and many of the new and often poorly paid jobs in the service sector are held by ethnic minority workers. Many workers are self-employed, part-time and non-unionised, or they are on short-term contracts with no 'job for life'. The care industry has the highest rate of growth investment and employment of any sector, and most of its workers are female (Gilroy 2008). This growth has been the result of the pressures of caring for a growing ageing population, demands for increased childcare provision, and a reduction in state provision for the disabled. Creating accessible environments, which are user-friendly for all age groups, is a key town planning issue (Greed 2011a, 2012). Over 80 per cent of single person pensioners lack access to a motorcar and 75 per cent of these carless pensioners are women (Age UK 2009; Help the Aged 2009).

Women and planning

Reappraisal of the social aspects literature

Let us now reappraise the social aspects of urban society set out in the last chapter, from a gender perspective. Women are scarcely visible in much of the nineteenth-century literature. If working-class women are mentioned, they are likely to be seen as those who caused the perceived problem of overpopulation because of low morals and poor hygiene (Richardson 1876). If upper- or middle-class women are mentioned, they are either presented as angels on a pedestal; or paradoxically as lazy, selfish, neurotic and contributing to the breakdown of society (Durkheim 1970 edition, originally 1897). Women and their needs are presented as a supporting cast to the main actors, not as people with problems and needs of their own in the new industrial society. Women were not entitled to own property for much of the nineteenth century, or to go into the professions, and so they had limited access to the world of property and planning, although many were active in the early housing reform movements (Atkins and Hoggitt 1984).

Tönnies, in defining his two models of society (see last chapter), the old and the new, as either *gemeinschaft* (community and private life) or *gesellschaft* (public life and business), left women in the awkward position of not quite fitting into either category. Even today, women's lives and work activities do not divide into 'public' and 'private' realms – work and home – in quite the way men's do, particularly if they are full-time housewives. Marx appears to have ignored women altogether, or perhaps he assumed they were included as 'workers' (Hartman 1981). Marx's whole worldview was founded on an arguably sexist emphasis on 'male' work and production, with little regard of women's role in production, reproduction and consumption, as homemakers, mothers and carers (Kirk 1980; Markusen 1981), all of which are forms of work necessary to the creation and sustaining of life itself. Over 1.5 million women were in domestic service during the nineteenth century but their work did not count, although their numbers actually exceeded men in manufacturing. Such attitudes had planning implications, for in the more 'socialist' areas of planning in the past women's needs were often not seen as related to production, and therefore as not a worthy subject for urban policy-making. But in fact women were likely to be undertaking domestic work in the home in order to 'create', care for, and feed the workforce in the first place, before they even got to the factory gates, as well as working themselves outside the home, in shops, offices and factories (McDowell 1983).

The first wave of feminism at the turn of the last century had a strong emphasis on the built environment (Gilman 1915; Boyd 1982; Greed 1990) which was reflected in model communities, and in co-operative housing ventures pioneered by women (Hayden 1981; Pearson 1988). 'Material feminism' existed in quite a different form from today, often tied up with utopianism, evangelical Christian reformism and the public health and housing movements. Ironically, notable individual women from this first wave, such as Octavia Hill (Hill 1956; Darley 1990) are often disparagingly seen as '*only a housing manager*'. Her ideas were influential over a wide range of land management issues, including rural planning, and regional economic policy (Cherry 1981, 53), and she played a major part in the setting up of the National Trust (Gaze 1988). Women were often criticised for being 'lady bountifuls', voluntary do-gooders. Indeed, since women did not really fit into male-defined class categories, they were always likely to be seen as either 'too posh to plan' or 'too common and uneducated' to join the professions. But women were not allowed to become professional town planners (or architects, surveyors, lawyers ...) until after the First World War when in 1919 the Sex Disqualification Removal Act was passed. Although women could now work in local authority planning departments, all women were required to leave upon marriage – there was no maternity leave either – so there were few senior women. It was not until after the Second World War that the marriage bar was lifted, which would enable women to continue in their jobs and reach positions of seniority. So there was only limited influence from women on the development of modern planning (Martin and Sparke 2003; Darling and Whitworth 2007).

The coming of the Welfare State in the 1940s did not entirely take into account the nature of women's lives. It was established to cater for the needs of the 'family' in which the man was seen as the breadwinner and the woman was seen as dependent wife and mother. For women it was 'only half way to Paradise'. The new Welfare State rendered them dependent upon the male breadwinner, with limited employment and pension benefits in their own right (Wilson 1980; 1991). Nevertheless women did have an influence on the development of town planning and housing policy but outside of the male-dominated public world of professional employment and academia. Some of the early urban social studies were by women (Bell 1911), but later as urban sociology became more formalised women were more likely to be mere assistants, as in Moore's study of Sparkbrook (Moore 1977), with some notable exceptions (Stacey 1960; Aldridge 1979). In Britain women appear in studies of working-class communities in a variety of over-simplified stereotypes, which are based on observing them as mono-dimensional residents tied to the area, rather than as people with jobs, interests and aspirations beyond its boundaries. Young and Willmott gave some emphasis to women in their study, but their fondness for seeing them in the role of 'Mum', as virtual tea machines, and almost as wallpaper to the main action of life, is open to question (Rose 1993). Their later work on the symmetrical family (Young and Willmott 1978) is seen as nothing more than wishful thinking by urban feminists (Little 1994).

Women's influence on the urban research and planning policy might be seen as somewhat stronger in North America. Although women could go to college in the United States, long before it was accepted in Britain, women were rapidly corralled into separate academic spheres (Little 2009; Jarvis *et al.* 2009, 56–8). The approach to urban studies was split between 'masculine' abstract urban science, and 'feminine' practical social work. So famous men created the grand theories of urban sociology and planning but excluded a woman's perspective. At best women were likely to end up as research assistants or professors' wives. Thus a gender perspective was generally left out of the famous studies of the Chicago School, such as the concentric zone theory, although, in contrast, great emphasis was put upon the ethnic minority dimension as a primary cause of urban spatial change. However, there were just a few indications of a wider gender perspective seeping in. For example, some Chicago sociologists did allow for the possibility of women being both workers and mothers, as reflected, for example, in the urban questionnaires used by Zorbaugh, one of the main researchers providing at least some 'space' for the concerns of ordinary American women (Bulmer 1984, 103). But in North American sociological studies of the suburbs, women, although presented as bastions of respectability, were seen as idle and lazy, thus reinforcing the sexist image of the 'stupid housewife' (Gans 1967). Such attitudes were soon to be challenged by the rise of feminism in the 1960s. For example, Betty Friedan wrote of the problems and dissatisfaction middle-class, college-educated women encountered in the American suburbs. They experienced what she called, 'the problem without a name', being stuck at home looking after the children all day, and with no chance of a career (Friedan 1963).

Meanwhile post-war British urban sociological studies concentrated mainly on working-class areas, for example, producing studies of deviants within the 'criminal area' of the inner city, in the genre of the Chicago School (e.g. Morris 1958). Such studies were extremely moralistic towards working-class young women. They tended to blame male juvenile delinquency on the mother's influence and perceived lack of responsibility. Identifying the inner city as a place of danger and conflict (Lawless 1989) created a threatening 'macho' image of the inner city, although over 54 per cent of inner-urban dwellers are women. Studies of race tended to concentrate upon black 'men', whilst studies of crime and deviance often seemed to have more interest in, even admiration for, the aggressors, usually young males, than in the victims who are usually women, children and the elderly. Children, especially toddlers and girls, were another 'minority' whose experiences of the built environment were often neglected, presumably because unlike some teenagers and male 'youth' they were not seen as a threat or as likely to cause trouble (Adams and Ingham 1998).

As explained in Chapter 8, the coming of neo-Marxist theory in the 1970s changed the nature of both planning and urban sociology. Traditional spatial and area-based considerations were supplanted by a new 'intellectual' interest in high-level structural theories of the city. The emphasis on impersonal macro-sociological forces in neo-Marxian sociology, combined with an occasional reference to an abstract working class, often gave the impression that there was no place for real people as individuals and families within the new urban theories. The urban sociologist Castells gave the impression that he saw the city as nothing more than 'a unit of labour power' (Castells 1977); not as consisting of the homes and lives of the inhabitants. In these debates the place of women was somewhat ambiguous, as they were neither 'land' nor 'society', and therefore invisible and irrelevant. Sometimes it seems in the literature that they are 'land' as the suburban housewife seems to be plumbed into the house along with the washing machine in much neo-Marxian theory on housing classes (cf. Bassett and Short 1980). But, there seemed to be little awareness of the lives or types of real women in terms of age, class, personal characteristics and planning needs (Photo 15.2).

It was considered bourgeois and trivial to raise community issues in this setting, let alone to

Photo 15.2   Women walking through the arcade of life

Will the future be sustainable for the next generation of young women in terms of equal opportunities? What are the implications for women in particular of current government cutbacks, unemployment and tax benefit changes?

mention 'women', with the prevailing emphasis being on political ideas, even revolution, rather than on individual people. There was considerable animosity from the male Left towards feminism in the 1960s, and women were likely to be told that they were 'selfish' and should be concerned with more 'serious' issues, such as male employment. If women workers complained about their needs being marginalised they were likely to be told to '*wait until after the Revolution*' or to '*go and make the tea*'.

Pioneer women who went into town planning in the 1960s and 1970s reported high levels of hostility, sexual harassment and open aggression (Greed 1994a). They were certainly not made welcome or seen as valuable people who had a unique insight to offer on how women in the community experienced the built environment. Ethnic minority planners – some of whom were women – experienced similar problems. However, gradually greater tolerance was being given to the needs of so-called minorities and equal opportunities policies were beginning to take effect; even in town planning departments (Reeves 2005; CIC 2009).

In due course (as explained in the last chapter), neo-Marxist theory put a greater emphasis on consumption, albeit defined in 'male' terms (Saunders 1985, 85). This opened the way for women to redirect attention the within urban politics to the significance of the domestic realm and the residential area, and to redefine production and consumption and their interrelationship from a feminist perspective (McDowell and Peake 1990; Little *et al.* 1988, ch. 2). It could be argued that men were only catching up with women urban sociologists such as Cockburn (1977) who had already produced a key book on the importance of community politics. Jane Jacobs had also raised many of the issues of concern to ordinary New Yorkers, including women, who were seeing their traditional neighbourhoods destroyed in the name of progress; but she was actually a journalist and not a self-avowed feminist writer (Jacobs 1964). Some would suggest that the second wave of urban feminism had grown as an offshoot from the radical politics of the 1960s and early 1970s, urban feminist theory being seen as a subset of post-Marxian theory. But much more of the impetus for change came from ordinary women who had been involved in various grass-roots community groups fighting the planners; some being concerned with design issues related to their traditional role as carers of children. As more women students entered higher education in the 1960s onwards they could not help but question much of what they were being taught in planning schools, and seek out material on 'women and planning'.

North American women architects and sociologists had not entirely lost the heritage of first-wave urban feminism (Jacobs 1964). A series of valuable books from North America dealing with a wide range of urban feminist issues, past and present, were appearing (including Hayden 1981 and Stimpson *et al.* 1981), which appear remarkably up to date in addressing still unresolved issues. Urban feminist studies were developing internationally, the ideas and current literature of British feminist geography being encapsulated in the work of the Women and Geography study group (McDowell 1983; WGSG 1984, 1997). A Canadian periodical entitled *Women and Environments* was established in the 1970s and is still going strong (WE 1999). Feminist academics were producing their own community studies of the inner city to rival some of the earlier male classics. For example, Campbell's study of working-class girls (Campbell 1984) made the link strongly between class, location and gender. Elaine Morgan's book (1974) may be seen as one of the first attempts in Britain to look at urban issues from the 'new' feminist perspective, followed by many others (Greed 1994a).

Many more women were entering professional and business areas in the 1980s (Spencer and Podmore 1980; Greed 1994a). This was to have an impact on the nature of professional practice and policy priorities. Concerns have been expressed both about 'women in planning' – that is women as fellow professionals; and 'women and planning' – that is the question of how to plan in a way that takes into account the needs of women in our towns and cities, as well as accommodating the needs of men. It would seem that ethnicity, and disability to some extent, were stronger initially than gender as factors which legitimated the need for the development of 'special' urban policies for groups who are seen as different. The issue of 'Equal Opportunities' was gaining prominence amongst local authorities, affecting their role as employers and policy-makers, especially in London. In spite of this apparent progress, black women urban feminists have pointed out that they are often squeezed out of the debate, commenting that many white people still assume that (as the saying goes) '*all black people are men, and all women are white*' (Mirza 1997), in theory at least. This is the very type of issue that policies based on 'interesectionality' theory have sought to address (in which a person can be many things at once, Cooper 2008;

Bagilhole 2009). Significantly 'intersectionality' was first developed as a concept by a black woman lawyer who experienced the overlap of different types of discrimination in her life (Crenshaw 1991). It is illegal to discriminate against people in the provision of public services on the basis of race (originally Section 20 of the Race Relations Act 1976, now found under the 2010 Equality Act). But research has shown that discrimination continues to exist (see De Graft-Johnson 1999, and as discussed further in the next chapter).

By the early 1980s, the women and planning movement was emerging more visibly (Foulsham 1990). This trend was greeted with complete misunderstanding by many men planners and surveyors, who made comments like, '*Women? That's not a land use issue*' and therefore were of the view that women's issues were *ultra vires*, that is outside the scope of planning law. Meanwhile the progressive Greater London Council (GLC) women's committee was producing a series of Women and Planning reports including the most comprehensive, *Changing Places* (GLC 1986). Women's committees were beginning to have a major influence in several cities in getting things done (J. Taylor 1990). 'Women and the Built Environment' became a fashionable topic and several of the main journals devoted a 'special' issue to the topic (IJURR 1978; Built Environment 1984 and again in 1996; Ekistics 1985; TCPA 1987). By the late 1980s a series of conferences were held, and working parties were established by the various built environment professional bodies, looking at women's needs as fellow professionals, as clients, and members of urban society. Some women set up in practice on their own or in groups. Matrix (1984), an all-women collective of architects, built, for example, the Jagonari Asian Women's Centre in Whitechapel, London. The Women's Design Service produced many reports (as listed on book's website) on all sorts of 'women and planning' matters, and comprised women architects, planners and surveyors, acting as both a consultancy service and pressure group.

The RTPI produced a Practice Advice Note (PAN) on 'Planning for Women', (RTPI 1995; Reeves 1996) which was circulated to all members. Subsequently a series of guidance documents and 'toolkits' were produced on 'mainstreaming' gender

issues into planning (RTPI 2003; RTPI 2007), along with a growing range of research projects and publications (Reeves 2005; Greed 2005a, 2005b). Much work was also achieved by the WGSG, that is the Women and Geography Study Group of the Royal Geographical Society (McDowell and Sharp (eds) 1997; Panelli 2004; Jarvis *et al*. 2009). There was also a strong international contribution on gender, especially on how to mainstream gender into global urbanisation policies, under the auspices of international organisations including the United Nations, Habitat and the Commonwealth (Reeves 2012). Whilst gender was high priority, 'women and geography' publications were more likely to link gender issues to environmental, European and disability issues, as well as sexuality, age and religion too, as the diversity agenda took hold. Indeed in recent years 'social geography' has strongly influenced planning education and, to a lesser extent, policy. In fact the whole field became a veritable growth industry, but whether all this actually changed the nature of town planning policy and urban form is another matter.

Women and land-use patterns

The context

The purpose of this section is to reconsider the development of the main land uses in cities from a 'women and planning' perspective and to suggest future trends and alternatives. Whilst much of 'women's planning' seems to be preoccupied with traditional women's issues such as childcare facilities, or with the problems of 'safety' and local design principles, to plan effectively for women would in the long run require the restructuring of our cities at the macro, city-wide, development plan level, in order to realign the relationships between the different land uses, and to introduce major changes in transportation systems.

Many of the problems women face in modern cities is a result of planners imposing strict zoning principles upon our towns and cities (as first mentioned in Part II on the history of planning). Planning theorists such as Geddes, Abercrombie and Le Corbusier saw the main components of the city as consisting of 'home areas, work areas, and leisure areas' (home, work, play) (Greed, 1994a). The division of cities into distinct home and work zones still continues today, in spite of demands for more sustainable mixed-use policies and more flexible urban regeneration schemes. Many women would argue that the division of work and home is meaningless for them, because it makes the fundamental mistake in equating work with what is done outside the home, and ignores all the 'home-making' and child-care work which occurs inside the home and the local neighbourhood. Also if 'play' and leisure are mainly defined in terms of playing fields and predominantly male sports facilities, there is little space for women or for that matter for children. Indeed, children, especially small children, are often seen as another overlooked 'invisible' group in planning (Adams and Ingham 1998; Gleeson and Sipe 2006).

This disregarded the fact that increasingly women were adopting two roles, that of home-maker and also worker; over 70 per cent of women with children work outside the home. From this attitude flows a whole series of flawed approaches to town planning. It seemed logical to planners to further encourage the separation of work and home by means of land-use zoning, which was meant to lead to greater efficiency, and less pollution from a public health viewpoint.

The separation of work and home, and the associated separation of business-related land uses and facilities from domestic work-related land uses such as food shops, schools and community facilities, increased the travel burden of women, the very ones who are far less likely to have access to a car in the daytime. To compound the problem, much transportation planning was based on the assumption that the 'journey to work' in the rush hour by car was the main category of journey in the urban area. In reality in some areas the majority of journeys are undertaken by women, at times spread throughout the day, and chiefly by public transport, and (of necessity) by walking, as shown in a survey undertaken by the GLC in London (GLC 1983) *On the Move* and this work on women and transport has been much developed subsequently (Hamilton *et al.* 2005; Uteng and Cresswell (eds) 2008). In the following sections the story of modern planning will be reappraised from a gender perspective, with reference to residential, employment and leisure activities, with frequent mention of the effects of zoning and the need for transport to join all the land uses together in a way that meets women's needs as well as men's.

Residential areas

The interwar period was characterised by the growth of mono-land-use suburban housing estates at relatively low density, consisting of both speculative private estates for the new middle classes and decentralised council housing estates. There was a preference for green-field sites, where land was cheaper. There was still quite an extensive system of public transport and urban life seemed to be more geared to the fact that few people had car. Transport was mainly by public bus, trams, cycles and suburban railways, and relatively speaking people without cars were better served then than they are today. Many food supplies were still delivered to the home by the butcher, baker and greengrocer, whereas all we have is home deliveries of milk and dairy goods. There was a greater level of provision and distribution of local shopping parades and other community buildings within the new housing estates: often built by the builder himself to attract buyers.

In the immediate post-war reconstruction period local authorities continued the building tradition of low-rise houses, in the form of dispersed council estates often miles from anywhere. Many housewives preferred the 'pre-fabs' (that is emergency housing built on a temporary basis, near existing centres on bomb-site land (see Chapter 6)). Inside they had all the 'mod cons' (modern conveniences) such as fitted cupboards and modern kitchen equipment. By the 1950s private house-building was back in business and many people aspired to own their own house. The building societies played a major role in offering finance and in perpetuating the 'image' of a home of your own, with publicity aimed at the 'breadwinner', encouraging the concept that 'an Englishman's home is his castle'. However, few wives really 'owned' their own houses jointly, as was to become painfully evident when the new, more liberal matrimonial laws in the 1960s led to a growth in the divorce rate and subsequently more 'homeless' wives and single parent families resulted. It was not until the 1980s that women began to 'be allowed' by building societies to get mortgages in their own right, and even then single women and wives in their own right found limitations. Even relatively well-off, single, working women had to rent. The housing stock and planning policy was not suited to providing for such groups, nor for the post-war growth of single young people seeking houses.

The quality of accessibility and transport to suburban areas, and within cities, was declining for those without cars in the 1960s because of the overemphasis by the planners on the motorcar. There were railway cutbacks on urban branch lines and rural routes, just at the time when outer suburban residential estates were growing. The growth of new large supermarket chains were putting smaller local shops out of business and making it more difficult for people without cars to shop locally (Bowlby 1989). There were other insidious trends towards greater efficiency (for whom?) in the siting and concentration of new health, school and social services facilities. The age of the out-of-town comprehensive school campus and hospital complex had arrived. Car drivers might want towns to be quite spread out with a high level of provision of roads, car parks and out-of-town centres, but pedestrians, and those dependent on public transport, might prefer their town to be close-knit with everything close together, and within easy walking distance. Again, it comes back to the question, 'How do you want to live?' (DoE 1972b). As public transport declined and essential social facilities became more decentralised, more people got cars until it no longer was considered economic to provide services or shops at the local community level. There was much criticism from consumer and women's groups and (even before the rise of 'feminism') in the 1960s about the fact that the planners gave planning permission for new developments with little consideration of how people would get to and from them. Many women did not have cars and far more women than men walked and undertook short local journeys to the shops, school and local facilities such as the post office, but, as mentioned in the transport chapter, 'walking' was not even counted as a means of transport in the 1960s and for that matter long after in many local planning authorities.

Many propose that because many land uses are far less 'noxious' in terms of pollution, and more compatible than they used to be, the arguments behind separating the land uses are out of date. Office development in particular could easily be decentralised back into the residential environment. The decentralisation of shopping and other community facilities to out-of-town locations reflects outdated land-use ideas about 'thinning out' cities and reducing congestion. Therefore, it is not surprising that many women planners press for strong policy statements on the provision of local shops at the local residential area level, and greater controls on out-of-town shopping centres, and a revitalisation of the food shopping component of central business area retail units for women office workers who can only shop in the lunch hour.

The move towards extensive apartment-building on brown-field sites around city centres has provided little suitable housing for families, mainly meeting the needs of young single males working in business and finance. Such properties are expensive and owner-occupied but they have many of the same problems that past, council blocks of flats manifested in terms of practicalities for families. The 1960s was marked by the relatively short but disastrous phase of the high-rise movement, which was far worse than traditional housing, although some estates were more central. Women, especially those with children, do not like high-rise blocks, or the small size of rooms in such schemes. If the flat is away from the ground floor all sorts of problems as to supervision of children, disposal of rubbish, finding safe storage space and drying washing arise. Many women architects and planners have suggested really quite simple solutions, such as increasing the level of lighting, improving visibility, etc., would help a great deal. Most important of all, listening to the people who actually live in the flats and who on a daily basis encounter all the 'little' problems and acting on their advice would solve some of the problems without creating the need for major upheavals. As with horizontal housing estates, many women are still concerned about the mono-use of the blocks, as well their condition.

To his credit, Le Corbusier originally designed in his *Unité d'Habitation* block, an integral play area, community and nursery rooms. It is not uncommon in other countries to find communal lounges, hobbies rooms, and launderettes integrated within the scheme. In North America there are quite upmarket residential high-rise blocks which often incorporate restaurants, sports facilities and child-care facilities for the residents, particularly in private-sector condominiums. There really is no point in piling people up together if there are no practical community facilities and nowhere for them to meet. Many women favour the addition of more caretakers and security staff, and a *concierge* system such as exists in France, including someone who can take in their parcels, keep an eye on the place, and screen visitors as is common in France. Some women would like to see more communal facilities within low-rise housing estates too. For example, the designation of, say, every house in 20 as a commu-nity area with a built-in crèche, and community centre, would be very useful. Dolores Hayden in her book *Redesigning the American Dream* (Hayden 2002, first published 1982) shows ways of converting exist-ing estates in this way. However as Roberts (1991) explains in her book on London County Council blocks, policies to meet the needs of women should not 'just' comprise policies about childcare and homemaking. These activities are likely to take up only a limited number of years until the children have left home. Rather 'women and planning' poli-cies should be concerned with the outside world of work, travel, safety and the environment too. These problems continue to today, still unresolved (Madariaga and Roberts (eds) 2013).

The development of the new towns has also been much commented upon from a 'women and plan-ning' perspective, especially in Scotland (Morris 1986). There are many problems associated with the concept of the 'neighbourhood'. It is based on the assumption that it is chiefly a women's zone, sepa-rated from the 'real' world of work into a world of community and children, in which men, who are presumably away at work, have little involvement in the daytime. In fact many of the women in new towns work, as cheap female labour was one of the factors which attracted light engineering and assem-bly industries to them. Whilst the planners might put the shops and school in close proximity within the neighbourhood, they were likely to put the factories outside it, creating major transport prob-lems, and much rushing to and fro between the different land uses (Attfield 1989).

The safety of the neighbourhood concept and the separation of pedestrian footpaths from main roads has been much criticised. For example, in Milton Keynes it was found that many women were unwill-ing to use the footpaths and cycle paths in the evening (Deem 1986). Many of the footpaths were designed in such a meandering manner that people made their own short cuts, or risked straying onto busy main roads. Many women prefer straight foot-paths, with good visibility on all sides, preferably in full view of houses and other buildings. This prob-lem is not just a characteristic of the new towns, but a feature of many design guides (Chapter 13). In their desire to create an interesting townscape, architects and planners unintentionally created a threatening environment for women, with blind corners, narrow alley ways, footpaths away from the houses, pedestrian underpasses (Photo 15.3), poorly lit back routes, and 'varied textures' of paved surfaces which ruin women's shoes and make the manoeuvre of pushchairs and wheelchairs hard going.

As described in Part II (history of planning), there was a gradual move away from the emphasis on new development, towards inner-city regeneration and urban conservation. Indeed regeneration, gentrifica-tion and sustainability have been continuing themes for over 30 years now, but seldom are these factors viewed from a gender perspective. Many women consider that recent attempts to make the city more sustainable by restricting traffic flow and reducing access to town centres are ill-thought-out as they lack a gender perspective and therefore discriminate against women, who are the ones most likely to have to use town centre shopping facilities. There is much need for further research on the gender aspects of the sustainability movement in respect of every aspect, including transport policy, waste disposal, shopping, cycling and house design (Oates and McDonald 2006). The whole sustainability move-ment requires critical analysis from a gender perspective, and is not so 'holy' that it is above analy-sis (Greed 2011a, 2011b). Many people are not free agents to change their transport patterns or mode. Many working-class families were moved out over the years into distant council estates, as working-class neighbourhoods were cleared or gentrified. Those who try to combine their work and caring duties without the use of a car find great difficulties

Photo 15.3   A typical, frightening pedestrian underpass

Although attitudes to urban design are now more enlightened and user-aware, still there is a vast backlog of dangerous underpasses, inaccessible pedestrian routeways and a generally depressing, poorly designed street environment.

because of poor public transport provision and employment opportunities being located a long commute away from home. An address in a 'bad' estate can reduce their chances of employment in the local area because of the alleged reputation of its residents, even if they are not individually the perpetrators of the activities that gave it a bad name in the first place (and of course this applies to the men too).

Employment areas

In discussing the issues of employment, both in respect of industry and office development, the illogicality for women of the separation of work and home becomes apparent. Yet this division is reinforced through zoning and a whole range of other public health, building, and office- and factory-related legislation. Large numbers of women work in the retail industry, although they are often marginalised in the debates, or their work is relegated to the realms of leisure for 'pin money' (for extras and fripperies, not necessities), although they may stand up for eight hours a day and work very hard. Many women work in factories, in routine office jobs and in (telephone) call centres. But they have frequently been excluded from the official figures and from the image of the working class in sociological literature. The post-war trend in town planning, towards both rezoning and decentralisation of industry on to green-field sites, created major problems for working women. This trend continues today as industry seeks to locate near motorway intersections on the edges of urban areas, and affects both upmarket high-tech science parks and more mundane light engineering and warehousing facilities.

Women office workers have constituted the largest single employment group in Britain in recent years, whilst jobs involving caring and cleaning are not far behind (Crompton and Sanderson 1990; Bilton *et al*. 2002). Women also comprise the majority of workers in the care industry, in cleaning, and in health work, which together comprise a set of industries with a larger workforce than manufacturing. Of course, social class is at work here too, as not all women are the same by any means. For example, 10 per cent of households employ cleaners, and many professional women employ nannies and other 'help' to solve their own childcare problems. Are the planners planning for the workforce on the basis of outdated stereotypes? And how does this affect transport policy, land-use and location decisions, and the level of accessibility to the built environment planned into new developments? Many women are concerned about the changes which are occurring in the nature of office work, especially its proletarianisation because of technological change. There has been an increase in the number of work-related illnesses and disabilities associated with computer use and with the pressures of call centres and data-inputting activities.

The separation of work and home creates major problems for women with children; indeed the whole ethos of the business world is unwelcoming to them. Much transport policy is still based upon 'the journey to work' which is assumed to be by car, an uninterrupted journey from home to work. But women workers often undertake intermittent, broken journeys, rather than radial journeys straight to and from the city centre. Such journeys are often undertaken outside the rush hour if they work part-time. For example, a woman's daily journeys might be as follows; home → school → work → shops → school → home, and may not necessarily be by car. Those women who work full-time and have cars are likely to break their journeys in a similar manner, and have to contend more with the pressures of achieving it all within the rush hour. Thus women trip-chain their journeys. In doing so they are actually being efficient and reducing their carbon footprint. Many women's journeys by car are not for their own benefit but they act effectively as public transport (where there is none) for members of their family too young or too old to drive as they ferry them to school, youth clubs, community centres, doctor's appointments and so forth, trip-chaining as

they go (Rosenbloom 1989; Darke *et al*. 2000; Uteng and Cresswell 2008; Hamilton 2000). Particular condemnation is levelled at the school run with the stereotype of rich mothers dropping their children off from their Range Rovers each morning. But only 8 per cent of women use their cars to participate in the school run, and over 70 per cent of all car journeys are still made by men. In fact many women have extreme difficulty getting their children to school and then themselves to work in the short time available in the morning rush hour (Coleman 2000; Hamilton *et al*. 2005). Additional concerns with both road safety and personal safety confront those women and their children who choose to walk or cycle instead (WDS 2005; Whitzman 2009, 2012), whereas travelling on public transport with a pushchair or small children can be extremely challenging (Lenclos 2002).

But what do women want instead? As an alternative to spread out, zoned, low-density cities, many women planners would like to see 'the city of everyday life', which they define as the city of short distances, mixed land uses and multiple centres as the ideal objective that would fully take into account gender considerations. Such a city structure would benefit all social groups, reduce the need to travel, and create more sustainable cities, that would be more accessible, whilst creating a higher quality of urban environment for all. It would provide more jobs and facilities locally and help revitalise declining areas overall (Skjerve 1993; Eurofem 1998).

Of course the problem is not just one of planning, although it is a major contributor, but the way society is organised as a whole. Many women experience problems because of lack of childcare, or simply in juggling office hours with school hours, and food shopping trips. Although on average 60 per cent of all workers in offices are women, and 80 per cent of all workers in the central area, including shop workers, are women, there is very little provision of childcare either in the office buildings themselves or out in the central business district. Many women planners argue there is a need for more childcare spaces than car parking spaces. A whole series of other policies would flow from this reallocation of space, further integrating work and home, and inevitably other land uses and facilities would gradually shift and realign in relation to this.

But the central business district and its offices may be doomed for the future, as more offices decentralise, and central areas become more congested and inconvenient. Increasingly business activity and routine office work is undertaken on the web. Many routine office functions have been computerised or even relocated to call centres overseas. Whilst the traditional argument still holds good that there has to be face-to-face contact in business, this only holds true for more senior people. In the future the trend may be to keep a central area headquarters but to decentralise office accommodation elsewhere, and this would be an ideal moment to suggest that it should be moved into the suburbs, rather than into the green-field out-of-town sites which are difficult to reach for those without transport and miles away from shops, schools and other facilities (Reeds 2011; Kunstler 1993). On the other hand, remote working may lead to the unification of work and home again as people work at home on their computers. But if this is going to become a more established 'mass' trend, then house design needs to be reconceptualised with more room for the 'home office'.

Retail development areas are both work areas to large numbers of women and essential areas to carry out shopping. But planners and developers often give the impression they see shopping as fun and leisure, and have little idea of the difficulties and time pressures which women operate under. The famous Lewis Mumford (1965) in his epic work on the development of the city in history, made much of the importance of man the noble hunter and food-gatherer at the dawn of history. The same Mumford, in another setting, had said, 'the daily marketing (shopping) is all part of the fun' (Mumford, 1930s) when commenting on women undertaking the same process of food-hunting and gathering in modern towns. It is now popular to put leisure facilities beside out-of-town shopping centres such as the Wonderworld at Merry Hill in Dudley, and Bluewater near Dartford, London. Although between 80 per cent of customers are likely to be female, still there has been little acknowledgement of the gender dimension of retail provision. In contrast, retail developers give considerable attention to the social class and disposable income of the catchment area population. Shopping policy has been bedevilled by the enthusiasm amongst planners for retail gravity models which have emphasised quantitative factors, such as the attraction of large centres to the car-borne shopper, as against qualitative factors, such as accessibility and provision of facilities such as public toilets, which may be a greater 'attraction' factor for women with small children and the disabled, whatever their social class or income level (Greed 2003b). Those shopping malls that are both centrally located within existing city centres, and provide good toilets, baby-care and access facilities, such as the Westfield centres in London, St David's Centre in Cardiff and Cabot Circus in Bristol, are increasingly more attractive to many shoppers than out-of-town solutions. In spite of the growth of online internet shopping, most shopping is still undertaken in the traditional way as people still seem to prefer actually seeing what they are buying, and having the opportunity to go out and see the shops. However, given the lack of public transport, poor parking, poor public toilets, lack of baby-care facilities and inaccessible built environment, many women with young families find internet shopping and home delivery more practical and less time-wasting. Cities need to be more welcoming and accessible for women, especially those with young families, and they need to be more 'legible' in terms of signage, so people know what is available and where it can be found, be it toilets, parking, disabled facilities, particular types of shops and social amenities.

To digress, the issue of public conveniences is another national problem. As long ago explained in the report *At your Convenience* (WDS 1990), facilities for women and children are underprovided for; in fact men have three times the amount of provision compared with women, according to an official survey of London (WDS 1990; Greed 2003b). Forty per cent of all public toilets have been closed in the last ten years, mainly because of government cutbacks as there is no statutory requirement for local authorities to provide them. Many men planners do not see this as a problem as they can always use a pub or club, and are unlikely to have childcare responsibilities. Subsequently greater attention was given to public toilet research as this is a matter that affects all women, and is one of the last frontiers of gender inequality within the built environment

(Greed 2003b). Research has continued to argue for increased toilet provision for women, not least to reduce the queues for the loo (Gershenson and Penner (eds) 2009; Penner 2013), as well as introducing the importance of a diversity and equality perspective to the topic which limits people's 'right to the city' (Molotch and Noren (eds) 2010; Cavanagh 2010). Likewise facilities are still very poor for those with disabilities and limit people's access to the city (Goldsmith 2000; Hanson *et al.* 2007), whilst the elderly may limit their travel because of lack of toilet provision (Age UK 2009). Indeed French urbanist academics have sought to apply Lefebvre's concept of 'the right to the city' to the issue of the effects of adequate toilet provision in French cities (Damon 2009) (as discussed towards the end of Chapter 8).

Leisure and play

There has been relatively little specific consideration of women's leisure needs in contrast to the immense amounts of land, money and effort which have been devoted to playing fields and sports centres primarily used by men, with considerable emphasis on football. Women's needs tend to get subsumed under the needs of their children for 'play areas'. Likewise the elderly may find a lack of quiet spaces to sit and may even be fearful of going outdoors (I'DGO 2009; Talen 2006, 2008). Provision specifically designed by men planners for 'women and children' have come in for much criticism from women planners. The fixation with providing generalised grassed open space and 'playing' fields for, apparently, the needs of all age groups and types of people, within both old and new neighbourhoods, has been questioned for many years (Jacobs 1964). The problems of 'open space as unpaid childminder' reflect deeper problems in society itself, in that Britain has one of the lowest levels of childcare provision in Europe. It also has a relatively small number of women in senior planning positions, unlike, for example, in Scandinavia.

Town and country planning has always been imbued with a reverence for the importance of lots of grass and trees to improve areas. Some local authorities have painted the walls of flats in problem estates green, presumably because of its associations with the countryside. It is often assumed that 'streets' are bad and 'open space' is good for children's play. In fact unless open space areas are adequately supervised they can rapidly become vandalised, and the potential location, or 'turf', of gangs of youths and dogs terrorising the smaller children. The provision of children's play areas, or even play streets within housing estates, can cause problems. It assumes that the mothers and other residents have little to do but 'keep an eye on the children'. Some planning guides suggest that kitchen windows should overlook the street or play area for this purpose. It takes no account of the noise and disruption that children make, which might be disturbing to people seeking to work at home. It is still assumed that childcare is a woman's job as the mother in the home – although most women work, whilst men who are parents and fathers too do not appear to see it as their problem.

To solve some of these problems many women planners suggest that what is needed is clearer definitions of different types of open space with different uses, and more supervision. Traditional parks with keepers and a range of activities within them are more useful than vague windswept unsupervised areas. Many would like to see better back-up facilities, such as public conveniences and distinct supervised safe play areas (WDS 1990), with suitable safe surfaces, instead of hard asphalt around the play equipment, or muddy grass. What are the open space needs of women themselves, assuming only some of them want 6 acres of playing field per thousand population? First, most women, most of the time are not accompanied by children, and those with dependent children are only a relatively small proportion of the female population. Many women on their own are very wary of public open space, but still welcome the existence of parks and green areas. However, in any landscaping or park scheme attention should be paid to security and surveillance factors. For example, the use of open railings rather than hedges around inner-city park areas enables women to see what they are walking into, whilst cities should be well signposted for pedestrians so people can easily 'read' their environment. Public conveniences and seating areas should be prominently positioned, not hidden behind bushes, and well signposted (Photo 15.4). Sports facilities should

Photo 15.4 The importance of signposts

It is important to have signposts in your own language, so that people know where facilities are located and how to get to them. This is as true 'physically' in terms of negotiating the city, as it is 'socially' in terms of knowing your way around the human rights and equality legislation and understanding what the information says.

provide crèches, and playing fields should be equipped with adequate changing facilities for women as well as men, although the 'sports pavilion' is usually seen as male territory. Many women feel intimidated by the 'Body Beautiful' image of the new leisure centres, or may have modesty, religious and ethnicity-related objections to mixed facilities, especially mixed swimming pools (Aitchison 2006; Al Sayyad and Massoumi 2010). It is not enough to say the facilities are there for everyone if they want to use them; careful programming and organisation of facilities is needed to cater for women as well as men.

Research has shown that younger women, and for that matter ethnic minorities, are less likely to use open space in the countryside for leisure compared with men. But to create healthy cities and a healthy population there is a need to enable people to feel safe and welcome in different locations (Barton and Tsourou 2006). Arguably, there exists a rather macho youth culture in the world of rural planning, and rural estate management, in which the emphasis on rock climbing, adventure sports, and fell walking rather marginalises women, although some women do undertake such activities (Hall 2006). Policy attitudes often appear imbued with contempt for and disparagement of people in cars and the provision of tourist facilities for the urban masses. In fact many women who do visit the countryside do so in the family car, bringing their childcare responsibilities with them in the back seat! Elderly people too, in coaches and cars, may want to look at the countryside through the vehicle window but have no inclination to do a 20-mile walk, although in their youth they may have been hikers too. The needs of all groups need to be respected. Forty-five per cent of the athletes competing in the 2012 Olympics were women and a fairer amount of the television coverage showed them competing. However, fewer women than men were shown when it came to the Paralympics; for example, women 'blade-runners' were not given the same prominence as their male counterparts. But normally only 5 per cent of televised sport comprises women's sports, and less than 1 per cent of newspaper sports reportage (Aitchison 2006).

The problem of policy implementation

As can be seen, women's use of the built environment is different from that of men, because of different lifestyles, duties, daily activity, work and travel patterns; and because of a range of diverse cultural, class, ethnicity, disability and age characteristics too. In seeking to change the nature of the built environment, and the planning policies which shape it, minority groups have found the UK planning system somewhat unyielding. Research undertaken on the extent to which gender was being mainstreamed (that is integrated) into planning policy by different planning authorities resulted in a very patchy picture of good, bad and indifferent (Greed 2005a, 2005b, 2006a). Legally, town planning is strictly speaking to do with physical, spatial matters, not social issues. Any conditions put on a planning permission must be for a 'genuine planning reason' (Duxbury 2013; Moore and Purdue 2013). However, there have been instances of planning authorities putting conditions on planning permission to achieve provision for women. Such instances, although relatively minor, are precedents which further confirm the argument that women's issues are material considerations in the granting of the planning permission, and have been valid under guidance originally set by Circular 1985/1, 'The use of conditions in planning permissions'.

Development control planners also have sought to use planning gain through Section 106 Agreements (Chapter 3) to get additional community facilities as part of the development control process. But planning gain agreements must only be used for the purpose of 'restricting or regulating the development or use of land' and must be 'reasonable' (Circulars 22/83 and 16/91, and see PPG1: all of which are now cancelled and replaced by the NPPF). An additional problem is that even if the developers are willing to build social facilities, someone has got to pay for their maintenance and management. Local authorities cannot afford to pay for all this with government cutbacks. Yet, provided there are clear policy statements as to what is expected on a site written into the relevant statutory plan, developers will be reasonably expected to provide related social facilities in order to obtain planning permission, without the need for complex planning agreements. The Department of Communities and Local Government (DCLG) has, until recently, appeared to prefer this approach than leaving it to the ad hoc imposition of complicated 'conditions of permission' at the planning permission stage, or to complex 'planning agreements'.

Policy planners have sought to use development plan policies as a means of achieving greater provision for women. But many planning policies that might benefit women have been seen as too 'social' and therefore as *ultra vires* (outside the scope of planning law) in that they were seen as 'not a land-use matter'. It is argued that the provision of such facilities is a 'land-use' matter, as it affects the way people 'use land', affecting accessibility in the first place, and affecting the nature of development itself (Cullingworth and Nadin 2006; Ricketts and Field 2012). But, policy requirements for the provision of crèches, toilets, baby-changing facilities, and other such social facilities as part of a development were likely to be seen as 'imposing quotas' and setting detailed space standard requirements which were not seen as being appropriate at the development plan level. Reeves identifies this as the 'strategic filter' problem, in that many women's policy requirements are seen as too detailed for the development plan level, but if they are not included at that level, they are 'filtered out' at the local plan level because there is no mention of them at the higher policy level (Reeves 2002).

London planning authorities, however, have always been more successful in these matters. Many of the London Borough Unitary Development Plans (UDPs) have contained 'women's policies' either within the main policy sections or as a separate chap-tcr in thcir Written Statement. Many of these were based upon the model Chapter VI of *Planning for Equality: Women in London* of the Greater London Development Plan (GLC 1984). Other London boroughs have threaded women's issues through the whole UDP document, adding relevant sections to each subject chapter. As accepted and approved policy, these 'women and planning' statements have the force of law when determining the planning application, but they have to be durable enough to stand up to a planning appeal, the fact they are 'good' is not enough. Subsequently the GLC was replaced by the Greater London Authority (GLA), which has continued the tradition of including gender issues in many of its documents. The GLA have the great advantage that they can include virtually any policy in their Supplementary Planning Guidance Documentation and as this receives approval under the unique powers of the Mayor in the London Assembly it can be taken as accepted planning policy. Thus the GLA incorporated many Equality and Diversity requirements into the London Mayor's Supplementary Guidance for the current London Strategic Development Plan (GLA 2007) and this trend seems to be continuing under subsequent updates under 'Boris' the Mayor of London. The situation in the UK, especially in London, is no doubt affected by wider European influences and linkages. Inspiration and examples from other EU countries where gender is taken into account more fully in the plan-making process are key in generating change (Madariaga and Roberts (eds) 2013).

A fundamental problem is that women's needs do not fit into the existing classifications of land use and development as embodied in planning law and development plans; although crèches for example now fall into Use D2. This use class covers non-residential institutions and inappropriately includes day nurseries and day centres, as well as museums and libraries. Some saw crèches as a potential element in the mixed B1 ('Business Use Class' (1995 Use Classes Order)) (Moore and Purdue 2006). Permission is not normally needed for the use by a householder of a room within a domestic house for childminding unless the use becomes dominant or intrusive. There has been no Circular or White Paper which specifically gives guidance on gender issues in town planning, and those which give indirect support are now somewhat dated. For example, Circular 22/84 (updated by PPG12, but now cancelled) stated that the unitary development plan system will 'provide authorities with positive opportunities to reassess the needs of their areas, resolve conflicting demands, and consider new ideas and bring forward appropriate solutions'. Many argue that 'women' *is* a material consideration in planning, because women and men use space in different ways (J. Taylor 1990: 98).

But in 2011 the clock was set back to zero. There is no mention of gender, or for that matter other minority issues, in the NPPF, which replaces existing guidance. Most of the existing PPGs and PPSs that have been used as a basis for including social considerations and minority needs in planning have now been cancelled. Complex planning gain agreements, and the negotiation of 'planning conditions', are to be replaced by a clearer, more open tariff system, through the application of the CIL (Community Infrastructure Levy) and other new measures introduced by the Coalition under the 2011 Localism Act, with little room for manoeuvre or the inclusion of non-developmental matters. The new planning system (Chapter 2) puts considerable emphasis upon the needs of the community and the importance of planning at neighbourhood level, but whether this will benefit women and for that matter other minority groups is yet to be seen. But the emphasis on speeding up the planning system and reducing imagined unnecessary restrictions does not bode well for anyone whose needs do not fit easily into this new streamlined system.

Currently, owing to local government cutbacks, public toilets and other local facilities such as libraries, respite care centres, and childcare facilities, are being closed across the country. But, as stated in Chapter 2, under the new localism regime, local communities are meant to be getting more powers to take over and run such facilities. Facilities Audits are to be undertaken which identify those facilities and buildings which local people want to retain as community assets. They then have the right to bid for these assets should they be under threat of closure or demolition under the Localism Act 2011. Indeed the Act gives parish and town councils 'General Powers of Competency' to do all sorts of things now! But the reality is that they lack the financial resources to do so, indeed many parish councils and for that matter neighbourhood forums have next to no spare money and what they have is being spent on producing their Neighbourhood Plan. Furthermore, as stated in Chapter 2, the neighbourhood forums that are meant to represent the community at local level in non-parished areas are only required to contain 21 residents, who are meant to represent on average 5000–10,000 people per local area. The chances of such a small group representing the diversity and variety found in many urban areas is highly unlikely, whereas in the rural parishes there has been a long tradition of predominantly white, older, articulate middle-class people serving on committees. Whilst some of these members are women, and are very aware of the effects of local cutbacks, they are a relatively unrepresentative group. But, they are willing and able to give their time often because they are retired. Whilst their enthusiasm for public service should not be undervalued, greater financial support to individuals and minority organisations wanting to be involved in the plan-making councils and forums would enable a wider range of types of people to come forward, particularly in deprived urban areas.

To conclude, although there has been a great deal of research, publication and effort put into getting 'women and planning' issues recognised and implemented, there is not, as yet, a commensurate level of approval and implementation. The Royal Town Planning Institute, Code of Professional Conduct, makes it illegal to discriminate on the basis of race, sex, or creed, and religion. This code should govern the individual planner's conduct, and it should make it 'his' duty to take gender and other equality issues into account. But lack of training and awareness, and a tick-box approach to equality matters, means that little has changed (Greed 2006a). The situation is very variable between different areas, and, at the coal face of development control, in some local authorities 'women and planning' conditions on a planning permission go through without question, whereas in others they are overturned (Greed 2005a, 2005b). This again reflects an ad hoc approach brought about by lack of strong central government guidance. In the final analysis, what happens in a particular local authority depends on the willingness and perspective of the local planners as to whether they are cooperative or negative in their support of such issues. However, arguably, a range of equalities legislation, over and above planning law, should be facilitating change. But, as will be explained in the next chapter, 'gender', as a valid equality issue, has been rather swamped by a range of other equalities issues under modern diversity practice. Indeed the tide has turned so much that whereas 20 years ago equality issues were scarcely mentioned in planning departments, it was found from the research that some local authorities had over 30 equality factors to take into account. These included the main sectorial categories of race, gender and so forth, but in addition differences including those based on class, income, housing type, location, education, caring responsibilities, religion and so forth. Gender was generally fairly low on the pecking order, way below matters of ethnicity, disability and sexuality. But in real people's lives gender cross-cuts and overarches many of these factors, and is arguably still one of the key factors to take into account when 'planning for people'.

For the tasks, further reading, additional photos, other resources and a list of WDS publications for this chapter, please visit www.palgrave. com/companion/greed.

16 Planning and the Built Environment Professions

The context

Reflecting on the nature of planning and the planners

This book has investigated the nature of planning policy, theory and practice. The last two chapters have looked at the 'planned' through the lens of the social aspects of planning. In this final chapter we look more closely at the nature of the planners themselves. First, the town planning profession will be set within the context of the other built environment professions and the wider construction industry of which planning is arguably one part (CIB 1996; Dainty *et al.* 2007). Comparisons will be made with other built environment professions, and the nature of the professionals therein, including surveying, architecture and construction (CIC 2009; Dainty and Loosemore (ed.) 2012). We will then look at the nature and composition of the planning profession and highlight some of the changes taking place which are reshaping it. Thus, both quantitative contextualisation (statistics) and qualitative (sociological) discussion will be included. For example, the ways in which the equality and diversity agenda is impacting on the built environment professions will be outlined.

This leads us on to a discussion of the nature of the professional subculture of planning, as to who is seen as acceptable to be a planner and who is excluded. It is argued that the personal perspective and worldview of the planners themselves shapes planning policy, and influences what is considered important to policy-making and what is marginalised or invisible. As demonstrated in this book planners have often initially missed the boat in respect of major societal and policy trends, for example in respect of environmentalism, women's issues and a whole range of equality and diversity consider-ations. To illustrate this, we will discuss one topical issue, namely the planners' apparent lack of aware-ness of the growing importance of religion in soci-ety, as manifest in the lack of policy recognition, and in the problems planners have dealing with planning applications for mosques and mega-churches. In the concluding section, we briefly review each chapter, in order to identify what other significant unresolved issues confront the planners for the future.

The spectrum of built environment professions

Planning is one part of a much wider spectrum of construction and built environment professions, each with their own professional body. At the 'hard' end of the spectrum are found the specialisms of construction, civil engineering and building site activities. The professional bodies associated with these include the various chartered engineering bodies such as the Institute of Civil Engineers (ICE) and the Chartered Institute of Building (CIOB). At the 'softer' end of the spectrum one finds profession-als involved in urban design, architecture, housing management, urban policy and research, and town planning, which are represented by bodies including the Royal Institution of British Architects (RIBA), the Chartered Institute of Housing (CIH) and of course the RTPI itself. There are also quasi-profes-sional academic groups and learned associations, of relevance to planning, which are concerned with urban sociology, social policy and urban renewal, who may be members of the British Sociological Association (BSA) and the Royal Geographical Society (RGS). Many academics study planning and urban issues but they are not necessarily planners as such and may not want to be so, but they do contribute to planning theory and knowledge.

In the middle ground of the spectrum one finds a range of other professional groups concerned with the more commercial business side of property development, valuation, estate agency, estate management and property portfolio assembly. Many of these activities are undertaken by members of the Royal Institution of Chartered Surveyors (RICS). There is a range of other specialist bodies concerned with aspects of property, which overlap with the RICS, such as the National Association of Estate Agents (NAEA) with around 10,000 membership, of which 15 per cent are women, and the Institute of Revenues, Ratings and Valuation (IRRV) which has taken on a new lease of life since the Incorporated Society of Valuers and Auctioneers (ISVA) amalgamated with the RICS.

There are many specialists in other professions dealing with built environment issues such as some solicitors, that is members of the Law Society, and barristers who specialise in town planning law within private practice (Ricketts and Field 2012). Interestingly both property law and planning law are attracting many women, whilst women now make up over 50 per cent of new solicitors. In the wider development process itself, there are many other professionals involved, such as accountants, economists and financial analysts concerned with the viability of the development. Urban geographers, statisticians, economists and sociologists may be called upon to have an input to the development. But in the real world it may not really matter what particular body you belong to, but what your proven expertise comprises.

The Royal Institution of Chartered Surveyors is one of the largest built environment professional bodies. Its membership includes quantity surveyors, building surveyors, valuers, estate managers, covering both urban and rural practice, and also contains a section for those specialising in planning and development (which is actually larger than the RTPI itself). At the end of 2012, RICS membership comprised 113,605 male members and 14,834 female members worldwide. In contrast, the RTPI has a membership of around 22,955, of whom 66 per cent are male and 34 per cent female. Therefore there are actually more surveyor-planners than there are planner-planners because 'planning and development' is a major specialism within the RICS, albeit

they deal with planning mainly from a commercial perspective, being employed in the private sector. We will discuss the chartered surveyors again later in the chapter.

Thus the RTPI is a small but significant organisation which may be seen to inhabit the middle ground of the spectrum, with members working in both the public and private sector. Town planners only comprise 6 per cent of the total membership of the built environment professions, because there are so many more engineers and surveyors. Yet, the power of the planners is disproportionate to their numbers (Greed 1994a, 21; 2000), because of their regulatory powers and managerial role over the built environment, through the auspices of the local government system. But the surrounding influence of the other built environment professions and the wider construction industry, of which town planning is officially one small part (CISC 1994; CIB 1996; CIC 2009, 2010), cannot be underestimated. The influence of construction professionals goes way beyond individual building projects; they are among the 'great and the good' being called upon to shape the built environment, at macro and micro levels, in a variety of capacities, posts and committees. For example, civil engineers may be heads of town planning departments, transportation planners, and planning inspectors and because of their technical backgrounds be unaware of social and accessibility issues (Greed 1999a).

The composition of the built environment professions

Most of the construction professions and occupations are not attractive to women (Photo 16.1) (CIC 2009). They are heavily male-dominated and 'white' even at building site level although Eastern European immigration of skilled construction workers has created a greater element of cultural diversity, albeit more at the trades rather than professional level (Thiel 2012; EHRC 2011). Few women are found in the manual trades, technical and site-based areas of employment, and few at professional level in the more technical, engineering end of the spectrum. The Institution of Civil Engineers (ICE) has 82,000 members, of which around 6 per cent are female (or 9 per cent if you include student

Photo 16.1   The building site

Building sites still present a foreboding, dirty, unattractive image to people considering construction as a career. In reality much of the work of chartered built environment professionals is similar to that done by lawyers, accountants, managers and designers in other sectors of the economy.

members). The Structural Engineers have around 26,000 members, of which around 5 per cent are female. The CIBSE (Chartered Institute of Building Services Engineers) has a membership of 18,000, of which around a thousand are female. The CIOB (Chartered Institute of Building) has a membership of 45,000, of which 2500 are female. The RIBA has a membership of around 45,000 too, of whom around 25 per cent are female, and around 30 per cent of students are women. But the exact number of women architects actually in employment is more difficult to calculate; probably less than half of those who are qualified to do so (De Graft-Johnson *et al.* 2005, 2006). A source of all sorts of useful information, data and comment on inequality in the construction professions (including planning and

architecture) is to be found at the website, constructingequality.co.uk, which is linked to the work of the Diversity Committee of the CIC (Construction Industry Council) which represents all the chartered built environment professional bodies.

It is estimated that the percentage of women architects actually working in practice comes down to around 10 per cent, with few women in senior positions and virtually no women 'starchitects' (big names like Norman Foster, Richard Rogers or Le Corbusier) except for the famous Zaha Hadid (a British-Iranian architect who designed the Olympic Aquatics Centre and many other famous buildings). However, there have been some quite spectacular changes at the top of the built environment professions in recent years.

The RIBA have had two women architect presidents, Ruth Reed and Angela Brady. The RTPI had its first woman president, Sylvia Law, in 1974 and then Hazel McKie in 1994 and Janet O'Neill in 2009, followed by Anne Skippers in 2010 and Catherine Ranson in 2014 (and Janet Askew as Vice President). This shows considerable progress in that 2014 is also the 100th Anniversary of the founding of the RTPI, which was entirely male-dominated in its early days. The ICE (Institute of Civil Engineers) even had a woman president, in spite of its extremely male-dominated membership profile, Jean Venables, in 2008. Women engineers are generally invisible to the general public but their work is all around us. For example, Julia Barfield in association with David Marks was responsible for the design of the London Eye, built in 2000. However, women remain generally underrepresented, especially at the more senior levels of employment. Many women opt for self-employment, consultancy and part-time work in order to manage the demands of their dual roles of planner and mother, and many fail to achieve promotion owing to career breaks.

Similar problems exist among the surveyors. Within the RICS the *Raising the Ratio* programme has attempted to increase diversity and equality, particularly in relation to women, but the RICS is also a very white institution (Ellison 2008). The Institute of Civil Engineers also has an extremely low number of both women and ethnic minorities relative to other professions. It has also undertaken initiatives to attract women, ethnic minorities, the disabled and gay people to the civil engineering profession. Many such initiatives continue for a couple of years and then fizzle out, so it is important to check the professional web pages to find out what is going on. There have been innumerable small groups set up to attract more women into construction, science and technology, engineering and for that matter planning and architecture, but few survive generally because of lack of funding and limited support from their professional body. Nevertheless, there have also been several useful reports promoting equality, particularly in construction.

Nationally there are various campaign organisations that are seeking to ensure that equality issues are enshrined in employment practice, such as Stonewall. There have been many attempts to increase the numbers of women in engineering and construction, and by association in surveying, architecture, property and planning. These include a Leadership Forum set up by the Equalities and Human Rights Commission (EHRC) in relation to women in engineering, to develop fairness, inclusion and respect at the strategic national level. The Royal Academy of Engineering's Diversity Unit and the RIBA's Architects for Change group are closely involved and in 2012 presented evidence to the Parliamentary select committee on Women in the Workplace. Even if more women are recruited, retention levels are low and promotion chances for both women and other minority groups are limited (CIC 2009; Greed,1993, 2000). There is concern at the continuing underrepresentation of minority groups and interests in the development process (Rhys Jones *et al.* 1996; Gale and Davidson 2006). In particular, there are relatively few women in the more technological areas of the built environment professions.

At the university level, the Athena-Swan project to get more women into STEM subjects (Science, Technology, Engineering, Medicine and Mathematics) is currently under way. This gives Gold, Silver or Bronze awards to educational institutions in recognition of the level of progress made. Athena-Swan http://www.athenaswan.org.uk/ is a subsidiary of the Equality Challenge Unit set up by the government in association with equalities and higher educational bodies including the UKRC (UK Resource Centre).

Greater problems, arguably, are experienced by ethnic minority people seeking to enter at the professional level. But, one cannot generalise as there are major class, culture and education variations between different groups. There is a great diversity of ethnic minority groupings, cultures and lifestyles, which is only beginning to be reflected in student composition, and hardly yet in professional meetings and offices (Uguris 2004; Baty 1997; CIC 2010; Thiel 2012). The planning profession still does not reflect the people for whom they are planning. For example, an overseas student from a relatively wealthy, and well-connected, family background, undertaking postgraduate research in a high-level university (and having to pay high tuition fees) cannot be compared with someone from an inner-city London background who has fought their way onto a professionally-qualifying course through a series of access courses whilst working part-time to support themselves. The problems are reflected in the case of Stephen Lawrence, who was all ready to be an architectural student before he was murdered by racist thugs in the inner city whilst waiting at a bus stop in 1993. Place of origin, and being 'in the wrong place at the wrong time', often cross-cuts with ethnicity, gender and class, in determining who 'has a chance' and who does not. The Society of Black Architects (SOBA) and the RIBA's internal group 'Architects for Change' have sought to increase diversity within the profession. It is estimated that around 18 per cent of all students on UK architectural courses may be classified as Black and Minority Ethnic (BME) although this includes significant numbers of both overseas students and Chinese and other Asian students (Sinha 2008; Ismail 1998; Perrons 2004).

We discussed the controversial issues of population levels and immigration in Chapter 14, and the issues identified are affecting the construction sector. Whereas in the 1960s everyone was told there were 'too many' people and families were advised to produce less children, partly as a result of such misguided past policies, we now have far fewer young people and people of working age. There has been a lack of adequately qualified people in the building trades, but many of the jobs have been filled by ready-trained skilled labour from Eastern European immigration. For example, 60 per cent of all those working on the Olympics site in manual, skilled and technician jobs were non-British as the Olympic Delivery Authority (ODA) sought to draw in people with specific levels of expertise from a very wide catchment area, but very few were recruited from the surrounding local area. But depending on foreign workers is a short-term solution, and to fail to train and recruit other ethnic minority groups (especially BMEs) and to expect the bulk of new workers to be young, male and white is storing up trouble and will make the building industry unsustainable in terms of future 'man' power provision. So there is a need to get more young people involved in the built environment sector at all levels. But older people should not necessarily be seen as a burden or

liability as over 30 per cent of the population are over 55 and many are still keen to continue working and have valuable skills to offer. On the downside, not everyone wants to work till they drop, especially not in physically demanding occupations.

Another key minority group are people with disabilities, who, at first sight, may not be considered suitable for built-environment-related employment. However people with disabilities are a very varied group indeed, and should not be discounted. Indeed in construction, disability, especially through building site injuries, is often seen as a reason for people leaving, rather than joining, the industry. Of course they may not be able to work at heights or run up and down ladders. But, it is often argued that many of the professional, administrative and computer-based jobs can be done by people with disabilities. Indeed, involving the disabled in the fields of architecture, urban design and planning provides a positive input into designing accessible, inclusive environments, from personal experience. Some of the greatest advances in inclusive design have been achieved through the work of disabled architects such as the late Selwyn Goldsmith (Goldsmith 2000) and the work of the Centre for Accessible Environments. But at present only around 0.3 per cent of all built environment professionals have declared they are disabled (Imrie 1996), although many want more 'visibility and involvement' (Chouinard *et al.* 2010). The participation of gay workers in the construction workforce and built environment professions has always been a difficult topic because of the dominant male, macho culture of the building world, although the planning profession has been open to accepting more diversity (Doan 2011). Particular problems centre around practical matters such as workplace toilets and privacy. This has always been a problem for women, who are a minority on building sites, but also for gay people, especially those who are transgendered, and the problems of 'which toilet to use' and being picked upon (Cavanagh 2010). Another important minority issue, which is often overlooked, is religion. There is a need to cultivate more flexible and sensitive work cultures to accommodate the needs of those who do not drink and who do not fit easily into the pub-centred drinking culture of many of the built environment professions. There is also a need for recognition of those who require time for prayer and religious festivals, be they Moslems, Evangelical Christians or Jewish people (Ahmed 1989). We will return to this aspect of the diversity agenda at the end of the chapter and consider its implications for planning practice.

The planners

Public or private sector planning?

Having given an overview of the context of the built environment professions of which planning is arguably one part, we will now look at the planning profession more closely. The world of the planning professional has been overtaken by some major cultural changes during the last 20 years and planning is no longer primarily part of the public sector or predominantly a local authority function. Arguably, all the professions have become more commercially-minded, although a sense of public service and responsibility to the wider community is still to be found in the codes of professional ethics produced by the professional bodies. In the 1980s, dynamic economic growth occurred in which property figured as a major commodity. The built environment professions have subsequently expanded since the 1990s, and become more diverse and entrepreneurial in membership. Whilst in the past the majority of planners worked in local government planning departments, increasing numbers are employed by private-sector consultancies.

The Big Bang (deregulation of financial services) in 1986 altered the financial world, sweeping away generations-old restrictions and barriers. A massive growth in property development and investment was one of the results. This provided new opportunities for the landed professions in the private sector, but it also meant that they were now undefended from invasion of part of their territory, in the areas of property portfolio management and investment analysis, from a range of other professionals, not least accountants, and from worldwide competitors. These included Japanese interests, and American banking and investment companies with substantially different corporate cultures. The 1980s 'enterprise culture' faded in the recession of the early 1990s, but New Labour continued with

policies of privatisation and deregulation of state control, as it attempted to speed up the planning system and reduce overheads. As a result, more planners were to be found in private-sector consultancies and less in traditional local planning departments, and many new graduates sought to get their first jobs in this new private arm of planning. However, increasing privatisation has had its drawbacks too, as planners can no longer depend upon 'a job for life' in local government, as the whole nation was rocked by the banking crisis which started in 2008. Government cutbacks have resulted in many local authority planning departments being reduced or amalgamated with other departments. This is a far cry from the 1960s under Labour governments when some planners imagined they were all powerful, and the nature of planning theory in the universities reflected this (cf. Chapter 8; Allmendinger 2002). But many would challenge the planners' power to control the property and land of others, not least property lawyers, and without political support the very concept of planning can become very vulnerable indeed.

The nature of planning practice has changed radically too, with a greater emphasis upon speed, efficiency and more business-like methods. Currently the Coalition is trying to speed up planning even more. Development control is referred to as development management, and applicants and users of the planning system are likely to be referred to as customers or clients, rather than simply members of the public, residents or 'the planned'. Few plans are likely to be produced on paper by traditional methods. Instead, much of the work of the planning department has been digitalised and is held electronically using GIS systems. Planners are more likely to be able to work more flexibly, whilst on the move and from home, because of the development of the internet, laptops and mobile phones. Likewise the general public find it easier to find out about what is happening in planning through consulting their local authority website or simply googling in key questions and phrases. But, paradoxically, the digitalisation and computerisation of planning has made the planners and planning process more remote from the people, if the only way to contact them is through websites and email. There have been attempts to cancel the weekly listing of planning applications in local newspapers, presumably to save money. If this does go ahead, those without access to a computer, or the skills to use it, will experience the negative effects of the digital divide, with plentiful internet access in cities. But many rural areas are not yet covered adequately by broadband, or experience very slow download speeds. So it is too soon to abandon all books and printed reports. This sits uneasily with the Coalition government's commitment to providing the community with a greater voice in local planning: not everyone has internet access, especially elderly and deprived groups. From an academic planning perspective, as books become less important, there is a danger that existing scholarship will be lost and reference will only be made to those sources and articles that have ended up on the web and are listed by the search engines.

The scope of planning

The RTPI was established in 1914 as a learned association (Ashworth 1968) consisting of architects, surveyors, public health officers and civil engineers who were concerned with town planning issues, but gradually town planning evolved as a separate profession with its own particular concerns and specialisations. There have been many changes in the organisation and activities of the planning profession, but many of the topics with which it is concerned have not changed that much. As can be seen from earlier chapters, the planning profession is concerned with both urban and rural issues, and with all types of land uses, including retail, residential, commercial, industrial, open space and other amenities. So there is no one simple definition of a planner as their roles and specialisms are many and varied. Whilst the planners' remit is still concerned with land use and development, that is with specific physical and geographical issues that are site- or area-specific, it is not limited to this. Planners are concerned with the social, economic, political and environmental factors that shape the built and natural environment. Town planning is a relatively broad profession, and incorporates a range of types of people with different areas of expertise. There are a number of people working in town planning who have dual professional qualifications, such as in architecture, law, civil engineering or surveying. One might find architects involved in those aspects of town planning which relate to conservation policy and design; lawyers involved in development control; and economists, statisticians and sociologists involved in the wider policy-making levels of the preparation of structure plan policies (Bayer *et al*. 2010).

With the growth of sustainability policy, there is a growing number of professional ecologists, environmentalists and landscape architects who offer expertise in the field of environmental assessment, which is now a planning requirement brought in by the European Commission (Nadin *et al*. 2010). Overall, there has been a widening of planning to take on the challenges of environmental planning, centred upon ecological issues, sustainability and pollution control. Many would say that the RTPI has missed out on this trend, in that many of the professionals involved in these specialisms do not necessarily belong to the RTPI, or consider themselves to be planners in the traditional sense, but belong to other newer professional bodies that sprang up in response to new ways of doing things and new areas of knowledge. However, everything goes in circles and if you wait long enough past trends come back into fashion, so, for example, the creation of 'healthy cities' is now an increasing concern of planners, reminiscent of the early origins of the profession which grew, in part, from the public health movement, over a hundred years ago (Barton and Tsourou 2006). Likewise urban design and social town planning have made a major comeback after years of a more impersonal, scientific, quantitative approach to the subject.

Universities offer a greater range of planning specialisms, such as environmental planning, transport planning and urban design degrees, rather than everyone doing just a plain planning degree. There are around 4000 planning students at any one time, ranging from undergraduate, to postgraduate, to full-time, distance learning and part-time. Over the years planning has also developed into a distinct academic discipline, with large numbers of planning researchers and theory-makers, who overlap with the work of geographers, economists, environmentalists and sociologists within our universities. Not all planning courses are the same, by any means, and one finds different specialisms and cultures in varied departments, as well as different specialisms being offered such as urban design, transport, sustainability and so forth. All this is a far cry from the days when most planners held perhaps a diploma at most and were likely to have come from the fields of engineering and surveying. Over the last 30 years there has been a huge increase in higher education and great emphasis is placed upon 'going to university', which has become essential just to get a typical middle-class job that 40 years ago people would get into straight from school. Sociologists term this trend the 'credentialisation' of society as you have to have a degree (credentials) to get anywhere (Collins 1979; Millerson 1964) and 'educational inflation' has affected all the built environment professions too (Gale and Davidson (eds) 2006). For example, in the 1960s, 80 per cent of people left school by 16, and only around 5 per cent went to university (most of whom were male), but many others trained on day-release or at technical colleges whilst working in local planning departments (Greed 1994a). But professionalisation was unstoppable, as the creation of special, exclusive professional bodies was a major factor in middle-class employment and in gaining recognition and status (Millerson 1964). It is a very British characteristic to have a 'chartered body', and a Royal one at that, to represent planning and to have such emphasis upon being a professional, whereas in other countries greater social status and legitimation might be placed upon being a scientist or an engineer (Collins 1979). There is a great deal of mystique associated with the English idea of a professional elite (and the ideal of the professional gentleman) which does not fit well the realities of the modern, international, competitive business world, nor with demands from a more educated population for greater involvement in the governmental decision-making process in town planning (Knox 1988). Whereas 17 per cent of the UK population were graduates in 1992, in 2013 38 per cent are now graduates, with six out of ten people in London having degrees (compared with three out of ten in the North East).

As a result of all this diversity in both education and practice, there is much debate as to what planning really comprises. Is town planning a real profession, such as law, architecture, medicine or civil engineering, and does it need to be? In fact all of these traditional professions have increasing levels of specialisation too and few professionals are jacks of all trades, and the all-rounder general practitioner is in decline. Planning may be seen as a composite of subjects put together for various administrative and political reasons, which nonetheless exudes a certain mystique. Thus, physical land-use planning is only a small component of the modern town planner's job, whereas once it was its *raison d'être*, its reason for claiming professional status. Nevertheless, regardless of the validity of its theoretical underpinnings (as discussed in Chapter 8), town planning remains a major bureaucratic function of local government, and an important component of the professional activities of the private-sector property development world. In addition to the main professional body, the RTPI, there are other influential town planning organisations. One of the main ones is the Town and Country Planning Association (TCPA), which is not a professionally qualifying body, but a prestigious pressure group originally founded at the beginning of the twentieth century to promote the idea of Garden Cities and Ebenezer Howard. There are also a range of additional organisations and interest groups catering to the needs of the different specialisms in planning, such as urban design, environment and sustainability, etc. These do not necessarily give professional qualifications, but provide forums, discussion groups, websites and conferences to enable their members to exchange ideas and keep up to date. Whilst voluntary pressure groups have played a major part in shaping public opinion and government policy towards planning, professional power has still been needed to implement and institutionalise the planning agenda.

It may appear from this book that planners are kings with absolute power over the built environment. This may have been the case in the past, particularly at times of increased state intervention such as in the Post-War Reconstruction period of the late 1940s, when private property rights were overruled by compulsory purchase powers and entire city centres, historical residential areas and local businesses were demolished to make way for the planners' grandiose plans. Looking back it is remarkable that this could have been done, and that the process was so undemocratic and totalitarian and overrode existing rights. As a real property lawyer once remarked in astonishment to me about planning powers, '*But you don't own it, so how can you plan it?*' Local authority planners have always had a high degree of power as operators of the development control system and creators of development plan policies. Nearly all development has to receive planning permission, and, therefore, to a degree, planning has had the upper hand over private-sector developers. But, to turn the argument around, planners cannot 'plan' unless the private property sector wants to develop and the location in question is likely to give reasonable financial returns. For example, developers are desperate to build in prosperous areas such as London and the South East and therefore planners can exert a considerable degree of additional control through planning gain agreements and negotiation (Chapters 2 and 3). But in some of the more economically depressed areas, such as the North East, the local authority may be desperate to get employment and business into the areas and will seek to entice developers through more amenable planning conditions.

So planners exist within a complex power situation in relation to the private sector and other professional bodies. However, planning definitely still does have a major role in the development of major projects (such as the Olympic site) and in shaping places, at many levels. There are definitely huge pressures to redefine or limit the role of planners. Few planners, or planning theorists, today would manifest the inflated ideas of the 1960s that they were legitimate controllers and saviours of society, but nevertheless planning is still powerful, because development cannot take place without it. Whilst in Britain many have become cynical towards and critical of the planners, planning itself is a force to be reckoned with globally. Urban planning is a major player in the modernisation of China, where huge, mega-cities are being built at a pace never encountered in the West (Logan 2009; Weiping Wu and Gaubatz 2012). However, different countries divide the professional cake up in different ways, so in some countries planning might be seen as part of architecture, or civil engineering, or even social policy, depending on the politics, history and culture of the country in question. Within Europe, under the EU there is a move towards increasing harmonisation of planning standards and procedures, to create a level playing field, which will affect the building industry, especially in the areas of 'public procurement' (that is public works contracts); building standards, construction products standards; and mutual recognition of professional qualifications and education. EC law increasingly affects all aspects of English law, including town planning and environmental law, because community law now takes precedence over national law in the member states. Likewise planning education has become increasingly harmonised across Europe (see AESOP website) and with the vast increase in international students in British universities it is essential for lecturers to have a more global perspective on urbanisation, and some knowledge of what is going on outside of the UK.

Comparisons with the surveyors

The nearest profession to planning is surveying; indeed planning grew out of it. The main professional body for surveying is the Royal Institution of Chartered Surveyors (RICS) whose roots go back over many centuries (Thompson 1968; Greed 1990). As outlined in the introduction, the RICS is a much larger body than the RTPI. The RICS contains within it a range of specialist groups, including general practice surveyors, land agents, land surveyors, minerals surveyors, quantity surveyors and building surveyors, which long have been seen as low on women (Avis and Gibson 1987). The Commercial and Residential division is the largest in which general practice surveyors, valuers, estate managers and housing managers are located (Wilkinson *et al.* 2008). Quantity surveyors make up nearly a third of the membership of the RICS and are therefore the second largest group. Please note the RICS, from time to time, change the way they divide up their membership, by specialism and category of work, so check the RICS website to see the current state of play.

As indicated, some RICS surveyors specialise in Planning and Development matters and primarily carry out town planning on behalf of developers and other private-sector clients. Some chartered surveyors may also belong to the RTPI. Likewise there are substantial numbers of people who hold joint membership of the RIBA and are planners (originally discussed by Nadin and Jones 1990, and check the web for modern updates). There is definitely an overlap in terms of planning practice between the two professions, but many surveyor-planners are to be found working in the private sector. But the planner's approach differs considerably from other built environment professionals. Whilst, for example, many surveyors may also specialise in planning, their remit is essentially commercial, to get the best return from the site for their client. RTPI planners are not only concerned with the individual developments and sites, but with the whole built environment, that is with the effects of development on that particular site on the city a as a whole, for example in terms of the traffic it will generate, the environmental implications and the social impact on the local residents. The majority of RICS surveyor-planners work in private practice, but they still have a major influence on the nature of local authority planning policy. They are the main advisers of the private sector, and thus, in a sense, 'the enemy'. They are the people on the 'other side of the fence' whose development activities local government town planners are there to control. Such surveyors represent interests which can often conflict with the objectives of the planning system. The commercial and valuation emphasis throughout the world of surveying colours the worldview of all surveyors and is distinctly different from that of the planners.

Likewise a feature of town planning work is that a wide range of people with different types of expertise work together as a large team, both in respect of the production of development plans and other planning policy documents within local government, and in the case of large-scale private-sector projects. This is rather different, relatively speaking, from the situation in surveying practice, where there is still more room for the sole practitioner, although in London many surveyors are members of very large firms which are subdivided into specialist offices and sections. Nevertheless, as a general principle, much of the work which goes on in the landed professions and the construction industry is strongly team-orientated. Although surveyors and planners both like to work in teams and are working on the 'same' issues, but from a different perspective, nevertheless the culture of the two professional groups is quite

different. Relatively speaking, the RTPI is known for having a more academic emphasis than the RICS, which has always prided itself on its practicality and common sense. Although this difference is arguably diminishing as both professional bodies are actively involved in more academic research activities and both require graduate entry, there has been a continuing growth and diversification of undergraduate and postgraduate education within the landed professions. People tend to choose their profession carefully in relation to future prospects and salaries, and at present it is noticeable that surveyors earn more than planners and have a higher, but more precarious, status in the private sector. One of the main reasons students give for choosing surveying is because (as would-be students often put it at interview) 'we don't want to be stuck in an office all day but want to get out and about'. But their office is likely to go out and about with them thanks to mobile internet access and remote working.

Cultural considerations

The planning subculture

Having looked at the way in which the planning profession fits into the wider built environment professional spectrum, let us go a bit deeper in terms of the qualitative, sociological aspects of the planning profession. In this final chapter, it is good to stand back and reflect on the nature of the planning profession, and to gain some sociological appreciation of its cultural peculiarities (Young and Stevenson (eds) 2012), thus becoming a 'reflective practitioner' (Schon 1995; Bourdieu 1986). As we have seen in Chapter 8, the concept of 'culture' has been recognised as an important factor in shaping society and the built environment (Williams 1981). It was often remarked in earlier chapters that planners were unaware of the changes around them, because of the dominance of certain attitudes and assumptions within the profession, that insulated them from seeing the needs of the people they were planning 'for', especially minority groups, women, and anyone unlike themselves. Even allowing for their small numbers in the past, disproportionately fewer women than men are reaching positions of seniority in local planning authorities or planning consultancies. Unless women reach the decision-making levels of the professions they will not be in a position to shape the future structure of the profession or influence the nature of the built environment through their professional activities and decisions. This is clearly the case with planning policy (Reeves 2005) but the lack of women on decision-making committees and working groups also affects the nature of Building Regulations and British Standards which shape the design of buildings, our surrounding environment and indeed just about everything that is 'designed', from urban transport systems to the details of housing interiors.

Such are the forces of professional socialisation that, even if planning students start off with different views, they become subject to pressures to subscribe to the values and attitudes of the profession in order to advance their careers. It is helpful to see the built environment professional bodies as possessing their own subcultural values and worldviews. 'Subculture' is taken to mean the cultural traits, beliefs and lifestyle peculiar to those, for example, in the planning tribe (Greed 1990, 1992). One of the most important factors seems to be the need for a person to fit in to the subculture. It is argued that the values and attitudes held by its members have a major influence on their professional decision-making, and therefore ultimately influence the nature of 'what is built'. The need for the identification with the values of the subculture would seem to block out the entrance of both people and alternative ideas, that are seen as 'different' or 'unsettling'. Therefore it is not only important to look at the sort of planning policies being promoted, but also the nature of the policy-makers. This is because the way in which the planners 'see' the world and their own life experiences undoubtedly shapes their policy priorities and perceptions of the city (Greed 1994a, 2000).

The concept of 'closure' in the relation to the power of various subcultural groups to control who is included in, or out, is a key factor in understanding the composition of the professions (as discussed by Parkin 1979, 89–90; and first developed by Weber 1964, 141–52, 236; and see Greed 1994a, 25). Even if individuals do enter professional courses with alternative views, and believe they can change it by 'joining in' and biding their time until they are in a position to alter the status quo, they soon find that

they are subjected to powerful professional socialisation processes (Knox 1988). Students, especially those from working-class backgrounds, all-girl schools, religious backgrounds and/or ethnic minority origins, often experience a measure of shock at the unexpected nature of the planning profession, with its fondness for football and beer! Also many 'outsiders' may have great difficulty with the subject matter, which may not be what they expected. They may experience considerable group pressure to 'believe' what they are told by authoritative lecturers and by fellow students. Disabled would-be students may never gain entrance in the first place. Rather it is often said that planners like to choose people like themselves, and until relatively recently this has been white, male, middle-class, able-bodied people like themselves. Indeed there has been little space for the consideration of such social issues within a profession that has historically put great emphasis upon physical land-use issues, and has manifested a veritable spatial fetishism, with little room for cultural, user- and value-related considerations. Thus it took time for movements such as 'women and planning', equality and diversity, and for that matter even environmental sustainability, to be taken on board by the planners because they did not 'fit' their schema of 'how the world should be'.

As stated earlier, most of the built environment professions are still predominantly white, middle class and male. Taking the land-use and construction professions together less than 6 per cent of those in professional practice are women. These factors may be irrelevant to urban policy-making, and to construction and architectural design, if women's needs are perceived to be the same as those of the men, or if it is believed that the professional man is equally capable of planning for all groups in society. But research and human experience have shown that women suffer disadvantage in a built environment that is planned chiefly by men, primarily for other men (Photo 16.2), and so changes need to be made, for women's different needs to be recognised and planned for (Hayden 2002; Reeves 2005; Jarvis et al. 2009), as explained in Chapter 15.

But even if we do get more women, more does not necessarily mean 'better', such are the forces of professional socialisation to the prevailing professional subculture. In particular, it does not follow

Photo 16.2   Planners planning

There is a need for the composition of policy-making and management meetings to change, as many minority groups are still underrepresented, and where men in suits dominate.

that women will be more socially aware than men, or for that matter more concerned with women's issues, as each is on a personal journey. But many would argue we simply need to get more young men and women into the built environment professions, come what may, to ensure the survival of these bodies. Most of the built environment professions have a preponderance of older members, and have failed to attract enough newer recruits. This is particularly a problem in construction, which has such a bad image of muddy building sites, whereas planning suffers from an image of low pay and limited prospects. This is part of a wider national demographic problem, as the population is ageing and has become unbalanced, with increasing numbers of pensioners and lower birth rates. It has been said that if every 16-year-old white boy went into construction there would still not be enough to 'man' the workforce at all levels, including the professional grades (Gale and Davidson

2006). Therefore in the next section we will return to the controversial issue of demographic change, the need for equality and diversity and the effects of an ageing population on the likely future nature of the planning profession.

Conceptualising change: critical mass?

In spite of many years of effort by minority groups, concerned with gender, age, ethnicity, disability and so forth, to change the culture and composition of the built environment professions, little has been achieved. Concepts which inform the investigation of change include (the ever popular but somewhat questionable) critical mass theory as to 'how many people are needed to change an organisational culture' (Greed 2000; Morley 1994, 195), an issue to which Bagilhole has given particular attention (Bagilhole *et al.* (eds) 2007; Bagilhole 2009). Kanter

(1983) suggests 15–20 per cent (minority composition) is needed to change the culture of an organisation, whilst Gale and Davidson (2006) suggest 35 per cent is necessary in the construction industry, and respondents have suggested the percentage should be much higher. Ironically town planning has one of the highest percentages of women in any of the built environment chartered professional bodies (except for housing) but commensurate change has not been manifested, in spite of the constant efforts and writings of 'women and planning' groups. A small well-organised group, or one or two totally dedicated charismatic individuals, may prove more effective than hundreds of new minority individuals, who appear confused and unsure of their role at a personal level, and who have such low expectations and high tolerance levels, that they may declare, '*I simply don't know what the problem is*', and who thus are easily socialised into the mainstream.

There is a range of theories which deal with such group dynamics, the role of individuals, and the significance of networks, which ensure either social inclusion or exclusion of 'new' or 'different' individuals. Actor network theory is of particular interest, which is concerned with asking 'what are the networks by which social power is maintained, or the pathways through which social change might be brought about?' (Callon *et al.* 1986; Murdock 1997). Such research is also concerned with the role of prime movers in detonating critical mass explosion (Kanter 1983, 296). Also, not to be dismissed, is the extensive range of New Age ideas and theories, which delve into more 'spiritual' realms as to how to create change, of which the Celestine series is a best-selling example (Redfield 1994). A resilient and influential minority of women exist within the construction and built environment professions who *are* likely to hold alternative viewpoints. This group is likely to increase as the present young cohorts of women professionals grow older and might contribute to the build-up of critical mass. Thus, much depends upon minority planners reaching senior decision-making levels, without losing their principles along the way. There is also a need for young urban professionals and students to engage in these issues, rather than imagining feminism is a thing of the past. But it often takes women, in particular, until their early thirties to realise the

situation is not fair, as they find out how difficult it is to juggle family and career responsibilities.

Generating change

A range of possibilities

A range of factors will now be discussed that might generate change within the composition and culture of the planning profession. Firstly, international influences can play a large part in changing the profession, and this has certainly been manifest in its adoption of United Nations derived policies on sustainability and the environment. Many of these global-level policies and directives have been transmitted down into British town planning through the role of the European Union, as we are now subject to EU Directives as a member state. The UN and EU also have provided a great deal of guidance and direction on equalities issues too. But these do not appear to be as readily adopted or agreed with by the UK planning profession. For example, the UN has set a series of Millennium Development Goals (Google MDGs and see Chapter 9) which include, along with environmental objectives, clean water, health, etc., the importance of gender equality, specifically mentioning women's needs. Such initiatives have been readily adopted by the Commonwealth Association of Planners.

Changes in the planning system may, or may not, lead to a more open approach to policy-making as part of the new localism agenda. The neighbourhood planning system is intended to give the community a greater say in policy-making. But there are serious questions as to whether a mere 21 people (the required number to comprise a neighbourhood forum) can encompass the diversity, concerns and policy issues of the 6000 average number of people living in a particular parish or neighbourhood area (jurisdiction). The new planning system is also meant to bring the planners and developers closer together too, not least by speeding up the system, with the objective of increasing growth and development: which usually boils down to more housing. Clearly, advanced 'people skills' are required on the part of the planners and the members of the neighbourhood to get the best out of the exercise, manage and maintain the momentum, and produce a plan that satisfies everyone involved. Already it is noticeable that the most articulate, well-resourced, professional middle-class groups within the community are better at 'playing the planning game'. Many people are just too busy, poor or unaware to be involved, as they fight to survive, to get on with their jobs and daily lives. Furthermore, within all groups, whether rich or poor, majority or minority population, women are less likely to get their views heard.

Mainstreaming equality

One means of integrating equality issues into planning is by means of gender mainstreaming and a wider agenda of equalities mainstreaming (Greed 2005a, 2005b; Reeves 2005). This requirement was originally stipulated by the EU as a result of the Treaty of Amsterdam, and required all member states to mainstream gender considerations into all aspects of policy-making, resource allocation and personnel matters at their local government level. As a result of EU Directives and also pressure for changes in UK Equalities legislation and guidance, equalities mainstreaming became a requirement to be undertaken by all local authorities, including planning departments. Central government further issued requirements that local authorities and all those bodies providing public services should be subject to a 'Gender Duty' to ensure that gender considerations had been taken into account. We undertook research for the RTPI to produce a Gender Mainstreaming Toolkit that might be undertaken by planners (who were mainly likely to be male and not necessarily sympathetic or aware of the issues) within development planning and development control departments (RTPI 2003, 2007 and see RTPI webpage). Dory Reeves has subsequently produced an international version of the gender mainstreaming toolkit for town planners (Reeves 2012). Gender mainstreaming may be defined as integrating gender considerations into all stages and aspects of plan-making. This is very different from 'gender proofing', a process in which normally the local authority is required to tick a series of boxes to confirm that equality considerations were taken into account 'after' the final policy documents have been produced.

In summary the gender mainstreaming toolkit stages may be boiled down to a series of questions

Textbox 16.1   A Toolkit Summary: how to mainstream gender into planning

Ask these questions:
Who is doing the planning?
Who are perceived to be the planned?
How are statistics gathered and who do they include?
How is the policy team chosen?
Is the team representative of women as well as men?
What are the plan values, priorities and objectives?
Who is consulted and involved in participation?
How is the draft plan evaluated?
Does gender mainstreaming reinforce other key policy areas?
Does it create better planning judged by fewer complaints?
How is the policy implemented, managed and monitored?

Key related stages:
 1. Setting goals and objectives
 2. Organising the institutional framework, resources and programme funding
 3. Collecting data inclusively
 4. Developing policy alternatives
 5. Public participation and consultation
 6. Evaluating policy alternatives
 7. Deciding which policies to adopt
 8. Monitoring progress, updating, revising policies
 9. Plan implementation
 10. Applying to development control

that planners must ask themselves at key plan-making stages which correspond to the traditional survey, analysis, plan approach (as written upon extensively by Greed 2003b, 2005a, 2005b, 2006a, 2006b, 2006d).

It was found from related research that in spite of this being a high-level requirement, as important as environmental assessment which had, in contrast, received unlimited support, most local planning authorities had failed to take these issues into account. But, there was a small group of more progressive authorities that were mainstreaming gender and other equalities issues into planning in an effective way, including several London boroughs and the Greater London Authority itself (GLA 2010).

However, one of the main issues was how to ensure that gender considerations were integrated into actual policy areas such as transport, housing, sustainability and employment, with specific changes and implications. To achieve this, Plymouth stood out because it had produced a Gender Matrix, a spreadsheet that sought to link back specific policy areas to specific policy issues (Plymouth 2001). However, it was found that most local planning authorities did have some form of equality proofing or mainstreaming but many had a rather superficial, generic approach. Indeed such was the perceived difficulty of the task that many authorities simply went for an 'after the event' gender proofing approach, which usually involved planners ticking a series of boxes to say they had taken gender into account. Some had great difficulty imagining how spatial planning policies would be changed by gender and instead tended to emphasise the personnel, human resources aspects of equality and failed to consider the physical land-use planning dimension.

The expanding equalities agenda: too much of a good thing?

Another problem that confronts local planning authorities is the sheer scale of equalities legislation and categories. Whilst the UN has prioritised gender considerations and this has been reiterated in EU Directives, many local authorities tried to cover a whole range of other categories all at once, including gender, ethnicity, sexuality, age, class, disability, religion and so forth. The only way of doing this was to introduce yet more equality forms, in which planners ticked the boxes to confirm they had taken all these issues into account – which is doubtful! We found in the research for the RTPI that some local authorities had 37 equality categories, so the whole thing became a purely bureaucratic exercise in which equality had become so diluted to become almost meaningless (Greed 2005a, 2005b). But it is a very difficult question to ask, how are local authorities meant to undertake such a difficult task? From the research, we argued that the trick was to concentrate on key major planning policies (rather than firstly on equality categories) and seek to work out how each policy in question might affect different minority groups. To do this there was a need for considerable survey work and public participation. However, these are all qualitative matters and there is little point in doing a massive quantitative survey which only asks bland yes/no questions that provide little space for understanding what people really think.

Therefore, in subsequent EPSRC-funded research, it was recommended that a 'cameo approach' was adopted, in which a selective representative range of focus groups was assembled, containing a cross-section of minority individuals and community groups, and in-depth discussion was undertaken to tease out the key issues (Hanson et al. 2007), particularly when dealing with detailed urban design considerations (Greed 2011a, 2012). Now this is not easy, and it requires long-term commitment and funding, and also an element of education to explain to participants the nature and limitations of planning policy and how to read maps. Otherwise there is a danger of raising unrealistic expectations and competing groups falling out. However, an area-based approach is nevertheless more realistic than vacuous, meaningless tick-box exercises. Of course individuals are usually a combination of minority characteristics, such as gender, race, colour, culture, age and so forth, and therefore it was helpful to refer to the principles of intersectionality (Bagilhole 2009; Cooper 2008). Indeed since everyone is sharing the same urban space within a particular locality or local plan area there is a need to achieve a balance between drawing out the distinct minority considerations as well as acknowledging the shared experiences, problems and issues.

New Labour put considerable emphasis upon the importance of social inclusion, equality and diversity issues, and a veritable equalities industry flourished under their administration. However, arguably not all equalities issues were treated equally, and gender and 'women and planning' issues often came low down on the pecking order relative to more media-attractive topics such as sexuality, culture and ethnicity. Gender cross-cuts, overarches and intersects with all other equality considerations (Reeves 2005). However, the old EOC (Equal Opportunities Commission) was merged with the Race Relations Commission and the Disability Rights Commission, into the Equalities and Human Rights Commission (EHRC) in 2006. A new Equalities Act was passed in 2010, which came into force in 2011 under the new Coalition government, which incorporated and amalgamated all the previous specific minority legislation such as the Disability Discrimination and Race Relations Acts. The new Act covers following 'protected categories': disability, gender reassignment, pregnancy and maternity, race, religion and belief, sex and sexual orientation. So the word 'gender' is not actually in the legislation but it is seen to be part of the category 'sex'. Also note that age is not included as such, nor is class, or for that matter socio-economic group, which were all in the draft bill and then taken out. This new legislation is meant to harmonise, simplify and strengthen previous legislation on all these issues. It covers a range of direct and indirect discrimination. It deals with the provision of goods and services, and for example planning policy, and is not just concerned with individual discrimination but with public policy and public facilities. So it draws on the model of institutional discrimination used under race equality law, and is more proactive in dealing with the effects of discriminatory organisations and their cultures. It is early days to see how this will all work out in application of the law, but arguably this Act extends the powers against discrimination more strongly into the realms of urban planning and public policy-making.

However, on the minus side, there is no longer a separate Gender Equality Duty as existed since 1997, but now all these duties are combined into a new Public Sector Equality Duty (PSED). There is no longer a requirement for local authorities to produce an 'equality scheme' as such. But now, given the stronger legislation, the duty is meant to be more of a monitoring role. Many minority group representatives are concerned that with the abolition of previous acts such as the Disability Discrimination Act (DDA), and Race Relation Acts (RRAs), everything has become too generalised. There is concern that the specific needs of their minority groups are going to be subsumed under a more general approach. Also it is felt that this will only increase the potential competition and conflict between different groups in bidding for funds, or for seeing specific changes made. The

Centre for Accessible Environments (CAE) is particularly concerned about this in respect of disability issues. As for gender, since there was never separate legislation on 'gender' as there was for example with race, disability and sexuality, there is great concern that women's issues will be sidelined even more. Age was not included in the new Equality Act, but this was compensated by the 2011 Employment Equality (Age) Regulations, which abolished the default retirement age, 65, as from 1 October 2011, and introduced increased controls on age discrimination in the workplace. All this is of relevance to planners as the workforce is getting older and therefore cities need to be more accessible, simply to enable people to get to work! But many elderly people are already retired and there are entire communities, particularly in the South West, where most residents are retired and much more elderly, and so developing economic regeneration strategies which emphasise employment is totally inappropriate in these localities. But all this may soon become history, for at the time of writing there was talk by the Coalition of greatly reducing the equality requirements and letting the Cabinet Office absorb and reduce the role of the EHRC.

A case study: religion and planning

It was noted in the first section of the chapter on the composition of the built environment professions that some groups were uneasy about joining the world of construction because of lack of flexibility or respect for their religious practices. It was also stated in the previous section that religion is now one of the protected categories under equalities. We have already illustrated the unrepresentative nature of the planning profession in respect of gender and ethnicity, and have demonstrated the problems of mainstreaming the needs of minority groups into planning policy. We will now make a brief digression into the topic of religion and planning, as an example of the apparent lack of application and impact of the equalities agenda in this respect upon the planning subculture and thus upon planning policy and practice. Again professional subcultural attitudes are at work, in that the planning profession is traditionally secular, somewhat scientific and frequently bureaucratic in character, and arguably out of touch with the changing needs of the planned.

The widening diversity agenda has allowed for a greater range of social and cultural issues to be included within urban sociological study, including religion. Religion has also grown in importance, not least because of the growth of Islam in the UK, as a valid equalities category enshrined in the 2010 Equality Act. But will planners be able to deal with religion, under the Public Sector Equality Duty, especially since they seem to have had such trouble with the more obvious topics of gender, race and disability? Will planners be able to deal with the 'new' categories of sexuality, religion and for that matter age, and how will they cope with conflicting demands from different minority groups? This is all a far cry from the olden days of 'top-down' planning! Does a pecking order already exist as to which topics planners imagine to be the most important? For example, inner-city problems are often 'seen' in terms of 'male black youth', which is racist and gives little attention to the needs of all the other groups that live in such areas. Many local planning authorities have a poor track record in dealing with planning applications from ethnic minority businesses and individuals, such as for minicab businesses, hot-food takeaways and new religious buildings. Rather than seeing these applications as a sign of increasing prosperity and community development, they are often seen as 'likely to cause problems' and there has, historically, been very little mutual understanding between planners and planned (Loftman and Beazley 1993; Gale 2008).

As we have seen in the historical chapters, planners' 'belief' about how the world should be has been a strong, but often silent and unacknowledged, influence on planning theory and policy in the past. It would seem that the modern, secular, humanist profession of planning may have difficulty appreciating and providing for the range of issues included in the new Equality Act, particularly in respect of recognising and meeting religious needs, as manifested in development control applications for premises. Yet within modern society religion is a growing phenomenon, and, as will be explained, applications for religious buildings are a growing component of the development control caseload. Goodness knows how all this will relate to the demands of the 2011

Localism Act and the involvement of the community in local planning; clearly a strong feat of complex juggling of interests is required by the planners.

Let us return to religion. By the end of the twentieth century, society was entering a post-secular phase (Gorringe 2002; Baker and Beaumont 2011; Al Sayyad and Massoumi 2010), manifested in renewed interest in spiritual matters and a concern for faith and religious issues in civil society and the city (Beaumont 2008) after the predominance of a secular, humanistic culture during the twentieth century (Cox 1965). But the planners have not caught up with this yet and, granted, this new phase of society does contain many paradoxes. Post-secularism is a complex phase, characterised by a contest between religious lobbyists (which have grown in strength with the resurgence of fundamentalist religions), and secular pressure groups who promote diversity and equality. Nevertheless, post-secularism has allowed some urban theorists to ask a new set of questions about the city, related to social justice, morality and whether the city is 'good'(Amin 2006). Planners have always prided themselves on being neutral and not there to make moral judgements (Sandercock 1997; Fewings 2008; Howe 1994). When women have complained that granting planning permission for uses such as lap dancing clubs and 24-hour bars may destabilise a neighbourhood and create possible dangers for women wishing to walk through the area unmolested, they are more likely to be dismissed as 'religious fundamentalists' or men-haters, than for their concerns to be taken seriously in terms of planning controls and design considerations. This is of particular concern to women who comprise the majority of many congregations and faith groups. But as stated in Chapter 3, moral and religious beliefs are not considered a material consideration in determining planning applications.

The planners' lack of religious awareness puts large sectors of the minority population at a disadvantage (Sandercock 2006; Engwicht 2007), especially Moslems, and Christians from non-traditional churches, especially black Pentecostal churches and immigrant congregations. Town planners have inevitably got involved in 'ethnic' issues, because of the sheer pressure of numbers involved with increased immigration, in terms of housing provi-

Photo 16.3   Traditional church in the background

Religion may be the next big 'ideology' with the resurgence of interest in the post-secular society. In spite of the growth in planning applications for new churches and mosques, many planners still have an outdated image of 'the church' as something there in the background, of little relevance to modern society.

sion and land-use strategy. Planners have also been faced with unfamiliar types of planning application. Immigration has had major implications for the planners, particularly in respect of problems of dealing with development control, dealing with planning applications, for example, for ethnic minority businesses including hot-food takeaways and minicab businesses which were likely to be met with accusations of smells, noise and disturbance. Applications for unfamiliar places of worship, with increased numbers of Moslems, such as mosques, were often refused on the basis of minarets and noise, along with black Pentecostal churches, especially those catering to the religious needs of African residents. According to the results of the 2011 Census, 59 per cent of the population of the UK is still Christian (albeit few attend church) and 4.8 per cent are Moslem (and only 0.5 per cent Jewish).

There has been a decline in religious affiliation and in church attendance within the traditional (white) denominations across European Christendom and church buildings are now merely seen as part of the historical and cultural background scenery of the city (Photo 16.3). But there has been a growth in church attendance in the developing world, especially in Africa and South America, and much of the rest of the world has not been yet affected by Western secularisation trends. As a result of increased immigration and globalisation (Fenster 2004), some of the largest churches in the United Kingdom comprise Pentecostal congregations which draw much of their membership from ethnic minority groups and in which women play a prominent role both as the majority of the congregations and in pastoral roles and in community development (Onuoha and Greed 2003). Many such faith communities have had great difficulty obtaining planning permission for church building (CAG 2008). For example, Kingsway International Christian Centre (KICC) comprises a mega-church with over 12,000 members of 46 different nationalities, and is one of the largest churches in Western Europe. KICC has been the subject of a long-running planning saga, because it failed to get planning permission for a new church building large enough to accommodate its congregation out on an industrial estate in Dagenham, East London. Its previous premises in Hackney were requisitioned as part of the Olympic site development. Because of their gracious willingness to move, KICC leaders imagined the planners would deal favourably with their application. But not so (DCLG 2009d). Both God and Gender (Faith and Feminism) share the misfortune of not being recognised as valid land-use issues within the UK planning system, although right at the start of modern planning, much reform and model town building was motivated by religious belief (Chapter 5).

In conclusion to this section, it is argued that much needs to change, not least the planners' understanding of the value of others' cultures, and life experiences so different from their own, especially in respect of gender considerations. In the post-secular age planners also need to acknowledge the importance of religion to planning: good and bad. They need to acknowledge the deeply sexist and esoteric religious roots of modern 'scientific', 'rational' planning principles, and, more positively, they need to understand the importance of faith to many sectors of the community today. Otherwise they will remain unaware and unable to meet the needs of the majority of society, including women, ethnic minority and religious groups within society (Narayanan 2014: Narayanan (ed.) 2015).

Unresolved matters and issues for the future

In the last section religion was identified as a neglected issue within the planning cultural agenda, but one which has major implications for planning practice, especially development control. In this final section we will retrace our steps through the chapters of the book, highlighting other issues and policy areas that are not yet resolved, that need watching for the future, or that need discarding from the planning agenda.

After the first introductory chapter, we plunged into the complexities of the nature of the planning system, charting recent changes and seeking to explain the Local Plans system developed by the Coalition government. A key problem that is not yet resolved is how to plan strategically at national level, which often requires a decisive hand, whilst maintaining local democracy and decision-making powers. At present it would seem that the promise of greater control by communities over what happens in their own area was fulfilled, because many of the key decisions as to the location of development were already being made at higher levels. It has always been a major issue in planning in how to get this balance right. There is also the structural question of how to organise the different levels of planning power, between national, regional, urban and local. After jettisoning the regional level, it would seem that this is gradually creeping back in, because there is always a need for high-level strategic guidance to set the agenda for future, especially for economic, development. It may be argued that the regional level is actually a key level at which the planning system might be organised in the future, providing the context for urban and local planning to operate effectively.

Several other unresolved issues came up in both Chapters 2 and 3. One was the question of whether it is possible to simplify planning. At first the Coalition government was keen to cut down massively on the vast amount of planning guidance that had been produced under previous Labour governments. But with time some of this guidance on specific topics began to return. National Planning *Practice* Guidance statements have begun to temper the austerity of the original National *Planning* Policy Framework in a thoroughly modern way under the auspices of the Planning Portal. Likewise in Chapter 3, the changes in planning law and the tweaks and simplifications directed at the Use Classes Order and other regulations were discussed. Attempts to speed up the planning system were soon seen to be very difficult to achieve, and likely simply to create another set of bureaucratic hoops and agencies. Faster planning might benefit developers in a rush (as time is money) but were likely to reduce the democratic rights, and rights of appeal of other concerned parties, and the community.

Other major debates were raised in the early chapters and emerged again and again throughout the book. These include the question of protecting the countryside, preserving the green belt, using brown-field land for new housing, and other spatial land-use considerations. None of this has been resolved and debates are likely to continue. But readers need to be aware that once land is built on, the area will never be the same and we only have a limited amount of land on our set of small islands. All new developments, whether it is a housing estate, a new set of wind turbines or a new out-of-town retail development, require more land to be taken for roads and other infrastructure to service them and change is never usually contained within the boundaries of the plots in question. In fact the impact of changes in land use and the sheer spatial, geographical aspects of development planning often seem to get lost in the political rhetoric that surrounds planning.

Part II of the book traced the historical development of towns and cities and their architecture. One lesson from the historical chapters is the importance of appreciating and understanding the heritage of the past, which continues to shape our cities, culture and very civilisation. Chapter 6 showed the foolishness of mass demolition and trying to create a shiny new future, which is a particularly twentieth-century habit. Indeed what is seen as modern in one generation often becomes jaded and out of fashion in the next. Chapter 7 brought the story of planning up to the present day, and discussed many of the conflicts, uncertainties and policy questions that planners face today. Much of this has been played out against the attitudes of central government towards planning, in particular the differences (and sometimes similarities) between Labour and Conservative (and more recently between New Labour and Coalition) approaches to planning.

Many of the policy issues were subsequently discussed within the specific topic chapters in Part III. Before this, in Chapter 8, the development of planning theory was discussed. This chapter demonstrated the alarming power that planning theory and planners can have if governments back them, particularly if planning is in tune with the ideologies and *zeitgeist* of the times. The change in attitude towards the planners was highlighted as both community groups, politicians and urban sociologists drew attention to the blind spots, biased attitudes and lack of awareness of the lives of ordinary people, often manifested by the planners.

In Part III, we investigated specific planning policy areas, including rural issues, sustainable development, urban regeneration, transport planning and urban design. In recounting, in each topic chapter, how policies developed, it soon became clear that planners have made some major policy mistakes and miscalculations, and we are still living with the results. These include the problems of high-rise council development, unnecessary demolition, out-of-town development, an over-enthusiasm for the needs of the motorcar, and the neglect of the planning needs of many social groups and minorities within society. But it is easy to be wise in retrospect and perhaps you can think of current policies that are seen as ideal, which may be questioned by future generations?

Chapter 9 stressed again the need to care for the countryside, as it is irreplaceable, but at the same time we need to be aware that change cannot always be stopped, but it can be managed in a productive manner. Chapter 10 on sustainability contained many of the most contentious and contested issues, including global warming, climate change, pollution, world health and population growth. One of the main lessons from this chapter is to remember that the concept of sustainability is not just about environmental sustainability, but also includes the need for social equality and economic well-being, without which environmental success is unlikely. The chapter also demonstrated that we live in a global village, within the same ecosphere and within an international economy, so we cannot adopt an isolationist attitude towards the rest of the world. Chapter 11 discussed urban regeneration and renewal, and looked at the main components of retail development, housing and the role of culture in creating vibrant cities, and was illustrated with case studies from East London. One of the key unresolved issues raised is the future of retail development, as many traditional High Streets are experiencing major decline. Modern shopping malls are still thriving but do not generally cater for local shopping needs or for those without a car. Overall more people are shopping on the internet and this is affecting the whole retail sector. We need to rethink the role of the town centre, High Street and out-of-town retail park too, as traditional land-use patterns are continuing to unravel, undermining many of the most basic town planning assumptions of what towns 'should' be like.

Chapter 12 on transport planning also raised many difficult issues, as we move from car-based transport systems towards a greater emphasis on the needs of the pedestrian, cyclist and public transport user. It was shown that we cannot deal with transport policy in isolation from sustainability considerations. But we also need to take into account urban design considerations too. However, it was advised that the policies of the new type of transport planners, who seek to control the motorcar in the name of sustainability, are not above reproach. The need to plan the city as a whole, to relocate land uses, and to provide adequate public transport options to enable people to get from home to work in a reasonable time and manner was stressed. There is no use condemning people for using their cars if there is no other sensible alternative available, particularly if they are living in the suburbs and there are no train stations or reliable direct bus routes available. A lack of gender awareness in policy-making is likely to penalise women who have more complex, multi-function journeys than men, more caring responsibilities and little time to undertake their journeys and tasks. Rather than being obsessed with trying to control individual journeys, especially by car, it is argued that there is a need to look again at where the traffic is coming from in the first place, and at what particular configuration of land uses generates the most commuter traffic. We need to re-plan our cities so that there is less concentration of employment in the city centre, and a greater level of decentralisation of jobs back into the surrounding residential suburbs where the majority of the working population lives. This strategy would complement policies that prioritise the provision of more housing development in city centres, a good strategy but one which is hardly family- or child-friendly.

In Chapter 13 on urban design we sought to show how the design agenda had moved over the years from doing housing layouts to creating quality spaces, which in turn contributed towards urban regeneration, city culture, accessibility and sustainability. The differences in opinion and perspective between the technically minded transport planner to keep the traffic moving, and the urban designer, who is concerned with place-making and quality environments, were highlighted. Again the need to look at the city as a whole was stressed. Dealing with one local area in isolation and pedestrianising and prettifying it, is only going to move traffic and in some cases employment to other localities. The danger of creating urban design schemes without reference to the needs of the people living in the area in question was stressed. Social inclusion, accessibility and mobility factors need to be taken into account both in urban design and planning policy-making, particularly as the population ages. But it would seem some local authorities are still writing large amounts of planning policy statements on employment as the basis of the future development of their area, and missing out on the importance of demographic changes, and wider cultural and leisure shifts shaping demand for new types of development. Planners and architects also need to be tuned into global trends in town planning and design as professionals share ideas across the globe (Photo 16.4).

In Part IV we looked at the social aspects of planning in more detail, seeking to right the balance towards planning for people to counter the arguably somewhat 'people-less' nature of much development and land-use planning. We traced the development of urban sociological issues past and present in Chapter 14 and considered the applicability of classical theories from the past to a changing, growing, diversifying, post-industrial Britain. We then re-ran the story, in Chapter 15, this time looking at the 'missing social groups', especially women and ethnic minorities, which were left out of a discourse, which for many years was focused on the needs of the traditional male working classes. In the final chapter we looked at the built environment professions and at the nature of the planners in particular. It was argued the professional subculture within planning not only leads to the exclusion of minority groups, but also shapes planning policy. A rather narrow worldview often seems to make the profession blind to the needs of others who are not like themselves. This was illustrated with reference to the problems faith groups are having in getting planning permission for worship and community buildings. Who knows

Photo 16.4   People travelling the world: Far East conference delegates

The world is on the move, and Britain is no longer isolated from international trends. Not only is there increased trade and migration, built environment professions from many countries are also travelling to each other's countries, for conferences and study tours, and in the process sharing ideas, architectural designs and urban planning policies.

what other issues planners will face in the future? What else is going to come out of nowhere and surprise the planners? It is important for the planners to be ahead of the game, to be able to read society and know what is going on. Otherwise planners will be stuck in a time warp as a traditional bureaucratic profession mainly concerned with land-use matters. It is hoped that in reading this book future planners will be more aware of the factors that generate the need for planning, will be able to anticipate future changes, and will be better able to deal with them.

For the tasks, further reading, additional photos and other resources for this chapter, please visit www.palgrave. com/companion/greed.

Bibliography

This extensive bibliography contains not only sources referred to within the printed version of this book but also references given on the book's website, especially in the E-Supplement that provides further reading advice for each chapter.

Abercrombie, P. (1944) *Greater London Development Plan* (London: HMSO).

Adams, E. and Ingham, S. (1998) *Changing Places: Children's Participation in Environmental Planning* (London: Children's Society).

Age Concern (1993) *Housing for All* (London: Age Concern).

Age UK (2009) *One Voice: Shaping our Ageing Society* (London: Age Concern and Help the Aged).

Ahmed, Y. (1989) 'Planning and Racial Equality', *The Planner*, 75(32), 1 December, 18–20 (London: Royal Town Planning Institute).

Aitchison, C. (2006) *Sport and Gender Identities: Masculinities, Femininities and Sexualities* (London: Psychology Press).

Aldous, T. (1972) *Battle for The Environment* (Glasgow: Collins).

Aldridge, M. (1979) *The British New Towns* (London: Routledge & Kegan Paul).

Alexander, A. (2009) *Britain's New Towns* (London: Routledge).

Alexander, C. (1965) *A City is not a Tree* (Harmondsworth: Penguin, available at www.rudi.net).

Allinson, J. (1998) 'GIS in Practice', *Planning*, May edition; 'Electronic Revolution: a Special Report', September 1998, 'Managing IT in a pressured environment', September 1998.

Allmendinger, P. (2001) *New Labour and Planning: From New Right to New Left* (London: Routledge).

Allmendinger, P. (2002) *Planning Theory* (Basingstoke: Palgrave Macmillan).

Allmendinger, P. and Tewdwr-Jones, M. (eds) (2002) *Planning Futures: New Directions for Planning Theory* (London: Routledge).

Allmendinger, P. and Thomas, H. (1998) *Urban Planning and the British New Right* (London: Routledge).

Allmendinger, P., Prior, A. and Raemaekers, J. (2000) *Introduction to Planning Practice* (London: Wiley).

Alonso, W. (1965) 'Cities and city planners', in 'Lynn and Daedalus', *The Professions in America* (Boston: Houghton Mifflin).

Al Sayyad, N. and Massoumi, M. (2010) *The Fundamentalist City* (London: Routledge).

Ambrose, P. (1986) *Whatever Happened to Planning?* (London: Methuen).

Ambrose, P. and Colenutt, B. (1979) *The Property Machine* (Harmondsworth: Penguin).

Amin, A. (2006) 'The good city', *Urban Studies*, 43(5-6), 1009–232.

Amin, A. and Thrift, N. (eds) (1995) *Globalisation, Institutions and Regional Development in Europe* (Oxford: Oxford University Press).

Anthony, K. (2001) *Designing for Diversity: Gender, Race and Ethnicity in the Architectural Profession* (Chicago: University of Chicago).

Armytage, W. (1961) *Heavens Below* (London: Routledge).

Armytage, W. (2007) *The New Towns of Britain: An Essay in Planning* (London: Routledge).

Arnstein, S. (1969) 'A ladder of citizen participation', *Journal of the American Institute of Planners*, 35, 216–24.

Arvill, R. (1969) *Man and Environment: Crisis and The Strategy of Choice* (Harmondsworth: Penguin).

Ashworth, W. (1968) *The Genesis of Modern British Town Planning* (London: Routledge & Kegan Paul).

Askew, J. (2009) *Review of Mobile Phone Operators: Permitted Development Rights* (Cardiff: National Assembly of Wales).

Association of Community Rail Partnerships (2012) Website (http://www.acorp.uk.com/) (accessed 14 July 2012).

Atkins, S. and Hoggitt, B. (1984) *Women and The Law* (Oxford: Blackwell).

Atkinson, R. and Helms, G. (eds) (2007) *Securing Urban Renaissance: Crime, Community and British Urban Policy* (Bristol: Policy Press).

Atkinson, R. and Moon, G. (1993) *Urban Policy in Britain: The City, the State and the Market* (London: Macmillan).

Attfield, J. (1989) 'Inside Pram Town, A Case Study of Harlow House Interiors, 1951–61', in J. Attfield and P. Kirkham (eds), *A View From The Interior: Feminism, Women, and Design* (London: Women's Press).

Attwood, L. (2011) *Gender and Housing in Soviet Russia: Private Life in Public Space* (Manchester: Manchester University Press).

Audit Commission (1999) *From Principles to Practice* (London: The Audit Commission).

Avis, M. and Gibson, V. (1987) *The Management of General Practice Surveying Firms* (University of Reading: Faculty of Urban and Regional Studies).

Backwell (2012) *Backwell Draft Neighbourhood Plan* (Backwell, Bristol: Backwell Parish Council), www.backwell-pc.gov.uk/backwell-draft-neighbourhood-plan.

Bacon, E. (1978) *Design of Cities* (London: Thames & Hudson).

Bagilhole, B., Green, S. and Dainty, A. (2007) (eds) *People and Culture in Construction: A Reader* (London: Taylor and Francis, Spon Research).

Bagilhole, B. (2009) *Understanding Equal Opportunities and Diversity: The Social Differentiations and Intersections of Inequality* (Bristol: Policy Press).

Bailey, J. (1975) *Social Theory for Planning* (London: Routledge & Kegan Paul).

Baker, C. and Beaumont, J. (eds) (2011) *Post-Secular Cities: Space, Theory and Practice* (London: Continuum).

Balchin, P. and Bull, G. (1987) *Regional and Urban Economics* (London: Harper & Row).

Ball, M. (1988) *Rebuilding Construction: Economic Change in The British Construction Industry* (London: Routledge).

Ball, S. (2012) *Liveable Communities for an Ageing Population: Urban Design Longevity* (London: Wiley).

Ball, S. and Bell, S. (1999) *Environmental Law*, 4th edn (London: Blackstone).

Bandarage, A. (1997) *Women, Population and Global Crisis* (London: ZED Books).

Banister, D. (2005) *Transport and Urban Development* (London: Earthscan).

Barker, K. (2004) *The Barker Review of Housing Supply: delivering stability, securing our future housing need* (London: TSO).

Barker, K. (2006) *The Barker Review of Land Use Planning: Final Report* (London: TSO).

Barlow Report (1940) *Report of The Royal Commission on the Distribution of The Industrial Population* (London: HMSO, Cmd. 6153).

Barrow, C. (2007) *Environmental Management for Sustainable Development* (London: Taylor & Francis).

Barthes, R. (1973) *Mythologies* (London: Paladin).

Barton, H. and Bruder, N. (1995*) Local Environmental Auditing* (London: Earthscan).

Barton, H. (1996) 'Planning for sustainable development', in C. Greed (ed.) (1996), *Investigating Town Planning* (Harlow: Longmans).

Barton, H. (1998) 'Design for Movement', in C. Greed and M. Roberts (eds) (1998), *Introducing Urban Design: Interventions and Responses* (Harlow: Longmans), Chapter 8, 133–52.

Barton, H., Davis, G. and Guise, R. (1998) *Sustainable Settlements: a guide for planners, designers and developers* (London: Earthscan).

Barton, H. and Tsourou, C. (2006) *Healthy Urban Planning* (Oxford: Spon).

Barton, H., Grant, M. and Guise, R. (2010) *Shaping Neighbourhoods for Local and Global Sustainability* (London: Routledge).

Barton, H. (2014) *City of Well-Being: a Guide to the Science and Art of Settlement Planning* (London: Earthscan).

Bassett, K. and Short, J. (1980) *Housing and Residential Structure: Alternative Approaches* (London: Routledge).

Bates, D.M. (2008) 'User perspective: blind people and shared surface developments', *Urban Design and Planning*, 161, Issue DP2, 49–50.

Baty, P. (1997) 'Is the Square Mile Colour Blind?', *Times Higher Education Supplement*, November, 6.

Bayer, M., Frank, N. and Valerius, J. (2010) *Becoming an Urban Planner: A Guide to Careers in Planning and Urban Design* (London: Wiley).

Bayman, B. (2008) *Underground: The Official Handbook* (London: Capital Transport).

BBC (2012) *The Secret History of Our Streets*, 6 episodes, transmitted June 2012 and can be found on the web (London: British Broadcasting Corporation).

BDOR (2011) *The Localism Bill and Neighbourhood Planning* (Bristol: BDOR Ltd). BDOR ceased trading 2012, now called Space Studio, Bristol.

Beaumont, J. (2008) 'Introduction: Faith-based organisations and urban social issues', *Urban Studies*, 45(10), 2019–34.

Beeching (1963) *The Beeching Report: The Reshaping of British Railways* (London: TSO).

Bell, C. and Bell, R. (1972) *City Fathers: The Early History of Town Planning in Britain* (Harmondsworth: Penguin).

Bell, C. and Newby, H. (1978) *Community Studies* (London: George, Allen & Unwin).

Bell, C. and Newby, H. (1980) *Doing Sociological Research* (London: George Allen & Unwin).

Bell, F. (1911) *At The Works* (London: Thomas Nelson).

Bell, J. (1996) *Doing your Research Project: A Guide for First-time Researchers in Education and the Social Sciences* (Milton Keynes: Open University Press).

Bell, Vicki (1999) *Performativity and Belonging* (London: Sage).

Bell, D. and Jayne, M. (2004) *City of Quarters* (London: Ashgate).

Belloni, C. (1994) 'A woman-friendly city: politics concerning the organisation of time in Italian cities', International Conference on *Women in The City: Housing Services and Urban Environment* (Paris: Organisation for Economic Co-operation and Development).

Benevelo, L. (1976) *The Origins of Modern Town Planning* (London: Routledge & Kegan Paul).

Benktzon, M. (1993) 'Designing our future selves: the Swedish Experience', *Applied Ergonomics*, 24(1), 19–27.

Bentley, I., Alcock, A., Murrain, P., McGlynn, S. and Smith, S. (1985 and 1992 new edition) *Responsive Environments: A Manual for Designers* (London: Architectural Press in association with Oxford Brookes University, Oxford).

BERR (2008) *Meeting the Energy Challenge – A White Paper on Nuclear Power* (London: TSO, BERR (Department for Business, Enterprise and Regulatory Reform)).

Betjeman, J. (1974) *A Pictorial History of English Architecture* (Harmondsworth: Penguin).

Bianchini, F. (1995) 'The twenty four hour city', *Demos*, Quarterly, Issue, 5.

Bianchini, F. and Greed, C. (1999) 'Cultural planning and time planning', in C. Greed (ed.), *Social Town Planning* (London, Routledge).

Biddulph, M. (2006) *Introduction to Residential Layout* (Oxford: Elsevier, Architectural Press).

Bilton, T., Bonnett, K., Jones, P., Skinner, D., Stanworth., M. and Webster, A. (2002) *Introductory Sociology* (London: Macmillan).

Birke, L., Himmelweit, S., Leonard, D., Ruehl, S. and Speakman, M. (eds) (1982) *The Changing Experience of Women* (Oxford: Basil Blackwell with Oxford: Open University).

Birkstead, J.K. (2009) *Le Corbusier and the Occult* (London: MIT Press).

Birmingham University (1987) *The Empire Strikes Back* (Birmingham: Centre for Continuing Cultural Studies).

Blowers A. (ed.) (1993) *Planning for a Sustainable Environment: A Report by The Town & County Planning Association* (London: Earthscan with TCPA).

Blowers, A. and Evans, B. (1997) *Town Planning in the 21st Century* (London: Routledge).

Blumer, H. (1965) 'Sociological implications of the thought of George Herbert Mead', in B. Cosin, I. Dale, G. Esland, D. MacKinnon and D. Swift (eds) (1977), *School and Society, A Sociological Reader* (London: Routledge & Kegan Paul).

Boardman, P. (1978) *The World of Patrick Geddes* (London: Routledge & Kegan Paul).

Boardman, A. (1991) 'Weavers of influence: The structure of contemporary geographic research', *Transactions of The Institute of British Geographers*, 16(1), 21–37.

Bodey, H. (1971) *Roads* (London: Batsford Books).

Bolsterli, M. (1977) *The Early Community At Bedford Park: The Pursuit of Corporate Happiness in The First Garden Suburb* (London: Routledge & Kegan Paul).

Booth, C. (1968, originally published in Series 1889–1906) *Life and Labour of The People in London* (Chicago: University of Chicago Press).

Booth, C. (1996) 'Breaking down barriers', in C. Booth, J. Darke and S. Yeandle (eds) (1996), *Changing Places: Women's Lives in The City* (London: Paul Chapman), Chapter 13, 167–82.

Booth, C. (1999) 'Approaches to meeting women's needs', *Gender Equality and the Role of Planning: Realising the Goal*, National Symposium, 1 July, Report of Proceedings (London: Royal Town Planning Institute).

Booth, C. and Gilroy, R. (1999) 'The role of a toolkit in mobilising women in local and regional development', paper presented at the *Future Planning: Planning's Future*, Sheffield, Planning Theory Conference, March.

Booth, C., Darke J., and Yeandle, S. (eds) (1996) *Changing Places: Women's Lives in The City* (London: Paul Chapman Publishing).

Booth, W. (1890) *In Darkest England and the Way Out* (London: Salvation Army).

Bor, W. (1972) *The Making of Cities* (London: Leonard Hill).

Bottomore, T. (1973) *Elites and Society* (Harmondsworth: Penguin).

Boulding, E. (1992) *The Underside of History*, Volume I (London: Sage).

Bourdieu, P. (1970 [2000 edition]) *Reproduction in Education, Society and Culture* (London: Sage).

Bourdieu, P. (1986) 'The forms of capital', in J. Richardson (ed.), *Handbook of Theory and Research for the Sociology of Education* (New York: Greenwood), 241–58.

Bourdieu, P. and Wacquant, L. (1992) *An Invitation to Reflexive Sociology* (Chicago: University of Chicago Press).

Bowlby, S. (1989) 'Gender issues and retail geography', in S. Whatmore and J. Little (eds) (1989), *Geography and Gender* (London: Association for Curriculum Development in Geography).

Boyd, N. (1982) *Josephine Butler, Octavia Hill, Florence Nightingale: Three Victorian Women Who Changed The World* (London: Macmillan).

Boyd, O. (2013) 'The way of the Dragon: China is Investing', *Construction Manager*, February, 12–17.

Boym, S. (1994) *Common Places: Mythologies of Everyday Life in Russia* (London: Harvard University Press).

Bradbury, R. (originally 1953) *Fahrenheit 451* (London: Flamingo 2008) (famous novel burning all books).

Bradley, S. (2007) *St Pancras Station* (London: Profile Books).

Bradshaw, G. (2012, originally 1863) *Bradshaw's Descriptive Railway Handbook of Great Britain and Ireland* (London: Old House).

Braidotti, R. (ed.) (1994) *Women, the Environment and Sustainable Development: Towards a Theoretical Synthesis* (London: Zed Books).

Brand, J. (1996) 'Sustainable development: the international, national and local context for women', *Built Environment*, 22(1), 58–71.

Brand, J. (1999) 'Planning for health, sustainability, and equity in Scotland', in C. Greed (ed.), *Social Town Planning* (London: Routledge).

Briggs, A. (1968) *Victorian Cities* (Harmondsworth: Penguin).

Brindley, T., Rydin, Y. and Stoker, G. (1996) *Remaking Planning: The Politics of Urban Change* (London: Routledge).

Brion, M. and Tinker, A. (1980) *Women in Housing: Access and Influence* (London: Housing Centre Trust).

Broady, M. (1968) *Planning for People* (London: NCSS/Bedford Square Press).

Brown, C. (1979) *Understanding Society: An Introduction to Sociological Theory* (London: John Murray).

Brown, L., Dixon, D. and Gillham, O. (2009) *Urban Design for an Urban Century: Placemaking for People* (London: Wiley).

Browne, K., Lim, J. and Brown, G. (2009), *Geographies of Sexuality* (Farnham: Ashgate).

Browne, K. and Bakshi, L. (2013) *Ordinary in Brighton?: LGBT Activisms and the City* (Farnham: Ashgate).

Brownill, S. (2000) 'Regenderation: women and urban policy in Britain', in J. Darke, S. Ledwith and R. Woods (eds), *Women and the City: Visibility and Voice in Urban Space* (Basingstoke: Palgrave Macmillan).

Brownill, S. and Downing, L. (2013) 'Neighbourhood plans: is infrastructure a localism issue?', *Town and Country Planning*, 82(9), September, 372–6.

Brundtland Report (1987) *Our Common Future*, World Commission on Environment and Development (Oxford: Oxford University Press).

Bruton, M. (1975) *Introduction to Transportation Planning* (London: Hutchinson).

BSI (2006) *BS6465 – Part 1: Sanitary Installations: Code of practice for the design of sanitary facilities and the scale of provision* (London: British Standards Institute).

BSI (2009) *BS8300 – Accessible Building Design: Improving the Built Environment, Code of Practice* (London: British Standards Institute).

BSI (2010) *BS6465 – Part 4: Sanitary Installations: Code of Practice for the Provision of Public Toilets* (London: British Standards Institute).

BTA (1999) *Better Public Toilets* (Winchester: British Toilet Association (BTA)).

BTA (2001) *Better Public Toilets: the provision and management of 'away from home' toilets* (Winchester: British Toilet Association).

BTA (2002) *Best Value Guide for Public Toilets* (Winchester: British Toilet Association).

Buchanan, C. (1963) *Traffic in Towns* (Harmondsworth: Penguin).

Buchanan, C. (1972) *The State of Britain* (London: Faber).

Buckingham-Hatfield, S. (2000) *Gender and Environment* (London: Routledge).

Buckingham-Hatfield, S. and Evans, B. (1996) *Environmental Planning and Sustainability* (Chichester: Wiley).

Buckingham, S. (2013) 'Gender, Sustainability and the Urban Environment', in I.S. Madariaga and M. Roberts (eds) (2013), *Fair Shared Cities* (London: Ashgate).

Building Regulations (2004 incorporating amendments of 2010 and 2013) *Approved Part M: Access and Use of Buildings* (London: DCLG).

Built Environment (1984) Special Issue on 'Women and The Built Environment', *Built Environment*, 10(1).

Built Environment (1996) Special Issue on 'Women and The Built Environment', *Built Environment*, 22(1).

Bulmer, M. (1984) *The Chicago School of Sociology* (London: University of Chicago Press).

Burdett, R. and Sudjic, D. (2011) *The Endless City* (London: Phaidon).

Burdett, R. and Sudjic, D. (2012) *Living in the Endless City* (London: Phaidon).

Burke, G. (1976) *Townscapes* (Harmondsworth: Penguin).

Burke, G. (1977) *Towns in the Making* (London: Edward Arnold).

Burke, G. and Taylor, T. (1990) *Town Planning and the Surveyor* (Reading: College of Estate Management).

Burton, E. and Mitchell, L. (2006) *Inclusive Urban Design: Streets for Life* (Oxford: Architectural Press).

CABE (2006a) *Design and Access Statements: How to Write Them* (London: Commission for Architecture and the Built Environment).

CABE (2006b) *The Principles of Inclusive Design: They Include You* (London: Commission for Architecture and the Built Environment).

CABE (2008) *Inclusion by Design: Equality, Diversity and the Built Environment* (London: Commission for Architecture and the Built Environment).

CABE (2010) *By Design: Urban Places in the Planning System: Towards Better Practice* (London: Commission for Architecture and the Built Environment).

Cabinet Office (2010) *The Coalition: our programme for government* (London: Cabinet Office).

Cadman, D. and Topping, R. (1995) *Property Development* (London: Spons).

CAE (monthly) *Newsletter* (London: Centre for Accessible Environments).

CAE (Centre for Accessible Environments) (1998) *Keeping up with the Past – making historic buildings accessible to everyone* (Video) (London: Centre for Accessible Environments).

CAE (2012) *Designing for Accessibility* (London: CAE in association with RIBA).

CAE (2013) *Access Audit Handbook* (London: RIBA Publishing).

CAG (2008) *Responding to the Needs of Faith Communities: Places of Worship: Final Report* (London: CAG, Cooperative Advisory Group Planning Consultants).

Callon, M., Law, J. and Rip, A. (1986) *Mapping The Dynamics of Science and Technology* (London: Macmillan).

Cameron, D. MP (2011) 'Big Society Speech', 23 May, http://www.number10.gov.uk/news/speech-on-the-big-society/ (accessed 10 July 2011).

Cameron-Blackhall, J. (2005) *Planning Law and Practice* (London: Cavendish).

Campbell, S. and Fainstein, S. (eds) (2003) *Readings in Planning Policy* (Oxford: Blackwell).

Campbell, B. (1984) *Wigan Pier Revisited: Poverty and Politics in the Eighties* (London: Virago).

Capon, A. (ed.) (July 2011) *Essays in Healthy City Design* (London: Arup in association with www.worldhealthdesign.com).

Carey, L. and Mapes, R. (1972) *The Sociology of Planning: A Study of Social Activity on New Housing Estates* (London: Batsford).

Carmona, M. and Tiesdell, S. (2006) *Urban Design Reader* (Oxford: Elsevier).

Carmona, M., Tiesdell, S., Heath, T. and Oc, T. (2010) *Public Places: Urban Spaces* (Oxford: Architectural Press).

Carson, R. (1962) *Silent Spring* (Harmondsworth: Penguin).

Carter, R. and Kirkup, G. (eds) (1989) *Women in Engineering* (London: Macmillan).

Castells, M. (1977) *The Urban Question* (London: Arnold).

Cavanagh, S. (2010) *Queering Bathrooms: Gender, Sexuality and the Hygienic Imagination* (Toronto: University of Toronto Press).

CEC (1990) *Green Paper on the Urban Environment*, Fourth Environmental Action Programme 1987–1992 COM(90) 218 CEC (Brussels: Commission of the European Communities).

CEC (1991) *Europe 2000: Outlook for the development of the Community's territory*, Directorate-General for Regional Policy and Cohesion, Brussels. COM(91) 452 (Brussels: CEC).

CEC (1992) *Towards Sustainability: Fifth Environmental Action Programme* (Brussels: CEC).

CEC (1994) *Communication from The Commission on The Recognition of Qualifications for Academic and Professional Purposes* (Brussels: CEC).

CEC (1997) *The EU Compendium of spatial planning systems and policies* (Luxembourg: Commission of the European Communities).

CEC (1999) *The European Spatial Development Perspective: towards balanced and sustainable development in the territory of the EU* (Brussels: CEC, Report of the Council of EU Ministers Responsible for Spatial Planning).

Chadwick, E. (1842) *Report on the Sanitary Condition of the Labouring Population of Great Britain* (London).

Chapin, F. (1965; and 1979 edition with J. Kaiser) *Urban Land Use Planning* (Illinois: University of Illinois Press), 12–25.

Chapman, D. (ed.) (1996) *Neighbourhoods and Plans in the Built Environment* (London: Spon).

Cherry, G. (1988) *Cities and Plans* (London: Edward Arnold).

Cherry, G. (ed.) (1981) *Pioneers in British Town Planning* (London: Architectural Press).

Chinoy, E. (1967) *An Introduction to Sociology* (New York: Random House).

Chouinard, B., Hall, E. and Wilton, R. (2010) *Towards Enabling Geographies: 'Disabled' Bodies and Minds in Society and Space* (Abingdon: Ashgate).

Christaller, T. (1966) *Central Place Theory* (London: Prentice Hall, originally 1933).

CIA (2014) *CIA World Fact Book* (Washington: Central Intelligence Agency), https://www.cia.gov/library/publications/the-world-factbook/.

CIB (1996) 'Tomorrow's Team: Women and Men in Construction', Report of Working Group 8 of Latham Committee, *Constructing The Team* (London: Department of The Environment, and Construction Industry Board (CIB)).

CIC (2009) *Gathering and Reviewing Data on Diversity within the Construction Profession*s (London: Construction Industry Council), in association with the University of the West of England, Bristol, by Ann de Graft-Johnson, Rachel Sara, Fiona Gleed and Nada Brkljac.

CIC (2010) *Building the Future: How Women Professionals Can Make a Difference* (London: Construction Industry Council).

CIOB (2006) *Inclusivity: The Changing Role of Women in the Workforce* (London: Chartered Institute of Building in association with Reading University, researcher Sonia Gurjao).

CISC (Construction Industry Standing Conference) (1994) *CISC Standards 1994: Occupational Standards for Professional, Managerial, and Technical Occupations in Planning, Construction, Property and Related Engineering Services* (London: CISC, The Building Centre, 26, Store Street, London, WCIE 7BT).

CITB (annual) *The Construction Industry: Key Labour Market Statistics* (King's Lynn: Construction Industry Training Board).

CITH (2010) *Manual for Streets 2: Wider Application of the Principles* (London: Chartered Institute of Highways and Transport).

Club of Rome (1972) *Limits to Growth* (New York: Universe Books).

Cockburn, C. (1977) *The Local State: Management of People and Cities* (London: Pluto).

Coleman, A. (1985) *Utopia on Trial* (London: Martin Shipman).

Coleman, C. (2000) 'Women, transport and cities: an overview an agenda for research', in J. Darke, S. Ledwith and R. Woods (eds), *Women and the City: Visibility and Voice in Urban Space* (Basingstoke: Palgrave Macmillan), 83–97.

Collar, N. (2010) *Planning Law: The Scottish System* (Edinburgh: W. Green).

Collins, M. (2011) *The Great Estate: The Rise and Fall of Council Housing*, BBC4 Film (London: BBC Publications).

Collins, R. (1979) *The Credential Society* (New York: Academic Press).

Competition Commission (2011) *Local Bus Services Market Investigation* (London: Competition Commission).

Conservative Party (2009) *Open Source Planning: Green Paper* (London: Conservative Central Office).

Cooke, P. (2007) *Creative Cities, Cultural Clusters and Economic Development* (Cheltenham: Elgar).

Cooper, D. (ed.) (2008) *Intersectionality and Beyond* (London: Taylor and Francis).

Corburn, J. (2010) *Towards the Healthy City: People, Places, Politics and Urban Planning* (London: MIT Press).

Corbusier, Le (1971, was 1929) *The City of Tomorrow* (London: Architectural Press).

Countryside Commission (1990) *Planning for A Greener Countryside* (Manchester: Countryside Commission Publications).

County Planning Officers Society (1993) *Planning for Sustainability* (London: CPOS).

Cowan, R. (ed.) (2008) *Design and Access Statements Explained, An Urban Design Group good practice guide* (London: Thomas Telford).

Cowell, R. and Owens, S. (2006) 'Governing Space: planning reform and the politics of sustainability: Environment and Planning', *Government and Policy*, 24, 403–21.

Cox, Harvey (1965) *The Secular City: Secularisation and Urbanisation in Theological Retrospect* (Harmondsworth: Penguin).

CRE (Commission for Racial Equality) (1989) *A Guide for Estate Agents and Vendors* (London: CRE).

CRE (1995) *Building Equality: Report of a formal investigation into The Construction Industry Training Board* (London: Commission for Racial Equality).

Crenshaw, K. (1991) 'Mapping the margins: intersectionality, identity politics, and violence against women', *Stanford Law Review*, 43(6), July, 1241–99.

CPRE (2012) *Inexpensive Progress? A Framework for assessing the costs and benefits of planning reform* (London: Campaign to Protect Rural England in association with the National Trust).

Crompton, R. and Sanderson, K. (1990) *Gendered Jobs and Social Change* (London: Unwin Hyman).

Crookston, M. (1999) 'The Urban Renaissance and the "New Agenda" in Planning', *Planning Law Conference* (London: Law Society), 26 November.

Crouch, S., Fleming, R. and Shaftoe, H. (1999) *Design for Secure Residential Environments* (Harlow: Pearson Education (Longmans)).

Cullen, G. (1971) *Concise Townscape* (London: Architectural Press).

Cullingworth, J.B. (1997) *Planning in the USA* (New York: Routledge).

Cullingworth, B. (1999) *British Planning: 50 years of urban and regional policy* (London: Athlone).

Cullingworth, B. and Nadin, V. (2006) *Town and Country Planning in the UK*, 14th edn (London: Routledge).

Dahrendorf, R. (1980) *Life Chances: Approaches to Social and Political Theory* (London: Weidenfeld and Nicolson).

Dainty, A. Green, S. and Bagilhole, B. (eds) (2007) *People and Culture in Construction* (London: Spon).

Dainty, A. and Loosemore, M. (eds) (2012) *Human Resource Management in Construction* (London: Routledge).

Damon, Julien (2009) 'Les Toilettes Publique: un droit a mieux amenagement', *Droit Social*, 1, 103–10.

Darke, J. and Brownill, S. (1999) 'A new deal for inclusivity: Race, Gender and Recent Regeneration Initiatives', paper presented at the *Future Planning: Planning's Future* (Sheffield: Planning Theory Conference), March.

Darke, J., Ledwith, S. and Woods, R. (eds) (2000) *Women and the City: Visibility and Voice in Urban Space* (Basingstoke: Palgrave Macmillan).

Darley, G. (1978) *Villages of Vision* (London: Granada).

Darley, G. (1990) *Octavia Hill* (London: Constable).

Darling, E. and Whitworth, L. (2007) *Women and the Making of the Built Environment* (London: Ashgate).

Davidoff, P. and Reiner, T. (1962) 'A choice theory of planning', *Journal of the American Institute of Planners*, 28, May (reprinted in Faludi (ed.) 1973, 277–96).

Davidson, R. and Maitland, R. (1999) 'Planning for tourism in towns and cities', in C. Greed (ed.), *Social Town Planning* (London: Routledge).

Davies, L. (1992) *Planning in Europe* (London: RTPI).

Davis, M. (2009) *Comrade or Brother? A History of the British Labour Movement* (London: Pluto Press).

Davies, L. (1998) 'The ESDP and the UK', *Town and Country Planning*, 67(2), March, 64–5.

Davies, L. (1999) 'Planning for disability: barrier-free living', in C. Greed (ed.), *Social Town Planning* (London: Routledge).

Davoudi, S. (2012) Resilience: a Bridging Concept or a Dead End?', *Planning Theory and Practice*, 13(2), 299–333.

DCLG (2005) *The National Strategy for e-government, e-transformation and e-planning*, (London: Department of Communities and Local Government).

DCLG (2007a) *Public Access to Toilets: A Strategic Guide* (London: DCLG).

DCLG (2007b) *Gender Equality Scheme*, Department of Communities and Local Government (London: DCLG).

DCLG (2008) *Lifetime Homes, Lifetime Neighbourhoods: a National Strategy for Housing in an Ageing Society* (London: DCLG).

DCLG (2009a) *Planning Policy Statement: Eco Towns – A supplement to Planning Policy Statement 1* (London: Department of Communities and Local Government Publications).

DCLG (2009b) *Approved Document M, Access to and Use of Buildings*, Building Regulation Part M (London: DCLG).

DCLG (2009c) *World class places: The Government's strategy for improving quality of place* (London: DCLG).

DCLG (2009d) *Appeal by Kingsway International Christian Centre and the London Development Agency* (London: Communities and Local Government), Ref: U0006.7/LBGH.

DCLG (2010a) *Use Classes Order* (London: DCLG), November.

DCLG (2010b) *Press Release John Healey: Green overhaul for planning system to cut emissions and bills*, http://www.communities.gov.uk/news/corporate/1499863 (accessed 10 March 2010).

DCLG (2011a) *National Planning Policy Framework* (London: Communities and Local Government Publications).

DCLG (2011b) *Community Infrastructure Levy: An Overview* (London: DCLG), http://www.communities.gov.uk/documents/planningandbuilding/pdf/1897278.pdf.

DCLG (2011c) *Local Authority Revenue Expenditure and Financing England*: 2012-1 (London: DCLG).

DCLG (2011d) *Press Release 3 January 2011 Pickles and Hammond to end the war on motorists*, http://www.communities.gov.uk/news/newsroom/1809347 (accessed 14 August 2012).

DCLG (2011e) *Public Sector Equality Duty* (London: DCLG and EHRC (Equality and Human Rights Commission)).

DCLG (2012) *Pre-application Consultation with Communities: a Basic Guide*, at http://www.communities.gov.uk/documents/ planningandbuilding/pdf/1854024.pdf.

DECC (2011) *The Carbon Plan: Delivering a Low Carbon Future* (London: Department of Energy and Climate Change).

DECC (2012) *The UK National Renewable Energy Action Plan* (London: Department of Energy and Climate Change).

De Graft-Johnson, A. (1999) 'Gender and Race', in C. Greed (ed.), *Social Town Planning* (London: Routledge).

De Graft-Johnson, A., Manley, S. and Greed, C. (2005) *Why Women Leave Architecture*, Study commissioned for the RIBA (London: RIBA in association with the University of the West of England).

De Graft-Johnson, A., Manley, S. and Greed, C. (2006) 'Diversity or the lack of it in the architectural profession: Why women leave architecture', *Construction Management and Economics*, 23(10), 1035–43.

De Graft-Johnson, A., Manley. S. and Greed, C. (2007) 'The gender gap in architectural practice: can we afford it?', in B. Bagilhole, S. Green and A. Dainty (eds), *People and Culture in Construction: A Reader* (London: Taylor & Francis/Spon Research).

Deem, R. (1986) *All Work and No Play?: The Sociology of Women and Leisure Reconsidered* (Milton Keynes: Open University Press).

DEFRA (2004) *Rural Strategy 2004* (London: Department of Environment, Food and Rural Affairs).

Delamont, S. (1985) 'Fighting familiarity', *Strategies of Qualitative Research in Education* (Warwick: ESRC Summer School).

Denington Report (1966) *Our Older Homes: A Call to Action* (London: HMSO).

Dennis, N. (1972) *Public Participation and Planners' Blight* (London: Faber).

Department of Health (1998) *Our Healthier Nation: A Contract for Health* (London: HMSO).

Department of Transport (1990) *Roads in Urban Areas* (London: HMSO).

DETR (1998a) *Modernising Planning* (London: HMSO, Department of Environment, Transport and the Regions).

DETR (1998b) *The Future of Regional Planning Guidance: Consultation Paper* (London: HMSO).

DETR (1998c) *A New Deal for Transport: Better for Everyone* (London: HMSO).

DETR (1998d) *Opportunities for Change: Consultation Paper on a Revised UK Strategy for Sustainable Development* (London: HMSO).

DETR (1999a) *Residential Roads and Footpaths Design Bulletin 32*, 2nd edn (London: DETR).

DETR (1999b) *Places, Streets and Movement: a companion guide to Design Bulletin 32 (Residential Roads and Footpaths Design)* (London: DETR).

DETR (1999c) *Leylandii and other High Hedges - Briefing note* (London: DETR).

DETR (1999d) *Modernising Planning: a Progress Report* (London: DETR).

DETR (1999e) *Design in The Planning System: a companion guide to planning policy note 1, General Policy and Principles* (London: TSO).

Devereaux, M. (1992) *European and National Planning* (Bristol: University of the West of England, Occasional Paper).

DfT (2000) *Public Transport Gender Audit* (London: Department for Transport, Mobility Unit).

DfT (2007) *Manual for Streets* (London: Thomas Telford publications in association with Institute of Highway Engineers), and see CIHT (2010) for *Manual for Streets 2*.

DfT (2009a) *Guidance on Local Transport Plans* (London: Department for Transport).

DfT (2009b) *Role of soft factors in patronage growth and modal split in the bus market in England* (London: Department for Transport).

DfT (2010) *Press Release, 20 October 2010: Transport spending review 2010*, http://www.dft.gov.uk/news/press-releases/dft-press-20101020 (accessed 14 August 2012).

DfT (2011a) *Design Manual for Roads and Bridges*, (DMRB) (London: Department for Transport), 15 volumes.

DfT (2011b) *Creating growth, cutting carbon: making sustainable local transport happen* (London: Department for Transport).

Department for Transport (2012a) *Vehicle Licensing Statistics*, https://www.gov.uk/government/statistical-data-sets/veh01-vehicles-registered-for-the-first-time (accessed 9 August 2012).

Department for Transport (2012b) *Light Rail and Tram Statistics* http://www.dft.gov.uk/statistics/series/light-rail-and-tram/ (accessed 05 September 2012).

Dixon, R. and Muthesius, S. (1978) *Victorian Architecture* (London: Thames & Hudson).

Doan, P. (ed.) (2011) *Queering Planning: Challenging Heteronormative Assumptions and Reframing Planning Practice* (Farnham: Ashgate).

Dobson, A. (2000) *Green Political Thought* (London: Routledge).

DoE (1970) *Sunlight and Daylight: Planning Criteria and Design of Buildings* (London: HMSO).

DoE (1972a) *Development Plan Manual: Structure Plans* (London: HMSO).

DoE (1972b) *How Do You Want to Live? A Report on Human Habitat* (London: HMSO).

DoE (1990a) *This Common Inheritance: Britain's Environmental Strategy* (London: HMSO), Command No. 1200.

DoE (1990b) *Roads in Urban Areas* (London: HMSO).

DoE (1992a) *Development Plans: Good Practice Guide* (London: HMSO).

DoE (1992b) *Land Use Planning Policy and Climate Change* (London: HMSO).

DoE (1993a) *The Good Practice Guide on Environmental Assessment of Development Plans* (London: HMSO).

DoE (1993b) *Schemes at Medium and High Density*, Design Bulletin (London: HMSO).

DoE/DoT (1993) *Reducing Transport Emissions Through Planning* (London: HMSO).

DoE (1994a) *Sustainable Development: The UK Strategy* (London: HMSO).

DoE (1994b) *Climate Change: The UK Programme* (London: HMSO) (Command No. 2427).

DoE (1994c) *Biodiversity: The UK Action Plan* (London: HMSO) (Command No. 2428).

DoE (1996) *Household Growth: Where Shall We Live?* (London: DoE).

Donnison, D. and Eversley, D. (1974) *London: Urban Patterns, Problems and Policies* (London: Heinemann).

Donnison, D. and Ungerson, C. (1982) *Housing Policy* (Harmondsworth: Penguin).

Dorey, P. (2005) *Policy Making in Britain* (London: Sage).

Dorling, D. (2008) *The No Nonsense Guide to Inequality* (London: New Internationalist).

Dorling, D. (2012) *The Population of Britain* (London: Sage).

Douglas, M. (1966) *Purity and Danger: An Analysis of the Concepts of Pollution and Taboo* (London: Routledge).

Dower Report (1945) *National Parks in England and Wales* (London: HMSO).

Dowling, J.A. (1995) *Northern Ireland Planning Law* (London: Macmillan).

Doxiadis, C. (1968) *Ekistics: An Introduction to the Science of Human Settlements* (London: Hutchinson).

Dresser, M. (1978) 'Review Essay' of Davidoff, L. *et al.* (1976), 'Landscape with Figures: Home and Community in English Society', *International Journal of Urban and Regional Research*, 2(3), Special Issue on 'Women and The City'.

Dresser, M. and Fleming, P. (2007) *Bristol: Ethnic Minorities and the City 1000–2001* (London: Phillimore, University of London Press).

Druker J. and White, G. (1996) *Managing People in Construction*, London: Institute of Personnel and Development.

Druker, J., White, G., Hegewisch, A. and Mayne, L. (1996) 'Between hard and soft HRM: human resource management in The construction industry', *Construction Management and Economics*, 14,405–16.

DTI (2004) *Driving Change: Retail Strategy* (London: Department of Trade and Industry).

DTI (2007) *Energy White Paper – Meeting the Energy Challenge* (London: Department of Trade and Industry).

DTLR (2001a) *Planning: Delivering a Fundamental Change*, (London: Department of Transport, Local Government and the Regions).

DTLR (2001b) *Planning Obligations: Delivering Fundamental Change* (London: DTLR).

Dudley Report (1944) *Design of Dwellings* (London: HMSO, Central Housing Advisory Committee of The Ministry of Health).

Dungey, J. and Newman, I (1999) *The New Regional Agenda* (London: Local Government Information Unit).

Dunham-Jones, E. and Williamson, J. (2011) *Retrofitting Suburbia: Urban Design Solutions for Redesigning Suburbs* (London: Wiley).

Dunleavy, P. (1980) *Urban Political Analysis* (London: Macmillan).

Durkheim, E. (1970, originally 1897) *Suicide: A Study in Sociology* (London: Routledge & Kegan Paul).

Durning, L. and Wrigley, R. (2000) *Gender and Architecture* (Chichester: Wiley).

Duxbury, R. (2013) *Telling and Duxbury's Planning Law and Procedure* (Oxford: Oxford University Press).

Dyos, H. (ed.) (1976) *The Study of Urban Form* (London: Edward Arnold).

Eade, J. (2011) 'From Race to Religion: Multiculturalism and Contested Urban Space', in C. Baker and J. Beaumont (eds), *Post-Secular Cities: Space, Theory and Practice* (London: Continuum), Chapter 9, 154–67.

EC (1999) *ESDP European Spatial Development Perspective: Towards Balanced and Sustainable Development of the Territory of the European Union* (Brussels: European Commission), Informal Council of Ministers responsible for Spatial Planning in Potsdam, http://ec.europa.eu/regional_policy/sources/docoffic/official/reports/pdf/sum_en.pdf.

EC (2010) The Urban Dimension in European Union Policies, on line at http://ec.europa.eu/regional_policy/sources/docgener/guides/urban/pdf/urbanguide1_en.pdf.

Edwards, T. (1921) *Good and Bad Manners in Architecture* (London: Dent).

Egan Report (1998) *Rethinking Construction: The Report of the Construction Task Force* (London: HMSO, The Egan Report, Construction Industry Council).

EHRC (2011) *Equality and Diversity: Good Practice for the Construction Sector* (London: Equalities and Human Rights Commission in association with the Construction Leadership Diversity Forum).

Ehrlich, P. (1971) *The Population Bomb: the End of Affluence and How to Survive* (London: Simon and Schuster, 1990 edition).

Ekistics (1985) 'Woman and Space in Human Settlements', *Ekistics: Special Edition*, 52(310), January.

Electoral Commission (2005) *The 2004 North East Regional Assembly and Local Government Referendums* (London: The Electoral Commission), http://www.electoralcommission.org.uk/_data/assets/pdf_file/0008/76994/NEreffullreport.pdf.

Elkin, T. and McLaren, D. (1991) *Reviving The City: Towards Sustainable Urban Development* (London: Friends of The Earth and Policy Studies Institute).

Elliot, D. (2008) *A Better Way to Zone: 10 Principles to Create More Liveable Cities* (Washington, DC: Island Press).

Ellison, L. (2008) *Raising the Ratio* (London: RICS (of women surveyors)).

Elson, M. (1986) *Green Belts* (London: Heinemann).

English Nature (1994) *Sustainability in Practice Issue 1: Planning for Environmental Sustainability* (Peterborough: English Heritage).

English Heritage (2004) *Countryside Quality Counts* (London: English Heritage).

English Heritage (2005) *Heritage Counts* (London: English Heritage).

English Partnerships (2007) *The Urban Design Compendium* (Oxford: Architectural Press).

Engwicht, D. (accessed 2007) '*The Connection between religion and urban planning*', research paper, Griffith University, Brisbane, at www.lesstraffic.com/Articles/places/religion.pdf.

Esher, L. (1983) *A Broken Wave: The Rebuilding of England 1940–80* (Harmondsworth: Penguin).

ESRC (2012) *Britain in 2013: The Nation in Focus* (Swindon: Economic and Social Research Council), www.esrc.ac.uk and www.ons.gov.uk.

Essex (1973) *A Design Guide for Residential Areas* (Essex: Essex County Council).

Essex (1997) *The Essex Design Guide for Residential and Mixed Uses* (Essex: Essex Planning Officers Association).

Essex (2005) *The Essex Design Guide* (Chelmsford: Essex County Council), updates available at www.the-edi.co.uk/downloads/19715_essexdesignguide.pdf.

Etzioni, A (1967) 'Mixed scanning: a third approach to decision-making', *Public Administration Review*, December (reprinted in Faludi (ed.) 1973, 217–29).

EUROFEM (1998) *Gender and Human Settlements: Conference Report on Local and Regional Sustainable Human Development from a Gender Perspective* (Hameenlina, Finland: Eurofem).

Evelyn, J. (1664) *Sylva: A Discourse of Forest Trees* (Cambridge: Cambridge University Press, 2013 reprint).

Eversley, D. (1973) *The Planner in Society* (London: Faber).

Evetts, J. (1996) *Gender and Career in Science and Engineering* (London: Taylor & Francis).

Fainstein, S. and Servon, L. (2005) *Gender and Planning* (London: Rutgers University Press).

Fainstein, S. and Campbell, S. (eds) (2011) *Readings in Urban Theory* (London: Wiley).

Falk, N. (2012) 'India's urban future: achieving smarter growth', *Town and Country Planning*, 81(10), October, 456–61.

Faludi, A. (1973) *Planning Theory* (Oxford: Pergamon Press (1992)).

Faludi, A. (ed.) (1973) *A Reader in Planning Theory* (Oxford: Pergamon).

Farnsworth, D. (2013a) 'Neighbourhood Planning: implications for planning practice', Proceedings of RTPI Conference, *Neighbourhood Planning: Experiences to Date* (Bristol: RTPI South West Branch). Available from Bristol Neighbourhood Planning Network at www.rtpi.org.uk/the-rtpi-near-you/rtpi-south-west.

Farnsworth, D. (2013b) 'Informed choice – the future for town planning', *Town and Country Planning*, February, 82(2), 85–7.

FCM (2006) *A City Tailored to Women: The Role of Municipal Governments in Achieving Gender Equality* (Montreal: Federation of Canadian Municipalities (FCM)), www.ville.montreal.qc.ca/femmesetville.

Fearns, D. (1993) *Access Audits: a guide and checklists for appraising the accessibility of buildings for disabled users* (London: Centre for Accessible Environments).

Fenster, T. (2004) *The Global City and the Holy City: Narratives in Knowledge, Planning and Diversity* (Harlow, London: Pearson).

Fenwick, J., McMillan, J. and Elcock, H. (2009) 'Local Government and the Problem of English Governance', *Local Government Studies*, 35(1), 5–20.

Fewings, P. (2008) *Ethics for the Built Environment* (London: Taylor and Francis).

Fincher, R. and Iveson, K. (2008) *Planning and Diversity in the City: Redistribution, Recognition, and Encounter* (Basingstoke: Palgrave Macmillan).

Finkelstein, V. (1993) 'Disability: a social challenge or an administrative responsibility?', in J. Swain, V. Finkelstein, S. French and M. Oliver (eds) (1993), *Disabling Barriers – Enabling Environments* (London: Sage Publications, in association with the Open University).

Fitch, R. and Knobel, L. (1990) *Fitch on Retail Design* (Oxford: Phaidon).

Fleck, J. (2003) *Accessible London: Achieving an Inclusive Environment: the London Plan (Spatial Development Strategy for Greater London); Draft Supplementary Planning Guidance* (London: Greater London Authority).

FOE (1988) *Environmental Charter* (London: Friends of the Earth).

Foley, D. (1964) 'An Approach to Urban Metropolitan Structure', in M. Webber, J. Dyckman, D. Foley, A. Guttenberg, W. Wheaton and C. Bauer Wurster (1964), *Explorations Into Urban Structure* (Philadelphia: University of Pennsylvania Press).

Forsyth, M. (2003) *Pevsner Architectural Guides: Bath* (London: Yale University Press) (and available other cities too, in various editions by various publishers).

Foulsham, J. (1990) 'Women's Needs and Planning: A Critical Evaluation of Recent Local Authority Practice', in J. Montgomery and A. Thornley (eds) (1990), *Radical Planning Initiatives* (Aldershot: Gower).

Frankenberg, R. (1970) *Communities in Britain* (Harmondsworth: Penguin).

Friedan, B. (1982, originally 1963) *The Feminine Mystique* (Harmondsworth: Penguin).

Friedman, M. (1975) *There's no such thing as a Free Lunch* (Chicago: University of Chicago).

Friedman, M. (1991) *Monetarist Economics* (London: Blackwells).

Friedman, M. (2002) *Capitalism and Freedom* (Chicago: University of Chicago).

Fudge, C. (1999) 'Urban Planning in Europe for Health and Sustainability', in C. Greed (ed.), *Social Town Planning* (London: Routledge).

Fulcher, J. and Scott, J. (2011) *Sociology* (Oxford: Oxford University Press).

FUN (Frauen Umwelt Netz) (1998) *European Seminar of Experts on Gender, Environment and Labour*, Frankfurt, December 1999, Conference Report.

Gabler, J. (2010) *Sociology for Dummies* (London: Wiley).

Gale, A. and Davidson, M. (2006) (eds) *Managing Diversity and Equality in the Construction Industry: Initiatives and Practice* (London: Taylor & Francis).

Gale, R. (2008) 'Locating Religion in Urban Planning: Beyond Race and Ethnicity', *Planning Practice and Research*, 23(1), 19–39.

Gallent, A. (2008) 'Strategic-Local Tensions and the Spatial Planning Approach in England', *Planning Theory & Practice*, 9(3), 307–23.

Gallent, A., Juntti, M., Kidd, S. and Shaw, D. (2008) *Introduction to Rural Planning* (London: Routledge).

Gallent, A., Morphet, J. and Tewdwr-Jones, M. (2008) 'Parish Plans and the Spatial Planning Approach in England', *Town Planning Review*, 79(1), 1–28.

Gans, H. (1967) *The Levittowners* (London: Allen Lane).

Gardiner, A. (1923) *The Life of George Cadbury* (London: Cassell).

Gardner, G. (1976) *Social Surveys for Social Planners* (Milton Keynes: Open University).

Garreau, J. (1991) *Edge City: Life on the New Frontier* (New York: Doubleday).

Gaze, J. (1988) *Figures in A Landscape: A History of The National Trust* (London: Barrie & Jenkins/The National Trust).

Geddes, P. (1968, originally 1915) *Cities in Evolution: An Introduction to The Town Planning Movement and to The Study of Civics* (London: Ernest Benn).

Gehl, Jan (2010) *Cities for People* (London: Island Press).

George, R. (2008) *The Big Necessity: Adventures in the World of Human Waste* (London: Portobello).

Gershenson, O. and Penner, B. (eds) (2009) *Ladies and Gents: Public Toilets and Gender* (Philadelphia: Temple University Press).

Gibberd, F. (1970) *Town Design* (Oxford: Architectural Press).

Gibbs, R. (2012) *Principles of Urban Retail: Planning and Development* (London: Wiley).

Giddens, A. (1989) *Sociology* (London: Polity).

Giddens, A. (1998) *The Third Way: The Renewal of Social Democracy* (Cambridge: Polity).

Gilg, A. (1999) *Perspectives on British Rural Planning and Policy* (Farnham: Ashgate).

Gilman, C. Perkins (1915 [1979]) *Herland* (London: Women's Press).

Gilroy, R. (1999) 'Planning to grow old', in C. Greed (ed.) (1999), *Social Town Planning* (London: Routledge).

Gilroy, R. (2008) 'Places that support human flourishing: lessons from later life', *Planning Theory and Practice*, 9(2), June, 145–63.

GLA (2007) *Planning for Equality and Diversity in London* (London: The London Mayor's Supplementary Guidance to the Greater London Strategic Development Plan, Greater London Authority).

GLA (2010) *The London Plan: Spatial Development Strategy for London, Draft Replacement Plan* (London: The Mayor's Office, Greater London Authority).

Glaister, S., Burnham, J., Stevens, H. and Travers, T. (2006) *Transport Policy in Britain: Public Policy and Politics* (Basingstoke: Palgrave Macmillan).

Glasson J., Therivel, R. and Chadwick, A. (2005) *Introduction to Environmental Impact Assessment* (London: Routledge).

Glasson, J. and Marshall, T. (2007) *Regional Planning* (London: Routledge).

GLC (Greater London Council) (1983) *On The Move* (London: GLC), now available from Greater London Authority (GLA).

GLC (1984) 'Planning for Equality: Women in London', Chapter VI of *Greater London Development Plan*, Draft Plan (London: GLC).

GLC (1986) *Changing Places*, Report (London: GLC).

Gleeson, B. and Sipe, N. (2006) *Creating Child-Friendly Cities: New Perspectives and Prospects* (London: Routledge).

Goffman, E. (1969) *Presentation of Self in Everyday Life* (Harmondsworth: Penguin).

Gold, J. and Gold, M. (2012) *The Making of Olympic Cities* (London: Routledge).

Goldsmith, M. (1972) 'Blueprint for Survival', *Ecologist Magazine*, January (reprinted Harmondsworth: Penguin).

Goldsmith, M. (1980) *Politics, Planning and The City* (London: Routledge & Kegan Paul).

Goldsmith, S. (2000) *Universal Design: a Manual of Practical Guidance for Architects* (Oxford: Architectural Press).

Gore, A. (1992) *Earth in The Balance: Forging a New Common Purpose* (London: Earthscan).

Gore, A. (2006) *An Inconvenient Truth: The Planetary Emergency of Global Warming and What We Can Do About it* (London: Bloomsbury).

Gore-Grimes, J. (2011) *Planning Law in Ireland* (London: Bloomsbury).

Gorringe, T.J. (2002) *A Theology of the Built Environment: Justice, Empowerment and Redemption* (Cambridge: Cambridge University Press).

Graft Johnson *see* De Graft Johnson.

Grant, B. (1996) *Building E=Quality: Minority Ethnic Construction Professionals and Urban Regeneration* (London, House of Commons).

Grant, M. (1998) *A Source Book of Environmental Law* (London: Sweet & Maxwell).

Grant, M. (2014) *Encyclopaedia of Planning Law* (London: Sweet & Maxwell).

Greed, C. (1990) *Surveying Sisters: Women in a Traditional Male Profession* (London: Routledge).

Greed, C. (1992) 'The Reproduction of Gender Relations Over Space: A Model Applied to The Case of Chartered Surveyors', *Antipode*, 24(1), 16–28.

Greed, C. (1993) 'Is more better?: Mark II – with reference to Women town planners in Britain', *Women's Studies International Forum*, 16(3), 255–70.

Greed, C. (1994a) *Women and Planning: Creating Gendered Realities* (London: Routledge).

Greed, C. (1994b) 'The place of ethnography in planning: or is it "real research"?', *Planning Practice and Research*, 9(2), 119–27.

Greed, C. (ed.) (1996a) *Implementing Town Planning* (Harlow: Longman).

Greed, C (ed.) (1996b) *Investigating Town Planning* (Harlow: Longman).

Greed, C. (1997) *The Composition and Culture of Construction*, End Report based on ESRC research on 'Social Integration and Exclusion in the Built Environment Professions'.

Greed, C. (1999a) *The Changing Composition and Culture of The Construction Industry* (Bristol: UWE, Faculty of The Built Environment), Occasional Paper.

Greed, C. (1999b) 'Can man plan: can woman plan better?', in J. Hughes and S. Sadler (eds), *Non-Plan: Essays on Freedom, Participation and Change in Modern Architecture and Urbanism* (Oxford: Architectural Press), 184–97.

Greed, C. (1999c) (ed.) *Social Town Planning* (London: Routledge).

Greed, C. (2000) 'Women in the construction professions: achieving critical mass', *Gender, Work and Organisation*, 7(3), July, 181–96.

Greed, C. (2003a) *Inclusive Urban Design: Public Toilets* (Oxford: Architectural Press).

Greed, C. (2003b) 'Gender mainstreaming within local planning authorities', *Municipal Engineer*, Special Issue on 'Social Inclusion' ISSN 0965 0903, 156, June Issue ME2, 119–27.

Greed, C. (2004a) 'Planning for Accessibility', in K. Bright (ed.), *Disability: Making Buildings Accessible* (London: Workplacelaw Network and Reading University), 37–47.

Greed, C. (2004b) 'Public toilets: the need for compulsory provision', *Municipal Engineer: Proceedings of the Institution of Civil Engineers* No.157, June Issue ME2, 77–85.

Greed, C. (2005a) 'Overcoming the factors inhibiting the mainstreaming of gender into spatial planning policy in the United Kingdom', *Urban Studies*, 42(4), 1–31.

Greed, C. (2005b) 'An Investigation of the effectiveness of gender mainstreaming as a means of integrating the needs of women and men into spatial planning in the United Kingdom', *Progress in Planning*, Manchester, 64(Part 4), 239–321.

Greed, C. (2006a) 'Social Exclusion: women in construction', in A. Gale and M. Davidson (eds), *Managing Diversity and Equality in the Construction Industry* (London: Spon Press), Chapter 4, 71–96.

Greed, C. (2006b) 'Women in Surveying: creating diversity', in A. Gale and M. Davidson (eds), *Managing Diversity and Equality in the Construction Industry* (London: Spon), Chapter 7, 128–50.

Greed, C. (2006c) 'The role of the public toilet: pathogen transmitter or health facilitator', *Building Services Engineering Research and Technology Journal*, 27(2), 127–40.

Greed, C. (2006d) 'Institutional and conceptual barriers to the adoption of gender mainstreaming within spatial planning departments in England', *Planning Theory and Practice*, 7(2), 179–97.

Greed, C. (2007) *A Place for Everyone: Report on Mainstreaming Gender into Spatial Planning Policy*, Briefing paper for Oxfam UK Poverty and Regeneration Programme: Regender (Oxford: Oxfam).

Greed, C. (2008) 'Are we there yet?: Women and Transport Revisited', in P.T. Uteng and T. Cresswell (eds), *Gendered Mobilities* (Aldershot: Ashgate), Chapter 16, 243–56.

Greed, C. (2011a) 'Planning for Sustainable Areas or Planning for Everyday life and Inclusion', *Journal of Urban Design and Planning*, 164, June Issue DP2, 107–19.

Greed, C. (2011b) 'A Feminist Critique of the Postsecular City: God and Gender', in C. Baker and J. Beaumont (eds) (2011), *Post-Secular Cities: Space, Theory and Practice* (London: Continuum), 104–19.

Greed, C. (2012) 'Planning and Transport for the Sustainable City or Planning for People', *Journal of Urban Design and Planning*, Proceedings of the Institution of Civil Engineers, 165, Issue DP4, 219–29.

Greed, C. (2013) 'A feminist perspective on planning cultures: tacit genders assumptions in a taciturn profession', Chapter 6 in G. Young and D. Stevenson (eds) (2013), *The Ashgate Research Companion to Planning and Culture* (Farnham: Ashgate).

Greed, C. and Reeves, D. (2005) 'Mainstreaming equality into strategic spatial policy making: are town planners losing sight of gender?', *Construction Management and Economics*: Special Issue on 'Diversity and Equality in Education', 23(10), 1059–70.

Greed, C. and Roberts, M. (eds) (1998) *Introducing Urban Design: Interventions and Responses* (Harlow: Longman).

Grieco, M., Pickup, L. and Whipp, R. (1989) *Gender, Transport and Employment* (Aldershot: Avebury).

Griffin, S. (1978) *Woman and Nature: The Roaring Inside Her* (London: The Woman's Press).

Grindrod, J. (2013) *Concretopic: A Journey Around the Building of Post War Britain* (Brecon: Old Street Publishing).

Gripaios, P. (2005) 'The Coherence of European Super-Regions: A UK Perspective', *The Political Quarterly*, 66(3), 170–6.

Grist, B. (1999) *An Introduction to Irish Planning Law* (Dublin: IPA).

Grover, R. (ed.) (1989) *Land and Property Development: New Directions* (London: Spon).

Guba, E. (1990) *The Paradigm Dialog* (Newbury Park, California: Sage Publications).

Guba, E. and Lincoln, Y. (1992) 'Competing paradigms in qualitative research', in N. Denzin and Y. Lincoln (eds), *Handbook of Qualitative Research* (Newbury Park, California: Sage Publications).

Guise, R., Barton, H. and Grant, M. (2010) *Shaping Neighbourhoods, Health, Vitality, Sustainability*, 2nd edn (London: Routledge).

Gunder, M. (2009) *Planning in Ten Words or Less: A Lacanian Entanglement with Spatial Planning* (Aldershot: Ashgate).

Habermas, J. (1979) *Communication and the Evolution of Society* (London: Heinemann).

Habermas, J. (1987) *The Philosophical Discourse of Modernity* (Cambridge: Polity Press).

Habermas, J. and Ratzinger, J. (2007) *The Dialectics of Secularisation: on reason and religion* (Rome: Ignatius Press).

Hague, C. (ed.) (2006) *Making Planning Work: a guide to approaches and skills* (Rugby: Practical Action Publishing).

Hall, M. (2006) *The Geography of Tourism and Recreation* (London: Routledge).

Hall, P. (1977) *Containment of Urban England* (London: Allen & Unwin).

Hall, P. (1980) *Great Planning Disasters* (London: Weidenfeld & Nicolson).

Hall, P. (1992) *Urban and Regional Planning* (London: Unwin Hyman), and earlier editions are referred to including 1989.

Hall, P. (1996) *Cities of Tomorrow: An Intellectual History of Urban Planning and Design in the Twentieth Century* (London: Blackwell).

Hall, P. (1999) *Sustainable Cities or Town Cramming?* (London: Town and Country Planning Association).

Hall, P., Gracey, H., Drewett, R. and Thomas, R. (1973) *The Containment of Urban England* (London: Allen and Unwin).

Hall, P. and Ward, W. (1999) *Sociable Cities: the Legacy of Ebenezer Howard* (London: Town and Country Planning Association & Wiley).

Hall, P. and Tewdwr-Jones, M. (2010) *Urban and Regional Planning*, 5th edn (London: Routledge).

Hall, P. with Falk, N. (2013) *Good Cities, Better Lives: How Europe Discovered the Lost Art of Urbanism* (London: Routledge).

Hall, S. and Jacques, M. (1989) *New Times: The Changing Face of Politics in The 1990s* (London: Lawrence & Wishart).

Hall, S. and Gieben, B. (1992) *Formations of Modernity* (Milton Keynes: Open University).

Hall, T. (2006) *Urban Geography* (London, Routledge).

Hall, T. (2007) *Turning A Town Around: A Proactive Approach to Urban Design* (Oxford: Blackwell).

Hambleton, R. and Sweeting, D. (1999) 'Delivering a new strategic vision for the capital', *Planning*, Issue 1347, 3 December, 16–17.

Hambleton, R., and Sweeting, D. (2004) 'US-style leadership for English local government, *Public Administration Review*, 64(4), 474–88.

Hampton, J. (2008) *The Austerity Olympics: How the Games came to London in 1948* (London: Aurum).

Hamilton-Baillie, B. (2008) 'Towards Shared Space', *Urban Design International*, 13(2), 130–8.

Hamilton, K. (2000) *Public Transport Audit* (London: DETR Mobility Unit), undertaken by University of East London, 2000.

Hamilton, K., Jenkins, L., Hodgson, F. and Turner, J. (2005) *Promoting Gender Equality in Transport*, Equal Opportunities Commission, Manchester, Working Paper No. 34.

Hammersley, M. (1995) *The Politics of Social Research* (London: Sage).

Hammersley, M. (1999) *Taking Sides in Social Research* (London: Sage).

Hammersley, M. and Atkinson, P. (1985) *Ethnography: Principles in Practice* (London: Tavistock).

Hammersley, M. and Atkinson, P. (2008) *Ethnography: Principles in Practice*, London: Routledge.

Hamnett, C., McDowell, L. and Sarre, P. (eds) (1989) *Restructuring Britain: The Changing Social Structure* (London: Sage with The Open University).

Hanhardt, C. (2013) *Safe Space: Gay Neighbourhood History and the Politics of Violence* (Durham, NC: Duke University Press).

Hanley, L. (2012) *Estates: An Intimate History* (London: Granta).

Hanson, J., Bichard, J. and Greed, C. (2007) *The Toilet Manual: The Role of the Toilet in Creating Accessible City Centres* (London: University College London), funded by EPSRC Vivacity Project.

Haralambos, M. (1995) *Sociology: Themes and Perspectives* (London: Unwin Hyman).

Hardill, I., Graham, D.T. and Kofman, E. (2001) *Human Geography of the UK* (London: Routledge).

Hardy, D. (1991) *From Garden Cities to New Towns* (London: Spon in association with the Town and Country Planning Association).

Harris, N. (2002) 'Collaborative Planning', in P. Allmendinger, and M. Tewdwr-Jones (eds), *Planning Futures: new Directions for Planning Theory* (London: Routledge).

Harrison, M. and Davies, J. (1995) *Constructing Equality: Housing Associations and Minority Ethnic Contractors* (London: Joseph Rowntree Trust).

Hartman, H. (1981) 'The unhappy marriage of Marxism and feminism', in L. Sergeant (ed.), *Women and Revolution* (London: Pluto).

Harvey, C. (2011) *Place, Identity and Everyday Life in a Globalising World* (Basingstoke: Palgrave Macmillan).

Harvey, D. (1975) *Social Justice and the City* (London: Arnold).

Harvey, D. (1985) *Consciousness and the Urban Experience* (London: Blackwell).

Harvey, D. (2007) A *Brief History of Neo-Liberalism* (Oxford: Oxford University Press).

Haskin, C. (2003) *Rural Delivery Review – A report on the delivery of government policies in rural England* (London: Department of Environment, Food and Rural Affairs).

Hass-Klau, C. (1990) *The Pedestrian and City Traffic* (London: Belhaven Press).

Hass-Klau, C. (1992) *Civilised Streets: A Guide to Traffic Calming* (London: Belhaven Press).

Hatt, P. and Reiss, A. (1963) *Cities in Society* (New York: Free Press).

Haughton, G., Allmendinger, P., Counsell, D. and Vigar, G. (2009) *The New Spatial Planning* (London: Routledge).

Hayden, D. (1976) *Seven American Utopias: The Architecture of Communitarian Socialism, 1790–1975* (London: MIT Press).

Hayden, D. (1981) *The Grand Domestic Revolution: Feminist Designs for Homes, Neighbourhoods and Cities* (Cambridge, Massachusetts: MIT Press).

Hayden, D. (2002, originally 1982) *Redesigning the American Dream*, 2nd edn (New York: Norton).

Haywood, R. (2009) *Railways, Urban Development and Town Planning in Britain: 1948–2008* (London: Ashgate).

Headicar, P. (2009) *Transport Policy and Planning in Great Britain* (London: Routledge).

Healey, P. (1983) *Local Plans in British Land Use Planning* (Oxford: Pergamon Press).

Healey, P. (1997, second edition 2006) *Collaborative Planning: Shaping Places in Fragmented Societies* (London: Macmillan).

Healey, P. (2007) *Urban Complexity and Spatial Strategies* (London: Routledge).

Healey, P., McDougall, G. and Thomas, M. (1982) *Planning Theory: Prospects for the 1980s* (London: Pergamon).

Healey, P., Mcnamara, P., Elson, M. and Doak, A. (1988) *Land Use Planning and the Mediation of Urban Change: The British Planning System in Practice* (Cambridge: Cambridge University Press).

Heap, D. (1991) *Outline of Planning Law* (London: Sweet & Maxwell) (and 1996 edition).

Helander, M. (ed.) (1981) *Human Factors Ergonomics: for Building and Construction* (New York: Wiley, at Department of Human Development, Penn State University).

Help the Aged (2007) *Nowhere to Go: Public toilet provision in the UK* (London: Help the Aged).

Help the Aged (2009) *Future Communities: Re-shaping our Society for Older People* (London: Help the Aged).

Herbert, J. (2008) *Negotiating Boundaries in the City* (Aldershot: Ashgate).

Herrington, J. (1984) *The Outer City* (London: Harper & Row).

Herrington, K. and Parker, G. (2012) 'Speed and Quality in Planning Decisions', *Town and Country Planning*, November, 81(11), 482–9.

Hewitt, S. (2009) 'We need to slow down: the case for a slow transport policy', *RTPI Branchout Newsletter*, Bristol, 141, Winter, 6.

Highways Agency (2012) *Annual Report and Accounts, 2011–12* (London: The Stationery Office).

Hill, M. (2005) *The Public Policy Process* (Harlow: Pearson).

Hill, W. (1956) *Octavia Hill: Pioneer of The National Trust and Housing Reformer* (London: Hutchinson).

Hillier, J. (1999) 'Culture, community and communication in the planning process', in C. Greed (ed.), *Social Town Planning* (London: Routledge).

Hillier, J. and Healey, P. (eds) (2010) *The Ashgate Companion to Planning Theory, Conceptual Changes and Spatial Planning* (Farnham: Ashgate).

HM Treasury and Office of the Deputy Prime Minister (2005) *The Government's Response to Kate Barker's Review of Housing Supply* (London: The Stationery Office (TSO previously HMSO)).

Hobhouse Report (1947) *Report of The National Parks Committee (England and Wales)* (London: HMSO).

Holloway, S., Rice, S. and Valentine, G. (2003) *Key Concepts in Geography* (London: Sage).

Hopkins, J. and Neil, P. (2012) *The Making of the Queen Elizabeth Olympic Park* (London: Wiley).

Hoskins, J. (1985) *Making of the English Landscape* (Harmondsworth: Penguin).

Houghton, T. (2010) (ed.) *Bristol Energy and Environment Plan* (Bristol: Bristol Energy Centre).

House of Commons (2004) *Session 2003–04 –Fifth Report – Reform of the National Lottery* (accessed 30 August 2009) Select Committee on Culture, Media and Sport, http://www.publications.parliament.uk/pa/cm200304/cmselect/cmcumeds/196/19603.htm.

House of Commons (2006) *High Street – 2015* (London: House of Commons, All-Parliamentary Small Shops Group).

House of Lords (1995) *Report from the Select Committee on Sustainable Development Vol. 1* (London: HMSO).

Howard, E. (1898) *Garden Cities of Tomorrow*, reprinted 1974 (London: Faber).

Howatt, H. (1987) 'Women in Planning – A Programme for Positive Action', *The Planner*, 73(8), August, 11–12.

Howe, E. (1980) 'Role Choices of Urban Planners', *Journal of The American Planning Association*, October, 398–401.

Howe, E. (1994) *Acting on Ethics in City Planning* (Rutgers, New Jersey: Center for Urban Research).

Hubbard, P. (2006) *City* (London: Routledge).

Hudson, M. (1978) *The Bicycle Planning Book*, Friends of The Earth (London: Open Books).

Hughes, J. and Sadler, S. (eds) (1999) *NonPlan: Essays on Freedom, Participation and Change in Modern Architecture and Urbanism* (Oxford: Architectural Press).

Hull, A. (2012) *Transport Matters: Integrated Approaches to Planning City Regions* (London: Routledge).

Hutchinson, M. (1989) *The Prince of Wales: Right Or Wrong?* (London: Faber and Faber).

Hutton, B. (2013) *Planning Sustainable Transport* (London: Earthscan).

I'DGO (2009) *Pedestrian Friendly Neighbourhoods* (Edinburgh: I'DGO (Inclusive Design for Getting Outdoors)), part of a series of research reports on older people's well being and getting outdoors at: http://www.idgo.ac.uk/useful_resources/publications.htm, EPSRC research headed by L. Mitchell and E. Burton.

IJURR (International Journal of Urban and Regional Research) (1978) *Women and The City*, Special Issue, 2(3) (London: Basil Blackwell).

Imrie, R. (1996) *Disability and the City: International Perspectives* (London: Paul Chapman).

Imrie, R. and Hall, P. (2001) *Inclusive Design: Designing and Developing Accessible Environments* (London: Spon).

Imrie, R. and Wells, P. (1993) 'Disablism, planning, and the built environment', *Environment and Planning C: Government and Policy*, 11, 213–31.

Infed (2012) 'Sustainable communities and neighbourhoods', at www.infed.org/community/sustainable_communities_and_neighbourhoods.htm.

Innes, J. (1995) 'Planning theory's emerging paradigm: communicative action and interactive practice', *Journal of Planning Education and Research*, 14(3), 183–9.

Ieropoulos, A., Greenman, J. and Melhuish, C. (2012) 'Urine utilisation by microbial fuel cells: energy fuel for the future', *Phys. Chem, Chem. Phys*, 14, 94–8.

Irigaray, L. (2007) *Je, Tu, Vu: Towards a Culture of Difference* (London: Routledge) (originally 1985).

Ismail, A. (1998) *An Investigation of the low representation of black and ethnic minority professionals in contracting* (Bristol: UWE), special research project.

Jackson, A. (1992) *Semi-detached London: Suburban Development, Life and Transport* (Oxford: Wild Swan Publications).

Jacobs, A. (2011) *The Good City* (London: Routledge).

Jacobs, J. (1964) *The Death and Life of Great American Cities: The Failure of Town Planning* (Harmondsworth: Penguin).

Jacobs, J. (1970) *The Economy of Cities* (Harmondsworth: Penguin).

Jarvis, H., Pratt, A.C. and Wu, P. (1988) *The Secret Life of Cities: The Social Reproduction of Everyday Life* (New York: Prentice Hall).

Jarvis, H., Cloke, J. and Kantor, P. (2009) *Cities and Gender* (London: Routledge).

Jayyousi, O. (2012) *Islam and Sustainable Development* (London: Gower).

Jenks, M., Burton, E. and Williams, K. (eds) (1996) *The Compact City: a sustainable urban form?* (London: Spon).

Johnson, L. (2009) *Cultural Capitals: Revaluing the arts, remaking urban spaces* (London: Routledge).

Johnson, W.C. (1997) *Urban Politics and Planning* (Chicago: American Planning Association).

Johnston, B. (1999) 'The province plans for the year 2025' by Bryan Johnston, *Planning*, Issue 1311, 26 March, 16–17.

Jones, O. (2010) *Chavs: The demonization of the working class* (London: Verso).

Jones, P. and Evans, J. (2008) *Urban Regeneration in the UK: Theory and Practice* (London: Sage).

Jones, R. (1982) *Town and Country Chaos: a critical analysis of the British planning system* (London: Adam Smith Institute).

Jones, R. (2011) *Beeching: 50 Years of the Axeman* (Horncastle: Morton's Media Group).

Joseph, M. (1978) 'Professional values: a case study of professional students in a Polytechnic', *Research in Education*, 19, 49–65.

Kandola, R. and Fullerton, J. (1994) *Managing the Mosaic: Diversity in Action* (London: Chartered Institute of Personnel and Development).

Kanter, R. (1972) *Commitment and Community: Communities and Utopias in Sociological Literature* (Cambridge, Massachusetts: Harvard University Press).

Kanter, R. (1983) *The Change Masters: Corporate Entrepreneurs at Work*, (Counterpoint, London: Unwin), 296, prime movers.

Keating, M. (1993) *The Earth Summit Agenda for Change: a plain language version of Agenda 21 and the other Rio Agreements Centre for our Common Future* (Geneva: UN).

Keeble, L. (1969) *Principles and Practice of Town and Country Planning* (London: Estates Gazette).

Keeble, L. (1983) *Town Planning Made Plain* (London: Longman).

Keller, S. (1981) *Building for Women* (Lexington, MA: Lexington Books).

Kelly, M. (1997) *The Good Practice Manual on Tenant Participation*, WDS (Women's Design Service, in association with DOE Special Grant Programme.

Killian Pretty Review (2004) *Planning Applications: A Faster and More Responsive System* (London: DCLG).

Kiminami, N., Button, K. and Nijkamp, P. (2005) *Public Facilities Planning* (Cheltenham: Elgar).

Kirk, G. (1980) *Urban Planning in a Capitalist Society* (London: Croom Helm).

Kirk-Walker, S. (1997) *Undergraduate Student Survey: A Report of The Survey of First Year Students in Construction Industry Degree Courses* (York: Institute of Advanced Architectural Studies) (Commissioned by CITB).

Kirton, G. and Greene, A.-M. (2003) *The Dynamics of Managing Diversity: A Critical Approach* (London: Butterworth/Heinemann).

Klosterman, R.E. (2003) 'Arguments for and against planning', in S. Campbell and S. Fainstein (eds), *Readings in Planning Theory*, 2nd edn (Oxford: Blackwell).

Knox, P. (1988) *The Design Professions and the Built Environment* (London: Croom Helm).

Kostoff, Spiro (2009) *The City Shaped: Urban Patterns and Meanings* (London: Thames & Hudson).

Kuhn, T. (1962) *The Structure of Scientific Revolutions* (Chicago: University of Chicago Press).

Kunstler, J. (1993) *The Geography of Nowhere: The Rise and Decline of America's Man-made Landscape* (New York: Touchstone).

Kyoto (1997) *The Kyoto Protocol: Towards Climate Stability* (New York: United Nations). The treaty came into force 2005.

Labour Party (1996) *The New Labour, New Life for Britain* (London: The Labour Party).

Labour Party (2005) *Britain: forward not back* (London: The Labour Party).

Lacey, A. (2004) *Designing for Accessibility* (London: Centre for Accessible Environments).

Lake, B. (1941, reprinted 1974) 'A Plan for Britain', special issue of *Picture Post*, 10(1), 4 January 1941 (Special Issue No 7, 1974) (London: Peter Way Ltd).

Lambert, C. (2002) Transforming city centres: post-recession gentrification and reurbanisation (London: AESOP).

Lancaster, Osbert (1956) *Pillar to Post: The Pocket-Lamp of Architecture: English Architecture without Tears* (London: John Murray).

Lane, P. and Peto, M. (1996) *Guide to the Environment Act 1995* (London: Blackstone).

Langford, D., Hancock, M., Fellows, R. and Gale, A. (1994) *Human Resources in The Management of Construction* (Harlow: Longman).

Lappé, F., Collins, J. and Rosset, P. (1998) *World Hunger: 12 Myths* (London: Earthscan).

Larsen, E. (1958) *Atomic Energy: The Layman's Guide to The Nuclear Age* (London: Pan).

Lavender, S. (1990) *Economics for Builders and Surveyors* (London: Longman).

Law Society (1988) *Equal in The Law: Report of The Working Party on Women's Careers* (London: The Law Society).

Lawless, P. (1989) *Britain's Inner Cities* (London: Paul Chapman).

Layard, A., Davoudi, S. and Baty, S. (2001) (eds) *Planning for a Sustainable Future* (London: Spon).

LDA (2008) *Inclusive Design Strategy* (London: London Development Agency), www.lda.gov.uk/server.php?show=ConWebDoc.2983.

Le Corbusier (1971, originally 1929) *The City of Tomorrow* (London: Architectural Press).

Leary, M. (2009) 'The production of space through a shrine and vendetta in Manchester: Lefebvre's spatial triad and the regeneration of a place renewed named Castleford', *Planning Theory and Practice*, 10(2), 189–212.

Leckie, J. (2009) *Development in an Insecure and Gendered World: The Relevance of the Millennium Goals* (Aldershot: Ashgate).

Lees, L. (2004) *The Emanicipatory City? paradoxes and possibilities* (London: Sage).

Lees, L., Slater, T. and Wyly, E. (2008) *Gentrification* (London: Routledge).

Leevers, K. (1986) *Women at Work in Housing* (London: Hera).

Lefebvre, Henri (1968) *Le Droit a la Ville* (Paris: Anthropos Press).

Lefebvre, H. (1974) *The Production of Space* (*La Production de l'espace*), in French 1974, original edition published by Anthropos, Paris, and translated into English in 1991 by Donald Nicholson-Smith, London.

Lenclos, M. (2002) *Inclusive Design: Access to London Transport* (London: Royal College of Art).

Leveson, R. (1997) 'Flexibility and professionals' *Flexible Working Briefing*, monthly review, Issue 9, 17 January, 2–4.

Levison, D. and Atkins, J. (1987) *The Key to Equality: The Women in Housing Survey*, Women in Housing Working Party (London: Institute of Housing).

Lewis, J. (1984) *Women in England 1870–1950* (Sussex: Wheatsheaf).

Lewisham (2008) *Report from Planning Committee (A) on Elizabeth Industrial Estate change of use of ground floor* (London: London Borough of Lewisham), Case File DE/237/C/TP, DCS Number 100-054-444 (see www.planningresource.co.uk).

LGMB (1993) *Framework for local Sustainability: a Response by The UK* (Luton: Local Government Management Board).

LGMB (1995) *Sustainability Indicators* (Luton: LGMB).

Lichfield, N. (1975) *Evaluation in the Planning Process* (London: Pergamon).

Lindblom, C. (1959) 'The science of muddling through', *Public Administration Review*, Spring (reprinted in Faludi (ed.)1973, 151–69).

Little, A.J. (2009) *Planning Controls and Their Enforcement*, 7th edn, loose leaf (London: Shaw & Sons).

Little, J. (1994) *Gender, Planning and the Policy Process* (Oxford: Elsevier Press).

Little, J. (1999) 'Gender and rural policy', in C. Greed (ed.) (1999) *Social Town Planning* (London, Routledge).

Little, J., Peake, L. and Richardson, P. (1988) *Women and Cities, Gender and The Urban Environment* (London: Macmillan).

Littlefair, P. (1991) *Site Layout Planning for Daylight and Sunlight: A Guide to Good Practice* (Watford, London: Building Research Establishment).

Littlefield, D. (2012) *Metric Handbook: Planning and Design Data* (Oxford: Elsevier, Architectural Press).

Liverpool Vision, 2010 Press Release: *Liverpool's New Lime Street Gateway officially opens* http://www.liverpoolvision.co.uk/News/Liverpool8217s_new_Lime_Street_Gateway_officially_opens.aspx (accessed 15 July 2012).

Lock, D. (2012) 'Off the Fence: Planning is Important for Investors', *Town and Country Planning*, 81(11), November, 479–81.

Loftman, P. and Beazley, M. (1993) *Race, Equality and Planning* (London: London Government Association).

Logan, J. (ed.) (2009) *Urban China in Transition* (London: Wiley).

Loew, S. (2012) *Urban Design Practice: An International Review* (London: RIBA Publishing).

Lo Piccolo, F. and Thomas, H. (2009) *Ethics and Planning Research* (Aldershot: Ashgate).

London Research Centre (1993) *London Energy Study: Energy Use and The Environment* (London: London Research Centre (LRC)).

Low, N. (1991) *Planning, politics and the state: political foundations of planning thought* (London: Unwin Hyman).

LPAS (1986) *Planning for Women: An Evaluation of Local Plan Consultation by Three London Boroughs*, Research Report No.2 (London: London Planning Aid Service).

LRN (1997) *Still Knocking at The Door*, Report of The Women and Regeneration Seminar, held May 1997, London Regeneration Network with London Voluntary Service Council.

LRN (1999) *Newsletter Monthly Newsletter*, London Regeneration Network, 356, Holloway Road, London N7 6PA. 0171 700 8119

Ludlow, D. (1996) 'Urban planning in a pan-European context', in C. Greed (ed.) (1996), *Investigating Town Planning* (Harlow: Longman).

LWMT (1996) *Building Careers: Training Routes for Women* (London: London Women and Manual Trades).

Lynch, K. (1968) *The Image of the City* (Cambridge: Massachusetts and London: MIT).

MacDonald, K. (2008) *Planning for Play Space* (Bristol: University of the West of England), unpublished MA Town and Country Planning.

Macey, J. and Baker, C. (1983) *Housing Management* (London: Estates Gazette).

Madariaga, I.S. and Roberts, M. (eds) (2013) *Fair Shared Cities* (London: Ashgate).

Maguire, D., Goodchild, M. and Rhind, D. (1992) *Geographical Information Systems: Principles and Applications* (London: Longmans).

Malthus, T. (1973, originally 1798) *Essay on The Principles of Population* (London: Everyman Dent).

Manchester (2008) *Design for Access 2* (Manchester: Manchester City Council), at www.manchester.gov.uk/downloads/designforaccess2.pdf.

Manley, S. (1999) 'Creating accessible environments' and 'Appendix 2: Disability', in C. Greed and M. Roberts (eds) (1998), *Introducing Urban Design* (Harlow: Longman).

Markusen, A. (1981) 'City Spatial Structure, Women's Household Work and National Urban Policy', in C. Stimpson, E. Dixler, M. Nelson and K. Yatrakis (eds) (1981),*Women and The American City* (London: University of Chicago Press).

Marriott, O. (1989) *The Property Boom* (London: Abingdon).

Marshall, S. (2009) *Cities, Design and Evolution* (London: Routledge).

Martin, B. and Sparke, E. (2003) *Women's Place: Architecture and Design 1860–1960* (London: Routledge).

Massey, D. (1984) *Spatial Divisions of Labour: Social Structures and The Geography of Production* (London: Macmillan).

Massey, D., Quintas, P. and Wield, D. (1992) *High Tech Fantasies: Science Parks in Society, Science and Space* (London: Routledge).

Massingham, B. (1984) *Miss Jekyll: Portrait of A Great Gardener* (Newton Abbott: David & Charles).

Matless, D. (1992) 'Regional surveys and local knowledges: the geographical imagination of Britain, 1918–39', in *Transactions*, 17(4), 464–80 (London: Institute of British Geographers).

Matrix (1984) *Making Space, Women and the Man Made Environment* (London: Pluto).

Matthew, H. (1993) 'The Liberal Age', in K. Morgan (ed.), *The Oxford Illustrated History of Britain* (Oxford: Oxford University Press).

Mawhinney, B. (1995) *Transport: The Way Ahead* (London: Department of Transport).

Mayer Hillman (ed.) (1990) *One False Move* (London: Policy Studies Institute).

McConnell, S. (1981) *Theories for Planning* (London: Heinemann).

McDowell, L. (1983) 'Towards an understanding of the gender division of urban space', *Environment and Planning D*, 1, 59–72.

McDowell, L. (1997) (ed.) *Undoing Place? A Geographical Reader* (London: Arnold).

McDowell, L. (2003) *Redundant Masculinities?: Employment Change and the White Working Class* (Oxford: Blackwell).

McDowell, L. (2013) *Working Lives: Gender, Migration and Employment in Britain 1945–2007* (London: Wiley/Blackwell).

McDowell, L. and Peake, L. (1990) 'Women in British Geography revisited: or The same old story', *Journal of Geography in Higher Education*, 14(1), 19–31.

McDowell, L. and Sharp, J. (eds) (1997) *Space, Gender, Knowledge: Feminist Readings* (London: Arnold).

McGillivray, D. (2006) *Blackstone's Environmental Law* (Oxford: Oxford University Press).

McLaren, D. (1998) *Tomorrow's World: Britain's Share in a Sustainable Future* (London: Earthscan with Friends of the Earth).

McLellan, D. (1973) *Karl Marx: His Life and Thought* (London: Macmillan).

McLoughlin, J. (1969) *Urban and Regional Planning: A Systems View* (London: Faber).

McMaster, R., Prior, A. and Watchman, J. (2013) *Scottish Planning Law* (London: Bloomsbury Professional).

Meadows, D.H. (1972) *The Limits to Growth* (London: Earth Island).

Meadows, D.H., Meadows, D.L. and Randers, J. (1992) *Beyond The Limits: Global Collapse or a Sustainable Future* (London: Earthscan).

Melia, S., Barton, H. and Parkhurst, G. (2010) 'Car free, low Car – What's the Difference?', *World Transport Policy and Practice*, 16(2), 24–32.

Meleis, A., Birch, E. and Wachter, S. (eds) (2011) *Women's Health and the World's Cities* (Philadelphia: University of Pennsylvania).

Merrett, S. (1979) *Owner Occupation in Britain* (London: Routledge & Kegan Paul).

Merrifield, H. (2006) *Lefebvre: A Critical Introduction* (London: Taylor & Francis).

Methorst, R. (2007) 'Shared Space: Safe or Dangerous? A Contribution to the objectification of a popular design philosophy', Toronto: *Walk 21*, Conference proceedings, October, 2007.

Mies, M. and Shiva, V. (1993) *Ecofeminism* (London: Zed Books).

Miles, M. and Huberman, M. (1996) *Qualitative Data Analysis* (London: Sage).

Millerson, G. (1964) *The Qualifying Associations* (London: Routledge & Kegan Paul).

Mills, C. Wright (1959) *The Power Elite* (Oxford: Oxford University Press).

Mirza, H. Safia (ed.) (1997) *Black British Feminism* (London: Routledge).

Mishan, E.J. (1973) *Cost Benefit Analysis* (London: George Allen & Unwin).

Mitchell, D. (2013) *The Right to the City: Social Justice and the Fight for Public Space* (New York: Guilford Press).

Mitchell, L., Burton, E. and Raman, S. (2004) *Neighbourhoods for Life* (Oxford: Oxford Centre for Sustainable Development, Oxford Brookes University and the Housing Corporation, London, 2004), at www.idgo.ac.uk/about_idgo/docs/Neighbourhoods.pdf.

Moody, S. and Melia, S. (2011) *Shared Space: Implications of Recent Research for Transport Policy* (Swindon: PFA Consulting Ltd in association with Bristol: UWE).

Molotch, H. and Noren, L. (2010) *Toilet: Public Restrooms and the Politics of Sharing* (New York: New York University Press).

Montgomery, J. (1994) 'The evening economy of cities', *Town and Country Planning*, 63(11), 302–7.

Montgomery, J. and Thornley, A. (eds) (1990) *Radical Planning Initiatives* (Aldershot: Gower).

Moore, V. and Purdue, M. (2013) *A Practical Approach to Planning Law* (Oxford: Oxford University Press).

Moore, R. (1977) 'Becoming a sociologist in Sparkbrook', in C. Bell and H. Newby(eds), *Doing Sociological Research* (London: George Unwin).

Morgan, E. (1974) *The Descent of Woman* (London: Corgi).

Morley, L. (1994) 'Glass Ceiling or Iron Cage: Women in UK Academia', *Gender, Work and Organisation*, 1(4), October, 194–204.

Morphet, J. (1993) 'Women and Planning', *The Planner*, Town and Country Planning School Proceedings supplement, 23 February 1990, 76(7), 58.

Morphet, J. (2010) *Effective Practice in Spatial Planning* (London: Routledge).

Morphet, J. (2013) *How Europe Shapes Britain* (Bristol: Policy Press).

Morris, A. and Nott, S. (1991) *Working Women and The Law: Equality and Discrimination in Theory and Practice* (London: Routledge).

Morris, A.E. (1972) *History of Urban Form: Prehistory to The Renaissance* (London: George Godwin).

Morris, E. (1986) 'An Overview of Planning for Women From 1945–1975', in M. Chalmers (ed.) (1986), *New Communities: Did They Get it Right?*, Report of a Conference of the Women and Planning Standing Committee of the Scottish Branch of The Royal Town Planning Institute, County Buildings, Linlithgow (London: RTPI).

Morris, P. (2005) *Methods of Environmental Impact Assessment* (London: Routledge).

Morris, T. (1958) *The Criminal Area* (London: Routledge & Kegan Paul).

Moser, C. (1993) *Gender Planning and Development: Theory, Practice and Training* (London: Routledge).

Mumford, L. (1965) *The City in History* (Harmondsworth: Penguin).

Munro, B. (1979) *English Houses* (London: Estates Gazette).

Murdock, J. (1997) 'Inhuman/nonhuman/human: actor network theory and the prospects of nondualistic and symmetrical perspective on nature and society', *Planning and Environment D*, 15(6), 731–56.

Myers, D. (2008) *Construction Economics* (London: Taylor & Francis).

Nadin, V. (2007) 'The emergence of the spatial planning approach in England', *Planning Research and Practice*, 22(1), 43–62 gives a good background to spatial planning.

Nadin, V. and Jones, S. (1990) 'A Profile of The Profession', *The Planner*, 26 January, 76(3), 13–24 (London: Royal Town Planning Institute).

Nadin, V., Duhr, S. and Colomb, C. (2010) *European spatial planning and territorial co-operation* (London: Routledge).

Narayanan, Y. (2014) *Religion, Heritage and the Sustainable City* (London: Routledge).

Narayanan, Y. (ed.) (2015) *Religion and Urbanism: Reconceptualising Sustainable Cities for South Asia* (London: Earthscan).

National Trust (2011) *Government reforms threaten green spaces*, http://www.nationaltrust.org.uk/main/w-chl/w-countryside_environment/w-planning-landing.htm (accessed 16 August 2011).

NAW (2012) *City Regions: Final Report* (Cardiff: National Assembly of Wales (Welsh Government)).

Network Rail (2012) Website http://www.networkrail.co.uk/ (accessed 14 July 2012).

New Economic Foundation (2004) *Ghost and Clone Town* (London: New Economic Foundation).

New Internationalist (1999) 'Green Cities: Survival Guide for the Urban Future', Special Edition of *The New Internationalist*, June 1999, No.313 (see also May 1996 edition on cities and cars) (Oxford: New Internationalist Publications).

Newby, H. (1982) *Green and Pleasant Land* (Harmondsworth: Penguin).

Newman, O. (1973) *Defensible Space: People and Design in the Violent City* (London: Architectural Press).

Norton-Taylor, R. (1982) *Whose Land is it Anyway?* (Wellingborough: Turnstone).

Novosti (1981) *Housing: The Soviet Union Today and Tomorrow* (Moscow: Novosti Press).

O'Toole, F. (2009) *Ship of Fools* (London: Faber & Faber).

Oates, C. and McDonald, S. (2006) 'Recycling and the domestic division of labour: is Green the new Pink?', *Sociology*, 30(3), 417–33.

Oatley, N. (1996) 'Regenerating cities and modes of regulation', in C. Greed (ed.) (1996), *Investigating Town Planning* (Harlow: Longman).

Oatley, N. (1998) (ed.) *Cities, Economic Competition and Urban Planning* (London: Chapman & Hall).

ODA (2008a) *Inclusive Design Strategy* (London: Olympic Delivery Authority), at www.london2012.com/documents/oda-equality-and-diversity/inclusive-design-strategy-september-2008.pdf.

ODA (2008b) *Sustainable Strategy for London* (London: Olympic Delivery Authority).

ODPM (2001) *Best Value Performance Indicators 2000/01* (London: Office of the Deputy Prime Minister).

ODPM (2003a) *Sustainable Communities: Building for the Future* (London: Office of the Deputy Prime Minister).

ODPM (2003b) *Sustainable Communities: Delivering through Planning* (London: Office of the Deputy Prime Minister).

ODPM (2004a) *Planning Policy Statement 22: Renewable Energy* (London: ODPM).

ODPM (2004b) *Planning Policy Statement 7: Sustainable Development in Rural Areas* (London: ODPM).

ODPM (2005) *Planning Policy Statement 1: Delivering Sustainable Development* (London: ODPM).

OECD (1994) *Women and The City: Housing, Services and The Urban Environment* (Organisation for Economic Co-operation and Development).

Office of Rail Regulation (2012a) Website http://www.rail-reg.gov.uk/ (accessed 14 July 2012).

Office of Rail Regulation (2012b) Passenger Journeys Chart, June 2012, http://dataportal.orr.gov.uk/displayreport/report/html/2dafd767-0d09-4bd5-90c9-291fe228a6e2 (accessed 15 July 2012).

Ogburn, William F. (1966, 1922) *Social change: With Respect to Cultural and Original Nature* (Oxford: Delta Books).

Oliver, M. (1990) *The Politics of Disablement* (London: Macmillan).

Oliver, P. (ed.) (1997) *Encyclopaedia of Vernacular Architecture of the World* (Cambridge: Cambridge University Press).

ONS (1998a) *The ESRC Review of Government Social Classifications* (London: Office of National Statistics in association with ESRC).

ONS (Office of National Statistics) (1998b) *Making Gender Count: Report of the Gender and Statistics Conference* (London: Gender Statistics Users Group, ONS).

ONS (2012) *Social Trends* (London: Office of National Statistics), also available online at: ONS – Social Trends – http://www.statistics.gov.uk/socialtrends/. You can also check for up-to-date figures by referring to the ONS website http://www.ons.gov.uk/.

Onuoha, C. and Greed, C. (2003) *Racial Discrimination in Local Planning Authority Development Control Procedures in London Boroughs*, Occasional Paper 15 (Faculty of the Built Environment, Bristol: University of the West of England).

Open University (1985) *Research Methods in Education and the Social Sciences*, No. DE304, Milton Keynes.

Osborn, R.J. and Whittick, A. (1967) *The New Towns: The Answer to Megalopolis* (London: Leonard Hill).

O'Toole, F. (2009) *Ship of Fools* (London: Faber & Faber).

Pacione, M. (2009) *Urban Geography* (London: Routledge).

Pahl, R. (1965) *Urbs in Rure* (London: Weidenfeld & Nicolson).

Pahl, R. (1977) 'Managers, Technical Experts and The State', in M. Harloe (ed.) (1977), *Captive Cities* (London: Wiley).

Palfreyman, T. and Thorpe, S. (1993) *Designing for Accessibility: An Introductory Guide* (London: Centre for Accessible Environments (CAE)). Address: CAE, Nutmeg House, 60, Gainsford Street, London SE1 2NY, tel: 0171 357 8182.

Panelli, R. (2004) *Social Geographies: From Difference to Action* (London: Sage).

Panelli, R. and Gallagher, L. (2003) '"It's your whole life really", negotiating work, health and gender', *Gender, Place and Culture*, 9(2), 95-105.

Pardo, V. (1965) *Le Corbusier* (London: Thames & Hudson).

Parker Morris Report (1961) *Homes for Today and Tomorrow* (London: Central Housing Advisory Committee).

Parkin, F. (1979) *Marxism and Class Theory: A Bourgeois Critique* (London: Tavistock).

Parkin, S. (1994) *The Life and Death of Petra Kelly* (London: Pandora).

PAS (2007) *Access all Areas: Planning for an Inclusive Environment* (London: Planning Advisory Service), http://www.ps.gov.uk/pas/aio/40475.

Pearson, L. (1988) *The Architectural and Social History of Co-operative Living* (London: Macmillan).

Penoyre, J. and Ryan, M. (1990) *The Observer's Book of Architecture* (London: Doubleday).

Penner, B. (2013) *Bathroom* (London: Reaktion Books).

Perrons, D. (2004) *Globalisation and Social Change – People and Places in a Divided World* (London: Routledge) (also she does gender and planning).

Pevsner, N. (1970) *Pioneers of Modern Design* (Harmondsworth: Penguin), and see Pevsner's pocket guides to England too (and see Forsyth).

Pharoah, T. (2010) 'Shared streets must find balance of user benefits', *Planning*, 28 May, Letters Page 8 (anti-blind people).

Phillips M. and Knowles, D. (2012) 'Performance and performativity: undoing fictions of women business owners', *Gender, Place and Culture*, 19(4), 416–37.

Phillips, M. and Phillips, T. (1998) *Windrush: The Irresistible Rise of Multi-Racial Britain* (London: HarperCollins).

Pickvance, C. (ed.) (1977) *Urban Sociology* (London: Tavistock).

Pinch, S. (1985) *Cities and Services: The Geography of Collective Consumption* (London: Routledge & Kegan Paul).

PINS (2010) *Annual Statistical Report: England* (Bristol: The Planning Inspectorate), Table 3.11 2009/10: Local Planning Authority Development Plan Documents Submitted. For updates see http://www.planningportal.gov.uk/uploads/pins/statistics_eng/annual_2012_13.pdf.

Pitman (Annual) *The Housing and Planning Year Book* (London: Pitman Publications).

Plato (5th Century BC) *Critias*, Translation (1929) by R.G. Bury (London: Heinemann).

Plymouth (2001) *Gender Audit of the Local Plan Review 2001 for the City of Plymouth* (Plymouth: University of Plymouth in association with City of Plymouth Council).

Portas Review (2012) *An Independent Review into the Future of our High Streets* (London: Department for Business, Innovation and Skills), in association with Mary Portas, retail consultant.

Power, A. (1987) *Property Before People: The Management of Twentieth-century Council Housing* (London: Allen & Unwin).

Poynter, G. and MacRury, I. (2009) *Olympic Cities: 2012 and the Remaking of London* (Farnham: Ashgate).

Preiser, W. and Ostroff, E. (2000) *Universal Design Handbook* (New York: McGraw-Hill).

Prescott, J. (2009) *Docks to Downing Street – My Story* (London: Headline Publishing Group).

Prince of Wales (1989) *A Vision of Britain* (London: Doubleday).

Prior, J. and Williams, C. (2008) *Sustainability through planning: Local authority use of BREEAM, Eco-Homes and the Code for Sustainable Homes* (London: Building Research Establishment, Garston, BRE Report BR498, May 2008).

Prizeman, J. (1975) *Your House, The Outside View* (London: Blue Circle Cement/Hutchinson).

PTEG (2012) Passenger Transport Executives Group: Annual Report (2012), http://www.pteg.net/Aboutpteg (accessed 15 July 2012).

Punter, J. (1990) *Design Control in Bristol: 1940–1990* (Bristol: Redcliffe Press).

Punter, J. (2009) *Urban Design and the British Urban Renaissance* (London: Routledge).

Purdue, O. (2013) *Belfast: Emerging City, 1850–1914* (Dublin: Irish Academic Press).

Qvistrom, M. (2010) 'Shadows of planning: on landscape and planning history and inherited landscape ambiguities at the urban fringe', *Geografiska Annaler: Series B, Human Geography*, 92(3), September, 219–35.

Race, S. (2012) *BIM Demystified* (London: RIBA Publishing).

Ramblers Association (2012) *Basics of Rights of Way Law*, http://www.ramblers.org.uk/rights_of_way/knowledge_portal/rights_of_way_law/basics_of_row_law#5._How_does_a_path_become_public_ (accessed 4 November 2012).

Rand, Ayn (1943) *The Fountainhead* (London: Penguin, 2001).

Ratcliffe, J., Keeping, M. and Stubbs, M. (2009) *Urban Planning and Real Estate Development* (London: Routledge).

Ratcliffe, J. and Stubbs, M. (1996) *Urban Planning and Real Estate Development* (London: UCL Press).

Ravetz, A. (1980) *Remaking Cities* (London: Croom Helm).

Ravetz, A. (1986) *The Government of Space* (London: Faber & Faber).

Rawnsley, A. (2001) *Servants of the People* (London: Penguin Books).

Reade, E. (1987) *British Town and Country Planning* (Milton Keynes: Open University Press).

Redfield, J. (1994) *The Celestine Prophecy* (London: Bantam).

Reeds, J. (2011) *Smart Growth: From Sprawl to Sustainability* (London: Green Books).

Rees, G. and Lambert, J. (1985) *Cities in Crisis* (London: Arnold).

Reeves, D. (1996) (ed.) 'Women and The Environment', Special Issue, *Built Environment*, 22(1).

Reeves, D. (2002) 'Mainstreaming gender equality: an examination of the gender sensitivity of strategic planning in Great Britain', *Town Planning Review*, 73(2), 197–214.

Reeves, D. (2005) *Planning for Diversity: Planning and Policy in a World of Difference* (London: Routledge).

Reeves, D. (2012) *Gender Equity Self-Assessment Tool for Local Government Planners* (London: Commonwealth Foundation).

Reith Report (1946) *New Towns Committee: Final Report* (London: HMSO).

Rex, J. and Moore, R. (1967) *Race, Community and Conflict* (London: Institute of Race Relations).

Rhys Jones, S., Dainty, A., Neale, R. and Bagilhole, B. (1996) *Building on fair footings: improving equal opportunities in the construction industry for women* (Glasgow: CIB).

RIBA (2009) *Inclusive Design: Creating a User's World* (London: Royal Institute of British Architects), available at www.youtube.com/ribavideo.

Richardson, B. (1876) *Hygenia, A City of Health* (London).

Ricketts, S. and Field, D. (2012) *Localism and Planning* (London: Bloomsbury Professional).

Robbins Report (1963) *Higher Education* (London: Ministry of Education).

Roberts, H. (1985) *Doing Feminist Research* (London: Routledge).

Roberts, J. (2003) *Environmental Policy* (London: Routledge).

Roberts, M. (1974) *Town Planning Techniques* (London: Hutchinson).

Roberts, M. (1991) *Living in A Man-Made World: Gender Assumptions in Modern Housing Design* (London: Routledge).

Roberts, M. and Eldridge, A. (2009) *Planning the Night-time Economy* (Routledge, London).

Roberts, M. and Greed, C. (eds) (2000) *Urban Design: A Primer* (Pearson: Harlow).

Roberts, M. and Turner, C. (2005) 'Conflicts of Liveability in the 24-hour City: Learning for 48 Hours in the Life of London's Soho', *Journal of Urban Design*, 10(2), 171–94.

Roberts, P. (1988) 'Women and Planning History: Theories and Applications', Paper given at *Women in Planning History: Theories and Applications*, Seminar of The Planning History Group (York: Institute of Advanced Architectural Studies).

Robson, O. (1953) *A Hundred Years of the Halifax: The History of the Halifax Building Society 1853–1953* (London: Batsford).

Rogers, B. (1983) *52%: Getting Women's Power Into Politics* (London: The Women's Press).

Rogers, R. (1999) *Towards an Urban Renaissance: Final Report of the Urban Task Force* (London: Urban Task Force).

Rose, G. (1993) *Feminism and Geography: The limits of geographical knowledge* (Cambridge: Polity Press).

Rosenbloom, R. (1989) 'Trip chaining behaviour: comparative and cross-cultural analysis of the travel patterns of working mothers', in M. Grieco, L. Pickup and R. Whipp (eds), *Gender, Transport and Employment* (Avebury: Oxford Studies in Transport), Chapter 4, 75–87.

Rowntree (1992) *Lifetime Homes* (York: Joseph Rowntree Foundation).

Rowntree, B. (1901) *Poverty: A Study of Town Life* (London: Dent).

Royal Commission on Environmental Pollution (1994) *Report of The Commission* (London: HMSO, Local Government Management Board).

Rozee, L. (2008) 'How planning can meet the challenges – in praise of Local Development Frameworks', *Town Planning Review*, 79(6), 593–622, Abercrombie Lecture.

RPG (Regional Planning Guidance) (1989) *Strategic Guidance for Tyne and Wear* (London: HMSO, Department of the Environment, RPG 1).

RTPI (1983) *Planning for A Multi-Racial Britain* (London: Commission of Racial Equality).

RTPI (1987) *Report and Recommendations of the Working Party on Women and Planning* (London: RTPI).

RTPI (1988) *Managing Equality: The Role of Senior Planners*, Conference 28 October (London: Royal Town Planning Institute).

RTPI (1991) *Traffic Growth and Planning Policy* (London: RTPI).

RTPI (1995) *Planning for Women Planning Advisory Note*, (London: Royal Town Planning Institute).

RTPI (1999) *Gender Equality and the Role of Planning: Realising the Goal*, National Symposium, 1 July, Report of Proceedings (London: RTPI) (paper by C. Booth).

RTPI (2003) *The Gender Mainstreaming Toolkit* (London: Royal Town Planning Institute), by Clara Greed and Dory Reeves and team, see www.rtpi.org.uk.

RTPI (2007) *Planning Advice Note 7: Gender and Spatial Planning* (London: Royal Town Planning Institute) (update on mainstreaming gender into planning).

RTPI (2010) 'Planning History', *The Royal Town Planning Institute Distance Learning Course* (Bristol: University of West of England and Leeds: Leeds Metropolitan University).

RTPI (2012) *The Handy Guide to Planning 2012* (London: RTPI in association with Planning Aid and the Urban Forum).

Rubenstein, D. (1974) *Victorian Homes* (Newton Abbot: David & Charles).

Ryder, J. and Silver, H. (1990) *Modern English Society* (London: Methuen).

Rydin, Y. (2003, originally 1998) *Urban and Environmental Planning in the UK* (Basingstoke: Macmillan).

Rydin, Y. (2011) *The Purpose of Planning, Creating Sustainable Towns and Cities* (Bristol: Policy Press).

Rydin, Y. (2013) *The Future of Planning: Beyond Growth Dependence* (Bristol, Policy Press).

Sandercock, L. (1997) *Towards Cosmopolis: planning for post-secular cities* (London: Wiley).

Sandercock, L. (2003) *Mongrel Cities: Cosmopolis II* (London: Continuum).

Sandercock, L. (2006) 'Spirituality and the Urban Professions – the paradox at the heart of urban planning', *Planning Theory and Practice*, 7(1), 69–75.

Sargent, L. (ed.) (1981) *Women and Revolution* (London: Pluto Press).

Saunders, P. (1979) *Urban Politics: A Sociological Interpretation* (Harmondsworth: Penguin).

Saunders, P. (1985) 'Space, The City and Urban Sociology', in D. Gregory J. and Urry (eds) (1985), *Social Relations and Spatial Structures* (London: Macmillan).

Scarman, Lord (1982) *The Scarman Report: The Brixton Disorders, 10–12 April 1981* (Harmondsworth: Penguin).

Scarrett, D. (1983) *Property Management* (London: Spon).

Scarrett, D. and Smith, M. (2008) *Property Valuation: the Five Methods* (London: Taylor & Francis).

Schon, D. (1995) *The Reflective Practitioner: How professionals think in action* (Aldershot: Ashgate).

Schuster Committee (1950) *Report on the Qualifications of Planners*, Cmd 8059 (London: HMSO).

Schuster, C. del Valle (2005) *Designing Public Toilets* (New York: Firefly).

Scott Report (1942) *Report of the Committee on Land Utilisation in Rural Areas* (London: HMSO).

Scott, N.K. (1989) *Shopping Centre Design* (New York: Van Nost Reinhold).

Scottish Office (1998) *Land Use Planning under a Scottish Parliament* (Edinburgh: Scottish Office).

Scottish Government (2013) National Planning Framework 3: A Plan for Scotland: Ambition, Opportunity, Place (Edinburgh: Scottish Government), http://www.scotland.gov.uk/Topics/Built-Environment/planning/NPF3-SPP-Review/NPF3.

Seeley, I. (1997) *Quantity Surveying Practice* (London: Macmillan).

Senior, D. (1996) 'Minerals and the Environment', in C. Greed (ed.) (1996), *Investigating Town Planning* (Harlow: Longmans), Chapter 8, 135–53.

SERPLAN (1988) *Housing, Land Supply and Structure Plan Provision in t he South East* (London: South East Regional Planning Council (SERPLAN), No 1070)

Service, A. (1977) *Edwardian Architecture* (London: Thames and Hudson).

Sewel, Lord (1997) 'Central and Local Government in Accord', Speech at the *Sustaining Change: Local Agenda 21 in Scotland Conference* (Edinburgh: The City of Edinburgh Council City Chambers, 21 November).

Shane, D.G. (2011) *Urban Design Since 1945: A Global Perspective* (London: Wiley).

Shaw, H. (2006) 'Food deserts: towards the development of a classification', *Geografiska Annaler B: Human Geography*, 88(2), 231–47.

Shaw, J. and Docherty, I. (2014) *The Transport Debate: Policy and Politics in the Twenty First Century* (Bristol: Policy Press).

Sheffield (1999) *Future Planning: Planning's Future* (Sheffield University: Planning Theory Conference, March).

Sheffield, E. (2012) *Universal Design: Creating Inclusive Environments* (London: Wiley).

Sheppard, A. and Britnell, S. (2013) 'Valuing a service brought in from the cold', *Town and Country Planning*, 82(6), 284–8.

Sheppard, A. and Smith, N. (2013) *Study Skills for Town and Country Planning* (London: Sage).

Shoard, M. (1981) *The Theft of The Countryside* (London: Temple Smith).

Shoard, M. (1987) *This Land is Our Land: The Struggle for Britain's Countryside* (London: Paladin).

Shoard, M. (1999) *A Right to Roam* (London: Blackwell).

Short, M. (2012) *Planning for Tall Buildings* (London: Routledge).

Sibley, D. (1995) *Geographies of Exclusion* (London: Routledge).

Silverman, D. (1985) *Qualitative Methodology and Sociology* (Aldershot: Gower).

Simmie, J. (1974) *Citizens in Conflict: The Sociology of Town Planning* (London: Hutchinson).

Simmie, J. (1981) *Power Property and Corporatism* (London: Macmillan).

Sinha, S. (2008) *Recognising Diversity in Architecture: teaching and learning in the context of diversity* (London: London Metropolitan University).

Sjoberg, G. (1965) *Pre-industrial City: Past and Present* (New York: Free Press).

Skeffington (1969) *People and Planning* (London: HMSO).

Skjerve, R. (ed.) (1993) *Manual for Alternative Municipal Planning* (Oslo: Ministry of The Environment).

Slater, A.-M. (2012) *Scottish Planning Law* (Dundee: Dundee University Press).

Smith, M. (1989) *Guide to Housing* (London: Housing Centre Trust).

Smith, N. (2000) *The New Urban Frontier: Gentrification and the Revanchist City* (London: Routledge).

Smith, N. and Williams, P. (1986) *Gentrification of the City* (London: Allen & Unwin).

Smith, R. (2006) *Planning Control: Development, Permission and Enforcement* (London: RICS).

Smith, S. (1989) *The Politics of Race and Residence* (Oxford: Polity).

SOBA (1997) 'Mentoring: to Tame Or to Free?', *Symposium*

Notes, Meeting of Society of Black Architects, 27 November, Prince of Wales's Institute of Architecture, London.

Song, S. (2012) *Urban Park Landscape* (London: Design Media Publishing Limited).

Speer, R. and Dade, M. (1994) *How to Stop and Influence Planning Permission* (London: RICS).

Speer, R. and Dade, M. (2011) *How to Get Planning Permission* (London: Ovolo).

Spencer, A. and Podmore, D. (1987) *In A Man's World: Essays on Women in Male-dominated Professions* (London: Tavistock).

Stacey, M. (1960) *Tradition and Change: A Study of Banbury* (Oxford: Oxford University Press).

Stamp, D. (1962) *Britain Structure and Scenery* (Harmondsworth: Penguin).

Stamp, D. and Coleman, A. (1960) *Land Utilisation Survey of England* (London: University of London).

Stanley, L. (ed.) (1990) *Feminist Praxis: Research, theory, epistemology in Feminist Sociology* (London: Routledge).

Stapleton, T. (2013) *Estate Management Practice* (London: Taylor and Francis).

Stark, A. (1997) 'Combatting the backlash: how Swedish women won the war', in A. Oakley and J. Mitchell (eds) (1997), *Who's Afraid of Feminism?: Seeing Through the Backlash* (London: Hamish Hamilton), 224–44.

Steiner, F and Butler, K. (2006) *Planning and Urban Design Standards: Student Edition* (London: Wiley). American planning book.

Stewart, W. (2000) *Mobile Phones and Health* (London: Independent Expert Group on Mobile Phones).

Stimpson, C., Dixler, E., Nelson, M. and Yatrakis, K. (eds) (1981) *Women and the American City* (Chicago: University of Chicago Press).

Stoker, G. and Young, S. (1993) *Cities in the 1990s: Local Choice for a Balanced Strategy* (Harlow: Longman).

Strauss, A. (ed.) (1968) *The American City* (London: Allen Lane).

Strauss, A. and Corbin, J. (1990) *Basics of Qualitative Research: Grounded Theory Procedures and Techniques* (London: Sage).

Summerson, J. (1986) *Georgian London* (Harmondsworth: Penguin).

SUSTRANS (2011) *DIY Streets, Cycle Paths* (Bristol: Sustrans) (previously Cyclebag).

Sutcliffe, A. (1974) *Multi-storey Living: The British Working Class Experience* (London: Croom Helm).

Swain, C., Marshall, T. and Baden, T. (2012) *English Regional Planning: 2000–2010* (London: Routledge).

Swain, J., Finkelstein, V., French, S. and Oliver, M. (eds) (1993) *Disabling Barriers – Enabling Environments* (London: Sage Publications, in association with the Open University).

Swartz, D. (1997) *Culture and Power: A Sociology of Paul Bourdieu* (Chicago: Chicago University Press).

Swenarton, M. (1981) *Homes Fit for Heroes* (London: Heinemann).

Talen, E. (2006) 'Design that enables diversity: the complications of a planning ideal', *Journal of Planning Literature*, 20(3), 233–49.

Talen, E. (2008) *Design for Diversity: Exploring Socially Mixed Neighbourhoods* (Oxford: Architectural Press).

Tallon, A. (2009) *Urban Regeneration in the UK*, 1st edn (London: Routledge).

Tallon, A. (2013) *Urban Regeneration in the UK*, 2nd edn (London: Routledge).

Tallon, A. and Bromley, R. (2002) 'Living in the 24 hour city', *Town and Country Planning*, November, 282–5.

Tarbatt, J. (2012) *The Plot: Designing Diversity in the Built Environment for Architects and Urban Designers* (London: RIBA Publishing).

Tawney, R. (1966) *Religion and the Rise of Capitalism* (Harmondsworth: Penguin), originally 1922.

Taylor, J. (1990) *Planning for Women in Unitary Development Plans: An Analysis of The Factors Which Generate 'Planning for Women' and The Form this Planning Takes* (Sheffield University: Town and Regional Planning Department, September, 1990, Unpublished MA Thesis).

Taylor, N. (1973) *The Village in The City* (London: Maurice).

Taylor, N. (1998) *Urban Planning Theory since 1945* (London: Sage).

Taylor, N. (1999) 'Town planning "social" not just "physical"', in C. Greed (ed.) (1999),*Social Town Planning* (London: Routledge).

Taylor Report (1990) *Hillsborough Stadium Inquiry: Final Report* (London: Home Office).

Taylor Report (2008) *Living Working Countryside: The Taylor Review of the Rural Economy and Affordable Housing* (London: DCLG).

Taylor Report (2012) *Review of Planning Practice Guidance* (London: DCLG).

TCPA (Town and Country Planning Association) (1987) 'A Place for Women in Planning', *Town and Country Planning*, 56(10), Special Issue (London: Town and Country Planning Association).

TCPA (1999) 'Land use planning under a Scottish parliament', *Town and Country Planning*, 68(6), June, 214, unattributed article.

TCPA (2005) *Planning for Accessible and Sustainable Transport* (London: Town and Country Planning Association).

TCPA (2009) *Applying Inclusive Design Principles to eco-town development: Eco-towns inclusive design worksheet* (London: TCPA), www.tcpa.org.uk/data/files/ecotwsinclusion.pdf.

TCPA (2009) *Eco-Towns Inclusive Design Worksheet: Applying Inclusive Design Principles to eco-town development* (London: TCPA), www.tcpa.org.uk/data/files/ecotwsinclusion.pdf.

TCPA (2012) *Creating Garden Cities and Suburbs Today* (London: Town and Country Planning Association).

Tetlow, J. and Goss, A. (1968) *Homes, Towns and Traffic* (London: Faber).

Tetlow King (2011) 'News items', http://www.tetlow-king.co.uk/news.php?item=190 (accessed 10 July 2011 and check for updates).

Tewdwr-Jones, M. (1996) *British Planning Policy in Transition: Planning in The 1990s* (London: University College London Press).

Tewdwr-Jones, M. (2002) *The Planning Polity* (London: Routledge).

Thames Valley Police (2010) *Compendium of Crime Prevention and Reduction in the Planning System* (London: Thames Valley Police).

Theniral, R. (1992) *Strategic Environmental Assessment* (London: Earthscan).

Thiel, D. (2012) *Builders: Class, gender and ethnicity in the Construction Industry* (London: Routledge).

Thomas, H. (1999) 'Social town planning and the planning profession', in C. Greed (ed.)(1999), *Social Town Planning* (London: Routledge).

Thomas, H. and Krishnarayan, V. (1999) *Race and Planning, the UK Experience* (Avebury: Ashgate).

Thomas, H. and Lo Piccolo, F. (1999) 'Best value, planning and race equality', Paper presented at the *Future Planning: Planning's Future: Planning Theory Conference*, March (Sheffield: University of Sheffield, Department of Planning).

Thompson, F.M.L. (1968) *Chartered Surveyors, The Growth of A Profession* (London: Routledge & Kegan Paul).

Thompson, D. (1955) *England in the Nineteenth Century* (London: Penguin).

Thornley, A. (1991) *Urban Planning and Thatcherism: the Challenge of the Market* (London: Routledge).

Toffler, A. (1970) *Future Shock* (London: Random House).

Tönnies, F. (1955) *Community and Association* (London: Routledge & Kegan Paul).

Transport for London (2008) *Central London Congestion Charging: Impacts Monitoring. 6th Annual Report, July 2008* (London: Transport for London).

Tricker, R. and Alford, S. (2012) *Building Regulations in Brief* (London: Routledge).

Tudor Walters Report (1918) *Report of The Committee on Questions of Building Construction in Connection with The Provision of Dwellings for The Working Classes* (London: HMSO).

Turner, T. (1996) *City as Landscape: A Post-PostModern (sic) View of Design and Planning* (London: Spon).

Uguris, T. (2004) *Space, Power and Participation: Ethnic and Gender Divisions in Tenants; Participation in Public Housing* (Aldershot: Ashgate).

UK Round Table on Sustainable Development (1996) *Defining A Sustainable Transport Sector* (London: HMSO).

UN (1992a) *The Rio Declaration: on Environment and Development*, Conference Proceedings Rio de Janiero (New York: United Nations).

UN (1992b) *Agenda 21* (New York: United Nations Commission on Environment and Development).

UN (2009) *United Nations Framework Convention on Climate Change*: http://unfccc.int/2860.php (accessed 30 August 2009) (New York: United Nations).

UNCED (United Nations Conference on Environment and Development) (1992) *Earth Summit – Press summary of Agenda 21* (Rio de Janeiro: UNCED).

UNESCO (2009) *The World's Heritage* (London: Harper Collins in association with UNESCO Paris).

Unwin, G. (1906) *Nothing Gained by Overcrowding* (London: Dent).

Urban Design Group (2002) *Urban Design Guidance* (London: Thomas Telford).

Urban Vision (2012) *Quick Guide to Neighbourhood Planning* (London: Urban Vision).

Uteng, T.P. and Cresswell, T. (eds) (2008) *Gendered Mobilities* (Aldershot: Ashgate).

Uthwatt Report (1942) *Report of The Expert Committee on Compensation and Betterment* (London: HMSO).

Vigar, G., Healey, P., Hall, A. and Davoudi, S. (2000) *Planning Governance and Spatial Strategy in Britain* (London: Macmillan).

Von Thunen, J. (2009) *The Isolated State in relation to Agriculture and Political Economy* (Basingstoke: Palgrave Macmillan, originally 1810).

Wales, Prince of (1989) *A Vision of Britain* (London: Doubleday).

Walker, G. (1996) 'Retailing development: in or out of town?', in C. Greed (ed.), *Investigating Town Planning* (Harlow: Longman).

Wall, C. and Clarke, L. (1996) *Staying Power: Women in Direct Labour Building Teams* (London: London Women and The Manual Trades).

Ward C. (1990) *The Child in the City* (London: Architectural Press).

Ward, S. (1994) *Planning and Urban Change* (London: Sage).

Ward, S. (2002) *Planning the Twentieth Century City: The Advanced Capitalist World* (London: Wiley).

Warren, K. (ed.) (1997) *Ecofeminism: Women, Culture and Nature* (Indianapolis: Indiana University Press).

Water Aid (2012) *Sanitation and Water for Poor Urban Communities* (London: Water Aid).

Watson, S. and Austerberry, H. (1986) *Housing and Homelessness: A Feminist Perspective* (London: Routledge).

WCED (World Commission on Environment and Development) (1987) *Our Common Future* (The Brundtland Report) (Oxford: Oxford University Press).

WDS (1990) *Children's Play Space* (London: Women's Design Service).

WDS (1998) 'Gender Issues within Planning Education', Broadsheet 28, London Women and Planning Forum (London: WDS).

WDS (2005) *Cycling for Women* (London: Women's Design Service).

WDS (2007) *What to do about Women's Safety in Parks* (London: Women's Design Service).

WDS (2010) www.gendersite.org searchable database on 'women and planning' (London: Women's Design Service).

WE (Women and Environments) (1999) *Women and Environments International Magazine* (Toronto: The WEED Foundation (Women, Environments, Education and Development Foundation)).

Weber, M. (1946) *The Methodology of the Social Sciences* (New York: Free Press).

Weber, M. (1964) (Introduction by Talcott Parsons) *Theory of Social and Economic Organisation (Wirtschaft und gesellschaft)* (New York: Free Press, originally 1905).

Weber, M. (1965) *The Protestant Ethic and the Spirit of Capitalism* (trans by Talcott Parsons) in 1935, originally 1905 (Harmondsworth: Penguin).

Wegener, M., Button, K. and Nijkamp, P. (2004) *Planning History and Methodology* (Cheltenham: Elgar).Weiping Wu and Gaubatz, P. (2012) *The Chinese City* (London: Routledge).

Wekerle, G., Peterson, R. and Morley, D. (eds) (1980) *New Space for Women* (Boulder: Westview Press).

Wellman, K. and Spiller, M. (2012, September) *Urban Infrastructure: Finance and Management* (London: Wiley).

WGSG (1984) *Geography and Gender* (London: Hutchinson, Women and Geography Study Group, Institute of British Geographers, London).

WGSG (1997) *Feminist Geographies: Explorations in Diversity and Difference* (Harlow: Longmans, Women and Geography Study Group of Royal Geographical Society and Institute of British Geographers, London).

Whatmore, S. and Little J. (eds) (1988) *Gender and Geography* (London: Association for Curriculum Development).

Whitehead, M. (2007) *Spaces of Sustainability* (London: Routledge).

Whitelegg, J. (1993) *Transport for a Sustainable Future: The Case for Europe* (London: Belhaven).

Whitelegg, E., Arnot, M., Bartels, E., Beechey, V., Birke, L., Himmelweit, S., Leonard, D., Ruehl, S. and Speakman, M. (eds) (1982) *The Changing Experience of Women* (Oxford: Basil Blackwell with Oxford: Open University).

Whitzman, C. (2009) 'The effectiveness of women's safety audits', *Security Journal*, 22, 205–18.

Whitzman, C. (2012) *Building Inclusive Cities: Women's Safety and the Right to the City* (New York: Routledge).

WHO (2011) *Healthy Urban Planning* (Copenhagen: World Health Organization).

Whyte, W. (1981) *Street Corner Society* (Chicago: University Press of Chicago).

Wiener, N. (1948) *Cybernetics: Control and Communication in the Animal and the Machine* (Cambridge, MA: MIT Press), reprinted 2010 by Kessinger Publications, London.

Wilkinson, S., Reed, R. and Cadman, D. (2008) *Property Development* (London: Taylor & Francis).

Williams, K. (2010) 'The conditions for, and challenges of, adapting England's suburbs for climate change', *Building and Environment*, 55, 131–40.

Williams, R. (1981) *The Sociology of Culture* (Chicago: Chicago University Press).

Williams, R.H. (1996) *European Spatial Policy and Planning* (London: Paul Chapman).

Williams, R.H. (1999) 'European Union: Social Cohesion and Social Town Planning', in C. Greed (ed.) (1999), *Social Town Planning* (London: Routledge).

Willetts, D. (2010) *The Pinch: How the Baby Boomers took their Children's Future and Why they Should give it back* (London: Atlantic books).

Wilson, D. (1970) *I Know it Was the Place's Fault* (London: Oliphants).

Wilson, E. (1980) *Only Half Way to Paradise* (London: Tavistock).

Wilson, E. (1991) *The Sphinx in the City: Urban Life, the Control and Disorder of Women* (London: Virago).

Wilson, E. and Piper, J. (2010) *Spatial planning and climate change* (London: Routledge).

Wood, D., Chynoweth, P., Adshead, J. and Mason, J. (2011) *Law and the Built Environment* (Chichester: Wiley/Blackwell).

Yin, J. and Farmer, P. (2012) *Urban Planning for Dummies* (London: Wiley).

Young, G. and Stevenson, D. (eds) (2013) *The Ashgate Research Companion to Planning and Culture* (Farnham: Ashgate).

Young, G. (2008a) *Reshaping Planning with Culture* (Aldershot: Ashgate).

Young, G. (2008b) 'The Culturization of Planning', *Planning Theory*, 7(1), 71–91.

Young, M. and Willmott, P. (1957) *Family and Kinship in East London* (Harmondsworth: Penguin).

Young, M. and Willmott, P. (1978) *The Symmetrical Family: Study of Work and Leisure in The London Region* (Harmondsworth: Penguin).

USEFUL PLANNING JOURNALS

Planning Theory, Urban Studies, Town Planning Review, Progress in Planning, Town and Country Planning Association Journal, The Planner, Planning Practice and Research, Environment and Planning, A,B,C and D, Planning Perspectives, International Journal of Urban and Regional Research.

Author and Name Index

Subject Index

361